The History of Sukkot in the
Second Temple and Rabbinic Periods

Program in Judaic Studies
Brown University
BROWN JUDAIC STUDIES
Edited by
Ernest S. Frerichs
Shaye J. D. Cohen, Calvin Goldscheider

Number 302
The History of Sukkot in the
Second Temple and Rabbinic Periods

by
Jeffrey L. Rubenstein

The History of Sukkot in the Second Temple and Rabbinic Periods

by

Jeffrey L. Rubenstein

Scholars Press
Atlanta, Georgia

THE HISTORY OF SUKKOT IN THE SECOND TEMPLE AND RABBINIC PERIODS

Copyright © 1995 by Brown University

All rights reserved. No part of this work may be reproduced or transmitted in any form or by any means, electronic or mechanical, including photocopying and recording, or by means of any information storage or retrieval system, except as may be expressly permitted by the 1976 Copyright Act or in writing from Brown Judaic Studies, Brown University, Box 1826, Providence, RI 02912.

Library of Congress Cataloging-in-Publication Data

Rubenstein, Jeffrey L.
    The history of Sukkot in the Second Temple and Rabbinic periods / by Jeffrey L. Rubenstein.
        p. cm. — (Brown Judaic studies ; no. 302)
        "Revision of . . . doctoral dissertation, submitted in October, 1992 to the Department of Religion of Columbia University" —P.
        Includes bibliographical references and indexes.
        ISBN 0-7885-0130-5 (cloth : alk. paper)
        1. Sukkot—History. 2. Sukkot in rabbinical literature.
3. Judaism—History—Post-exilic period, 586 B.C.–210 A.D.
4. Judaism—History—Talmudic period, 10–425. I. Title.
II. Series.
BM695.S8R83   1995
296.4'33'09014—dc20   95-18812
                                                      CIP

Paperback edition published 2006 by Brown Judaic Studies
ISBN 1-930675-33-X (paperback : alk. paper)

Printed in the United States of America
on acid-free paper

Table of Contents

Preface and Acknowledgements ix

Abbreviations xi

Introduction 1

1. The Origins and Ancient History of Sukkot 13
   - I. Legal Traditions 13
   - II. Narrative Traditions 18
   - III. General Theories 20
   - IV. Origins of the Sukka and Lulav 25

2. The Second Temple Period 31
   - I. Ezra-Nehemiah 31
   - II. Zechariah 14 45
   - III. Jubilees 50
   - IV. 1-2 Maccabees 56
   - V. Qumran Scrolls 64
   - VI. Philo 69
   - VII. Pseudo-Philo 73
   - VIII. Josephus 75
   - IX. Christian Scriptures 84
   - X. Plutarch 94
   - XI. Numismatics and Iconography 97
   - XII. Conclusions 99

3. The Sukkot Temple Festival: Rabbinic Traditions 103
   - I. The Willow-Procession 106
   - II. The Water Libation 117
   - III. The Cultic Background of the Libation 122
   - IV. *Simḥat Beit Hasho'eva* (Rejoicing at the Place of Water Drawing) 131
   - V. SBH in the Light of Hellenistic Religions 145
   - VI. Extra-Rabbinic Evidence of SBH 148
   - VII. The Lulav and the Hallel 152
   - VIII. Conclusions 159

4. Sukkot and Rain in Tannaitic Sources 163
   I. Sukkot, Judgment and Rain 165
   II. Interpretations of the Lulav 169
   III. Rain and the Liturgy 171
   IV. Conclusions 178
5. History of Tannaitic Halakha 181
   I. The Endurance of the Lulav and the Sukka 181
   II. The Four Species 191
   III. The Rabbinic Lulav Ritual 197
   IV. Skhakh (Sukka-Roofing) 203
   V. Skhakh: The Essence of the Sukka 212
   VI. The Sukka 216
   VII. Dwelling in the Sukka 225
   VIII. Conclusions 235
6. Tannaitic Midrashim: The Clouds of Glory 239
   I. The Biblical Background 243
   II. Clouds of Glory in the Midrashim 245
   III. Clouds of Glory and the "Desert Motif" 256
   IV. The Halakha and the Aggada 260
   V. Conclusions 270
7. Sukkot in the Amoraic Midrashim 273
   I. Eschatology 275
   II. Rejoicing and Atonement 290
   III. Protection and the Clouds of Glory 301
   IV. Unity 302
   V. The Lulav as Sign 305
   VI. Rain and Agriculture 311
   VII. Miscellaneous 314
   VIII. Conclusions 315
8. Conclusions 319

Bibliography 327

Index 337

Scriptural Index 343

Preface and Acknowledgments

This book is a revision of my doctoral dissertation, submitted in October, 1992 to the Department of Religion of Columbia University. To address a wider audience I have omitted several chapters of the dissertation that focused on specific questions pertaining to Sukkot but distracted attention from the overall historical development of the festival. Similarly, I have added several sections not found in the dissertation in order to complete the historical picture. I have also omitted detailed analyses of several passages from both second temple and rabbinic sources that were overly technical.

I am very conscious of the immense debt I owe to all my teachers, in my youth, at Oberlin College, the Jewish Theological Seminary, Hebrew University and Columbia University. At every stage of my education I profited from enthusiastic and sensitive instructors. Three professors deserve special acknowledgment. Professor Richard Freund introduced me to the critical study of Jewish sources during my freshman year at Oberlin College. He stirred in me the passion for Judaic Studies, academic life, scholarship and teaching. For the past decade, he has been a treasure teacher, adviser, colleague and friend. Professor Seymour Siegel ז'ל took me under his wing when I first arrived at the Jewish Theological Seminary. The long hours we often spent in this office discussing both academic and practical matters, especially Jewish Ethics, were exhilarating intellectual experiences. I profited immeasurably form his comprehensive knowledge of all fields of Judaism – rabbinics, Hasidism, mysticism, ethics, history, theology. Yet Professor Siegel always stressed the limits of scholarship and the importance of real life. His death was a loss for us all. Professor David Weiss-Halivni, who directed my doctoral research, has been much more than my adviser over the past five years. He has been a teacher, mentor and role model. He is in large part responsible for my textual, analytical and scholarly abilities, and for whatever merits this book displays. I hope some day to emulate his sensitivity as teacher, devotion to students and willingness to give of his time to discuss any concern.

Professors Menahem Schmelzer, Raymond Scheindlin, Seth Schwartz, Richard Kalmin, Eliezer Diamond, Alan Segal, Victor Horowitz, Michael Satlow, Harry Fox and Mark Hirshman read chapters of the dissertation. I thank them for their helpful and insightful comments. I thank Professor Shaye J.D. Cohen, editor of the Brown Judaica Series, who reviewed the manuscript, for his comments and advise. I am extremely grateful to Professor Robert Goldenberg who closely read the revised manuscript. His searching questions, insightful suggestions and perceptive criticisms have substantially improved this study. The librarians at the Jewish Theological Seminary and at the Annenberg Research Institute assisted me through the project. My colleagues in the Skirball Department of Hebrew and Judaic Studies at New York University offered constant support and encouragement. My thanks to all of them.

Special thanks are due to all my friends, relatives and colleagues who constantly gave me moral support and encouragement: Tali Frank, Rachel Tessler, Bill Hamilton, Debbie Block, Michael Friedland, Tom Friedman, John Perlman, Beth Perlman, Jeff Segelman, Burt Appel, David Bergman, Robert Kahn, Gordon Kunin, Richard Camras, Mark Richter, Brad Hirschfield, Hal Hirschfield, Adam Wohlberg, Judy Heicklen, Marisa Joss, Mychal Springer, Jack Brauner – and many others. Thanks to them, I never felt like I was working alone.

Generous funding from numerous sources has made this book possible. Columbia University furnished me with a President's Fellowship. I received a scholarship through the Interuniversity Program of Hebrew University to study in Israel. The Memorial Foundation for Jewish Culture helped support two years of research and writing. Temple Har Zion of Penn Valley Pennsylvania, where I served as Scholar-in-Residence, provided two years of generous financial, moral and administrative support. The Skirball Department of Hebrew and Judaic Studies at New York University contributed funds to the publication of the manuscript. I deeply thank these institutions.

My parents, to whom this study is dedicated, have given me unflagging love, devotion and support. For them my love and thanks are boundless.

JEFFREY L. RUBENSTEIN
NEW YORK, NY
JULY 20, 1994
12TH OF AV, 5754

Abbreviations and References

Throughout the book, "sukka" and "sukkot" refer to booths; "Sukkot" (capitalized) to the festival. "Lulav" generally refers to the three or four species taken together. "Palm" or "palm branch" designates the palm independent of the myrtle and willow.

Translations of Josephus, Philo and other classical authors, except where noted, are from the Loeb Classical Library series. I have modified the translations occasionally. Translations from the Pseudepigrapha are from J.H. Charlesworth, ed., *The Old Testament Pseudepigrapha* (2 vols; Garden City, N.Y.: Doubleday, 1983-85).

Abbreviations of Books of the Bible and Apocrypha, and Journals follow the *Society of Biblical Literature, Membership Directory and Handbook, 1992*, pp. 212-213.

References to rabbinic texts provide the page numbers of the editions used in parentheses following the citation. Thus *Sifre Num.* §150 (196) = *Sifre* to Numbers, paragraph 150, p. 196 in Horovitz's edition.

References in the footnotes often utilize a short form. Complete publication information, including the editions of rabbinic texts, appears in the bibliography.

Hebrew transliteration is phonetic: ṣ=צ; ḥ=ח; ʾ=א; ʿ=ע. Complete vocalization is only provided when necessary.

Where Hebrew transcriptions are called for, capital letters are used: Ṭ=ט; Y=י, W=ו, Š=ש

Transliteration of Greek follows the system of the *Society of Biblical Literature, Membership Directory and Handbook, 1992*, p. 212.

Abbreviations

AJ	Antiquitates Judaicae (Antiquities of the Jews) (Josephus)
ARNA	'Avot deRabbi Natan, version A (ed. Schechter)
ARNB	'Avot deRabbi Natan, version B (ed. Schechter)
AuS	Arbeit und Sitte (G. Dalman)
b	Babylonian Talmud
BaR	Bamidbar Rabba
BHM	Beit Hamidrash (ed. Jellinek)
BJ	Bellum Judaicum (The Jewish War) (Josephus)
BMM	Baraita demelekhet hamishkan (ed. Kirschner)
BR	Bereisheet Rabba (ed. Theodor-Albeck)
BT	Babylonian Talmud
CD	Cairo (Geniza) text of the Damascus Covenant
Col.	Column
CTgA,B,C,D	Targums from *Masoreten des Westens* (ed. Kahle)
DQS	*Diqduqei Soferim* (Rabinovicz)
DR	Devarim Rabba (ed. Lieberman)
ER	Seder Eliyahu Rabba (ed. Ish-Shalom)
EZ	Seder Eliyahu Zuta (ed. Ish-Shalom)
H	The Holiness School
JPS	New Jewish Publication Society translation of the Bible
Jub	Jubilees (ed. Wintermute)
l., ll.	line, lines
LamR	'Eicha Rabba (Lamentations Rabba)
LCL	Loeb Classical Library
LXX	Septuagint (ed. Rahlfs)
m	Mishna
Mekhilta	Mekhilta d'Rabbi Ishma'el (ed. Horovitz-Rabin)
Mekhilta RSBY	Mekhilta d'Rabbi Shimon ben Yoḥai (ed. Epstein-Melamed)
MG	Midrash HaGadol (ed. Margoliot et al., cited by volume and page)
MLH	*Mavo lenusaḥ hamishna* (J. Epstein)
MM	Midrash Mishlei (ed. Vizotsky)
MS,MSS	Manuscript, Manuscripts
MT	Masoretic text
MT	Mishneh Torah (Maimonides)
MTeh	Midrash Tehillim (ed. Buber)
nn.	notes
OG	'Oṣar HaGeonim (ed. Lewin)

PR	Pesiqta Rabbati (ed. Ish-Shalom)
PRE	Pirqei d'Rabbi Eliezer (Jerusalem, 1980)
PRK	Pesiqta d'Rav Kahana (ed. Mandelbaum)
Ps.-Sol.	Psalms of Solomon
PT	Palestinian Talmud
P.-W.	*Paulys Real-encyclopaedie der klassischen Altertumwissenschaft.*
QohR	Qohelet Rabba (ed. Hirshman [chapters 1-4])
RH	Rosh Hashana
RR	Ruth Rabba
SA	Shmini ʿAṣeret
SBH	simḥat beit hasho'eva (rejoicing at the place of water-drawing)
ShR	Shir HaShirim Rabba
Sifre Num.	Sifre to Numbers (ed. Horovitz)
Sifre Deut.	Sifre to Deuteronomy (ed. Finkelstein)
SOR	Seder ʿOlam Rabba (ed. Ratner)
SR	Shmot Rabba
SZ	Sifre Zuta (ed. Horovitz)
t	Tosefta (ed. Lieberman or Zuckermandel)
Tan	Tanḥuma (Berlin, 1927)
TanB	Tanḥuma (ed. Buber)
TDNT	*Theological Dictionary of the New Testament*
TK	*Tosefta Kifshuta* (Lieberman)
TN	Targum Neofiti (ed. Diez-Macho)
TO	Targum Onkelos (ed. Sperber)
TR	*Tosefet Rishonim* (Lieberman)
TY	Targum Pseudo-Jonathan (ed. Clarke)
TYG	Targum Yerushalmi (ed. Ginsburger)
VR	Vayiqra Rabba (ed. Margoliot)
y	Yerushalmi (Palestinian Talmud)
Yalqut	Yalqut Shimoni (Jerusalem, 1970)
YK	Yom Kippur

Tractate

(If no tractate abreviation appears, the reference is to Tractate Sukka; m1:4 = Mishna Sukka 1:4)

Ah	'Ahilot (Ohalot)	Mid	Middot
Ar	ʿArakhin	MQ	Moʿed Qatan
AZ	ʿAvoda Zara	MS	Maʿaser Sheni
BB	Bava Batra	Naz	Nazir
Bekh	Bekhorot	Ned	Nedarim
Ber	Berakhot	Nid	Nidda
Bes	Beṣa	Par	Para
Bik	Bikkurim	Pe	Peʿa
BM	Bava Mesia	Pes	Pesaḥim
BQ	Bava Qama	Qid	Qiddushin
Dem	Demai	RH	Rosh Hashana
Ed	ʿEduyot	Sanh	Sanhedrin
Eruv	ʿEruvin	Shab	Shabbat
Git	Gittin	Sheq	Sheqalim
Hag	Ḥagiga	Shev	Sheviʿit
Hal	Ḥalla	Shevu	Shevuʿot
Hul	Ḥullin	Sot	Sota
Kel	Kelim	Suk	Sukka
Ket	Ketubot	Ta	Taʿanit
Kil	Kilayim	Tam	Tamid
Ma	Maʿaserot	Ter	Terumot
Mak	Makkot	Toh	Tohorot
Makh	Makhshirin	Yad	Yadayim
Me	Meʿila	Yev	Yevamot
Meg	Megilla	Yom	Yoma
Men	Menaḥot	Zev	Zevaḥim

Introduction

This study analyzes the history of the festival of Sukkot during the second temple and rabbinic periods. While the Jerusalem temple stood Sukkot was the preeminent festival and primary pilgrimage. The cult observed the festal week with sacrifices, processions, fertility rites and other temple rituals. The destruction of the second temple in 70 CE left rabbinic Judaism with the question of how to celebrate Sukkot, a temple festival, without a temple. Which elements were retained from the legacy of cultic rituals and which were abandoned? What does the rabbinic Sukkot festival share with its antecedent of temple times and in what does it differ? How did Sukkot evolve in the later rabbinic periods as memories of the temple receded? The following pages address these issues by tracing the development of the festival over the course of a millennium.

The destruction of the second temple posed a major challenge to Judaism. Jews thought of the temple as God's terrestrial abode, the place in which he dwelled among his people. There the God of their ancestors, in tangible if not material form, could be found. More than symbolizing the existence of God, the temple marked in concrete, physical space the real presence of God on earth. Heaven and earth intersected at the temple, for the summit of the temple mount reached up to the clouds while its foundations extended to deep subterranean realms. According to this mythic worldview, at the time of creation God selected Mt Zion to be his future abode. The temple, then, was not only the house of God, but God's house: invulnerable, eternal and permanent. Its destruction meant that God had abandoned his house, and presumably his people. The Romans were only divine agents, the instrument by which God accomplished his design to remove his presence from his worshippers. Why did God abandon his temple and permit its destruction?

Beyond the theological questions there were practical issues. For centuries the religious, cultural and economic life of Jews focused on the Jerusalem temple, the priesthood and associated institutions. Each day the priests brought the sacrifices God had commanded and thereby maintained the connection between the nation and the deity. Biblical law mandated that tithes be set aside for the priests and Levites, and that a portion be taken to Jerusalem and consumed in a sacrificial meal there. Peasants carried the first fruits of their crops to the temple and presented them before the altar. Traders established markets in the temple courtyards to provide animals for those who desired to offer a sacrifice. For much of this period the high priest was an important political figure – under the latter Hasmoneans he doubled as king – so the political and diplomatic administration was concentrated there as well. Jews from the diaspora aspired to journey to Jerusalem and worship in the house of their God, and so set the temple as the focus of their religious lives. The destruction of the temple put an end to these institutions.

The practical effects of the destruction impacted the festival cycle in a particularly acute fashion. Pesaḥ, Shavuot and Sukkot, the three harvest festivals, were *ḥagim*, pilgrimages to the temple. Pilgrims flocked to Jerusalem to observe the priests perform the service, participate in popular celebrations, and partake of sacrificial meals. Josephus, the first century Jewish historian, describes throngs of worshippers bringing a Pesaḥ sacrifice and partaking of a ritual feast.[1] Shavuot, celebrated for one day, marked the wheat harvest with a ritual presentation of two loaves of bread before the altar. On Yom Kippur, vast crowds watched from the courtyards as the high priest performed intricate purification rites, sacrificed the scapegoat and other offerings, and eventually entered the Holy of Holies to confess the sins of the people. The declaration of each new month, which established the dates of upcoming festivals, took place at the temple and was communicated to Jews throughout the country.

Sukkot, of all the festivals, suffered the repercussions of the destruction most acutely. The autumnal harvest concluded the lengthy Israelite agricultural year. After the grapes, fruits and remaining grain had been harvested, an arduous task in and of itself, preparation of wine and threshing grain entailed rigorous labor. Having completed this work, peasants could look forward to several months of relative calm. Now was the time to celebrate and give thanks for the fruits of the land. The fall festival was therefore the most joyous festival of the year and the best attended pilgrimage. Sukkot became known as *heḥag, the* festival, an appellation found in both the Bible and rabbinic sources. The week of festivities in Jerusalem included a panoply of colorful temple rituals and popular celebrations. At no other time did the worshippers enthusiastically participate in celebrations lasting throughout the night.

---

[1] *BJ* 2:10; 6:423-24.

In addition to giving thanks for the completed harvest, the people prayed that their crops would thrive during the next year. Fall marked the beginning of the rainy season, which determined whether the crops would flourish or wither, hence whether the people would prosper or suffer. To ensure abundant rain the cult performed elaborate rainmaking ceremonies and the people participated in prayers and other rites. The destruction of the temple and concomitant cessation of cultic worship abruptly prevented cultic celebration of the festival. The temple festival *par excellence* no longer had a temple.

Post-temple Judaism faced the question of how to celebrate Sukkot, the primary cultic festival, in a world without a temple. This book is about the rabbinic response to this challenge. How did the rabbis, founders of the Judaism that became normative, observe Sukkot after the destruction? What did the festival mean to them? How does this compare to its celebration and meaning in temple times? As the centuries passed and memories of the temple faded, did the rabbinic understanding of Sukkot change?

One thing was certain: the festival could not be celebrated as before. The centralization of the cult legislated by the Book of Deuteronomy had become an axiom of rabbinic faith. To perform sacrifices anywhere but in the temple of God was unthinkable. At best, the non-sacrificial rituals and ceremonies could have been continued after the destruction in new places of worship. The rabbis could have found exegetical support to justify the performance of water libations outside of the cult in order to replicate modes of temple worship in their basic forms. Although this course was possible theoretically, it was not feasible in practice. As we shall see, the rituals depended too heavily on the temple context and the mythic understanding of the power of the cult. Libations influenced the rain supply because cultic worship ultimately ensured the proper workings of the natural world. The hydraulic processes which determined the water cycle depended on the temple and its location above the ancient floodwaters. Fertility rites worked through the power of the cult to influence the forces of creation. To perform such rituals after the destruction of the temple would not have made religious sense.

Yet several other responses were possible. If the temple rituals themselves could not be continued, the rabbis could have attempted to preserve the general orientation of the festival. New forms could have been created to express and transmit inherited conceptions and beliefs. A different set of rituals, which did not depend on the cult for their coherency, might have been instituted to replace the temple ceremonies. Despite the fundamental incongruity of a temple festival without a temple, the opportunity for continuity was there. On the other hand, the architects of a post-temple Judaism could have seized upon this vacuum radically to reinterpret the festival. They might have opted to sever the connection between Sukkot and the temple by transforming the festival into a celebration of something else. Medieval Judaism appended the celebration of Simhat Torah, "Rejoicing with the Torah," to Sukkot, and there is no reason for this not to have occurred in an earlier age. The festival that expressed cultic joy might well have evolved into the highest expression of the joy of Torah or another ideal of rabbinic piety.

Or the rabbis could have eschewed both possibilities, neither reinterpreting the festival nor developing new ritual forms. They could have chosen to preserve a few fragments of the temple celebrations and to retain the traditional conception of the festival. In the extreme case they might have abandoned all rituals as intrinsically connected to the cult and observed Sukkot much like a Sabbath, refraining from prohibited work, enjoying a ritual feast, and performing liturgical worship of some sort. This lack of innovation essentially transpired in the case of Shavuot. While Shavuot received a novel historical dimension as the commemoration of the revelation at Sinai, no rituals replaced the two loaves presented as a wave-offering or the presentation of other first-fruits; observance of the festival consisted of liturgy and feast.

The modes of extra-temple piety practiced before the destruction probably influenced this choice to some extent. The destruction of the temple did not leave a vacuum in religious life. Like all cultures, Israel always had a popular religion, which, to the consternation of the prophets, often deviated from "official" prophetic and priestly ideology. Sukkot originated, in part, as an agricultural festival celebrated in the vineyards and fields after the harvest. From time immemorial farmers rejoiced immediately upon completion of the labors of the gathering season. Local festivities undoubtedly continued even as the cult centralized worship and observed the official national festival in the temple. Despite the importance placed on the pilgrimage to Jerusalem to worship in the official cultic context, all Israelites could not journey each year to the temple. Those who lived at some distance from the temple, or, after the Hasmonean conquests, in the Galilee, must have observed the biblically ordained festivals in some fashion. Whether they imitated aspects of the temple rituals or possessed ancient local customs is difficult to determine. At all events, the destruction did not end the observance of Sukkot in popular religion.

In addition to local traditions, during the century preceding the destruction movements had developed seeking to popularize and democratize aspects of the cult. The Pharisees and other schools devised methods of complex exegesis and collected extra-scriptural traditions, thereby establishing a religious authority that competed with the priestly

Introduction

hierarchy. Study and interpretation of Torah now served as modes of piety in and of themselves, an alternative to participation in the cult. The "Fellowship" *(ḥavura)* adopted the practice of eating foods in the state of purity previously demanded only of priests serving in the temple, and thus extended cultic piety to popular practice. The trajectory of the rise of the synagogue is debated, but it is likely that prior to the destruction some form of structured, communal worship flourished alongside the temple cult.

The Qumran sect had already rejected the cult as corrupt and retreated to the hills beside the Dead Sea. While they idealized cultic worship and ultimately hoped to return to a purified Jerusalem temple, they nevertheless created a rich religious life for their temporary exile. The Qumran scrolls yielded an abundance of liturgical texts, descriptions of rituals and legal traditions. Exactly how the Qumran community observed the festivals is unclear, but fragments of the scrolls indicate that they possessed a highly developed liturgy and ritual. Nor should we ignore the greater diaspora, the Jewish communities that prospered during this time in Rome, Alexandria, Cyrene and elsewhere. From Philo's writing it is evident that these communities, although far from the temple, observed the law and celebrated the festivals. The destruction of the temple entailed cessation of the cult, but not of Judaism, of the dominant and official mode of worship, but not of the totality of religious life, of the festival pilgrimages, but not of the pilgrimage festivals. The rabbis had to grapple with popular modes of piety when they considered post-temple observance of Sukkot. For this reason it is all the more necessary to examine sources from the second temple period.

How to celebrate Sukkot after the destruction of the temple was therefore an open question. We cannot point to any inevitable or "natural" course that had to be taken. The choices made and the ways not taken should reveal much about rabbinic religion. What rituals did the rabbis carry over from temple times and what did these rituals mean to them? What do the main festival symbols represent? What, in essence, did Sukkot commemorate? By comparing rabbinic observance of Sukkot with second temple worship we can assess to what degree the rabbis reinterpreted Judaism in the post-temple world and to what degree they perpetuated older conceptions and rituals. The answers to these questions provide a perspective from which to evaluate the nature of rabbinic Judaism and its relationship to the Judaism of temple times.

Focus on "the rabbis" does not ignore the fact that the challenge of how to observe Sukkot faced all Jewish communities, most of which were not rabbinic. It would be interesting to compare the rabbinic celebration to those that developed spontaneously in various communities before the spread of rabbinic influence. Unfortunately, we are limited by the extant sources. Apart from the meager iconographic and numismatic evidence, literary sources devolve exclusively from rabbinic circles. Only occasional hints survive about contemporary practices opposed by the rabbis. This study, perforce, concentrates on rabbinic literature and the rabbinic festival.

In *The Origins of the Seder*,[2] the late Baruch Bokser adopted this type of approach to study the rabbinic observance of Pesaḥ. Bokser compares the seder described in the Mishna and Tosefta to the Pesaḥ sacrifice and meal in temple times, identifying points in common while elucidating the differences between the rituals. He demonstrates how the Mishna's seder constitutes a "remything" of salvation. In particular, Bokser documents that the Mishna elevates the status of the matzah such that it becomes the primary ritual symbol. In the post-temple world, meaning was transferred from the Paschal lamb to the unleavened bread. The narration of mythic history with symbols and rituals combines the central institutions of rabbinic piety: "blessings, study, acts of lovingkindness and fellowship."[3] Thus Bokser provides an insightful study of the nature of the rabbinic seder and how it developed from earlier forms.

Bokser limited his study to the seder as described in Mishna-Tosefta – essentially to a single chapter – choosing not to analyze the tannaitic halakhic midrashim or the larger corpus of midrashic materials. Nor did he analyze other components of the festival such as the search for ḥameṣ or the ritual of its removal and assess how these contributed to the "remything" of the rabbinic celebration. This made for a controlled and methodologically rigorous study: at issue was how one source redacted at one time portrayed one ritual. Bokser avoided difficult questions such as the relationship between different rabbinic sources, the fact that they derive from various – and to a great extent – unknown times and places, the identity of the authors and the degree to which the source reflected "real" life or purely theoretical discussions of the editors. Yet the tradeoff for such limited scope and methodological rigor was not insignificant, for Bokser excluded many interesting questions. How did other rituals of the festival contribute to the seder experience or combine with it to produce something larger? How important is the seder within the overall observance of Pesaḥ? Does the rabbinic aggada, especially the exegesis of the Pesaḥ story, reflect a similar "remything" of Pesaḥ? How do later rabbinic sources interpret the Pesaḥ symbols and rituals? To gain that wider perspective, in this study I gather sources from all extant

---

[2]Baruch Bokser, *The Origins of the Seder* (Berkeley and Los Angeles: University of California Press), 1984.
[3]P. 99

literature, halakhic and aggadic, tannaitic and amoraic, of Babylonian and Palestinian provenance, and evaluate the festival of Sukkot in its entirety. The range of sources raises those questions that the limited and controlled study avoids, but the tradeoff should yield a comprehensive view of a rabbinic festival.

This type of study is important because it approaches these question from an integrated perspective. Two methods have dominated the study of rabbinic Judaism. The first attempts to understand rabbinic Judaism by analyzing rabbinic theology: what did the rabbis say about God, the commandments, suffering, gentiles, etc?[4] The second method describes the worldview of rabbinic Judaism (or Judaisms) through analysis of the Mishna and subsequent documents, focusing on the evolution of rabbinic traditions. How does the Mishna (Tosefta, Bavli, etc.) express a system of holiness, and of what does that system consist?[5] Both approaches have contributed a great deal to the interpretation of rabbinic Judaism. At the same time, these studies are limited to one perspective and mode of analysis. They rarely extend beyond the sources to consider the individual rituals and practices – the Sabbath, the mezuza, the evening service – and what their observance meant. The focus on history of traditions and theology has preempted study of the actual components of the religious life of the authors of the documents. Questions about the nature of the religious experience of particular rituals are often overlooked. In this study I utilize a more synthetic approach in order to consider how the celebration of a festival developed over the course of time. The method is eclectic, but closer to history-of-religions and not simply history-of-traditions or theology. In evaluating the rabbinic Sukkot festival I assess both halakhic and aggadic sources and discuss

---

[4]Solomon Schechter, *Aspects of Rabbinic Theology* (New York: Macmillan, 1909); George Foote Moore, *Judaism in the First Centuries of the Christian Era* (Cambridge: Harvard University Press, 1927); C.G. Montefiore and H. Loewe, A *Rabbinic Anthology* (London: Macmillan, 1938); E. Urbach, *Hazal: pirqei 'emunot vedei'ot* (Jerusalem: Magnes, 1969) (= *The Sages: Their Concepts and Beliefs*, trans. I. Abrahams [Jerusalem: Magnes, 1979]); E.P. Sanders, *Paul and Palestinian Judaism* (Philadelphia: Fortress Press, 1977). The works of Max Kadushin, *Organic Thinking: A Study in Rabbinic Thought* (New York: Jewish Theological Seminary, 1938) and *The Rabbinic Mind* (New York: Jewish Theological Seminary, 1952) pursue a related, if somewhat idiosyncratic, approach.

[5]Jacob Neusner, "The History of Earlier Rabbinic Judaism: Some New Approaches," *History of Religions* 16 (1977), 225-236; idem, *Judaism: The Evidence of the Mishna* (Chicago: University of Chicago Press, 1981); idem, *Judaism in Society: The Evidence of the Yerushalmi* (Chicago: University of Chicago Press, 1983); idem, *Judaism: The Classical Statement: The Evidence of the Bavli* (Chicago: University of Chicago Press, 1986); A.J. Avery-Peck, *Mishnah's Division of Agriculture: A History and Theology of the Seder Zeraim* (Chico: Scholars Press, 1985).

the relationship between the two realms. My goal is to venture beyond the confines of these strict categories and attain a wider perspective.

The focus on Sukkot in rabbinic times distinguishes this study from much of the previous work on Sukkot.[6] Scholars have analyzed Sukkot as celebrated during second temple times, both describing the festival in its entirety[7] and attempting to reconstruct the individual rituals.[8] To a great extent these studies depend on the descriptions of temple rites preserved in the Mishna and later rabbinic sources, but they focus on the second temple period, rather than the rabbinic festival. Similarly, biblical scholars studied Sukkot as described in later sources to shed light on the royal temple festivals of the Israelite monarchy.[9] New Testament scholars have examined Sukkot in order to elucidate scriptural passages

---

[6] For full survey of scholarship see Jeffrey L. Rubenstein, *The History of Sukkot during the Second Temple and Rabbinic Periods: Studies in the Continuity and Change of a Festival* (Dissertation, Columbia University; Ann Arbor: University Microfilms, 1992), 27-35.

[7] The most comprehensive study of this type is S. Safrai's work on the pilgrimage, *'Aliya leregel biyeme bayit sheini* (Tel-Aviv: 'Am hasefer, 1965). Chapter Six contains a section devoted to Sukkot. Other general discussions of the second temple Sukkot festival include L. Finkelstein, *Thle Pharisees: The Sociological Background of Their Faith*[3] (Philadelphia: Jewish Publication Society, 1962 [1938]), 102-115, 700-708; D. Flusser, "Ḥag hasukkot bevayit sheini," *Maḥanayim* 50 (1960), 28-31; S. Zeitlin, *The Rise and Fall of the Judean State* (3 vols; Philadelphia: Jewish Publication Society, 1962-78), 3 :247-52.

[8] Primarily the water libation and *simhat beit hasho'eva* ("rejoicing at the place of water-drawing"): A. Geiger, *Lehr- und Lesebuch zur Sprache der Mischnah* (Breslau: Leuckart, 1845), 22-24, 131; L. Venetianer, "Die Eleusinische Mysterien im Tempel zu Jerusalem," *Populär Wissenschaftliche Monatsblätter* 17 (1897), 170-81; D. Feuchtwang, "Das Wasseropfer und die damit verbundenen Zeremonien," *MGWJ* 54-55 (1910-11), 535-52, 713-29, 43-63; J. Hochman, *Jerusalem Temple Festivities* (London, 1911); Raphael Patai, *Hamayim* (Tel Aviv: Devir, 1936), 55-65; idem, *Man and Temple* (New York: Ktav, 1947), 24-54; H. Fox, "Simḥat beit hasho'eva," *Tarbiz* 55 (1985), 173-213.

[9] P. Volz, *Das Neujahrsfest Jahwes (Laubhüttenfest)* (Tübingen: Mohr, 1912); S. Mowinckel, *Psalmenstudien II. Das Thronbesteigungsfest Jahwes und der Ursprung des Eschatologie* (Skrifter Utgitt av Det Norske Videnskaps-Akademi i Oslo, II. Hist.-Filos. Kl., 1922); reprint: *Psalmenstudien I-VI* (Amsterdam: P. Schippers, 1961); idem, *The Psalms in Israel's Worship*, trans. D.R. Ap-Thomas (2 vols; Oxford: Blackwell, 1962), original title: *Offersang og Sangoffer* (Oslo: H. Aschenhoug, 1951); H. Schmidt, *Die Thronfahrt Jahves* (Tübingen, 1927); N.H. Snaith, *The Jewish New Year Festival, its Origins and Development* (London, 1948). The Myth-and-Ritual school has also devoted attention to Sukkot in their reconstruction of Israelite mythic-cultic religion. See the essays collected in *Myth and Ritual*, ed. S.H. Hooke (London: Oxford University Press, 1933) and *Myth, Ritual, and Kingship*, ed. S.H. Hooke (Oxford: Clarendon Press, 1958); W. Oesterley, "Early Hebrew Festival Rituals," *Myth and Ritual*, 111-46; T. Gaster, *Thespis* (Connecticut, 1956).

Introduction 9

and issues concerning early Christianity.[10] Again the focus is not on Sukkot for its own sake, nor on the rabbinic festival, but on New Testament issues. Studies that address rabbinic concerns have concentrated on the individual sources and given but cursory attention to the festival as a whole.[11] I have profited immensely from these studies, and my debt to their authors and many others will be apparent on each page. My study aims to synthesize this legacy in a comprehensive examination of the rabbinic festival. It reverses the previous trend in that it examines earlier sources in order to provide a perspective with which to assess rabbinic developments.

Outline

The first task is to understand the roots of the Sukkot festival and its antecedents in the biblical period. Chapter One presents the older biblical sources and general theories of the development throughout the first temple period. Biblical passages are also important in that later exegetes, both of the second temple and rabbinic periods, interpret these texts in order to determine how the festival should be observed properly. Biblical legislation, in other words, became as important a factor in determining the nature of Sukkot in later times as the tradition of actual celebrations in previous years. Ambiguities in biblical verses became the substance of dispute among later generations and produced substantial variation in ritual observance.

Chapters Two and Three examine the celebration of Sukkot during the second temple period. The second chapter attends to non-rabbinic sources that antedate the destruction of the temple in 70 CE. These include the later biblical passages found in Zechariah 14 and Ezra-

---

[10]H. Strack and P. Billerback, *Kommentar zum Neuen Testament aus Talmud und Midrasch* (4 vols.; Munich: Beck, 1922-28), "Laubhüttenfest," 2:774-812; H. Riesenfeld, *Jésus transfiguré* (Acta Seminarii Neotestamentici Upsaliensis, vol. 16; Copenhagen, 1947); J. Jeremias, "Golgotha und der heilige Felsen," *Angelos* 2 (1926), 74-128; H. Ulfgard, *Feast and Future: Revelation 7:9-17 and the Feast of Tabernacles*, Coniectanea Biblica: New Testament Series, vol. 22 (Stockholm: Almqvist & Wiksell, 1989). Numerous analyses of specific New Testament passages, primarily John 7 and Rev 7 and 24, touch on Sukkot and its themes. See Chapter 2,IX.

[11]J.N. Epstein, *Mevo'ot lesifrut hatana'im*, ed. E.Z. Melamed (Jerusalem: Magnes, 1957), 350-54; H. Albeck, *Mishna* (6 vols.; Jerusalem and Tel Aviv, 1954-59), 2:473-79; J. Neusner, *Sheqalim, Yoma, Sukkah* (Leiden: Brill, 1982), 125-75; J. Heinemann, "The Art of Composition in Leviticus Rabba," *Hasifrut* 2 (1971), 832-33 (Hebrew); J. Heinemann, *Prayer in the Talmud: Forms and Patterns*, trans. R. Sarason (Berlin and New York: De Gruyter, 1977), 139-150. Thus Ulfgard, *Feast*, 108 n. 45, observes, "there is a remarkable lack of scholarly literature on the Feast of Tabernacles in post-biblical times and in Jewish literature."

Nehemiah, and intertestamental literature, including the Book of Jubilees, 1 and 2 Maccabees, Josephus, Philo, the Temple Scroll and other Qumran texts. From these sources a picture emerges of how the festival was celebrated in temple times. Rabbinic traditions describing the Sukkot temple festival are analyzed in Chapter Three. These sources preserve the most detailed accounts of the rituals carried out during the seven days of festivities in Jerusalem. Since the rabbinic documents were redacted several generations after the destruction of the temple, and may have been influenced by rabbinic views of history, they must be treated separately. Having analyzed the two types of sources in this way, we may then compare the two portrayals of Sukkot in order to attain as complete an understanding of the festival as possible. The overall results provide a basis for comparing whether the later rabbinic observance of the festival continues or departs from elements of earlier times.

Chapter Four begins our discussion of Sukkot in rabbinic times. We first address the question of Sukkot as a rain festival. Sukkot falls in autumn, at the beginning of the rainy season, and was the opportune time to ensure that rain was plentiful. Both second temple and rabbinic sources suggest that the temple rituals were directed to this end. The destruction of the temple presented the rabbis with difficult questions regarding the rain-making dimension of Sukkot. Could Sukkot retain its function of influencing the rain supply? Or would the rabbis jettison this element of the festival and seek to provide for rain in other ways? Here then is the first test of the relationship between rabbinic and temple understandings of Sukkot.

The following two chapters are devoted to the tannaitic traditions which present the initial rabbinic construction of Sukkot. The Mishna, Tosefta and other tannaitic sources preserved in the talmuds contain numerous halakhic traditions about the lulav, the sukka and proper observance of the festival. Attributed to authorities who lived from temple times until the end of the second century, the traditions cover almost two centuries. As a whole, the legal prescriptions reveal the various components of the rabbinic festival and to what extent the post-temple observance continues or departs from the temple celebration. Placing the traditions in a rough chronological sequence allows us to trace the development within this period. Did rabbinic practices diverge farther from the temple roots as time passed?

In contrast to the plethora of halakhic sources, there remain few tannaitic aggadic traditions about Sukkot. Chapter Six analyzes the dominant aggadic motif, the booths as symbol of the "clouds of glory," the divinely bestowed clouds that surrounded the Israelite camp during the wandering in the desert. This symbolism reveals a great deal about

Introduction

the tannaitic conception of the festival and sheds light on the religious experience of residing in the sukka.

The paucity of tannaitic aggada is more than offset by the richness of amoraic midrashim. Chapter Seven collects the interpretations of the lulav and sukka in these sources. Here we find a stunning array of symbolisms which reflect the spectrum of conceptions and beliefs evoked by Sukkot. Essentially the aggadot express what the festival symbols, and therefore the festival itself, meant to the rabbis.[12] Chapter Eight presents the conclusions that emerge from this study.

---

[12] I have not discussed amoraic halakhic sources or the development of halakha in amoraic times, since there is little innovation. The amoraim primarily take their agenda from the halakhic categories established in tannaitic sources, explaining and adjudicating disputes and adding further refinements. One amoraic halakhic innovation, the concept of the sukka as a temporary dwelling, is discussed in "The Sukka as Temporary or Permanent Dwelling: A Study in the Development of Talmudic Thought," *HUCA 64* (1993), 137-66

1

The Origins and Ancient History of Sukkot

I. Legal Traditions

This preliminary chapter surveys the biblical sources pertaining to Sukkot and the major theories concerning its origin and development in the first temple period. While this era of Israelite history antedates the periods of our study, it is important to appreciate the nature of the autumnal festival during this time. The second temple Sukkot festival descended from its first temple counterpart and probably retained much of the content. Moreover, scholars of the second temple period appeal to biblical passages to shed light on Sukkot as celebrated during later times. Biblical scholars, for their part, routinely adduce sources from the second temple and even rabbinic periods to reconstruct the festival of the biblical and pre-biblical eras. The theories surveyed here provide the background for our study and introduce some of the sources to be analyzed at length in later chapters.

The earliest biblical sources do not use the appellation "the festival of Sukkot." Exod 23:16 and 34:22, assigned to the JE source and usually dated to the tenth century BCE, call the autumnal festival the "the festival of ingathering (ḥag ha'asif)."[1] Exod 23:16 notes that the ingathering festival occurs "at the end of the year when you gather in the results of your work from the field," while Exod 34:22 sets the festival "at the turn of the year." The term "ingathering" probably refers to the final harvest, the ingathering of fruit, although it may refer to the post-harvest labor of

---

[1] The Gezer calendar of the tenth century BCE mentions two months of 'asif, probably corresponding to September and October. See H. Donner and W. Röllig, *Kanaanäische und aramäische Inschriften* (Weisbaden: Otto Harrassowitz, 1962-64), 1:32, no. 182, and 2:181-182.

ingathering wine from the vat and grain from the threshing floor.² Beyond the title, the verses supply no information other than commanding all male Israelites to appear before God at this time. The vague designation the "turn of the year" indicates no calendrical date had been fixed. Peasants apparently celebrated after the completion of their labors, a time which varied from year to year with normal climatic fluctuations. Many scholars connect this festival to two celebrations described in the Book of Judges.³ Jgs 9:27 tells how the residents of Shechem, a Canaanite village, "went out into the fields, gathered and trod out the vintage of their vineyards, and made a festival." They then entered the temple of their god, ate, drank and rejoiced. Jgs 21:19-21 refers to "the annual feast of YHWH now being held at Shiloh," and mentions that women danced in the vineyards. These descriptions point to a vintage festival of primitive agricultural character.⁴ Note that the fall festival is the annual "feast of the Lord," an indication of its importance already in early times. Deut 16:13-15 first connects the fall festival to booths (*sukkot*):

> (13) After the ingathering from your threshing floor and your vat, you shall hold the Festival of Sukkot for seven days. (14) You shall rejoice in your festival, with your son and your daughter, your male and female slave, the Levite, the stranger, the fatherless, and the widow in your communities. (15) You shall hold the festival for YHWH your God seven days, in the place that God will choose; for the Lord your God will bless you in all your crops and all your undertakings, and you shall have nothing but joy.

---

²The *'asif* months mentioned in the Gezer calendar (see previous note) probably correspond to September and October, by which time the harvest would have been completed, but the processing of wine and oil could have continued. Exactly when the *'asif* festival was celebrated is unclear. An early date, derived from D and P which set the festival in the middle of the seventh month, generally sometime in September, would link *'asif* with the fruit harvest and vintage. Indeed, Deut 16:13 explicitly mentions the winepress and threshing floor (see below). A later date suits the olive harvest and processing of oil. W.F. Albright, "The Gezer Calendar," *BASOR* 92 (1943), 22 n. 30 advocates the latter dating and the connection to the olive harvest. However, links between Sukkot and olives are tenuous at best: see Wellhausen, *Prolegomena*, 95-97 and Dalman, *AuS*, 4:193. S. Talmon, "The Gezer Calendar," *JAOS* 83 (1963), 183 n. 46, suggests that *'asif* originally referred to the fruit havest, and only later became a general term which could also be applied to the olive harvest. On the Palestinian agricultural cycle see mPe 8:1; yYev 15:2, 14d; Dalman, *AuS*, vol. 1, parts 1-2.

³Wellhausen, *Prolegomena*, 94; de Vaux, *Israel*, 495, 501-502; MacRae, *Tabernacles*, 252; Pedersen, *Israel*, 2:418-419.

⁴Wellhausen, *Prolegomena*, 94-96; de Vaux, *Israel*, 496 and others suggest the autumnal festival is the annual pilgrimage to which 1 Sam 1:3 alludes. Eli may have assumed Hanna was drunk from the wine typically consumed at such vintage festivals (1 Sam 1:14). Like Jgs 21:19, the festival took place at Shiloh.

Deuteronomy links the "ingathering" specifically to that of grain and wine from the processing places. No explanation is given for the title "the festival of Sukkot (booths)." It may derive from the booths that sheltered watchmen in the fields throughout the summer. During the busy harvest season field workers camped out in booths and, when they had completed the labor, celebrated the festival there. This explanation of the sukka, however, is not universally accepted. Some suggest pilgrims stayed in booths during the celebrations at cult sanctuaries or at the Jerusalem temple, and the booths therefore have no connection to the harvest. Below we consider this question in greater detail.[5]

Verse 15 instructs to "hold the festival for YHWH your God," reminiscent of "the festival of YHWH" of Jgs 21:19. Again the title suggests that the autumnal Sukkot festival was special, distinguished from its sister festivals. Deuteronomy emphasizes the joyous character of the festival, a reflection of the happiness at successfully concluding the arduous tasks and excitement at new stores of grain and wine. Here the seven day length of the festival is prescribed.

Deut 31:10-13 designates Sukkot as the date of the septennial *haqhel* ("Assembly") ritual when the entire people gathers to hear a public reading of the Torah. It is unclear if this ritual was actually practiced in biblical times or whether it is part of utopian Deuteronomic legislation. In any case, the selection of Sukkot for the time of the ritual suggests that Sukkot was recognized as the preeminent festival and primary pilgrimage. At Sukkot the Deuteronomistic authors expected the entire people to gather at the central sanctuary.

Lev 23:33-44 and Num 29:12-34 present the most detailed legislation concerning the festival. Scholars now agree the Leviticus passage is composite, the first section deriving from the Priestly source (P) (23:33-38) and the second section from the Holiness School (H).[6] P designates the fifteenth of the seventh month as the date that the festival of Sukkot commences and legislates that the celebration last for seven days. Some scholars claim the fixed date reflects a later era when the festivals became institutionalized; the earlier sources leave the date open since completion of the harvest varied from year to year.[7] P also prescribes an additional

---

[5]P. 25.
[6]I follow the analysis and dating of I. Knohl, "The Priestly Torah Versus the Holiness School: Sabbath and the Festivals," *HUCA* 58 (1987), 65-117." See too Jacob Milgrom, *Leviticus 1-16 (AB* 3; New York: Doubleday, 1991), 13-42.
[7]Wellhausen, *Prolegomena*, 101; de Vaux, *Israel*, 498; Kraus, *Worship*, 62. Weinfeld, *Institutions*, 117-18, in his massive attack on Wellhausen, cites examples from ancient Near East texts which designate specific dates for festivals, showing that fixed dating is not a late development. Nonetheless, it is hard to argue with the biblical evidence: JE set no date; D and P do.

gathering on the eighth day, later known as *Shmini 'aṣeret*. Work is prohibited on the first day and on the gathering on the eighth.

Numbers 29, also P, details the sacrifices for each day of the festival. The first day requires thirteen bulls, two rams and fourteen lambs, and on each succeeding day the number of bulls is reduced by one. The sacrifices for the eighth day, one bull, one ram and seven lambs, deviate from the pattern. Since the eighth day is not mentioned in earlier legislation or, as we shall see, in earlier narrative sources, it apparently comprises a later development. The precise nature of the gathering and its relationship to Sukkot are unclear.[8]

H, which postdates P,[9] is the latest of the major Pentateuchal sources. H emphasizes the holiness of the land, as opposed to P which limits holiness to the sanctuary and cult. For H God dwells in the land as well as in the temple, which gives non-priests and those not immediately connected to the temple the privilege and responsibility for maintaining its sanctity. H adds several new components to the directives for Sukkot:

> (39) Mark, on the fifteenth day of the seventh month, when you have gathered in the yield of your land, you shall observe the festival of YHWH [to last] seven days; a complete rest on the first day, and a complete rest on the eighth day. (40) On the first day you shall take the product of *hadar* trees, branches of palm trees,

---

[8]Licht, *Sukkot*, 178 discusses *Shmini 'aṣeret* but neglects to make any suggestions as to its purpose. Knohl, *Priestly*, 94-98 advances a creative and ingenious argument. He proposes that the *'aṣeret* should be connected to agricultural concerns, as are the gatherings of 2 Kgs 10:19-20, Isa 1:13 and Joel 1:14, 2:15. The sacrifices prescribed in Num 29:36 for the *'aṣeret*, one bull, one ram, and seven lambs, are identical to those prescribed for the first and tenth of the seventh month, the *yom teru'ah* and *yom kippurim* (Num 29:2,8). This suggests that there is a thematic connection between the days. Now *'aṣeret* appears together with "fast" and "trumpet" in Joel 2:15: "Blow a trumpet in Zion, solemnize a fast, proclaim an assembly (*'aṣeret*)." The context is the attempt to arouse God's mercy and compassion, and blessings of rain and fertility are mentioned as well (2:21-27). Knohl concludes that the eighth day gathering was a type of ritual assembly akin to a fast, the purpose of which was to arouse the mercy of God for the people. At this season the people prayed that God have compassion in granting them bountiful rain for the coming year. However, no horn is prescribed for the eighth day, nor a fast ordained. The sacrifice analogy is interesting but inconclusive. Weinfeld, *Institutions*, 119 also considers *Shmini 'aṣeret* a rain festival based on Hittite parallels. Both Weinfeld and Knohl cite TY to Lev 23:36, "gather to pray before God for rain," but the targum obviously reflects rabbinic ideas.

[9]Knohl dates P to the early eighth century. He suggests the Holiness School began to develop during this time, and continued throughout the exilic period and into the second temple period. See *The Conception of God and Cult in the Priestly Torah and the Holiness School* (Dissertation: Hebrew University, 1988) (Hebrew). Milgrom, *Leviticus*, 27-28 claims H was redacted during the exile. He dates P to "not later than the middle of the eighth century (ca. 750 BCE)."

boughs of leafy trees, and willows of the brook, and you shall rejoice before YHWH your God seven days. (41) You shall observe it as a festival of YHWH for seven days in the year; you shall observe it in the seventh month as a law for all time, throughout the ages. (42) You shall live in booths seven days; all citizens in Israel shall live in booths, (43) in order that future generations may know that I made the Israelite people live in booths when I brought them out of the land of Egypt, I the Lord your God.

Like D and JE, H employs the title "the festival of the Lord," and refers to the ingathering. Like P it assigns the date to the fifteenth of the seventh month and prescribes complete rest for the first and eighth day. The ritual described in v. 40, known as the lulav and *etrog* (citron) in rabbinic literature, first appears here. Scholars still debate the meaning of the first species, rendered here in the translation of the Jewish Publication Society as "the product of *hadar* trees." The phrase is typically understood as "fruit of goodly trees," later specified as the citron by the rabbis. The JPS translation, on the other hand, reflects proposals that the clause refers in a general way to tree *products*, not necessarily fruit, probably intending to include all types of foliage.[10] Processions with branches characterize agricultural festivals, so the ritual is most likely a fertility rite of some sort.[11] The ritual takes place "before YHWH," which might point to local cultic sanctuaries or even to the Jerusalem temple. Recall that Jgs 21 places the annual celebration at Shiloh, an early Israelite shrine.

H commands that all Israelites reside in booths for seven days. D and P used the title "the festival of booths" but did not shed any light on the function of the booths. Nor did these sources explicitly command the Israelites to reside in the booths. This suggests the festival originally took its title from a common practice, not a religious obligation. The booths served a utilitarian function, whether providing shelter for peasants during the labors of the harvest and ingathering, or for pilgrims during their sojourns at cultic shrines. But if most peasants and pilgrims occupied booths as temporary shelters, some would have sufficed without. Those who lived close enough to the fields or cult centers would lodge at their houses. That is, the title "festival of booths" had a

---

[10]On this vexing question see A.B. Ehrlich, *Randglossen zur hebräischen Bibel* (Hildesheim: G. Olms, 1968 [1908-14]), 2:84; R. Kittel, *Geschichte des Volkes Israel* (Stuttgart: W. Kohlhammer, 1923-29), 3:593; Y. Avishur, "Peri ʿeṣ hadar," *Beit Mikra* 34 (1989), 138-39; H. Ginsburg, "Lemilon leshon hamiqraʾ," *Hanokh Yalon Jubilee Volume*, ed. S. Lieberman et al. (Jerusalem, 1963), 167-172; S. Tolkowsky, "The Meaning of 'Peri ʿeiṣ Hadar' (Lev. 23:40)," *JPOS* 8 (1928), 17-23; idem, *Hadar*, 13-68; Issac, *Citrus* and Chapter 5,II. Some Samaritans interpreted the verse as an instruction to bring the fruit of any beautiful tree. See S. Hanover, *Das Festgesetz der Samaritaner nach Ibrahim ibn Jakub* (Berlin, 1904), 50.

[11]W. Mannhardt, *Antike Wald und Feldkulte* (Berlin, 1877). See below, p. 29.

descriptive, rather than prescriptive, sense in earlier sources. H transforms what had been an aspect of the festival into a religious obligation. Booths no longer serve a utilitarian function, but constitute a central ritual of the festival.[12]

H also appends an historical explanation. The festival booths commemorate the booths in which the Israelites dwelled during the desert sojourn.[13] The ritual reenacts an experience from the times of the ancestors. This historical explanation is somewhat strange in that the Pentateuchal narratives of the exodus trek never place the Israelites in booths. Suddenly H refers to an historical event unknown to the rest of the Bible. This anomaly, we shall see, directed the rabbis to a particular understanding of this verse and of the symbolism of the sukka.

Recently Israel Knohl analyzed the approach to the festivals of the Holiness School.[14] He shows that while H postdates P, it regularly incorporates primitive agricultural rituals of popular religion. Both the festal bouquet and the commandment to dwell in booths represent attempts to institutionalize popular festival rituals of ancient Israelite provenance. The Holiness School evidently aspired to preserve rituals that became less common with increasing urbanization, population growth, and division of labor, and to give these rituals divine charter. Their historical explanation for the building of booths provided a theological grounding for every Israelite to reside in booths, not simply the peasants or pilgrims who actually needed them.

Ezekiel 45:25 prescribes sacrifices for the seven days of "the Festival." The seven bulls, seven rams and one goat required for each day differ somewhat from the list in Numbers. The date is set on the fifteenth of the seventh month. No "eighth day" gathering is mentioned.

II. Narrative Traditions

Narrative biblical passages that mention Sukkot complement the legal passages and present an additional cultic dimension. In 1 Kgs 8 (=2 Chr 5:2-7:10) Solomon dedicates his temple at "the Festival" in the seventh month.[15] This title echoes the name "the Festival of YHWH" in

---

[12]See Knohl, *Priestly*, 97; Auerbach, *Feste*, 12 n. 2. Milgrom, *Leviticus*, 27-28 suggests the commandment to dwell in booths demonstrates that H was composed during the exile. "Thus this H tradent effectively resuscitates the Sukkot festival for his fellow exiles and, subsequently, for Jews everywhere." So Ehrlich, *Kultsymbolik*, 54 n. 138.

[13]Only Kaufmann, *Toledot*, 1:578 considers this historical explanation an early element of the festival. All other scholars consider it late, and probably exilic.

[14]Above n. 6.

[15]1 Kgs 8:2, assuming the MT text. A. Geiger, *Hamiqra Vetargumav*, trans. Y. Baruch (Jerusalem: Bialik, 1949), 47-48 n.1, claims "the Festival" here refers to

legal sources. The date in the seventh month and the seven day celebration (1 Kgs 8:65) point to the autumnal festival. Although the dedication of the temple constitutes an independent festival – Solomon celebrated for fourteen days: seven for the festival and an additional seven specifically for the dedication (1 Kgs 8:65) – that he coordinated it with the autumnal festival indicates that this was the occasion for pilgrimages to cult sites.[16] The biblical authors imagined the scene in terms of their experiences at Sukkot celebrations. The mass gathering, copious sacrifices and extensive celebrations (1 Kgs 8:62-66) provide a glimpse of the joyous cultic festivities.[17]

The significance of the autumnal gathering emerges from the efforts of Jeroboam to prevent Israelites of the northern kingdom from making the pilgrimage to Jerusalem. Jeroboam instituted "a festival on the fifteenth day of the eighth month." In imitation of the festival in Judah, he established a parallel celebration at the northern shrine at Bethel (1 Kgs 12:32). Although Jeroboam had set up cult centers in the north (1 Kgs 12:26-31), he feared that his people would still travel to Jerusalem to celebrate the annual autumnal festival, and deemed it necessary to introduce a similar festival. The Jerusalem temple festival evidently attracted large numbers of pilgrims and presumably involved elaborate cultic rites. The date in the eighth month deviates from the seventh month designated by other sources. Either Jeroboam wished to sever any associations between his new festival and the Jerusalemite precedent

---

Solomon's dedication festival, while the words "in the seventh month" are a gloss based on 2 Chr 5:3, and do not appear in the LXX Kings. While some scholars agree the words "the seventh month" in v. 2 are a gloss, they nonetheless take "the Festival" to refer to Sukkot. See e.g. Martin Noth, *Könige* (BKAT IX/1; Neukirchen-Vluyn: Neukircher Verlag, 1983), 176; John Gray, *I and II Kings* (London: SCM Press, 1970), 206-208. For comprehensive discussion see Bernhard Stade and Friedrich Schwally, *The Book of Kings* (Baltimore: John Hopkins Press, 1904), 98-100. Similarly the words in 1 Kgs 8:65, "observed the Festival at that time before the Lord our God, seven days *and again seven days, fourteen days in all,"* may be a gloss based on 2 Chr 7:8-10; they too are lacking in the LXX. See de Vaux, *Israel*, 498-99; Stade, 109 and all major commentaries. Even so, the words "the Festival" would seem to refer to Sukkot, not the temple dedication festival, or rather the combination of the two: the autumnal festival that served to celebrate the dedication as well. So Gray, 234; Pedersen, *Israel*, 2:422. The Chronicler may have objected to Solomon using the autumnal festival to celebrate the temple dedication, and so created an independent festival.

[16]See previous note. Even if the double seven-day celebration derives from the Chronicler, the point remains. 1 Kgs 8 still places the dedication at the time of the autumnal celebration.

[17]The post-exilic retelling of the dedication in 2 Chr 7:9 adds that the gathering on the eighth day was duly observed. This additional day apparently was added to the festival after the redaction of Kings and before Chronicles.

or scribes changed the original "seventh month" to "eighth month" to emphasize the corruption of religion Jeroboam perpetrated.[18] From Jeroboam's concern we learn that the autumn temple festival attracted pilgrims from near and far, and was central to Israelite religious life.

The post-exilic passages Ezra 3, Neh 8 and Zech 14 will be treated in the following chapter.

III. General Theories

The designations "Festival of YHWH" or "the Festival" in both narrative and legal sources indicate the importance of Sukkot, and the accounts of Solomon and Jeroboam confirm that Sukkot was the primary annual pilgrimage. However, apart from the rites described in Leviticus, these passages tell us little of the content of the festival. To fill in the gap, biblical scholars have proposed general theories concerning the origin and nature of the festival. The two main theories are the "enthronement festival" and the "covenant renewal festival."

The enthronement festival *(Thronbesteigungfest)* was proposed by Sigmund Mowinckel at the beginning of this century.[19] He argued that the autumnal festival was originally a New Year festival that celebrated the "enthronement of YHWH." In the cyclical, mythic view of time, each year the forces of chaos threaten to overwhelm the order of creation.

---

[18]Mowinckel, *Psalms,* 1:119 n. 43 claims that the autumnal festival was originally celebrated in the eighth month, as do A. Cooper and B. Goldstein, "The Festivals of Israel and Judah and the Literary History of the Pentateuch," *JAOS* 110 (1990), 22-28. The convoluted calendrical shifts necessary for these reconstructions make them unlikely. See Snaith, *New Year,* 50-52; de Vaux, *Israel,* 499; Kraus, *Worship,* 55; S. Talmon, "Divergences in Calendar-Reckoning in Ephraim and Judah," *VT* 8 (1958), 54-58. Ehrlich, *Kultsymbolik,* 53 suggests that the harvest occurred one month later in the north due to climatic differences.

[19]Mowinckel, *PsSt.* A similar reconstruction was proposed independently by Paul Volz, *Das Neujahrsfest Jahwes* (Tübingen: Mohr, 1912). In his introduction Mowinckel relates how he was informed of Volz's work while still writing his opus. He refrained from reading Volz until he had finished the manuscript. In 1927 Hans Schmidt published *Die Thronfahrt Jahves am Fest der Jahreswende im alten Israel* (Tübingen: J.C.B. Mohr, 1927) and reconstructed the autumnal festival along similar lines. Like Mowinckel he focused on the festival of the first temple, whereas Volz concentrated on the celebration in second temple times. Schmidt accepted Mowinckel's general approach to the Psalms but emphasized the festal processions as the crucial cultic acts. The "Myth and Ritual" school carried these basic reconstructions to the extreme. See the three collections of essays edited by S. Hooke, *Myth and Ritual* (London: Oxford University Press, 1933); *The Labyrinth* (New York: Macmillan, 1935); and *Myth, Ritual, and Kingship* (Oxford: Clarendon Press, 1958). See too Riesenfeld, *Jésus;* Gaster, *Thespis.* For criticism of this school, see the excellent review of C. Hauret "L'interpretation des Psaumes Selon L'ecole 'Myth and Ritual'," *Revue de science religeuse* 33,34 (1959,60), 321-42; 1-34.

God and the powers of good struggle anew against this onslaught. The cult dramatizes the annual battle, which culminates with the victory of God and his (re-)coronation as king. Support for this theory derives from form-critical study of Psalms and other biblical passages identified as the liturgy that accompanied the festival rituals.[20] The evidence, then, is implicit, deriving from biblical passages that do not explicitly mention Sukkot, but that are connected to the festival on other grounds. Mowinckel marshaled some further support from parallel festivals in Babylonian religion.

The heart of the reconstructed festival involved a procession with the ark of the covenant to dramatize the enthronement of YHWH, in which the Israelite king, the representative of YHWH on earth, played the leading role.[21] Worshippers acclaimed YHWH as king and celebrated the initiation of his reign. Other rites included the sounding of trumpets and the shofar signaling the coronation, a torch and light festival connected to the creation of the world and the autumnal equinox, repentance and purification before the advent of YHWH, reconsecration of the temple, libations, feasting, dancing and sacrifices. The enthronement assured the re-invigoration of the natural world, hence the festival included elements of agricultural and harvest celebrations. Fertility rites such as water libations and processions with willows sought to ensure copious rainfall and the blessings of YHWH in the subsequent harvest season. At this time YHWH sealed the fates for the coming year. In addition, the festival gave expression to fundamental beliefs of the Israelites: the revelation and theophany, salvation of Israel, the exodus, renewal of the covenant, and the inviolability of Jerusalem. Rituals and beliefs that eventually coalesced into three independent observances on the first, tenth and fifteenth of Tishrei, later known as Rosh Hashana, Yom Kippur and Sukkot, all took place during this festival.[22] The original Israelite autumnal festival, the ancient Sukkot festival, embodied this panoply of myth and ritual.

The Babylonian New Year festival, the Akitu festival, served as a model for the reconstruction.[23] Observed from the first through eleventh

---

[20]Whereas Volz (see previous note) employed no overarching method, but based his claims on brilliant and imaginative interpretations of biblical verses, rabbinic sources and occasional forays into comparative religion, Mowinckel argued from his "form-critical" or "cult-functional" approach to Psalms, which built on Herman Gunkel's form critical method. See Mowinckel, *Psalms*, 1:5-41.

[21]*PsSt*, 127-9; *Psalms*, 1:125.

[22]*PsSt*, 83-89; Volz, *Neujahrsfest*, 24-25.

[23]On the Akitu festival, see S. Pallis, *The Babylonian Akitu Festival* (Copenhagen, 1926); H. Zimmern, *Zum Babylonischen Neujahrsfest*^{2} (Leipzig: B.G. Teubner, 1918); H. Tadmor, "The New Year in Mesopotamia," *'Ensiqlopedia Miqra'it* (Jerusalem:

of Nisan, the Akitu celebrated the annual enthronement of the god Marduk. Priests read the Babylonian creation story detailing the triumph of Marduk over the primordial gods and his acclamation as king. Statues of other gods were brought to Babylon to pay homage to Marduk. A procession of the statue of Marduk along the "sacred way," accompanied by great rejoicing and the cry "Marduk is king," to a temple known as the "Akitu-house" outside of the city dramatized the enthronement.[24] Additional rites of confession and a ritual humiliation of the king took place, for at this time Marduk determined the destinies of gods and men for the coming year. The enthronement festival was thus an Israelite version of the Babylonian Akitu festival. Where the Babylonians acclaimed Marduk as king the Israelites championed YHWH. Hence the phrase ""YHWH has become King," of Psalms and the appellation "festival of YHWH" for Sukkot.[25]

Bialik, 1976), 7:305-11 (Hebrew) and the bibliography there; Pedersen, *Israel*, 2:747-50 with bibliography. See also Levenson, *Creation*, 70-72. The Akitu was celebrated variously in spring or autumn.

[24]The next day the statue was returned. Exactly what took place in the Akituhouse is not known. Scholars conjecture a ritual combat dramatized the battle between Marduk and Tiamat. Some suggest priests acted out the death and rebirth of Marduk. Others claim a *hieros gamos* of Marduk and Zarpanitum his consort was dramatized, either physically by the king and high priestess or symbolically; so Pallis, ibid., 226-41; contra: Tadmor, ibid., 309.

[25]Pss 47 (*'elohim malakh*), 93, 96, 97, 99. Parallels to Israelite myth and ritual are evident. Recitation of the Babylonian creation story (*enuma elish*) recalls the allusions to creation and foundation myths in the Psalms; the fixing of destinies recalls Rosh Hashana as the Day of Judgment; the king's atonement and confession ceremony parallels that of the high priest on Yom Kippur; the procession and enthronement of Marduk correspond to the procession with the ark and enthronement of YHWH; the cry "Marduk is king" parallels "YHWH is king." Mowinckel never explained the precise relationship between the Akitu and enthronement festival. He generally avoided the claim that Mesopotamian religion actually had influenced Israelite worship. He seems to have believed, rather, that a common cultic tradition existed in both places, hence the nature of the Babylonian celebration had implications for the Israelite. See, however, *Psalms* 1:125: "the rich temple cult in Jerusalem, *highly influenced* as it was from Canaan..." and 1:136, "We may, then, conclude that both ancient Canaanite and Babylonian-Assyrian ideas and customs have contributed elements to the Israelite harvest, new year, and enthronement festival." But he proceeds to say: "In Israel, however, the old, originally Canaanite festival has become something entirely new and *sui generis*." Volz actually adduces Babylonian parallels less frequently than Mowinckel, but one senses that the Akitu festival served as his general model and inspiration. His first sentence reads: "The Israelite-Jewish people reached the climax of their cultic and national life in the pilgrimage feasts, such as the Babylonians held when they went up to the city of their god in honour of their principal deity Marduk, and the Greeks when the state and nation assembled for Panegyric festivals." (Translation from the citation in Kraus,

This reconstruction emphasizes the temple cult as the context of the festival. Cultic worship preserves the world order instituted at creation and perpetuates the blessings of rain, sun, crops, fertility, health, strength and everything good. Life is a perpetual struggle between the forces of good and evil, and only the cult assures the continuation of the world. What happens in the cult really happens, so to dramatize creation is simultaneously to effect it. By rehearsing foundation events and the enthronement, the cult secured the continuation of good fortune under the dominion of YHWH. At Sukkot cultic worship reached its acme.[26]

The second theory emerged from the school of form-criticism that gave primacy to legal traditions and sought to reconstruct ancient Israelite institutions on that basis. These scholars find the origin of Sukkot in the ancient Israelite covenant-renewal celebration.[27] The context is likewise the cult, but the radically different understanding of the Israelite cult produced a distinct reconstruction of the festival. Antedating the establishment of temples and sanctuaries in Israel, the cult reached back into the ancient desert period. In the cult the Israelites reenacted the historical events of the exodus, the covenant at Sinai and the conquest. The *haqhel* ritual (Deut 31:10-13) provided the paradigm for this covenant-renewal ceremony. Now *haqhel* took place during the festival of Sukkot, so these scholars concluded that the covenant-renewal ceremony originally took place at this point. At this ceremony the Israelites renewed their tribal compact and religious institutions under the rule of their God and thereby became "a holy people."

The agricultural rituals that characterize Sukkot in Pentateuchal legislation represent the second stage of the festival's development. In the nomadic period the Israelites dwelled in tents at the tribal

---

Worship, 7.) The "Myth and Ritual School" explicitly modeled their reconstructions after Babylonian precedents.

[26]There appears to be as yet no *communis opinio* with respect to Mowinckel's enthronement festival. For general criticism see Snaith, *New Year;* Kaufmann, *Toledot,* 1:580-85; Kraus, *Worship,* 16-19; N. Sarna's introduction to M. Buttenweiser, *The Psalms* (New York: Ktav, 1969 [1938]), xxvii-xxix; M.Z. Brettler, *God is King* (JSOT 76; Sheffield: Sheffield Academic Press, 1989), 157-58. P. Welten, "Königsherrschaft Jahwes und Thronbesteigung," *VT* 32 (1982), 297-310 reviews and questions the evidence adduced from Babylonian and Assyrian sources. Levenson, *Creation,* 166 n. 23 ("one need not accept the whole myth-and-ritual scenario in order to see a large element of truth in it") and H.H. Rowley, *Worship in Ancient Israel: Its Forms and Meaning* (London, 1967), 190 accept the festival, albeit with reservations. The issue has become marginalized rather than settled, since literary approaches now dominate the study of the Psalms.

[27]Alt, *Essays,* 123-71; Noth, *Traditions,* 59-62; Beyerlin, *Origins;* G. von Rad, *The Problem of the Hexateuch and Other Essays,* trans. E.W.T. Dicken (New York: McGraw-Hill, 1966), 35-39. See Cross, *Canaanite,* 79-90 and 79 n. 3 for bibliography and further references.

gatherings.²⁸ After the settlement they adopted the agricultural lifestyle and festival calendar of their Canaanite neighbors. Pilgrims to the annual covenant-renewal festivals dwelled in the now familiar booths of the agricultural culture.²⁹ Such customs reflect the later, sedentary lifestyle and relate but tangentially to the origin and inherent nature of the festival.

Both theories consider the ancient autumnal festival to be a cultic festival at heart. Different conceptions of the early cult lead to mutually exclusive reconstructions of the festival. The question of the origins of Sukkot therefore becomes inextricably intertwined with larger questions of the nature and origin of the ancient Israelite cult. Yet the theories tend to converge as we move away from origins to the festival as practiced in the middle and end of the first temple period. Proponents of the covenant-renewal hypothesis concede that in the later monarchy, with the growth of temples, centralization, and the increasing importance of the king, the covenant-renewal festival evolved into a royal-temple festival along the lines of the enthronement festival.³⁰ While neither

---

²⁸See Beyerlin, *Origins*, 120-22. A. Alt, "Zelte und Hütte," *Kleine Schriften* (Munich: C.H. Beck, 1959), 3:233-42, however, suggested that Israelite warriors stayed in sukkot during military campaigns (cf. 2 Sam 11:11) and occupied the same sukkot at the covenant renewal ceremony: "Heergemeinde und Kultgemeinde waren ja in Alt-Israel grundsätzlich identisich" (p. 241).

²⁹This process, it seem to me, is discussed superficially and not explained satisfactorily. See Alt, ibid., 3:241-42; Kraus, *Worship*, 64, 131-34; Beyerlin, *Origins*, 121. Beyerlin, 158 cursorily notes the "attempts of the cult to absorb and master Canaanite practice in the matter of festivals and sacrifices" when the Israelites made the transition to an agricultural life style. M. Noth, *Leviticus*, trans. J.E. Andersen (Philadelphia: Westminster Press, 1965), 176 acknowledges that the custom of booths "goes back to the original natural situation of the feast, with its dwelling in 'booths' in the midst of the orchards and vineyards at the time of fruit- and grape-harvest." In *A History of Pentateuchal Traditions*, trans. B. Anderson (Englewood Cliffs, N.J.: Prentice-Hall, 1972 [1948]), 60, Noth states that the covenant-renewal ceremony "was somehow combined with the old Canaanite feast of tabernacles which was celebrated about the same time and belonged to the ancient Canaanite agricultural tradition." How? See too his confused account in *The History of Israel*, trans. S. Goodman (New York: Harper & Brothers, 1958), 97-99.

³⁰G. von Rad, *The Problem of the Hexateuch and Other Essays*, trans. E.W.T. Dicken (New York: McGraw-Hill, 1966), 39-43; idem, "The Origin of the Concept of the Day of Yahweh," *JSS* 4 (1959), 103-108. For an alternative reconstruction of an enthronement-type autumnal festival, see Kraus, *Worship*, 209-222 and his important monograph, *Gottesdienst in Israel: Studien zur Geschichte des Laubhüttenfestes* (Munich: Chr. Kaiser, 1954). Kraus refuses to accept Babylonian parallels or information from later rabbinic sources, and insists one must stick "consistently to what the passages really say" (*Worship*, p. 209). His autumnal festival included a procession of the ark to the temple mount, retelling of the election of David and Zion, delivery of an oracle of YHWH by a cult prophet,

theory completely ignores the agricultural aspect of the festival, neither sees the harvest as the essence of the celebration.[31] Thanksgiving for the harvest, prayers for the upcoming year and fertility rites become minor components of a larger New Year or covenant-renewal festival. Throughout the first temple period, the autumnal festival, which came to be known as Sukkot, was a cult festival of tremendous importance.

IV. Origins of the Sukka and Lulav

Whatever the merit of these reconstructions of Sukkot, the Bible prescribes but two rituals besides the obligatory sacrifices: the taking of the 'four species' of Lev 23:40, later known as the lulav, and the sukka. Thus canonized in scripture, these two rituals received particular attention in post-exilic interpretations of Sukkot. Ironically, although they probably did not constitute the essence of the first temple celebrations, by virtue of their memorialization in scripture, their importance increased in the second temple and rabbinic constructions of Sukkot. The origins of the sukka and the lulav deserve special comment.

The sukka, we noted, probably derives from the booths commonly built in the fields and vineyards for protection from the elements.[32] Peasants used the booths throughout the harvest and gathering season, so the festival was named for them. But what was the precise function of the booths and how exactly did they relate to the festival?[33] At this point consensus breaks down. Some scholars suggest that the entire family slept out in the fields during the harvest, taking shelter in crude booths or huts.[34] Fields were located at some distance from the village, so to

---

procession to the sanctuary with singing of psalms and blasts of the shofar, and finally "the mighty official proclamation of the sacred cultic name of Yahweh," at which point the pilgrim performed an "act of adoration." All in all, an enthronement festival with a more pronounced Israelite stamp. For full discussion see Rubenstein, *Dissertation*, 56-61. The "Myth and Ritual" school, on the other hand, went in the opposite direction and played up the Babylonian and Near East influences on the Israelite festivals. Their reconstructions of the festival, however, are speculative and unconvincing. See the collections of essays edited by Hooke and the critical review of Hauret, above n. 19.

[31] For the covenant-renewal approach, agricultural elements entered after the settlement of Canaan and the assumption of a sedentary life-style.

[32] Isa 1:8, 4:6; Jon 4:5; Job 27:18; Matt 21:33. See Dalman's observations cited below.

[33] Some scholars address this question in the vaguest of terms. Thus Pedersen, *Israel*, 2:421: "The use of booths doubtless belonged to the early Canaanite feast and to that part of it which took place in the vineyards." Cf. M. Noth, *Leviticus* (Philadelphia: Westminster Press, 1965), 176.

[34] Driver, *Deuteronomy*, 197.

return home each night during the gathering season was impractical.[35] Others propose that the temporary shelters were set up to house migrant grape-gatherers hired especially for the harvest.[36] For others sukkot were found in olive groves and used by watchmen to guard the olive harvest.[37] It is also possible the booths were used to protect the produce of the harvest, and not as shelters for peasants or watchmen.[38]

One potential problem with these explanations is that they relate to the harvest. But if the harvest was completed before the celebration commenced, why remain in the shelters for additional days? Moreover, some scholars claim that the "ingathering" is not the harvest or vintage, but the ingathering from the winepress and threshing floor.[39] They question the relevance of booths to this process and find the origin of the custom elsewhere.[40] Yet Gustaf Dalman, who traveled through Palestine in the early nineteenth century, observed that Arab peasants slept over in arbors in vineyards from August until October to guard the harvested fruit. He inferred that the biblical "festival of ingathering" marked the conclusion of this period; after the completion of the harvest a thanksgiving celebration took place in the sukkot before the peasants returned home to store the produce away.[41] Similarly MacRae suggests that a "joyous thanksgiving celebration would begin on the spot and the huts might serve as a cultic symbol of the celebration itself."[42] This phenomenon is known from other harvest celebrations where festivities begin at the scene of the harvest in booths or temporary shelters.[43] In this

---

[35]MacRae, *Tabernacles*, 255. So J. Morgenstern, "The Festival of Jerobeam I," *JBL* 83 (1964), 112.
[36]Thackeray, *Septuagint*, 61.
[37]Auerbach, *Feste*, 11. Auerbach apparently believes the sukkot were not used during the grape harvest or the gathering from the threshing floor. He believes that these took place at the end of August, whereas the olive harvest occurred somewhat later. See Dalman, *AuS*, 4:190-91.
[38]H. Cazelles, *Études sur le Code de L'Alliance* (Paris, 1946), 99.
[39]See n. 2 and text thereto.
[40]Tur-Sinai, *Halashon*, 3:81; Licht, *Sukkot*, 175. See below.
[41]Dalman, *AuS*, 1:161-64; 4:337. Deut 16:13, however, speaks of ingathering from the winepress and threshing floor (not from the fields), but the dates (at least of P) cohere.
[42]MacRae, *Tabernacles*, 255. Weinfeld, *Deuteronomy*, 218 suggests the booths were set up in vineyards where festal dances took place. Cf. Jgs 21:19-22.
[43]J. Harrison, *Prolegomena to the Study of Greek Religion*[3] (Cambridge: Cambridge University Press, 1922), 146, describes the sports conducted on the threshing floors during the Greek Haloa festival: "The sports held were, of course, incidental to the business of threshing; but it was these sports that constituted the actual festival. To this day the great round threshing-floor that is found in most Greek villages is the scene of the harvest festival. Near it a booth (*skéné*) is to this day erected, and in it the performers rest, and eat and drink in the intervals of

way the booths played a role in the festival even though the harvest had been completed. Part of this confusion results from the fact that the commandment to reside in booths appears only in H, which, we noted, regularly introduces popular customs into the festival legislation.[44] The title "festival of booths" of D and P may simply indicate that the festival followed the period of gathering during which booths were used in one of the capacities mentioned, but need not imply that the booths served a ritual function during the actual celebration. H subsequently legislated that the booths be occupied for a seven day postharvest festival in an effort to restore popular agricultural practices.[45]

A second theory claims the festival sukka originated as the temporary shelters erected by pilgrims for their sojourn during pilgrimages to central sanctuaries. Demand for accommodation outstripped supply and necessitated that sleeping quarters be improvised.[46] We noted that the covenant-renewal theory espouses a version of this model.[47] On Sukkot, at the original covenant-renewal ceremony, the Israelites erected their tents around the sacred tent of the central sanctuary, and over the course of time the tents became booths. The main objection to this etiology is the fact that Sukkot was not the only pilgrimage festival. If booths were the customary shelters of pilgrims why did the autumnal pilgrimage, and not Pesaḥ or Shavuot, acquire this title and ritual?[48] Moreover pilgrims probably stayed in tents; booths are always associated with fields and vineyards.[49]

---

their pantomimic dancing." See also Nilsson, *Geschichte*, 1:779-780. E. Robinson, *Biblical Researches in Palestine* (Boston, Crocker and Brewster, 1856), 2:81 reports the same of Palestine in 1838: "The vintage is a season of hilarity and rejoicing to all; the town is then deserted, and the people live among the vineyards in the lodges and in tents." See, however, Wensinck, *New Year*, 27-28 who questions the force of Robinson's report.

[44]Knohl, *Priestly*, 65-105, especially 94-98.
[45]Knohl, *Priestly*, 97 and n. 103; cf. Auerbach, *Feste*, 11-14.
[46]Ehrlich, *Hamiqra*, 1:237-38 (to Lev 23:43); Licht, *Sukkot*, 175; Knohl, *Priestly*, 94; H.L. Ginsberg, *The Israelian Heritage of Judaism* (New York: Jewish Theological Seminary, 1982), 60. See too Volz, *Neujahrsfest*, 20-21. Ehrlich suggests that the command to reside in sukkot outside of Jerusalem only emerged when the people ceased to make the pilgrimage to Jerusalem because of overcrowding and the difficulty of constructing sukkot. Disturbed that many would no longer celebrate the festival, the prophets instructed that sukkot should be erected in rural dwelling places as well.
[47]Beyerlin, *Origins*, 123; Kraus, *Worship*, 63-64 (see above, p. 26); See too Volz, *Neujahrsfest*, 20 and W. Eichordt, *Theology of the Old Testament*, trans. J. Baker (London: SCM Press, 1961), 1:122.
[48]Knohl, *Priestly*, 95 and Licht, *Sukkot*, 175 argue that the autumnal festival entailed a lengthy sojourn of seven days and therefore the booths were associated

Proponents of the enthronement festival generally understand the ritual dwelling in the sukka as the imitation of a cultic ritual. The Israelites entered tents or booths to imitate God revealing himself in a tent as dramatized during the New Year festival.[50] Others argue the booths represent the bridal chamber of the purported sacred marriage.[51]

---

with it. Ehrlich, *Hamiqra*, 1:237 explains that the autumnal pilgrimage was the most important.

[49] See above, p. 25 and n. 32. However, Licht, *Sukkot*, 175 cites parallels from Greek festivals where pilgrims dwelled in booths, not tents.

[50] Volz, *Neujahrsfest*, 21-22: "Weil die Gottheit im Zelt erscheint, wohnen an ihrem Erscheinungstag auch die Kultgenossen in Zelt bezw. in Zweighuetten."

[51] Hooke, *Myth*, 12; Oesterley, *Rituals*, 139-40; C.J. Gadd, "Babylonian Myth and Ritual," 56 in Hooke, *Myth*. Thackeray, *Septuagint*, 69 comments to Ps 76:3, "His tabernacle (*sukko*) is in Salem" that the verse "happily recalls the thought which could not fail to occur to every pilgrim at the Feast of Booths. Jahweh himself is present with his worshippers, Himself observing the festival in the immemorial fashion; He, too, has His *Sukkah* in the Holy City." Riesenfeld, *Jesus*, 148-64 subscribes to a similar explanation, that the rite took place in YHWH's special sukka, and through a process of "democratization" the entire people took to residing in booths; cf. Pedersen, *Israel*, 2:741-42. It is strange that Mowinckel wrote less about the sukka than the other festival rites. He suggests: "the people lived in tabernacles is not only a survival from the stay in the vineyard during the grape gathering, but is connected with the May-branches, the well-known restorative of fertility in nearly all parts of the earth." Thus the sukka originated in the harvest setting but functions as a fertility charm; so *Psalms*, 1:187. In *PsSt*, 103 n. 1, however, he claims that the sukka was one of the latest elements of the festival, and developed from the branches carried in festivities (the lulav). It was originally a Jerusalemite urban practice made orthodox by Deuteronomic legislation. E.G. Kraeling, "The Real Religion of Ancient Israel," *JBL* 47 (1928), 150 argues that camping in sukkot was thought to effect a magical renewal of vegetation.

Less plausible theories of the origin of the sukka are included here simply for the sake of completeness. Tur-Sinai, *Halashon*, 3:84, considers the sukka the symbolic equivalent of the Cherubim above the ark. Both represent the *sukkat he'anan*, the cloud-canopy in which God rides through the heavens, and in which guise God preceded the camp in the desert (the pillar of cloud.) Lev 23:43 commands the Israelites to live in sukkot as an imitation of this guiding cloud. The Israelites entered *sukkot* in autumn, at the beginning of the rainy season, in order to arouse God to enter his cloud in heaven and send forth rain. Patai, *Hamayim*, 51 also considers sukkot as symbols of celestial clouds. So Grunwald, *Sukkothrituals*, 435. Wensinck, *New Year*, 33-41 and L.I. Pap, *Das Israelitische Neujahrsfest* (Kampen, 1933), 40-41 believe the Israelites considered their houses taboo or subject to demons at certain times. Cf. Riesenfeld, *Jesus*, 177. They were forced to set up sukkot as temporary quarters during these periods. J.B. Segal, *The Hebrew Passover* (London: Oxford University Press, 1963), 151-52 posits a ritual exodus during which the people left the cities to seek powers of vegetation in the desert, "just as the goddess of the myth, in its varied forms, went out with her faithful companion to seek the dead god and restore him to life." Segal concedes that the Bible contains no trace of this myth. He adds that the ritual exodus may be better

The Origins and Ancient History of Sukkot

Even if these last theories are discounted there is no consensus as to the provenance of the sukka. Two mutually exclusive approaches can be discerned. According to one the sukka derives from rural vineyards and fields and only later became a fixture at central sanctuaries. According to the second the sukka originated as a shelter for pilgrims at central sanctuaries and only later became a festival obligation practiced throughout the land. My sense is that the agricultural origin is more plausible. Biblical passages set sukkot in vineyards and fields, and do not suggest pilgrims resided in sukkot until Ezra-Nehemiah. Ezra's community builds sukkot in Jerusalem in order to comply with what they found written in the law, an allusion to Lev 23:42. That passage, we have seen, is part of H's attempt to reintroduce popular rituals. The sukka undoubtedly was an ancient practice, but the obligation to dwell in sukkot for a seven day festival is H's innovation. The restoration community observed that commandment, and thereafter sukkot became the practice in Jerusalem as well.

The consensus of scholarship views the four species mentioned in Lev 23:40 as some sort of ancient fertility rite.[52] The custom is only mentioned in H but its "primitive" character points to an ancient practice. How the fertility charm worked receives various answers. According to some, the palm was the "tree of life" throughout the Near East. Willows grow near water and symbolize moisture.[53] "Boughs of leafy trees" and fruit symbolize general growth and fertility. Taken together the bundle symbolized life, vegetation, fertility and moisture, and functioned as a magic charm to stimulate the growth of crops.[54] For others, the green branches and fruit express the power of fertility and hence the power of God. By touching the lulav this power of life is transferred to human beings. Processions with these boughs spread the power over the temple, city and country.[55] The lulav expresses the "life-

---

explained as an attempt to hasten the rains by a magical process or by the feeling that "it was right to leave the artificial luxuries of the city for the simple existence of the desert." So Pedersen, *Israel*, 2:421: "...men leave their customary habitations and become at one with nature together with which they are to be sanctified through the feast."

[52] The verse mentions *kapot temarim*, "branches of palm." The rabbis interpreted the phrase to refer to the *lulav*, the immature palm frond, the stage before the leaves unfold. As *pars pro toto*, "lulav" also refers to the four species in rabbinic sources.

[53] Scholars debate the identification of the *'arava* of Lev 23:40. See Chapter 5,II n. 33.

[54] Oesterley, *Rituals*, 140-46; Volz, *Neujahrsfest*, 34. Oesterley also suggests the etrog symbolized fertility, but here he has retrojected a later practice to biblical times. See too Grunwald, *Sukkothrituals*, 441-48.

[55] Mowinckel, *PsSt*, 104.

force" (*Lebenskraft*) through its healthy, green color and ability to grow quickly.[56] In part, the lulav was a means of "identifying the worshipper with the trees, or getting for him the numen inhering in trees."[57] Still others adopts the rabbinic explanation that the four species were a rain charm.[58] Palms grow at desert oases and beside streams and ponds on the plains and in the valleys.[59] "Willows of the brook" obviously recalls the rivers and streams where they grow.[60] The cluster thus symbolizes plants, water and rain.

This dispute about ancient origins should not obscure the scholarly consensus that throughout the first temple period the autumnal festival was the paramount Israelite celebration. The rise of the monarchy and the establishment of royal temples placed the king and the cult at the center of national religious life. On Sukkot, as the festival came to be called toward the end of this period, the nation directed its energy to the temple celebrations.

This connection to the temple and monarchy, however, works both ways. As long as these institutions flourished, Sukkot was the primary pilgrimage festival celebrated with magnificence and pomp. But as these institutions decayed, the festival inevitably suffered. The general deterioration by the end of this period and the collapse of the monarchy seriously disrupted the celebration of the festival. The Babylonian conquest together with the destruction of the temple in 587 BCE and the deportation of the nobility and leading priests essentially brought Sukkot to an end. Neither temple, nor cult, nor priesthood functioned in the ensuing half-century. Actually the break was even longer: although Cyrus allowed the exiles to return in 538 BCE and gave permission to rebuild the temple, resumption of structured religious life took much longer. How would the festival be celebrated in the second temple period?

---

[56]Volz, *Neujahrsfest*, 34.
[57]Goodenough, *Symhols*, 4:149.
[58]Patai, *Hamayim*, 55; so Ehrlich, *Kultsymbolik*, 55-56 and A. Schaffer, "The Agricultural and Ecological Symbolism of the Four Species of Sukkot," *Tradition* 20 (1982), 128-40 (although phrased in terms of prayer and petition, not charm and magic.) Cf. bTa 2b. Grunwald, *Sukkothrituals*, 435 suggests the lulav was shaken in order to produce rainstorms which shake the branches of trees.
[59]Zohary, *Plants*, 60.
[60]"Willow are rather common along the banks of permanent streams and near fresh-water springs, in the coastal plain, on the mountains, and in the upper Jordan Valley"; Zohary, *Plants*, 131.

2

The Second Temple Period

While the ancient history of Sukkot and its celebration in first temple times remains obscure, the nature of the festival in the second temple period stands in sharper relief. The Bible is no longer our exclusive source: different texts spanning the centuries of the second temple period describe aspects of Sukkot celebrations. Besides the late biblical books of Ezra-Nehemiah and Deutero-Zechariah, the Books of Jubilees and Maccabees, the philosopher Philo, the historian Josephus and other sources provide important information. Rabbinic literature preserves additional descriptions of the celebration of Sukkot in temple times. The variety of perspectives offered by such diverse sources yields a more balanced and controlled study. Because we are not dependent exclusively on one author or one type of source, there is less chance that a particular bias skews the picture of the festival in any way. The nature of Sukkot in the second temple period is important for it provides the point of departure for assessing the question of change or continuity in rabbinic religion. The first generations of rabbis recalled the second temple Sukkot festival, either from personal experience or oral tradition, and had to decide what they would retain after the destruction. This chapter analyzes non-rabbinic sources while the following chapter addresses rabbinic traditions concerning second temple rites. We start with Ezra-Nehemiah and Zechariah 14, and continue chronologically through the sources.

I. Ezra-Nehemiah

The Jewish community that received permission from Cyrus to rebuild the temple in 538 BCE faced the challenge of restructuring temple worship after a period of radical discontinuity. The Babylonian conquerors already began to deport the elite in 597 BCE, and leading priestly families were certainly included.[1] Religious life was undoubtedly seriously disrupted during these times. Fifty years passed from the destruction of the first temple in 587 BCE until the beginning of the resettlement, and the resumption of organized worship would require still more time. Even after the completion of the temple some time would pass before the institutionalization of worship took root. Given these disruptions, as well as changed social, cultural and political conditions, the form of the renewed cult was very much an open question. Nothing guaranteed that the reconstituted mode of worship would resemble its first temple antecedent.[2] The nature of the temple service in general, and the observance of the festivals in particular, was liable to change. However, several factors exerted a "conserving" influence: the community possessed the Pentateuchal legislation which prescribed sacrificial protocol and various rituals;[3] oral traditions provided some direction as to how the festival should be observed; and the elderly who had worshipped at the first temple in their youth could describe what they had seen with their own eyes.[4] Nonetheless, the lack of continuous religious experience for two generations and the absence of the mimetic tradition of regular ritual life entailed the possibility of major innovations.[5]

In this respect the situation of the restoration community evokes some parallels to that of the rabbis six centuries later. The rabbis also faced the challenge of reconstituting religious life after the destruction of the temple. They too possessed the Pentateuchal legislation and oral traditions. The two groups differed of course, in that the restoration community built a temple, whereas the rabbis constructed a new system of piety. As much as they prayed, hoped and longed for the rebuilding of the temple, the project never came to fruition. Yet the rabbis prepared for the ultimate rebuilding by devoting a tremendous amount of thought to temple matters. How the community of early second temple times

---

[1] 2 Kgs 24:8-16. According to 2 Kgs 24:14, only the poor were left behind. 2 Kgs 25:12 notes that only vine dressers and farmers remained in the land.

[2] E. Janssen, *Juda in der Exilszeit* (Göttingen, 1956), 39-42, suggests that those who remained in Palestine set up a temporary altar of sorts. Nonetheless, one can hardly speak of a functioning cult. See too P. Ackroyd, *Israel under Babylon and Persia* (London: Oxford University Press, 1970), 17-19.

[3] Assuming, of course, that the Pentateuch had been redacted by this point. Some believe the final redaction took place after the exile. If not the Pentateuch, the community possessed other such sources.

[4] Ezra 3:12 relates that some of the older priests and Levites who had seen the first temple wept at the much inferior altar and foundations of the fledgling second temple. Cf. Hag 2:1-5.

[5] Moreover, many of those who participated in the rebuilding returned from Babylonia where they had been subject to foreign cultural influences; Ezra 2:1-70.

The Second Temple Period

reestablished Sukkot worship may prove instructive for understanding the rabbinic period.

The Books of Ezra-Nehemiah reveal that the community that attempted to rebuild the temple experienced numerous difficulties and frustrations. They managed to set up the altar, resume minimal sacrificial worship, and lay the foundations of the temple, but did not succeed in rebuilding it for some time (Ezra 3). Crop failures, the urgency of building houses, the hostility of the Samaritans and internal conflict interrupted the work for twenty years until the reign of Darius (520 BCE). The temple was finally completed and dedicated in 515 BCE (Ezra 6:13-18). Yet when Ezra and Nehemiah returned from Babylonia in the mid and late fifth century BCE, they found the city in poor shape, morale low, the cult in disarray and the temple sanctity compromised. Nehemiah lamented, "How is it that the House of God has been neglected?" (Neh 13:11). The discontinuity between first temple and second temple worship was more pronounced than appears at first glance.

Ezra 3:1-6 briefly narrates the resumption of the sacrifices on the altar and mentions the observance of Sukkot. At the beginning of the seventh month the people gathered in Jerusalem (3:1). Yeshua the High Priest and Zerubavel, grandson of the last king, then built the altar in order to offer the obligatory sacrifices. They began to sacrifice the daily offering on the first day of the month (3:3,6) and then celebrate "the Festival of Booths as it is written" with the appropriate offerings (3:3-4). The passage emphasizes that the Sukkot sacrifices inaugurated the regular functioning of the cult; thereafter Sabbaths, new moons and other festivals would be observed in the proper way (3:4-5).[6] The initiation of the festival cycle on Sukkot recalls the dedication of Solomon's temple, and the parallel serves to confer legitimacy on the restored cult. Just as God responded to the dedication of the first temple by Solomon, so the efforts of Yeshua and Zerubavel should receive divine favor.

The passage emphasizes that the community observed Sukkot "as it is written" and brought sacrifices "in the proper quantity as is prescribed for it" (Ezra 3:4). The latter phrase derives from Num 29:12-35, which

---

[6]The chronology in the passage is somewhat confused, for the summary in 3:6 asserts, "From the first of the seventh month they began to make burnt offerings to the Lord." But according to 3:2 they built the altar only after the people had assembled on the first day. Verses 4-5 make it clear that the regular functioning of the cult only began after Sukkot. On the internal composition of Ezra 3:1-6 see A. Gunneweg, *Esra* (Gütersloh: Gerd Mohn, 1985), 73; Ackroyd, *Chronicler*, 145-46.

details the Sukkot offerings and repeats this formula for each day.[7] Reference to the "written" law and insistence that the restored cult followed the dictates of Pentateuchal legislation serve as means to legitimate the renewal of sacrifices.[8] The constant tension over temple matters that pervades Ezra-Nehemiah and the latter prophets reveals deep divisions over the workings of the cult, so the author wished to emphasize that the renewed sacrificial order conformed to the commandments of God. At the same time, the reference to the Torah suggests that those who resumed sacrifices required a source of instruction and turned to scripture. Authoritative traditions preserved at least the basic cultic protocol and attenuated the potential deviation of the restored cult from its predecessor.

The passage mentions no other Sukkot rituals. This may be because the passage focuses on the resumption of sacrifices, not the festival of Sukkot for its own sake or the accompanying temple rituals. Yet it seems that at this early stage cultic observances consisted of sacrifices alone. Years would pass before the temple itself was erected, the priestly orders reorganized and the religious lives of the people oriented around the Jerusalem temple. The restoration of the cult, therefore, did not immediately bring about the renewal of the full celebration of the festivals in all their glory. Sukkot, as celebrated in the second temple period, rose from something of a vacuum.

Neh 8 narrates a later stage of the renewal of Sukkot festivities. This chapter is one of the most inscrutable in the Bible and raises numerous difficulties that have yet to receive satisfactory explanations. Here we only address the major issues pertaining to the development of Sukkot. The chapter describes the events of the mid or late fifth century BCE,[9] at some point in the career of Ezra.[10] In the seventh month the people gather together in "the square before the water gate" (8:1) and ask Ezra to read from the Torah of Moses. There follows a description of the

---

[7]Num 29:18, 21, 24, 27, 30, 37. Ezra 3:4 is singular (*bemispar*) whereas the Pentateuchal legislations adopts the plural form (*bemisparam*). See Shaver, *Chronicler*, 100; Fishbane, *Interpretation*, 112, n. 21.
[8]Presumably the "as it is written" refers to the sacrifices, since Neh 8 suggests that the ritual building of booths was only reinstituted then; see below.
[9]The date of Ezra's return, and whether he came before or after Nehemiah, is one of the most vexing scholarly questions. Nehemiah's return can be dated to 445 BCE, the twentieth year of the reign of Artaxerses I (Neh 2:1). The traditional date of Ezra's return is 458 BCE. Some scholars suggest Ezra came after Nehemiah, arriving in 428 BCE, while still others propose 398 BCE. See John Bright, *A History of Israel*[3] (Westminster Press: Philadelphia, 1981), 391-402; and D.J.A. Clines, *Ezra, Nehemiah, Esther* (Grand Rapids: Eerdmans, 1984), 16-24 for discussion. Clines inventories the proponents of each date.
[10]Although the passage was probably composed later. See n. 21.

reading, after which the people weep, but are told to stop crying and to celebrate the festival (8:2-12).[11] At this point the narrative mentions that on "the second day" the leaders gathered together to listen to the reading:

> (14) They found written in the Torah that the Lord had commanded Moses that the Israelites must dwell in booths during the festival of the seventh month, (15) and that they must announce and proclaim throughout all their towns and Jerusalem as follows, "Go out to the mountains and bring leafy branches of olive trees, pine trees, myrtles, palms and [other] leafy trees to make booths, as it is written." (16) So the people went out and brought them, and made themselves booths on their roofs, in their courtyards of the House of God, in the square of the Water Gate and in the square of the Ephraim gate. (17) The whole community that returned from the captivity made booths and dwelt in the booths – the Israelites had not done so since the days of Joshua[12] son of Nun to that day – and there was very great rejoicing. (18) He read from the scroll of the Teaching of God each day, from the first to the last day. They celebrated the festival seven days, and there was a solemn gathering on the eighth, as prescribed.

After hearing the commandment the people immediately make preparations. This may imply the festival commenced on the second of the month, although the narrative does not specify the dates the festival was observed, so it is possible observance did not begin until the fifteenth.[13] In any case, the community was completely unaware of the ritual of building booths, and presumably knew nothing of the festival itself. The editor considers the mass building of booths such a watershed that he asserts the community had not done so since the time of Joshua. What stands out is that the community learned to observe the festival from the Torah. They do not celebrate with spontaneous harvest festivities or familiar local traditions. Rather, they consciously perform the rituals prescribed by scripture.

The absence of other rituals does not imply that the festival was celebrated exclusively by building booths. The main concern of Ezra-Nehemiah is not the description of a Sukkot celebration but that the community hears the law and obeys. Observance of Sukkot serves as a paradigmatic example of this theme: the people rush to build booths as prescribed in scripture. So we should not really expect the author to detail other rituals the community may have observed. Yet the

---

[11]Some scholars suggest the weeping points to an atonement ceremony, a type of precursor of Yom Kippur, that formed part of the original autumnal festival complex. See Mowinckel, *Studien*, 3:44.
[12]MT has Jeshua.
[13]See Blenkinsopp, *Ezra*, 290-91; Ryle, *Ezra*, 245, Welch, *Judaism*, 264; J.M. Myers, *I and II Esdras* (Garden City, New York: Doubleday, 1974), 156.

deterioration of religious life coheres with everything we know about this period. If the narrative presents an idealized and highly dramatic version of a religious renewal, it probably reflects the essential course of events. Ezra, Nehemiah and the "scribal" movement eventually influenced the community to observe the rituals prescribed in the Torah. They filled the religious vacuum by turning to the Torah as the source of instruction. At the outset of the second temple period Sukkot was less a harvest or temple festival than a "scriptural" observance. That is, the community learned how to celebrate the autumnal harvest from scripture.

This account presupposes some form of Lev 23:39-43, the Holiness Code, for only H explicitly mentions the obligation to dwell in sukkot, to collect species of plants, and to assemble on the eighth day. But three differences between the Levitical legislation and the Nehemian account are apparent. First, Lev 23 describes two distinct rituals: a) that certain plant species and fruits be collected and there be rejoicing before God (23:39-41); b) that all Israelites dwell in sukkot (23:42-43). Whatever the precise nature of the festivities with the species, the passage does not command explicitly that the booths are to be made from them.[14] Neh 8:15, however, instructs the people to "bring" the plants "to make sukkot." Second, the plant species listed do not cohere. And Leviticus requires fruit (*peri*), while the Nehemian species are exclusively leafy branches.[15] Third, Neh 8:15 seems to claim that two commandments were found "written in the Torah of Moses," both to dwell in sukkot and to issue a proclamation to gather the species to make sukkot. While the former commandment appears in Lev 23:42 (although not verbatim), the latter is not found anywhere.

It may be that the community inherited an alternative version of the Pentateuch which reflects the different manner of celebrating the

---

[14]This understanding of the verse is not a reflection of my rabbinic bias; it is the consensus of scholarship that the "taking" pertains to a ritual bouquet of sorts, not to the construction of the sukka. That the *sensus literalis* of Lev 23:40 does not refer to the sukka can be seen from the Qaraite Joseph Haro'eh's tortuous arguments. A good Qaraite, Haro'eh' wished to prove the verse pertained to the building of sukkot, as per Qaraite tradition. A good biblical scholar, he knew it did not. He concedes the verse "on the face of it" says nothing of constructing a sukka, and is forced to conclude: "however, he who prefers to see the implication of the building of the booth in the verse *And you shall take for yourselves* says that while Scripture does not expressly direct its building, it is impossible that the ordinance of its building should not be manifestly indicated in Scripture; we must therefore say that this verse does direct its building, by implication." Haro'eh's interpretation is cited by Aaron b. Elijah; Nemoy, *Karaite*, 178-79.

[15]Cf. Ibn Ezra to Lev 23:40. Neh 8:13 specifies "leafy branches" (*'alei*) of palm while Leviticus prescribes palm "branches" (*kapot*).

festival.¹⁶ The discrepancies in observance result from divergent textual traditions. Several scholars, however, suggest that the community possessed essentially the same text and their practice reflects an interpretation of the Pentateuchal passage.¹⁷ They might have

---

¹⁶A. Bertholet, *Leviticus* (Tübingen: J.C.B. Mohr, 1901), 71; Ehrlich, *Hamiqra*, 2:426; Mowinckel, *Studien*, 3:166ff; Gunneweg, *Nehemia*, 115, n. 15; C. Houtman, "Ezra and the Law: Observations on the Supposed Relation Between Ezra and the Pentateuch," *OTS* 21 (1981), 111. The lack of explicit mention of the celebration of New Year's Day or the Day of Atonement as prescribed in the Pentateuch also suggests that the author of Ezra-Nehemiah did not possess MT Leviticus. Cf. Blenkinsopp, *Ezra*, 291: "This inconsistency between the historical narrative in Ezra-Nehemiah and Pentateuchal law in one of several indications that the latter had not yet attained its final form." And see de Vaux, *Israel*, 407-409. Kellermann, *Nehemiah*, 27, 34 suggests the reading of the law is a New Year's Day celebration.
Other scholars emend Neh 8:15 by deleting "and that" of verse 15. In this case the proclamation to gather the species and build booths is what Ezra (or the leaders) said, not what Ezra found written in the Torah. See L.W. Batten, *A Critical and Exegetical Commentary on the Books of Ezra and Nehemiah* (ICC 12; New York: Scribner, 1913), 361; Kaufmann, *Toledot*, 4:327, n. 34; Ackroyd, *Ezra*, 297; H. Schneider, *Die Bücher Ezra und Nehemiah* (Bonn: Peter Hanstein Verlag, 1959), 210; W. Rudolph, *Esra und Nehemia* (Tübingen: Mohr, 1949), 150; F. Fensham, *The Books of Ezra and Nehemiah* (Grand Rapids, Michigan: Eerdmans, 1982), 220. (The LXX adds "and Ezra said" before the command). While this emendation obviates the problem of the commandment to make a proclamation, the contradictions in the modes of celebration and types of species remain.
¹⁷Kaufmann, *Toledot*, 4:327-28 suggests that the ritual in Nehemiah is the result of an early midrash-halakha. Faced with the commandment to build sukkot (Lev 23:42), but learning nothing explicit from Leviticus about how they should be constructed, Ezra concluded from the previous verses (23:40-41) that the sukkot were to be built out of the species. Fishbane, *Interpretation*, 110-11 also attempts to resolve the difficulties by appealing to a midrash-halakha. The decision to build sukkot out of the species was an "etymological exegesis" of the word *sukkot* in Lev 23:42. The levitical interpreters derived *sukkot* from the verbal stem *SKK*, "to cover over [with branches]." The plant species mentioned in Nehemiah were simply those found in the attempt to comply with the directive to build sukkot – they bear no relation to the species of Lev 23:40. So Nehemiah makes no reference whatsoever to the species of Leviticus! Fishbane explains the presence of ואשר ("and that"), the elusive direct citation (problem three), by suggesting that the interpreters felt so strongly that their interpretation was implied in the text of Leviticus that they described it as "written" in the Torah. See too Blenkinsopp, *Ezra*, 292 and Albeck, *Jubiläen*, 18. Other scholars call the proclamation of Ezra a "paraphrase" rather than a "midrash." Thus Ryle, *Ezra*, 247 comments: "But there is no reason on that account to suppose a corruption in the text... The fact is that the writer only refers in a general way to the substance of the passage in Lev 23, relating to the Feast of Tabernacles. The mention of "Jerusalem" is alone sufficient to show the spirit of free adaption in which the reference to the law is made." And see Ibn Ezra to Lev 23:40 and Yehuda Hadasi, *'Eshkol Hakofer* (Westmead, England: Gregg International Publishers, 1971 [1836]), 122.

understood that the booths must be made from the plant species prescribed in the previous verses.¹⁸ The species they collected were likewise based on an interpretation of Lev 23:40.¹⁹ This question,

---

¹⁸See previous note. The lack of mention of the lulav should not be taken as evidence that the practice was unknown to Ezra-Nehemiah. This account of Sukkot celebrations is not comprehensive, and hardly mentions the temple ceremonies at all. Neh 8:18, "They celebrated the festival seven days and there was a solemn gathering on the eighth, as prescribed," informs the reader that the sacrifices and other ceremonies were also carried out. See too Hoffmann, *Vayiqra*, 2:201. Childs, *Introduction*, 630-31 comments on the "highly selective use of source material" by the authors. The account also neglects to mention observance of YK on the tenth. True, some scholars take this as proof YK did not exist at this time, and others see the weeping of Neh 8:9 as a type of YK observance (Mowinckel, *Studien*, 3:44). But the lack of mention can be attributed to the fact that the holiday is extraneous to the author's purposes. The author wishes to illustrate the community's rededication to the law, not narrate the precise manner they observed the autumnal festivals for historical interest. Weinfeld, *Institutions*, 111-16 has demonstrated that YK should not be considered a late observance. Cf. Kaufmann, *Toledot*, 1:217-18.

¹⁹The difference in species is most problematic for this approach. Particularly difficult is the mention of fruit in Lev 23, for fruit does not make good building material. See the attempts to harmonize the passages cited by the Qaraite Aaron ben Elijah (d. 1369) in Nemoy, *Karaite*, 179-182, which anticipate most of the following interpretations of modern scholars. A.B. Ehrlich, *Randglossen zur hebräischen Bibel* (Hildesheim: G. Olms, 1968 [1908-14]), 2:84 suggests reading פרי (fruit) as פורי or פארי, from פאר, "beauty, glory." (R. Kittel, *Geschichte Des Volkes Israel* [Stuttgart: W. Kohlhammer, 1923-29], 3:593 accepts this conjecture, as does Auerbach, *Feste*, 13.) Ehrlich takes הדר with עץ, "the glory of the *hadar* tree," not with פרי, "beautiful fruit of the tree." The verse may then be read as "the glory of a beautiful tree," i.e., its branches, not its fruit, since beautiful trees may yield ugly fruit, but they always have beautiful branches. Ehrlich also suggests emending הדר to הדס (myrtle), which coheres more closely with Neh 8 where the myrtle is mentioned explicitly. Y. Avishur, "Peri 'eṣ hadar," *Beit Mikra* 34 (1989), 138-39 suggests they interpreted פרי עץ as "the *products* of beautiful trees," a general category, referring to the three following species: palm branches, branches of leafy trees and willows of the brook. Avishur takes הדר with the following phrase: פרי עץ—הדר כפות תמרים, and claims that פרי and הדר and ענף are synonyms, all referring to branches. H. Ginsburg, "Lemilon leshon hamiqra'," *Hanokh Yalon Jubilee Volume*, ed. S. Lieberman et al. (Jerusalem, 1963), 167-72, makes a similar argument. What is important is not whether these scholars are "correct " but that they advance plausible interpretations. The restoration community may well have interpreted the verse in one of these ways. Note that "branches of leafy trees" and even "willows of the brook" are general categories, and the particular species detailed in Nehemiah may have been considered specific examples of the general directives. It is perhaps significant that bSuk 32b, in interpreting the "branches of leafy trees" as the myrtle, argues that the reference cannot be to the olive. Apparently the rabbis sensed that someone (Ezra!) did interpret the "leafy trees" as the olive or wild olive. Hoffmann, *Vayiqra*, 2:200 aptly characterizes all efforts to harmonize the species in Lev 23

unfortunately, is impossible to settle, and involves other issues such as the date of redaction of the Pentateuch and stability of the text. More telling is the fact that the Nehemian community brought the program of the Holiness School (H) to fruition. As we noted in the previous chapter, H wished to restore popular agricultural rituals to a central focus of the festivals. Apparently this program had not succeeded; the legislation, like much of the Pentateuch, remained theoretical or utopian. Neh 8 reveals that observance of such rituals had been neglected, exaggerating the hiatus back to Joshua and the conquest. Now the community returned to the primitive agricultural rituals H advocated so as to fulfill the "teachings of the Lord." Dwelling in booths thus became a ritual in its own right. We noted that the precise relationship of booths to the festival is debated, and that while Deut 16:13-15 calls the autumnal festival the "Festival of Booths," it does not command the Israelites to reside therein. Whether booths served as temporary shelters for pilgrims during their sojourn at the temple or as shelters in the fields during the harvest or ingathering, the dwelling was not understood as a religious ritual. The booths primarily served a practical rather than ritual function, providing shelter for those who needed it. Those who lived in Jerusalem or had houses in the fields had no use for booths. Neh 8, following the program of H, made the dwelling in booths a ritual obligation.[20] The entire community built and dwelled in booths to fulfill the dictates of the Torah, whether they required the shelter or not. Whatever the original connection of the booths to agricultural culture and its harvest festivals, in this period scripture served as their source. Continuity between the first temple festival and Sukkot in the second temple period was mediated primarily by the Torah.

To this point we have assessed the Nehemian passage primarily from a historical perspective. An equally important question is whether the account sheds light on the themes and motifs the editor of Ezra-Nehemiah associated with Sukkot. The remarkably dramatic yet somewhat confused narrative, the juxtaposition with the Torah reading

---

and Neh 8 as "futile excuses." An alternative is to assume minor textual variations are responsible for the differences. But then we are approaching the idea that Ezra possessed a different text, and must justify why we postulate minor textual differences but reject a more substantial one.

[20]See Licht, *Sukkot*, 176. This seems to be the innovation the author intends by his claim that the Israelites had not observed Sukkot since the time of Joshua. Prior to the settlement of the land the entire people required the temporary shelter booths provide. After the settlement, while booths may have been a feature of the festival, it was not the case that the entire people inhabited them. Only in the time of Ezra did the entire community dwell in booths again. However, the allusion to Joshua also makes a theological point; see p. 41.

assembly, and the editorial comments suggest that the observance of Sukkot serves larger theological purposes.[21] Why did the editor frame

---

[21]The internal composition of the chapter is confused. In Neh 8:1-4 the people gather before "Ezra the Scribe." He reads from the Torah (8:3), flanked by 13 leaders. Then in 8:5 Ezra opens the book – from which he had been reading two verses earlier! Neh 8:7 provides a different list of the 13 names which includes "the levites," and "they," not Ezra, read from the book (8:8). Nehemiah suddenly appears with Ezra in 8:9, although in no other passage do the two appear in tandem. Here Ezra is described as "the Priest and the Scribe." A second assembly occurs in 8:13 at which the elders alone are present. At this assembly the verse concerning Sukkot is found, and the people set out to comply with the dictates of the verse. Thus the authors creatively wove together accounts of an assembly for reading the law (8:1-12) with that of an assembly that culminated in the celebration of Sukkot (8:13-18), or even invented an assembly as the context for the Sukkot observance modeled on the assembly for reading Torah. (Note that the parallel in 1 Esdr 9 contains the first assembly, but not the second, although this may be due to a deficient manuscript; one could also argue the first assembly was modeled on the Sukkot assembly.) The vivid description of the reading appears to be based on synagogue practice: all rise as the Torah is opened (v. 5); they recite an opening prayer (v. 6); the people answer "Amen, Amen," raise their hands, and then bow down; and the interpreters expound the passage for the people. The authors apparently have retrojected the pattern of worship of their time to the assembly in order to produce a colorful narrative. See Kellermann, *Nehemiah*, 30; Gunneweg, *Nehemia*, 110; In der Smitten, *Esra*, 39-45. Cf. Kaufmann, *Toledot*, 1:218. For these reasons scholars believe Neh 8-9 has been substantially reworked by the Chronicler. See Kellermann, *Nehemiah*, 26-31, 90-92; Kapelrud, *Ezra*, 92-95; Ackroyd, *Chronicler*, 332-34; Blenkinsopp, *Ezra*, 285-86. The placement of Neh 8, and actually the entirety of Neh 8-10, provides additional warrant to pay close attention to the theological uses of the passage. The reemergence of Ezra as the protagonist has led to the almost unanimous conclusion that these chapters were originally connected with the Ezra narrative, and were later transferred to their present place. In 1 Esdr 9, the beginning of the parallel to Neh 8 follows the parallel to Ezra 10, the pledge of these who married foreign wives to divorce them. Most scholars believe Neh 8 originally followed Ezra 8. See Mowinckel, *Studien*, 3:7-17, 152; Kapelrud, *Ezra*, 14; Kellermann, *Nehemiah*, 31; C. Torrey, *The Composition and Historical Value of Ezra-Nehemiah* (Giessen, 1896), 29-35; O. Eisfeldt, *The Old Testament: An Introduction*, trans. Peter Ackroyd (New York: Harper and Row, 1965), 548. J.M. Myers, *I and II Esdras* (Garden City, New York: Doubleday, 1974), 152 summarizes the different theories. So the Chronicler moved the chapters, presumable for good reason. He felt the chronological sequence was less important than the theological concern. The editor felt that only after the full restoration of the wall and settlement of the people was it fitting that there be a full restoration of other communal institutions. In Neh 8-12 the Chronicler portrays the coalescing of an ideal community of faith, and the observance of Sukkot must be understood in light of this canonical development. As the fully restored community they immediately act upon the commandments found in the Torah. See Childs, *Introduction*, 630-31. In addition to these factors, the editorial comment in 8:17 invoking Joshua and insistence that the entire community observed the festival "as prescribed" (8:18) signal that the editor means to shape his traditions to make certain points.

the account as he did, and what does it indicate about the meaning of the festival? Since most scholars believe the Chronicler edited Ezra-Nehemiah, we are now dealing with Sukkot as understood in the age of the Chronicler, generally dated to the mid-fourth century BCE.[22]

The association of festivals with important historical events is a familiar biblical motif. Blenkinsopp points to six examples: the dedication of the first temple (Sukkot, 2 Chr 5-7), the completion of Hezekiah's reforms (Pesaḥ, 2 Chr 30), the completion of Josiah's reforms (Pesaḥ, 2 Chr 35:1-19), the completion of the first return (Sukkot, Ezra 3:1-6), the completion of the second temple (Pesaḥ, Ezra 6:19-22) and the completion of Ezra's reforms (Sukkot, Neh 8:13-18).[23] The account of the Josianic reforms, in particular, reveals marked parallels to Neh 8 (2 Kgs 23:22; 2 Chr 30:26; 35:18). Under Josiah the promulgation of a new law book led to extensive changes in practice. The new compact was observed communally through the celebration of Pesaḥ as dictated by the new law. In Nehemiah rededication to the Torah is demonstrated by daily readings throughout the festival and observance of the Sukkot rituals in conformity with the commandments of scripture.

The parenthetic comment that Sukkot had not been celebrated since the time of Joshua (8:17) should be understood in this light. A favorite

---

However, I would not go as far as In der Smitten, *Esra*, 46 who considers the whole passage an "unhistorischer Bericht des Chronisten." Rather the Chronicler inherited a tradition of the restoration community's reinstitution of Sukkot. He then wove it into a larger narrative and colored it to serve his theological and pedagogical purposes. Of course the Chronicler edited all of Ezra-Nehemiah, including Ezra 3:1-6 analyzed above, but the editorial hand is particularly heavy in Neh 8. See Ackroyd, *Chronicler*, 333: "the Chronicler has integrated into what now appears as a continuous narrative, elements which do not originally belong together. The fact that we may detect Ezra traditions of the receiving and acceptance of the law and of the action on foreign marriages suggests that, viewing the moment of Ezra's action as most significant, he has incorporated this (and thereby reinterpreted) other traditions which were similar in general purport."

[22]The Chronicler combined earlier sources, including an "Ezra Narrative" and a "Nehemiah Narrative," with Aramaic documents, lists and other traditions. Since Chronicles reflects no consciousness of Hellenism or the shift from Persian to Greek hegemony, the work typically is dated prior to the conquest of Alexander in 333 BCE. (However, Ackroyd, *Chronicler*, 9-10, cautions against this *argument ex silentio*; dates as late as the late 3rd century BCE are not uncommon.) Nehemiah's first term lasted from 445-433 BCE, and he served a second term of unknown duration (Neh 13:6-7), while Ezra is variously dated to 458, c. 420 or 398 BCE (see n. 9), so the Chronicler must have lived after this time. See Bright, *Israel*, 395-98 and D.J.A. Clines, *Ezra, Nehemiah, Esther* (Grand Rapids: Eerdmanns., 1984), 9-14. On the Chronicler's editing of Ezra-Nehemiah, see Blenkinsopp, *Ezra*, 47-54.

[23]Blenkinsopp, *Ezra*, 290.

device of the Chronicler is to link two historical events by asserting that a festival had not been celebrated from the time of the earlier until the latter. 2 Chr 30:26 remarks that prior to Hezekiah's Pesaḥ, "since the time of King Solomon son of David of Israel nothing like it had happened in Jerusalem." 2 Chr 35:18 notes of Josiah's Pesaḥ that "since the time of the Prophet Samuel, no Pesaḥ like that one had ever been kept in Israel." Here the Chronicler makes the same assertion about Ezra's Sukkot and Joshua. The statement is programmatic to a certain extent. A correlation is created between a later innovation and an earlier, authoritative precedent from hoary antiquity. The correlation links the return of Ezra, the resettlement of the promised land, with the conquest of Joshua, the initial settlement. The editor evokes the assembly of Josh 24, when the whole people accepted the Torah in perfect harmony, to frame the restoration assembly. Just as their forefathers had journeyed to the promised land with the Torah which they had received on Mt Sinai, so the returned exiles returned to the promised land and rededicated themselves to that Torah. In this way a paradigm of former greatness is connected with the efforts of the restoration community, as is tacit divine sanction.[24]

With these motifs in mind, it is instructive to compare the role of Sukkot in the two passages we have addressed, Ezra 3:1-6 and Neh 8. Both passages associate Sukkot with foundational assemblies and events. Both introduce the accounts with identical verses (Ezra 3:1 = Neh 7:72),

---

[24]See Blenkinsopp, *Ezra*, 290-91; Ackroyd, *Chronicler*, 333; Gunneweg, *Nehemia*, 109, 117; idem, *Esra*, 45. (Here, ironically, the rabbinic apologetic in bAr 32b is on the right track.) This interpretation is superior to understanding the editor's comment as accurate historical information. Scholars who do so – apart from mistaking historiography with history – must then define *what* had not been celebrated since the time of Joshua, for the celebration of Sukkot *in toto* could hardly have begun with Nehemiah. The spectrum of solutions betrays the futility of this approach: never had it been celebrated in "this strict way" (Ryle, *Ezra*, 247); never had the whole people celebrated it around a central sanctuary (W. Rudolph, *Esra und Nehemia* [Tübingen: Mohr, 1949], 152-53; H. Schneider, *Die Bücher Esra und Nehemiah* [Bonn: Peter Hanstein Verlag, 1959], 210); never before had the feast been observed with booths (Kapelrud, *Ezra*, 91; Kellermann, *Nehemiah*, 30); never had booths been constructed in this way (Blenkinsopp, *Ezra*, 292-93); never before in Jerusalem itself (de Vaux, *Israel*, 497; In der Smitten, *Esra*, 44); never with such widespread participation and splendor (Hoffmann, *Vayiqra*, 2:201). Kaufmann, *Toledot*, 4:328 believes that there had never been the combination of sukkot in Jerusalem, since Deut 31 mentions pilgrimages to Jerusalem, but not making sukkot, while Lev 23 ordains that sukkot be made in one's place, but does not know of a pilgrimage. See Fishbane, *Interpretation*, 110, for objections. If there is a new element, I suggest it is the resolve to observe what had been ancient folk customs as divinely ordained rituals. This was not new since Joshua, but completely new. See n. 20.

which may indicate that the two traditions concern one original founding assembly; at the least it indicates that the redactor associated one event with the other, and suggests the reader do likewise.[25] Yet the two accounts display a manifest shift in concern.[26] Ezra 3:1-6 associates the resumption of the festival sacrifices with the festival of Sukkot because the founding of Solomon's temple took place on Sukkot (1 Kgs 8). Neh 8 associates Sukkot not with the foundation of the cult, but the foundation of the authority of scripture.[27] There is no explicit mention of the numerous Sukkot sacrifices which had been the concern in Ezra 3, nor of other temple rites. Rather the community observes the festival by means of the rituals found written in the Torah. While mention of Sukkot in Ezra 3 expresses continuity with earlier times by casting the establishment of worship in the same mode as the dedication of Solomon's temple, Sukkot in Neh 8 points forward to the growing importance of Torah and its study.

The juxtaposition of a Sukkot celebration and a Torah reading assembly recalls the Deuteronomic *haqhel* ceremony. Due to this precedent, the author of our account felt Sukkot was the appropriate festival on which to place the foundational gathering.[28] He directs, in the spirit of Deut 31:12, "Gather the people, the men, women, children, and strangers in your communities" and relates that "men and women and all who could listen with understanding" (Neh 8:2) were present at the assembly. Intricate calculations which seek to prove that this assembly indeed occurred during the Sabbatical year – apart from being largely unconvincing – miss this point.[29] The emphasis on the reading of the Torah, not the mandatory Sabbatical assembly, led the editor to associate Sukkot with the assembly of the acceptance of the law.[30]

---

[25] 1 Esdr 9:37, parallel to Neh 7:72, is worded differently. This may indicate that the original wording in Nehemiah was altered later to match that of Ezra 3:1.
[26] See Welch, *Judaism*, 263.
[27] Gunneweg, *Nehemia*, 110; Welch, *Judaism*, 262-64. As noted above, the emphasis on carrying out the sacrifices in accordance with the "scripture" and the "law" in Ezra 3:4 already points to this theme.
[28] The author related that the Torah was read every day of the festival (8:18), whereas Deuteronomy prescribes one reading. Fishbane, *Interpretation*, 113, suggests that Ezra interpreted the command in Deut 31:10, to read the Torah "on the festival" (*behag*), as "during the festival," that is, throughout the festival, and not only once.
[29] J. Morgenstern, "The Three Calendars of Ancient Israel," *HUCA* 1 (1924), 79; A. Pavlovsky, "Die Chronologie der Tätigkeit Esdra. Versuch einer neuer Lösung," *Biblica* 38 (1957), 273-305, 428-56.
[30] It should be noted that the assembly resembles the "covenant-renewal" festival that Alt, von Rad and Kraus claimed was the original essence of Sukkot, adducing Deut 31:10-13 as evidence. See Chapter 1, III n. 27 and text thereto.

Thus the importance of Sukkot for the editor of Neh 8 (presumably the Chronicler) derives primarily from its association with the reading of the law. Sukkot, the time specified for the Deuteronomic septennial Torah reading, was the appropriate festival upon which to portray the culmination of the efforts of restoration community to rededicate themselves to the Torah. Just as other historical events occurred on the festivals, notably Josiah's promulgation of a new scroll found in the Temple, so too the restoration community assembled on Sukkot to pledge their allegiance to the Torah. To dramatize the resolve of the community the editor depicts their immediate response of gathering branches and building sukkot in order to comply with the commandments. The primary significance of Sukkot stems from its association with reading of the Torah, and its observance demonstrates immediate, unconditional performance of the commandments.

In sum: celebration of Sukkot in the early second temple period therefore reveals continuity with first temple times. Yeshua and Zerubavel dedicated the altar on Sukkot and brought the numerous sacrifices as prescribed. As Solomon dedicated the first temple on Sukkot, so Yeshua and Zerubavel resumed cultic worship with the Sukkot offerings. The fact that the people gathered in Jerusalem in the seventh month indicates that the autumnal festival remained an important pilgrimage as in monarchic times. Thus to a certain extent Sukkot remained the leading temple festival and pilgrimage. A second element of the festival, the dwelling in booths, also reflects continuity. In this case the scriptural passages detailing festival rituals are primarily responsible for continuity in observance. From scripture the community learned to celebrate the festival by building and dwelling in booths. This communal observance resurrected an ancient folk custom that had been a feature of the autumnal festival. Yet the understanding of the dwelling in booths as an obligatory ritual constitutes a new element, or at least a transformation of an older practice. The commanding power of scripture converts an ancient feature of the festival into a primary ritual. Ironically, the "Festival of Booths" became a more appropriate title in the second temple period.

This scriptural inspiration for communal Sukkot observance is crucial to the Chronicler, the editor of the Ezra-Nehemiah traditions, and illuminates the meaning of Sukkot in the mid-fourth century BCE. He associates Sukkot and its rituals with the authority of the Torah, with the reading of the law and rededication of the community to the commandments. While the Deuteronomic *haqhel* ceremony provides some precedent, this association is innovative. Celebration of Sukkot rituals as prescribed demonstrates the community's allegiance to scripture. The immediate building of sukkot serves as a paradigm for how the redactors believe the community ought to behave. In this respect the depiction of Sukkot serves the historiographic and theological purposes of the editor. A community which had neglected the law, violated the commandments and intermarried reformed itself under Ezra, Nehemiah and scribal authority.[31] That community assembled to hear the Torah, agreed to separate from their foreign wives and pledged to follow the prescriptions of scripture. Since the rabbis shared similar beliefs about the primacy of scripture and its interpretation, we should keep this perspective in mind when we analyze rabbinic conceptions of Sukkot.[32]

II. Zechariah 14

The last chapter of Zechariah contains a brief but critical reference to the festival of Sukkot. Scholars concur that the second half of Zechariah, chapters 9-14, derive from a later anonymous prophet, and were appended to the original prophecies of Zechariah ben Berechiah. Because of the pronounced apocalyptic outlook of chapters 12-14, some even distinguish "Trito-Zechariah" from "Deutero-Zechariah" and suggest an extremely late date, as late as the second century BCE.[33] Recent scholarship tends to place the chapters somewhat earlier, in the late fourth century, probably after the conquest of Alexander the Great and the beginnings of Hellenism.[34] The prophecy sheds light on ideas current in the period following the Chronicler and the final editing of the Ezra-Nehemiah traditions.

Zech 14 depicts a battle in which the nations assault and destroy Jerusalem. God then appears as the divine warrior with his heavenly retinue and they triumph over the enemy forces (14:3-5).[35] God transforms the surrounding territory, first crushing the Mount of Olives to make his approach, then miraculously creating the eschatological Jerusalem (14:4, 8-11). The countryside flattens such that Mt Zion towers

---

[31]See Childs, *Introduction*, 635-37.
[32]The Chronicler's retelling of the dedication of Solomon's temple, 2 Chr 5:2-7:10 (= 1 Kgs 8), adds little to the account except for the insistence that *Shmini 'aṣeret* was observed on the twenty-third (2 Chr 7:9). See Chapter 1, II nn. 16-17 and text thereto.
[33]See the survey of scholarship in H. Mitchell, *Haggai, Zechariah and Malachi* (ICC 56; Edinburgh: T. & T. Clark, 1912), 232-59; D.A. Witt, *Zechariah 12-14: its Origins, Growth and Theological Significance* (Dissertation; University Microfilms, 1991), 1-16, 126-27; Hanson, *Apocalyptic*, 287-92; Schaefer, *Composition*, 393 n. 65.
[34]Schaefer, *Composition*, 392-94. Hanson, *Apocalyptic*, 400 prefers a somewhat earlier date, between 475-425 BCE, as does Meyers, *Zechariah*, 26-28.
[35]On the Divine Warrior see Cross, *Canaanite*, 91-111; Hanson, *Apocalyptic*, 292-334.

above the rest of the land, and a stream of living waters flows from the city to fertilize the entire country. The victory establishes God's sovereignty firmly upon the earth (14:9). Thereafter the nations must acknowledge that sovereignty by an annual pilgrimage to Jerusalem on Sukkot when they "bow low to the King Lord of Hosts" (14:16-19):

> (16) All who survive of all those nations that came up against Jerusalem shall make a pilgrimage year by year to bow low before the King Lord of Hosts to observe the Festival of Sukkot. (17) Any of the earth's communities that does not make the pilgrimage to Jerusalem to bow low to the King Lord of Hosts shall receive no rain. (18) However, if the community of Egypt does not make this pilgrimage, it shall not be visited by the same affliction with which the Lord will strike the other nations that do not come up to observe the Festival of Sukkot.[36] (19) Such will be the punishment of Egypt and all other nations that do not come up to observe the Festival of Sukkot.

The prophet envisions the celebration of Sukkot as the central festival of the restored temple. Failure to perform the Sukkot pilgrimage and obligatory rituals is tantamount to rebellion against God and receives due punishment. That the prophet placed this ultimate test of faith on Sukkot rather than Pesaḥ or another festival demonstrates the importance of Sukkot in his time. In his experience, specifically on Sukkot crowds of pilgrims journeyed to the temple. On Sukkot, temple worship reached its apex as the people faithfully appeared to worship their God. Projected into eschatological time and universalized, Sukkot becomes the point at which all nations, not only Israelites, journey to the temple.

In contrast to the difficulties rebuilding the temple and reconstituting religious life described in Ezra-Nehemiah, Zech 14 implies that Sukkot had once again become the leading temple festival of a flourishing cult. The vision recalls the autumnal festival of first temple times and evokes the description of the mass gathering of all Israelites to celebrate the dedication of the temple under Solomon. The prophecy of a universally observed pilgrimage on Sukkot justifies the title "festival of YHWH"

---

[36]Because Egypt depends on the Nile for its water, and not on rain, a special punishment awaits her. The targum warns that the Nile will not provide its waters. Some emend the text to "it shall be visited by the same affliction," meaning visited by the plague mentioned in vv. 12-15. Meyers, *Zechariah*, 408 translates: "And if the family of Egypt does not go up and does not come in, then no [rain will be] for them; there will be the plague with which Yahweh smites the nations that do not go up and celebrate the Feast of Booths." For thorough textual notes and commentary, see Schaefer, *Zechariah*, 223-32; Meyers, 407-507. See too W. Harrelson, "The Celebration of the Feast of Booths According to Zech. XVI. 16-21," *Religions in Antiquity: Essays in Memory of Erwin Ramsdell Goodenough*, ed. J. Neusner (Leiden: Brill, 1968), 88-96.

employed by earlier biblical sources. On this festival he prophecies "YHWH shall be king over all the earth; in that day YHWH will be one with one name" (14:9), for all nations celebrate the "festival of YHWH." Such exalted images suggest that in the time of the prophet a thriving religious life surrounded the second temple. The community had overcome the difficulties of re-establishing the cult. Temple structures were now institutionalized and accepted by the population. That the prophet predicts destruction probably results from his judgment of the contemporary temple institutions as inherently corrupt. He feels that the situation had deteriorated to such an extent that the temple could only be restored by the direct intervention of God, and only after the nations send part of the city into exile (14:2). The apocalyptic character of the vision stems from the prophet's despair of changing firmly entrenched, successful temple institutions.[37] In any case, Sukkot clearly ranked first in importance among the temple celebrations. Despite the discontinuity in worship before the ascent of the second temple cult, celebration of Sukkot quickly took on its ancient character.

The prophet presupposes a link between Sukkot and rain. Nations that fail to perform the annual pilgrimage to Jerusalem on Sukkot are denied rain in the ensuing year (14:19). The belief that Israel's annual rainfall is determined at the autumn festival, an idea found explicitly in rabbinic sources, grounds this universalized vision of the impact of the celebration of Sukkot upon all nations. Most scholars believe that rain-making rituals always constituted a major element of the festival.[38]

---

[37] I am following the basic line of thought of Hanson, *Apolcalyptic*, 372-95, and, to a certain extent, Otto Plöger, *Theocracy and Eschatology* (Oxford: Basil Blackwell, 1968). Hanson has been criticized for positing too radical a distinction between the 'visionary' and 'heirocratic' parties; see P. Caroll, "Twilight of Prophecy or Dawn of Apocalyptic," *JSOT* 14 (1979) 19-35 and Ackroyd, *Chronicler*, 137-38. (However, Plöger, 107 writes of the 'cultic community' and the 'eschatological group,' and even Ackroyd acknowledges "sharp hostility both from outside the community but also from within.") Still, his reconstruction best accounts for the apocalyptic motifs. For my argument the precise social and religious divisions are less important than the fact of a firmly established cult with impressive festival celebrations, a picture which also emerges from the Chronicler's descriptions of joyous worship (2 Chr 5:2-7:10). The alternative explanation, that Zech 14 expresses the hopes for future restoration of a seer demoralized by a fledgling temple and neglected cult (Meyers, *Zechariah*, 493-506) does not satisfactorily account for the violence, divine intervention and apocalyptic elements, nor explain the importance of Sukkot. How does the Sukkot festival of a dilapidated cult become the model for glorious eschatological worship? If this reconstruction is correct, it would still imply Sukkot was the primary temple festival, and not substantially affect my claims.
[38] Patai, *Hamayim*, 48-62; Mowinckel, *Psalms*, 1:94, 119; 147 n. 124; 2:233; Snaith, *New Year*, 62-63; Volz, *Neujahrsfest*, 15. See too Weinfeld, *Institutions*, 119; E.O.

Primitive agricultural festivals around the world routinely attempt to influence nature to provide ample rain. Ancient Israel, which depended almost exclusively on rain as a source of water, could not have been different. Ironically, the relatively late Zech 14 provides the first explicit testimony of that connection, and demonstrates that in the mid second temple period an important element of Sukkot continued to be the impact on the rain supply.

The connection between Sukkot and rain emphasizes the nature of Sukkot as a temple festival. The entire vision conceives of the temple as controlling the forces of nature. This background explains the transformations of the temple mount and the surrounding terrain. Jerusalem rises above the other mountains, the rest of the country flattens, and a perpetual stream of fresh water flows down from the temple (14:8-11).[39] Since the cult functioned to restore fertility, in the eschatological temple fresh water actually flows out from the temple to fertilize the land. Water flows from high to low, so the temple mount becomes the highest mountain. To fail to observe Sukkot meant that the blessings of the temple – restored fertility of the earth – would not be enjoyed.

Yet this cultic understanding of the festival rites has been overlaid with a prophetic perspective. God withholds rain in order to punish the recalcitrant nations. Their sin is the failure to acknowledge God as King, not the failure to perform a rain-making ritual. The prophecy does not unambiguously suggest that the rites of the festival themselves directly secure rainfall while their neglect results in the absence of rain. The underlying conception is the prophetic idea of reward and punishment.[40] God rewards obedience with ample rain and punishes disobedience with drought. The link to Sukkot therefore is not explained by internal necessities of the prophecy; had the prophet fixed the mandatory date for the pilgrimage at some other point his vision would be no less intelligible. Yet he has set the date on Sukkot, and clearly presupposes some connection between the festival and the rain supply. It is in the

---

James, *Myth and Ritual in the Ancient Near East* (London: Thames and Hudson, 1958), 66-97; Mowinckel, *Psalms*, 1:161-62, 188; A.R. Johnson, "The Rôle of the King in the Jerusalem Cultus," *The Labyrinth*, ed. S. Hooke (New York: Macmillan, 1935), 85-86. Given that Sukkot falls at the beginning of the rainy season, this conclusion is undoubtedly correct, although we lack firm evidence in the sources. For difficulties in demonstrating the connection between Sukkot and rain based on earlier biblical sources, see Rubenstein, *Dissertation*, 277-81.

[39] For this reason God crushes the Mount of Olives, which is taller than Mt Zion, when he attacks the nations (14:3).

[40] So Pedersen, *Israel*, 2:425. Meyers, *Zechariah*, 473-74 sees both "covenantal" and "agrarian" aspects.

background, then, that we see glimmerings of the idea that the rituals of Sukkot impact the upcoming rainfall.

The prophetic perspective complicates the relationship between Sukkot and rain by introducing a powerful relationship between rain and judgment, a relationship that tannaitic literature would delineate more clearly. In this passage motifs of judgment form the background of the prophecy but do not appear in full expression. The "day of the Lord" and the battle against the enemies (14:1,3) evoke the image of God coming to judge the world and the nations. God becomes king over the whole world (14:9) and punishes the peoples who fought against Jerusalem (14:12) and who do not make the yearly pilgrimage. Such punishment points to the idea of an annual divine reckoning. These motifs are refracted through an eschatological lens and emerge more as punishment than verdict. Nonetheless, punishment presupposes judgment, so the background of the prophecy is easily uncovered: On Sukkot God judges Israel (and the nations). Based on Israel's conduct, God determines the rainfall for the approaching year.

Finally, a word must be said about Sukkot and eschatology. Often it is asserted that Sukkot always possessed an eschatological character, and Zech 14 adduced as primary evidence.[41] Yet, while the vision is undoubtedly eschatological, the precise function Sukkot serves in the eschatological arena must be defined carefully. The heart of the vision prophesies a restored city and temple. Having abandoned hope of any historical rectification of the problems, the prophet defers deliverance to the eschatological future. We noted that the despair over the current institutions produces the apocalyptic outlook whereby no restoration is possible short of a radical upheaval through divine intervention.[42] The transformations of the temple mount and the city of Jerusalem similarly manifest despair over the current situation. Only in eschatological time, and through miraculous acts of God, can the temple and city be rebuilt. The eschatological focus thus centers on the restored city, mountain and temple. The prophet visualizes worship in that eschatological temple in

---

[41]Comblin, *Liturgie*, 39-40; Riesenfeld, *Jésus*, 29-54; C.W.F. Smith, "No Time for Figs," *JBL* 79 (1960), 315-27; Daniélou, *Symbols*, 2-3 and *Liturgy*, 334; Daniélou even traces the eschatologizing tendency back to Isa 32:18, "Then my people shall dwell in peaceful homes, in secure dwellings, in untroubled places of rest." He comments, "From this time on, the liturgy of the feast, while remaining a figure of the past, became also a symbol of the future." Even if the verse mentioned "tents" (as Daniélou translates) it would be completely unsatisfactory evidence for this claim. See too the paltry evidence adduced by Schaefer, *Zechariah*, 226.

[42]This point remains whether the despair is caused by alienation from a powerful priestly group controlling a healthy cult (Hanson, *Apocalyptic*, 376-78, 391-92), or by the inability of the prophet and his circle to bring the temple to the glorious state it deserves (Meyers, *Zechariah*, 495-502).

terms of the acme of temple worship – the festival of Sukkot. The eschatological celebration differs from historical Sukkot rituals in its universal perspective; all nations are obligated to bow in the temple now that God has established his sovereignty over the whole earth.[43] But the annual date occurs precisely at this point because Sukkot was the outstanding temple festival, the high point of temple worship, hence the appropriate model for eschatological worship. The annual celebration of the festival contained no inherent eschatological aspect. Rather, the restored temple is the key eschatological concept, rebuilt upon the transformed natural order and purified from its current state of spiritual and moral ruin. Because of its strong association with the temple the festival of Sukkot finds a place in the eschatological vision.

Great care therefore must be taken before asserting that Sukkot possesses inherent eschatological associations. Those who celebrated Sukkot annually at the temple probably experienced no eschatological longings. They came on pilgrimage to the house of their deity, brought sacrifices, witnessed the temple rituals, and celebrated the bounty of the harvest and restored fertility of nature. Their focus was not on the eschatological future but the past harvest season and the fertility of the upcoming year. On the other hand, those groups who could not participate in temple worship because of their hostility toward the contemporary priesthood, or who were disappointed with the state of the cult, visualized a restored temple and a legitimate priesthood. In that temple Sukkot, the paramount annual festival, was naturally celebrated. Hence the "eschatological associations" of Sukkot are reflexes of the festival's deep temple associations. Zech 14 indicates that Sukkot was the temple festival *par excellence*, not that it possessed eschatological motifs.

III. The Book of Jubilees

The Book of Jubilees, usually dated to the early or mid-second century BCE, consists of a retelling of Genesis. The festivals are extremely important to the author for two reasons. First, part of his agenda was to emphasize that the patriarchs observed all Jewish laws

---

[43]Hanson, *Apocalyptic*, 381 also claims that the split of the Mount of Olives creates an "immense processional way" through which God and his heavenly minions enter Jerusalem in triumphal glory. This motif derives from what Hanson calls "the ritual pattern of the conflict myth." The "ritual pattern" stems, at least in part, from the great royal New Year or enthronement festival celebrated at the temple. As we sketched in Chapter 1, III, the central rite of this festival was supposedly the procession of YHWH to his throne in the temple celebrating his annual advent. Thus elements of the vision itself may emerge from the annual autumnal celebration. On the universal aspects of the vision see Hanson, 391-93.

and rituals. Although the Pentateuch sets the revelation on Mt Sinai, and only ascribes isolated practices to the patriarchs (such as circumcision), Jubilees retrojects many more laws to patriarchal times, including the festivals. Second, Jubilees is obsessively concerned with the calendar, which became a major point of controversy among different Jewish groups of the second temple period.[44] Jubilees presupposes a solar calendar that fixes the festivals on the same days of the week each year, as opposed to the lunar-solar mode of reckoning of the Pharisees and rabbis in which the dates of the festivals vary from year to year. The author stresses that the patriarchs celebrated the festivals on the proper days and thus provides the correct precedent for posterity. Two passages in Jubilees describe the festival of Sukkot. Jubilees 16 attributes the first Sukkot celebration to Abraham and his household. Jubilees 32 briefly alludes to Jacob's celebration of Sukkot before pointing out that Jacob first observed "the Addition" on the eighth day.

Jubilees 16 provides the more extensive account of Sukkot celebrations. Abraham builds an altar and celebrates "near the altar" (16:20). The sacrifices listed (16:22-23) deviate somewhat from those prescribed by Num 29:12-40, as occurs regularly in Jubilees.[45] Here the author apparently wishes to emphasize the number seven, inspired perhaps by the seven-day festival in the seventh month, as well as his overarching calendrical scheme of seven-year cycles, so he prescribes seven sheep among the burnt offerings; seven rams, kids, sheep and goats as thank offerings; and seven spices for the concoction of incense. Jacob also brings copious sacrifices on the fifteenth of the seventh month: fourteen bulls, twenty-eight rams, forty-nine sheep, seven lambs and twenty-one goats (32:4; note the multiples of seven.) The number of sacrifices far exceeds the sacrifices brought on other festivals in Jubilees, and points to a temple celebration of great proportions.

Jubilees repeatedly emphasizes joy and rejoicing: Abraham builds the altar to God "who was making him rejoice" and celebrates "a festival of joy" (16:20). He "rejoices with all his heart" along with his household (16:25), again "blessed and rejoiced" (16:27), and calls the festival "the festival of the Lord, a joy acceptable to the most high" (16:28). Israel

---

[44]See Jub 6:32-35 and CD 3:14-15; J. van Goudoever, *Biblical Calendars* (Leiden: Brill, 1959); S. Talmon, "The Calendar of the Covenanters of the Judean Desert," *Scripta Hierosolymitana* 4 (1958), 167-74; L. Schiffman, *The Halakhah at Qumran* (Leiden: Brill, 1976), 84-133.

[45]M. Delcor, "La Fête Des Huttes dans le Rouleau Du Temple et dans le Lovres Des Jubilés," *RQ* 57-58 (1991), 188-91 analyzes the different sacrificial prescriptions in greater depth. See too J.C. Vanderkam, "The Temple Scroll and the Book of Jubilees," *Temple Scroll Studies*, ed. G.J. Brooke (Sheffield: Sheffield Academic Press, 1989), 211-236.

accordingly is commanded to celebrate Sukkot with joy (16:29). And the author concludes that Abraham "praised and gave thanks to his God for all things in joy" while holding the species during the circumambulations (16:31). The almost palpable enthusiasm is in good keeping with the summary of the nature of the festival of Deut 16:15, "you shall have nothing but joy" and the injunction "to rejoice" with the four species of Lev 23:40. Yet the striking repetition suggests that the author draws on intense emotions he experienced personally. The passage indicates again that in the second temple period Sukkot was a very joyous time. Note that Abraham names Sukkot "the festival of the Lord," following biblical terminology, reinforcing the picture of Sukkot as the most joyous feast.[46]

The booths themselves are an unexplained feature of the festival. Abraham builds booths for himself and for his servants (16:21), and the heavenly tablets instruct Israel to dwell in booths (16:29). No reason for this ritual is given. Since Jubilees retrojects the celebration to the time of Abraham it could not justify the ritual by paraphrasing Lev 23:43 which connects the booths to the exodus. The omission of this explanation may indicate that Sukkot was not considered a commemoration of the exodus in the Jubilees circle. It was primarily a cultic and agricultural festival, not a celebration of an historical event. Jubilees then commands that the festival be celebrated in succeeding generations:

> (16:29) Therefore it is ordained in the heavenly tablets concerning Israel that they will be observers of the festival of booths seven days with joy in the seventh month which is acceptable before the Lord (as) an eternal law in their generations throughout all (time), year by year. (30) And there is no limit of days for this because it is ordained forever regarding Israel that they should celebrate it and dwell in booths, and set wreaths upon their heads, and take leafy boughs, and willows from the brook. (31) And Abraham took branches of palm trees, and the fruit of goodly trees, and every day going round the altar with the branches seven times [a day] in the morning, he praised and gave thanks to his God for all things in joy.[47]

---

[46]The passage asserts that Abraham was the first to celebrate the "festival of Sukkot" (16:21). But Abraham himself calls Sukkot "the festival of the Lord, a joy acceptable to the most high God" (16:27). The injunction on the heavenly tablets refers to the "festival of Sukkot." See also Jub 32:28-29 discussed presently.

[47]I have adopted the translation of v. 31 of R.H. Charles, *The Book of Jubilees* (London: Adam and Charles Black, 1902), 118; E. Kautzsch, *Apokryphen und Pseudepigraphen des alten Testaments* (Tübingen: J.C.B. Mohr, 1900), 2:71; A. Kahana, *Hasefarim haḥisonim* (Tel Aviv, 1936), 1:256. O.S. Wintermute in Charlesworth, *Pseudepigrapha*, 89 translates: "...each day of the days he used to go around the altar with the branches. Seven times per day, in the morning, he was praising and giving thanks to God for all things." This translation places the stop after "branches" and begins a new sentence with "seven days." This reading can be understood two ways: 1) Abraham circled the altar but once each day, while

The Second Temple Period

This is the only source to prescribe the wearing of wreaths or crowns on Sukkot.[48] This custom is routinely found at agricultural festivals, and serves as a second means of rejoicing with flora, a variation of the festal bouquet. Hints of this practice appear in the Bible (Isa 28:1-5), and it was a common custom at religious processions throughout the Greco-Roman world.[49] Rabbinic sources mention "sukka-wreaths" and allude to customs of hanging wreaths from the roofing of the sukka.[50] The mention of wreaths in Jubilees suggests that many diverse customs and modes of celebration took place during Sukkot festivities.[51] Lev 23:40 prescribed one of the various agricultural rituals practiced by the Israelites, and this "canonized" ritual became the most prominent rite

---

he praised and gave thanks seven times. 2) Identical to Charles's translation, reading the second sentence as explaining the first: Abraham praised and gave thanks seven times each morning *by* circling the altar. While the first interpretation avoids contradicting the rabbinic practice (mSuk 4:5; see below), it leaves the difficult question of what Abraham did to praise and thank God *seven* times each morning (seven prayer-services?). Unless we understand this sevenfold praise as a hyperbolic figure meaning "a great deal" (cf. Lev 26:18), the only plausible reading requires a sevenfold circumambulation of the altar each day, however the verse is punctuated.

[48]In a painting of the Dura synagogue (3rd century CE) which may depict the procession to the temple in the time of Solomon, some figures hold lulavs while the figures bearing the ark wear wreaths. The dedication occurred at the time of Sukkot (1 Kgs 8), so the artist may have portrayed the celebrants with the ritual objects of the festival. The wreaths evoke this Jubilees passage, and perhaps indicate that standard Sukkot dress included wreaths. See C. Kraeling, *The Synagogue* (New Haven: Yale University Press, 1956), 113-17. However, this interpretation of the painting has been challenged. R. Wischnitzer, *The Messianic Theme in the Painting of the Dura Synagogue* (Chicago: University of Chicago Press, 1948), 53-55 claims the scene depicts "Joseph's bones carried to Canaan," not Solomon's Sukkot festival, while I. Sonne, "The Paintings of the Dura Synagogue," *HUCA* 20 (1947), 306-308 argues it is Aaron's coffin and burial procession.

[49]The participants in Judith's triumphal procession wear wreaths; Jdt 15:13. See too T. Levi 8:9; Tacitus *Hist.* 5:5. For general discussion and other sources see Riesenfeld, *Jésus*, 48-51; K. Berger, *Das Buch der Jubiläen* (Jüdische Schriften aus hellenisch-römanischer Zeit II/3; Gütersloh: Gerd Morn, 1981), 419; and Goodenough, *Symbols*, 7:135-71, esp. 164-65. mBik 3:3 describes a wreath (*'atara*) of olive leaves on the ox bearing first fruits, and R. Zera mentions the same of a lamb, yBik 3:3, 65c. S. Lieberman, *Hellenism in Jewish Palestine* (New York: Jewish Theological Seminary, 1950), 144-46 discusses this practice.

[50]ySuk 1:1, 51d; yBes 1:1, 60b (*'iturei sukka*). See too M. Hadas, "Jub. 16:30," *AJSL* 33 (1933), 338, for what may be a reference to this custom in a scholiast to Aristophanes. In rabbinic sources wreaths also appear at wedding celebrations; mSot 9:14; bSot 49b; ySot 9:16, 24b-c.

[51]See too the Temple Scroll 17:1 (Yadin, *Scroll*, 2:72): "[the] priests; and they shall put wrea[ths(?)] =(*'at[arot]*)." If Yadin's reconstruction is correct, the scrolls document wreaths in the temple context.

among groups that based observance upon scriptural prescriptions. Jubilees alludes to another of the manifold agricultural rites that probably characterized Sukkot during this time.

The passage presents a confusing account of the four species. The heavenly tablets command all Israel to take leafy boughs and willows from the brook (16:30). Abraham himself took branches of palm trees and the fruit of goodly trees for his circumambulations of the altar (16:31). While these are the very species listed in Lev 23:40, in Jubilees they serve in two distinct rites. Only the fruit and palm are held during processions around the altar. The willows and leafy boughs are not used for this purpose but are to be "taken," just as Lev 23:40 specifies. The author does not describe the "taking" in detail,[52] but he probably pictures the carrying of a festal bouquet in the manner of the rabbinic lulav ritual. It appears then that the author of Jubilees wished to paraphrase Lev 23:40, to remain true to his biblical source, yet he knew of two rituals in which flora was carried, so he distributed the biblical species among the two rites. He designates the first two (palms and fruit) for a ritual procession around the altar and the second two (leafy boughs and willows) for a folk ritual not necessarily connected to the temple service. The fact that the branches and willows appear in tandem with the booth and wreath, and not in connection with Abraham's altar rituals, may point to extra-temple celebrations. Whether in Jerusalem or in rural areas, leafy boughs, willows, crowns and other flora served as decorations, adornments, perhaps props for dancing, and symbols of life and joy in sukkot and at private banquets.

Now the circumambulations of the altar corresponds to the ritual which rabbinic sources call 'arava, the willow procession.[53] Ps 118:27,

---

[52]Fishbane, *Interpretation*, 112 n. 20 claims that the willows and leafy boughs are to be used to build the sukkot. I do not think that this is clear from the text. Albeck, *Jubiläen*, 17, claims they are to be carried in the hand.

[53]Full discussion in Chapter 3, I. mSuk 4:5 claims a seven-fold circumambulation took place only on the last day of Sukkot; on the preceding days only one revolution occurred. The Mishna does not specify precisely how the ritual was performed, and the amoraim dispute the matter in bSuk 43b. According to some amoraim willows were erected beside the alter and then the participants circumambulated with lulavs. Other amoraim claim the participants held the willows and subsequently set them up beside the altar. Jubilees corresponds better to the opinion that the circumambulations were with lulavs, but still differs from the rabbinic description, for Jubilees says nothing of the willows for the altar. See L. Finkelstein, *The Pharisees: The Sociological Background of Their Faith*[3] (Philadelphia: Jewish Publication Society, 1962 [1938]), cv. Finkelstein also points out that the author of Jubilees enjoins the procession for seven consecutive days, and therefore rules that the procession takes precedence over the Sabbath. According to mSuk 4:2 the lulav is only taken on the Sabbath if the Sabbath coincides with the first day of Sukkot, while the willow takes precedence over the

"Bedeck the festival with branches at the corners of the altar" may allude to the same ritual.[54] We need not make too much of the inconsistency whereby Jubilees prescribes palms and fruit for the altar procession, and rabbinic sources the willow. The author of Jubilees probably wished to find biblical precedent for both rituals, and divided the plant species mentioned in Lev 23:40 between them. Actual practice may have included all four species, or various combinations of these and other flora, in both rituals.

The verbatim paraphrase of the biblical verses may indicate that at this stage all types of plants were used, that the four kinds had not been interpreted to refer to the specific four types of the rabbinic rite. Thus the *peri 'eṣ hadar* of Lev 23:40 remains "fruit of goodly trees" in Jubilees, not "citrons," and the phrase *'anaf 'eṣ 'avot* is translated "leafy boughs," not myrtle. The author also follows the biblical text by mentioning *"branches of palm,"* not just one palm branch, and "willows *of the brook,"* not just "willow." The rabbis accept various types of willows but require one immature palm frond *(lulav)*, not any branch of the palm. It appears, then, that Jubilees is unaware of the rabbinic interpretation of Lev 23:40. However, the priority of the author may have been to quote the biblical terminology directly. He may have known of (what would become) the rabbinic interpretation, but intended here to employ the biblical phrases. We shall return to this matter in our discussion of the lulav.[55]

That Abraham offered "praise" and "thanks" while he circumambulated the altar points to a liturgical recitation. This may be the aforementioned Ps 118 if the allusion in v. 27 is indeed to the ritual. This Psalm, moreover, comprises part of the group of Psalms known as the Hallel, which rabbinic sources claim was recited each day of Sukkot during the temple service.[56]

The second passage, Jub 32, narrates Jacob's celebration of Sukkot. The author interpreted Gen 33:17, where Jacob builds sukkot for his animals, to imply that Jacob observed the festival. Here Sukkot serves primarily as a framework for other laws and events and a prelude to *Shmini 'aṣeret*. The author is less concerned with informing the reader of the rites of the festival, as he was in Jub 16, and does not make Jacob the

---

Sabbath on the seventh day alone. This Jubilean law is difficult to reconcile with the otherwise extremely stringent Sabbath law (See Jub 50). It is possible that the Jubilean calendar did not count the intermediate Sabbath as a day of the festival. See Rubenstein, *Dissertation*, 271-77 (= "The Sadducees and the Water Libation," *JQR* [forthcoming, 1995]).
[54] See Fishbane, *Interpretation*, 112; Petuchowski, *Psalm*, 268.
[55] Chapter 5, II.
[56] According to mSuk 3:9 the lulav was held during the recitation of the Hallel and shaken at certain times.

paradigmatic precedent-setting worshipper. In fact, the passage does not even mention the festival of Sukkot by name, merely stating that Jacob brought copious sacrifices on the fifteenth of the seventh month and for the following seven days (32:4-6). Jacob is the first to observe *Shmini 'aṣeret*, which Jubilees calls "Addition," and the heavenly tablets command subsequent generations to observe this day.

The passage continues with a series of laws and events that strongly imply a relationship to Sukkot. Jacob sets aside tithes and brings burnt offerings from them, while his son Levi serves as priest for the first time (32:8-9). The laws of tithes found on the heavenly tablets are narrated. Jacob then resolves to build a sanctuary around the altar with a courtyard and wall. God reveals himself to Jacob, blesses him and sends an angel to give Jacob seven tablets containing secrets of the future. The patriarch finds instructions on one of the tablets not to build the sanctuary as planned, because God has selected a special place elsewhere. Now the author of Jubilees is so concerned about setting events in the proper time and specifying their dates that it cannot be coincidental that these events occur on Sukkot. Rather there must be a substantive connection to the festival. Since the "second tithe" must be consumed in Jerusalem "before the Lord," Jubilees appropriately pronounces this law on Sukkot when most people could be expected to journey to Jerusalem. At that time they should remember to bring their tithes so as to fulfill the law and enhance their festival celebrations.[57] The initiation of the priesthood is a prerequisite for institutionalized temple worship, and logically occurs on the great temple festival. Jacob's intention to build the sanctuary at this time recalls Solomon's dedication of the temple on Sukkot.[58] These associations confirm that the author knew Sukkot as the primary pilgrimage and temple festival.

IV. 1-2 Maccabees

Several passages in 1-2 Maccabees relate Sukkot to the festival of Hanukka. The earliest reference appears in a letter cited at the beginning

---

[57]Thus Tobit 1:6-7 proudly recounts how he traveled to Jerusalem at the festivals with his first-fruits and tithes.

[58]Both the tithing commandments and account of Jacob's intention to build a sanctuary respond to issues in the biblical text (Gen 28). When Jacob awakens from his dream he promises to "take a tithe for God" if God keeps him safe on his journey (Gen 28:22). So Jubilees has Jacob actually separate tithes and provides the commandment for posterity. Jacob also promises, "this stone, which I have set up as a pillar, shall be God's abode." And yet he never builds a temple. Jubilees solves the difficulty by explaining that Jacob had planned to build the temple before the heavenly tablets instructed him that God reserved another place for the sanctuary.

The Second Temple Period

of the book of 2 Maccabees. A group of Jerusalem Jews sent the letter in 124 BCE[59] to "their brethren, the Jews that are throughout Egypt," reporting their deliverance after the outrages of Jason, who had usurped the office of high priest, and calling on their coreligionists to celebrate the new festival.

> And now we ask you to celebrate the Days of Sukkot[60] in the month of Kislev (2 Macc 1:9).

They name the festival, which ultimately became known as Hanukka, after Sukkot.[61] A second letter preserved in 2 Macc 1:1-2:18 also links the two festivals:

> Inasmuch as we are about to celebrate, on the twenty-fifth of Kislev, the Purification of the Temple, we thought we ought to let you know, so that you, too, might celebrate [it as Days] of Tabernacles and [Days] of Fire, [as] when Nehemiah, the builder of the temple and the altar, brought sacrifices (2 Macc 1:18).[62]

This passage appears in a forged letter supposedly written in 164 BCE by a triumphant Jerusalem group to the Egyptian communities, but actually written much later.[63] The letter shares a common purpose with the

---

[59]Taking the date in 1:10 as part of this letter, not the following one. See Goldstein, *II Maccabees*, 24, 138-41.
[60]The letter, preserved in Greek, employs the standard Greek name for Sukkot, *skēnopēgia*, the regular translation of "the festival of Sukkot" in the LXX.
[61]Zeitlin would have us translate "...keep the days *like* the feast of Tabernacles in the month of Kislev," suggesting that the term *isa* has dropped out of the text. (See Zeitlin, *First Maccabees*, 54 and *Second Maccabees*, 103). But the text is clear, and it is dangerous to emend against all known witnesses, especially when there are no syntactical or philological difficulties. He claims the Purification festival is "like Tabernacles" in that it lasts for eight days. This datum, however, is not mentioned in the letter. Cf. the translation of E. Kautzsch, *Die Apokrypha und Pseudepigrahen Des Alten Testaments* (Tübingen: J.C.B. Mohr, 1900), 1:86: "So feiert denn nun die Tage [der Tempelweinahe nach Art] des Laubhüttenfest im Monat Kislev."
[62]The text of this passage is elliptical and requires some additions. This translation follows Goldstein, *II Maccabees*, 154, although I have added brackets to clarify the supplemented words. Other translations make similar adjustments. Thus Zeitlin, *Second Maccabees*, 115: "We thought it only right to tell you, so that you too may celebrate [these days like] the Feast of Tabernacles, and the day of the fire, [commemorating the time] when Nehemiah, who rebuilt both the Temple and the altar offered sacrifices" (my brackets), See too Habicht, *2 Makkabäerbuch*, 203; Kautzsch, ibid., 1:87 note "c" on various proposed emendations and Wacholder, *Letter*, 112. Goldstein, *II Maccabees*, 171 claims that "Purification" is the name of the festival, a proper noun, although this point is not universally accepted.
[63]This forged letter cites the authentic earlier letter (2 Macc 1:7-9). Goldstein, *II Maccabees*, 164 dates the letter to 103/2 BCE. Bickerman dates the letter no earlier

previous letter: to encourage Egyptian Jews to adopt the new festival. At the conclusion of the letter the author returns to this goal: "We write you inasmuch as we are about to celebrate the Purification, [asking] if you will also please observe these days" (2 Macc 2:16). Note that this letter does not name the festival after Sukkot, but compares its celebration to Sukkot.

What can we learn about Sukkot from these references? The titles of the festival and its immediate associations indicate again that the authors knew Sukkot as the primary temple festival. That the first letter names a festival celebrating the purification of the temple "the Sukkot of the month of Kislev" shows that Sukkot celebrations centered around the temple. If the second letter instructs the Egyptian community to celebrate the "Purification" festival like Sukkot, then the Sukkot rites must be appropriate for such a celebration. The allusions to Nehemiah and subsequent allusions to Moses and Solomon (2 Macc 2:8) reinforce this point. Nehemiah, "the builder of the temple and altar," probably refers to the initiation of sacrifices under Jeshua and Zerubavel found in Ezra 3:2-4.[64] It seems that according to the author's tradition Nehemiah was involved with that rededication, although the Bible places his advent somewhat later. The author relates that Nehemiah consecrated the altar with the remains of the sacred fire the priests hid away before they went into exile (2 Macc 1:19). This fire was preserved in a liquid state – apparently petroleum – and miraculously changed back into fire, consuming the sacrifices and burning upon the altar. That dedication, as we noted, took place at the time of Sukkot, so the author instructs his

---

than 67 BCE; so M. Hengel, *Judaism and Hellenism*, trans. J. Bowden (Philadelphia: Fortress, 1981), 1:100. Zeitlin, *Second Maccabees*, 36 and a few others argue that 2 Macc opens with one letter, not two, but W. Grimm and O.F. Fritzche, *Kurzgefasstes Exegetisches Handbuch zu den Apokryphen des Alten Testamentes* (Leipzig, 1851-60), 36 already calls this view a "curiosity." On this issue and on the question of a forged or authentic letter see also E. Bickerman, *Studies in Jewish and Christian History* (Leiden: Brill, 1980), 2:136-58; Habicht, *2 Makkabäerbuch*, 199; B. Niese, *Kritik der Beiden Makkabäerbücher* (Berlin: Weidmann, 1900), 13; Attridge, *Historiography*, 182 n. 66; Wacholder, *Letter* and the references there, 89 nn. 1-2 and 90-91 nn. 6-7.

[64]Rabbinic (and presumably proto-rabbinic Jewish) historiography routinely places figures from different historical periods together. For example, Haggai, Zechariah and Malachi reportedly sat on "the Great Assembly" together with Ezra, Nehemiah, and Mordechai (See targum to Song 7:3; Ginzberg, *Legends*, 6:447-49; Ira Schiffer, "The Men of the Great Assembly," in *Persons and Institutions in Early Rabbinic Judaism*, ed. W.S. Green [Missoula, 1977], 237-76). Nehemiah easily could have been considered a contemporary of Jeshua and Zerubavel, and assumed to have taken part in building the altar and temple. Goldstein, *II Maccabees*, 174 suggest Nehemiah was Zerubavel's Hebrew name according to tradition, although there is no evidence of this.

readers to celebrate "[as Days] of Tabernacles and [Days] of Fire." The new temple-purification festival should resemble its precedent, the festival associated with dedication of the second temple altar.[65]

After relating the miracle of Nehemiah's time, the letter alludes to Moses's dedication of the Tabernacle (Lev 9:23-24) and Solomon's dedication of the temple, careful to point out that sacred heavenly fire appeared at both dedications. The Tabernacle dedication lasted eight days and the author claims Solomon also observed an eight-day festival to celebrate the dedication (2 Macc 2:12).[66] The author clearly means to link the "Purification" to the dedication of Solomon, and the eight day celebration provided good precedent for an eight-day festival.[67] In this way he presents the "Purification festival" as the last link in a chain of dedication ceremonies. Solomon and Nehemiah dedicated the temple and altar on Sukkot. The new dedication festival celebrating the Hasmonean triumph continues in this august tradition. It should not be seen as a new, unprecedented festival, but as a divinely sanctioned commemoration that rests on solid biblical and post-biblical tradition. Thus the letter constitutes a piece of propaganda aimed at legitimating the celebration of the Hasmonean triumph and persuading Egyptian

---

[65]The reference to fire relates exclusively to Nehemiah and previous dedications. There is no need to read in an allusion to *simḥat beit hasho'eva* (SBH), the all-night celebration described in rabbinic sources (see Chapter 3, III), as does Zeitlin, *Second Maccabees*, 41 and "The Bet Ha-Shoebah and the Sacred Fire," *JQR NS* 43 (1953), 217-223. Cf. O.S. Rankin, *The Origins of the Festival of Hanukkah* (Edinburgh: T. & T. Clark, 1930), 91-129 for critique of this suggestion. Moreover, Fox has recently disproven the view of SBH as a fire festival; see Fox, *Sho'eva*. Wacholder, *Letter*, 113-14 suggests the reference to "[days of] Fire" pertains to the eight-day commemoration of the burnt offering mentioned in *Megilat Ta'anit*: "From the first to the eighth of Nisan not to fast, for the burnt offering was instituted" (H. Lichtenstein, "Die Fastenrolle," *HUCA* 8-9 [1931-32], 318.) I think this interpretation less likely because the author nowhere states the Purification festival lasts eight days. He implies this length in his claim that Solomon observed an eight-day festival at the dedication of the first temple. Still, to find precedent for this length was a secondary concern at best. If the author means to refer to this commemoration of the burnt offering, he does so on account of the motif of instituting sacrifices or initiating the altar. In any case, the nature of the commemoration mentioned in *Megilat Ta'anit* is disputed; there may never have been an actual festival, but simply a prohibition against fasting. See Yoram Erder, "The First Date in *Megilat Ta'anit* in Light of the Karaite Commentary on the Tabernacle Dedication," *JQR NS* 82 (1992), 263-83.
[66]While in 1 Kgs 8 Solomon observes seven days of a dedication festival and seven days of Sukkot, 2 Chr 7:9 notes that the king dismissed the people on the 23rd of the month, which allows for an eight-day celebration.
[67]It is odd that this letter never explicitly states the festival should last eight days. The length is mentioned only in 2 Macc 10:6.

Jewish communities to celebrate the new festival.[68] The association with previous dedications that took place on Sukkot and the appearances of sacred fire were effective propagandistic devices. Sukkot, the classic temple-dedication festival, served as a model for a new temple-purification festival of Kislev.[69]

A second point of contact between Sukkot and the new festival appears in a passage from the body of 2 Maccabees. This book is an epitome of a five volume history written by Jason of Cyrene, who probably lived in the early first century BCE.[70]

---

[68] Why should the Egyptian community have been so reluctant to accept the new festival? First, it was not traditional Jewish practice to spontaneously institute festivals. Jewish festivals were commanded by God and recorded plainly in the Bible. Purim, which like Hanukka seems to lack the divine imprimatur, at least had been canonized in the biblical corpus. And despite this fortuitous event, the propagandizing letters at the end of Esther insisting that all communities of Jews accepted the obligation as Mordechai prescribed (Esth 9:27-32), that now all Jews are "irrevocably obligated" to observe the days, suggest that some rejected the innovative commemoration. Moreover, the Egyptian Jewish communities were probably influenced by the Oniad priestly dynasty. The Oniads considered themselves the rightful high priests, and considered the Hasmoneans no more legitimate than Jason and the Hellenists they replaced. To observe a purification festival sanctioning the rededication of worship under an illegitimate priesthood was obviously an anathema. As the Hasmoneans became progressively more Hellenized the Oniad suspicions would only become more compelling to Egyptian Jews. In this hostile environment the author composed his letter to defend the legitimacy of the Hasmonean dynasty and their dedication festival. He points out that Moses, Solomon and Nehemiah had their deeds sanctioned by providence. Now Judah has purified the temple once again. The author suggests this event parallels those of his predecessors and subtly cautions the Egyptian communities to understand the consequences of ignoring a divinely approved festival. See Goldstein, *II Maccabees*, 24-25, 138-53, 161-67; Attridge, *Historiography*, 183. (Goldstein considers the letters to be propaganda directed specifically at the Oniad priests and their schismatic temple. This interpretation exaggerates and necessitates overreading the text. But he correctly identifies the source of resistance to the new festival.) S. Zeitlin, "Hanukkah: Its Origin and Significance," *JQR NS* 29 (1938/9), 21-23 attributes the Egyptian communities' reluctance to accept the festival to the fact that they experienced neither the persecution nor the Hasmonean triumph. They would not celebrate a festival commemorating a military victory, but could be impressed by a miracle of sacred fire.

[69] So M. Liber, "Hanoucca et Souccot," *REJ* 63 (1912), 25: "Entre Souccot et Hanoucca le lien le Temple; les deux fêtes sont des fêtes de Dédicace, des fêtes du Temple."

[70] The dates of Jason and his epitomist are disputed. While some claim Jason was an eyewitness to the Hasmonean triumphs, others date his work as late as the middle of the first century. See Hengel, *Hellenism*, 1:96 and the notes there for a survey of the views; Schürer, *History*, 3/1:180-85; Habicht, 2 *Makkabäerbuch*, 173-77 and Attridge, *Historiography*, 177. Goldstein, *II Maccabees*, 83 suggests Jason

On the very same date on which the temple was profaned by foreigners occurred the purification of temple, on the twenty-fifth of the ninth month (that is, Kislev). Joyfully they held an eight-day celebration, after the pattern of Sukkot, remembering how a short time before they spent the festival of Sukkot like wild beasts, in the mountains and in the caves. Therefore holding wreathed wands, and graceful branches, and palm fronds, they offered songs of praise to Him Who had victoriously brought about the purification of His Place. By vote of the commonwealth they decreed a rule for the entire nation of Jews to observe these days annually. (2 Macc 10:5-8)[71]

Jason does not name the festival after Sukkot but draws parallels between Sukkot rituals and the Hasmonean celebration. He ignores the association with founding of temples and altars; historical precedents for dedications on Sukkot are not his interest. Rather he suggests that the new festival originated as a substitute for a missed Sukkot celebration. Fighting the guerrilla war against the forces of evil, the faithful Jews could not observe Sukkot in its proper manner. After their victory in Kislev they replicated the festivities neglected two months previously. For this reason, Jason informs us, they celebrated eight days and rejoiced by holding wands (lulavs) and singing hymns. Yet he does not explicitly direct that the annual observance should be conducted in this way.

This new explanation seems to be another attempt to legitimate the innovative festival. Branches were commonly held and waved during parades, victory celebrations and other festivities. The account of the celebration after Simon conquered the Jerusalem citadel in 1 Macc 13:51, for example, describes the people bearing palm branches without any reference to Sukkot: "Simon's men entered the citadel...with utterances of praise and palm branches and to the music of lyres and cymbals and lutes and hymns and songs." Jason probably pictured the celebratory parade after the rededication of the temple in similar terms, and drew a parallel to the Sukkot rituals. In this way he provided a clearer explanation of the name "Sukkot in the month of Kislev," which the first letter did not explain, and the second letter associated with temple dedications. Apparently the festival was known by several names for some years until the title "Hanukka" (Dedication) became dominant: Josephus calls the festival "Lights" (*phota*), while the letters at the beginning of 2 Maccabees employ "Purification," and "Sukkot in the month of Kislev."[72] Familiar with the latter title but unclear as to what

---

wrote by 86 BCE, and the epitomist between 78/7 and 63 BCE. Few support Zeitlin, *Second Maccabees*, 27-30, who dates the epitomist to the reign of King Agrippa, 41-44 CE.
[71] Translation from Goldstein, *II Maccabees*, 374. I have substituted "Sukkot" for "Tabernacles."
[72] 1 Macc 4:56 (Dedication); 2 Macc 1:18 (Purification).

the festival had to do with Sukkot, Jason devised this explanation.⁷³ The artificial explanation served Jason's purpose of promoting the new Hasmonean festival. Jason points out that the commonwealth ordained that all Jews observe a similar festival each year. The victory celebration was not a one-time make-up for a neglected Sukkot festival, but precedent for an annual festival to commemorate the triumph of Judah and to honor "Him Who had brought about the purification of his place." God delivered the whole Jewish people, not only the Jews of Judea, hence "the entire nation" ought to observe the festival.⁷⁴

Whether contrived by Jason or commonplace, the explanation of Hanukka as a make-up Sukkot again reveals a strong link between Sukkot and the temple. In this case the associations derive not from the motif of Sukkot as paradigmatic dedication festival but from the nature of annual Sukkot celebrations. Fugitives in the mountains and denied access to the temple, pious Jews could not observe Sukkot. True, they could not celebrate Pesaḥ, Shavuot or other festivals, but these were of

---

⁷³Goldstein, *I Maccabees*, 274-80 takes the reference to Sukkot far too seriously, and confuses history with historiography. He suggests Judah Maccabee wanted to dedicate the altar on Sukkot, and since they had missed two intercalations while the Hellenists held power, the calendar was two full months off, and the twenty-fifth of Kislev (of the "defective" calendar) was actually the fifteenth of Tishrei, only ten days after the appropriate time for the festival. Judah found biblical sanction for prolonging Sukkot beyond its set time based on Solomon extending Sukkot (according to the hypothetical Hasmonean text of Chronicles) and Hezekiah delaying Pesaḥ. The Hasmonean festival thus *really was* a Sukkot celebration. Judah expected a miracle of divine fire like that which occurred in the time of Solomon, and since none took place, everyone tried to forget that the original festival was meant to be a Sukkot celebration. All this is far too speculative. The author of 1 Maccabees had no problems with a newly instituted Hasmonean festival, and shows no awareness of a relationship to Sukkot. Indeed, he suggests the festival was observed on the twenty-fifth of Kislev because that was the same day Antiochus had first profaned the temple (1 Macc 4:52-55). On the other hand, the authors of 2 Maccabees and of the letters attempt to defend the legitimacy of the Hasmonean festival by tying in Sukkot. What Judah himself thought is unknown. For less complicated reconstructions that share the view of the first Hanukka as a Sukkot celebration see R. Leszynsky, "Das Laubhüttenfest Chanukka," *MGWJ* 55 (1911), 400-18; M. Liber, "Hanoucca et Souccot," *REJ* 63 (1912), 24-26 (with further references there 24 n. 1.) Contra this position see Geiger, *Urschrift*, 24; Zeitlin, *First Maccabees*, 52-54 who claims, however, that the pious Jews actually celebrated Sukkot together with the dedication festival. I think it more likely to see the use of Sukkot as a later legitimizing device.

⁷⁴Attridge, *Historiography*, 182: "While the epitome of Jason's work is thus primarily a didactic reflection on history which preserves some valuable data, 2 Maccabees in its final form may well have been designed for a specific cultic purpose. The two introductory letters, as already noted, call upon Egyptian Jews to observe the festival of the rededication of the temple."

The Second Temple Period

less importance. Victorious in battle and having purified the temple, they were able to celebrate Sukkot properly. For Jason, inability to celebrate Sukkot was a principal consequence of losing the temple; resumption of its celebration the essential benefit of the temple's purification. Sukkot again is the temple festival *par excellence*.

The phrase "wreathed wands, and graceful branches, and palm fronds" clearly alludes to the four species of Lev 23:40. The author employs the Greek word *thyrsoi*, a most appropriate term for the ritual bouquet. *Thyrsoi* were actually wands carried by worshippers in celebrations dedicated to the Greek god Dionysus. They were generally fashioned from a shaft wreathed with ivy and vine leaves, with a pinecone on top,[75] but were occasionally made from different flora.[76] By employing this technical term the author designates a specific ritual function, for *thyrsoi* were cultic artifacts, and generally not used in political ceremonies or other festivities.[77] Josephus, we shall see, uses this very term for the lulav. The palm fronds recall the "branches of palm" of Leviticus, and "graceful branches" parallel the "branches of leafy trees" and perhaps allude to the "beautiful (= graceful) fruit" as well.[78] Note that the author does not refer to myrtles or citrons, which would identify the biblical species specifically.

The final reference to Sukkot appears in 1 Macc 10:21.[79] The author briefly notes that "Jonathan put on the sacred vestments in the seventh month of the year 160,[80] on the festival of Sukkot." The Seleucid King Alexander Balas, who was engaged in a power struggle with his rival Demetrius, attempted to form an alliance with Jonathan and so appointed him high priest. Meanwhile Jonathan had already assumed de facto power in Jerusalem and needed no Seleucid appointment. To

---

[75] Liddell-Scott, s.v. *thyrsos*.
[76] F. van Lorentz, "Thyrsos," in P.-W., 6:A,1:747-52; A. Reinach, "L'Origine de Thyrse," *RHR* 66 (1912), 27-38.
[77] The use of the term in Jdt 15:12, a non-cultic context, is an exception. See the sources quoted in Reinach, ibid., 18-19.
[78] Jason's terminology is close to the LXX to Lev 23:40. Graceful branches, *kladous hōraious*, echoes *karpon ksulou hōraion*, the translation of *peri 'eṣ hadar*. The term *kladous* (branches) corresponds to the third species in Leviticus, *kladous ksulou daseis* (branches of leafy trees). And the "palm fronds," *phoinikas*, of course alludes to the "branches of palm trees," *kallunthra phoinikōn*. We might even take Jason's latter two terms as explanations of the first: "wreathed wands, i.e., graceful branches and palms," despite the interposing particle "and."
[79] Goldstein, *I Maccabees*, 62-63, places 1 Maccabees later than the last decade of second century BCE but earlier than 63 BCE. Seth Schwartz, "Israel and the Nations Roundabout: I Maccabees and the Hasmonean Expansion," *JJS* 52 (1991), 16-38 argues for a much earlier date.
[80] 152 BCE.

demonstrate his authority Jonathan donned the high priest's vestments during the festival of Sukkot. The passage implies that Sukkot was the appropriate time to assume the high priesthood, not that Sukkot happened to be the time of year when Jonathan received the appointment or independently consolidated his power. Sukkot was certainly an appropriate time for such public demonstrations of authority, when masses came on pilgrimage and the high priest had the opportunity to feature in the elaborate Sukkot ceremonies.[81] Dedication of temples, altar, and priestly dynasties consistently gravitate to Sukkot.

V. Qumran Scrolls

The Qumran (Dead Sea) Scrolls have contributed a great deal to the study of Judaism in the second temple period. Unfortunately, few texts mention Sukkot specifically, and the occasional references are not very informative.

Most references to Sukkot occur in the Temple Scroll, which provides detailed instructions about the dimensions of the temple, its chambers and utensils, together with lists of the appropriate sacrifices.[82] Cols. 27:10-29:1 detail the sacrifices required for the second, third and fourth days of Sukkot; prescriptions for the other days have been lost. The passage is in close agreement with Num 29:12-25, the main difference being that the kid for the purification-offering is listed with the other sacrifices that require a drink and meal offering.[83] In Numbers the kid is listed separately.[84]

---

[81] Note that in *AJ* 18:93-95 Josephus relates that the Roman governors kept the high priest's garments and gave them to the high priest seven days before the three yearly festivals and the fast day.

[82] The Temple Scroll (11QTemple) deals with laws of Sukkot in Cols. 11:13, 27:10-29:13, 42:10-17, 44:6-16. Yadin summarizes the implications of this text for Sukkot in *The Temple Scroll*, 1:134-136.

[83] Yadin, *Temple*, 1:135, 143. G.A. Anderson, "The Interpretation of the Purification Offering in the *Temple Scroll* (11QTemple) and Rabbinic Literature," *JBL* 111 (1992), 24-30 explains the exegesis that led to these requirements for the purification offering. For an inventory of the other minor differences see M. Delcor, "La Fête Des Huttes dans le Rouleau Du Temple et dans le Lovres Des Jubilés," *RQ* 57-58 (1991), 183-85.

[84] The lulav is not mentioned in these columns. The absence is because the passage deals exclusively with the obligatory sacrifices, not other rituals. Booths are not mentioned here either. They receive attention in cols. 42 and 44 only because the frameworks of the sukkot were permanent fixtures, hence part of the temple structure itself. The lack of explicit mention of the lulav therefore does not imply the rite was unknown to the author of the Temple Scroll. Note that there is no commandment to eat unleavened bread on Pesaḥ, although the laws of the paschal sacrifice appear in col. 17 (2:73-74).

The Second Temple Period

The instructions for the construction of the temple prescribe that sukkot be built upon the top story of the edifice:[85]

> And on the roof of the third [story] you shall make columns, roofed over by beams, (stretching) from one column to another; (this will serve as a) place for booths; eight cubits high (shall be the height of the columns), and the booths shall be built on them every year on the Festival of Sukkot, for the elders of the congregation, for the leaders, for the heads of the fathers' houses of the children of Israel, and for the commanders of the thousands and for the commanders of the hundreds, who will come up and sit there until the sacri[fi]cing of the festival burnt offering – that of the Festival of Sukkot; (thus they shall do) every year.[86]

The scroll instructs that beams be placed on columns atop the rooms of the third and outer courtyard, and that booths be built there each year. Apparently the beams were permanent structures that served as the framework for the roofing of the sukkot. The passages about the divisions of areas of the temple also lists sukkot among the chambers and rooms allotted to each tribe (col. 44:6-10.) Here too the sukkot, or at least the beams, are fixed structures perched on the columns. The author mentions one booth for the fifty-four chambers of Judah, and two sukkot for the one hundred and eight chambers of Levi. He pictures long sukkot stretching across the extent of the roof. The meaning of the directive to build the sukkot each year presumably refers to the special roofing, the *skhakh*. Each year the "skeletal structures," as Yadin calls them, the beams and columns, were covered with the requisite roofing.[87] Later we will discuss the relevance of other aspects of this passage to the halakhic development of the sukka.[88]

These sukkot serve the congregation of Jews (or at least their leaders) who journey to the temple. The instruction that they sit in the sukkot until the completion of the sacrifice is interesting. This seems to constitute a specific obligation to dwell in a sukka throughout the temple service. Not only was one to eat and sleep in a sukka, but one stayed in a sukka while the sacrificial rite was performed.[89]

---

[85] On the structure of the temple in the Temple Scroll, see Johann Maier, "The Temple Scroll and Tendencies in the Cultic Architecture of the Second Commonwealth," *Archaeology and History in the Dead Seas Scrolls*, ed. Lawrence H. Schiffman (Sheffield: Sheffield Academic Press, 1990), 67-82.
[86] Col. 42:3-17; Yadin, *Temple*, 2:179-180.
[87] Yadin, *Temple*, 1:135.
[88] Chapter 5, IV and VI. Yadin, *Temple*, 136 notes that the prescription to build sukkot within the temple complex echoes the description in Neh 8:16 that sukkot were built "in the courts of the house of God."
[89] I. Knohl, "Post-Biblical Sectarianism and the Priestly Schools of the Pentateuch: The Issue of popular Participation in the Temple Cult on Festivals," *The Madrid Qumran Congress*, ed. J.T. Barrera and L.V. Montaner (Leiden: Brill, 1992), 2:606-

The fragmentary state of many of the scrolls makes it difficult to arrive at solid conclusions. A recently published fragment seems to refer to the four species.[90] The fragment contains a list of times for praising God, and mentions several of the group's festivals documented in other scrolls. The last preserved line reads:

> [...] Praise and bless and thank
> [...Praise and bless] and thank with branches of a [leafy] tree (*'anfei 'eṣ 'avot*)

---

607 reads this precept as a polemic against the popular "procession ceremonies" celebrated by the folk and the Pharisees. The Sadducean/Boethusian author of the Temple Scroll felt participation of the laity compromised the holiness and purity of the cult. He insists the folk remain in booths in the outer courtyards during the sacrificial service, watching passively and not engaging in any ritual activity. I think Knohl has overinterpreted the passage, which, for a polemic, is quite restrained. Moreover the passage only requires the leaders to sit in the booths, not the masses who would most offend the sanctity of the temple. And they need only remain in booths until the completion of the offering of the festival sacrifice. Could they not then carry out the "procession ceremonies"? The purported Sadducean/Boethusian opposition to the water libation (tSuk 3:16; bSuk 48b; ySuk 4:8, 54d) challenged a sacerdotal ritual, not a popular procession. Most importantly, opposition to the willow ritual focused on violations of the Sabbath, not the ritual per se. tSuk 3:1 carefully notes: "For the Boethusians do not admit that the beating of willows takes precedence over the Sabbath." See Chapter 3, n. 23 and the corresponding text, and Rubenstein, *Dissertation*, 254-62; contra Knohl, 604 n. 10. In fact, the opposite argument could be made: the sukkot for Israelites reflects a policy of including non-priests in cultic worship. It supplies a ritual act for Israelites parallel to the priestly sacrificial rites.

There may be a fragment related to this law of building sukkot in the temple preserved in a midrash-halakha found in *Sifra Deut.* §140 (193): "*You shall make the Festival of Sukkot for yourselves for seven days (Deut 16:13).* For the layman. How do I know even for God? (*gavoah*; or "for the temple"). It teaches: *The Festival of Sukkot for the Lord seven days (Lev 23:34).* As long as you make a sukka, I consider it as if you made it for God." The midrash is difficult, as shown by the wide range of explanations found in the commentaries. It seems that this midrash has been reworked by later hands. The original midrash ended with the citation from Leviticus. Focusing on the tension between Deut 16:13, that describes the festival "for yourselves," and Lev 23:34, that proclaims the festival is "for the Lord," the midrash derives two commandments, to make sukkot both "for yourselves" (layman), and "for God," i.e., for the temple. Recall that Neh 8:16 notes the community made sukkot "in the courtyards of the House of God." I suspect a midrash-halakha similar to that of the *Sifre* underlies the Temple Scroll's sukkot within the temple compound and the commandment to sit in them during the sacrifices. In this way one makes a "Festival of Sukkot for God."

[90] E. Qimron, "Times for Praising God: A Fragment of a Scroll from Qumran (4Q409)," *JQR NS* 80 (1990), 341-47.

Perhaps the beginning of the second line read "on the days of Sukkot," thus listing the festival and its associated ritual.[91] This fragment is extremely significant for it refers to the ritual of Lev 23:40. The term "branches of a leafy tree" corresponds to the rabbinic term "lulav," that is, the four species together. While the rabbis used the palm as the *pars par toto* for the four species, the text here adopts the biblical phrase "branches of a leafy tree,"[92] which the rabbis interpreted as the myrtle. In any case, we have good evidence that the Qumran community interpreted Lev 23:40 as a festal bouquet.

Finally a very fragmentary text, 4Q502, contains several suggestive phrases.[93]

[ידם] [מ].[ם.. [   ] [יבר]ך להם] [לאחיות] [אשר חבב] [בבית ה
[לולבי]ם [ד לפניו כו]ל [שבעת ימי]ם [ברוך אל] [חת כבוד] [ומהללים]
[שלום] [ה לשמחת] [קו]דש קודשי]ם [ד לק]ים [שמחה]

The second line, "...lulavs[94]...before him all...seven days...bless God...honor...and praise" is highly suggestive. True, "lulav" serves as a generic term for "palm" and other plant products, and need not refer specifically to the festival bouquet as in rabbinic literature. However, Joseph Baumgarten proposes the mention of "seven days" and "praise" indicates the text pertains to Sukkot.[95] Reference in the following line to

---

[91] This would parallel the instructions for other festivals: "[...Praise and bless] in the days of the wood festival with offering of] wood for sacrifices [and bless his name. Praise and bless] on the day of commemoration by acclamation [with the shofar]." But as can be seen from the brackets, this pattern of festival and means of praise is partially reconstructed in each case.
[92] Qimron, ibid., 346 notes that the fragment reads "branches," in the plural, whereas Lev 23:40 reads "branch." He points out that later Hebrew routinely adopts the plural for nouns used collectively in biblical Hebrew. The Samaritan Pentateuch also has the plural, "branches." Perhaps the Qumran text had this reading too.
[93] The text was published by M. Baillet in *Discoveries in the Judean Desert 7* (Oxford: Clarendon Press, 1982), p. 94, fragments 94-99 1. 2. It is dated on paleographic grounds to the beginning of the first century BCE. Baillet calls this text "Rituel de Mariage," and suggests that it comprises the liturgy for a marriage ceremony, although the final portions are so fragmentary as to preclude identification with any certainty.
[94] All that can be read from the photograph (plate xxxii) are the letters ולב (hence the transcription should read [ל.]ולב[ם.) But see Baillet's note, p. 94: "Sur le bord droit on devine le contour du premier *lamed*."
[95] Baumgarten, 4Q502. Baillet, who conjectured that the text comprised the liturgy of a marriage ritual, commented on the mention of the lulav: "Sagit-il du 'lulab', branche de palmier traditionellement employée pour la fête des Tabernacles? ...Il est vrai que la palme puvait figurer dans d'autres cérémonies." If Baillet is correct, the use of the lulav at marriage ceremonies may have derived from Sukkot practice, and may indirectly confirm that the lulav was practiced on

"joy" also recalls a familiar characteristic of Sukkot.[96] If this is correct, then we have evidence of the term lulav in an extra-rabbinic source.

This text comprises the liturgy for a ritual gathering of some sort. Baumgarten notes that the larger fragments repeatedly mention "mature men and women," and "elderly men and women," (*'ashishim, 'ashishot, zeqeinim, zeqeinot*) as well as "young men and women, brothers and sisters" (*ne'arim, ne'arot, 'ahim* and *'ahayot.*) The ritual thus included men and women, and gave special prominence to the elderly. He suggests that the text served as the liturgy for a popular gathering on Sukkot, that these features "bring to mind the popular Sukkot celebration known as *simhat bet ha-so'ebah*," the all-night celebration in the temple courtyard. We shall discuss this celebration in more detail in the following chapter. Even if the 4Q502 gathering is not to be identified specifically with SBH, that it reflects popular Sukkot celebrations seems likely.

The data is admittedly meager, but the scrolls do provide some interesting information. If the liturgical texts reflect the practices of the Qumran community, as seems likely, then we have additional evidence that the Sukkot rituals were practiced outside of the temple. Presumably the men of Qumran held or shook the four species during their prayer services. While one text calls the ritual bouquet after biblical terminology, consistent with the general tendency of the Qumran community to remain close to the biblical world, 4Q502 employs the post-biblical term *lulav*, known from rabbinic sources. If the identification of 4Q502 as a popular Sukkot celebration is correct, it is further indication of popular participation in Sukkot rites.[97]

Sukkot. On the other hand, other sources of the celebratory use of flora are equally possible. Baumgarten criticized Baillet's analysis of the text, noting that the joyous celebration of a marriage is incompatible with the Qumran-Essene ideal of celibate monasticism.

[96]Fragment 8 contains the phrases פרי עצה and Fragment 9 ומי תהומיה and וכול יבולה. These references point to prayers for fertility and rain appropriate for Sukkot.

[97]The only other references to Sukkot in the (to date published) scrolls are the Mishmerot texts, which list the priestly courses designated to serve on the festival of Sukkot. See B.Z. Wacholder and M.G. Abegg, *A Preliminary Edition of the Unpublished Dead Sea Scrolls* (Washington, D.C.: Biblical Archeology Society, 1991), 64-66, 71-73: Mishmerot A Fragment 4 iii:9; iv:4, 13; v:7; vi:2; Mishmerot B^a Fragment 2 ii:2, 7; iii:2, 6, 9. Other such texts were published by R.H. Eisenman and M. Wise, *The Dead Sea Scrolls Uncovered* (Rockport, Massachusetts: Element Books, 1992), 109-128. CD 7:10 (C. Rabin, *The Zadokite Fragments*² [Oxford, Clarendon Press, 1958], 28) and 4QFlor (T. Gaster, *The Dead Sea Scriptures*³ [Garden City, N.Y.; Anchor Press, 1976], 447) offer explanations of Amos 9:6, "I will raise up the fallen sukka of David," but provide no information about the festival. The reference to the sukka in CD 11:8 has nothing to do with Sukkot. In the context of Sabbath law, the document rules: "One may not carry [anything] from his house to the outside, or from the outside to his house. If he is in a sukka

The Second Temple Period

VI. Philo

Philo, who was one of the leaders of the Alexandrian Jewish community, lived from about 20 BCE to 50 CE. His main discussion of Sukkot appears in *Special Laws* 2:204-214, his treatise of explanations, commentary and analysis of much of biblical law. Philo calls the festival *skēnai*, a Greek word that can mean either "tents" or "booths,"[98] and asserts that the festival occurs at the autumnal equinox. This dating of the festival is peculiar to Philo and at odds with the rabbinic calendar, according to which the fifteenth of Tishrei does not fall at the equinox. It is possible that Philo has interpreted Exod 34:22, "the turn *(tequfa)* of the year," to refer to the equinox.[99] On the other hand, Philo notes that Pesaḥ occurs in the month of the vernal equinox, so perhaps he simply means that Sukkot falls near the equinox. Philo learns from the equinox that "we should honor equality and hate inequality" – a lovely thought, but one that tells us little about Sukkot. From the *autumnal (metōporinē)* setting Philo then learns a lesson about thanksgiving. Playing on the etymology of this word, Philo points out that the festival follows the ripening *(meta tēn opōran)*. Once the ripened fruits are gathered in it is appropriate to thank God, the source of all good.

Philo then mentions the commandment to stay in booths / tents / *skēnas*. His first explanation for the ritual is as follows:

---

he may not carry [anything] from it nor bring [anything] inside." (אל יוצא איש מן הבית לחוץ ומן החוץ אל הבית: ואם בסוכה יהיה — אל יוצא ממנה ואל יבא אליה). Both Rabin, 54-55 and L. Schiffman, *The Halakhah at Qumran*, (Leiden: Brill, 1976), 113 interpret this law to require that every family build its own sukka. (Rabin actually translates the law: "Even if he be in a booth *for Tabernacles*, let him not take..." [his italics.]) They claim the same law is reflected in Josephus who states that "Moses bids each household to fix up booths" (*AJ* 3:244, cited below. Rabin translates: "that each family must have its own private booth for Tabernacles.") Josephus, however, loosely paraphrases biblical legislation, and hardly intends to rule that one may not use a booth belonging to other families. Rabin also coordinates this ruling with R. Eliezer's opinion, bSuk 27b (Rabin's reference bSuk 9a is errant) that each man must possess his own sukka. (The sages permit one to dwell in a sukka belonging to another.) But CD 11:8 does not state that each family must possess its own sukka. The law simply gives a booth the status of a house with respect to the laws of carrying on the Sabbath. In any case, nothing in the scroll indicates that a *festival* sukka is at issue. Booths were used for a variety of purposes including storage and shelter for animals.

[98] The standard Greek term, found in the LXX, 2 Maccabees and Josephus is *skēnopēgia*, "pitching tents/booths." Philo's name *skēnai* is not found elsewhere.

[99] The LXX reads *mesounto tou eniautou*, the "middle of the year," which Philo may have understood as the "midpoint" or equinox. On Sukkot as an equinoctial festival, see Chapter 3, III n. 133. Goodenough, *Symbols*, 4:159-161 reads in a mystical element to this and the other explanations of Philo.

The reason of this may be that the labour of the husbandmen no longer requires that they should live in the open air, as nothing is now left unprotected but all the fruits are stored in silos or similar places to escape the damage which often ensues through the blazing sunshine or storms of rain. For when the crops which feed us are standing in the open field, you can only watch and guard the food so necessary to you, by coming out and not shutting yourself up like a woman who never stirs outside her quarters. And if while you remain in the open air you encounter extreme cold or heat, you have the thick growth of the trees waiting to shade you, and sheltered under them you can easily escape injury from either source. But when all the fruits are being gathered in, come in yourself also to seek a more weatherproof mode of life and hope for rest in place of the toils which you endured when laboring on the land.

During the harvest season the laborer must venture outside to tend to the crops and remain for long periods of time in the fields and orchards. Although no man-made shelters are located there, the growth of trees provides a measure of protection against the elements, both shade from the sun and shelter from wind and cold. However, when the harvest labors have been completed, one naturally returns to more "weatherproof" domiciles, to *skēnas*. There one rests from the arduous work of the ingathering. Here Philo attempts to relate the stay in sukkot to the harvest, to find an explanation for the practice linked to the agricultural cycle. Because the festival follows the harvest, he is loath to explain the *skēnas* as protective shelters for field workers. Rather they serve as the dwellings to which farmers return after the agricultural labors have been completed. It appears that Philo conceives of the *skēnē* as a firmly constructed tent able to provide solid shelter, not a booth or hut for temporary protection against the elements; *skēnē* in and of itself admits both meanings. For this reason I am hesitant to routinely translate Philo's *skēnē* as "booth."[100] We noted in Chapter One that biblical scholars struggle with this very question of the original function of the booths. Living in Alexandria and unfamiliar with Palestinian agricultural life, Philo did not appreciate that booths provided shelters in the fields during the harvest and simultaneously a place for festivities to commence. Ironically, whereas for H the sukka resuscitates a primitive agricultural rite, for Philo the ritual relates more to culture than nature, marking the return from the natural agricultural world to the type of solid dwellings that characterize the city.

Philo then provides a second explanation for residing in tents: the tents recall the journeys of the forefathers in the desert, who resided in

---

[100]Following the LXX, Philo regularly uses *skēnē* for the tents of the Israelites in the desert (see e.g. *Life of Moses* 1, 169, 200, 289, 313) and for the Tabernacle (*mishkan*).

tents at various stopping points. This reason derives from Lev 23:43, although Philo does not frame his comments in terms of God causing the Israelites to dwell in tents. For him the Israelites naturally stayed in the typical dwellings of desert travelers. From this Philo learns another moral lesson: one should remember old misfortunes in times of prosperity. This awareness is not only a great pleasure, but leads to a life of piety, for one becomes grateful for the present good fortune and fears a change for the worse. Philo notes that they thank God for this prosperity "with songs and words of praise and beseech Him and propitiate Him with supplications that they may never repeat the experience of such evils." Perhaps here he alludes to a festival liturgy including psalms and thanksgiving litanies (*hikesiai* = *hosha'anot*) practiced in the diaspora on Sukkot.

To explain why the festival occurs on the fifteenth of the month Philo again appeals to the equinox. At this time moonrise immediately follows sunset, so the day is never without "the glorious light which nature gives." Philo makes similar remarks about Pesaḥ and the vernal equinox, emphasizing the continual light provided by the sun and moon.[101] He calls *Shmini 'aṣeret* the "closing" festival because it concludes both Sukkot and the cycle of annual festivals. Philo ends his comments on Sukkot with an interpretation of the eight day length of the festival. Eight is the first cubic number, and begins a "higher category of solids." Likewise the autumnal festival is a "complement" and "conclusion" to the other festivals, and has more "stability" and "fixity." At the conclusion of the agricultural year, there remains no anxiety about the upcoming harvests. Sukkot is therefore the most "solid" festival, when heightened experiences of joy, celebration and thanksgiving occur.

These moral lessons are consistent with Philo's general tendency to interpret biblical passages for pedagogic purposes, usually in an allegorical fashion. They probably say little about how the festival was actually celebrated or what it meant to most Alexandrian Jews. However, in *Flaccus* §116-24, Philo provides a partial account of a Sukkot celebration in Alexandria. He relates that Gaius Flaccus, the Roman governor who had made life miserable for the Jews, met his downfall during Sukkot. Philo compares the misery the Jews experienced before Flaccus's arrest with the outpouring of joy afterward:

> For the Jews were holding then the national feast of the autumn equinox, in which it is the custom of the Jews to live in *skēnas*. But nothing at all of the festal proceedings was being carried out. The rulers were still suffering...

---

[101] *Special Laws* 2:155.

> All night long they continued to sing hymns and songs of praise and at dawn pouring out through the gates, they made their way to the parts of the beach near at hand, since their meeting-houses had been taken from them, and standing in the most open space cried out with one accord...

Here Philo states unequivocally that it was the custom to dwell in *skēnas* in Alexandria. They failed to observe the rite while Flaccus held power because he had abused the leaders and upset the Jews to such an extent they were in no mood to celebrate. This brief allusion supplies the clearest evidence of the ritual sukka in the diaspora; the passage in *Special Laws* comprises scriptural exegesis and does not indicate whether diaspora communities actually observed the commandments. The gathering at the beaches does not seem to be a typical festival ceremony or type of water-ritual parallel to the water libations. Philo states that they were forced to gather at the beaches because they had no access to their meeting-places *(proseuchai)*. Ordinarily they would gather in their regular assembly halls. Note that Philo again sets Sukkot at the equinox.

In his summary of sacrifices for all the festivals, *Special Laws* 1:189-90, Philo details the sacrifices for Sukkot, following Num 29:12-34. He also mentions the sacrifices for *Shmini ʿaṣeret*. Other references to Sukkot in Philo are inconclusive[102] or uninformative.[103]

---

[102] In *Life of Moses* 2:41 Philo mentions that a festival *(panēgyris)* is celebrated annually on the island of Pharos. The festival honors Pharos for there the Torah was first translated into Greek by the "Chaldean sages" invited by Ptolmey Philadelphus. Philo describes the festival thus: "But, after the prayers and thanksgivings, some fixing tents (or booths; *pēksamenoi skēnas*) on the seaside and others reclining on the sandy beach in the open air feast with their relations and friends, counting that shore for the time a more magnificent lodging than the fine mansions in the royal precincts." Does Philo depict here a type of Sukkot observance? The phrase *pēksamenoi skēnas* brings to mind the common Greek term for the festival of Sukkot, *skēnopēgia*. Josephus describes the building of sukkot with the same terminology: *pēgnusthai skēnas* (*AJ* 3:244). But this interpretation, while possible, is not necessary. The phrase is often employed for the erection of a tent or booth in any context (Michaelis, *Skēnē*, 368, 390). Moreover, booths or tents were sometimes set up at Greco-Roman festivals to provide shelter. Deissman, *Light*, 115 even claims *skēnopēgia* was a technical term in the Hellenistic world for such tent-festivals, although this has been disputed (Michaelis, 390 and n. 2). Philo depicts a common practice at outdoor festivals, and need not allude to a Sukkot celebration. Note that only some of the people build booths; the others recline on the beach without shelter. The booths/tents were for convenience, not as a rite of the festival. Hence no reference to Sukkot should be understood from this passage.

[103] In *On the Migration of Abraham* §202 Philo notes that seventy bulls are sacrificed on Sukkot in addition to the other prescribed offerings. The context is the importance of the number seventy. He makes the same observation in *On Flight and Finding* §186.

The Second Temple Period

From Philo we learn that the Jews in Alexandria, and probably in the rest of the diaspora, built sukkot. Dwelling in the sukka was not limited to pilgrims who journeyed to Jerusalem, but was now firmly entrenched in popular religion. His interpretation of sukkot in terms of a return to a more solid shelter after the harvest is *sui generis*, although he also notes that the sukka commemorates the sukkot of the exodus. Philo does not mention the lulav and etrog, which raises the possibility that prior to the destruction these were specifically temple rituals, and not practiced outside Jerusalem.[104] On the other hand, he may have thought that the lulav smacked of paganism and intentionally omitted it.[105] Philo only acknowledges a connection between Sukkot and the temple in his list of sacrifices. He conveys no hint that Sukkot was a special temple festival or included elaborate cultic rituals. This is probably because Philo lived in the diaspora and wrote for a diaspora audience which had little direct knowledge or contact with the temple. It is difficult to know, as always with Philo, whether his allegorical interpretations were widespread Alexandrian traditions or his alone.

VII. Pseudo-Philo

An explicit link between Sukkot and rain appears in the *Biblical Antiquities* of Pseudo-Philo, generally dated to the first half of the first century CE.[106] This work comprises a paraphrase of much of the Pentateuch into which the author incorporated later traditions. He paraphrases Lev 23:40 as follows:

> And you will take for me the beautiful fruit[107] of the tree and the palm branch and the willow and the cedar *(cedrum)* and branches of myrtle. And I will remember the whole earth with rain, and the measure of the seasons will be established, and I will fix the stars and command the clouds, and the winds will resound, and lightening bolts will rush about, and there will be a thunderstorm. And this will be an everlasting sign; and the nights will yield dew, as I said after the flooding of the earth...[108]

---

[104]So Allon, *Filon*, 459; contra: Albeck, *Mishna*, 2:254-55 n. 6.
[105]So Epstein, *Tannaim*, 349. Goodenough, *Symbols*, 4:161 suggests the lulav and etrog "were too particularly Jewish to attract the gentile readers he was addressing in this series of writings."
[106]Harrington, *Pseudo-Philo*, 299. For a full discussion of dating considerations, see Feldman's prolegomenon to the reprint of M.R. James, *The Biblical Antiquities of Philo* (Ktav: New York, 1971 [1917]), xxviii.
[107]Harrington, *Pseudo-Philo*, 321 translates "branch." But the Latin *fructum* corresponds better to "fruit." See the translation of James, ibid., 114.
[108]Pseudo-Philo 13:7 (Harrington, p. 321).

Pseudo-Philo describes in rich detail the atmospheric consequences of performing the festival rituals. The four species function as a type of rain charm, an idea also expressed in the rabbinic sources. They have the momentous theurgic effect of arousing God to bless the earth with rain. That which was implicit in Zech 14 and John 7 is stated explicitly here: the Sukkot rituals produce rain.

This text offers the earliest testimony that the four species prescribed in the Bible were identified with specific plants. First, the generic "branches of leafy trees" of Lev 23:40 has been interpreted as "branches of myrtle." Second, the Latin text reads *cedrum*, "cedar," an obvious anomaly, which brings the total to five species. Here the translator probably read the Greek *kitron (citron)* as *kedron* (cedar) and translated *cedrum* in place of *citrum*.[109] In later Hellenistic times the Greeks erroneously believed that the citron came from the cedar-tree, which led to the citron being called the *kitron* or *kitria*, as opposed to its earlier name, the "Persian apple."[110] Hence there is ample reason for the confusion. With this emendation of *citrum* for *cedrum* the passage still lists five species, and includes both "pleasant fruit" and "citron." Does this imply they took pleasant fruit of all sorts and citrons in addition? Now two manuscripts omit the term *cedrum*, which suggests that the word originated as an explanatory gloss that mistakenly entered the text.[111] If so we are left with a fairly close translation of Lev 23:40, the only deviation being the specification of the myrtle, congruent to the rabbinic interpretation. Or was the reference to citron originally an appositive for the fruit: "take for me beautiful fruit of the tree, citrons,..."? Or should we understand the Latin *fructum* as "products," a general category: "take for me beautiful products of the tree: the palm branch and the willow and the citron and branches of myrtle"? Because of these questions it is difficult to base firm conclusions on this passage. However, the explicit mention of myrtle and the possible allusion to the citron may point already to the rabbinic interpretation of the ritual.

---

[109] Although probably composed in Hebrew, the Latin text is a translation of a (lost) Greek translation. See Harrington, *Pseudo-Philo*, 298-99.
[110] See Athenaeus, *Deipnosophists*, 3:83d. "I maintain that the word 'citron' (*kitrion*) is not found in ancient writers, but the thing itself is described by Theophrastus of Eresus in his *History of Plants* in such a way that I am forced to understand his description as referring to the citron." He then cites the passage in which Theophrastus describes the "Persian or Median apple," the original term for the citron. Josephus uses both terms.
[111] See *Pseudo-Philo's Liber Antiquitatum Biblicarum*, ed. G. Kisch (Indiana, 1949), 150, apparatus to 13:7, note n.

VIII. Josephus

The historian Josephus is the only source for much of our knowledge of the history of Judaism throughout the second temple period. He supplies information about Sukkot in his paraphrases of biblical passages and in accounts of post-biblical celebrations of Sukkot, both in the past and of his own day.

Where Josephus paraphrases the Bible he sometimes restructures the biblical accounts, embellishes the text with additional details, or deletes elements found in the Bible. These changes often reflect Josephus's own opinion or the conditions of his time. In a lengthy section of *The Jewish Antiquities*, Josephus paraphrases the passages from Lev 23 about the festivals. He cites the Sukkot legislation as follows:

> On the fifteenth of the same month, when the cycle of the year turns and approaches the wintry season, he [Moses] bids each family to fix up booths [*skēnas*], apprehensive of the cold, and for protection against the year.[112] And whenever they should have won their fatherland, they were to repair to that city which they would in honor of the temple regard as their metropolis and there for eight days keep festival: they were to offer burnt-offerings and sacrifices of thanksgiving to God in those days, bearing in their hands a bouquet [*eiresiōnē*] composed of myrtle and willow with a branch of palm, along with citrons.[113] On the first of those days their burnt sacrifices...such are the rites, handed down

---

[112]The translation of the first sentence follows A. Schalit, *Flavii Josephis Antiquitates Judaicae in linguam hebraicam vertit* (Jerusalem, 1963), 1:99. Thackeray, in the LCL edition, translates: "the turning point to the winter-season is now reached, Moses bid each family to fix up booths, apprehensive of the cold and for protection against the year's inclemency."

[113]*tou mēlou tou tēs perseas*. Thackeray translates "the fruit of the Persea," followed by Schalit, ibid., "the fruit of the Peach!" Josephus clearly intends the citron. Schalit's translation is erroneous, as the Greek for peach is *mēlon tou tēs persikon*. And while persea can refer to a Persea-tree (see Liddell-Scott, 1395), here *perseas* comes from *Persēs* (accusative: *Persēn* or *Perseā*) meaning "Persian," and should be translated: "The Persian apple" or "Persian fruit." Indeed, *mēlon tou tēs persikos* (or *mēdikos*) was the original Greek term for the citron. Early Greek writers called the citron the "Persian apple" or "Medean apple," following Theophrastus, who claimed that the citron originated in Medea and Persia. See Chapter 5, II n. 45 and text thereto. In his only other reference to the citron, *AJ* 13:372, Josephus employs the term *kitria*, the standard latter Greek term (in Latin, *citreum*). See Atheneus, *Deipnosophists*, 3:83; Hehn, *Kulturpflanzen*, 333-35; Tolkowsky, *Hadar*, 63-64 and above, p. 74 on the change in terminology. The difference may be due to Josephus's sources. R.P. Gallant, *Josephus' Expositions of Biblical Law: an Internal Analysis* (Dissertation: Yale University, 1988), 100-101 points out that Josephus carefully phrased the description of the species. He links the myrtle and willow with the particle *kai*, and connects these two to the palm with *sun* ("myrtle and willow *with* a branch of palm.") This suggests that the palm is the principal element of the cluster. Josephus indicates the citron is independent of these three with the term *prosontos*, "along with" or "in addition."

from their forefathers, which the Hebrews observe when they erect their booths...(AJ 3:244-47 = Lev 23:33-44).

The first statement appears to deviate completely from Lev 23. Josephus claims Sukkot marks the onset of winter. Because of the anticipated change in climate, Moses commands the people to erect booths. Lev 23:43, on the other hand, commands Israelites to reside in booths to commemorate those in which God caused their forefathers to dwell during the exodus. Apparently Josephus felt uncomfortable with this fanciful notion, which implies that God supplied the booths for the Israelites, an idea that his Hellenistic audience might have ridiculed. He replaced the biblical explanation for the booths with an appeal to climatic changes.[114] But this explanation appears to be illogical. Houses obviously provide more protection from cold and rain than booths or even tents. Only if one lacks a house would one construct a booth for winter shelter. It is likely that Josephus speaks here of the desert generation which left Egypt in the temperate month of Nisan / Xanthicus (= April), and presumably had no need for shelters until winter. At the approach of the first cool weather, Moses bid the Israelites to construct booths for protection, houses or firmer shelters being unfeasible. Note that Josephus projects the laws of the lulav into the future – "when they were to win their fatherland" – as opposed to the commandment of the sukka that applies here and now, that is, to the period prior to the conquest.[115]

Now in two other passages Josephus refers obliquely to the custom of building sukkot. Both of these are almost parenthetical remarks. The first, in the account of the struggle between Antigonos and Aristobolos, notes: "when Antigonos had come in pomp from a campaign to attend the festival at which, according to national custom, they make sukkot for God" (BJ 1:73, AJ 13:304). In the second passage Josephus observes: "Four years before the war, when the city was enjoying profound peace and prosperity, there came the feast at which it is the custom of all Jews to make sukkot for God..." (BJ 6:301). The vague idea that sukkot are erected "for God" or "to God" ("in God's honor"?)[116] is not the clearest explanation of the rite, but it is significant that Josephus does not adduce

---

[114]The explanation bears some similarity to Philo's explanation that the *skēnē* provides shelter after the completion of harvest; *Special Laws* 2:206-207. But Philo only suggests the booth / tent offers better protection than the open air of the fields; he does not claim it suffices in the cold of winter, as does Josephus.

[115]Compare the laws of Pesaḥ where Josephus states that "our lawgiver... ordained that we should *year by year* offer the same sacrifice which, as I have already said, we offered then on a departure from Egypt" (AJ 3:248). Thus the Pesaḥ sacrifice was celebrated during the desert period as well.

[116]So Thackeray translates the dative, BJ 1:73.

the climatic explanation. Therefore it seems that Josephus's climatic rationale is indeed meant to explain the reason the Israelites built booths in the desert. Josephus regularly provides rational explanations of the commandments, and here he explains why the desert generation built sukkot.[117] Subsequent generations, on the other hand, build sukkot in honor of God, not to prepare for the approaching winter.[118] Thus Josephus replaces the biblical explanation that sukkot commemorate the booths of the exodus with the simple assertion that the Sukkot are built "for God."

It is significant that Josephus restricts the observance of the lulav to a future time when Jerusalem should become the capital city and place of the temple. Unlike the sukkot, which Moses commands to build immediately, the lulav is deferred until pilgrimages are carried out. This suggests the lulav is not to be practiced outside of the temple, that it was used exclusively in cultic ceremonies. In fact Josephus implies the lulav is some sort of ceremonial prop or sacrificial accouterment rather than an independent ritual. Worshippers hold the bouquet for eight days while

---

[117]D. Goldenberg, *Halakhah in Josephus and in Tannaitic Literaute: A Comparative Study* (Dissertation; Philadelphia: Dropsie College, 1978), 209-10 notes that Josephus consistently offers "a reason or rationalization of a law." His examples include *AJ* 4:260-63; 4:265; 4:266; 4:269; 4:275; 4:288.
It is instructive to compare the explanation of the Qaraite Aaron ben Elijah in Nemoy, *Karaite*, 187-88. Aaron is attempting explain why Sukkot is celebrated in the seventh month if it commemorates the booths the Israelites built in the desert. Did they not build the booths immediately upon leaving Egypt in the first month? He explains: "It is possible to say also that the reason was that the children of Israel did not make any booths in the wilderness until the time of Tishri, because they had no need for booths until the arrival of winter, when such would serve as a shelter from the rains; and the beginning of the arrival of winter and cold is the time of Tishri." See too Ibn Ezra to Lev 23:43.

[118]R.P. Gallant, *Josephus' Expositions of Biblical Law: an Internal Analysis* (Dissertation; Yale University, 1988), 95-96 suggests that Josephus found the biblical explanation of the commemorative aspect of the booths problematic. "There is a temporal incongruity between the commemoration – a holiday of limited duration occurring at one point in the year, and that which it commemorates – a continuing historical condition whose origin is associated with a different point in the year – Passover." Josephus accordingly provided a different reason: the booths commemorate "a historical practice occurring at one point in the year – the erection of booths beginning on the fifteenth of the seventh month, in preparation for winter." Here Gallant seems to have overinterpreted Josephus, for Josephus gives the booths no commemorative aspect. Josephus does not say that Jews build booths to commemorate the booths Moses ordered to be built. They serve the practical function of providing protection against the cold. This practical function only makes sense in the desert setting, not in Josephus's time. Rather than reading in a commemorative aspect, I prefer to limit the explanation to the desert period, especially given Josephus's other comments.

they offer sacrifices. Those who did not participate in the temple service presumably should not take the lulav.

Josephus calls the lulav an *eiresiōnē*, a technical term for the wand of laurel wound with wool held by worshippers in various Greek cults. This term accurately expresses the nature of the lulav. It was not a generic collection of fronds intended for decoration or homage, but a cultic wand used in cultic rituals.[119]

Josephus provides the first complete identification of the biblical species. With the exception of Pseudo-Philo, all previous sources replicated the biblical terminology or paraphrased the biblical phrases without specifying the types of plants. Josephus presupposes that the fruit of Lev 23:40 is the citron and the "branches of leafy trees" are myrtles. Here Josephus is in full agreement with the rabbinic interpretation of the ritual. The historian confirms that the rabbis inherited the identification of the species from earlier times.

We proceed now to Josephus's paraphrases of biblical narratives that mention Sukkot. In his retelling of Solomon's dedication of the temple, Josephus adds a telling phrase: "At this same time happened to fall the festival of Sukkot[120] *which is considered especially sacred and important by the Hebrews.*"[121] Josephus wishes to explain why Solomon dedicated the temple at this time. He informs his readers that Sukkot "is considered especially sacred and important" and therefore Solomon selected this festival for the dedication. At the same time, Josephus reveals the status of Sukkot during his life. It was still the preeminent religious festival in the first century. Unfortunately Josephus adds little to the already sparse biblical description of Sukkot. For both the Bible and Josephus the focus of the passage is the dedication of the temple, not the festival of Sukkot.

Josephus makes subtle yet illuminating changes to the biblical account of King Jeroboam's northern shrines.[122] According to Josephus, it was "when the feast of Sukkot was about to take place," that Jeroboam decided to establish competing temples, concerned lest the pilgrims to Jerusalem return their allegiance to the Judean king. In 1 Kgs 12:27 the more general concern that the people will perform sacrifices in the Jerusalem temple motivates Jeroboam. Whenever they wish to sacrifice, whether to fulfill a vow, observe a festival or worship their God, they may be inclined to journey to the magnificent temple in Jerusalem.

---

[119]On the related term *thyrsos*, see p. 82.
[120]Josephus call the festival *skēnopēgia*, following the regular LXX usage. Where 1 Kgs 8:2 designates the time as "month of Etanim, on The Festival," Josephus deletes the ancient Hebrew name of the month, long forgotten by his time, and explains "The Festival" as "the festival of Sukkot."
[121]*AJ* 8:100-123 = 1 Kgs 8.
[122]*AJ* 8:225-231 = 1 Kgs 12:25-33.

Josephus then relates that Jeroboam wished to observe "the festival" of the seventh month, just as it was observed in Jerusalem, and therefore built an altar and performed the sacrifice. In the Bible Jeroboam establishes the festival in the eighth month, also "like the festival" in Judea, albeit one month later (1 Kgs 12:32). By setting Jeroboam's festival in the seventh month Josephus makes it clear that the festival was a surrogate for Sukkot. Jeroboam, according to Josephus, wished to celebrate Sukkot in the north exactly as it was celebrated in Jerusalem. It seems that Josephus interprets the story in light of his own experience. As the outstanding festival of the year, when almost everyone could be expected to journey to Jerusalem, the festival of Sukkot in particular preoccupied Jeroboam. He was not concerned about the occasional pilgrim who embarked on the arduous journey to Jerusalem at any given time of year, but he was worried about the great pilgrimage of Sukkot. The reworking of the passage suggests again that Sukkot was the paramount festival in Josephus's day.[123]

---

[123]Other Josephan biblical paraphrases are less informative. Josephus quotes Deut 31:10 at *AJ* 4:209. This is his only reference to the Deuteronomic *haqhel* ceremony. Following scripture he prescribes that the ceremony take place on Sukkot. His description of the ceremony differs slightly from that of the Mishna. The account gives the impression that Josephus drew from his memory (although perhaps flawed) of actual practice. We learn nothing of other rituals of the festival. In *AJ* 11:75-78 Josephus paraphrases Ezra 3:1-6 (or 1 Esdr 5:47-49), the description of the building of the altar and the resumption of sacrifices. This occurred in the seventh month (Ezra 3:1), so the festival of Sukkot was observed according to the law. Josephus adds nothing relevant to Sukkot to the biblical text.
Josephus paraphrases the account of Neh 8 in *AJ* 11:154-58. In this case Josephus has performed major surgery on the biblical text to clarify the obscure biblical chronology. Neh 8:2 claims the people gather on the first of the seventh month, presumably on Rosh Hashana (or proto-Rosh Hashana.) The Torah is read on this festival, and the ensuing lament occurs then. At a second gathering on the "second day" the people discover the passage about Sukkot and immediately set out to the mountains to gather branches, build booths, and observe the festival. What day they celebrate Sukkot is not stated explicitly, but it could be understood that the celebration began on that day (see n. 13). Attempting to simplify the vague chronology (and correct the problematic omission of Yom Kippur), Josephus sets the whole course of events on Sukkot and condenses two readings into one. Here too he probably refracts the biblical account through the lens of his experience. Rosh Hashana was not a pilgrimage festival, and there would be no reason for a "multitude" to appear in Jerusalem. Sukkot, when all endeavored to make the pilgrimage, was the logical time for a mass gathering. Perhaps Josephus also reworked this passage in light of Deut 31:10 which places *haqhel* and its reading of the Torah on Sukkot. In the Josephan account the observance of Sukkot no longer functions as the paradigmatic example of the community's rededication to the law. It serves as the occasion for the mass

Consistent with his paraphrases of biblical passages, Josephus's accounts of post-biblical celebrations of Sukkot portray Sukkot as the most important festival. In Book 13 of the *Antiquities*, Josephus tells how Antiochus Sidetes, the Seleucid King, invaded Judea and besieged John Hyrcanus in Jerusalem (c. 135 BCE). As provisions dwindled, Hyrcanus expelled some people from the city, but Antiochus refused to allow them to depart. Caught in no-man's land, they suffered terribly until Sukkot:

> Just then, however, the festival of Sukkot came round, and those within the city took pity on them and admitted them again. And Hyrcanus sent to Antiochus requesting a truce of seven days on account of the festival, which Antiochus, deferring to his piety toward the Deity, granted and moreover sent a magnificent sacrifice, consisting of bulls with gilded horns and cups of gold and silver filled with all kinds of spices. And those who were at the gates received the sacrifice from the men who brought it, and took it to the sanctuary, while Antiochus feasted his army...(*AJ* 13:242)

The festival affords grounds for ending the stalemated siege. Josephus is not interested in the nature of the Sukkot festivities. He only mentions the sacrifice and gifts Antiochus Sidetes sends to underscore the ruler's piety, justify his title Eusebes (the Pious) and explain why Hyrcanus subsequently agreed to terms. How the Jews themselves celebrated is omitted. But we learn the high regard in which the festival was held. Neither party wished to be held accountable for preventing the celebration of Sukkot, either out of concern for divine punishment or political backlash.

Sukkot also played a role in the conflict between Aristobolos I, the son of John Hyrcanus who followed his father as high priest and ruler, and his brother Antigonos (104-103 BCE).

> But one day when Antigonos had returned from a campaign illustriously at the season of the festival during which they erect sukkot for God, it chanced that Aristobolos fell ill, and Antigonos, arrayed in great splendour and with his heavy armed soldiers about him, went up to the temple to celebrate the festival and pray earnestly for his brother's recovery; thereupon the unscrupulous men who were bent on disrupting the harmonious relation between them, found in Antigonos' ambitious display and in the successes he achieved a pretext to go to the king and maliciously exaggerate the pomp [*pompēn*] of his appearance at the festival...(*AJ* 13:303-308)[124]

It is not clear whether Antigonos desisted from his campaign in order to celebrate Sukkot in Jerusalem or whether the campaign chanced to end at

---

gathering in Jerusalem. The reference to 1 Macc 10:21 in *AJ* 13:46 adds little to the source.

[124] Cf. the parallel at *BJ* 1:73.

the time of Sukkot. The latter seems more likely, but the vague wording leaves open the former possibility. If this is the case the event highlights the significance of Sukkot. Even a military general ceased hostilities to attend the crucial festival of the year. That Antigonos appeared "arrayed in utmost splendor" and made a magnificent display points to the elaborate pageantry that characterized Sukkot. The display was not inappropriate for the festival, but inappropriate for a substitute high priest, at least in the eyes of his detractors, so troublemakers adduced the ostentatiousness as proof of disloyalty and ambition; otherwise such grandeur suited the expected tenor of day.

To serve as a high priest on Sukkot was evidently a dangerous affair. It contributed to the death of the Hasmonean scion Aristobolos III at the hands of Herod in 35 BCE.

> When Sukkot came around – this festival is observed by us with special care – he [Herod] waited for these days to pass, while he himself and the rest of the people gave themselves to rejoicing. But it was the envy arising from this very occasion and clearly working within him that led him to carry out his purpose more quickly. For Aristobolos was a youth of seventeen when he went up to the altar to perform the sacrifices in accordance with the law, wearing the ornamental dress of the high priests and carrying out the rites of the cult, and he was extraordinarily handsome and taller than most youths of his age...and they (the people) called out to him good wishes mingled with prayers...(*AJ* 15:50).

The parenthetical remark "this festival is observed by us with special care" again emphasizes the status of Sukkot. Aristobolos made a magnificent impression because he acted as high priest on the central festival of the year, when the greatest crowd was present, and the people most careful about the observances. This caused Herod such consternation that he felt it necessary to eliminate the priest, but had to wait until after the important festival. During Sukkot, Herod and the people "gave themselves to rejoicing," consistent with the celebratory character of the festival. The motif of magnificent displays of Sukkot ceremonies followed by suspicion of ambition recalls the account of Aristobolos and Antigonos. Josephus reveals that Sukkot is the festival on which pomp, intrigue and political machinations take place. Because of the great numbers and impressive temple rituals, the high priest received such honor that his rivals felt threatened.

Josephus mentions the sacrifices and "rites of the cult," for the splendid execution of these rituals affected the crowd so deeply. Unfortunately he does not describe the rites more precisely. Does he mean the libations and willow processions detailed in rabbinic sources? Once again the author focuses on the political fallout from religious events and alludes to the rituals only to the extent they bear on politics.

Yet we must assume the array of rituals was sufficiently impressive to provoke fierce jealousy.

One of Josephus's most famous stories is the account of the people pelting Alexander Jannaeus with citrons:

> As for Alexander, his own people revolted against him – for the nation was aroused against him – at the celebration of The Festival,[125] and as he stood beside the altar and was about to sacrifice, they pelted him with citrons, it being a custom among the Jews that at the festival of Sukkot everyone holds wands *(thyrsous)* made of palm branches and citrons – these we have described elsewhere...(AJ 13:372).

If the reading "The Festival" is correct, Josephus uses the same terminology as the Bible, Jubilees and rabbinic literature.[126] Josephus is not summarizing a biblical passage here, so his use of the title indicates that it was a common name in his time, and confirms again the preeminent status of Sukkot. The report that everyone held lulavs and etrogs is significant. Josephus mentions this in a matter-of-fact fashion, explaining to his readers why the people happened to be armed with etrogs. Josephus employs here the term *thyrsos,* as opposed to the term *eiresiōnē* he had adopted in an earlier passage. This extremely apt term, as we have seen, refers to the wand carried by worshippers in Dionysian celebrations.[127] Readers familiar with the Greek cult would immediately understand the ritual function of the lulav. If the description is historically accurate we have the earliest attestation of the citron as the "fruit of goodly trees" of Lev 23:40, and can date their ritual use to the time of Jannaeus, about the first decade of the first century BCE.[128] On the other hand, Josephus may have retrojected the custom of his own time, the mid-first century, to the time of Jannaeus. Would that Josephus had said more about the performance of the lulav ritual; the skeletal account only informs us that the lulav was held during sacrifices. This coheres with the paraphrase of Leviticus at *AJ* 3:244-47 where Josephus implies the lulav is symbiotically connected to the offerings. While sacrifices are performed, the lulav is held. Although this picture arguably is not meant to be comprehensive, the evidence suggests the lulav was exclusively a cultic rite.

---

[125]Some manuscripts omit "The." The Latin has *festivitas tabernaculorum.*

[126]Some manuscripts have "a festival" instead of "the festival." The parallel in *BJ* 1:88 reads, "After his reduction of these places to servitude, the Jewish populace rose in revolt against him on a festival, for it is on these festive occasions that sedition is most apt to break out."

[127]See above, pp. 63 and 78.

[128]Jannaeus ruled from 103-76 BCE. Josephus places the insurrection near the beginning of his rule.

In another passage Josephus relates how Malichus, supporter of Hyrcanus and murderer of Antipater, persuaded Hyrcanus to bid Herod not to enter Jerusalem with his foreign troops during "the festival."[129] Malichus claimed the foreigners would disturb the people in their "state of ritual purity." Although Herod ignored the order, the attempt implies people took great pains to purify themselves so as to celebrate Sukkot in Jerusalem, and to be rendered impure was reason for disappointment and distress.

In the accounts of Sukkot during the great revolt of 67-70 CE, Josephus sheds more light on the festival. He relates that the Roman general Antipatris Cestius advanced to Lydda on Sukkot and found the city almost deserted (*BJ* 2:515). With the exception of fifty people, all the residents had journeyed to Jerusalem. This account provides reliable evidence that most Jews (or at least Judeans) actually traveled to the temple on Sukkot. Josephus is not making exaggerated religious claims about the devotion of the Jews to their law or the magnificence of the temple rites. He simply explains in passing why Cestius found so few residents in Lydda. Moreover, Josephus relates that when Cestius neared Jerusalem, the Jews rushed to fight him since they felt great confidence in their numbers.[130] However, Lydda was only about twenty miles from Jerusalem, so we cannot be sure that those from the Galilee or at greater distances journeyed to the temple in equal numbers.

In sum, the Josephan evidence reveals that Sukkot was the dominant pilgrimage festival. In his paraphrase of biblical passages, Josephus assumes that it was a surrogate Sukkot celebration Jeroboam devised to prevent the populace from journeying to Jerusalem. He reveals no surprise at the magnificent Sukkot celebration and temple dedication of Solomon; he even adds in passing the explanation that Sukkot "is considered especially sacred and important by the Hebrews" (*AJ* 8:100). Josephus adds a similar remark – that Sukkot is observed "with special care" – to explain why Herod had to bide his time before murdering Aristobolos and why his jealousy increased. That his comment is again parenthetical is crucial: Josephus does not boast here about how faithfully the Jews observe their laws, nor attempt a bathetic description

---

[129] *AJ* 14:285-86; *BJ* 1:229-230. In *BJ* it is less clear that Sukkot is meant.
[130] Josephus remarks that they rushed to fight on the Sabbath "with no thought for the seventh day of rest, for it was the very Sabbath which they regarded with special reverence" (*BJ* 2:517). The reference to a special Sabbath is puzzling. To the best of my knowledge the intermediate Sabbath of Sukkot is not distinguished substantively from other Sabbaths in any other source. Perhaps Josephus simply means that being both the Sabbath and the festival of Sukkot, the day was doubly holy. Or that the Sabbath was particularly important on account of Sukkot, the preeminent festival.

of how the magnificence of the Jews was destroyed by the Romans. He states a fact to make his account comprehensible to his audience. That Lydda was almost deserted on Sukkot confirms the "special care" with which the Jews observed the festival. The accounts of Hyrcanus and Antiochus, Aristobolos and Antigonos, and the Herodian intrigue, provide glimpses of the grandeur and pomp that characterized Sukkot celebrations at the temple.

The passages about the lulav and sukka are less clear, obscured by the Josephan tendency simultaneously to reorganize, reformulate, reinterpret and paraphrase biblical passages. He seems to consider the lulav exclusively a temple ritual. His explanation of the sukka is curious. Sukkot are erected "for God," not to commemorate the exodus.[131]

IX. Christian Scriptures

In contrast to Pesaḥ, which features prominently throughout the Christian Scriptures, and Shavuot (Pentecost), on which Acts 2-6 sets the outpouring of the spirit, pilgrimage to the temple and the subsequent drama, Sukkot is only mentioned explicitly in John 7.[132] Perturbed by this underemphasis and the apparent lack of a Tabernacles commemoration in early Christian sources – could it be that the first Christians ignored the most important Jewish festival? – some scholars have argued that Sukkot motifs form the background to several passages of the Christian Scriptures. Most of these are highly speculative, and provide little information about the festival even if the identification is correct.[133] Three cases, however, rest on more solid ground and provide

---

[131] The Bible describes several observances as "to God" or "for God," such as the Paschal offering (Exod. 12:11; 23:5), the festival of Pesaḥ (Exod 12:14), the Sabbath (Exod 16:23; Lev 23:3), and the festival of Sukkot itself (Lev 23:34, 41). So Josephus is, in part, paraphrasing biblical language. But he omits the explicit historical explanation in favor of this general notion.

[132] John 7:2, "Tabernacles" (*skēnopēgia*); 7:8, 7:10-11, 14, "the feast" (*tēn heortēn*); 7:37, "the last day of the feast, the great day" (see below).

[133] Several attempts have been made to interpret the transfiguration, Mark 9:2-8 = Matt 17:1-8 = Luke 9:28-36, against a Sukkot background. See H.B. Swete, *The Gospel According to St. Mark* (London, 1898), 179; F.J. Badcock, "The Time of the Transfiguration," *JThSt* 24 (1922/3), 169-70; I. Abrahams. *Studies in Pharisaism and the Gospels*; ed. H. Orlinsky (reprint; New York: Ktav, 1967 [1917-24]); 2:52-53; E. Lohmeyer, "Die Verklärung Jesu Nach dem Markus-Evangelium," *ZNW* 21 (1922), 185-213; G.H. Boobyer, "St Mark and the Transfiguration," *JTS* 41 (1940), 119-40; Daniélou, *Liturgy*, 339. Thus K. Stendahl, "Matthew," *Peake's Commentary on the Bible*, eds. M. Black and H.H. Rowley (London: Thomas Nelson and Sons, 1962), 788: "The basic pattern of the transfiguration is that of the Feast of Tabernacles (e.g. the three booths) as the inauguration of the New Age with Jesus enthroned as a high-priestly Messiah." The most comprehensive of these is Riesenfeld's *Jésus Transfiguré*. Riesenfeld draws attention to the following motifs:

some substantive information about Sukkot. The sources technically date from after the destruction of the temple, but since they depend on older traditions, and describe the events of temple times, they are included in this chapter.

---

1) The booths (*skēnas*), 2) the cloud, identified with the clouds of glory, the rabbinic interpretation of the exodus sukkot, 3) the shade/shadow provided by the cloud, just as the sukka provides shade, 4) the deep eschatological sense, including Elijah, the high mountain, the shining face and the revelation of Jesus's sonship. In addition to these, the heavenly voice, the figures of Moses and Elijah, the "rest" and suffering are all related to Sukkot (pp. 243-280). Riesenfeld depends heavily on the enthronement festival theory of the origin of Sukkot in the radical form of the "Myth and Ritual" school, proposing that the original festival experienced "disintegration," "democratization," and "spiritualization," which gave it a dominant eschatological character. He interprets the "booths" in terms of the sukkot the righteous would inhabit in the World to Come, the sukkot made of the skin of Leviathan, and/or the sukka of the Messiah, motifs that appear in amoraic midrashim, and whose roots Riesenfeld attempts to trace back to the biblical period. Likewise the cloud is the cloud-canopy that covered the temple, originally God's sukka (in which the sacred marriage was consummated), which would return in eschatological times. The meaning of the transfiguration is to be understood through the combination of these traditional motifs that are realized in Jesus. The eschatological and messianic hopes that the Jews associated with Sukkot are new fulfilled in Jesus (pp. 277-280). Yet for all of Riesenfeld's impressive learning, each motif individually, as well as the complex of themes in its entirety, can be explained without reference to the festival. For example, let us take the "booths," the strongest evidence of a Sukkot background. The Greek term is *skēnas*, which can mean booth, tent or tabernacle. According to Michaelis, *Skēnē*, 369, in the LXX *skēnē* translates אהל 330 times, משכן 93 times and סוכה 25 times. He points out that the Christian Scriptures use *skēnē* with this variety of meanings. Taking issue with Riesenfeld, he rejects any connection to festival booths (pp. 379-80). The cloud would then derive from the pillar of cloud found by the Tabernacle in the Israelite desert camp, while the divine voice and figure of Moses relate to the same idea. Thus even the *skēnas* are not necessarily Sukkot booths, and the other motifs have likewise received a plethora of interpretations. See E. Dombrowski, *La Transfiguration de Jesus* (Rome: Institut Biblique Pontifical, 1939), 90-99; J. van Goudoever, *Biblical Calendars* (Leiden: Brill, 1959), 253 and the various interpretations of the figures of Moses and Elijah surveyed in M.E. Thrall, "The Transfiguration: Elijah and Moses in Mark's Account of the Transfiguration," NTS 16 (1969-70), 307-11. Therefore I hesitate to draw far-ranging conclusions about the symbolism and meaning of Sukkot based on this passage. As V. Taylor, *The Gospel According to St. Mark*[2] (London: Macmillan, 1966), 386 observes: "The interpretation of this narrative presents a very difficult problem and few will claim that they can give an explanation which completely satisfies them." E. Schweizer, *The Good News According to Mark*, trans. D. Madvig (Richmond, Virginia: John Knox, 1970), 180 comments: "It is no longer possible to explain the history of the tradition of this passage." For summary of the history of the interpretation of the transfiguration, see Dombrowski, 113-56; Taylor, 386-88.

According to John 12, Jesus journeys to Jerusalem just before Pesaḥ."[134] However the description contains several elements that suggest a Sukkot setting.

> (12) The next day a great crowd who had come to the feast heard that Jesus was coming to Jerusalem. (13) So they took branches of palm trees and went out to meet him, crying, "Hosanna! Blessed is he who comes in the name of the Lord, even the King of Israel!" (14) And Jesus found a young ass and sat upon it; as it is written, (15) "Fear not, daughter of Zion; behold, your king is coming, sitting on an ass's colt!"

The people take branches of palm trees, or, translating the definite article literally, "*the* branches of palm trees" *(ta baia tōn phoinikōn)*, that is, the palm branches they had cut beforehand. Palm trees were never found in abundance at Jerusalem, so the people could not have spontaneously cut down branches from a nearby palm. Nor, on Pesaḥ, was there any reason for having prepared palm branches. If the entry took place on Sukkot and the branches identified with the lulav, this difficulty disappears. The cry of "Hosanna" derives from the phrase *hoshi'a na* ("deliver us") of Ps 118:25, one of the Hallel psalms associated with Sukkot.[135] According to rabbinic tradition, the lulav should be shaken as these words are recited.[136] Although it can be argued that waving palms is a typical sign of homage,[137] unrelated to Sukkot, and the cry "hosanna"

---

[134]"The next day" is the day after Jesus came to Bethany, which occurred "six days before the Passover" (John 12:1). In the other Gospels the events also seem to take place before Pesaḥ, assuming that not much time has elapsed between the entry and the date given in Mark 14:1 = Matt 26:2 = Luke 22:1-2. Some scholars, however, claim these passages relate to a second journey to Jerusalem, and the "triumphal entry" took place on Sukkot. For discussion see C.W.F. Smith, "No Time for Figs," *JBL* 79 (1960), 316.

[135]The Hallel was recited on Pesaḥ while the lambs were slaughtered at the temple and during the *seder* as well. But the Hallel was most closely associated with Sukkot, recited each day of the festival, and the lulav was shaken precisely at Ps 118:25 (mSuk 3:9). So in conjunction with the palm branches the liturgical expression points to a Sukkot background.

[136]mSuk 3:9; see Chapter 3, VI.

[137]W.R. Farmer, "The Palm Branches in John 12, 13," *JTS* 3 (1952), 62-66, Schnackenburg, *John*, 1:374 and many other commentaries who do not even mention Sukkot, interpret the lulav as a symbol of nationalism or power. It should be noted that the Gospel parallels lack mention of the palm branches. In Mark 11:8 the people "spread their garments on the road, and others spread leafy branches which they had cut from the fields." In Matt 21:8 they act similarly, while in Luke 19:36 they spread garments but no mention is made of branches. The Sukkot imagery is therefore weaker; the generic branches and garments are traditional expression of homage. (On spreading garments see 2 Kgs 9:13.) Yet the tradition of John 12, not the parallel, is at issue. On the relationship of the Gospel parallels to John, see Brown, *John*, 1:459-61. F.C. Burkitt, "Ω and Θ: Studies in the Western Text of St Mark," *JTS OS* 17 (1916), 142-45 claims the entry

is a routine sign of acclamation,[138] not a festival liturgy, the appearance of both elements together appears to be more than mere coincidence.

If the original tradition placed Jesus's entry on Sukkot, as seems likely, what do we learn about the festival? First, the practice of the lulav appears to have been common. The people carry the palm branches about, and seem to hold the fronds throughout the day. Second, the large crowds and the advent on Sukkot indicate again that Sukkot was the leading pilgrimage.[139] Sukkot was the appropriate time for Jesus to make his public appearance.[140]

The "Tabernacles complex," John 7:1-8:59, relates the events of the last year of Jesus's life that take place during Sukkot at the temple. Throughout his Gospel the Evangelist structures major events around the Jewish holy days such as the Sabbath, Pesaḥ and Dedication

---

took place on Hanukka, since 2 Macc 10:6 describes festivities with palms and hymns during the Hasmonean triumphal procession. Brown, *John*, 1:457 concludes that there may be some Sukkot symbolism, but the matter "is beyond the possibility of proof."

[138]The Greek reads *hōsanna*, a simple transliteration of the Hebrew, rather than *sōson dē* ("save now") as the LXX translates Ps 118:25 and parallels. Cf. the LXX to 2 Kgs 19:19; 2 Sam 14:4; Ps 86:2, 16; Isa 37:20; Jer 17:14. On this question, see Burkett, ibid., 139-42; Brown, *John*, 1:457; E. Freed, "The Entry Into Jerusalem in the Gospel of John," *JBL* 80 (1961), 329-38; E. Werner, "'Hosanna' in the Gospels," *JBL* 65 (1946), 113-121; C.W.F. Smith, "Tabernacles in the Fourth Gospel and Mark," *NTS* 9 (1962), 130-36; H. Anderson, *The Gospel of Mark* (New Christian Bible. London: Oliphants, 1976), 263; W.L. Lane, *The Gospel According to Mark* (Grand Rapids, Michigan: Eerdmans, 1974), 397; J. van Goudoever, *Biblical Calendars* (Leiden: Brill, 1959), 261-62. See Werner, 99-112 for a summary of scholarship.

[139]Only later, as Jesus became identified with the sacrificial lamb, did the Church shift the advent to Pesaḥ.

[140]Is there a specific eschatological or messianic association with Sukkot? Of course the passage contains the messianic motif of Jesus riding on the ass in fulfillment of Zech 9:9. But one wonders whether this theme derives from Sukkot or from the general messianic orientation of the entire Christian scriptures. The Gospels (and their antecedent traditions) narrate the life of Jesus, the son of God and Messiah, so the nature of the literature is consistently eschatological. The question is whether Sukkot possessed prior eschatological associations of its own which the Christian tradition appropriated and developed. Was the lulav, for example, always considered a messianic signal which the tradition conveniently applied to Jesus? My sense is that this is not the case. The tradition had Jesus approach the temple at the most appropriate time, on the leading pilgrimage festival, and portrayed the people greeting him with the palms and cries typical of Sukkot. Indeed, according to John, even the messianic-ass symbolism was lost on Jesus's disciples (John 12:16)! The disciples themselves did not realize the Messiah was at hand, and clearly neither they nor the people took the lulav and cried "hosanna" from eschatological excitement.

(Hanukka.)[141] Consistent with our expectations, the events associated with Sukkot take place at the temple. Indeed, when Sukkot approaches, the disciples encourage Jesus to go to Judea "that your disciples may see the works you are doing. For no man works in secret if he seeks to be known openly. If you do these things, show yourself to the world" (7:3-4). They realize that Jesus will have the greatest audience at the great autumnal festival. Jesus arrives during the "middle of the festival" and proceeds to teach (7:14-36). The climax occurs on the last day:

> (36) On the last and greatest day of the festival, Jesus stood up and cried out:
> (37) If anyone thirst, let him come [to me]
> (38) and let him drink, who believes in me. As the scripture says, "From within him shall flow rivers of living water."[142]
> (39) (Here he was referring to the Spirit which those who come to believe in him were to receive. For there was as yet no Spirit, since Jesus had not been glorified.)
> (40) Some of the crowd who heard [these words] began to say, "This is undoubtedly the Prophet."
> (41) Others were claiming, "This is the Messiah." But an objection was raised: "Surely the Messiah isn't to come from Galilee?"

By "last day" it is unclear whether the Gospels mean the seventh and last day of Sukkot itself, later known as *Hoshana rabba*, or the Eighth Day Festival, *Shmini 'aseret* (= SA). Scholars are divided on this issue, and no

---

[141]Sabbath, 5:1-47; Pesaḥ, 6:1-71; Dedication, 10:22-39; preparations for and Pesaḥ, 12:1ff.
[142]The translation is that of Brown, *John*, 305 who follows the "western" or "Christological" interpretation adopted by the Latin Church Fathers. Altering the punctuation slightly results in a different reading whereby the water emerges from the believer, not from Jesus: "If anyone thirsts, let him come to me and drink. He who believes in me, as the Scripture says..." Both the Church Fathers and modern scholars are divided as to the correct reading. I follow Brown who suggests that the Eastern interpretation derives in great part from the influence of Origen, who in turn was influenced by Philonic ideas, considerations extraneous to the text. Other punctuations that result in slightly different interpretation have also been proposed; see Brown, 321; J. Blenkinsopp, "John vii 37-39: Another Note on a Notorious Crux," *NTS* 6 (1958-60), 95-98; G.D. Kilpatrick, "The Punctuation of John VII. 37-38," *JTS NS* 11 (1960), 340-43; J.N. Sanders, *A Commentary on the Gospel According to St. John*, ed. B.A. Mastin (London: Adam & Charles Black, 1968), 213. This issue is of some consequence, for the two interpretations point to different scriptural passages as the basis for the saying. But these differences pertain more to Christian theology than the nature of Sukkot. On this issue, see J.B. Cortés, "Yet another Look at Jn 7, 37-8," *CBQ* 29 (1967), 75-86; D.C. Allison, "The Living Water (John 4:10-14; 6:35c; 7:37-9)," *St. Vladimir's Theological Quarterly* 30 (1986), 143-57; Schnackenburg, *John*, 2:152-54; Brown, 320-24, 331 and the literature listed there.

decisive argument has been made.¹⁴³ All assume the allusion is to the water libation, which would seem to favor the seventh day, since it is not clear that the libation was performed on SA.¹⁴⁴ Furthermore, the seventh day, according to rabbinic sources, included a sevenfold circumambulation of the altar, a type of culmination of the libations and rituals held on each day of the festival. But the designation "last day" better suits SA, this being the regular term in tannaitic sources.¹⁴⁵ On the other hand, SA is never called the "greatest day," while this appellation recalls the name Hoshana Rabba, the "great hoshana [day]," as the seventh day came to be called, albeit in later times. This question is better left undecided, for the entire passage should be treated for its testimony as to the themes associated with Sukkot rather than strict historical data.

The scripture Jesus cites, "From within him shall flow living water," does not appear in the Bible, which has led to a futile search for the citation.¹⁴⁶ The expression appears to be a composite of several verses and themes;¹⁴⁷ the Evangelists routinely cite the Hebrew Scriptures in combinations or adaptations of the originals. Given the Sukkot-temple context, it seems that the author meant to allude to Zech 14 or Ezek 47.¹⁴⁸

---

¹⁴³Brown, *John*, 320 favors the seventh day, as does Sanders, ibid., 212 and Schnackenburg, *John*, 152. J.H. Bernard, *The Gospel according to St. John*, ed. A.H. McNeile (ICC 29; New York: Scribner, 1929), 280-81 argues for SA. See the survey of opinions in B. Lindars, *The Gospel of John* (London: Marshall, Morgan & Scott, 1972), 297-98.
¹⁴⁴Only R. Yehuda asserts the libation was performed on the eighth day as well; mSuk 4:9.
¹⁴⁵Actually "last festival day," *yom tov ha'aharon*: mSuk 2:6, 4:8, Ta 1:1, 1:2; tSuk 1:7, 4:17, Bes 3:9, Hag 2:10, MQ 2:13. Technically SA is an independent festival.
¹⁴⁶No biblical verse corresponds to his words precisely. There is no end to suggestions about the underlying verse; proposals include Isa 4:14, 6:35, 18:11, 54:3, 55:1, 58:11, Prov 5:15, 9:4, 18:4, Sira 24:19-21, 30-33, 51:23-4, Ps 46:4, 105:40-1, Ps 78:15-6, Jl 3:18, Zech 14, Ezek 47, as well as hypothetical targums to these verses. See Brown, *John*, 320-3 and the exchange of Grelot and Boismard in the literature cited there, 331, and the references in n. 142. Whatever the original context of the saying, the Gospel author has placed it in the temple on Sukkot. The Evangelist understood the scripture cited by Jesus to pertain to Sukkot themes, and bids his audience to make the same associations by placing it at this time and place. Therefore the allusion to water should be understood in relation to water on the festival and/or in the temple. Interpretations that take the water as a metaphor for wisdom and seek the source in Proverbs should be ruled out.
¹⁴⁷M.E. Boismard, "De Son Ventre Couleront Des Fleuves D'eau (Jo., VII, 38)," *RB* 65 (1958), 545.
¹⁴⁸Brown, *John*, 327; P. Grelot, "Jean, VII, 38: Eau du rocher ou source du Temple," *RB* 70 (1963), 43-51; D.C. Allison, "The Living Water (John 4:10-14; 6:35c; 7:37-9)," *St Vladimir's Theological Quarterly* 30 (1986), 143-57; B. Grigsby, "Washing in the Pool of Siloam – A Thematic Anticipation of the Johannine

Zechariah's eschatological transformation of Jerusalem envisions "living water" flowing out of the city to the east and west (14:8).[149] Ezek 47 prophesies a stream of enormous force flowing out of the temple. These waters too are "living waters"; they "heal" the salty water of the Dead Sea (47:8), cause every creature that comes in contact with them to live (47:9), and spawn plentiful fish and eternally verdant trees (47:10,12).

The Sukkot-temple context elucidates the point of the saying. Jesus asserts that he is the source of those living waters.[150] Whereas Ezekiel and Zechariah prophesied living waters flowing from the temple or rebuilt Jerusalem, Jesus claims that the waters flow from his belly.[151] Raymond Brown calls attention to the "replacement" motif prevalent in the Gospel of John whereby Jesus systematically replaces Jewish institutions.[152] Here Jesus replaces the temple and city as the fount of life; his body becomes the new temple and new city, his spirit the new waters of life. The eschatological hopes for an unceasing supply of water have been realized in the person of Jesus himself, hence the people conclude that the man before them is the Messiah (v. 41).[153]

Cross," *NovT* 27 (1985), 227-35; A. Feuillet, "Les Fleuves D'eau Vive," *Parole de Dieu et Sacerdoce*, ed. E. Fischer (Paris, 1962), 107-120.

[149]Living water," incidentally, is the best evidence that Zech 14:8 forms the background to the actual saying, not just to the Evangelist's understanding. Zech 14:8 is one of the few passages outside of the Levitical purity laws that mentions "*living* water." The phrase also appears in Gen 26:19; Lev 14:5, 50, 51, 52, 15:13; Jer 2:13, 17:13; Song 4:15, but only in Zech 14:8 do living waters "go out" i.e. flow from the source, as in the Gospels.

[150]See Grelot, ibid.; Brown, *John*, 327. I am not convinced by Grelot (and following him, Brown, 323, 327) that the allusion is *also* to Moses striking the rock and bringing forth water. Grelot makes too much of the allusion to the mythical well of the desert sojourn in tSuk 3:11, the extended midrash on Ezek 47. There is no proof that the well was actually associated with Sukkot or its rituals, and even if this is true of the Tosefta, it does not follow that such an interpretation was known to John. The connection of the *well* to the *rock* is also weak.

[151]Cf. John 4:10-14 where Jesus asserts that whoever drinks from the waters he offers will never thirst again: "but the water that I will give him will become in him a well of water springing up into eternal life." The motif of water runs throughout the fourth gospel: see 2:1-11, 3:5-6, 4:10-14, 6:35, 7:37-40, 19:34.

[152]*John*, cxliii and 104: "Jesus is the real Temple; the Spirit he gives will replace the necessity of worshipping at Jerusalem; his doctrine and his flesh and blood will give life in a way that the manna associated with the exodus from Egypt did not; at Tabernacles, not the rain-making ceremony but Jesus himself supplies the living water; not the illumination in the temple court but Jesus himself is the real light on the feast of Dedication, not the temple altar but Jesus himself is consecrated by God."

[153]Note that the eschatological focus of the passage derives primarily from the role of the temple. Because Jesus replaces the temple, the eschatological conception of the temple as source of living water is transferred to him. Sukkot figures in this equation by virtue of its status as the outstanding temple festival.

The Second Temple Period

The passage provides some evidence of the association between Sukkot and rain. Both Hoshana Rabba and SA included rain-making ceremonies.[154] By setting the scene at that time, the Evangelist reflects an understanding of the function of the festival and its rituals as ensuring a sufficient supply of water. Concerns for water, rain and a fruitful year were paramount for those who came to celebrate the festival. The advent of Jesus promises in perpetuity the waters the Sukkot rituals attempted to guarantee annually.

Rev 7:9-17 employs the most vivid Sukkot imagery in the Christian scriptures. The visionary depicts a scene of heavenly worship:

> (9) After this I looked, and behold, a great multitude which no man could number, from every nation, from all tribes and peoples and tongues standing before the throne and before the Lamb, clothed in white robes with palm branches in their hands, (10) and crying out with a loud voice, "Salvation belongs to our God who sits upon the throne, and to the Lamb!" (11) And all the angels stood round the throne and round the elders and the four living creatures, and they fell on their faces before the throne and worshipped God, (12) saying, "Amen! Blessing and glory and wisdom and thanksgiving and honor and power and might be to our God for ever and ever! Amen." (13) Then one of the elders addressed me, saying, "Who are these, clothed in white robes, and whence have they come?" (14) I said to him, "Sir, you know." And he said to me, "These are they who have come out of the great tribulation; they have washed their robes and made them white in the blood of the Lamb. (15) Therefore are they before the throne of God, and serve him day and night within his temple; and he who sits upon the throne will shelter them with his presence. (16) They shall hunger no more, neither thirst any more; the sun shall not strike them, nor any scorching heat. (17) For the Lamb in the midst of the throne will be their shepherd, and he will guide them to springs of living water; and God will wipe away every tear from their eyes."

Consider the following elements: first, the assembled multitude carries palm branches or lulavs. Second, they cry "salvation," *sōteria*, which may correspond to "deliver us" of Ps 118:25,[155] at which point the lulav was shaken (mSuk 3:9). Third, the great assembly which crowds around the throne of God, bows (7:11) and worships (7:15) suggests a pilgrimage to

---

Rituals and modes of worship of the preeminent temple festival are realized in Jesus and no longer necessary. Imagining the eschatological temple, the author pictured the quintessential temple festival, Sukkot.

[154] The sevenfold circumambulation of the altar was probably a petition for rain. Rabbinic liturgy adds the petition for rain on SA (See Chapter 4, I).

[155] Elsewhere the Christian Scriptures transliterate the phrase as *hōsanna*, and in these contexts the word may express acclamation, not a petition for deliverance. See above p. 86. That the phrase is translated here as *sōteria* suggests that the passage alludes to the Sukkot liturgy. Some scholars, however, suggest the phrase in Revelation evokes different biblical verses. See Ulfgard, *Feast*, 91.

the temple. Fourth, the phrase "he who sits on the throne will shelter (or 'tabernacle'; *skēnōsei*) them with his presence" evokes the image of a divine sukka or covering. The verb comes from the same root as the Greek for "booth" or "tent." This divine shelter recalls Isa 4:5, the prophecy of a divine cloud that forms a sukka over the temple. Fifth, the promise of "springs of living water" recalls the water associations of the festival. Finally, in the ensuing verses, the angels sound trumpets. The Mishna relates that trumpets were sounded during the procession bringing the water libations to the temple. Some scholars even suggest the creatures and angels around the throne recall the circumambulation around the altar,[156] the white robes symbolize the priests at the temple and the multitude from all nations reflects the universal thrust of Sukkot.[157] One may quibble with each element individually – the palms may be mere victory symbols and *sōteria* may allude to other biblical verses – but taken together the vision reflects a Sukkot celebration.[158]

The Sukkot celebration, like the rest of the book, is set in eschatological time. The author essentially fleshes out the prophecy of Zech 14 of the nations making a pilgrimage to Jerusalem to celebrate Sukkot.[159] He imagines that very celebration in terms of his Christian-apocalyptic perspective and thus fuses Christian images (e.g., Christ the lamb) with Sukkot motifs. Daniélou connects the passage to Jesus's entrance to Jerusalem in John, which, as we have just concluded, also involves Sukkot imagery. "We have here [Rev 7:9-17], on the second level of eschatology, the projection of the first fulfillment which was, on the level of the Gospel, the episode of Palm Sunday."[160] In the Gospels the advent of Jesus as Messiah took place on Sukkot and initiated the eschaton. The author of Revelation offers a secondary development of that idea.

---

[156]Draper, *Tabernacles*, 138-39.
[157]McKelvey, *Temple*, 163-65.
[158]This has been acknowledged by many scholars, beginning in 1719 by C. Vitringa in *Anakrisis Apocalypse I*, 295-319 (cited in Draper, *Tabernacles*, 133 with further references), Daniélou, *Liturgy*, 341; Riesenfeld, *Jésus*, 278 nn. 67-68; McKelvey, *Temple*, 75-76; Comblin, *Liturgie*, 38-39; Draper, *Tabernacles*; Ulfgard, *Feast*; A. Farrer, *The Revelation of St. John the Divine* (Oxford, 1964), 111; W.J. Harrington, *Understanding the Apocalypse* (Washington: Corpus Books, 1969), 131 and further references in R.H. Charles, *A Critical and Exegetical Commentary on the Revelation of St. John* (ICC 44; Edinburgh, 1920), 1:211. Charles, however, held the opposite opinion: "There is no grounds for seeing in the text a reference to a heavenly Feast of Tabernacles."
[159]Draper, *Tabernacles*, convincingly argues that this passage comprises a midrash on Zech 14.
[160]Daniélou, *Liturgy*, 342. His view of the overall eschatological character of Sukkot in second temple times is questionable.

The key to understanding the role of Sukkot in the vision is to appreciate the importance of the temple throughout Revelation.[161] Chapters 4 through 20 comprise an extended description of the heavenly temple, while 21-22 expand the focus to the new Jerusalem. Rev 7:9-17 is one of the seven visions of eschatological worship that punctuate the lengthy description.[162] So in the wider context, the passage depicts a scene of eschatological worship in the heavenly temple.[163] The multitude is accordingly described in sacerdotal terms: "therefore they are before the throne of God, and serve him day and night within his temple." The Sukkot imagery – the palms, the cry of "salvation", the trumpets, the bowing before the throne and the "service" by day and night – replicates festival worship at the temple. Sukkot was the paramount temple festival, so worship in the eschatological temple resembles the Sukkot ritual. Like the prophet of Zech 14, when the visionary imagined worship in the heavenly temple, he instinctively pictured Sukkot.[164] Primarily on Sukkot pilgrims journeyed to the temple, experienced the divine presence and made their obeisance.

Because of the overall eschatological perspective of the book, and because the heavenly temple is an eschatological concept, the Sukkot celebration too occurs in eschatological times. But it is important to see that this link is a by-product of the festival's association with the temple and not due to purported ancient eschatological associations of Sukkot. The chain of association moves from eschatology to temple to Sukkot. That is, the eschatological vision of the author includes a temple, and since Sukkot was always the outstanding temple celebration and most popular pilgrimage, he portrayed worship in that temple in terms of Sukkot. Similarly, the protective, "tabernacling" presence of God derives primarily from the eschatological vision of the temple. God's presence was always to be found in the terrestrial temple, concentrated in the holy of holies. In the heavenly, eschatological temple that sheltering presence becomes a constant, living reality. Isaiah already envisioned the future temple covered by a cloud by day and a canopy by night as shelter from shade and protection from rain (4:5-6). Rev 7:15-17 describes the

---

[161]See McKelvey, *Temple*, 151-178.
[162]McKelvey, *Temple*, 161-62. The other visions: 4:2-11; 5:8-14; 11:15-19; 14:1-5; 15:2-4; 19:1-8. E. Schüssler-Fiorenza, *The Book of Revelation – Justice and Judgment* (Philadelphia: Fortress, 1985), 171 provides a slightly different list, including 12:10 and 20:4-6.
[163]For Temple imagery (especially the altar) see 4:2-11, 6:9, 8:3-6; 9:13, 11:1-3, 14:1-5; 15:5-8; and Fiorenza, ibid., 99. Cf. McKelvey, *Temple*, 162: "What is this but the ancient motif of the festal gathering at Zion put to Christian use."
[164]Thus I am in substantial agreement with Draper, *Tablernacles* (above, n. 159.) Both visions depict an eschatological temple. Cf. McKelvey, *Temple*, 161.

worshippers at that temple under the same protective presence.[165] As in John 7:37-38, the temple serves as the essential link through which eschatological motifs become associated with Sukkot. But whereas John saw the temple fulfilled in Jesus, the author of Revelation pictures a heavenly, eschatological temple in which the lamb-Christ resides along with God.[166]

X. Plutarch

Plutarch, a well-traveled and well-read priest of Delphi, lived in the last half of the first century and beginning of the second century CE. His work *Quaestiones Convivales* was written in his advanced years, probably in the first decade of the second century.[167] I include it here because he deals with Sukkot as celebrated when the temple stood, and probably relies on an earlier source. In Book IV 6,2 of this work Plutarch reports a discussion in which the disputants debate the identity of the God of the Jews.[168] Symmachus asserts the Jews worship Dionysus and supports

---

[165] Isa 4:6. Ulfgard, *Feast*, 97 notes the importance of this text ("The reader cannot but notice the strong resemblances between Isa 4:6 and Rev 7:16"), but does not consider the implications. Temple motifs, rather than the "exodus pattern," generate the protective presence.

[166] Here we may briefly address Rev 21:1-22:5, the description of the new Jerusalem. Comblin, *Liturgie*, 27-40 argues that this vision embodies the full development of Rev 7:9-17. Motifs in common include: the twelve tribes (21:12), the throne of God (22:1-3), worship (22:3), God's "tabernacle" ($sk\bar{e}n\bar{e}$ = sukka?; 21:3), living water (21:6, 22:1), the wiping away of tears (21:4), and the sign on the forehead (22:4). He also claims the imagery here, like that of 7:9-17, derives from Sukkot. The stream of living water expresses the "eschatological symbolism" of the water libation, while the imagery of light (21:23, 22:5) derives from the "illumination ceremony" of Sukkot, i.e. *simḥat beit hasho'eva*. But these are weak and unconvincing parallels. The passage actually lacks unambiguous Sukkot motifs. The imagery in the passage devolves primarily from the temple. In the eschatological temple one finds the throne and presence of God, his sheltering presence, and divine light, glory and life (21:4, 21:33, 22:5). The paradise imagery (22:1-2) also derives from the mythic identification of the temple, Mt Zion and garden of Eden. See Ezek 16:14; 28:13-14; Ps 36:8-10, 50:2. The stream of living water reflects the mythic view of the temple as the source of water for the entire world, as found in Zech 14:8-9 and Ezek 47:8-11. In eschatological time the mythic view becomes reality, and the temple eternally provides living water. To be sure the water libation on Sukkot tapped into that mythic view by attempting to stimulate the temple's hydraulic resources (see Chapter 3, I). So Sukkot imagery forms the background of the vision only to the extent that it too shares in mythic temple imagery. (Evidence does not support the existence of an "illumination ceremony" on Sukkot. See Chapter 3, III.)

[167] Stern, *Authors*, 1:545 n. 2.

[168] Stern, *Authors*, 1:553-58.

this claim by adducing parallels between Jewish festivals and Dionysian rites. He describes Sukkot in the following passage:

> First, he said, the time and character of the greatest, most sacred holiday of the Jews clearly befit Dionysus. When they celebrate their so-called Fast, at the height of the vintage, they set out tables of all sorts of fruit under booths *(skēnais)* and huts *(kaliasin)* plaited for the most part of vines and ivy. They call the first [day] of the feast "Booth."[169] A few days later they celebrate another festival, this time identified with Bacchus not through obscure hints but plainly called by his name, a festival that is a sort of 'Procession of Branches' or 'Thyrsus Procession' in which they enter the temple each carrying a thyrsus. What they do after entering we do not know, but it is probable that the rite is a Bacchic revelry, for in fact they use little trumpets to invoke their god as do the Argives at their Dionysia...[170]

In assessing this passage we must be careful not to take Plutarch as an unimpeachable historical source. Much of his information is obviously erroneous, including the overall claim that the Jews worship Dionysus, as Tacitus already realized.[171] If he errs on this point, how much the more so with the details of Sukkot rituals. At the same time, he (or his source) clearly had some reliable information about the festival.

The description "the greatest, most sacred holiday" must refer to Sukkot, not "the fast" (Yom Kippur), since Symmachus bases his claim of Jewish Dionysian worship on the rituals of Sukkot.[172] But he is somewhat confused about the relationship between the two festivals, and implies that the first day of "the Fast" is called "Booth" or that "the Fast," "Booth," and "another festival" are different days of a larger annual festival.[173] In any case, that Plutarch calls Sukkot "the greatest and most sacred festival" and knows something of its rituals confirms the status of Sukkot during the second temple period. Plutarch places the festival at the "height of the vintage," which, together with the Dionysian parallels, provides some evidence for the association of Sukkot with the vintage in post-biblical times.[174]

---

[169]The name *skēnē* (Booth) for the festival appears only here, although Philo uses *skēnai* (Booths or Tents). See above, n. 98.
[170]Translation from Stern, *Authors*, 1:557-58, taken from H. Hoffleit in the LCL series. I have altered *skēnais* from "tents" to "booths" and changed "they call the first days of the festival Tabernacles" to "they call the first [day] of the feast Booth."
[171]Historae 5:5 (= Sterns, *Authors*, 2:226, no. 281.)
[172]So Stern, *Authors*, 1:560.
[173]For ways to emend the passage, see Büchler, *Cabanes*, 193.
[174]Jgs. 9:27 and 21:19 suggest the autumnal festival was primarily related to the vintage. See Chapter 1, I.

Plutarch refers to booths plaited with vines and ivy. This description of the booths resembles that found in rabbinic sources; mSuk 1:3 considers the status of a sukka upon which one has trained ivy, vines or gourds. Plutarch's claim that fruit is placed on tables appears to be a similar means of decorating the sukka, and also has rabbinic parallels.[175] tSuk 1:7 rules fit the roofing of a sukka upon which one hangs fruit, nuts and grape clusters. Plutarch does not mention where the booths are located. If "height of the vintage" has a locative dimension, we may conclude the booths were out in the vineyards. That the booths are described separately from the temple rites, which Plutarch actually considers to belong to an independent festival, also suggests booths were erected not only by pilgrims in Jerusalem but outside the temple as well. To the extent that Plutarch can be trusted, we have one of the few allusions to extra-temple observance of the festival rituals.[176]

The "procession of branches" or *thyrsoi* probably refers to the lulav. 2 Macc 10:7, we noted, uses the same term for the lulav.[177] Büchler suggests the "procession of branches" refers to the willow procession on the seventh day of Sukkot, since Plutarch claims this rite occurs on "another festival."[178] This interpretation, while possible, gives excessive credence to the source; we noted that Plutarch's chronology is confused. Plutarch vaguely knows of a procession in which flora of some sort are carried, so he describes it literally as a "procession of branches" and then with the more technical term "thyrsos-procession" to capture the Dionysian and cultic character. Reference to the willow rite is possible but uncertain.[179] More significant is that the description of a

---

[175]Büchler, *Cabanes*, 192 points out that the laws of tithing appear in Jub 32, the passage describing Jacob's celebration of Sukkot (see p. 55). He suggests the fruit Plutarch mentioned was brought as second tithe to be eaten in Jerusalem and was set upon tables in sukkot.

[176]See above on Philo, *Flaccus*, §116-124, above p. 71. Contra Büchler, *Cabanes*, 193 who argues the description of booths pertains exclusively to the temple and Jerusalem. Having reasoned the fruit on the tables was brought as tithes to the temple (see previous note), he is forced to claim the sukkot are located in Jerusalem.

[177]See too *AJ* 13:372; above, pp. 78 and 82.

[178]Büchler, *Cabanes*, 186-87, refers the *thyrsos* to the lulav, the *kradē* to the willow. Stern, *Authors*, 2:561 points out this term itself implies no connection to the willow.

[179]The passage seems to imply the thyrsos-procession occurs only at "another festival," a one-time affair, not each day. Büchler, *Cabanes*, 185 makes the plausible suggestion *heortē* should be translated "ceremony," not "festival (day)," the sense of the passage being that they observe "another ceremony" each day of the festival. But once again we should hesitate before embarking on such attempts to reconcile Plutarch with biblical and rabbinic sources. We cannot expect Plutarch or his source to know such details accurately.

procession[180] with flora recalls the description in Jubilees (and rabbinic literature) of a procession circumambulating the altar.[181]

XI. Numismatics and Iconography

No discussion of the sources that relate to Sukkot is complete without reference to the festival symbols in ancient Jewish art. The lulav and etrog appear on several Jewish coins and many other objects. This material has been collected by Goodenough in his monumental work, *Jewish Symbols in the Greco-Roman Period*.[182] Unfortunately, the interpretation of iconography is fraught with danger, for it is difficult to determine the exact meaning of a piece of art.[183] To avoid that insoluble debate, I will suffice with a summary of the evidence and a brief survey of the prevailing theories.

The lulav and etrog first appear on coins of the first revolt against the Romans, 66-70 CE.[184] According to Kadman's inventory, of the five years in which coins were minted, all the coins with Sukkot symbols bear the imprint "year four," i.e., 69-70 CE.[185] The slogan changed from "Freedom for Zion" of years two and three to "Redemption of Zion" for year four. Several scholars conjecture that this change in terminology reflects a shift in aspiration from political freedom to messianic redemption, and the

---

[180]*eis to hieron eisiasin*. However, Plutarch does not employ the term *pompē*, the technical term for a religious procession in the Hellenistic world.

[181]Plutarch reports they "use little trumpets to invoke their deity." While the Levites sounded trumpets each day at the temple, on Sukkot special blasts marked points of the procession that returned to the temple with the water libation (mSuk 4:9, 5:5). If lulavs were held during this procession as well – the lulav, like the libation, serving as rain charm – Plutarch's description would be fitting. Büchler, *Cabanes*, 186, suggests the trumpet blasts are those sounded when the willows were erected beside the altar, mSuk 4:5.

[182]Goodenough, *Symbols*, 4:145-55, 12:86-88. Riesenfeld, *Jésus*, 48-56 and Ulfgard, *Feast*, 131-47 also discuss iconography in great detail.

[183]Criticism of Goodenough's interpretation has been severe. See the review of criticism and general summary in M. Smith, "Goodenough's Jewish Symbols in Retrospect," *JBL* 86 (1967), 53-68.

[184]For many years several coins with lulavs were assigned to Simon Maccabeus. See e.g. F.W. Madden, *History of Jewish Coinage and of Money in the Old and New Testament*, ed. H. Orlinsky (New York: Ktav, 1967), 47-49. The consensus now assigns these coins to the second revolt and Simon bar Kochba. See Avi-Yonah's prolegomenon in Madden, xx-xxii.

[185]Other motifs on coins of the first revolt: chalice, three pomegranates, amphora, vine leaf, palm tree between two baskets of fruit, three palm branches tied together, wreath of palm branches. See L. Kadman, *The Coins of the Jewish War* (Jerusalem, 1960), 84.

Sukkot symbols therefore possess a messianic message.[186] One scholar even advances the dubious and unprovable assumption that the Roman general Vespasian's temporary cessation of military activity was perceived "as a godsend by the rebels" and the "Redemption of Zion" slogan refers to that event.[187] But this interpretation is pure speculation.

In the coins of the Bar-Kochba revolt of 132-135 CE, lulavs and the combination of a lulav with an etrog appear among the following motifs: a temple facade, amphora, vine leaf, wreath, bunch of grapes, palm branch, palm tree, pair of trumpets and lyre.[188] Again some scholars propose that the Sukkot symbols, as in the coins of the first revolt, point to a hope for redemption or messianic deliverance.[189] Others claim the lulav (of both revolts) is a victory symbol, a motif encountered in the Books of Maccabees and that will reappear in later midrashim.[190] Undoubtedly the proponents of the second revolt hoped for victory, political independence and to rebuild the temple. Yet this does not prove the symbols imprinted on their coins expressed these ideas. Would we say the amphora and vine leaf have a similar meaning? Rather the lulav and etrog seem to be either general symbols of nature and fertility, like the bunch of grapes, vine leaf and palm, or symbols related to the temple that point again to conception of Sukkot as a temple festival.

Lulavs and etrogs appear frequently on Jewish tombstones and in catacomb decorations.[191] They are found on oil lamps from the first and

---

[186] Kadman, ibid., 94: "It seems, therefore, that the representation of the lulab and ethrog together with the legend *for the redemption of Zion* on the coins of year four symbolized not only the Feast of Tabernacles, but also the messianic hope of final redemption." So Ulfgard, *Feast*, 134-37; M. Dacy, "Sukkot in the Late Second Temple Period," *Australian Journal of Jewish Studies* 6, 2 (1992), 105-106.

[187] Ulfgard, *Feast*, 135. See there n. 572 for further references.

[188] See Avi-Yonah in F.W. Madden, *History of Jewish Coinage and of Money in the Old and New Testament*, ed. H. Orlinsky (New York: Ktav, 1967), xxxvii-xxxix. For photographs of the lulav coins see Y. Meshorer, *Jewish Coins of the Second Temple Period*, trans. I.H. Levine (Tel-Aviv: Am Hassefer, 1967), plate XX, nos. 161-63.

[189] Kadman, *Coins*, 93-4; A. Reifenberg, *Ancient Jewish Coins*² (Jerusalem: Rubin Mass, 1947), 37. Reifenberg claims that the amphora depicted was precisely that used for the water libation. It is true that Bar-Kochba requisitioned the four species for this soldiers (see Chapter 5, II n. 40). That this was for messianic reasons, rather than simply to observe the festival commandments , is unclear.

[190] See 1 Macc 13:51 and probably 2 Mac 10:5-8. Goodenough, *Symbols*, 4:145-46.

[191] See J.B. Frey, *Corpus Inscriptionum Judaiacarum* (New York: Ktav, 1975 [1936]), 1:663, index, s.v. "loulab," "ethrog"; Goodenough, *Symbols*, index to vols. 3 and 12, s.v. "lulab." The inscriptions range from the third century BCE to the sixth century CE. It should be noted that in many of these cases it is not clear that the figure is specifically a lulav or simply a palm branch.

The Second Temple Period 99

second centuries,[192] on glass and other objects,[193] on synagogue mosaics, sarcophogi and tombs. Exactly what this means – other than that the lulav was a popular symbol – is difficult to determine.[194] The sukka does not appear as much in art, presumably because its is difficult to depict, and easily could be confused with a house, tent, shack or any square object.[195]

XII. Conclusions

After the destruction of the first temple over a century elapsed before religious life was re-established on a solid foundation under Ezra and Nehemiah. For at least fifty years no sacrifices were offered, and for another twenty years the lack of a temple prevented the cult from developing to any great extent. During this period the festival of Sukkot bore little resemblance to its first temple antecedent. The account of the assembly in Nehemiah 8 makes it clear that the community no longer

---

[192] V. Sussman, *Neirot ḥeres me'utarim* (Jerusalem: Bialik, 1972), 42-43 and plates 8-13 (pp. 64-66). See also plates 84-85 which Sussman claims depict the willows adorning the altar.

[193] See Goodenough, *Symbols*, index to volume 3, s.v. "lulab."

[194] Goodenough concludes they served originally as funerary emblems, and, like the menora, symbolized immortality; *Symbols*, 4:147; 12:86-88. So J. Daniélou, "Le symbolisme eschatologique de la Fête des Tabernacles," *Irénikon* 31 (1958), 28-29. Goodenough surveys the literary sources, especially Philo, in an effort to prove the heavily mystical and otherworldly nature of the festival. And he notes that palms are also found on pagan and Christian graves as symbols of immortality, 4:165. But this interpretation derives from his discredited thesis of a mystical, syncretistic, non-rabbinic Judaism, in which he discerns a "very mystical approach to Tabernacles" and should be treated with skepticism. However, there are certain points of contact with amoraic midrashim in which the lulav is associated with new life. PRK 27:3 (407-408) suggests that God "created anew" the generations on the verge of death, and as a response the people joyously carry their lulavs. The lulav symbolizes the anticipated new life, or life-after-death. Since most of the midrashim focus on the nation as a whole, the eschatological themes are expressed in more general terms; see Chapter 7, I. On a grave, however, the motif may point to personal immortality.

[195] J.Z. Smith, *Imagining Religion* (Chicago: University of Chicago Press, 1982), 15 tabulated 944 inscriptions from Rome, Beth Shearim and Egypt collected by Goodenough. He found 41 instances of a lulav, 30 of an etrog, 111 of a menora, 27 of a flask, 18 of a shofar and 6 of the Ark. One could argue that since about half the symbols are lulavs or etrogs, the festival and its symbols must have been extremely important. On the other hand, Smith notes that this pictorial range is not impressive, that Jewish iconography "exhibits an extremely limited vocabulary." It seems to me that the popularity of the lulav and etrog, like that of the shofar and menora, has more to do with the fact that they lend themselves easily to pictorial representation. It is much harder to depict a Torah scroll, temple, or piece of matzah in an asthetic and easily recognizable manner. For this reason the sukka also appears infrequently.

observed the popular festival rituals. Both the official cult and popular religious life had deteriorated. To cope with this discontinuity Ezra[196] attempted to reconstitute the festival based on scriptural traditions. The essence of the festival consisted of observing the Torah's commandment to build booths, to dwell in them for seven days and to fulfill the other obligations of the holy days.

During the period of relative stability in the fourth and third centuries BCE the temple cult flourished. Sukkot again became the main pilgrimage and primary temple festival, and retained this status until the destruction in 70 CE. The prophet of Zech 14 already pictures worship in the eschatological temple as a Sukkot celebration. Likewise the author of Revelation models worship in the heavenly temple after Sukkot. 2 Maccabees names the new temple-rededication festival after Sukkot and portrays it as a replacement for a missed Sukkot celebration. New Testament traditions have Jesus appear in the temple on Sukkot so that he address the widest audience. Jubilees prescribes a plethora of sacrifices for Sukkot, and associates the institutionalization of the priesthood and tithing obligations with this festival. Josephus points out that Sukkot is "considered especially sacred and important by the Hebrews," and observes that they observe the festival "with special care." Wars, political disputes and rivalries were suspended to allow the celebration of the festival. The accounts of the downfall of several high priests after their public appearances on Sukkot opens a small window to the magnificent pageantry that took place. The high priest became the center of attention and admiration as large crowds watched him perform the elaborate festival rites.

Several sources testify to the observance of the rituals of the sukka and lulav, the commandments specified in scripture. Nehemiah 8 implies that, although the sukka ritual had not been observed for many years, the community which resolved to fulfill the Torah built sukkot to dramatize their new faith. They make the sukkot from branches of palms and other flora gathered from the surrounding countryside. Jubilees notes that Abraham built booths for his household, and directs his descendants to do likewise. The Temple Scroll describes long sukkot on the roof of the temple and prescribes the leaders to dwell in sukkot during the sacrificial service. Philo remarks that the Alexandrian community usually set up booths (or tents) during the festival. Several times Josephus notes that the people build booths "in honor" of God. Plutarch's source described the booths as plaited with ivy and vines, a description consistent with rabbinic sources. The Temple Scroll probably assumes that foliage will be placed each year on the permanent

---

[196]That is, the Ezra of the narrative.

frameworks of beams and columns to fashion booths. Thus the sources even provide some information as to the appearance of the booths. The popularization of this ritual throughout Palestine and as far as Alexandria demonstrates the success of the program of the Holiness School and the restoration community that first adopted the prescribed rite. In this way the festival acquired a popular dimension not connected with the temple celebrations.

The ritual taking of the four species prescribed in Lev 23:40 seems to have been widely observed.' The heavenly tablets of Jubilees command all Israelites to celebrate with "leafy boughs and willows of the brook," a clear allusion to the biblical verse. Jason of Cyrene explains that they celebrated the rededication of the temple by bearing wands and palms as is the custom on Sukkot. Plutarch's source also mentions a "thyrsus-procession," into the temple, which probably refers to the lulav. These sources may imply that a formal procession with the lulav took place, although they may simply mean that as pilgrims approached the temple they carried the festal bouquet. Josephus confirms that worshippers at the temple generally carried ritual wands and citrons. And several New Testament passages describe the crowds holding palm-branches at the Jerusalem temple and in the eschatological temple.

Narrative sources place the lulav in the context of temple worship.[197] Recall that Josephus even reformulates the biblical passages to link the lulav to the sacrifices. This suggests that the lulav was practiced only within the temple precincts as a mode of cultic worship. Philo, we noted, omits mention of the lulav. On the other hand, a Qumran liturgical text formulated a blessing for the "branches of leafy trees," apparently the lulav, which suggests that the Qumran community practiced the rite.[198] A second text mentions the "lulav" in what appears to be a description of a popular celebration. Since these Qumran texts are fragmentary and ambiguous, we may conclude that the lulav was basically a cultic rite.

Josephus identifies the four species as citrons, palms, willows and myrtles, as would the rabbis. Pseudo-Philo knows of the myrtle and quite possibly the citron. So this tradition dates at least to the mid-first century CE. If Josephus (or his source) accurately reports the tradition that Alexander Jannaeus was pelted with citrons, and did not refract it through later custom, then the tradition can be pushed back to the early first century BCE. I will return to this topic in Chapter 5,II in the analysis of rabbinic sources.

---

[197]Jubilees, which paraphrases the biblical legislation, is the only possible exception, although Abraham does celebrate around an altar.
[198]Unless the blessing is intended specifically for those who worship in the temple.

These pre-rabbinic sources unfortunately yield but scanty information about the temple rituals and customs not explicitly contained in scripture. Zech 14 and John 7 reveal a connection between observance of Sukkot and the rain supply. Pseudo-Philo provides the clearest expression of this idea, interpreting the lulav as a means of entreating God for rain. He probably transferred (or at least added) the function of other rituals to the lulav, constrained as he was by the genre of his work as a paraphrase of scripture, and thus precluded from mentioning non-scriptural rites. We may assume that there were cultic rituals directed to produce rains, but there remains no solid information about them. Jubilees describes Abraham circumambulating the altar seven times each day with palms and fruit, a rite which is not prescribed by the Torah. Since this coheres with rabbinic sources, we may safely conclude that a procession of this sort took place around the altar. Jubilees also mentions the wearing of crowns, probably garlands of flora typical of harvest festivals. Finally a fragmentary Qumran text seems to contain a liturgy of popular celebrations with lulavs involving men and women, elderly and youths alike. For more information about the festival rituals we must turn to rabbinic sources.

3

The Sukkot Temple Festival: Rabbinic Traditions

Rabbinic literature preserves detailed traditions of the rituals performed in the temple on the festival of Sukkot. The earliest rabbinic document, the Mishna, depicts three main rituals: water libations, the willow procession (*'arava*), and *simḥat beit hasho'eva* (rejoicing at the place of water-drawing; henceforth SBH), an all-night festivity celebrated in the temple courtyards. The Mishna also describes how worshippers practiced the lulav ritual in temple times, and contains several allusions to other cultic rituals. Further details of these rituals are preserved in the Tosefta, a companion – and sometimes commentary – to the Mishna which includes tannaitic traditions that the Mishna omitted. The Babylonian and Palestinian Talmuds contain some additional information as well as interpretations of the Mishnaic and Toseftan traditions. These sources paint a much richer picture of the temple festival than we gain from the limited pre-rabbinic sources analyzed in the previous chapter. However, several considerations complicate the use of rabbinic literature as a source for the history of the second temple period.[1] The Mishna was redacted in about 200 CE, over a century and a

---

[1] Jacob Neusner has repeatedly set forth these issues, and repeatedly denied the reliability of Mishnaic traditions pertaining to temple times. See Neusner, *Judaism*, 14-22; idem, *Method and Meaning in Ancient Judaism* (Missoula, Montana: Scholars Press, 1979), 6-8; idem, "The Modern Study of the Mishnah," *The Study of Ancient Judaism I*, ed. J. Neusner (New York: Ktav, 1973); idem, "The Use of the Later Rabbinic Evidence for the Study of First-Century Pharisaism, in *Approaches to Ancient Judaism I*, ed. W.S. Green (Missoula, Montana: Scholars Press, 1978), 215-28; idem, *Reading and Believing: Ancient Judaism and Contemporary Gullibility* (Atlanta, 1986); etc. etc. The issues are presented clearly in W.S. Green, "What's in a Name – The Problematic of Rabbinic 'Biography'," in *Approaches to Ancient Judaism I*, 77-96 and Strack, *Talmud*, 63-66.

quarter after the destruction of the temple, and the Tosefta somewhat later. This lengthy interval casts doubt on the accuracy of the information preserved. While many traditions are attributed to sages who lived during temple times and witnessed the temple service themselves, we cannot be certain that these attributions are correct.[2] Later sages may have retrojected their ideas to earlier predecessors in order to augment the authority of their traditions. Even if the attributions are correct, there remains the possibility that the traditions changed, consciously or subconsciously, as they were passed down from generation to generation.[3] Moreover, the rabbis were not historians, and the Mishna was not intended as an historical work. The Mishna regularly sets out the laws that govern the ideal society imagined by the rabbis, not the laws actually in force at the time. The Mishna consequently tends to describe the temple in an idealized fashion, prescribing how worship should take place, not necessarily how the cult actually functioned during its existence. Therefore scholars have questioned the reliability of traditions that purport to describe matters related to the temple. To what extent do rabbinic traditions of Sukkot temple rituals accurately reflect the forms of worship in earlier times?

To this point scholarship had not developed methods that allow this question to be answered with certainty. Recent research has tended to show that the rabbis accurately transmitted traditions from much earlier periods. An halakhic document found among the Qumran Scrolls known as *Miqṣat Maʿaseh HaTorah* or MMT contains a list of halakhic disputes between the Qumran group and their opponents.[4] The topics cohere closely with rabbinic traditions of disputes between the Pharisees and the Sadducees in temple times.[5] Rabbinic literature even uses the same technical terms and phrases as in the Qumran text.[6] Other Qumran texts display similar affinities to the legal traditions preserved in rabbinic

---

[2] See Neusner, *Judaism*, 14-22; Green, *What's in a Name?*, 77-96.
[3] The fact that Mishnaic traditions appear in a limited number of forms indicates that the original traditions have been recast and reformulated. See Green, *What's in a Name?*, 81-83 and his references there n. 21. It does not necessarily follow, however, that the tradition is artificial or invented.
[4] On MMT see E. Qimron and J. Strugnell, "An Unpublished Halakhic Letter from Qumran," *Biblical Archaeology Today*, ed. J. Amitai (Jerusalem, 1985), 400-407; Y. Sussmann, "The History of Halakha and the Dead Sea Scrolls: Preliminary Observations on Miqsat Maʿase ha-torah (4QMMT)," *Tarbiz 59* (1989/90), 11-76 (Hebrew); L. Schiffman, "The New Halakhic Letter (4QMMT) and the Origins of the Dead Sea Sect," *BA 53* (1990), 64-73.
[5] Sussmann, *MMT*, 23-27.
[6] Ibid., 26.

materials.⁷ All this has led Joseph Baumgarten, the leading scholar of early Halakha, to conclude that "[i]n the sphere of Halakha, the rabbis were trustworthy preservers of tradition."⁸ These studies do not prove that rabbinic traditions can be trusted absolutely, but they do suggest that the traditions are not absolutely untrustworthy.⁹

Corroboration in non-rabbinic sources clearly provides a sound basis for establishing the reliability of a rabbinic tradition. However, in the case of Sukkot, non-rabbinic sources provide limited information as to the temple rituals. At the same time, the general recognition of the importance of the temple and the clues that point to the existence of certain practices furnish some evidence for the basic picture that emerges from rabbinic materials. In addition, several internal considerations help to assess the reliability of a rabbinic tradition. One can usually sense where rabbinic literature takes on a mythic perspective and an idealized tone, or reports miracles and other supernatural phenomena, and should be considered less historical than legendary. While these legendary traditions share the same basic forms with other rabbinic materials, their *content* is marked by exaggeration, hyperbole and folkloristic motifs. Where rabbinic sources interpret earlier materials, and do not preserve independent traditions from temple times, the source must be scrutinized more carefully. A nuanced and careful study can differentiate between traditions of greater and lesser historical worth.

This is not the place for a comprehensive treatment of methodology for the study of rabbinic sources. Nor should we be interested solely in historical questions. The nature of rabbinic memory and historiography is also important. What is the rabbinic conception of Sukkot and how does it compare with that of other sources? What is the significance of

---

⁷See the review of evidence in Joseph Baumgarten, "Recent Qumran Discoveries and Halakhah in the Hellenistic-Roman Period," *Jewish Civilization in the Hellenistic-Roman Period*, ed. Shmaryahu Talmon (Sheffield: Sheffield Academic Press, 1990), 147-158.

⁸Ibid., 155-156.

⁹David Goodblatt, "Towards the Rehabilitation of Talmudic History," *History of Judaism: The Next Ten Years*, ed. B. Bokser (Chico, California, 1980), 33-43 also argues for the possibility of writing history based on rabbinic sources. E.P. Sanders, *Jewish Law from Jesus to the Mishnah* (Philadelphia: Trinity Press, 1990), 244 in a searching critique of Neusner's relentless critique of rabbinic methodology, writes: "The model for historical research, however, should not be that of the courtroom, in which there are only two possibilities, and in which one side must bear the burden of proof – early until proved late, *or* the reverse. That is too crude for the information gained from our discipline. I am hopeful that a new generation of scholars will continue the search for the Pharisees, and in doing so will carefully *sift* and *weigh* the extremely difficult evidence" (italics in the original). See too Baumgarten's criticism of Neusner, "Recent Qumran Discoveries," 150, 152-53.

the fact that the Mishna transmits descriptions of cultic rituals no longer practiced? How do these compare to the rituals the rabbis actually observed? The purpose of this chapter is to appreciate both this aspect of the rabbinic understanding of Sukkot, namely the view of the Sukkot of the past, and to gain additional insights into the festival as celebrated in second temple times.

I. The Willow Procession

Mishna Tractate Sukka consists of five chapters. The first two chapters contain rulings for the construction of the sukka and the obligation to dwell therein. The third chapter defines the four species and the proper way to observe the ritual. The fourth and fifth chapters describe the rituals observed in temple times. These latter chapters comprise an independent composition that focuses on the festival of the past rather than the contemporary mode of observance. Jacob Epstein concluded that these chapters were "essentially redacted during the time of the temple," although he concedes that later hands made additions in a few places.[10] While the dating to temple times is questionable, the bulk of the material probably comprises an early tannaitic source, perhaps composed soon after the destruction. The unit begins with a Mishna that sets forth the framework for the following materials:

[A] The lulav and the willow – six or seven [days].
[B] The Hallel [psalms] and the rejoicing – eight [days].
[C] The sukka and the water libation – seven [days].
[D] And the flute – five or six [days].

(mSuk 4:1)

This Mishna lists the rituals practiced in temple times and reports how many days each was observed. The following mishnayot take up each ritual in turn, and explain the prescribed durations.[11]

mSuk 4:3,5-7 describe the willow ritual:

[A] The willow for seven days – how so?

---

[10]*Tannaim*, 350; see following note.

[11]The lulav and willow rituals were not observed when the Sabbath coincided with an intermediate festival day. If the first day of Sukkot fell on the Sabbath, the lulav ritual was nevertheless observed, which resulted in a seven day ritual (mSuk 4:2, tSuk 3:1; see below, section VI.) If the seventh day of Sukkot fell on a Sabbath, the willow ritual took place, again making a seven day ritual (tSuk 3:1). This formal structure and focus on the temple celebrations, including the return to the lulav and sukka that had been discussed in the tractate's previous chapters, indicate that Epstein correctly characterized the materials as an independent unit (see previous note).

[B] If the seventh day of the willow fell on the Sabbath – the willow [takes place] seven [days].
[C] And [if it fell] on all other days – six [days].
(mSuk 4:3)

[A] The commandment of the willow – how so?
[B] There was a place below Jerusalem named Moṣa.[12]
[C] They would go down there and collect from there branches[13] of willows, and come and erect them at the sides of the altar, and their tops bent over the altar.
[D] They sounded an extended blast [on the trumpet], a quavering blast, an extended blast.
[E] Each day they circle the altar once and say: "O [Lord] deliver us, O [Lord] deliver us."[14]
[F] R. Yehuda says: "אני והוא,[15] deliver us. אני והוא, deliver us."
[G] That day they circle the altar seven times.[16]
(mSuk 4:5)

[A] Its practice on the Sabbath was the same as on weekdays.
[B] Except they would gather them on the eve of the Sabbath, and leave them in golden troughs so that they would not wither.
[C] R. Yohanan b. Beroka says: They used to gather branches of palm and beat them on the altar.[17]
[D] And that day was called the day of beating branches.
(mSuk 4:6)

[A] Immediately the children snatch their lulavs and eat their etrogs.
(mSuk 4:7)

---

[12]Probably identical to *Hamoṣa* mentioned in Jos 18:26. bSuk 45a and ySuk 4:3, 54b state that its name was Colonia, presumably because it was occupied and settled by Roman troops following the destruction. Edward Robinson, *Biblical Researches in Palestine* (Boston: Crocker and Brewster, 1856), 1:463 and n. 3 mentions a village called Kulônieh, "an hour and a half from Jerusalem," a few miles to the north-west. This was apparently Moṣa; see Adolphe Neubauer, *La Géographie du Talmud* (Hildesheim: Georg Olms, 1967), 152-53. The village was abandoned after Robinson's journeys, and following the establishment of the state of Israel, a new settlement was founded nearby and named Moṣa. See Pinhas Ne'eman, *'Enṣiqlopedia lage'ographia talmudit* (Tel Aviv: Joshua Chachik, 1970), 2:132. The personal name *Moṣa* appears in 1 Chr 2:46, 8:36-37, 9:42-43.
[13]*murbiot*, or "young trees." bSuk 45a and ySuk 4:3, 54b cite tannaitic traditions that the willow branches were eleven cubits tall so as to droop over the ten-cubit tall altar.
[14]Ps 118:25.
[15]Transcription: 'NY WHW'. For variants see Fox, *Succah*, 131. Some manuscripts have אני והו in place of אני והוא. Fox, 137-38 convincingly argues the variant is simply one of spelling, not of content.
[16]That is, the seventh day.
[17]Some versions of the Mishna read "beat them *on the ground*" and some "beat them on the sides of the altar." See Fox, *Succah*, 141 and *DQS* to bSuk 45a.

A baraita preserved in bSuk 45b reports the liturgical recitation upon completing the ritual:[18]

[A] When they depart, what do they say? "Beauty is yours, *(yofi lakh)*, O altar. Beauty is yours, O altar."
[B] R. Eliezer says: "For Yah and for you, O altar. For Yah and for you, O altar."

The Tosefta relates that the Boethusians believed the willow ritual should not be observed on the Sabbath:

[A] The lulav takes precedence over the Sabbath at the beginning [of the festival], and the willow at the end.
[B] Once the Boethusians pressed heavy rocks upon it [the willows] on the eve of the Sabbath.
[C] The folk *('amei ha'areṣ)* saw them, and came and dragged them away, and took them out from under the stones on the Sabbath.
[D] For the Boethusians do not admit that the beating of willows takes precedence over the Sabbath.

(tSuk 3: 1)

The basic contours of the ritual are apparent although the particular details sketchy. They collected willows from Moṣa, a nearby town, and then came to Jerusalem and assembled around the altar. The Mishna does not explicitly state whether the gathering and bringing of willows constituted an intrinsic part of the ritual or simply the preliminary provisioning, nor whether the journey to Jerusalem took place as a formal ritual procession. Now mSuk 4:3 claims they did not perform the ritual on the Sabbath (except on the seventh day), while 4:6 suggests they did set the willows around the altar, having gathered them beforehand. This implies that the gathering and procession from Moṣa to Jerusalem were omitted on the Sabbath, but otherwise they comprised an intrinsic part of the ritual. Processions to temples, altars and other holy places are widespread religious phenomena – the libation, as we shall see, also included a procession – so it is likely that the trek from Moṣa to Jerusalem took this form.

The nature of the circumambulations of the altar is also unclear. mSuk 4:5C reports that they erected the willows beside the altar and sounded the trumpet, and then 4:5E mentions the circuits. We would expect that if the ritual centered on the willows the worshippers would carry the willows around the altar prior to placing them at its side. In the BT the amoraim disagree on this question. Some claim that they

---

[18]bSuk 45b. The baraita has been appended to some texts of the Mishna, including printings of bSuk 45a. See *DQS*, ad loc. and Fox, *Succah*, 139 and the references there.

circumambulated with willows and then erected them beside the altar, while others claim they set the willows beside the altar and circumambulated with lulavs.[19] The different opinions in this case reflect different interpretations of the Mishna, rather than independent oral traditions about the ritual. Most likely the circumambulations were performed with willows – the description says nothing whatsoever of the lulav – but we should not advance solid historical claims where the traditions are silent. A second important point is that the circuits around the altar required the celebrants to enter the main temple courtyard, and even to enter into the area between the sanctuary and the altar, a domain from which they were normally excluded.[20] So festive was the occasion and so popular the ritual that the normal prohibition banning non-priests from the inner temple precincts was suspended.[21]

The Mishna's ruling that the ritual be performed on the Sabbath indicates that the rabbis considered the ritual an essential element of temple worship. The full ritual was conducted if the Sabbath fell on the seventh day (4:3B), and a limited observance took place on intermediate festival days that coincided with the Sabbath (4:6A-B). Cultic activity on the Sabbath constituted a perennial difficulty in temple times, and was a constant point of conflict among different Jewish groups. The rabbis and their precursors, the Pharisees, ruled that the essential temple service such as the daily and communal festival offerings should be performed

---

[19] bSuk 43b. According to MTeh 17:5 (128-29) willows were carried (but see the variants in Buber's n. 36), according to MTeh 26:5 (217) lulavs. See 'Or Zaru'a (Zitomir, 1862-90), 2:69a; A. Aptowitzer's note in Sefer Ravyah (Jerusalem: Harry Fischel Institute, 1964), 2:397 n. 9 and J. Rubenstein, "Cultic Themes in Sukkot Piyyutim," PAAJR 59 (1993), 204-207.

[20] The amoraim, as well as medieval commentators, struggle with the problem that non-priests generally were limited to the outer temple courtyards and could not approach the altar. In Mishnaic theory, Israelite men were allowed into the main courtyard (the "court of priests"; mKel 1:8) when they presented sacrifices, but not beyond, and even priests with blemishes could not enter the area between the altar and the "porch" (the front of the sanctuary; mKel 1:9). Both ySuk 4:3, 54c and bSuk 44a recognize that the procession entailed a relaxation of the normal restrictions on entry, but imply that only priests with blemishes were allowed to participate, although normally prohibited from entry to the inner court. Traditional commentaries accordingly conclude that only priests performed the circuits while the rest of the people watched from the outer courts. However the description in the Mishna places no limits on the participants, implying that all performed the circuits. One medieval jurist, Ibn Ghiyyat, Sha'arei simḥa, 114a, recognized this fact and ruled that Israelites were allowed into the inner court for the sake of the ritual. See too Safrai, 'Aliya, 191 and nn. 164-65.

[21] See too I. Knohl, "Post-Biblical Sectarianism and the Priestly Schools of the Pentateuch: The Issue of Popular Participation in the Temple Cult on Festivals," The Madrid Qumran Congress, ed. J.T. Barrera and L.V. Montaner (Leiden: Brill, 1992), 2:603.

on the Sabbath, while festival offerings of individuals and voluntary offerings should not be sacrificed. In all cases they attempted to limit compromising the sanctity of the Sabbath, as in our example, where the Mishna rules that the full willow ritual is not to be conducted. Other Jewish groups ruled that the Sabbath required the suspension of all (or almost all) cultic activity.[22] According to the Tosefta, the Boethusians believed that no part of the willow ritual may take place on the Sabbath. They tried to prevent its observance by placing heavy rocks on the willows that had been prepared beforehand and placed in the temple on Friday.[23] The Tosefta claims that the "common folk" supported the

---

[22]The Bible prescribes offerings for the Sabbath, so it cannot be that the dissident groups forbade all cultic activity. They apparently ruled that the daily offering *(tamid)* should not be offered. CD 11:17 commands that "no one should offer on the altar on the Sabbath, except the burnt offering of the Sabbath; for thus it is written 'apart from your Sabbath offerings' (Lev 23:38)." By restructuring the calendar they attempted to prevent the confluence of the Sabbath and festivals so as not to offer the obligatory festival offerings on the Sabbath. The solar calendars of Jubilees and the Temple Scroll (and possibly MMT; see Sussmann, *MMT*, 24 and n. 61) were constructed to avoid as much as possible the confluence of the festivals and the Sabbath, as regularly occurs according to the rabbinic solar-lunar calendar. See J. van Goudoever, *Biblical Calendars* (Leiden: Brill, 1959), 63; S. Talmon, "The Calendar of the Covenanters of the Judean Desert," *Scripta Hierosolymirana 4* (1958), 167-74; L. Schiffman, The *Halakhah at Qumran* (Leiden: Brill, 1976), 84-133. See too S. Talmon, "Yom Hakkippurim in the Habakkuk Scroll," *Biblica* 32 (1951), 549-63, who suggests the Habakkuk Scroll shows that the sect observed Yom Kippur on a different day than the "official" fast, and the "Wicked Priest" interfered with their observance. Such controversies are not unknown among the rabbis themselves, as the famous account of mRH 2:8-9 attests. Since Pesaḥ and Sukkot last a full week, at least one day inevitably coincides with the Sabbath. For suggestions how these groups coped with this problem, see Y. Erder, "Precedents Cited by ʿAnan for the Postponement of Passover that Falls on Sabbath," *Zion* 52 (1987), 153-75 (Hebrew); idem, "When did the Karaites First Encounter Apocryphic Literature akin to the Dead Sea Scrolls?" *Cathedra* 42 (1987), 57-60 (Hebrew).

[23]Nothing in the sources implies the Boethusians opposed the ritual per se, but only its performance on the Sabbath, as the Tosefta explicitly says: "For the Boethusians do not admit that the beating of willows *takes precedence over the Sabbath."* Albeck, *Mishna*, 2:255 suggested the Boethusians rejected the entire ritual on the grounds that it is not explicitly written in the Torah. But this conception of the Sadducees / Boethusians is no longer accepted; see Sussmann, *MMT*, 47 n. 185 and Rubenstein, *Dissertation*, 254-262. Cf. mMen 10:3. The Mishna rules that the ʿomer offering (Lev 23:9-14) should be cut on the day after Pesaḥ even if this is a Sabbath, and explains that the elaborate ceremony preceding the cutting flaunts the Boethusians who believe "that the ʿomer is not cut on the day after the festival." The Boethusians interpreted the ambiguous "the day after the Sabbath" of Lev 23: 15 (which the rabbis interpreted as the day after Pesaḥ) to refer to the Sunday following the first Sabbath after the conclusion of Pesaḥ. (This is now clear from the calendar of the Temple Scroll; but see bMen

rabbinic / Pharisaic policy and thwarted these attempts to prevent the ritual by removing the boulders.

The sources distinguish the willow procession of the seventh day from that of the first six days of the festival. Besides this distinction of full or partial observance on the Sabbath, the days differ in the number of circumambulations. On the seventh day they circled the altar seven times, not just once as on previous days (mSuk 4:5G).[24] Clearly the ritual built to its climax on the seventh day of Sukkot. Recall that John 7:37 has Jesus make his proclamation on "the last and greatest day of the festival."

The liturgical expressions have sparked much debate [4:5E-F]. The first expression, "O [Lord] deliver us, O [Lord] deliver us," derives from Ps 118:25, one of the Hallel psalms mentioned in the Mishna.[25] Now in the same psalm, verse 27 has been translated "Bind the festal procession with branches up to the horns of the altar,"[26] or "Bedeck the festival with [willow-] branches at the corners of the altar."[27] The psalm probably

---

65a-b, and see Sussmann, *MMT*, 30-31 n. 81a.) Their motivation, in part, was to prevent the confluence of the *'omer* offering and the Sabbath as occurs periodically according to the rabbinic calendar. For the same reason tRH 1:15 asserts the Boethusians hired witnesses to deceive the sages about the sighting of the new moon.

[24]Jubilees prescribes a sevenfold circumambulation each festival day. See p. 116 and Chapter 2, III.

[25]So the *communis opinio*. However, Fox, *Succah*, 134-37 claims that both the tradition cited anonymously and that of R. Yehuda derive not from the Hallel but from ancient piyyutim that were part of the temple liturgy. The Mishna refers to the piyyut by its first or last line, and the disagreement concerns which piyyut was recited during the ritual. Fox notes that a variant textual tradition of R. Yehuda's liturgy reads אני והוא והושיעה נא, which does not correspond to the verse. He also rejects the association with Ps 118:25 since most manuscripts of the Mishna omit the divine name ("O deliver us" instead of "O Lord deliver us.") See too Heinemann, *Prayer*, 139-42 and the discussion of the Hallel below. This is an interesting theory, and I accept, with Heinemann, the antiquity of the *hoshaʿanot*. But the manuscript evidence is divided (although Fox claims the best manuscripts support his theory), and the precedents he cites for piyyutim with these refrains derive from geonic times. There is also the difficulty that the Palestinian amoraim no longer understood the thrust of this ruling, as evident from their farfetched explanations of R. Yehuda's statement (see below). Yet only a continuous custom of reciting such piyyutim would explain their appearance in geonic times. The great advantage of this theory is that it obviates the problem of explaining R. Yehuda's obscure phrase אני והוא (see below).

[26]RSV translation. LXX and all versions interpret *'avotim* as boughs, not cords. See Petuchowski, *Psalm*, 267-68; C.A. and E.G. Briggs, *A Critical and Exegetical Commentary on the Book of Psalms* (ICC 15; New York: Scribner, 1906-7), 2:409. bSuk 45a already finds biblical precedent for the willow ritual based on this verse.

[27]Fishbane, *Interpretation*, 112.

served as the liturgy for this very ritual, the "branches" being the willow branches carried around the altar and then placed beside it. Most likely, the psalm was recited in its entirety during the procession.[28] R. Yehuda provides an alternative recitation: "אני והוא, deliver us. אני והוא, deliver us,"[29] usually understood as "I and He, deliver us. I and He, deliver us." The comments of the Palestinian amoraim indicate that they took the phrase as a petition that God should save himself together with Israel: "deliver us," that is, deliver me (= the worshipper) and Him [= God].[30] Since God shares in the suffering of Israel, by saving the people he simultaneously delivers himself from suffering. Hai Gaon explains that "He" refers to the altar, the petition being to save the individual and the altar on which he atones for sin.[31] These interpretations, however, cohere better with rabbinic theologies than cultic liturgies. Like the previous opinion in the Mishna, R. Yehuda's tradition was probably a petition for salvation, and אני והוא an appellation for God. It has been proposed that R. Yehuda simply provides the pronunciation of Ps 118:25 which the Mishna (4:5E) designates as the liturgical phrase. Rather than pronounce the name of God explicitly, אנא ה', the worshippers adopted the surrogate אני והוא.[32] Recently Joseph Baumgarten has adduced compelling evidence to support this interpretation, although והוא need not be understood as an alternative pronunciation of the tetragrammaton, but simply the third person singular pronoun.[33] This pronoun is used as a substitute for the

---

[28]See Petuchowski, *Psalm*, 269-71; Amos Ḥakham, *Sefer tehilim* (Jerusalem: Rav Kook, 1970), 2:371 n. 31. Note further v. 24: "This is the day which YHWH has made; let us rejoice and be glad in it." The verse points to a special day, a festival, probably the "Festival of YHWH," and the emphasis on rejoicing suits Sukkot. Cf. Friedrich Baethgen, *Die Psalmen* (Göttingen, 1897), 347, who links the psalm to Sukkot (but ignore his overly zealous historicizing claim that Ezra composed the psalm specifically for the observance of Sukkot in 444 BCE).
[29]See Fox, *Succah*, 137-138, and the literature cited there; Epstein, *MLH*, 276-77. Later traditions connected this phrase to the seventy-two letter names of God derived from Exod 14:19-21. See Rashi, bSuk 45a, s.v. *'ani*.
[30]ySuk 4:3, 54c.
[31]*OG, Sukka, teshuvot* §§170-171, to bSuk 45a (66).
[32]Geiger, *Qevusat ma'amarim* (Berlin, 1877), 103; Urbach, *Sages*, 128 ("a mumbled version of *'Anna* and the Name); and Eliezer Ben-Yehuda, *Milon halashon ha'ivrit* (Berlin, 1915), 3:1263-65 advocate this explanation with minor points of difference. Both Urbach and Geiger considered the formula as a conscious attempt to conceal the divine name. For Ben-Yehuda no deliberate camouflage took place; this was the "natural" pronunciation of the time. G. Allon, *Meḥqarim betoldot yisra'el* (Tel Aviv, 1957-58), 1:200 and L. Blau, *Das altjüdische Zauberwesen* (Budapest, 1895), 131 offer similar interpretations. Ben Yehuda summarizes explanations of the *rishonim*.
[33]Joseph Baumgarten, "A New Qumran Substitute for the Divine Name and Mishnah Sukkah 4.5," *JQR* 83 (1992), 1-5.

divine name in several Qumran texts.³⁴ In 4Q266, an early manuscript of the *Damascus Document*, the blessing formula praises God as און הו, strikingly parallel to אני והוא.³⁵ R. Yehuda's tradition thus reflects a divine cognomen popular during second temple times. The evidence of the Qumran scrolls demonstrates once again the reliability of the tannaitic traditions.

The concluding liturgies reported in the baraita are also obscure. Literal translation yields an expression of praise for the altar: "Beauty is yours, O altar." Presumably the beauty consists of the adornment with willows. Such farewell acclamations are attested elsewhere in rabbinic and Hellenistic literature.³⁶ A second scholarly trend interprets the term יופי (YWPY) as an epithet for the tetragrammaton (YHWH).³⁷ mSanh 7:5 implies that יוסי (YWSY) served as a divine appellation in popular parlance. Reluctance to enunciate the tetragrammaton led to the substitution of terms with similar intonation and form. In addition, the "Prince of the Torah," a semi-divine figure in ancient Jewish mysticism,

---

³⁴This suggestion was made by L. Ginzberg, *An Unknown Jewish Sect* (New York: The Jewish Theological Seminary, 1970), 40-41 and H. Yalon, *Qiryat Sefer 28 (1952)*, 71, (both refer to our Mishna.) Yalon and Moshe Greenberg, "The Hebrew Oath Participle ḤAY/ḤÉ," *JBL* 76 (1957), 29-38 refer to scholars who claim הוא occasionally substitutes for the name of God in the Bible, and Greenberg claims the same for אני, also referring to our Mishna.

³⁵The sense of און is debated. Baumgarten considers it may mean "power," as in Isa 40:26, but prefers to understand it as a form of אנא, a result of the tendency to "disguise" the divine name, as Urbach argued (n. 32). It seems more likely that these variants reflect popular pronunciation rather than deliberate attempts to "disguise" the name. Both Greenberg and Baumgarten refer to the saying attributed to Hillel at SBH, "To the place my heart loves, there my legs carry me. If you come to my house, I will come to your house. If you do not come to my house, I will not come to your house, as it says, *In every place that I make my name known I will come to you and bless you (Exod 20:20)*." The "I" here is generally interpreted as Hillel putting words in God's mouth (so Tosafot, bSuk 53a, s.v. *'im* and references in Lieberman, *TK*, 4:888 and n. 3). Given the use of "he," "I" may be another divine name. See Hochman, *Festivities*, 105 n. 74, and the previous note.

³⁶S. Lieberman, *Hellenism in Jewish Palestine* (New York: Jewish Theological Seminary, 1950), 11 interprets the obscure phrase קלון דיאו of yAZ 1:2, 39c as καλον δυε, "Set well," and refers to a similar phrase in a Greek magical papyrus. In the talmudic midrash Adam speaks this phrase "as an acclamation to the sun, a kind of farewell to it." The Greek *kalos* corresponds exactly to *yofi*, and the farewell to the altar parallels the farewell to the sun. See too Lieberman, "Qalos qilusin," *Alei Ayin: The Salman Schocken Memorial Volume* (Jerusalem, 1951), 75-82. *PRK* 5:8 (91) perhaps sheds some light on the expected results of the praise: "At each and every praise *(kol qilos veqilus)* with which Israel praises the Holy One, He has his presence abide among them."

³⁷A. Marmorstein, *The Old Rabbinic Doctrine of God* (London: Oxford University Press, 1927), 31, based on Blau, *Zauberwesen*, 115; Urbach, *Sages*, 1:128.

is called *yofi'el*.³⁸ Greek magical papyri invoke ιωφη, ιωπη among other divine beings.³⁹ Patristic literature reports that the Samaritans pronounced the divine name Ἰαβε or Ἰαβαι, which, assuming the common interchange of labials, may be related.⁴⁰ However, the liturgical phrase, "YHWH, the altar is for you," is barely intelligible, although it does parallel somewhat the alternative tradition of R. Eliezer, "For Yah and for you, O altar. For Yah and for you, O altar." Yet this tradition also appears to be a type of acclamation. The sense is: we pay homage to You, God, and to the altar. Thus bSuk 45b explains: "To Yah we give thanks, and to you [the altar] we give praise; to Yah we give thanks and to you we give acclaim." It seems more likely, then, that the liturgical phrases were acclamations of praise for the altar and its powers of fecundity. That the petitions for salvation ("deliver us") and invocation of divine appellations occurred during a fertility rite suggests they served as prayers or even magical formulae to effect the purpose of the ritual. In any case, rabbinic sources testify that a highly developed liturgy accompanied the willow ritual.

In mSuk 4:6C R. Yohanan b. Beroka appears to bring an alternative tradition concerning the ritual. He claims that they gathered palm branches and struck them on the side of the altar. Although ostensibly a strange rite, there are parallels in other cultures, especially in rituals designed to produce rain.⁴¹ This ritual may reflect an alternative interpretation of Lev 23:40. While the dominant rabbinic tradition interpreted the "branches of palm" as immature palm fronds to be placed in the floral bouquet, this tradition interpreted the phrase as solid palm branches, which were "taken" for striking upon the altar.⁴² Yohanan

---

³⁸Blau, *Zauberwesen*, 131; G. Scholem, *Gnosticism*, 12, nn. 6-7.
³⁹Blau, *Zauberwesen*, 131.
⁴⁰References in S. Lowy, *Samaritan Exegesis*, 273-75. However Lowy suggests the terms are "faulty transcriptions of incantatory formulae."
⁴¹See n. 17. Patai, *Temple*, 37 suggests beating with green branches was believed to promote the growth of plants. He cites *BR* 10:6 (79): "R. Simon said: There is no single grass which has not its *mazal* (guardian angel) in the firmament, which beats it and says to it: grow!" He also refers (n. 59) to G. Frazier, *The Golden Bough*³ (New York: Macmillan, 1935), 9:64 who reports that the New Caledonians beat their plants to make them grow. In our case, however, the altar is beaten with the plants, which suggests that the ritual depends on the powers of the altar, unlike the cross-cultural parallels. For other parallels see Patai, *Hamayim*, 55 and n. 1. There he suggests wet branches were beaten on the altar, and the drops of water that sprayed upon it functioned like the water libation. See too idem, "The 'Control of Rain' in Ancient Palestine," *HUCA* 14 (1939), 277 and n. 137; Dalman, *AuS*, 1,1,149.
⁴²bSuk 45b suggests R. Yohanan b. Beroka found scriptural warrant by expounding the plural: "*branches of palm* (Lev 23:40). One for the lulav and one for the altar." The exegesis, however, need not be based on the plural form, but on

calls "that day" (the seventh day, 4:6D) the "day of beating branches," which some understand to dispute the previous tradition, in which "that day" involved a sevenfold circumambulation associated with the willow.[43] However, Yohanan can be interpreted as mentioning an additional ritual, not a replacement.[44] Note that the Mishna provides no name for "that day" based on the willow, so no explicit dispute appears. The Toseftan tradition combines the two rituals by referring to the "beating of willows" (t3:1D) . It seems that numerous rituals were practiced over the course of the festival, only a few of which rabbinic sources preserve in detail. Besides the willow procession, palm branches (or willows) were gathered and struck against the altar, and other such rituals probably took place as well.[45] Rabbinic literature tends to confer a uniform, legal character on what was governed by custom and popular practice. Worshippers probably marched with lulavs, palm branches or other assorted foliage, in keeping with the general character of floral processions. In tannaitic times the precise order and details of the rituals were naturally not remembered perfectly, thus the confusion in the sources.

If Ps 118 was connected to the willow procession then of course we have documentation of the ritual in a non-rabbinic source. Jubilees, we

---

the *sensus literalis* of the phrase. "Branches" may be interpreted as the developed palm branches (the *ḥaruta* or *ḥaraya*; see bSuk 32a; *BR* 40:17 (388); Löw, *Flora*, 2:329-330), not the immature frond, the lulav, as indeed the term *kapot* suggests. The striking on the altar would be the interpretation of the commandment to rejoice, the purpose of the undefined "taking."

[43] So Bertinuro to m4:6 and Tosafot, bSuk 45b, s.v. 'aḥat, who explain that Yohanan also disagrees about the previous days; each day of Sukkot they performed the ritual with a palm branch, not a willow. *Tiferet Yisra'el, Yakhin* suggests he only disputes the Sabbath protocol, fearing the willows would wither if left overnight, and therefore substituting firm branches.

[44] See the last lines of the Tosafot, ibid.

[45] Here we should mention the *haqhel* ceremony that Deut 31:10-13 prescribes for Sukkot of the Sabbatical year. This ceremony is not mentioned in Mishna-Tosefta Sukka, but mSot 7:8 and tSot 7:13-17 map out its protocol. Josephus mentions the ceremony but once, in his paraphrase of Deuteronomy, *AJ* 4:209-211. Whereas Deuteronomy does not specify who reads from the Torah, Josephus writes that it is the high priest. This may be pure exegesis, but it seems more likely that he reports the practice of his day. Tannaitic sources, on the other hand, rule that the king reads and transmit the famous (and perhaps legendary) tradition of King Agrippa shedding tears upon reading the verse "You may not set a foreigner over you, one who is not your kinsman" (Deut 17:15). See Safrai, *'Aliya*, 196-98; D.R. Schwartz, *Agrippa I* (Tübingen: J.C.B Mohr, 1990), 159-163. See too the manuscript variants of mSot 7:8, some of which set *haqhel* on SA; bSot 41a; Albeck, *Mishna*, 3:388; and B.M. Levin, "Ḥiluf minhagim bein bnei bavel uvein bnei 'ereṣ yisra'el," *Sinai* 11 (1942), 3. On the wine libation see Rubenstein, *Dissertation*, 229-246.

noted, also refers to a procession around the altar independent of the lulav. Abraham takes palms and fruit and circles the altar seven times each day. The Mishna has one circuit each day (apart from the seventh day), but the two sources clearly allude to the same ritual.[46] Plutarch's reference to a "thyrsos-procession" together with trumpets provides an apt description for the willow procession and its trumpet blasts (4:5D). The general description of the festivities in 2 Macc 10:7-8, the rejoicing with "wreathed wands, and graceful branches, and palm fronds" while reciting psalms, may also relate to processions of this sort.

The reference in m4:7 to children points to yet another Sukkot custom. At the completion of the circumambulations around the altar on the seventh day, and perhaps together with the beating of palm branches, children apparently engaged in some game with their lulavs and ate their etrogs. Exactly what they did with their lulavs is unclear. The Mishna could mean that they threw them down, or they snatched them from one another, or they untied the band that held the species together.[47] These gestures seem to have been another expression of gaiety or festal joy. When the ritual use of the objects was completed, children were allowed to have fun in whatever ways they enjoyed.

---

[46]Jub 16-29-31. Jubilees has a particular predilection for the number seven, and prescribes Sukkot sacrifices in multiples of seven at the expense of contradicting the biblical text (see Chapter 2, III text at n. 45). The Jubilean sevenfold circumambulation may be related to this phenomenon.

[47]Margoliot, in his comments to *VR* 37:2 (858), derives the verb *shomtin* from the Syriac *shamota*, a thief: the children "grabbed" lulavs from each other. Bertinuro suggests the children threw down their lulavs. Others explain that children "loosened" the band, or pulled apart the tie; see Tosafot, bSuk 45a, s.v. *miyad*. Rashi, ibid., s.v. *miyad* claims the adults grabbed the lulavs from the hands of children and ate their (the children's) etrogs. This interpretation understands *miyad* not as a temporal adverb ("immediately") but as a prepositional phrase: "from the hands." However, *miyad* typically means "immediately" in the Mishna; see Kosovsky, *'Osar leshon hamishna*, 826-27. This too would seem to be a game or joyful play. From the objections attributed to Resh Laqish and R. Yohanan in bSuk 46b, it appears they understood that the children ate each others' etrogs, and presumably the children, not the adults, snatched (or whatever) the lulavs. Patai, *Temple*, 162-64 explains the children threw both the lulavs and the etrogs. He claims that children are a symbol of innocence and therefore lead rain-making rituals in various cultures. For children *throwing* as opposed to eating etrogs, Patai refers to *VR* 37:2 (858), which he translates as "ethrogs which the children threw on the day of Hoshana." However, in Margoliot's edition the text reads "etrogs which are taken from the children," and the variants have "which the children carry" or "which the children break (*meqalqlin*)." Apparently Patai took *meqalqlin* from the verb *QLQ*, to throw – a doubtful interpretation. See the apparatus, Margoliot's comments; Albeck, *Mishna*, 2:476-77; and Urbach, *Sages*, 440.

The Mishna does not reveal the overall purpose of the willow ritual. Like the shaking of the lulav, it served as a general expression of joy and fertility. The processional aspect allowed the folk to participate in the ritual together with the priests. Patai has convincingly argued that the ritual was specifically directed to producing rain. He suggests that the "altar covered with green branches stands for the earth itself,"[48] and the verdant covering "serves to accentuate its identity with the thirsty earth."[49] The ritual attempts to produce a parallel blossoming of nature throughout the country. Circumambulations are common rain-making rituals in many cultures.[50] The willow, moreover, is a particularly apt symbol of the need for rain, since willows require copious amounts of water, and rapidly wither in times of drought.[51] Trumpet or shofar blasts served as general cries of alarm, especially when rain was desperately needed. For this reason the public prayers for rain that accompanied the series of fasts prescribed by Mishna Ta'anit for periods of drought included repeated shofar blasts.[52] The liturgical cry "O Lord deliver us" is a most appropriate plea for rain. Without rain crops wither, animals die and people suffer. Prayers for rain were essentially prayers for survival, for "deliverance."

II. The Water Libation

Zech 14 and John 7 presuppose a connection between Sukkot and rain. Rabbinic accounts of the water libation provide the ritual background. The framework Mishna, mSuk 4:1, prescribes the libation for seven days, and mSuk 4:9-10 supplies a more detailed description:

[A] The Water Libation for seven days, how so?
[B] He would fill a golden flask that contained three *log* from the Siloam.
[C] When they reached the Water Gate, they sounded an extended blast [on the trumpet], a quavering blast, an extended blast.
[D] He ascended the ramp and turned to his left.
[E] Two silver bowls were there.

---

[48]Patai, *Temple*, 34-35. So Ehrlich, *Kultsymbolik*, 57. Cf. Patai, *Hamayim*, 54. On the cosmic significance of the altar see Jeremias, *Golgotha*, 105-106.
[49]R. Patai, "The 'Control of Rain' in Ancient Palestine," *HUCA* 14 (1939), 275. See too Mowinckel, *PsSt*, 36, 102-104, who also saw the willow branches as general symbols of fertility, and Dalman, *AuS*, 1,1,150.
[50]Patai, *Temple*, 35; Ehrlich, *Kultsymbolik*, 56-57 and n. 148.
[51]Thus the observation of *VR* 30:10 (708) that the "willow dries up before the other three species."
[52]mTa 2:5, 3:1, 3:3. Patai, *Hamayim*, 51, claims trumpet blasts imitate (and bring about) the sound of thunder. So W. Robertson Smith, *Lectures on the Religion of the Semites*³, ed. S.A. Cook (London: A & C Black, 1927), 231. Dalman, *AuS*, 1,1,153 suggests the trumpet gets God's attention.

[F] R. Yehuda says they were plaster bowls. But they had been blackened because of the wine.
[G] They had openings like two slender snouts,[53] one wide, the other narrow, so that the two would empty simultaneously.
[H] The western [bowl] was for water, the eastern [bowl] for wine.
[I] If he poured [the libation] of water into [the bowl] for wine or the [libation] of wine into the [bowl] for water, he fulfills [the obligation].
[J] R. Yehuda says he used to pour a libation consisting of one *log* all eight days.
[K] And they say to the [priest] pouring the libation, "Raise your hand!"
[L] Since once he poured the libation on his feet, and the entire people stoned him with their etrogs.

(mSuk 4:9)

[A] Its practice on the Sabbath was the same as on the weekdays.
[B] Except that on the eve of the Sabbath he would fill a golden jug that had not been consecrated[54] from the Siloam, and leave it in a [temple] chamber.
[C] If it spilled out or was uncovered,[55] he would fill [the flask] from the laver.
[D] For water and wine that became uncovered are unfit for the altar.

(mSuk 4:10)

The Tosefta adds a few additional details: tSuk 3:14-15 notes that the libations flowed from the bowls through a pipe at the base of the altar and down into the *sheetim*, the channels beneath the temples. tSuk 3:16 adds the important datum that they poured the libations with the morning *tamid* offering. It identifies the priest who poured the libation at his feet as a Boethusian (mSuk 4:9K-L). tSuk 3:18 explains the purpose of the libation:

---

[53] According to Rashi, bSuk 48b, s.v. *kemin*, the bowls had snouts protruding from them, and the snouts had holes of different sizes at the end. The libations descended from the bowls through the snouts out the holes and onto the altar. The altar in turn had two holes into which the libations flowed, and from there descended into the channels (*sheetim*; see below). Tosafot, ibid., s.v. *kemin*, allude to the parallel expression "openings like two slender snouts" in mMid 3:2: "at the south-western corner [of the altar] there were two openings, like two slender snouts." The Tosafot explain the libation bowls did not have snouts but two holes *like* perforated snouts, from which the liquids flowed directly into the openings of the altar. See too tZev 6:11, tSuk 3:14 and the sources cited by Lieberman, *TK*, 4:879-80.

[54] Liquid that remained overnight in consecrated vessels was considered unfit for the altar; bSuk 50a; ySuk 4:9, 54d. Cf. the other explanations in the talmuds.

[55] Uncovered liquids were considered dangerous, and hence unfit for the altar; see bSuk 50a; ySuk 4:9, 54d.

R. Akiba said: The Torah said...bring a water libation on Sukkot [since it is the season for rains][56] in order that the rain waters may be blessed for you...[57]

The narrative of the ritual is interrupted by various halakhic details, but the general procedure emerges clearly. The libations were drawn from the Siloam pool constructed in first temple times. Fearing an Assyrian siege, in 700 BCE King Hezekiah built the famous tunnel to convey water from the Gihon spring, which flowed outside the western wall of the city, within the city walls (2 Kgs 20:20; 2 Chr 32:30). A channel that flowed from the Gihon was known as the Siloam stream, so the pool Hezekiah built to receive the waters took on the same name.[58] Rabbinic and Christian traditions attribute miraculous powers to the waters of the pool, probably a result of its use as the source for the libation.[59] According to the Tosefta the libations were poured with the daily morning offering *(tamid)* sacrificed soon after sunrise.[60] The distance from the Siloam, which lies at the southern tip of the city of

---

[56]The words "since it is the season for rains" are found in MS Erfurt of tSuk 3:18, and MSS London and Erfurt of tRH 1:12. They are omitted in MS Vienna of both tSuk and tRH. See *TK*, 4:885.

[57]See Chapter 4, text to nn. 6 and 22 for the full source and analysis.

[58]The Gihon served as the primary water source for Jerusalem in Jebusite and early Israelite times. Archaeological evidence suggests that Solomon built a channel from the Gihon which flowed along the western side of Jerusalem to irrigate his royal gardens. The channel became known as the *shelah* or *shiloaḥ* (Siloam), probably meaning "sending," and is mentioned in Isa 8:6, "the gently flowing waters of the *shiloaḥ*." After building the tunnel, Hezekiah stopped up the Gihon to deny the Assyrian army a source of water. Soon the Gihon was forgotten. Where the Gihon is mentioned in 1 Kgs 1:33 the targum reads *shiloha* – correctly identifying what became of the Gihon's waters (cf. Rashi ad loc. "the Siloam is a spring and its name is Gihon.") Hence from Hezekiah's time onward the libation must have been taken from the Siloam pool, although prior to Hezekiah, if the libation was practiced, it may have been taken from the Gihon. See M. Hecker, "Haspaqat mayim birushalayim bimei qedem," *Sefer Yerushalayim*, ed. M. Avi-Yonah (Jerusalem: Devir, 1956), 191-99; Y. Shiloh, *Excavations at the City of David 1*, (Qedem 19; Jerusalem: The Hebrew University of Jerusalem, 1984), 24 and now D. Gill, "How They Met: Geology Solves Mystery of Hezekiah's Tunnelers," *BAR* 20,4 (1994), 20-33. R. Reich, "'From Gad Yawan to Shiloaḥ'– on the History of the Gihon Spring," *'Ereṣ-yisra'el* 19 (1987), 330-33 (Hebrew) and R. Amiran, "Mei hashiloah veta'alat ḥizqiyahu," *'Iyyunim besefer yishayahu*, ed. B. Luria (Jerusalem, 1981), 243-66 reconstruct this history along slightly different lines. (The Siloam channel was modified during Hezekiah's reign, but still served to irrigate the surrounding area for some time.)

[59]Josephus, *BJ* 5:410 (cf. tAr 2:6; tPar 9:2 and S.J.D. Cohen, *Josephus in Galilee and Rome: His Vita and Development as a Historian* [Leiden: Brill, 1979], 254-55); *BJ* 5:140; tTa 1:8; yHag 1:1, 76a; targum to Qoh 2:5; *ARNA* §35, (105). According to mPar 3:2 the ashes of the red cow were mixed with waters from the Siloam.

[60]t3:16. Cf. mYom 2:5.

David, to the temple is about one half mile. Therefore the ritual must have commenced with the priest drawing water into a golden vessel at dawn.

mSuk 4:9C reads "when they reached the Water Gate." This gate, the Tosefta notes, received its name from the ritual, a fact which illustrates the importance of the Sukkot ceremonies.[61] "They reached" suggests the libation was conveyed in a ritual procession.[62] The priest who drew the water was undoubtedly escorted by other priests, trumpeters, and throngs of worshippers eagerly participating in the important ritual. The trumpet was also sounded during the willow ritual (mSuk 4:5D) and presumably signaled the arrival of the procession at its goal, or marked a station along the way. From the Water Gate the procession proceeded to the temple courtyards where the people assembled. The priest with the flask ascended the ramp leading up to the altar.[63]

A libation of wine accompanied the morning and evening daily offerings throughout the year.[64] On Sukkot the water libation supplemented that libation. According to the Mishna the priest poured the libations into bowls perched on the south-east corner of the altar. The libations descended simultaneously onto the altar before they drained off through a pipe. The tradition of the priest pelted with etrogs for incorrectly performing the libation indicates the rabbis pictured crowds of people intently watching the ritual. Worshippers eagerly anticipated the pouring of the libation and attached great importance to the rite.

The Mishna portrays the libation ritual on the Sabbath in a similar fashion as the Sabbath willow ritual. They drew water on Friday and stored it overnight within the temple confines. On the Sabbath the libation was poured on the altar, but no procession from the Siloam, trumpeting or associated rites took place. In contrast to the willow, no day was singled out for an enhanced ceremony. R. Yehuda even reports

---

[61] tSuk 3:3. The identification of this gate, like that of most gates, is disputed. mSheq 6:3 and mMid 2:6 place it as the most eastern gate on the south side. See Hochman, *Festivities*, 114 n. 100. A "water gate" is mentioned in Neh 8:1, but this may have been a gate of the city, not the temple.

[62] Cf. Hochman, *Festivities*, 113 n. 97.

[63] Or gave the flask to a different priest. Recall that Jonathan assumed the high priesthood on Sukkot (1 Macc 10:21), Alexander Jannaeus, while sacrificing on Sukkot in his capacity as high priest, was pelted by etrogs (*AJ* 13:372), and Aristobolus III, high priest under Herod, likewise performed the Sukkot sacrifices (Josephus, *AJ* 15:50). ySuk 4:8, 54d also identifies the priest who was pelted as a high priest. So it is plausible that the high priest generally offered the Sukkot sacrifices and performed the libation.

[64] Exod 29:40; Num 28:7ff; mZev 6:2.

The Sukkot Temple Festival: Rabbinic Traditions 121

that the libation took place on SA, generally considered an independent festival.

No non-rabbinic source explicitly mentions the libation.⁶⁵ Zechariah 14 and John 7 indicate a connection between Sukkot and rain, but neither illuminates the specific rituals. Some scholars find extra-rabbinic evidence in the Josephan story of the people pelting Jannaeus with etrogs as he stood to sacrifice on the altar (*AJ* 13.372).⁶⁶ According to argument, the Josephan story and the Mishnaic account (mSuk 4:9K-L) refer to the same event, so Josephus confirms the existence of the libation.⁶⁷ Actually the striking similarities cast doubt on the authenticity of the rabbinic tradition. The rabbis probably adapted a popular Josephan tale about Sukkot for their own purposes. Whereas Josephus attributed the violent reaction to Jannaeus's general cruelty and the charge that he descended from a proselyte and should not serve as priest, the rabbis framed the conflict in terms of a legal dispute, and incorporated the popular motif of etrog-pelting.⁶⁸ To fully resolve this issue requires a comprehensive

---

⁶⁵See n. 168 for some attempts to find references to a water ritual.

⁶⁶See Chapter 2, VIII text at n. 125.

⁶⁷The Mishna claims that a priest was pelted for spilling the libation at his feet. The talmuds identify the priest as a Sadducee (bSuk 48b; ySuk 4:8, 54d; in tSuk 3:16 he is a Boethusian), and Jannaeus purportedly was opposed by the Pharisees (so Schürer, *History*, 1:222, based largely on later rabbinic traditions; but C. Rabin, "Alexander Jannaeus and the Pharisees," *JJS* 7 [1956], 5-7 shows there is no evidence the Pharisees, in particular, opposed Jannaeus), presumably because he sided with the Sadducees. The Sadducees (according to argument) rejected the Pharisaic oral tradition, including the water libation, which has no explicit source in scripture. For this reason Jannaeus refused to pour the libation on the altar. Therefore the two sources must refer to the same event, and Josephus testifies to the libation. But this argument cannot stand up to scrutiny. Several tannaitic sources indeed find a scriptural source for the libation (*Sifre Num.* §150 [196]; tSuk 3:18), so it is unlikely the Sadducees would have opposed it on those grounds. Moreover the view that the Sadducees rejected "the Oral Torah" and that this comprised the essential debate between the groups oversimplifies matters. In fact, there is absolutely no evidence in rabbinic sources that the priest (or the Sadducees) rejected the legitimacy of the libation. At best the sources indicate a difference in opinion as to how the ritual should be performed. For a comprehensive treatment of the libation controversy, see Rubenstein, *Dissertation*, chapter 6 and "The Sadducees and the Water Libation," *JQR* (forthcoming).

⁶⁸Etrog-pelting appears to have been a stock literary motif. According to bQid 73a the citizens of Mahoza pelted R. Zeira with etrogs when he insulted them with his homily. G. Allon, "The Attitude of the Pharisees," *Jews, Judaism and the Classical World*, trans. I. Abrahams (Jerusalem: Magnes, 1977), 33 n. 34 argues that the stories in Josephus and rabbinic tradition do not refer to the same incident. He explains the common trope of etrog-pelting by suggesting "that it was a daily occurrence for the people to pelt with etrogs anyone whom they wished to insult," and cites as evidence the R. Zeira incident. Another example can be found in *Tan Qedoshim* §8 (443); *TanB*, 3:77 (in three MSS; see Buber's n. 43);

study of all parallels between Josephus and rabbinic stories.[69] In any case, Josephus does not mention the libation, and cannot be cited as outside proof.

III. The Cultic Background of the Libation

Water libations, found in many religions, are rain-making rituals, as R. Akiba already realized.[70] R. Akiba, however, explains the power of the libation in terms of "blessing"; God sees the libation, remembers his people, and blesses them with ample rain. But as a ritual of the temple, the working of the libation should be understood primarily in cultic

---

Yalqut §615. The midrash tells of a man who brought dates and apples to Hadrian hoping to receive a reward, but the emperor ordered his soldiers to slap the man's face with them. He returns home and tells his wife to be thankful that he did not bring etrogs, for in that case they surely would have pelted his face and entire body with them. This tale suggests that pelting with etrogs was a standard expression of disgust.

[69] For some preliminary work, see S.J.D. Cohen, "Parallel Historical Tradition in Josephus and Rabbinic Literature," *Proceedings of Ninth World Congress of Jewish Studies – 1985*, B/1 (1986), 7-14.

[70] For water libations in other cultures see G. Frazier, *The Golden Bough*[3] (New York: Macmillan, 1935), 1:248ff; Feuchtwang, *Wasseropfer*, 548-49; Hochman, *Festivities*, 59, 84 (Egypt), 123 n. 144 (Babylonia) and 117 n. 109; Grunwald, *Sukkothrituals*, 450; Patai, *Temple*, 35-36. An astonishing parallel to the water libation took place at the temple of the goddess Atargatis at Hieropolis, described by Lucian, *De Dea Syria*, §13: "What happened after this, however, is the subject of a story told by the inhabitants of the Holy City, and we may rightly be amazed at it. They say that in their land a great chasm was formed and it took in all the water. When this happened, Deucalian set up altars and built over the chasm a temple sacred to Hera. I myself saw the chasm. It is beneath the temple and quite small. Whether it was large of old, and now such a size as it is, I do not know. In any case the one that I saw is small. As a symbol of this story they do this: Twice each year water from the sea is carried to the temple. Not only priests, but the whole of Syria and Arabia brings it and from beyond the Euphrates many men come to the sea and all bring water. First they pour it out in the temple. Afterwards it goes down into the chasm, and the chasm, though small, takes in a great deal of water. In doing these things they claim that Deucalion established this custom in the sanctuary as a memorial both of the disaster and of the divine favor." (Translation from *De Dea Dyria*, ed. H.W. Attridge and R.A. Oden [Missoula, Montana: Scholars Press, 1976], p. 21; see also §48). On the authenticity of Lucian's account see R.A. Oden, *Studies in Lucian's De Syria Dea* (Missoula, Montana: Scholars Press, 1977), 24-32, 41-45. This parallel is cited by Feuchtwang, 548, Hochman, 85, Patai, 56-57. However, while these scholars understand the Syrian ceremony as a rain producing rite, Oden claims it served to restrain the floodwaters, much as the legends of David and the shard (below, p. 127.) W.F. Albright, *Archaeology and the Religion of Israel* (Baltimore: John Hopkins Press, 1968), 194 n. 7 also suggests the rite was connected to the "fertility-bringing fresh water in the Great Deep."

rather than theurgic terms. That is, the water libation worked through the power of the cult to influence the forces of nature and ensure the fertility of the earth. That power derived from the functions of the temple and cult in a *mythic* worldview. By "myth" or "mythic" I mean a nonhistorical understanding of reality that views phenomena and symbols in terms of their essential, cosmic significance.[71] The temple, for example, is not simply an edifice that stands on a certain mountain in Jerusalem, but the central point of the earth, the link to heaven and the seat of divine government. Mythic events relate to founding acts of the past through which the present reality came to be. In mythic, as opposed to historical thought, these foundation acts are not merely past events that established the nature of the present, but are constantly occurring episodes, reenacted annually in a cultic drama. For in mythic thought, the forces of chaos constantly threaten to overwhelm the ordered cosmos: "The present world order established by a victory in the past does not continue automatically. It must be constantly activated in the drama of the cult."[72] Herein lies the tremendous importance of ritual. Ritual acts, generally those of the cult, constantly reactualize primordial time and ensure the continued order of the world.[73]

Biblical and rabbinic mythic worldviews picture the temple as the fundamental source of fertility, an epicenter from which streams of water flow forth to irrigate the earth.[74] Those waters ultimately derive from the "Deep" *(tehom)*, the primordial floodwaters separated and confined by God at the time of creation.[75] The flood resulted when "the fountains of the Great Deep *(tehom rabba)* burst open" (Gen 7:11), when God released the Deep from its subterranean confinement, and ceased when "the

---

[71]Childs, *Myth*, 17-21; Levenson, *Zion*, 102-105; M. Eliade, *The Sacred and the Profane* (New York: Harper & Row, 1961), 80-113.
[72]Childs, *Myth*, 20.
[73]Childs, *Myth*, 20; Levenson, *Zion*, 103; Eliade, ibid., 68-95.
[74]Ps 36:8-10, 133; Isa 33:20-24 (in which God blesses the earth from Zion). See Ohler, *Mythologische*, 191-95. This mythic trope is also expressed through the identification of the garden of Eden with Mt Zion. See Levenson, *Zion*, 127-32 and idem, *Theology of the Program of Restoration of Ezekiel 40-48* (Cambridge, Mass: Scholars Press, 1976), 11-14, 25-36; Childs, *Myth*, 86-87; Ohler, *Mythologische*, 152, 159, 183-89; H.J. van Dijk, *Ezekiel's Prophecy on Tyre* (Rome: Pontifical Biblical Institute, 1968), 116; W.H. Propp, *Water in the Wilderness: A Biblical Motif and Its Mythological Background* (Atlanta, Georgia: Scholars Press, 1987), 99; H.N. Wallace, *The Eden Narrative* (Atlanta: Scholars Press, 1985), 77, 85-86.
[75]Isa 51:9-10, "It was You who hacked Rahab in pieces, that pierced the dragon. It was You who dried up the Sea, the waters of the great Deep." See Ps 29, 33:7, 74:13-15, 77:17-20, 89:10-11, 93, 104:5-9, 106:9, 114:1-8; Isa 11:15; Nah 1:4; Job 26:12-13, 38:8-11; H. Gunkel, *Schopfung und Chaos* (Göttingen, 1895), 91-111; Patai, *Hamayim*, 132-34, 150-52; Otzen, *Myths*, 67-68; Ohler, *Mythologische*, 81-116; Levenson, *Creation*, 1-50.

fountains of the deep and the floodgates of the sky were stopped up" (Gen 8:2).[76] That God "stops up" the deep assumes the waters flow from the underworld through channels.[77] Under normal circumstances the waters of the Deep ascend through these channels and fertilize the earth. Thus Deut 33:13, "Blessed of the Lord be his land with the bounty of dew from heaven and of the Deep that couches below," understands the Deep as a source of blessing, namely a flow of waters into streams and rivers parallel to rain (or dew)[78] from heaven.[79] The visions of Zechariah and Ezekiel indicate that the channels from which the subterranean waters emerge are located beneath the temple.[80] Zech 14 prophesies that the temple will produce a source of "living waters" (or "waters of life") that heal and purify. A stream emerges from the temple and divides into two halves, one of which flows east to the Mediterranean, the other west to the Dead Sea. Ezekiel prophesies that a stream will trickle from the base

---

[76] The Deep retains the potential to flood the earth at any moment. See Ps 46:2-4; Pedersen, *Israel*, 457; Otzen, *Myths*, 37, 54-58. This mythic view conflicts with the covenantal idea that God promised never to flood the earth again (Gen 9:12-17.)

[77] Similarly, when God brings forth waters from the Deep, the Bible employs verbs such as "break open," *(BQ'*; Ps 74:15, Prov 3:20, Gen 7:11.)

[78] TO and some variants read "with the bounty of heaven above," reading *me'al* for *mital*. The reference would thus be to rain from above and waters from below.

[79] Cf. Gen 49:25, "The God of your father who helps you, and Shaddai who blesses you with blessings of heaven above, blessings of the deep that couches below, blessings of the breast and womb," and Deut 8:7, "a good land, a land with streams and springs and fountains *(tehomot)* issuing from plain and hill." (Fountains also spurt forth from the Deep in Gen 7:11.) Here *tehomot* refers to the fountains themselves, parallel to "springs" and "streams," all of which derive from the subterranean waters. See P. Reymond, *L'eau, Sa Vie, et Sa Signification dans L'Ancient Testament* (Leiden: Brill, 1958), 200-202. The magical fertility of the garden of Eden depicted in Ezek 31:1-9 results because "Waters nourished it, the Deep made it grow tall, washing with its streams the place where it was planted, making its channels well up more than for all the trees of the field" (31:4).

[80] Zech 13:1, 14:8-21; Ezek 47:1-12. A similar vision is found in Joel 4:18 where a fountain emerges from the temple and irrigates the nearby plain. Technically these visions are eschatological, not purely mythic. Yet the two are closely related. Eschatological visions fuse mythic and historical modes of thought by projecting elements of myth to the end of historical time. The prophets pictured the nature of things at the end of time – a future, blessed era free of the woes of the present – in terms of idealized mythic conceptions. Many elements of the messianic age are drawn from myths about creation and the paradisiacal era, the timeless period before history began. The lines of myth and history meet in eschatology. Cf. Cross, *Canaanite*, 144; S. Mowinckel, *He That Cometh*, trans. G.W. Anderson (New York: Abingdon Press, 1954), 162. J. Levenson, *Theology of the Program of Restoration of Ezekiel 40-48* (Cambridge, Mass: Scholars Press, 1976), 5-54 delineates the mythic traditions behind the eschatological vision of the temple in Ezek 40-48. See too H. Schmidt, *Die Thronfahrt Jahves am Fest der Jahreswende im alten Israel* (Tübingen: J.C.B. Mohr, 1927), 9.

The Sukkot Temple Festival: Rabbinic Traditions

of the future temple, grow into mammoth proportions and quickly reach such a depth that it cannot be crossed (Ezek 47:1-12).[81] The river transforms the countryside into an Eden-like paradise and the Dead Sea into a sea of life teeming with fish.[82]

Rabbinic sources provide a more developed picture of this mythic worldview.[83] The center of the cosmos is marked by the 'even shtia, the "foundation stone," pictured variably beneath the temple or at the place of the altar.[84] The stone is the cosmic center[85] where heaven, earth and

---

[81] It is interesting to note that J.Z. Smith, in his masterful study of ritual *To Take Place* (Chicago: University of Chicago Press, 1987), meticulously analyzes Ezek 40-48. He omits from his discussion Ezek 47:1-12 on the grounds that it reflects "a quite different ideological perspective" (p. 151 n. 49.) Indeed, this chapter comprises the myth upon which the ritual is based. Cf. Ps 104:5-13 and Ohler, *Mythologische*, 85-87. Yet another version of the eschatological vision appears in Rev 22:1-5.

[82] The projections of the prophets depict the eschatological era in mythic terms when the temple becomes a real source of blessing and fertility. Thus in the eschatological prophecies of Isa 51:3 and Ezek 36:35 the entire land of Israel becomes "like the garden of Eden." For other eschatological associations with water see Jer 31:7-14; Isa 35, 41:17-20, 48:21, 49:10; Ps 107:33-38. The same conception underlies the numerous rabbinic traditions celebrating the fecundity of the land of Israel, location of the temple and altar: once three buds of mustard produced nine *kab* of mustard and wood sufficient for the roofing of a hut; every vine in Israel requires the whole city to harvest; peaches are as large as pots (bKet 111b-112a, which contains other such traditions.)

[83] As do numerous sources in the Apocrypha and Pseudepigrapha: see Jub 8:12,19 (the center or navel of the world); 1 En 17, 18, 24-26 (garden of Eden on Mt Zion, Mountain as *axis mundi*); 2 En 28 (creation of world). This worldview is not the only one reflected in biblical, apocryphal or rabbinic sources; Judaism never had an official mythology or theology, and tended to absorb and digest numerous external conceptions. The worldview is *one* of those reflected in Jewish literature which seems to be particularly prominent and long lived, and which best coheres with the libation ritual.

[84] On the 'even shtia in general, see the pioneering essay by Feuchtwang, *Wasseropfer*, 718-29; 44-58, who was the first to explore this mythic view and relate it to the water libations. See too Jeremias, *Golgotha*, 91-108; Wensinck, *Navel*; Levenson, *Zion*, 133-35; Ginzberg, *Legends*, 5:14-17, 292; P. Schäfer, "Tempel und Schöpfung," *Studien zur Geschichte und Theologie des Rabbinischen Judentums* (Leiden: Brill, 1978), 125-28; M. Michlin, "Der Tempelberg oder Eben Shettija," *Yerushalayim* 11-12 (1916), 137-236; J.Z. Smith, *To Take Place* (Chicago: University of Chicago Press, 1987), 83-85. PRE §10 (26b) places the stone in the Deep *(tehom)*, below the temple. Cf. BR 55:7 (591); bEruv 19a; bSuk 32b; bYom 54b; yYom 5:4, 42c and PRE §35 (82b). For the identification with the altar see Jeremias, 105-106; Wensinck, 40-42 and M. Fishbane, *Text and Texture* (New York: Schocken, 1979), 118. According to mYom 5:2 the 'even shtia stands in the Holy of Holies in the second temple at the place where the ark had stood in the first temple. The high priest placed the incense censer upon the stone during his Yom Kippur ritual. In this view too the stone functions as a center, since the Holy of Holies was situated

underworld intersect, and the point at which God began to create the world.⁸⁶ Most significantly, it is the capstone that contains the waters of the Deep.⁸⁷ When God subdued the ancient flood waters of the Deep, he imprisoned them beneath the earth.⁸⁸ The waters are always poised to erupt from their subterranean realm, as they did during the flood, and only the capstone beneath the temple prevents this calamity:⁸⁹

---

in the middle of the temple complex, which was in the center of Jerusalem, Israel and the world (see *Tan Qedoshim* §10 [444], *TanB* 3:78.) This stone may have biblical roots in the cornerstone mentioned in Isa 28:16. Note in the next verse the threat that flood waters will sweep away the shelter. Jer 51:26 prophesies the complete destruction of Babylonia with the image of the lack of a cornerstone.

⁸⁵Also known as the "navel of the earth." See *PRE* §35 (82b); *MG* 1:508 to Gen 28: 18; *Breisheet Rabbati*, ed. H. Albeck (Jerusalem, 1940), 139. Josephus, *BJ* 3:52, claims that many call Jerusalem the navel of Judea. Jub 8:19 places Mt Zion at the center of the navel of the earth. Cf. 1 En 26:1-6.

⁸⁶tYom 2:14, bYom 54b; Lieberman, *TK*, 4:772-73 (Lieberman was partially anticipated by Jeremias, *Golgotha*, 97.) See too bTa 10a and *Sifre Deut.* §37 (69-71). The etymology of *shtia* is unclear. Maimonides to mYom 5:2 comments: "The explanation of *shtia* is foundation (*yesod*). In truth the place of the cult is the foundation of the earth." David Kimhi, *Sefer hashorashim*, ed. J. Biesenthal and F. Lebrecht (Jerusalem, 1966), 379 offers a similar explanation, and derives the term from the root שתה. Kohut, '*Arukh*, 8:180 relates the stone to the *sheet* (see below) and explains both as foundation. Lieberman suggests the etymology derives from שתי, to weave, (the world was "spun out" from the stone) and suggests that this was the Palestinian (and original) tradition, whereas the Babylonian tradition explained *shtia* based on "found." See, however, the critique by P. Schäfer, "Tempel und Schöpfung," *Studien Zur Geschichte und Theologie Des Rabbinischen Judentums* (Leiden: Brill, 1978), 125-128. If the *'even shtia* did grow out of the Isaian cornerstone (Isa 28:16), a type of "foundation" stone, then this etymology should be favored. The fact that *shtia* probably relates to *sheet*, the foundation of the temple, supports this derivation. See below.

⁸⁷bSuk 53a-b and ySanh 17:2, 29a; *TY* to Exod 28:30. See below. Jeremias expresses this idea in almost poetic terms: "Höchste Stelle der Erde, Stätte der Gegenwart Gottes und des zukünftigen Paradieses, Pforte zum Himmel – der Sinn der verschiedenen Vorstellungen ist derselbe: *der heilige Felsen ist der Eingang zur Himmelswelt*... Verschusstein der Urflut, Ursprung der Gewässer, Eingang ins Totenreich – der Sinn der Vorstellungen ist derselbe: *Der heilige Felsen ist der Eingang in die Unterwelt*." See *Golgotha*, 94, 98 and Wensinck, *Navel*, 23-35. Some of the rabbinic sources adduced by Jeremias and others, including many of the most explicit, are considerably late, appearing in the medieval midrashim. But the many early rabbinic traditions in addition to the remarkable consistency with biblical and apocryphal materials demonstrate that the later sources simply retell ancient traditions in more detailed forms.

⁸⁸*BaR* 18:22, bBB 74b; *SR* 15:22 depict God's struggle against personified (deified?) waters. See S. Daiches, "Talmudisches und Midraschische Parallelen Zum Babylonischen Weltschöpfungsepos," *Zeitschrift für Assyriologie* 17 (1903), 394-99; Ginzberg, *Legends*, 5:26-27.

⁸⁹Cf. *BR* 33:1 (299-300); *PRK* 9:1 (147) and parallels: "The mountains press down the Deep in order that it not rise up and flood the earth." *PR* 194b has Leviathan

When David came to dig the foundations[90] of the temple, he dug fifteen hundred cubits but did not find the Deep. Finally he found a shard and wished to lift it. It said to him, "You cannot." He said to it, "Why?" It said, "Because I press down the Deep here." He said to it, "From when were you here?" It said to him, "From when the Merciful One made his voice heard from Sinai, 'I am the Lord your God.' Then the earth shuddered and sank, and I am placed here to press down the Deep." Nonetheless, he did not listen to it. As soon as he lifted it the Deep rose and wished to flood the earth...[91]

A similar legend appears in the BT:

> When David was digging the foundations *(sheetim)*, the Deep rose and tried to flood the earth... He wrote the Name [of God] on a shard and threw it into the Deep and the Deep receded sixteen thousand cubits. When he saw that it had descended so far, he said, "the more it is raised, the more the earth is irrigated." He said the fifteen 'Songs of Ascent' (Pss 120-134) and raised it fifteen thousand cubits and left it one thousand cubits [below the temple.][92]

Other traditions identify the shard with the *'even shtia*, and have God seal off the Deep with it at the time of creation.[93] The source of the earth's fertility, as the BT tradition makes clear, stems from the waters of the Deep.[94] They rest below the *sheetim*, the subterranean channels, also considered to be the temple's foundations, which serve as their conduit to the earth.[95] If the waters descend too far they cannot flow upward into streams and rivers and fructify the earth.

---

press down the Deep lest it flood the earth. The Deep rose up and destroyed the Egyptians at the Red Sea in *Mekhilta, Beshalakh* §5 (132).

[90] *temeliosim = themelion*; J. Levy, *Wörterbuch über die Talmudim und Midraschim*² (Berlin and Vienna: B. Harz, 1924), 4:651.

[91] ySanh 17:2, 29a. Cited by Feuchtwang, 547; Patai, *Temple*, 57. See Ginzberg, *Legends*, 4:96, 6:258 for comments and parallels.

[92] bSuk 53a-b; cited by Feuchtwang, *Wasseropfer*, 547; Jeremias, *Golgotha*, 95-96; Patai, *Temple*, 56; Levenson, *Zion*, 134.

[93] M. Gaster, *The Exempla of the Rabbis (Sefer Ma'asiot)* (reprint; New York: Ktav, 1968 [1924]), §155. The tension in these views results from the mythic conception in which God constructed the temple on Mt Zion as opposed to the more historical view of David and Solomon as its builders. In both traditions the Deep lurks in a subterranean realm contained by a stone / shard. At the center of the world, the stone separates the waters of chaos from the mountain and the temple, the outstanding symbols of cosmic order.

[94] Cf. the variants of *TYN* to Gen 50:1.

[95] The great confusion as to the nature of the *sheetim* results from the inconsistency of the rabbinic sources themselves. Non-mythic sources describe them as channels; mythic sources as foundations. See Rashi, bEruv 19a, s.v. *ma'ayan vs.* bSuk 49a, s.v. *sheetim*; M. Michlin, "Der Tempelberg oder Eben Shettija," *Yerushalayim* 11-12 (1916), 169-171; Feuchtwang, *Wasseropfer*, 544; Jeremias, *Golgotha*, 102 and 105. Hochman, *Festivities*, 117-18, n. 110 exemplifies the confusion. The stam, bSuk 49a-b already sensed two contradictory views. See

The cultic workings of the water libation now become clear.[96] Recall that t3:14-15 relates that the libations flowed from the altar down through a pipe and into the channels / foundations *(sheetim)*. The Tosefta then cites a tradition of R. Yose: "The foundation *(sheet)* was bored down to the Deep." So (in the mythic view) the libations flowed from the altar through the pipe down to the foundations of the temple and into the Deep. Merging there with the primordial waters, the libation set in motion a process through which the earth was fertilized. According to R. Eliezer:

> When they pour the water libation on the Festival, the Deep says to its companion, "Let your waters spring forth. I hear the voice of two friends," as it says, *Deep calls to Deep in the roar of your ducts (ṣinorekha)* (Ps 42:8).[97]

The "two friends" are the libations of water and wine. The "ducts" correspond to the "pipe,"[98] the conduit through which the libations flow downward to the foundations and the Deep. Libations stimulate the personified Deep to let its waters flow forth and supply streams, rivers and springs with water.[99] Here the libations function as a sign to the Deep that it is the appropriate time to irrigate the world. The Deep also seeds the rain clouds:

> R. Yehuda said: Once each month ducts rise from the Deeps and irrigate the whole earth, as it says, *And a flow would well up from the ground and water the whole surface of the earth (Gen 2:6)*. The clouds make the lakes hear the noise of their ducts, and the lakes make the Deeps hear the voice of their ducts, and Deep calls to Deep to raise water and to give it to the clouds, as it says, *Deep calls to Deep in the roar of your ducts (ṣinorekha) (Ps 42:8)*. And the clouds draw water from the Deeps as it

---

too *OG, Sukka, perushim* §312, to bSuk 49a (103); E. Slomovic, "Patterns of Midrashic Impact on the Rabbinic Midrashic Tale," *JSJ* 19 (1988), 75-83 and the literature cited there; J. Heinemann, *'Aggadot Vetoldoteihem* (Jerusalem: Keter, 1974), 26-29.

[96]Feuchtwang, *Wasseropfer*, 544-52 was the first to reconstruct this process. (Although Etlinger in *'Arukh laner* to bSuk 49a [93b], s.v. *'al* already sensed the basic mechanism.) He was followed by Jeremias, *Golgotha*, 100-104; Patai, *Temple*, 54-65.

[97]bTa 25b.

[98]The Greek loanword *silon* corresponds to the Hebrew *ṣinor*.

[99]Gen 49:25 mentions the "blessings of the Deep that crouches beneath," translated in *TYN* as "the blessing of the springs of the Deep that come up from the earth from beneath." (Cf. *TY* ad loc; *Sifre Deut*. §353 [413]). Cf. *BR* 13:17 (125-26); yTa 1:3, 64b. In *TYN* to Num 21:6 and Deut 32:10 the mythical well that supplies the Israelites water in the desert rises from the Deep.

says, *He makes clouds rise from the ends of the earth (Ps 135:7)* – they shower rain in the places where God commands them to rise up.[100]

The source depicts the complete hydraulic system of the earth. A monthly effusion from the Deep is the ultimate source of water. This occurs when clouds communicate to the lakes that they are ready to receive water, and the lakes transmit the message to the Deep. The clouds then descend and receive their water from the Deep. As evident in the legend of David reciting the Songs of Ascent in order to raise the level of the Deep, the higher the water level, the more easily clouds fill with water and the more plentiful the rain.[101] That clouds garner their water from the oceans or Deep, not the heavens, is a widespread rabbinic conception. Thus R. Yosef states, "Even though the rain descends from heaven, it is created exclusively from the earth."[102]

Besides the "signal" the libations communicate to the Deep to raise its waters, there seems to be a type of sympathetic magic at work. Pouring water on the ground is believed to produce a corresponding "pouring" of water from heaven. Here too the mythic cosmology plays a part. According to R. Levi, "it is the way of the world that when rain descends, the Deep rises."[103] Similarly, "R. Shimon b. Elazar said: There is no handbreadth [of rain] that descends from above for which the earth does not discharge two handbreadths [of water.]"[104] These statements assume that rain, having fallen, ultimately finds its way into the Deep and causes its level to rise. The libation flowing into the Deep mimics the rain that flows into the Deep, and, given the logic of sympathetic magic, produces that flow of rain.[105]

---

[100]*PRE* §5 (12b-13a); *Yalqut Hamekhiri*, ed. S. Buber (reprint; Jerusalem, 1965 [1899]) to Ps 42:8 (1:246).
[101]This conception of clouds gathering water from the ocean or Deep derives from Job 38:8-9: "Who closed the sea behind doors, when it gushed forth out of the womb, when I clothed it in clouds, swaddled it in dense clouds." Cf. Gen 2:6, Job 26:8.
[102]*BR* 12:11 (110). Cf. bTa 9b (=BR 13:10 [119]) according to R. Eliezer and *BR* 13:11 (120) according to Resh Laqish; bSuk 11b; Eruv 45b; Men 69b and Rashi s.v. *sheyardu*; ySuk 1:5, 52b; *PRE* §5 (12b-13a). Cf. 2 En 28:2 (version A) and Patai, *Hamayim*, 144-45. The notion that the clouds absorb waters from the heavens is also found.
[103]*BR* 32:7 (294).
[104]tTa 1:4; *BR* 13:13 (122).
[105]In some rabbinic conceptions there is an upper Deep in the heavens parallel to the lower Deep. Thus Rabba, bTa 25b: "I saw Ridya (the angel of rain). He looks like a three year old calf with a split lip. He stood between the lower Deep and the upper Deep. He said to the upper Deep, 'Pour forth your waters.' He said to the lower Deep, 'Let your waters spring up.'" Similarly, the aforecited tradition of R. Eliezer refers to the Deep and its companion. (On Ridya, see bYom 21a.) Other references to an upper and lower Deep: *BR* 13:10-13 (119-23); bTa 9b-10a;

The workings of water libations therefore should be understood in mythic-cultic terms. Their efficacy derives from the mythic hydraulic structure that places the temple as the source of fertility. The ritual was not primarily a symbolic gesture or accompaniment to prayers that God send abundant rain. Rather the ritual in and of itself produced an effusion of waters from the subterranean Deep that fertilized the earth and seeded the clouds with rain.[106] For this reason the destruction of the temple made the libation ritual obsolete. No other place contained the fertilizing power of the temple or gave access to the Deep. To perform libations in the post-temple world would have been religiously unintelligible.

One final note: this mythic view of the temple may shed light on a second dimension of the willow ritual. As the point of access to the *sheetim* and the Deep, the altar essentially controls the sources of fertility. The altar, in other words, can be considered the true "capstone" of the subterranean waters and Deep. Several sources therefore identify the altar and the foundation stone.[107] Other rabbinic traditions call the altar a winepress,[108] while a Qumran text designates the altar the "vineyard of

---

Patai, *Temple*, 62-65; and nn. 32-40; idem, *Hamayim*, 135-37, 143. In this view, the rising of the level of the lower Deep is related to the upper Deep sending forth its rain. The libation therefore mimics the upper Deep raining down its water to the lower Deep and was considered to effect the same result.

[106]Mary Douglas refers to this concept of ritual as "instrumental efficacy"; *Purity and Danger* (New York: Ark, 1966), 68.

[107]See Jeremias, *Golgotha*, 105-106; Wensinck, *Navel*, 40-42 and Fishbane, *Text and Texture*, 118-119. Thus Jellinek, *BHM*, 5:63: "Where is the navel? That is Jerusalem. The navel itself is the altar. And why is it called the foundation stone? Because the earth was founded from it." Note too the exegesis of Gen 29:2-3 in BR 70:8 (807-808): "*There before his eyes was a well in the open. This is Zion. Three flocks of sheep were lying there beside it. These are the three pilgrimage festivals. For the flocks were watered from that well. From there they drew forth the Holy spirit. The stone on the mouth of the well was large. This is simḥat beit hasho'eva... When all the flocks gathered there. "Coming from Lebo-hamath to the Wadi of Egypt"* (= 1 Kgs 8:65). *The stone would be rolled from the mouth of the well and the sheep watered. Since from there they drew forth the holy spirit. Then the stone would be put back on the mouth of the well. Set back in its place until the next festival.*" According to Jeremias, 104, the interpretation is as follows: At each festival Israel comes to Zion, identified with a well, a source of water. The stone rolled away at the beginning of the festival allows Israel to "draw forth." This stone represents the altar, which gives access to the Deep. Thus the altar provides the main conduit to the subterranean waters. Note that the verse introduced from 1 Kgs 8:65 relates to the celebration of Sukkot under Solomon.

[108]tSuk 3:15; tMe 1:16. Recall that the water libation was poured together with a wine libation, and both flowed down into the channels beneath the altar. The daily wine libations also descended to the channels. The residue of wine contributed to the notion of the altar as a winepress.

God."[109] Such traditions understand the altar to be responsible for the vintage, and ultimately the growth of all vegetation, by virtue of its fertilizing power.[110] To adorn the altar with willows attempted to draw on its fertilizing waters and to stimulate its power to rejuvenate the earth.[111]

IV. Simhat Beit Hasho'eva

Simḥat beit hasho'eva, the "rejoicing at the place of water-drawing," (henceforth SBH) is the most obscure of the Sukkot temple rituals. Its name and purpose have long been subjects of controversy. Rabbinic sources describe the ceremony in grandiloquent terms, creating the impression that this was the outstanding annual celebration, the acme of the temple worship. In contrast to the descriptions of the libation and willow ritual, the rabbinic traditions assume a particularly legendary color. Yet extra-rabbinic sources are all but silent. The Mishna provides an uninterrupted narrative description of the ritual.

[A] The flute – five or six days.

---

[109]4Q500. See J. Baumgarten, "4Q500 and the Ancient Conception of the Lord's Vineyard," *JJS* 40 (1989), 1-6: "4Q500 is a blessing addressed to God expressing the hope for the flourishing of his vineyard. The latter was exegetically understood to embrace not only the community of Israel, but the Temple mount and more specifically the altar and the streams of sacrificial fluids which flowed out from the precincts of the Sanctuary as a source of fructification for the gardens of the area."
[110]Baumgarten, ibid., 2 refers to Ezek 47: 1-12. The stream that flows from the temple produces "all kinds of trees for food...their leaves will not wither nor their fruit fail; they will yield new fruit every month, because the water for them flows from the Temple." This vision is related to the libation by tSuk 3:3-12. (And could there be a connection between the place 'Arava, to which the waters flow [47:8], and the willow ['arava]?) *Tan Qedoshim*, §10 (444) explains that Solomon produced orchards and gardens (Qoh 2:5) with trees from every land because he could identify the streams that branched from the subterranean temple waters to fertilize the whole world.
[111]Mowinckel, *Psalms*, 1:18-19 argues that creation myths and rituals are simultaneously soteriological: "That life is thus *created* through the cult means salvation from that death and destruction which would befall, if life were not renewed. For existence is an everlasting war between the forces of life and death, of blessing and curse... Thus it is "the fact of salvation" which is actualized in the cult... The very fact that the cult is creative led to this first salvation being generally conceived as the first creation of life, of the 'land/world' (the Hebrew word *'ereṣ* means both). Creation is salvation." The prayers for "deliverance" or "salvation" recited at the altar, albeit primarily associated with rain, when coordinated with the libation and its mythic cosmogonic background, may be understood on this basis.

[B] This is the flute of the *beit hasho'eva* (place of water-drawing), which does not supersede either the Sabbath or the Festival-Day.
[C] They said: whoever has not seen *simḥat beit hasho'eva* (rejoicing at the place of water-drawing) never saw true rejoicing.

(mSuk 5: 1)

[A] On the eve following the first Festival-Day they would go down to Court of Women and make a great precaution.[112]
[B] There were golden lamps there, with golden bowls at their tops.
[C] There were four ladders at each lamp
[D] Four boys from the Young Priests, with full pitchers of oil that held one hundred-twenty *log* in their hands, would pour into each and every bowl.

(mSuk 5:2)

[A] They made wicks from the worn-out undergarments and belts of the priests, and kindled [the lamps] with them.[113]
[B] There was no courtyard in Jerusalem that was not illuminated from the light of the *beit hasho'eva* (place of water-drawing).

(mSuk 5:3)

[A] Pious Men and Men of Deed[114] used to dance before them with torches and recite praises before them.
[B] The Levites [stood] with lutes, lyres, cymbals and innumerable instruments of every sort on the fifteen steps that lead down from the Court of Israelites to the Court of Women,
[C] which correspond to the fifteen "Songs of Ascent" of the Psalms, upon which the Levites stand for the Song.[115]

(mSuk 5:4)

---

[112]See n. 128.

[113]mSheq 5:1 refers to an officer of the temple responsible for wicks (*paqi'a*). One opinion in bYom 23a connects this to SBH. But see Albeck's notes, *Mishna*, 2:462.

[114]*Ḥasidim ve'anshei ma'ase*. mSot 9:15 notes that when Hanina b. Dosa died, the Men of Deed ceased. Hanina was known as a healer (mBer 5:5) and miracle worker; apparently it is this type the Mishna has in mind. See G. Vermes, "Hanina Ben Dosa," *JJS* 23 (1972), 28-50 and 24 (1973), 51-64. For the somewhat unconvincing argument that these titles refer to specific social groups, and efforts to identify them, see S. Safrai, "Teaching of Pietists in Mishnaic Literature," *JJS* 16 (1956), 15-33; idem, "Ḥasidim ve'anshei ma'ase," *Sinai* 50 (1985), 133-54, and see the references for other opinions.

[115]The syntax is difficult. [C] is paralleled in mMid 2:5, and may be a gloss here. The point is that during SBH the Levites stood on the same steps upon which they normally stood for the Song. The "Song" is the psalm the Levites recited each day in the temple service. See mMid 2:5, mAr 2:6 and mTam 7:4. Some versions read "the Levites stand and recite the Song"; see Fox, *Succah*, 176, 179.

The Sukkot Temple Festival: Rabbinic Traditions

[A] Two priests stood at the Upper Gate that leads down from the Court of Israelites to the Court of Women, with two trumpets in their hands.
[B] When the cock[116] crowed, they sounded an extended blast, a quavering blast, an extended blast.
[C] When they reached the tenth step, they sounded an extended blast, a quavering blast, an extended blast.
[D] When they reached the courtyard, they sounded an extended blast, a quavering blast, an extended blast.
[E] They would walk and sound [the trumpet] until they reached the gate that leads out to the east.
[F] They reached the gate that leads out to the east,[117] and turned to face west, and said:
[G] "Our ancestors were in this very place, with their backs to the Temple of the Lord and their faces to the east; they prostrated themselves to the sun in the east. But we are Yah's, and our eyes [turn] to Yah."[118]
[H] R. Yehuda says: They repeat it, saying: "We are Yah's, and our eyes [turn] to Yah."[119]

(mSuk 5:5)

The Toseftan traditions form a commentary to this block of Mishna, and add additional details to the account.

[A] At first, when they would watch at *simḥat beit hasho'eva*, men would watch from within and women from without.

---

[116]The term *gever* seems to refer to the cock here, although this usage is atypical. The same phrase appears in mYom 1:8 and mTam 1:2. In bYom 20b Rav interprets the *gever* as a human being, which the talmud identifies as the "cryer" (*keruz*) an officer of the temple mentioned in mSheq 5:1. There, however, the cryer is named Gevini, although the officer responsible for locking the gates is named Ben Gever. Albeck, *Mishna*, 2:465 (to mYom 1:8) points out that mTam 1:2 implies the *gever* and the officer should not be identified. See too tSheq 2:14 and Lieberman, *TK*, 4:691.
[117]On the identification of this gate and the "Upper Gate" see Joshua Schwartz, "Once More on Nicanor's Gate," *HUCA* 62 (1991), 259-61.
[118]This liturgy alludes to Ezek 8:16: "Then he brought me to the inner court of the House of the Lord, and there, at the entrance to the Temple of the Lord, between the portico and the altar, were about twenty-five men, their backs to the Temple of the Lord and their faces to the east; they were bowing low to the sun in the east." See n. 133.
[119]On [G]-[H] see Fox, *Succah*, 183-85. In the Palestinian textual tradition, the first opinion at [G] reads, "We turn our eyes to Yah" (אנו ליה עינינו), and R. Yehuda disagrees, claiming that the word "to Yah" was repeated: We are Yah's, and to Yah our eyes [turn] (אני ליה וליה עינינו). The Babylonian textual tradition has the same phrase for both the first opinion and R. Yehuda. Apparently R. Yehuda insists the phrase was repeated. They said "We are Yah's, and our eyes turn to Yah. We are Yah's, and our eyes turn to Yah." bSuk 53b explains this as: "we bow to Yah, and our eyes hope in Yah."

[B] When the court saw that they behaved irreverently, they made three balconies in the courtyard, facing the three sides.
[C] There the women sat and watched *simḥat beit hasho'eva*, and they did not mingle.

(tSuk 4:1)

[A] Pious Men and Men of Deed used to dance before them with torches and recite praises before them. [= mSuk 5:4A]
[B] What would they say?
[C] "Blessed be he who never sinned, and whoever sinned, may he be forgiven."
[D] Some would say, "Blessed be my childhood that did not shame my old age" – these were the Men of Deed.
[E] Some would say, "Blessed be my old age that made atonement for my childhood" – these were the penitents.

(tSuk 4:2)

[A] Hillel the elder says,
[B] "To the place my heart loves, there my legs take me. If you come to my house, I will come to your house. If you do not come to my house, I will not come to your house, as it says, *In every place where I cause my name to be mentioned I will come to you and bless you (Exod 20:21)*."

(tSuk 4:3)

[A] Once Rabban Shimon b. Gamaliel was dancing with eight flaming torches, and not one of them touched the ground.
[B] When he bowed down he put his finger to the earth on the floor, bowed, kissed and stood upright immediately.[120]

(tSuk 4:4)

[A] R. Yehoshua b. Hanania said: "All the days of *simḥat beit hasho'eva* we never went to sleep.
[B] We awoke for the daily morning offering, from there to the synagogue,[121] from there to the additional *(musaf)* offerings, from there to eating and drinking, and from there to the House of Study, from there to the daily evening offering, from there to *simḥat beit hasho'eva*."

(tSuk 4:5)

---

[120]Hochman, *Festivities*, 76 suggests the prostration "consisted in bending over to kiss the ground while standing on the great *toes*, and resuming the upright position without using one's hands," translating *'eṣba'o* as "toe." Quite a gymnastic feat!

[121]It is doubtful that the temple contained a synagogue. See Zeitlin, "There Was No Synagogue in the Temple," *JQR NS* 53 (1962), 168; Lieberman, *TK*, 4:888. The version in y5:2, 55b has "from there to prayer" in place of "to the synagogue." Cf. the version in bSuk 53a.

The Sukkot Temple Festival: Rabbinic Traditions

[A] The Levites with lutes, lyres, cymbals and instruments of every sort [= m5:4B]
[B] Some would say, "*A song of ascents. Now bless [the Lord all you servants of the Lord who stand nightly in the house of the Lord]* (Ps 134:1)."
[C] Some would say, "*Lift your hands toward the sanctuary and bless the Lord* (Ps 134:2)."
[D] When they took leave of one another, they would say, "*May the Lord bless you from Zion...and live to see your children's children* (Ps 128:5-6)."

(tSuk 4:7-9)

The phrase that introduces the narrative, "whoever has not seen SBH never saw true rejoicing," reveals that the rabbis recalled the celebration in an idealized manner.[122] The festival represented ideal worship, the unbridled joy of temple times. The ensuing description portrays the celebration in hyberbolic terms. Before we assess the purpose of the ritual, we must be sensitive to the exaggerated elements. That every courtyard in Jerusalem was lit up from the light of the SBH is a clear overstatement (m5:3B). The 30 *log* (about 15 gallons) of oil held by each young priest as he ascended the ladder is an impossibility.[123] Levites stand with "innumerable" instruments (m5:4B). The description of the Pious *(hasidim)* dancing and the people watching is probably distorted. An important characteristic of popular festivals of this sort was that all who came to celebrate could participate in the rejoicing.[124] The mingling of sexes and irreverent behavior that required precautionary measures (t4:1) occurred during the ecstatic dancing, not while the people stood as idle spectators.

The Tosefta and talmuds internalize the ideal tone of the Mishna and continue the process of idealization. t4:2-3 portrays the "Pious and Men of Deed" who danced at festivities as rabbinic heroes.[125] In this way the Tosefta "rabbinizes" the celebration by placing rabbinic sages as the leaders of temple festivities, while relegating the priests to standing idly

---

[122] mSuk 5:1C. So too the baraita, bSuk 51b, "He who never saw SBH never saw true rejoicing. He who never saw Jerusalem in her glory, never saw a beautiful city. He who never saw the temple never saw a beautiful building."
[123] Assuming the 120 *log* was divided among the four priests. ySuk 5:2, 55b asks, but does not resolve, whether each priest carried 30 or 120 *log*! bSuk 52b (see DQS) was well aware of the heroic strength required, claiming the young priests displayed greater strength than the son of Mirta b. Baitos, who carried with one hand two thighs of a valuable bull (= tYom 1:14).
[124] For other examples of popular celebrations of this type, see Jdt 15:12, mTa 4:8. Maimonides may have sensed this, for he rules in *MT*, Laws of Lulav 8:13 that everyone plays musical instruments or sings. However, in 8:14 Maimonides limits the dancing to the elite.
[125] Cf. the slightly expanded traditions, ySuk 5:4; 55b-c, bSuk 53a.

on the stairs. Their purported praises are rabbinic wisdom sayings and apothegms, not the types of songs or liturgies one would expect at a temple festival.[126] That R. Shimon b. Gamaliel juggled eight(!) torches simultaneously and acrobatically prostrated while supporting himself on his fingers alone obviously exaggerates (t4:4).[127] bSuk 53a comments on the prostration that "no human being can do this." Where m5:3 alludes obliquely to a "great precaution," t4:1 elaborates that they set up balconies to prevent improprieties between the sexes.[128] The version of

---

[126] ySuk 5:4, 55b reformulates the saying attributed to Hillel in tSuk 4:3, translates it into Aramaic, and provides a new context. "When Hillel saw them behaving wildly he would say, [Even if] we are here, who is here? Does He need their praises?... When he saw them behaving properly he would say, If we were not here, who would be here? Even though many bring praises before Him, He enjoys the praises of Israel most." So his saying becomes social commentary, a response to the behavior of the people. Neusner, *Pharisees*, 1:235-36, points out that the Tosefta's formulation is a general proverb about the temple and lacks any inherent connection to SBH. The editor of the Tosefta has imposed a context by placing it in the narrative of SBH. A variant of the tradition appears in *ARNA* 12 and *ARNB* 27 (28a). *ARNA* makes no connection to SBH, interpreting the "place my heart loves" as the synagogue and *beit midrash*, while *ARNB* invokes SBH as "another interpretation." It is fairly certain that the "original" saying (or the early form of the tradition) was not connected to SBH. The tradition in its extant forms reveals the understanding of SBH of later rabbis, not Hillel himself. See too David I. Brewer, *Techniques and Assumptions in Jewish Exegesis before 70 CE* (Tübingen: J.C.B. Mohr, 1992), 50-52.

[127] While the Tosefta reads "flaming torches", y5:4, 55c has "torches of gold."

[128] There is great confusion as to the *tiqqun*. Both bSuk 51b and y5:2, 55b cite mMid 2:5: "Before the Courtyard [of Women] was free and [afterward] they surrounded it with a gallery so that the women should watch from above and the men from below and they should not mingle together." This implies the gallery was a permanent fixture, whereas m5:1 states that the *tiqqun* was made each year on the eve following the first day, just prior to the celebration. Cognizant of this difficulty, Rashi explains that the "gallery" was a wall-bracket (*ziz*) upon which the planks women stood on were placed each year. Meiri (to b51a) suggests they actually constructed brackets and built balconies from the walls, and that "a little work" was permitted despite the prohibition against building on a festival. Cf. Lieberman, *TK*, 4:886. Maimonides, *MT*, Laws of the Lulav 8:12, shifts the construction of the balcony back to the day before Sukkot, contradicting m5:2. Albeck, *Mishna*, 4:477 and Safrai, *'Aliya*, 194 suggest that the structure was permanent, but each year the "precaution" was taken that the men and women remain in their respective places; cf. y5:2, 55b. A similar explanation was proposed by Herzfeld, *Geschichte*, 3:170. This confusion makes attractive the suggestion of A. Geiger, *Lehr- und Lesebuch zur Sprache der Mischnah* (Breslau: Leuckart, 1845), 23-24 that *tiqqun gadol* means "great preparation," presumably the organization of the lanterns, oil, instruments and perhaps food and drink. So Hochman, *Festivities*, 102-103 n. 63. However the root TQN in the *pi'el* generally means "repair" in the Mishna. Only occasionally does it mean "prepare," e.g. mBM 10:5, Shab 12:1, Avot 3:16. Fox lists one textual witness to the *hiph'il* here,

t4:1 in b51b reads that "the sages ordained *(hitqinu)* that the women sit above and the men below." Thus the precaution becomes a formal legislative act.[129] This version also relates an additional stage: first the men were inside the courtyard and the women outside, then the women outside and men inside, and finally the women above and men below. Josephus does not mention any galleries in the women's court. Rabbinic sources seem to have imagined progressively firmer barriers to behaviors they found objectionable. The talmuds also embellish the brilliance of the lamps. The Mishna already claimed that the light illuminated every courtyard in Jerusalem, and a baraita adds that "A woman was able to separate wheat by the light of the *beit hasho'eva*.[130] In the PT we find the lamps pictured even more miraculously.

> Bar Kappara said, "they [the lamps] were 100 cubits tall."[131] But it has been taught: Anything that stands 100 cubits requires a base of 33. Now a ladder on this side requires 33 cubits, and a ladder on that side requires 33 cubits. It was taught: The whole courtyard was only 187 cubits long by 135 wide. A teaching was found: Their place was subject to a miracle!"

That is, the bases of the lamps and ladders required a space of over 135 cubits, but fit into an insufficient space miraculously. In bSuk 52b the lamps are only(!) 50 cubits high.

Despite the idealized tone and rabbinization we still gain a fairly good idea of the celebration. Indeed, once these colorings are identified they can be filtered out with some confidence. SBH was a nocturnal festival that took place in the temple courtyards. Worshippers danced,

---

compared to eleven for the *pi'el*. In any case, the nominal form *tiqqun* refers to the "ameliorative results" of legislation, as noted correctly by Jaffee, *Taqqanah*, 207 n. 7. In the Mishna it occurs only here and in the phrases *tiqqun 'olam* (mGit 4:2-7,9; 5:5, 9:4, mEd 1:13) and *tiqqun hamizbeah* (mGit 5:5, mEd 7:9; in tYev 6:8 we find *tiqqun valad*), which mean "precaution for the general good" and "precaution for the benefit of the altar." Hence the "great tiqqun" would seem to be a "great precaution" and not a "great preparation." But see Hochman's philological observations.

[129]Jaffee, *Taqqanah*, has shown that this use of *hitqinu* is better understood as a rabbinic literary device, not historical fact. At all events, a legislative act is promulgated once, whereas the Mishna implies the *tiqqun* occurred each year. For another example of a revision of earlier traditions that augments the authority of the sages, see Baruch Bokser, "Todos and Rabbinic Authority in Rome," *Religion, Literature, and Society in Ancient Israel, Formative Christianity and Judaism I*, ed. J. Neusner et. al (New York: University Press of America, 1987), 117-30.

[130]bSuk 53a, y5:3, 55b.

[131]The walls of the sanctuary were 100 cubits high (mMid 4:6), and the Mishna claims that all of Jerusalem was illuminated by the light. Hence Bar Kappara reasons the lamps must have been 100 cubits tall.

sang, fraternized, and, at times, their enthusiastic rejoicing culminated in wild or lewd behaviors that offended the particularly pious. Torches and lamps supplied light. Levites provided music with their array of instruments, and the priests led liturgical recitations including psalms. The fifteen "Songs of Ascent," Pss 120-134, comprised the main liturgy.[132] At dawn the priests sounded trumpets to signal the beginning of the procession. They marched across the courtyard to the "gate that leads out to the east" where the sun was about to rise. There they recited a brief liturgy professing their faith in God.[133]

---

[132] Ps 134, the last of these psalms, which t4:7-9 has the Levities recite antiphonally, contains the apt phrase: "Bless the Lord all you servants of the Lord who stand nightly in the house of the Lord." In the aforecited legend of David and the foundations of the temple (bSuk 53a-b), David recites these fifteen Songs of Ascent to make the Deep ascend so that its waters have access to the earth. A reflex of the legend probably explains the superscription to Ps 120:1 in the targum: "a Psalm recited on the steps of the Deep." Now SBH was connected to the libation, a rain-making ritual, and the legend suggests the Songs of Ascent were related to this goal. H. Graetz, "Die Halleluja- und Hallel-Psalmen," *MGWJ* 23 (1879), 245 based on t4:7, argues the assembly continued with Pss 135-46 after the Levites concluded the Songs of Ascent. Ps 135 indeed seems appropriate for this setting. The opening call, "Halleluyah, Praise the name of the Lord, give praise you servants of the Lord who stand in the house of the Lord in the courts of the house of our God," could refer to those celebrating the vigil in the courtyards. Subsequent verses relate to God as bringer of rain: "He makes clouds rise from the end of the earth; He makes lightning for the rain; He releases the wind from his vaults" (v. 7).

[133] It is difficult to believe that they actually recited the liturgy prescribed by m5:5G. Why mention the pagan tendencies of their forefathers at a time like this? Professions of faith do not usually demean the customs of the ancestors. Even if they wished to make clear that their sunrise ritual did not constitute sun-worship, they need not have revealed that their forefathers worshipped the sun. On the other hand, it seems unlikely that the rabbis would invent such a bizarre recitation. Urbach, *Sages*, 1:60 comments: "Although the passage from Ezekiel is cited, it is not to be assumed that 'our ancestors who were in this place' refers to the men whom Ezekiel saw, and it is almost certain that the celebrants did not mean to say that their forefathers were sun-worshippers, but there is preserved here an allusion to a custom of praying towards the sun as an expression of reverence for light... it is not impossible that the prostration to the sun contained an expression of reverence to the Creator of light." But why then quote Ezekiel which clearly refers to pagan abominations? bSuk 53b understood the Mishna very well to mean that the ancestors corrupted the temple, and even exaggerated the offensiveness of the ancient practice, claiming that they defecated toward the sanctuary. The amoraim in ySuk 5:5, 55c suggest they bowed both to the sun and to the sanctuary.

Urbach acknowledges that the ritual alludes "to the custom of praying toward the sun as an expression of reverence for light." That is, the rabbis sanitized the temple practice where they indeed bowed to the sun. Scandalized that the Mishna implies they actually worshipped the sun, Urbach suggests they

The Sukkot Temple Festival: Rabbinic Traditions

Why did the rabbis idealize the celebration of SBH to such a degree?[134] First, there is a general tendency in rabbinic literature to

---

worshipped God as its creator. But need this be the case? Josephus's famous description of the Essenes suggests sun-worship was not unknown: "Before the sun is up they offer no word on mundane matters, but offer to him certain prayers, which have been handed down from their forefathers, as though entreating him to rise" (*BJ* 2:128). Morton Smith, "Helios in Palestine," '*Erez Yisra'el* 16 (1982) 199-214 marshals a mass of evidence that suggests sun-worship was prevalent throughout the second temple period, although he does not refer to this liturgy. (Jacob Milgrom, "Challenge to Sun-Worship: Interpretation of Temple Scroll's Gilded Staircase," *Biblical Archaeology Review* 11, 1 [1985], 70-73 partially responds to Smith's contentions.) And see L. Ginzburg, *Perushim vehidushim birushalmi* (New York: The Jewish Theological Seminary, 1941), 3:373-76. Other scholars too have claimed sun-worship featured prominently in the temple Sukkot celebrations. See n. 141 and Thackeray, *Septuagint*, 62; Volz, *Neujahrsfest*, 26; McKelvey, *Temple*, 81 n. 2; Riesenfeld, *Jesus*, 278; Gaster, *Thespis*, 65-66; Snaith, *New Year*, 90-93; Ehrlich, *Kultsymbolik*, 57 n. 149; F.S. Hollis, "The Sun-cult and the Temple of Jerusalem," in Hooke, *Myth*; Joshua Schwartz, "Once More on Nicanor's Gate," *HUCA* 62 (1991), 261-62; H.G. May, "Some Aspects of Solar Worship at Jerusalem," *ZAW* 55 (1937), 269-279. J. Morgenstern, "Gates of Righteousness" *HUCA* 6 (1929), 1-27 believes that the worshippers gathered in the temple forecourt early on New Year's morning "to watch the victorious sun of righteousness rise with healing in its wings." Much of the evidence for these claims is weak, depending on an overreading of Gospel traditions or the assumption that SBH was a fire (hence sun) festival. More likely, sun-worship could have been connected to the autumnal equinox, which many scholars believe to have been part of the ancient biblical festival; see Mowinckel, *Psalms*, 1:18; Pedersen, *Israel*, 2:775; Morgenstern, "Supplementary Studies in the Calendars of Ancient Israel," *HUCA* 10 (1935), 7-11 and already Philo, *Special Laws*, 2:204-206. Gaster, 65 considers *tequfat hashana* of Exod 34:22 as the equinox. Further research is needed to settle these issues.

[134]H. Graetz, *Geschichte der Juden*[5], ed. M. Brann (Leipzig, 1905 [1857]), 3:140 suggested that the glorified festival represented an anti-Saducean or anti-Boethusian polemic. Since the rabbis believed that the Sadducees / Boethusians denied the legitimacy of the libation, they played up the ritual and romanticized its preparatory nocturnal festival. He believed SBH and the libation were not observed from Hyrcanus's defection to the Sadducees until the reign of Salome, who restored the temple to the control of the Pharisees. The triumphant Pharisees began to celebrate their neglected festival with special vigor. Graetz points to a parallel case in mMen 10:3 which describes an elaborate ceremony prior to the cutting of the Omer sheaf including a thrice repeated ritual dialogue. The Mishna then remarks: "Why all this? Because of the Boethusians who used to say: the Omer is not reaped on the day after the Festival (Pesaḥ)." This explanation is not completely satisfactory. Graetz failed to realize that the rabbinic descriptions themselves are exaggerated. The historiography requires explanation, not the history. The idealization continues in the Tosefta and the talmuds, texts redacted long after the fall of the Sadducees, when such polemic was not urgent. Moreover, the Mishna does not claim that the Sadducees opposed the libation, and the perspectives of the Tosefta and talmuds are complicated. See "The Sadducees and the Water Libation," *JQR*, forthcoming.

idealize the temple and temple worship. mAvot 5:5, for example, lists ten miracles that obtained at the temple. The sacrificial meat never spoiled, a fly was never seen and rain never extinguished the fire upon the altar. According to mTam 3:8, various activities of the temple, including the voice of the high priest, could be heard in faraway Jericho.[135] That is, rabbinic traditions sometimes assume a *mythic* character of the sense I described in connection with the libation. They perceived the temple in terms of its cosmic significance as the divine abode and a conduit between heaven and earth. Mythic memory exaggerates all its qualities: the splendor of the priests, the sounds of the music, the majesty of the building, and naturally the joyous celebrations.[136]

Second, rabbinic sources link *simḥa*, festal joy, the obligation to rejoice on the festivals, with rejoicing in the temple. True rejoicing involved the priestly service, the levitical choirs, and culminated in the sacrificial meal. The name of the ceremony, "*rejoicing* at the place of water-drawing," pointed to a particularly joyous time. If *simḥa* was associated with all festivals by definition, a ritual named specifically for its joyous character must have been extraordinary. Not that this was completely fabricated – Sukkot is consistently described as the time for rejoicing, the festival *par excellence,* and genuine historical memories of great joy undoubtedly lingered. By rabbinic times those memories tended to grow to mythic proportions.

That SBH was a popular celebration, and not exclusively conducted by priests and Levites, contributed to the idealization. Here was an opportunity to stress the prominence of the rabbinic founders and the participation of the entire people. As opposed to other ceremonies, where the rabbis / Pharisees could at best direct the priests to conduct the ritual properly, but never perform the rituals themselves, at SBH rabbinic heroes took center stage.[137] Hillel, Shimon b. Gamaliel and other

---

[135]Cf. the commentary on this Mishna in *ARNA* 35 (52a). See too mTam 2:2 (the priests never neglected to clear the ashes from the altar); bAr 10b-11a (*magrefa* of the temple played 1000 songs); bYom 21a (the fragments of earthen vessels broken in the temple disappeared in their places, as did the waste from the bird offerings, inner altar and the candelabra; the show-bread was still warm when it was removed from the table after a week, etc.); bMeg 10b (= bBB 99a: the ark did not detract from the space of the inner sanctuary); tSot 13:7; bYom 21b, 38a, 39a, 54a; bSuk 51b; yYom 6:3, 43c.
[136]Cf bPes 109a: "R. Yehuda b. Betera says: While the temple stood, there was no rejoicing except with (sacrificial) meat, as it says, *You shall sacrifice there offerings of well-being and eat them, rejoicing before the Lord your God (Deut 27:7)."* See too the exaggerated memory of the daily offerings sacrificed on Sukkot in *BR* 65:17 (729): they were so big that even two camels could not carry them easily!
[137]See e.g. mYom 1:1-8 and tYom 1:8.

"Men of Deed" led songs and praises. They put on the elaborate celebrations before the people while the priests passively stood at attention. Rabbinic tradition naturally embellished the magnificence of the celebrations. The founding fathers featured in one of the greatest celebrations of the year, not in a minor ritual of little significance.

What was the overall focus of the ritual? Here we come to the vexing question of the title *simḥat beit hasho'eva*, generally translated as "rejoicing at the place of water-drawing." This designation seems inappropriate, for the account of the ritual takes place exclusively in the temple courtyards and makes no mention of water-drawing.[138] Abraham Geiger therefore rejected the traditional understanding of *sho'eva* as a reference to drawing water. He called attention to the manuscript variant *she'uva* and explained the term as a Hebrew form of the Syriac *shova*, a torch. Geiger claimed this was the correct reading, and related this title to the unusual prominence of torches in the description of the festivities.[139] SBH was a fire celebration, and had no connection to water.[140] Of course this explanation of the etymology of *sho'eva* raised an even larger question: why was such a fire festival part of the Sukkot temple celebrations? – a question never satisfactorily answered by Geiger and those who accepted his thesis.[141] This conjecture found wide acceptance in the scholarly

---

[138] Even the term *beit is* problematic: if it means the "place of water-drawing" why was no water-drawing performed there? Maimonides to mSuk 5:1 explains *beit* as the "place at which they prepared for the celebration, and it was so called because of the verse *and you shall draw water in joy* (Isa 12:3)." He alludes to ySuk 5:1, 55a which interprets the verse metaphorically in terms of drawing the "holy spirit," not the water. Herzfeld, *Geschichte*, 1:179 interprets *beit* as "time" based on *TO* to Gen 40:20 where *beit valda* means birthday, criticized appropriately by Hochman, *Festivities*, 59, who inappropriately explains *beit* as vessel – the festivity celebrated around the vessel for the drawn water (or the water-drawing.) See too Epstein, *MLH*, 321.
[139] A. Geiger, *Lehr- und Lesebuch Zur Sprache der Mischnah* (Breslau: Leuckart, 1845), 22-24, 131. This etymology is also suggested in Kohut, *'Arukh*, 2:85. Epstein, *MLH*, 322 n. 3 and Fox, *Sho'eva*, 173-78 catalog those who embraced Geiger's interpretation.
[140] Geiger, ibid., 23: "Mit wasserschöpfen hat diese Freude der Beleuchtung gar keinen Zusammenhang." S. Zeitlin, "The Bet Ha-Shoebah and the Sacred Fire," *JQR NS* 43 (1953), 218: "The Mishna speaks separately of the libation, ניסוך המים, and the *Bet ha-Shoebah*, בית השואבה, which makes it evident they were not identical." Maimonides seems to have considered the rituals as unrelated, for he sets forth the laws of the libation in *MT*, Laws of Daily and Additional Offerings 10:7-10 and those of SBH in *MT*, Laws of Lulav 8:12-15, and makes no connection between them.
[141] Thackeray, *Septuagint*, 62 explained the fire festival as a legacy of Israelite sun-worship. He also suggested a relationship to the autumnal equinox, which occurs around the time of Sukkot. Zeitlin, ibid., 217-23 mixed in elements of Hanukka and other dedication festivals and invented a celebration of the

world, although some who subscribed to the etymology rejected the supposed fire festival.[142] In any case, Harry Fox has shown this interpretation to be fallacious by demonstrating that the purported manuscript variant does not, in fact, exist.[143] Fox emphasizes that all ancient traditions indeed connect the festival to water. A century of confusion on this issue has been resolved, leaving us with the original puzzle: what was the SBH?

Consistent with the designation "water drawing," the nocturnal festival must be associated with the libation.[144] It was a preparatory festival that directly preceded the drawing of water. Note that the Mishnaic narratives of the two rituals are incomplete. The filling of the vessel at the Siloam seems to pick up in the middle of the libation ritual. How did they get to the Siloam? Did they assemble there spontaneously? Or did they arrive in a procession not mentioned in the Mishna? The account of SBH leaves off after the recitation of the ritual formula at the "gate that leads out to the east." Did the people just disband at this point or did the procession progress further? When combined together, the two almost complement each other. As for time, the libation account begins early in the morning,[145] just when the SBH description ends. As for location, the SBH account progresses across the courtyard, from the "Upper Gate" to the "gate that leads out to the east," while the libation narrative begins at the Siloam. It seems reasonable to assume that the procession moved from the gate to the Siloam, although this datum is not given in either account. The alternative possibility, that the procession disbanded at the gate after such a brief march and then

---

initiation of fire upon the altar. Patai, *Temple*, 85 explained the kindling of lamps both as a commemoration of the first creation of light and as the "kindling anew of the cosmic light at its proper place, the temple, the source of the light of the world." For him, the lamps function as an important ritual focus in their own right and bear cosmic significance. (Volz, *Neujahrsfest*, 28 proposes a similar explanation.) Elsewhere Patai suggested the blazing light represents lightning, and, like the libation, serves as a charm to create this desired effect (*Hamayim*, 51).
[142]See the survey in Fox, *Sho'eva*, 173-79.
[143]Ibid, 178. Hochman, *Festivities*, 54-60 already rejected the association with fire on etymological grounds.
[144]Rashi and most rishonim relate the two: "All this rejoicing was exclusively on account of the water libation" (bSuk 50a s.v. *beit*.) Meiri to mSuk 4:1 comments that the sounding of the trumpet at the SBH was a "sign that they should go to draw water from the Siloam." Cf. Fox, *Sho'eva*; Epstein, *Tannaim*, 351; Feuchtwang, *Wasseropfer*, 543; Herzfeld, *Geschichte*, 1:187-89; A. Halevi, *'Erkei ha'aggada vehahalakha* (Tel Aviv: Devir, 1979-82), 2:211.
[145]This datum is not specified in the Mishna, but emerges from t3:16 that specifies the libation was poured with the morning *tamid* offering.

spontaneously reassembled at the Siloam (or that a completely separate group assembled at the Siloam), seems far less likely.[146]

Several considerations bolster the conclusion that the two accounts describe one and the same ritual. The phrase "they reached," governs both the libation procession (m4:9C) and the SBH procession (m5:5, four times.) Moreover, in both accounts the priests sound the same series of trumpet blasts ("a sustained, a quavering, a sustained blast") at designated points (m4:9, 5:5). m5:6, which details the forty-eight trumpet blasts sounded on the Friday of Sukkot, mentions three blasts "for the filling with water."[147] Trumpeting was clearly an essential part of the procession which accompanied the ritual from start to finish. In addition, m5:1 refers to the "flute of the *beit hasho'eva*," the very flute m4:1 prescribed for five or six days. Yet the account of the nocturnal celebration mentions no flute despite the description of Levites with lutes, lyres and cymbals. Most likely the flute was played at the Siloam when the priests drew the water for the libation.[148] The "rejoicing at the

---

[146]Herzfeld, *Geschichte*, 1:187-89 hedges by claiming that some of the worshippers joined the priest who headed toward the Siloam, while others apparently disbanded. He was troubled by the fact that the libation ritual also included a procession, but since he considered SBH a fire festival, he rejected an organic connection between the two events. Although Hochman connects SBH to the libation, he claims a different procession formed to accompany the priest to the Siloam; *Festivities*, 79. Patai, *Temple*, 27-30 suggests the same procession continued to the Siloam.

[147]This detail is omitted from m4:9-10, the narrative of the libation. Both bSuk 54a and y5:6, 55c explain that m5:6 and 4:9-10 were taught by different tannaim. t4:10 confirms the tannaim disputed the details of the trumpet blasts. See Epstein, *Tannaim*, 352.

[148]Thus TY to Deut 16:14: ותיחדון בחג בשאובתא וחלילא, "you shall rejoice on the Festival with the water-drawing and the flute." Both Meiri to bSuk 42b (155) and R. Yehuda b. Binyamim (RiBBaN, in *Ginzei rishonim: masekhet sukka*, ed. M. Hershler [Jerusalem, 1962], 269) comment that the Levites played the flute along with other instruments while the water was drawn. Ritba to m4:1, b42b (396) suggests they played the flute while they proceeded to the Siloam for the water-drawing: החליל. פי' שהיו מנגנין בו בשמחת בית השואבה כשהולכין להביא מים לניסוך. But to m5:1, b50a (457) he suggests the flute was played at the time of the libation itself: פי' שהיו מזמרין בו בבית השואבה בחלילין וכלי זמר בשעת נסוך המים. (This language is somewhat problematic: he seems to refer to the libation, which took place at the altar, as the *beit hasho'eva*; see the editor's note, p. 396, n. 8.) R. Yehonotan of Lunel (in *Ginzei rishonim*, 220) also implies the flute played when the water was drawn: "they used to rejoice in honor of the drawing of water and pipe on flutes and lutes." However Rashi, bSuk 50a, s.v. *vezehu* (as in *DQS*, ad loc., n. א), suggests the flute played during the nocturnal celebration: שהיו מחללין להרבות שמחה לשמחת בית השואבה. (So too b50b s.v. *'aval*.) He cites the following Mishna which describes the Levites and their instruments. Maimonides too rules that a flute was played at night during SBH (*MT*, Laws of Lulav 8:12). Apparently this is the flute of *beit hasho'eva*; Maimonides lists it first in the order of instruments that

beit hasho'eva" took place in the temple courtyard, while the "flute of *beit hasho'eva*" accompanied the water-drawing itself and escorted the libation procession to the temple.[149]

It seems that SBH spontaneously developed out of popular celebrations that prevailed throughout the city during the festival week. These eventually coalesced around the libation procession that took place each morning (except the Sabbath) and gradually assumed a semi-institutionalized character.[150] This conclusion tallies with the etymology

---

created the "rejoicing." This explanation is problematic since, as we have seen, mSuk 5:4 lists several instruments that were played during SBH, but does not mention the flute. Moreover the flute is that of *beit hasho'eva*, not of *simḥat beit hasho'eva*. It is worth noting that the narrative account of the libation gives no description of what occurred while the libation was actually drawn. The mention of trumpet blasts at the filling in m5:6 provides the only detail. But such an important ritual must have involved more than the sounding of the trumpet followed by a silent scooping of water. If an entire night was devoted to joyous festivities in anticipation of the libation, we should expect that the priest actually filled the vessel with commensurate pomp. That a special flute was played during the ritual, and perhaps other instruments as well, fills in some of the missing ceremony. Undoubtedly a liturgical recitation took place. It seems likely that the flute was also played during the procession from the Siloam to the temple, since flutes were choice instruments for ritual processions. When rural townsmen brought their firstfruits to Jerusalem in a festive procession, "the flute was played before them until they drew near to Jerusalem," and again "until they reached the Temple Mount" (mBik 3:3-4). The "favorite" (*ḥaviv*) of musical instruments (ySuk 5:1, 55a), the flute came to serve as the prime expression of festival joy.

[149]Scholars claim SBH took place on five or six nights based on mSuk 4:1, "The flute five or six..." (If the first day of Sukkot fell on the Sabbath, SBH could be held each intermediate night, six nights in all. In other years the festival was held each night except Friday night, five in all.) But the nocturnal celebration may have been a one-night affair. While the flute accompanied the drawing of the libation five or six days, SBH perhaps took place only one night. The narrative description begins "On the eve after the first Festival-Day they would go down to the Court of Women" (m5:2), and says nothing of other nights. In t4:5, R. Yehoshua b. Hanania speaks of "All the days (*kol yemei*) of SBH," and narrates the time from the morning sacrifice on the first day of Sukkot until SBH that night. This source appears in both talmuds (y5:2, 55b; b53a) with minor variations. The phrase "all the days of SBH" could mean "all five or six days each year we celebrated SBH." On the other hand, it could mean, "all the days when SBH was practiced," i.e., "each year, on the day we celebrated SBH." The version in BT in fact begins: "when we used to rejoice at SBH, we never saw sleep..." Both talmuds accept the first interpretation. Note that the first intermediate day of Pesaḥ is distinguished by the '*omer* ritual, which would parallel the first intermediate day of Sukkot marked by SBH. (I thank Robert Goldenberg for this observation.) On this matter see Rubenstein, *Dissertation*, 175-81.

[150]Yet the connection between the rituals was loose. The water-drawing and libation procession that took place on the first festival day of Sukkot was not

of *sho'eva*, which, as Fox has demonstrated, alludes to the drawing of water. SBH comprised the preparatory celebration. Excitement built up during the all-night festivities in anticipation of the morning procession to the Siloam.[151] These long and magnificent festivities enhanced the significance of the libation ritual.

V. SBH in the light of Hellenistic Religions

A review of the general practice of the "all-night festival," the *pannychis*, in Hellenistic religion helps to explain elements of SBH, the libation and the relationship between the two rituals. *Pannychis* is a technical term for a religious celebration that lasted throughout the night. These celebrations were fairly common in Greek religion, and often occurred during festivals that continued for several days.[152] Because nights were considered particularly appropriate times for merrymaking and revelry, *pannychides* were exclusively celebrations of great joy. All *pannychides* involved extensive singing and dancing; some featured races, carousing and ritual practices such as the bearing of myrtle branches.[153] The cover of night and ecstatic joy encouraged men and women "to mix together without timidity."[154] Wine and drinking-bouts often took place.[155] To keep awake all night was not an easy matter, and to sustain this sort of energy even more difficult. The Greek author Athenaeus (2nd

---

preceded by SBH, which commenced only on the second night. Hochman, *Festivities*, 63 suggests that "in all probability the celebration originally consisted merely of a procession to and from Siloa led by a flute. This will explain why the festivity is denoted by החליל." It also explains why SBH and the libation are related but not indispensable to each other.

[151]t3:16 claims the libation was performed with the morning *tamid*, which was offered immediately after sunrise. But we must allot some time for the procession to reach the Siloam and return. Even if they started out at dawn, it would have been difficult to return to the temple in time for the *tamid*, for the Siloam Pool lay at the southern tip of the city of David, about one half mile from the temple. See p. 120. (This problem obtains even if we assume the libation had no connection to SBH. Time would still be needed to proceed from the Siloam to the temple, and it is unlikely this could be done between dawn and the *tamid*.) Perhaps the *tamid* was delayed slightly on the morning following SBH.

[152]On the *pannychis* see L. Ziehen, "Pannychis," P.-W., 18,1,2, 629-632; Nilsson, *Feste*, 215, 377-78; Parke, *Festivals*, 49-50; Wilamowitz, *Glaube*, 2:353-54; Burkert, *Religion*, 232; M. Vassits, *Die Fackel in Kultus und Kunst der Griechen* (Belgrade, 1906), 19, 66.

[153]Nilsson, *Feste*, 378.

[154]Wilamowitz, *Glaube*, 2:353-54. Cf. Ziehen, ibid., 632. Nilsson, *Feste*, 377-78, conjectures that the *pannychis* of Aphrodite may have involved orgiastic rites, but these are not documented in the sources.

[155]Plutarch, *The Roman Questions*, §55; *On Being a Busybody*, §3; *Progress in Virtue* §5; Athenaeus, *Deipnosophists*, 6:250.

century CE) mentions that prizes were awarded to those who stayed awake the longest, and that the participants attempted to keep themselves awake by dancing.[156] The parallels to SBH are clear. The rabbinic descriptions of singing, dancing and allusions to mixing of the sexes can be understood as typical elements of rejoicing characteristic of nocturnal celebrations. Similarly, the juggling and acrobatics that made such an impression on the later tannaim parallel the games and contests that entertained the people and kept them from falling asleep.

A second feature of Greco-Roman religions that illuminates the temple festivities is the *pompa (pompē)*, the technical term for a cultic procession.[157] Processions were so characteristic of Greek religion that "hardly a festival is without its *pompē*."[158] In Hellenistic times processions became even more popular and spread throughout the Hellenistic world.[159] Ubiquitous rituals of this type always exhibit great diversity, but the typical characteristics of a procession appear consistently. The *pompa* always proceeded towards a place of importance to the cult, generally a sanctuary where sacrifices were offered. The starting point was sometimes a different sanctuary, although in certain cults a specific area or building served as a set place where the procession formed.[160] Priests, musicians, men, women and children, animals for the sacrifices, occasionally performers and acrobats, all participated in the procession. Herein was one important characteristic of the ritual: the entire people could play an active role. Often the participants carried in their hands branches and wands;[161] fruit, oil, cloth and other offerings; weapons, incense burners, phallus-poles, and miscellaneous cultic implements. They offered prayers and sang special procession-hymns as they walked and during the rests along the way.[162] Processions facilitated mass participation in the festivities and served as expressions of festal joy. In time they tended toward extravagant show, and thus *pompa* came to mean any display of "pomp."

---

[156]*Deipnosophists*, 14:647, 15:668.

[157]For general discussion of the *pompa* see Bömer, *Pompa* (= P.-W., 21,2: 1878-1994); Nilsson, *Prozessiontypen*; Eitrem, *Prozessionem*; Burkert, *Religion*, 99-101; Parke, *Festivals*, 22-25. See also Nilsson, *Feste*; Simon, *Festivals*, 32, 60-61, 90. Other types of *pompae* include bridal, burial, military (= triumph), royal and private processions.

[158]Burkert, *Religion*, 99. So Nilsson, *Geschichte*, 1:780: "Die grosste Schaustellung an den Festen war die Prozession, die wohl niemals fehlte."

[159]Bömer, *Pompa*, 1895.

[160]Simon, *Festivals*, 32.

[161]C. Böttlicher, *Der Baumkultus der Hellenes* (Berlin: Weidmann, 1856), 403-405; Nilsson, *Prozessiontypen*, 322.

[162]Burkert, *Religion*, 102.

The libation ritual consisted of a *pompa*. The description in the Mishna is somewhat sketchy, and provides only a brief glimmer of the parade. But the priests with trumpets, the bearing of the libation flask, the sound of the flute and the culmination at the altar with the libation and sacrifices are characteristic processional elements. The willow-ritual which consisted of carrying the willows from Moṣa to Jerusalem and up to the altar can also be designated a *pompa*.

In many cases the *pannychis* and *pompa* were connected.[163] The worshippers celebrated a *pannychis* throughout the night and set out in procession at dawn. Thus an Athenian document reads: "The Hieropoioi who manage the yearly Panathenaia are to make the all-night service (*pannychis*) as well as possible in honour of the goddess and are to send the procession at sunrise."[164] Throughout the night excitement increased as the worshippers prepared for the next day's colorful procession. SBH and the libation procession should be understood in this way. The all-night festivities, dancing, singing and the memorable blazing of lamps rallied the celebrants for the morning ritual procession. Now SBH concluded with a short march across the women's court to the "gate that leads out to the east" where the short prayer was recited. But it seems likely that the libation procession was the real culmination of the night long festival. This minor jaunt, we have suggested, was simply the beginning of the procession to the Siloam, and the pause at the gate one of several stops along the way. The festivities that lasted throughout the previous night focused energy on this important ritual and thereby magnified its significance.

The *pannychis* also helps to understand the curious prominence of fire at a celebration linked with a water libation, which led scholars mistakenly to understand SBH as a fire festival. In Greco-Roman religion torches were regularly carried at *pannychides*, processions and almost every celebration that occurred at night.[165] First, the people simply needed to see. In antiquity torches were the primary means of illumination after dark for those who moved from place to place, while lamps remained in fixed posts. Second, burning flames made for a vivid,

---

[163] Burkert, *Religion*, 232; Wilamowitz, *Glauben*, 2:353-54; Bömer, *Pompa*, 1887; L. Ziehen, "Pannychis," P.-W., 18,1,2, 631.
[164] Parke, *Festivals*, 49. The document dates from 335 BCE.
[165] M. Vassits, *Die Fackel in Kultus und Kunst der Griechen* (Belgrade, 1906) provides an exhaustive list of the use of torches in Greek cults. His introductory remarks suggesting that the torch always serves a "kathartisch-apotropäisch" function, at least in public rituals, is overstated. See Nilsson's comments, *Feste*, 396-97, n. 4. See too Mau in P.-W., 12:1947-1952 (s.v. "Fackeln"); Nilsson, *Prozessiontypen*, 313, 332 and C. Daremberg and E. Saglio, *Dictionnaire des antiquités grecques et romaines* (reprint: Paris: Hachete, 1926-1931 [1873-1919]), II/2, 1027-29.

powerful experience. Thus Nilsson writes of the Eleusinian Mysteries: "It may be added that the Mysteries were celebrated by night in the light of many torches, which added to their impressiveness."[166] The torches and lamps served a utilitarian rather than ritual function by providing light and creating an intense ambience. We need not overinterpret the lamps and torches of SBH. Their prominence is somewhat exaggerated in the exuberant rabbinic descriptions. As in the other nocturnal rites, they simply supplied illumination and contributed to the power of the festival experience.[167]

VI. Extra-Rabbinic Evidence of SBH

As with the libation and the willow, there is no explicit mention of SBH in extra-rabbinic sources of the second temple period.[168] We noted

---

[166]M. Nilsson, *Greek Popular Religion* (New York: Columbia University Press, 1940), 43. See too idem, *Feste*, 396-97 n. 4. Nilsson astutely points out that there were fire-cults and apotropaic rituals in which torches played an important ritual role. But not every use of torches serves this function. L. Venetianer, "Die Eleusinische Mysterien im Tempel zu Jerusalem," *Populär Wissenschaftliche Monatsblätter* 17 (1897), 174-178 emphasizes the parallel use of torches in the Eleusinian mysteries and SBH without considering what purpose the torches served. There is nothing extraordinary that in both cases the torches provided light. To suggest that SBH was an imitation of the mysteries based on this type of parallel is futile.

[167]This investigation of Greco-Roman parallels is not meant to suggest that SBH was borrowed from Hellenistic religions. Dance, song and rejoicing are universal religious phenomena. Comparison with parallel practices of the Hellenistic world sets simply SBH in a wider context. The connection between a night long celebration and the ensuing procession can be understood in light of other such rituals.

[168]Some have attempted to find evidence in various biblical passages. The talmuds connect the name SBH to Isa 12:3, "You shall draw waters in joy from the waters of salvation"; bSuk 50b; ySuk 5:1, 55a. Fox, *Sho'eva*, 203-206 proposes, with appropriate reserve, that these Isaian passages point to the existence of a water festival and procession. He suggests that Isa 12 is intrinsically connected to the Hallel Psalms and may allude to the libation itself. Hochman, *Festivities*, 81 briefly suggested that "Isaiah xii:3 might point to some festive ceremony of water-drawing as underlying, and so making intelligible, its metaphor," but does not link the chapter to the Hallel. For other scholars who link Isa 12 to Hallel Psalms see Fox, 203 n. 193; and add Mowinckel, *Psalms*, 1:123 nn. 58 and 131. Volz, *Neujahrsfest*, 30 also connects Isa 12:3 to the libation. The Hallel, of course, featured prominently on Sukkot, and perhaps certain portions were recited during the libation procession. What all this tells us of SBH is less clear. Even if we grant Fox's arguments, biblical testimony of a water festival does not confirm the existence of a preparatory, all-night celebration such as SBH. Others cite Isa 30:29 as evidence of nocturnal festivities "For you, there shall be singing / As on a night when a festival is hallowed / There shall be rejoicing as when they march with flute / with timbrels, and with lyres / To the Rock of Israel on the Mount of

that a fragmentary Qumran scroll seems to contain the liturgy of a popular celebration associated with Sukkot.[169] The references to rejoicing, men and women, youths and elderly, led Baumgarten to suggest that the ritual resembles SBH. Would that the text had been preserved in its entirety! Slightly stronger evidence may be found in a second century CE papyrus from Alexandria.[170] The papyrus contains an expense account which lists among other expenses a payment by a certain Ismaelos of 100 drachmae for an "all-night celebration for the Festival of Sukkot."[171] The papyrus unfortunately gives no clue as to what he purchased with the money, nor how the celebration was observed. We discussed aspects of the *pannychis* of Greco-Roman cults, but this was a private affair, or possibly that of the synagogue sponsored by Ismaelos. Yet this papyrus confirms that diaspora communities practiced an all-night festival on Sukkot, probably an imitation of SBH.

There may be a reflex of SBH in the striking description of a Jewish *pannychis* that appears in Philo's *The Contemplative Life*.[172] In his

---

the Lord" (JPS translation). See Weinfeld, *Institutions*, 120-22, Mowinckel, *PsSt*, 91; Kraus, *Worship*, 218; Volz, *Neujahrsfest*, 26, who also mentions Ps 57:9, 92:3 and 134:1; H. Schmidt, *Die Thronfahrt Jahves am Fest der Jahreswende im alten Israel* (Tübingen: J.C.B. Mohr, 1927), 27-28. The flute is regularly mentioned in the Bible and undoubtedly was played at festivals (1 Sam 10:5, Isa 5:12, 1 Kgs 1:40; cf. mAr 2:3, mTam 3:8), so its mention is not exceptional. H. Graetz, "Die Halleluja- und Hallel-Psalmen," *MGWJ* 28 (1879), 244 and W. Oesterley, *The Psalms* (London, 1953), 537 (and see A. Weiser, *The Psalms*, trans. H. Hartwell [Philadelphia: The Westminster Press, 1959], 786) claim that Ps 134:1, "Bless the Lord, all you servants of the Lord who stand at night in the house of the Lord," mentioned in tSuk 4:7, refers to the nights of SBH (see n. 132). But other scholars understand the psalm as a farewell blessing offered by departing pilgrims to the temple personnel or as an allusion to the standard nightly watches. See Levenson, *Creation*, 91.

[169]Chapter 2,V, text to n. 93.
[170]*Corpus Papyrorum Judaicarum*, eds. V. Tcherikover and A. Fuks (Cambridge: Harvard University Press, 1957-64), 3:5-6, no. 452a. The editors refer to SBH in the note to line 15. The papyrus is dated on paleographic grounds.
[171]*pannychis tēs skēnopēgias*.
[172]See Baumgarten, 4Q502, 131 and Chapter 2,V. Fox, *Sho'eva*, 206 and n. 206 suggests that a passage from Philo's *Flaccus* §116-124, cited in Chapter 2, VI alludes to the festival. The nocturnal celebration with hymns and songs recalls SBH. The procession to a source of water at dawn and the assembly with prayers perhaps derives from a type of water festival parallel to the libation ceremonies. However, these festivities perhaps were nothing more than victory celebrations at Flaccus's death; the fact that he dies on Sukkot mere coincidence. Philo does not write that they celebrated all night "as was their custom" or offer any indication that the descent to the water was an annual rite. On the contrary, he explains that they were forced to gather on the beaches because their meeting-places had been confiscated, not because it was standard practice. Fox is inclined to see a "conflation" of SBH and rejoicing at the demise of the enemy. (Of course SBH

panegyric of the Theraputae, the group he admires so much for their religious devotion, spirituality and piety, Philo praises the all-night celebrations they observed. These feasts occurred every seven weeks.[173] After prayers and a meal at which men and women sat separately, the Theraputae listened in complete silence while the president conducted a discussion of scripture. After the discourse the president sang a hymn and all joined in the refrains. Philo continues:

> After the meal they hold the sacred *pannychis*, which is celebrated in the following manner. They all rise up in a body and at the center of the refectory they first form two choirs, one of men, the other of women, the leader and precentor chosen for each being the most highly esteemed among them and the most musical. They sing hymns to God composed in many meters and melodies, now chanting together, now chanting antiphonally,[174] now moving hands and feet in concordant harmony, and full of inspiration they sometimes chant processional odes, and sometimes the lyrics of a chorus in standing position as well as executing the strophe and antistrophe of the choral dance...

> Modeled above all on this, the choir of the Theraputae, both male and female, singing in harmony, the soprano of the women blending with the bass of the men, produces true musical concord. Exceedingly beautiful are the thoughts, exceedingly beautiful are the words, and august the choristers, and the end goal of thought, words and choristers alike is piety. Thus they continue till dawn intoxicated with this exquisite intoxication and then when, not with heavy head or drowsy eyes, but more alert than when they came to the banquet, they stand with their faces and whole body turned to the east, and when they behold the rising sun, with hands stretched heavenward they pray for a joyous day, truth, and acuity of thought. And after the prayers they retire each to his own sanctuary once more to ply the trade and cultivate the field of their wonted philosophy.[175]

This astonishing celebration has much in common with the rabbinic descriptions of SBH, including the idealized, adoring tone ("exceedingly beautiful the thoughts, exceedingly beautiful the words..."). Most prominent are the hymns, song and praises recited both at the meal and during the *pannychis*. The "hymns of earlier poets" parallel the psalms recited during SBH, the Hallel recited during the libation and sacrifices,

---

was only celebrated at the temple. These Alexandrian ceremonies would have to be considered as vicarious diasporic "imitations" of the temple festivities, as in the papyrus.)

[173]See Baumgarten, *Studies*, 135-36; *Philo of Alexandria, The Contemplative Life, The Giants and Selections*, trans. by D. Winston (New York: Paulist Press, 1981), 320 n. 38 and the references there.

[174]Winston, ibid., 56 inadvertently omitted this phrase *(tē de kai antiphōnois)* in his translation.

[175]*The Contemplative Life*, §§83-89. Trans. Winston, ibid., 55-57.

and perhaps the psalms recited during the procession. Particularly noteworthy is the "antiphonal harmony"; t4:7-9 depicts the Levites reciting psalms antiphonally at SBH, as was common temple practice.[176] Hymns and songs composed by the Theraputae themselves echo the "songs and praises" recited by the sages. The gesticulating and choric dancing[177] recall the dancing and acrobatics of rabbinic sources. Both Philo and the rabbis emphasize the separation of the sexes. The men and women of the Theraputae finally join together in song,[178] and perhaps they danced together as well. The rabbis remembered that the mingling of the sexes had necessitated precautionary measures to keep them apart. Philo compares the rapture of the Theraputae to the Bacchic revelries of the Dionysian cult, and employs the image of "intoxication" with religious enthusiasm. Both ancient authors and modern scholars noted the similarities between Dionysian mysteries and Sukkot celebrations.[179] This energy and enthusiasm of the Theraputae resemble the ecstatic celebrations of SBH. Finally both celebrations include a prayer at dawn. The Theraputae face east toward the rising sun while the rabbis claim the procession, having proceeded eastward in the direction of the sun, faces west for the prayer, but the similarity is clear.[180] It may be that these periodic celebrations originated as vicarious imitations of the Sukkot

---

[176]Heinemann, *Prayer*, 139-55. F.C. Conybeare, *Philo: About the Contemplative Life* (Oxford: Clarendon Press, 1895), 252 notes that the "choral refrain" (*akroteleutia*) is the proper term for the refrains in Psalms such as "for his mercy endures forever," of Pss 136 and 118, both recited in the Sukkot liturgy. The recitation of the Levites at SBH mentioned in t4:7-9 reflects an antiphonal choral recitation. The Tosefta relates that "some would say" Ps 134:1, "others would say" Ps 134:2, and that "When they took leave of one another, they would say," Ps 128:5-6. That is, they would all join together. It seems two Levitical choirs sang alternate verses of Psalms, and joined in unison at the end.

[177]Winston, ibid., translates *epixēronomountes kai eporxoumenoi* as "moving the hands and feet"; more literally: "gesticulating and dancing." In his commentary to Philo, Conybeare, ibid., 254 mentions SBH as an example of Jewish all-night dancing.

[178]Cf. *Life of Moses I* §180 (6:369), Philo's description of two choirs at the Song of the Sea, and *Life of Moses II* §256 (6:577) on the beautiful harmony produced when male and female voices mingle.

[179]Plutarch, *Quaes. Conv.* IV 6, 2 (Stern, *Authors*, 2:553-562; see Chapter 2,X); Büchler, *Cabanes*; Epstein, *Tannaim*, 349; L. Venetianer, "Die Eleusinische Mysterien im Tempel zu Jerusalem," *Populär Wissenschaftliche Monatsblätter* 17 (1897), 170-81.

[180]mSuk 5:5E-G. The ritual of the Theraputae, in fact, seems to be the very type of worship the rabbinic liturgy disavows.

temple festivities. Perhaps the entire all-night celebration developed from such an imitation of SBH.[181]

VII. The Lulav and the Hallel

The chapters of the Mishna devoted to temple rituals only mention the lulav briefly. Because the rite continued to be practiced in post temple times, most of the tannaitic traditions pertain to the contemporary ritual, and were collected in chapter 3 of the tractate. However, m4:1 notes that the lulav was practiced six or seven days during temple times. m4:2 and 4:4 explain:

[A] The lulav seven days – how so?
[B] If the first Festival-Day of the Festival fell on the Sabbath, [the] lulav [takes place for] seven [days].
[C] If [it fell] on all other days – six [days].

(mSuk 4:2)

[A] The commandment of the lulav – how so?
[B] The entire people brings their lulavs to the temple mount.[182]
[C] And the overseers receive [them] from their hands, and lay them out on the roof of the stoa.[183]
[D] The elders leave their [lulavs] in a [temple] chamber.
[E] They instruct them to say: whoever ends up with my lulav – behold, let it be [given] to him as a gift.
[F] The next day they wake up and arrive, and the overseers throw [the lulavs] before them.
[G] They snatch and strike each other.

---

[181]Philo's statement that the poets of an earlier age have bequeathed "hymns suited for processions, libations, and the altar," in and of itself, may be an allusion to the libation ritual. Wine libations were performed daily on the altar, but the combination of procession, libation and altar fits Sukkot best. The description may refer to the psalms recited during the procession from the Siloam to the altar. We know little about the origins and history of the Theraputae, but they seem to be related to the Essenes / Qumran community. Philo perceived an affinity between the groups, as he juxtaposed his discussions of the two, attributing to the Theraputae the "contemplative life" and to the Essenes "the active life" (*The Contemplative Life* §1). A second point of contact is the system of Pentacontad feasts of the Theraputae, perhaps related to the firstfruit festivals of wheat, wine and oil of the Temple Scroll, which also occurred at fifty-day intervals. Baumgarten, *Studies*, 137 and n. 23, considers the Theraputae as an "Egyptian off-shoot" of the Essenes. Perhaps the ceremony described in the fragmentary Qumran scroll is related to this Theraputae banquet.

[182]Some versions of the Mishna read: "If the first Festival-Day falls on the Sabbath, the entire people..." See Fox, *Succah*, 125-26 and the references there.

[183]Other objects are placed on the "roof of the stoa" in mSheq 8:4 and mPes 1:5. Cf. bSuk 44b-45a.

[H] When the court saw that they might get hurt, they ordained that each should take [the lulav] at home.

(mSuk 4:4)

m4:2B asserts that the lulav took precedence over the Sabbath on the first day of Sukkot. (Later rabbinic sources provide the exegetical basis for the priority of the first day.[184]) m4:4 then depicts how this was carried out so as least to compromise the sanctity of the Sabbath. Lulavs were brought to the temple on Friday, stored there overnight and reclaimed on the next day. Since each person must own his lulav (m3:13), the authorities directed the worshippers to say that they give their lulav to whomever winds up with it, and thus each would own the lulav he takes on the next day. The Mishna explains that this plan proved untenable. Either the worshippers desired so ardently to reclaim their own lulav or the provision did not forestall a mad rush to get their hands on any lulav that some became injured in the scuffling. Therefore the court decided that the lulav ritual should be performed at home and not in the temple courtyard.[185]

This Mishna contains thematic parallels to those that addressed the willow and libation ritual on the Sabbath (m4:6; 4:10). In each case the concern is how to perform the ritual given the Sabbath prohibitions. Just as the willows and libation water were brought to the temple Friday and left overnight, so too the lulav was initially left overnight in the temple confines. The lulav presented a unique problem in that it was a popular ritual. While the one libation jug and the few willows needed to adorn the altar presented no logistical problem, the multitude of people struggling to find their own lulav was unworkable in practice. On the other hand, while the libation and willow required the altar, the lulav involved no direct connection to a cultic object, and could be performed outside the temple. Thus the different nature of the rituals led to different solutions to the problems presented by the Sabbath.

The historicity of this Mishna is debatable. It bears a striking similarity to mSuk 3:13, which describes the parallel phenomenon in post-temple times. They brought the lulav to the *synagogue* before the Sabbath and on the next day reclaimed their own lulavs.[186] The

---

[184]*Sifra, 'Emor*, 16:3 (102b): *The first day* (Lev 23:40) – even on the Sabbath. *The first day*. They supersede the Sabbath [by taking the lulav] only on the first day [of the festival]. Cf. bSuk 43a.
[185]The summary statement of a seven-day lulav ritual (m4:2, when the Sabbath coincided with the first day) is therefore deceptive. After the purported change the ritual took place six days within the temple and one day at home.
[186]The account also resembles tEruv 3:6: "At first they would leave weapons in the house nearest the wall (after returning from a battle on the Sabbath). Once

suggestion that "the court" legislated this change appears to be a retrojection to temple times of the rabbinic decision-making body. As in other cases, the rabbis portray the court of sages as the ultimate authority over temple matters. On the other hand, tSheq 2:14 lists among the temple officials, "Ben Diphai over the lulav," apparently referring to this Mishna. Was he (or that priestly family) the overseer responsible for collecting the lulavs on Friday? If so, then the ritual may have taken place as described at the outset of the Mishna, while the later ordination of the court is ahistorical, either reflecting the practice in post temple times or the opinion of Pharisaic or other pietistic groups. To the extent that the traditions dealing with the libation and willow on the Sabbath can be trusted, we would expect the lulav ritual to have elicited similar concern.[187] It is plausible that different strategies were adopted to cope with Sabbath observance of the lulav. In any case, the tradition points to the importance of the ritual to the masses of worshippers. Priests performed the primary cultic ceremonies, but every worshipper could participate actively in the festivities by bearing the lulav. Hence the Mishna recalls the great significance each placed upon rejoicing with the lulav he had acquired.

Pre-rabbinic sources do not associate any specific ritual gesture with the lulav. In Maccabees and Josephus the people "bear" or "hold" the palms or branches.[188] In Jubilees Abraham "took" branches and "went" around the altar. Pseudo-Philo instructs to "take for me," following Lev 23:40, "and you shall take." The Gospels portray the crowd holding or taking palm branches in the quasi-Sukkot rituals.[189] Most rabbinic sources assume the ritual of the lulav is performed by "taking" the species in the hand or "shaking" them, as we shall presently discuss. But one tradition hints at a different interpretation of the ritual. That tradition echoes in the description of the "Men of Jerusalem" in tSuk 2:10. The precise identity of this group is unclear, but the associated circle of traditions relates primarily to temple times.[190]

[the enemies] returned, and they struggled to take their weapons, and killed each other. They ordained that each should return [his weapons] to his home."
[187]Cf. mBes 1:5: "The House of Shammai say: One may not carry the child or the lulav or the Torah scroll in a public place, and the House of Hillel permit it." This debate pertains to Festival Days, not the Sabbath.
[188]2 Macc 10:8: *exontes phoinikas*; *AJ* 3:246: *pheronta en tais xersin*; *AJ* 13:372: *exein ekaston thyrsous*. 1 Macc 13:51 reports that the people entered the temple with palm branches (*meta...baiōn.)*
[189]John 12:13: *elabon ta baia*; Rev 7:9: *kai phoinikes en tais xersin autōn*.
[190]The "Men of Jerusalem" are mentioned in mSuk 3:8, mKet 4:12, mMakh 1:6; tSuk 2:3, 2:10, tSot 7:15 (MS Erfurt); *Sifre Deut*. §218 (251); *Sifre Num*. §116 (130). The usages are not uniform. *Sifre Num*. uses the phrase to designate the inhabitants of Jerusalem during the time of the first temple. In *Sifre Deut*. Zeiri

[A] R. Elazar b. R. Sadoq said: This was the custom of the Men of Jerusalem.
[B] He entered the synagogue with the lulav in his hand.
[C] He stood to translate [the Torah into Aramaic] or to pass before the ark with the lulav in his hand.
[D] If he read from the Torah or performed the priestly benediction he set it on the ground.
[E] He left the synagogue with the lulav in his hand.
[F] He visited the sick and comforted mourners with the lulav in his hand.
[G] When he entered the House of Study he gave it to his son or his servant and returned it to his house.[191]

(tSuk 2:10)

Apparently the Men of Jerusalem believed that the proper way to fulfill the commandment of Lev 23:40 was to hold the lulav in one's hand throughout the day. One "took" the lulav by hand, carrying it all day long, holding it as one went about one's activities. The ritual was not expressed (only) through a specific gesture during worship, but applied throughout the day. This interpretation flows naturally from the verse itself, which simply commands to take the species "and rejoice before the Lord your God seven days." It seems that this understanding of the commandment was abandoned after the destruction. The tannaim do not even present the tradition of the Men of Jerusalem as a different interpretation of the ritual. The tradition does not appear in a dispute, and is probably transmitted solely because of its association with the previous statement in which R. Meir mentions another custom of the Men of Jerusalem (with which he indeed seeks to prove his side of a dispute.) bSuk 41b claims that R. Elazar b. R. Sadoq preserved the

---

relates three of their legal traditions to R. Yehuda b. Betera, who agrees with two of them. (Cf. *Midrash Tannaim*, 103.) In mKet 4:12 they are used in opposition to "the Men of the Galilee." In mMakh 1:6, and in the m-tSuk examples (including our case) later tannaim cite their customs. R. Yohanan quotes an assorted series of traditions in their name in bPes 113a. In m-tSuk their customs are transmitted by R. Elazar b. Sadoq and R. Meir, tannaim of the first and third generations.

[191]Lieberman, *TK*, 4:865-66, discusses the details of the passage and explains why the lulav had to be set down during certain actions. This daily routine has a somewhat legendary character in that it includes a sequence of quintessential acts of piety. ySuk 3:14, 54a adduces the baraita to explain the opinion of R. Yose in m3:14 that one who carries his lulav on the first day of the festival that coincided with the Sabbath is not liable, "since he took it out with permission." The talmud points out that the lulav was held at times other than its technical ritual use during the Hallel. Therefore one who forgets that it is the Sabbath and continues this supererogatory practice is not liable. There is good reason to trust the accuracy of this tradition, or at least some basic historical kernel. No tanna would invent a tradition that conflicted with standard rabbinic practice and had no real legal force.

tradition exclusively to demonstrate how enthusiastically the Men of Jerusalem fulfilled the commandments.[192] That is, he did not intend to transmit a legal position or competing tradition, but only to portray exemplary behavior. What Elazar originally intended is difficult to determine, but the talmud probably sensed the intention of the editor of the Tosefta accurately. There is no hint in our sources that any tanna believed one fulfilled the commandment to "take the lulav" in this way.

The accounts of Maccabees, Jubilees and the Gospels essentially agree with the practice of the Men of Jerusalem in describing the lulav held in the hand. The Tosefta implies the Men of Jerusalem held the lulav throughout the day, and the extra-rabbinic sources should be interpreted in this light. Festal joy was experienced both through the symbolic value and the extended connection felt by physically grasping the bouquet.

Apart from the account of the Men of Jerusalem all rabbinic sources assume the lulav is to be "taken" or "shaken" (נטל or נענע) at specific times. The earliest source, a debate between the House of Hillel and the House of Shammai, defines the points at which the lulav should be shaken during the recitation of the Hallel:

> [A] When did they shake it?
> [B] At *Praise the Lord*, at the beginning and the end [of Ps 118; = 118:1, 118:29].
> [C] Also at *O Lord deliver us (Ps 118:25a)*. These are the words of the House of Hillel.
> [D] The House of Shammai say: Also at *O Lord, let us prosper (Ps 118:25b)*.
> [E] R. Akiba said: I watched Rabban Gamaliel and R. Yehoshua. The entire people shook their lulavs, but they shook only at *O Lord, deliver us*.
>
> (mSuk 3:9)

This Mishna appears in the third chapter, not in the section of the tractate that pertains exclusively to temple matters, for the issue relates equally to the lulav ritual in post temple times. That the traditions are attributed to the Houses of Hillel and Shammai, and to Rabban Gamaliel and R. Yehoshua, who lived during temple times, suggests the Mishna describes the practice at the temple.

According to all opinions in the Mishna the lulav was shaken at some point or points during Ps 118. This Psalm, we noted above, is one

---

[192]מאי קמ'ל. להודיעך כמה היו זריזין במצוות; bSuk 41b. The same sugya contains the following: "Mar b. Maremar said to Rav Ashi, 'My father used to pray with it (the lulav).'" Rashi explains that the lulav was so dear to him that he held it in his hand during prayer. Perhaps this is a vestige of the custom of the Men of Jerusalem.

of the Hallel Psalms (Pss 113-118), which the framework Mishna (m4:1) prescribed for all eight days of the festival. No further information about the Hallel appears in chapters four and five. In the temple service the Hallel was recited on the eve of Pesaḥ (during the slaughter of the paschal lambs), the first and last day of Pesaḥ, Shavuot and the eight days of Sukkot.[193] While the Hallel features on all festivals, it was most closely associated with Sukkot; unlike Pesaḥ, it was recited each day of the festival.[194] mAr 2:3 reports that temple musicians played the flute as the Levites recited the Hallel.[195] Recall that the flute featured in the SBH, and represents a second link between the Hallel and Sukkot.

The account of the willow ritual reports that the assembly recited, "O [Lord] deliver us" (Ps 118:25) when they circumambulated the altar, the same verse the House of Hillel assign for the waving of the lulav. Above we noted that some amoraim asserted the circumambulations were performed with lulavs and the willows were erected beside the altar, while others claimed the circumambulations involved willows.[196] Perhaps the mass of worshippers held lulavs and waved them at the same time as the priests made their circuits with the willows. In this way the same verse became associated with the two rituals. The entire Hallel was probably recited as the willow procession made its way from Moṣa to the temple courtyards.[197] The ritual reached its climax when they arrived at the altar to the final verses of Ps 118, perhaps repeating 118:25 over and over.[198] The worshippers cried for deliverance – thinking of

---

[193]tSuk 3:2, mPes 5:7; see Büchler, *Tempelpsalmen*, 116-18. tSuk 3:2 also prescribes the Hallel for the eight days of Hanukka, but this probably relates to post-temple rabbinic liturgy. See, however, mTa 4:4 and Louis Finkelstein, "The Origin of the Hallel," *HUCA* 23,2 (1950-51), 321-22. In any case, the recitation on Hanukka would be a reflex of the Sukkot practice. mAr 2:3 notes that the flute was played twelve days a year before the altar (at the slaughtering of the Pesaḥ sacrifice and the Second Pesaḥ, on Pesaḥ, Shavuot and the eight days of Sukkot.) The flute accompanied the Hallel (Rashi, bAr 10a, s.v. *velo hayah*), so the Hallel was probably limited to these twelve days.
[194]See *PRK*, "Alternative Parsha" (458): "Thus you find that on all seven days of the Festival we read the Hallel, but on Pesaḥ we only read the Hallel on the first day and its eve." And see I. Abrahams, "The Hallel," *Festival Studies* (London, 1906), 159-66.
[195]See n. 193.
[196]Above, n. 19.
[197]Büchler, *Tempelpsalmen*, 131-35 claims only the last chapter (118) was recited on Sukkot, and the other chapters divided between the Pesaḥ sacrifice and meal. See too Amos Ḥakham, *Sefer tehilim* (Jerusalem: Rav Kook, 1984), 2:353, 372-377.
[198]Heinemann, *Prayer*, 148 believes the *Hoshaʿanot* piyyutim originally accompanied the willow ritual: "It is hard to believe that the worshippers in these processions would merely repeat the same line again and again, be it "We beseech Thee, O Lord, save now", or ^{a}nî w^{e}hô, save now!" (Mishnah Sukkah IV,

rain – and waved their lulavs. The tannaitic traditions suggest the waving was not exclusively limited to this phrase, but that some waved during other verses, or perhaps whenever the spirit moved them. Later sources refer to the lulav as an *hoshaʿana*, based on this phrase, *hoshiʿa na* (deliver us), at which point the waving took place.[199]

Rabbinic traditions describing the recitation of the Hallel shed some light on the custom at the temple:

> [A] [Rabbi Akiba expounded...]
> [B] How did they recite the Song?[200]
> [C] As a minor who leads the Hallel at school, and they answer each and every phrase after him.
> [D] Moses said, *I will sing to the Lord (Exod 15:1)*, and Israel said, *I will sing to the Lord.*
> [E] Moses said, *The Lord is my strength and my might (Exod 15:2)*, and Israel said, *The Lord is my strength and my might.*
> [F] R. Eliezer the son of R. Yose the Galilean said:
> [G] As an adult who leads the Hallel in the synagogue, and they answer the first phrase after him.
> [H] Moses said, *I will sing to the Lord (Exod 15:1)*, and Israel said, *I will sing to the Lord.*
> [I] Moses said, *The Lord is my strength and my might (Exod 15:2)*, and Israel said, *I will sing to the Lord.*
> [J] Moses said, *The Lord, the Warrior... (Exod 15:3)* and Israel said, *I will sing to the Lord."*[201]
>
> (tSot 6:2-3)

The Tosefta reports the custom of tannaitic times. When a minor led the Hallel each worshipper repeated the words verbatim, since a minor cannot fulfill an adult's obligation. When an adult led the Hallel the worshippers responded to each verse with the initial verse of the chapter. Both modes of recitation probably derive from temple times. In his masterful study of prayer, Joseph Heinemann demonstrates that stereotyped responses of this sort characterized temple liturgy. The simple, repetitive response allowed the entire assembly of worshippers to participate actively in the recitations without requiring a deep knowledge of the prayers. For this reason responsorial liturgies

---

5), but they probably did recite numerous short petitionary sentences, each of which would be followed by the above refrain, as became the medieval custom." See too Fox, *Succah*, 134-137.

[199]bSuk 37a, 37b. In bSuk 30b-31a *hoshaʿana* refers to the myrtle. Apparently the term applied to each of the four species as well.

[200]I.e., how did the Israelites recite the Song of the Sea (Exod 15:1-17)?

[201]tSot 6:2, according to MS Vienna. See Lieberman's apparatus and *TK*, 6:668 for variants. And see tPes 10:7; bSuk 38b.

accompany processions in many religions.[202] It is more likely the Hallel recited in the temple was conducted in the manner of an adult leading the Hallel in tannaitic times. The procession leader or Levitical singers sang each line of the Hallel Psalms, and the entourage repeated the refrain "Halleluyah" (Ps 113:1).[203] The first four verses of Ps 118 conclude with the formula "His steadfast love is eternal," undoubtedly a response of the followers. The brief phrase *hoshi'a na* (deliver us), the "Hosanna" of the Gospels, constitutes another such response.

VIII. Conclusions

Sources from the second temple period consistently portray Sukkot as a temple celebration of great significance. Descriptions of the Sukkot celebrations in rabbinic literature cohere with this picture. While second temple sources rarely describe the rituals in detail, and much of our sense of the festival derives from general associations, rabbinic traditions preserve detailed traditions. If extra-rabbinic sources depict the forest, rabbinic literature illustrates the trees. When extra-rabbinic sources do mention or hint at specific rituals, there is typically substantive overlap with those of rabbinic literature. The circumambulations of the altar in Jubilees parallel the circumambulations following the willow ritual. The lulav mentioned by Josephus and Jubilees, and alluded to in 2 Maccabees, appears in the temple celebrations narrated by the Mishna. The rain-making rituals that form the background of Zech 14 and John 7 come to the fore in the libation and SBH. Processions, as in 2 Maccabees and Plutarch, feature in the willow ritual and water libations. Both bodies of literature leave the distinct impression that a wide variety of rituals, some popular, others priestly, took place over the course of the festival, yet were not preserved in the sources. Jubilees's reference to the wearing of crowns and the Mishna's stray reference to a palm-beating ceremony point to a diversity of fertility rites. In general the two bodies of evidence are far more complementary than in tension.

Actually there is a curious paradox in assessing the nature of Sukkot in the second temple period. The earliest sources – Jubilees, Maccabees, Philo, the Qumran scrolls – provide scanty information. The later rabbinic traditions, on the other hand, furnish detailed descriptions of the ceremonies connected with the temple. Little would be known of the

---

[202] Heinemann, *Prayer*, 46 n. 12 provides references.
[203] Heinemann, *Prayer*, 145 suggests "Halleluyah" was the only response throughout the entire Hallel. Indeed, mSuk 3:10, which relates to the post-temple tannaitic ritual, prescribes: "If an adult read him [the Hallel], he answers 'Halleluyah' after him." Tosafot, bSuk 38b s.v. *mikan*, based on a statement of Rava, suggests that they responded with the first verse of each psalm.

diverse temple rituals were it nor for rabbinic traditions. We would probably not have concluded that Sukkot was the major festival in second temple times nor appreciated the connection to rain. Josephus's parenthetic remark that Sukkot "is considered especially sacred and important by the Hebrews" (*AJ* 8:100) would have been considered a curiosity. At best we would have concluded that Sukkot was the primary festival, but not known the reason. In light of the rabbinic evidence Josephus's comment is fully understandable.

This does not mean that the extra-rabbinic sources guarantee the historical accuracy of rabbinic traditions. There is no escape from the lack of explicit attestation of libations or SBH outside rabbinic literature. Rather, the rabbinic rituals conform to the expectations generated by other descriptions. They allow us to understand why extra-rabbinic sources designate Sukkot as "the festival," why Josephus informs that it is "considered especially sacred," and why Jubilees would expatiate so exuberantly about the joy of the festival. To what extent rabbinic traditions can be trusted historically becomes, to a certain extent, a subjective issue, a function of scholarly predispositions.[204] I have tried in each case to point out elements of the rabbinic descriptions that seem exaggerated, either distorted by the general rabbinic view of the past or historically suspect for other reasons. Those who adopt a skeptical view of the reliability of rabbinic literature will not draw firm historical conclusions about the actual details of temple celebrations. Those who have some faith that rabbinic traditions preserved information about temple protocol will reconstruct the celebrations along the lines of our discussion, accepting the general picture even if rejecting various details. Given the general agreement with extra-rabbinic sources, it seems that the rabbinic materials acquire a presumptive plausibility once the obvious historiographic tendencies are filtered out.

That rabbinic literature provides narratives of temple rituals is noteworthy in its own right. The rabbis reveal their conception of Sukkot as a temple festival characterized by elaborate cultic rituals. This point is strengthened if we take the traditions as prescriptive or programmatic rather than descriptive. The message is that the proper observance of Sukkot involves libations and other temple ceremonies. At all events, this conception reflects a continuity of religious ideas from earlier periods. Despite the destruction of the temple, there remains a conception of Sukkot as a temple festival in essence. At the same time, we should recall that Mishna Sukka contains three full chapters devoted to the sukka and the lulav. Traditions from temple times did not exhaust

---

[204] Assuming there has been careful text-criticism, judicious evaluation of the evidence and rigorous argument.

everything the rabbis had to say about the festival. What these contribute to the rabbinic conception of Sukkot will be analyzed in Chapters 5 and 6. But first we must assess the connection between Sukkot and rain as worked out in other rabbinic sources.

4

Sukkot and Rain in the Tannaitic Period

The vision of Zechariah reveals a widespread belief that the observance of Sukkot influenced the supply of rain. Most scholars assume this idea dated back to ancient times; rain festivals are found universally in agricultural societies and stem from the most essential religious urges.[1] Pseudo-Philo makes this conception explicit by interpreting the lulav as a sign for God to send rain. Water libations, circumambulations with willows and other rain-making rituals conducted at the temple indicate that rain was a central, if not the central, focus of the festival.

The destruction of the temple entailed the potential cessation of this orientation of Sukkot. Rain-making rituals, we noted in the previous chapter, rested on the mythic conception of the temple as the seat of fertility and the ability of the cult to stimulate the powers of nature. Apart from this general notion of the power of the temple, the individual Sukkot rituals depended on a mythic structure that no longer obtained. Water libations worked because they stimulated the subterranean waters of the Deep lurking directly beneath the altar. To pour water libations after the destruction of the temple would have been religiously unintelligible. The water could not reach the Deep nor set in motion the hydraulic processes that originated from the flow of the primordial waters. The destruction of the temple required a reconceptualization of the processes of rejuvenation of the natural world in ways that played

---

[1]Mowinckel, *Psalms*, 1:95, 147 n. 124, 164, 2:233; Oesterley, *Rituals*, 128, 137; Licht, *Sukkot*, 173; Snaith, *New Year*, 62-63; Knohl, *Priestly*, 94-98; E.O. James, *Myth and Ritual in the Ancient Near East* (London: Thames and Hudson, 1958), 66-67; A.R. Johnson, "The Rôle of the King in the Jerusalem Cultus," *The Labyrinth*, ed. S. Hooke (New York: Macmillan, 1935), 65.

down the role of the cult. No longer could temple rituals be seen as the crucial means to restore the earth's fertility. Fortunately mythic-cultic conceptions coexisted with other religious ideas in both biblical and rabbinic thought. The lack of any official or systematic theology here proved to be a great advantage, for the rabbis inherited a plethora of religious conceptions from which to draw. They possessed ample theological resources with which to construct a post-temple worldview. However, nothing guaranteed that the religious ideas that came to the fore would give Sukkot a function related to rain. Indeed, given the conspicuous absence of biblical testimony to this relationship, a new construction of Sukkot without such a component was a distinct possibility.

In this respect the destruction of the temple presented the opportunity for a deliberate reinterpretation of the festival. Some have suggested that the absence of biblical testimonies to the connection between Sukkot and rain reflects the uneasiness of the biblical authors toward mythic and magical ideas.[2] For example, the creation account of Gen 1 eliminates such myths as YHWH's struggle with other gods or the ancient sea-monsters (theomachy), the formation of the earth from the body of the defeated gods, the creation of the primordial temple and so forth. Fragments of these myths in other biblical passages reveal that they were widely known yet deliberately suppressed by the authors of Gen 1.[3] Likewise, festival legislation in the Pentateuch is largely purged of mythic conceptions. For this reason, evidence of the complex of myth and ritual expressed at the ancient Israelite festivals must be reconstructed from Psalms.[4] Even Zech 14, the one biblical passage that explicitly links observance of Sukkot and rain, involves clearer notions of divine judgment and reward than myth and cult. Just as biblical authors may have toned down the association between Sukkot and rain, the rabbis might have exploited the cessation of the cult to eliminate that dimension of the festival.

Rabbinic views on the connection between Sukkot and rain thus provide an excellent opportunity to evaluate the extent of continuity or discontinuity from second temple to rabbinic times. In this case we find strong evidence of continuity together with signs of subtle shifts in thought. Tannaitic sources express the link between Sukkot and rain in

---

[2] Licht, *Sukkot*, 174. Licht also proposes there was no need to mention the element of rain because it was obvious to all. On the general biblical aversion to myth, see Levenson, *Zion*, 120-22.
[3] Kaufman, *Toledot*, 1:419-422; Levenson, *Creation*, 1-99.
[4] Thus Mowinckel and other proponents of the enthronement festival depend ultimately on the form-critical analysis of Psalms for their primary evidence.

three ways: by notions of the divine judgment concerning rain, through interpretations of the festival rituals, and through the liturgy.

I. Sukkot, Rain and Divine Judgment

Conceptions of divine judgment and the calendrical position of the festival underlie the tannaitic view of Sukkot and rain. As in Zech 14, the operative factor is not the proper observance of the festival but divine judgment that takes place on the festival. God determines the amount of rain that will fall based on the behavior of the people, and that judgment is assigned to Sukkot on account of its calendrical position.

[A] At four times in the year the world is judged:
[1] at Pesaḥ, on grain;
[2] at Shavuot, on the fruits of the tree;
[3] On Rosh Hashana, all human beings pass before Him like a body of soldiers,[5] as it is written, *He who fashions the hearts of them all, who discerns all their doings* (Ps 33:15);
[4] and on the Festival [of Sukkot] they are judged on water.
(mRH 1:2)

[B] R. Akiba[6] said: The Torah said:
[1] Bring an *'omer* of barley on Pesaḥ, since it is the season of barley, in order that grain will be blessed for you.
[2] Bring wheat [and][7] first fruits on Shavuot, since it is the season of trees, in order that the fruits of the trees will be blessed for you.
[3] Bring the libation of water on Sukkot, [since it is the season for rain],[8] in order that the rainwaters will be blessed for you.
[4] Say before him verses of kingship (*malkhuyot*), verses of remembrance (*zichronot*) and verses of the shofar (*shofarot*)...
(tRH 1:12)

[A] Everything is judged on Rosh Hashana, and its sentence sealed on Yom Kippur. These are the words of R. Meir.
[B] R. Yehuda says:[9] Everything is judged on Rosh Hashana, and its sentence is sealed in its time. (1) On Pesaḥ, on grain. (2) On Shavuot, on the fruit of the tree. (3) On Sukkot, on water. (4) And the sentence of human beings is sealed on Yom Kippur.
(tRH 1:13)[10]

---

[5] See MS Kaufmann, MS Vienna of tRH 1:11 and *TK*, 5:1022.
[6] bRH 16a reads, "R. Yehuda said in the name of R. Akiba."
[7] So MS London. MS Vienna omits the "and." MS Erfurt has only "wheat." See *TK*, 5:1024.
[8] So MSS London, and Erfurt; MS Vienna omits. In the parallel at tSuk 3:18, MS Erfurt has the phrase; MSS Vienna and London omit. Alfasi to bRH 16a reads "because the Festival is the season of rains of the year." See *DQS* ad loc, n. א and see below, n. 21.
[9] MS Erfurt adds: "in the name of R. Akiba."
[10] Cf. bRH 16a; *Sifre Num.* §150 (196); *Sifre Deut.* §40 (81-82). yRH 2:3, 57a brings these and other opinions without attributions.

According to the Mishna, God renders judgment at four different times throughout the year. The Mishna itself provides little explanation as to why the respective judgments occur at these times. The reasoning appears in the two Toseftan passages, which point out that these festivals fall at the time of year appropriate for the item judged – "the season of" (barley, trees, etc.), in the words of R. Akiba (tRH 1:12), or "in its time," in the words of R. Yehuda (tRH 1:13B).[11] The judgment that determines the scope of the "grain" crop occurs at Pesaḥ, since spring is the season of the barley harvest, and Pesaḥ is the spring festival. God judges the amount of fruit on Shavuot, the time when fruits begin to ripen. Human beings pass before God on RH. Although judgment of their actions is not specifically mentioned, it is clear from the first line of the Mishna that they come before God for this purpose. The simile of troops standing for inspection before their general paints a graphic picture of judgment, and the verse from Psalms reinforces the image. Here there is no "organic" or natural connection to the time of year; unlike grain and fruit human beings do not ripen at any particular time.[12] In the theological calendar RH and YK are simply designated days of judgment of human behavior. On Sukkot God determines the amount of rain for the coming year. For the first time the calendrical justification is explicit: the rainy season occurs around the time of Sukkot, hence judgment for rain takes place at the festival.

mRH 1:2 does not define the nature of the judgment. Apparently "the world is judged" (ha 'olam nidon) means "all human beings of the world" are judged.[13] That is, God judges the behavior of human beings and rewards or punishes them by means of grain, fruit and rain, either gracing the earth with ample quantities or withholding these blessings.[14] This theology renders Sukkot and its rituals of secondary importance.

---

[11] The connection between first-fruits and Shavuot is weak. In his commentary to the Mishna, Bertinuro cites tRH 1:12, with which he wishes to prove that these are the appropriate times. But the Tosefta itself requires some explanation (see below). Rashi, bRH 16a, s.v. shtei and other rishonim explain that first-fruits cannot be brought before Shavuot (mBik 1:3). Therefore Shavuot begins the season for first-fruits, although most ripen later. And see TK, 5:1024, ll. 42-43.

[12] RaN (to Alfasi, bRH 16a) cites PRK 23:1 (333-334) (as do many other commentators), as well as other interesting and tortuous explanations to justify why RH should be the day of judgment. And see previous note.

[13] 'olam has this meaning in other mishnayot; see mSanh 4:5, mAvot 3:15.

[14] See Meiri to bRH 16a (155). According to Lieberman, TK, 5:1025, yRH 1:3, 57a interprets the Mishna that each person is judged as to his share in water, crops and fruit. But see Yafe 'einayim to mRH 16a and Allon, Filon, 456.

Divine judgment determines rainfall, not proper observance of the festival rites.

The explanation attributed to R. Akiba in t3:12 coheres with the unattributed Mishna as to the times of judgment. He introduces a new element in the equation: the rituals of the seasonal holidays. R. Akiba argues for substantive connections between ritual and reward. He offers a series of reasons for the commandments *(ta'amei hamiṣvot)* which addresses both the functions of the rituals and the seasons when they are performed. Festival rituals have the momentous theurgic effect of causing God to bless the rains and sources of food. They must be performed at the festivals because the seasonal festivals and concomitant judgments are linked with agricultural or natural phenomena. Thus the calendrical position of each festival is crucial. While R. Akiba speaks of blessing, not judgment, the theological outlook complements that of the Mishna. The water libation must be carried out on Sukkot since God determines the extent of the rainfall then, and the ritual serves to influence God in a favorable direction. To the Mishna's idea that God renders judgment of rain on Sukkot R. Akiba adds a ritual that influences the outcome.[15]

tRH 1:13 presents two views that conflict with the Mishna.[16] Both views distinguish judgment from sentence, a distinction foreign to the Mishna. According to R. Meir, RH is the exclusive time of judgment, and YK that of sentence. R. Yehuda agrees with R. Meir that judgments take place on RH, but claims that sentences are rendered at four separate times, essentially those listed in mRH 1:2 (except for YK.) The theological motivation underlying these opinions is clear. As noted above, crops, fruit and rain ultimately depend on the conduct of human beings, which is judged on RH and YK. How then can it be said that natural phenomena are judged at other times?[17] Due to this inexorable logic, R. Meir concentrates the judgments and sentences on RH and YK. R. Yehuda attempts to mediate between theological necessity and the idea that natural phenomena are judged in their appropriate season. While he wishes to preserve the connection between the festivals and the seasonal cycle of nature, he cannot ignore the rabbinic belief that RH is the time of

---

[15]The interpretation of the water libation will be discussed presently; here our interest is simply the general importance of Sukkot to rain.

[16]See bRH 16a. BT attributes the Mishna to the school of R. Ishmael (or Samuel, according to the version of R. Hananel.) And see yRH 1:3, 57a and *TK*, 5:1025.

[17]See RaN to Alfasi, bRH 16a: "Since a man is judged on RH, certainly he is judged with respect to all his circumstances. He is judged as to his crops and fruit and all his dealings. Since this is the case, all things are judged on RH." See too bBer 16a, and *Kitvei Ramban*, ed. C. Chavel (Jerusalem: Rav Kook, 1963), 1:223.

judgment. He compromises by divorcing judgment from sentence, placing the former on RH and the latter at the appropriate festival.

The Mishna's view would thus seem to reflect an older tradition. Zechariah already anticipates the Mishna's idea of connecting to Sukkot a judgment for rain. Based on a baraita, bRH 16a attributes the Mishna to the school of R. Ishmael,[18] and we have seen that it agrees with R. Akiba in tRH 1:3. The generation of R. Akiba and R. Ishmael[19] thus transmit traditions connecting divine judgments to each festival, whereas their students, R. Meir and R. Yehuda, assign the primary role to RH and YK. R. Akiba's position bears some affinity to the "priestly" or cultic worldview whereby rituals performed for specific ends automatically effect results. He avoids a purely mechanical notion of ritual by formulating the effect in terms of the object (crops, fruit, rain) being "blessed for you." No mechanical power over nature inheres in the ritual; rather God is moved to bless the rain, crops or fruit. His explanation combines cultic ideas with the notion of reward and punishment. R. Yehuda compromises between the old tradition that natural and agricultural phenomena are determined at their associated festivals and the developing theology of RH as the day of judgment. R. Meir abandons the older tradition in favor of the emergent theology.[20]

A second tension at work is the tension between post-temple and temple worldviews. Construed strictly, the position of R. Akiba implies that rain and crops can no longer be blessed since water libations, first-fruit offerings and the ʿomer ceased with the destruction of the temple. For this reason other tannaim may have avoided any overt link to the cultic rituals prescribed for the festivals. R. Yehuda retains a connection

---

[18]R. Ishmael's opinion is identical to the Mishna, except that human beings are judged on RH and sentenced on YK. This tradition appears in a baraita, bRH 16a.
[19]Assuming the school of R. Ishmael transmits his opinions.
[20]It is possible, however, that the two traditions simply express two different perspectives and should not be charted diachronically. Jubilees actually polemicizes against the idea that the determination of rain takes place on RH, a belief in line with R. Meir (Jub 12:16-18). yRH 1:3, 57a brings four unattributed opinions concerning the times of judgment and sentence: 1) All are judged and sentenced on RH; 2) All are judged on RH and sentenced on YK [= R. Meir]; 3) All are judged on RH and sentenced in their time [= R. Yehuda]; 4) All are judged in their time and sentenced in their time. The lack of attestation perhaps indicates that all four opinions coexisted. These two basic outlooks essentially reflect "prophetic" and "priestly" perspectives to varying degrees. The prophetic – that God rewards and punishes on the basis of individual merits and sins: the priestly – that the temple and its rituals ensure the right order of the cosmos and bring blessings to the world. (I use these terms as convenient designations; the relationship between the prophets and the cult is far more complex.) The tension between these two perspectives can be sensed in all four opinions.

to the festivals based on the their calendrical position, while R. Meir eliminates even that connection.

In sum, the unattributed Mishna, R. Akiba, R. Yehuda and the school of R. Ishmael associate Sukkot with rain. The association principally derives from the calendrical position of Sukkot as the festival closest to the rainy season. Divine judgment forms the substance of the connection. Because rain and all divine blessings are granted by God, the determination of the amount of rain is rendered through judgment. Only in the opinion of R. Akiba does a more immediate connection between the rituals of Sukkot and the rain supply appear. Yet even R. Akiba accepts the divine judgment or blessing as the determinative factor; the ritual is primarily symbolic, a means to ensure divine favor. All human beings can do is to try to influence God through the performance of the appropriate rituals. Despite the mythic-cultic legacy of the festival, theology becomes paramount in the rabbinic period. Rain results when God judges his people favorably, not from any automatic, magical ritual, nor from any rejuvenation of creation by the cult. The rabbis thus maintain the conception of Sukkot as the festival that influences the upcoming supply of rain but express that connection in terms of standard rabbinic theology, not through a mythic-cultic worldview.

II. Rabbinic Interpretations of the Festival Rituals

A second link between Sukkot and rain explicit in tannaitic sources stems from interpretations of the water libation and lulav. We noted in tRH 1:12 R. Akiba explained that the Torah prescribes a water libation on Sukkot in order that the rainwaters be blessed. A parallel tradition appears in tSuk 3:18 together with a prooftext:

> R. Akiba said: The Torah said...bring a water libation on Sukkot [since it is the season for rains][21] in order that the rainwaters may be blessed for you. And the Torah states, *Any of the earth's communities that does not make the pilgrimage to Jerusalem to bow low to the king, Lord of Hosts, shall receive no rain. However if the community of Egypt does not make the pilgrimage it*[22] *shall not be upon them* (Zech 14:18).

R. Akiba cites Zech 14 to prove his view that rainfall depends upon the proper celebration of Sukkot. Although the prophecy ostensibly makes no reference to the water libation, R. Akiba appears to have "read in" the ritual. He understands that the punishment of the nations results from

---

[21] The words "since it is the season for rains" are found in MS Erfurt of tSuk 3:18, and MSS London and Erfurt of tRH 1:12. They are omitted in MS Vienna of both tSuk and tRH. See *TK*, 4:885.

[22] In this context, their "rain" shall not be upon them, meaning the water supply of Egypt, the Nile, will be reduced commensurately. See Chapter 2, II n. 36.

their having neglected to make the pilgrimage and perform, or at least bow while the priest performs, the water libation.[23] The punishment is the lack of rain, hence the verse demonstrates the water libation ensures the rain supply. What is important here is not whether R. Akiba provides the "correct" interpretation of the water libation, but rather its appearance in tannaitic sources. For R. Akiba, the importance of Sukkot and its rituals inhered in their influence on rain.

According to R. Eliezer the lulav served to entreat God for rain:

> R. Eliezer said to him: These four species only come to obtain the favor [of God] about water. Just as it is impossible for these four species [to subsist] without rain, so it is impossible for the world [to subsist] without water.[24]

This source occurs in the context of a debate over the liturgical "mention" of rain and will be discussed in depth below. R. Eliezer explains that the species of the lulav, dependent upon rain for their ability to grow, petition God to supply the necessary precipitation. This explanation essentially coincides with the standard anthropological interpretation of the rite. R. Eliezer would probably not have used the term "rain charm" favored in some anthropological discussions. He offers a more rational theological explanation – that the ritual demonstrates nature's profound need for rain such that God should notice and respond. The PT version of his statement places more emphasis on the symbolic value than on the petitionary function: "Because these four species grow from water, therefore they come [in connection with] matters of water."[25] Indeed, palm trees mark oases in the desert and grow around sources of water in arid lands.[26] Willows cluster around rivers, marshes and fresh-water springs.[27] The Bible often associates the verdant growth of myrtles with rain, as in Isa 41:17-19: "I will open up streams on the bare hills and fountains amid the valleys; I will turn desert into ponds, the arid land into springs of water; I will plant cedars in the wilderness, acacias and myrtles and oleaster."[28] And the rabbis believed that the citron grew exclusively beside sources of water.[29] This interpretation is almost identical to that of Pseudo-Philo, and is undoubtedly of considerable antiquity. While the water libation

---

[23]See *Hidushei HaRashbaṣ* to bRH 16a, cited in Lieberman, *TK*, 4:885.
[24]bTa 2b. See p. 173 for the full context and parallels.
[25]yTa 1:1, 63c.
[26]Thus Zohary, *Plants*, 60: "The date palm is primarily a tree of the desert oases...wild date palms are widely dispersed near brackish rivers and springs."
[27]Ibid., 131.
[28]So too the promise of rain entails the blooming of myrtles in Isa 55:10-13.
[29]bSuk 35a; ySuk 3:5, 53d; *VR* 30:8 (707).

Sukkot and Rain in the Tannaitic Period

ceased with the destruction of the temple, the lulav continued to be practiced. R. Eliezer's explanation reveals not only the tannaitic understanding of the temple festival celebrations, but also the interpretation of the festival and rituals as practiced in their time. The tannaim believed that when they shook the lulav they entreated, and perhaps influenced, God to bless the earth with rain.

III. Rain and the Liturgy

Tannaitic liturgy also expressed the close association between Sukkot and rain:

[A] From when does one mention the 'powers of rain'?[30]
[B] R. Eliezer says: from the first Festival-Day of Sukkot.
[C] R. Joshua says: from the last Festival-Day.
[D] R. Joshua said to him: since rain is not the sign of a blessing on the Festival,[31] why should they make mention of it?
[E] R. Eliezer answered: He only says, 'Who makes the wind blow and the rain descend' in its due season.[32]
[F] He said to him: If so one should always make "mention."

(mTa 1:1)[33]

Both R. Eliezer and R. Joshua agree that beginning at some point during Sukkot the *tefila* (the "Eighteen Blessings,") the central prayer of the tannaitic liturgy, must include a reference to God as the provider of rain. Henceforth the *tefila* was to include the phrase "Who makes the wind blow and the rain descend." The debate centers on that starting point. R. Eliezer rules the phrase must be included starting with the first day of the festival. He argues that the additional line does not amount to a prayer for rain, but only a confession of God's power over rain.[34] One

---

[30]I.e., when does one add the phrase, "Who makes the wind blow and the rain descend" to the second paragraph of the *tefila*, the "Eighteen Blessing?" Cf. mBer 5:2.
[31]So all manuscripts and early printings. See Diamond, *Ta'anit*, 93-99 and Rosenthal, *Ta'anit*, 261 n. 1 for full apparatus. Printed versions of the Mishna have "since rain is only the sign of a curse." See *DQS* ad loc., n. ד. The "curse" is explained in mSuk 2:9.
[32]אף הוא אינו אומר אלא משיב הרוח ומוריד הגשם בעונתו. So most MSS. According to Diamond, *Ta'anit*, 100-103 and Rosenthal, *Ta'anit*, 265, n. 9, this is the best text. Contra Albeck, *Mishna*, 2:331 and Epstein, *MLH*, 715. See too Malter, *Ta'anit*, 1 and Heinemann, *Tefila*, 81, n. 12.
[33]I have only listed the most important variants. For complete apparatus see Diamond, *Ta'anit*, 88-111. I doubt whether the actual dialogue should be attributed to R. Eliezer and R. Joshua. See below p. 174.
[34]Or later tannaim attributed this reasoning to him. The baraitot cited below imply that the original rulings of R. Joshua and R. Eliezer were transmitted in several formulations.

does not ask for rain by reciting this line, but only mentions God's mastery of rain at the beginning of the appropriate season. R. Joshua rules the phrase should be added on the last Festival-Day (i.e., on *Shmini 'aṣeret*). He argues that mentioning God as provider of rain constitutes a prayer. But rain interferes with the actual celebration of Sukkot when people are residing in booths; to pray for rain during Sukkot invites disaster. Only on SA, when people no longer dwell in booths, are prayers for rain appropriate. He rejects R. Eliezer's claim that the phrase contains only a mention of rain, not an actual prayer. If the phrase but acknowledges God's mastery over rain, then the phrase should be included throughout the year.

This final objection is left unanswered; the Mishna stops short of providing a complete justification of R. Eliezer's position. R. Eliezer concedes to R. Joshua that rain is not desirable on Sukkot, but only in its "due season," after the festival. So why indeed begin to mention the "power of rain" specifically on Sukkot? His opinion, however, is easily understood even without the explicit justification found in baraitot and the talmud.[35] Rain is the central focus of the festival. As mRH 1:2 affirms, God determines the rainfall on Sukkot.[36] It is most appropriate, then, that from the outset of the festival the liturgy reflect this major concern.[37]

A different version of the disagreement between R. Eliezer and R. Joshua appears in a baraita found in both bTa 2b and yTa 1:1, 63a.

---

[35]See below, and see yTa 1:1, 63a.

[36]Cf. bTa 2a where this Mishna is considered a "continuation" of mRH 1:2.

[37]Gilat, *Eliezer*, 312 refers to *MG* 3:657 to Lev 23:35: *"The first day' (Lev 23:35).* But is it not the fifteenth day? Yet you say *the first day*. R. Eliezer said: The first day for rainfall. This teaches that it is fit [to pray] for rain from the beginning of the festival just as we stop from the beginning of Pesaḥ. But out of respect for Israel, so as not to cause them inconvenience by it raining in the temple during the festival [of Sukkot], and also because it would prevent dwelling in the sukka, therefore we do not mention rain until the end of the festival." The conclusion contradicts R. Eliezer's opinion in the Mishna, that one mentions rain on the first festival day. Thus it is likely that R. Eliezer's statement here consists only of "The first day for rainfall," and the rest of the midrash reflects a different opinion. The attribution to R. Eliezer is suspect given that the source is so late, but it provides a plausible exegetical basis for his opinion. Gilat also refers to fragments of an unknown midrash published by L. Ginzberg, "Three Incomplete Homilies from an Unknown Midrash," *Tarbiz* 4 (1933), 328 (Hebrew). The version of the "unknown midrash" is difficult, but seems to confirm that R. Eliezer only stated the first sentence.

Sukkot and Rain in the Tannaitic Period

bTa 2b[38]

[A] It was taught: From when does one mention the 'powers of rain'?
[B] R. Eliezer says: From the time the lulav is taken.
[C] R. Joshua says: From the time it is put away.
[D] R. Eliezer said to him: These four species only come to obtain the favor [of God] about water. Just as it is impossible for these four species [to subsist] without rain, so it is impossible for the world [to subsist] without water.
[E] R. Joshua said to him: Is not rain during the festival only a sign of a curse?
[F] R. Eliezer said: I did not say ' to ask' [for rain] but 'to mention'.[40]...[41]
[G] R. Akiba says: On the sixth day of the festival he 'mentions'.
[H] R. Yehuda ben Betera says: On the second day of the festival he 'mentions'.[42]
[I] R. Yehuda [says] in the name of R. Joshua: The one who passes before the ark on the last day of the festival – the second [to pass before the ark, to lead the musaf service] mentions, the first [to pass before the ark, to lead the morning service] does not mention. On the first festival day of Pesaḥ, the first mentions, the second does not mention.

yTa 1:1, 63c[39]

[A] It was taught:

[B] R. Eliezer says: From the time when the lulav is taken.
[C] R. Joshua says: From the time he sets it down.
[D] What is the reason of R. Eliezer: Because these four species grow from water, therefore they come [in connection with] matters of water.[43]

---

[38]See Diamond, Ta'anit, 256-66 for variants.
[39]These two paragraphs occur at different points in PT. I have lined them up in parallel with the BT material.
[40]The commentaries debate whether R. Eliezer means one must mention, or only that one may mention. See Rashi, bTa 2b, s.v. kakh; Tosafot, bTa 2a, s.v. 'im. The sense of the passage, as well as the Mishna, suggest that we should follow the Tosafot and understand that the mention is obligatory on the first day.
[41]The next section of the baraita is interpreted by the stam and all rishonim as a continuation of the dialogue. But see Halivni, Meqorot, 4:428-29 who argues that

Although the first section of the baraita [A-C] does not appear in tannaitic documents, the fact that it appears in both talmuds strongly suggests that it is an authentic tannaitic tradition. In this section the definitions provided by R. Eliezer and R. Joshua for the time to begin mentioning the 'power of rain' differ from those in the Mishna. Here they define the starting point in relation to the lulav.[44] The explanation that R. Eliezer provides for linking the 'mention' of rain to the lulav [D] seems to be authentic as well. It appears in both talmuds with but minor changes in the wording. The main difference is that the explanation appears as a self-contained baraita in PT while in BT that baraita has been incorporated into a longer baraita. This is not an uncommon phenomenon, and only suggests that originally the two BT baraitot were independent, not that they are pseudepigraphic.[45] The baraita supplies R. Eliezer's reasoning which the Mishna omitted. R. Eliezer rules that "mention" begin on the first day of the festival, when the lulav is taken,

---

it is an independent debate, unrelated to R. Eliezer and R. Joshua. And see Rosenthal, *Ta'anit*, 267 and n. 28. For a different opinion, see Diamond, *Ta'anit*, 319.

[42]On the authenticity of these baraitot, see Diamond, *Ta'anit*, 319-22, 335.

[43]This explanation appears as the first statement in the talmud, which suggests it comments on the Mishna directly. But the Mishna makes no mention of the lulav. It must be understood in connection with the disagreement in the baraita [I], which occurs a few lines below.

[44]The two definitions of R. Eliezer are equivalent, for 'the time of taking up the lulav' is 'the first Festival-Day.' It is not clear whether the time of 'setting down the lulav,' R. Joshua's definition in the Mishna, is equivalent to the 'last Festival-Day,' R. Joshua's definition in the baraita. Generally the lulav is not needed after the morning of the seventh day, and is 'put away' then. By this interpretation the 'mention' should begin immediately thereafter, still on the seventh day. (So Rabenu Gershom [printed as Rashi to the first three pages in bTa; see Halivni, *Meqorot*, 4:428, n. 2], bTa 2b, s.v. *misha'at* and 3a s.v. *'ela*). But technically the entire day is fit for taking the lulav, so the time of "setting down" the lulav may designate the time after the seventh day, at the evening prayer of the eighth day. In this case R. Joshua's definitions in the Mishna and baraita would coincide. (So Rav Mani in yTa 1:1, 63a; Rashi, bTa 4a s.v. *rabbi*; Tosafot, bTa 2b, s.v. *misha'at*.) See too Rosenthal, *Ta'anit*, 268-69 n. 32.

[45]Or, alternatively, it is possible that the BT preserves the original form of the baraita. The long baraita was broken into sections, as is wont to happen, and the PT transmits but one section. Even if the second baraita cannot be attributed to R. Eliezer, the first baraita, in which he defines the time for "mention" in relation to the taking of the lulav remains. While it is possible that this formulation simply serves as a convenient shorthand for "the morning of the first day," I think it unlikely. The definition suggests that R. Eliezer indeed connected the lulav to rain in a substantive way. He refers to the lulav not merely as a designation of the time, but because he understood the lulav to be connected to rain. See too Diamond, *Ta'anit*, 307.

because the lulav itself entreats for rain. It is appropriate that the liturgy acknowledge rain at this time.

The third section of the baraita [G-H] presents two further opinions of the starting point of the liturgical addition. R. Akiba places it on the sixth day, R. Yehuda b. Betera on the second. The BT connects these seemingly arbitrary opinions to the tannaitic midrashim concerning the Pentateuchal source of the water libation. These halakhic midrashim build on irregularities in the otherwise identical formulation of the sacrificial instructions for the days of Sukkot (Num 29:12-28), by which the second and sixth days are distinguished.[46] Eliezer Diamond argues that these are the authentic tannaitic midrashim grounding their opinions.[47] He suggests that R. Akiba and R. Yehuda ben Betera derived the starting point for "mention" of rain from the day of Sukkot on which the Torah "mentioned" the water libation. They connected the liturgical reference to rain to the libation, the temple ritual directed to this end – although they linked the liturgy not to the day of its performance but to the Pentateuchal source. R. Eliezer had understood the lulav to entreat for rain, and linked the liturgical mention of rain to the first performance of the ritual. R. Akiba and Ben Betera interpreted the water-libation as a rain ritual, and connected the liturgical mention to the scriptural source of the rite.[48]

---

[46]*Sifre Num.* §150 (196): "R. Yehuda b. Betera says: It is written on the second [day of Sukkot], *and their libations (Num 29:19; WNSKYHM)*, and on the sixth day *and its libations (29:31; WNSKYH)*, and on the seventh day *according to their laws (29:35; KMŠPTM)*. Behold, [the three extra letters], M, Y, M – here is *mayim*, water. From this there is a hint of the water libation from the Torah. R. Akiba says: On the sixth day of the festival he 'mentions'. For it says [in the sacrificial instructions] on the sixth day, *and its libations (29:31)*. The verse speaks of two libations. One is the water libation and one is the wine libation."

[47]Diamond, *Ta'anit*, 319-24. It is interesting to note that *TN* to Num 29:31, which lists the sacrifices for the sixth day, adds: "and a flask of water which is offered on the sixth day upon the altar as a good memorial of the fructification of the rain (its *minhah*) and its libations, and the libation of water." The text is somewhat confused, but clearly prescribes the water libation for the sixth day. This view appears to derive from R. Akiba's exegesis that "mention" of rain should begin on the sixth day. Perhaps the targum reasoned that since R. Akiba derived "mention" of rain from the "mention" of the libation on the sixth day, then the libation itself must have taken place on the sixth day alone. *TY* has a similar reading. See B.J. Bamberger, "Halakic Elements in the Neofiti Targum: A Preliminary Statement," *JQR* 65 (1975), 33.

[48]If the baraitot are later attempts to provide a justification for R. Akiba and R. Yehuda b. Betera, and even if their opinions that "mention" begins on the second or sixth day are pseudepigraphic, it does not vitiate, but only delay, this conclusion. Then it is not the tannaim who connect "mention" to the scriptural source of the water libation, but the amoraim or stammaim.

In the final portion of the baraita [I] R. Yehuda cites an alternative version of R. Joshua's statement, according to which the precentor of the additional service on the "last day" (= SA) initiates the addition.[49] In mTa 1:1 R. Joshua ruled the addition occurs on "the last day" without specifying whether the precentor of the morning or additional service made the addition. If the morning service is meant (as we assume when no specification is given), then we have two traditions concerning R. Joshua's opinion. All in all there are five formulations for the time when "mention" should begin: R. Eliezer, R. Joshua, R. Yehuda in the name of R. Joshua,[50] R. Akiba and R. Yehuda b. Betera.[51]

Different liturgical customs apparently were practiced in the tannaitic period.[52] Perhaps R. Eliezer, known for his allegiance to older traditions, transmits the older custom. If so, we again detect a conflict between a hard "liturgical logic" and a temple-centered tradition.[53] Logically, petition or even acknowledgment of rain should follow the festival, upon which rain is an annoyance at best and an indication of divine displeasure at worst. But during temple times the whole festival of Sukkot, and especially the libation performed each day, was associated with the rainfall of the upcoming season. R. Eliezer's opinion reflects this legacy and begins "mention" of God as master of rain on the first day of Sukkot. R. Akiba and R. Yehuda b. Betera represent intermediate positions. R. Joshua, in view of the fact that rain was not actually desired on the festival, defers mention to the last festival day. Here he almost severs the connection between Sukkot and rain, for SA is technically a separate festival.

Even R. Joshua's opinion precedes the times the tannaim actually expected rain. tTa 1:3 brings three opinions as to when the first rain should fall – the third, seventh or seventeenth of Heshvan. Reflecting these opinions, mTa 1:3 rules that the "request" for rain proper *(she'eilat geshamim)*, added to the ninth blessing of the *tefila*, enters the liturgy on

---

[49]mTa 1:2 attributes this opinion to R. Yehuda (without mention of R. Joshua) according to most variants. See Diamond, *Ta'anit*, 110-11. Some Palestinian amoraim apparently read R. Yehuda in the name of Ben Betera. See Malter, *Ta'anit*, 2-3; Halivni, *Meqorot*, 4:437-38; Epstein, *MLH*, 251, 825 n. 1, 1183; Albeck, *Mishna*, 2:492.
[50]So R. Yehuda in mTa 1:2. See n. 49.
[51]The five formulations may translate into but three different times, depending on the interpretation of [A]; see n. 44. R. Nahman b. Isaac, bTa 3a, determines that the R. Joshua here is R. Joshua b. Betera.
[52]See Gilat, *Eliezer*, 312; Heinemann, *Tefila*, 81.
[53]So Gilat, *Eliezer*, 311-12.

the third or seventh.[54] The reason given is that "they 'request' rain only near the time for rain."[55] Thus the tannaim did not expect or pray for rain until this time.[56] Why then add "mention" of God as master of rain at any point close to Sukkot? Why not wait until rain was actually

---

[54] See, however, mBM 8:6 which seems to define Sukkot itself as the beginning of the rainy season (in the context of leases). tToh 7:8 claims the rainy season begins whenever the "second rain" falls.

[55] mTa 1:2. This mishna speaks of "requesting rain," *sho'alim 'et hageshamim*. bTa 4b gives two interpretations of this term. The first explains that the clause refers to the ninth blessing of the *tefila*. A second interpretation suggests the clause also pertains to the "mention" of the rains. This unattributed Mishna would therefore rule like R. Joshua in mTa 1:1. But in mTa 1:3 "requesting rain" clearly pertains to the ninth blessing, and that is undoubtedly the meaning here too, the second interpretation notwithstanding. We must therefore explain either that the clause has simply been misplaced, and belongs after mTa 1:2 and before mTa 1:3 (Malter, *Ta'anit*, 3, n. 4 and 40-41, n. 48), or that the clause points out that although R. Eliezer and R. Joshua disagree about "mention," they agree that one only asks for rain later (Heinemann, *Tefila*, 82, n. 17; Albeck, *Mishna*, 2:331). See too Halivni, *Meqorot*, 4:435 n. 7. Rosenthal's reconstruction is too hypothetical; *Ta'anit*, 265-70.

[56] I am reading the Mishna as do the Babylonian amoraim. Heinemann, *Tefila*, 79-85 claims that the Palestinian amoraim interpreted mTa 1:1-3 such that "mention" and "request" for rain entered and left the liturgy at the same time. When the Mishna refers to one or the other, it means both. Only R. Eliezer distinguishes the two, beginning the "mention" on the festival itself. So the Palestinian amoraim rule that one begins to "mention" and "request" rain simultaneously. Heinemann follows R. Tanhum bar Hiyya, yTa 1:2, 64a, and assigns mTa 1:3 to temple times in order to avoid a contradiction with the opinions in mTa 1:1: in temple times the request for rain was delayed in deference to pilgrims so they could return home without being rained upon. But rain was really expected and/or desired as soon as mention of rain was added to the liturgy. After the destruction, with pilgrims no longer an issue, they changed the practice and added the "request" at the same time as the "mention." (According to the Babylonian reading, mTa 1:3 deals with the "request" for rain and mTa 1:1 with "mention," so there is no contradiction). While Heinemann focuses on the way the amoraim read the Mishna, and does not propose to analyze its original meaning, he does suggest that "perhaps the Palestinian interpretation is superior and more satisfactory" (p. 83). I disagree with Heinemann for two reasons. First, it is difficult to accept that the two terms, *mazkirin* and *sho'alim*, are used interchangeably. These are technical terms and clearly pertain to different liturgical elements. Second, Heinemann follows R. Tanhum bar Hiyya, who assigns mTa 1:3 to temple times. Yet tannaitic sources themselves give no reason mTa 1:3 pertains exclusively to the pre-destruction practice. R. Tanhum's consideration is external, not internal. Indeed, mTa 1:1 would seem to be the earlier Mishna, since R. Joshua and R. Eliezer predate R. Gamaliel, and since R. Eliezer is known for his affinity to the old halakha. It is more plausible that the liturgy requested rain on or immediately after Sukkot in temple times, when the water libation was performed, than that the liturgy specifically avoided mention of rain in deference to pilgrims.

expected? Moreover the Babylonian communities delayed their "request" for rain (*she'eilat geshamim*) until sixty days after the equinox on account of the agricultural circumstances that prevailed there.[57] Because they wished to retain the connection between the festival and rain, they made no such adjustment with the "mention" of rain.[58] The fact that the date of the festival did not tally strictly with climatic conditions was of lesser importance.

This liturgical addition also reflects the transition from temple religion to rabbinic piety. The temple had been the focus of rain-oriented ceremonies, both through the Sukkot rituals and throughout the rest of the year. Hence the classic biblical rain ceremonies – even when they include prayer – are set in a cultic context. Samuel's prayer for rain at Gilgal (1 Sam 12:17-18), Elijah's performance on Mt Carmel (1 Kgs 18) and Zechariah's vision reflect a cult setting. Parallel to the temple ceremonies there may have been prayers for rain, either in the official priestly liturgy or later among proto-rabbinic or Pharisaic groups. That R. Eliezer connects "mention" of rain with the lulav and R. Akiba and R. Yehuda b. Betera connect it with the water libation reveals the nexus of prayer and cult. Even if the liturgical "mention" of rain developed after the destruction, this connection to Sukkot rituals represents a desire for continuity with temple practices.[59] Just as the festival temple ceremonies were directed towards rain, so the liturgical "mention" oriented the rabbinic celebration of the festival towards rain. With the destruction of the temple prayer became the main vehicle for petition, and was no longer ancillary to cultic ritual.

IV. Conclusions

In the tannaitic period Sukkot retained its significance as the critical time for ensuring the rain supply for the coming year.[60] Ironically, rabbinic traditions express the link between the festival and rain more

---

[57] Hananya, the nephew of R. Joshua transmits the tradition, bTa 10a. On Hananya, see Hyman, *Toledot*, 503. He was a tanna, and spent time in Babylonia, so the practice appears to have prevailed in Babylonia in tannaitic times.

[58] Cf. Heinemann, *Tefila*, 83.

[59] Thus the three rabbinic worship services correspond to the times of sacrifices (according to one explanation), bBer 26b. The same is true of the *ma'amadot*; see mTa 4:2-3. See too mRH 1:1-4.

[60] The importance of rain is repeatedly stressed in tannaitic literature. The series of fasts and mourning practices instituted if rain does not fall soon after Sukkot dramatizes this fact. See too bTa 7a, "The day of rain is more important than the day of resurrection;" bTa 7b, "The day of rain is as important as the day on which heaven and earth were related." And see bTa 2b, 6b, 8a; bBM 85a. The tannaim claimed that the prayer the high priest recited in the Holy of Holies included a prayer for rain, yYom 5:3, 42c.

clearly than does the Bible.[61] The temple was destroyed, water libations had ceased, and SBH no longer celebrated. Yet with the lulav and through prayer the tannaim sought to influence God to send abundant rain. The motif of divine judgment becomes a factor in the equation. This element, visible to some extent in Zech 14, recurs repeatedly in amoraic midrashim.[62] Sukkot is the appropriate time to propitiate God, but the mere performance of the rituals is no guarantee. Only if God judges the people favorably will rain descend.

Thus taken together, biblical and rabbinic literature manifest a remarkable continuity in the significance of the festival. In ancient Israel, throughout the second temple period, and even after the destruction of the temple, the connection of Sukkot to rain remained in force. The forms changed from libations and temple rites to prayers – although the lulav continued to be practiced. And to some extent the connection weakened as certain tannaim shifted the judgment of rain to RH and others deferred liturgical additions to SA. But despite these minor adjustments the overall conception of Sukkot as the time to ensure the rain supply for the coming year endured. This continuity reveals that the absence of the cult and the destruction of the temple did not undermine the mythic worldview of the temple as the source of blessing and the key to the hydraulic structure. Mythic conceptions lived on without their original ritual underpinnings and despite the loss of its sacred space.

---

[61]Indeed, rabbinic literature is indispensable for understanding the nature of the biblical autumnal festival. Biblical passages, ancient Near Eastern parallels and anthropological insights are wholly inadequate to demonstrate a relationship between Sukkot and rain. Only when these obscure hints are examined against the explicit testimony of rabbinic sources can they can be adduced with any measure of confidence. Were it not for rabbinic literature, this aspect of the festival would be completely lost. On the other hand, the biblical evidence, weak as it is, simultaneously confirms the rabbinic traditions of water libations and SBH. Viewed together with biblical material, the larger context of the ceremonies described in rabbinic texts can be seen and their existence confirmed.

[62]Rain and judgment are linked in biblical sources independent of Sukkot. Thus Deut 11:13-17, which comprises part of the *Shema*, a cornerstone of rabbinic liturgy, states: "If you obey the commandments that I enjoin upon you this day, loving the Lord your God and serving Him with all your heart and soul, I will grant the rain for your land in its season, the early rain and the late...Take care not to be lured away to serve other gods and bow to them. For the Lord's anger will flare up against you and he will shut up the skies so that there will be more rain, and the ground will yield no produce; and you will soon perish from the good land that the Lord is giving you."

5

The Tannaitic Period: Legal and Ritual Developments

I. The Endurance of the Lulav and the Sukka

The destruction of the second temple presented the tannaim with the question of how to celebrate Sukkot, a temple festival, without a temple. Sacrifices, libations, SBH and the willow procession were cultic rites that depended on the temple context. Tannaitic theology forbade offering sacrifices and performing the associated rituals except at the Jerusalem temple. Given the mythic-cultic background that grounded the temple rituals, this policy was all but inevitable. What, then, would become of Sukkot?

The first three chapters of Mishna Tractate Sukka provide a wealth of legislation concerning the sukka and the lulav. Rabbinic Judaism celebrated Sukkot with these two rituals together with the liturgy and worship of the Beit Midrash and synagogue. Why did these rituals survive?

Dwelling in sukkot was not inherently connected to the cult. Ritual use of the sukka probably originated from the shelters built in fields for protection against the elements, and some undoubtedly continued local celebrations even after centralization of the cult. Even if the custom originated from the temporary booths occupied by pilgrims while attending autumnal festivals at central sanctuaries, and even if during the second temple period the majority of people performed the ritual near the Jerusalem temple, the dwelling itself was not a cultic rite. The ritual involved no priest, no altar and no sacrifice. Moreover scripture explains the booths as a commemoration of the sukkot God provided for the Israelites during the exodus from Egypt, a symbolism that divorces the ritual from the temple context. To dwell in a sukka anywhere at all ritually commemorates the exodus. Therefore the destruction of the temple did not affect the ritual logic of the sukka. Dwelling in booths naturally became a cornerstone of the tannaitic Sukkot festival.

That the lulav would survive the destruction of the temple was less assured. Ritual, exegetical and historical considerations might have limited the practice to the temple. Unlike the sukka, the lulav ritual took place in the context of cultic worship. A fertility symbol and rain charm, the festal bouquet served a function similar to that of libations and the circumambulations of the altar, and was related to the power of the temple as the ultimate source of fertility. After the destruction the lulav might have shared the fate of these rituals, and for the same reason: the absence of the mythic-cultic structure rendered the rituals religiously unintelligible. Scriptural exegesis could have supported this conclusion easily. The scriptural source directs that the rejoicing take place "before the Lord" (Lev 23:40), a phrase that probably refers to the temple, or at least to local sanctuaries. We noted that Josephus reflects this understanding in his biblical paraphrase by detaching his account of the lulav from that of the sukka, deferring the lulav to future celebrations in Jerusalem.[1] Josephus interpreted the Bible to ordain the lulav specifically for festivities at the temple. Straightforward exegesis of the biblical text leads to the conclusion that the ritual not be practiced without a temple or cult center.

Historically, it seems likely that the lulav was practiced almost exclusively at the temple. The rejoicing with flora in 2 Macc 10:5-8 occurred at the temple and celebrated its purification. The Gospel scenes of worshippers bearing palms occur when Jesus approaches the temple.[2] The sole narrative passage in which Josephus mentions the lulav – the account of the pelting of Jannaeus – takes place at the temple.[3] Only the Jubilees reference is ambiguous. Abraham takes palm branches and fruit to circumambulate the altar. Yet all Israelites are commanded to take leafy boughs and willows. It is unclear what they do with the flora, although there seems to be no specific link to the temple.[4] Rabbinic traditions themselves testify to the temple as the primary context for the lulav:

> [A] At first the lulav was taken for seven days at the temple, and one day in the country.

---

[1] *AJ* 3:244-47. See Chapter 2, VIII.
[2] In John 12:13 the people emerge from Jerusalem to greet Jesus. In Mark 11:11 the people greet him near the Mount of Olives, as he approaches Jerusalem. They were presumably carrying their palms to the temple. Cf. Chapter 2, IX.
[3] *AJ* 13:372.
[4] See Chapter 2, III n. 52 and text thereto.

[B] After the temple was destroyed R. Yohanan b. Zakkai ordained that the lulav be taken in the country for seven days, in memory of the temple.

(mSuk 3: 12)[5]

The Mishna claims that during temple times the lulav was practiced for but one day in the "country" *(medina)*, the area beyond the temple. The single-day practice is difficult to reconcile with the biblical passage which commands a seven-day observance.[6] In all likelihood, this practice represents a secondary development: the lulav ritual of the temple gradually attained a measure of popularization and spread throughout the country to a limited extent. After the destruction the tannaim resolved to perform the ritual for seven days in all places. Yet they realized that the week-long practice depended on the temple rite, that they performed the ritual throughout the week not because the Torah commanded it, but as a memory of the temple practice.

Gedaliah Allon proposed that originally the lulav was limited to the temple.[7] He adduced the passages from Josephus and Maccabees as evidence, but based his claim primarily on the fact that Philo omits mention of the species in his rehearsal of the laws of Sukkot. Dwelling in sukkot is the only ritual Philo relates. Allon concluded that the lulav was hardly practiced outside of the temple at this time, so Philo had no need to mention it. According to Allon, during the "last days" of the temple they began to observe the lulav throughout the country as "a type of reminder of the temple," the very motivation given by the Mishna for the post-destruction practice. I think that Allon's thesis is essentially correct, although the *argumentum ex silentio* from Philo is inconclusive, and far less compelling than the Josephan evidence.[8] Except for the obscure

---

[5]Parallels in mRH 4:3; *Sifra 'Emor* 16:9 (102d).
[6]However, there is an exegetical linchpin for distinguishing the first day. Lev 23:40 reads "You shall take on *the first day* beautiful fruit...and you shall rejoice before the Lord seven days." To the sensitive scribal ear, the phrase "the first day" is superfluous (obviously if one rejoices for seven days he must take the species already on the first). According to the halakhic midrash related to the Mishna, "the first day" teaches that the ritual be performed everywhere on that day, while "seven days" refers to the temple practice. It seems most likely that the popularization of the practice engendered the exegesis, that the halakhic midrash was formulated to justify the practice (or to support the Mishna that prescribes the practice.) For other midrashim that address "the first day," see *Sifra 'Emor* 16:3 (102d); bSuk 43a; y3:13, 54a; *VR* 30:7 (704); *MG* 3:586 to Lev 23:40.
[7]Allon, *Filon*, 457-59. So Safrai, *'Aliya*, 190-91.
[8]Epstein, *Tannaim*, 349 claims that Philo omitted mention of the lulav because it resembled Bacchanalian rites. He points out that Jason of Cyrene, author of 2 Maccabees, knew about the lulav, so the diaspora was well aware of the custom. Albeck, *Mishna*, 2:254-55, n. 6 points out that Philo both omits mention of other

description of Jubilees, all sources set the lulav in the context of temple celebrations. The Mishna's view of the past basically concurs. The strong association between the lulav and the Hallel Psalms, the central component of the temple festival liturgy, bolsters this conclusion. I would add to Allon's reconstruction that we must take into account the fact that Sukkot was the main pilgrimage festival, and, at least during the last years of the temple, pilgrimages were almost universally attended.[9] Most celebrating took place at the temple simply because the population congregated there, especially those who took the festal obligations seriously.

It is even possible that the Mishna exaggerates the extent of the pre-destruction practice outside of the temple. The lulav may have been practiced exclusively at the temple and only spread to the "country" when the destruction made it impossible to perform the ritual at the temple. However, the gradual popularization of cultic piety characterizes movements at the end of the second temple period. The Pharisees, for example, adopted elements of priestly and temple practices to their private observance. Pharisees transferred purity laws from the temple cult to everyday life, eating their food only in the state of purity required of priests.[10] They sought to participate vicariously in temple worship through the ma'amadot, "courses" of Israelites parallel to the Priestly and Levitical divisions.[11] According to tannaitic sources the Israelite ma'amadot, like the priests serving in the temple, fasted and were forbidden to cut their hair or wash their clothes (mTa 2:7; 4:2.) Those unable to go to Jerusalem congregated in their localities to read the story of creation. One mishnaic tradition implies that the ma'amadot recited

---

extra-temple commandments and mentions certain commandments limited to the temple. Allon was aware of this objection and made an unsatisfactory attempt to answer it. In the last sentence of his article he notes that although Philo mentioned the sounding of the shofar on the New Year, he did so only because this was an "independent commandment" (מצווה לעצמה), unlike the lulav which was but one element of the Sukkot ritual.

[9]Philo, *Special Laws*, 1:69: "Countless multitudes from countless cities come, some over land, others over sea, from east and west and north and south at every feast." Josephus, *BJ* 2:515 relates that when Cestius arrived in Lydda (Lod) he "found the city deserted, for the whole population had gone up to Jerusalem for the festival of Sukkot." See also *BJ* 1:253; *AJ* 17:214; 17:254; 20:106. And see Safrai, *'Aliya*.

[10]Neusner, *Pharisees*, 3:288-300.

[11]mTa 4:2-3, tTa 2:2-3, mMeg 3:6. See Safrai, *'Aliya*, 217-20; Elbogen, *Hatefila*, 180; Schürer, *History*, 2:293; Albeck, *Mishna*, 2:495 and Malter, *Ta'anit*, 210, n. 230. mBik 3:2 assumes each ma'amad was coordinated with a specific geographical area.

Hallel,[12] so it is plausible that on Sukkot they took the lulav in imitation of the temple liturgy.[13] Tannaitic traditions concerning the *ma'amadot* may not be completely reliable,[14] but they are evidence enough to show that some Jews began to adopt and imitate elements of the temple worship. In this way, the Pharisees and other such groups probably started to take the lulav, at least for the first day, independent of the temple. For the bulk of the population, however, the lulav remained a temple ritual.

Given these historical, ritual and exegetical factors, how are we to explain the endurance of the lulav in tannaitic times? First, although the lulav took place in the temple, it had a much looser connection to the cult than libations or the willow ritual. Josephus portrays the lulav as an accouterment to the sacrifices, a prop held in the hand while priests perform the cultic rituals. Libations were poured on the altar, the willows carried around the altar and set about it, but the lulav had no such intrinsic connection to other cultic artifacts. The lulav functioned primarily through its symbolism. Fertility symbols could survive the destruction of the altar and temple where cultic rituals could not. [15] To pour a libation without an altar made no ritual sense, but to take a lulav continued to symbolize renewed fecundity. Only a slight reinterpretation of the ritual would be required as tannaitic conceptions of the process of rejuvenation shifted away from the mythic view of the temple.[16]

---

[12]mTa 4:4. The Mishna reads, "Every day on which Hallel is recited, there is no *ma'amad* at the morning service." (Here *ma'amad* refers not to the assembly but to the reading of scripture.) Commentators disagree as to whether the Mishna pertains exclusively to the Israelite assemblies at the temple in Jerusalem (Rashi, Bertinuro, Malter, *Ta'anit*, 400, n. 78) or even to those in the outlying areas (Ritba, Rashash.)

[13]Elbogen, *Hatefila*, 181 conjectures that the liturgy of the *ma'amadot* included Psalms, like those sung by Levites, and petitionary prayer. Cf. Heinemann, *Prayer*, 127, 129-131.

[14]There are no demonstrably early traditions concerning the *mishmerot* and *ma'amadot*, which raises the possibility that the tannaitic traditions embellished the historical truth. But the Qumran sect also knows of 26 *mishmerot* of priests, Levites and Israelites (1QM 2:2-4), so there seems to be some historical basis to the conception.

[15]To put this argument in other words: the overall rabbinic policy to discontinue sacrificial worship was decisive. Like all offerings brought directly to the altar, libations and the willow ritual were considered part of the sacrificial cult. The lulav, on the other hand, was not an offering of any sort. I am not claiming cultic rituals did not function symbolically as well, or that the symbolism of the lulav was unrelated to the cult.

[16]Theoretically, of course, the tannaim could have reinterpreted the libations in a way that no longer depended on the temple context and continued to practice the

Second, the lulav was closely linked with the Hallel, shaken at the recitation of various verses. Since the tannaim incorporated the Hallel into the rabbinic liturgy, the lulav may have entered tannaitic piety by virtue of this connection.[17]

Third and most importantly, the fact that the Torah explicitly prescribed the lulav gave the ritual special significance. No scriptural passage explicitly commanded the performance of libations, SBH, the willow and other such rites. While some tannaim eventually grounded these practices in exegeses of biblical verses,[18] and others may have considered them part of the "Oral Torah,"[19] the rituals would not make the same impression as an explicit commandment. Reflecting the lesser status, later amoraim consider the willow ritual a "custom of the prophets,"[20] and SBH an "additional" expression of joy.[21] But I focus here less on theoretical legal categorizations of the rituals than the direct impact of scriptural prescriptions. As we have seen, the tannaim interpreted the Torah to mandate the seven day observance of the lulav only in the temple, yet decided to adopt this practice throughout the country after the destruction. They did so, I believe, because they wished to fulfill as much as possible scriptural dictates of festival observance. The question whether the ritual would be considered a "rabbinic enactment" (derabanan) or more authoritative was secondary. That

---

rite after the destruction. But this would have required a much greater degree of reinterpretation than that required by the lulav.

[17] If worshippers held lulavs during the willow ritual when hoshaʿanot were recited, the liturgy again may have brought the lulav with it. Recitation of hoshaʿanot and circumambulations became part of rabbinic liturgy, although it is unclear how early this development can be dated. The dominant stream of medieval Jewish thought considered these circumambulations a "memory" of the temple, which reflects an awareness that proper performance of the ritual requires the cult. On this topic see J. Rubenstein, "Cultic Themes in Sukkot Piyyutim," PAAJR 49 (1993), 185-209.

[18] Libation: Sifre Num. §150 (196); bTa 2b (and parallels); yRH 1:3, 57b (and parallels). Note tSuk 3:18: "R. Akiba said, The Torah said...bring a water libation on Sukkot..." Willow: Sifra ʾEmor 16:6 (102d); bSuk 34a, 44a.

[19] bSuk 34a, 44a and parallels; ySuk 4:1, 54b (assuming the attributions are correct. Most traditions associating these rituals with the Oral Torah are attributed to amoraim, not tannaim.)

[20] bSuk 44a, which also contains the opinion that the willow "has a basis in the prophets" (yesod neviʾim), apparently a lesser degree of authority than "a custom of the prophets." This sugya recognizes the greater weight of an explicit scriptural source. On this basis R. Zevid in the name of Rava explains why the lulav is practiced seven days "in memory of the temple" whereas the willow is not, even for those who consider the willow Toraitic and hence of equal authority to the lulav. He observes that the lulav has a "root in the Torah" whereas the willow does not.

[21] simḥa yetera; bSuk 51a.

scripture explicitly prescribed the lulav influenced the tannaim to incorporate the ritual into emergent rabbinic Judaism.

Let us glance at a parallel case that exemplifies this phenomenon. The commandment to eat bitter herbs on Pesaḥ occurs in Exod 12:8 and Num 9:11. In both cases the context relates to the Pesaḥ sacrifice; "they shall eat it (the sacrifice) roasted over fire, with unleavened bread and bitter herbs" (Exod 12:8). Clearly the bitter herbs merely accompany the sacrificial meat. Scripture imposes no independent commandment to eat the herbs; if the Pesaḥ sacrifice is not carried out, the bitter herbs need not be consumed. This indeed was the conclusion of the amoraim.[22] Yet rabbinic piety transformed the bitter herbs into an essential component of the Pesaḥ *seder,* and formulated a blessing asserting that the eating fulfills a divine commandment. Again, to focus on this incongruity or the precise categorization on the obligation to eat the herbs as rabbinic or Toraitic misses the essential point. That scripture prescribed the herbs as a festival practice influenced the rabbis to preserve the ritual even after the destruction precluded the Pesaḥ offering. So too the scriptural designation of the lulav as a Sukkot ritual was largely responsible for its persistence in post-destruction times.

We thus see a gradual popularization of the lulav ritual, which was originally associated exclusively with temple celebrations. Pharisees and others who sought to incorporate temple practices into their own personal piety probably conducted a partial observance of the ritual even outside of the temple.[23] After the destruction, R. Yohanan b. Zakkai and his followers "ordained" that the lulav be taken on each of the seven days.[24] This cannot really be called a "democratization" of ritual, since

---

[22] Rava in bPes 120a; cf. Ramban to Exod 12:8.
[23] mSuk 4:4 offers a possible course of development. The Mishna claims that in temple times, when the first day of Sukkot occurred on the Sabbath, the people brought their lulavs to the temple beforehand (since they could not carry them to the temple on the Sabbath.) Due to the commotion and violence that resulted when each tried to find his own lulav, "they ordained" *(hitqinu)* that each person should take the lulav at his home. In this way the connection between the lulav and the temple weakened; a temple ritual was transferred to the home. However, it is hard to judge the historical accuracy of this source. The historicity of *taqqanot* in rabbinic sources has been challenged. Jaffee, *Taqqanah,* argues that the *taqqana* in the Mishna is a literary device which rarely reflects historical reality. But even if there was no formal *taqqana* – if the practice of taking the lulav at home developed because the particularly pious did not wish to carry their lulavs to the temple – the development may have occurred along these lines. The custom of the "Men of Jerusalem" to hold the lulav throughout the day also indicates the ritual began to take on an identity of its own: it was carried in the hand outside of the temple; see Chapter 3, VI, text to n. 190 and see below.
[24] Except for the Sabbath. See the previous note on the historical accuracy of the rabbinic *taqqana*. It is possible that taking the lulav for seven days was becoming

the lulav had not been performed exclusively by priests, but by all who took part in the temple celebrations. The process is part of the trend by which Judaism became more "portable" and less dependent on the temple, Jerusalem or the land of Israel. Sukkot henceforth would be celebrated in each local community, presumably in the synagogue or Beit Midrash, with the lulav and etrog.[25]

In this respect the approach of the tannaim parallels that of the restoration community depicted in Neh 8. Both the tannaim and the Nehemian assembly confronted the challenge of religious discontinuity by turning to scripture to learn how to observe Sukkot. Both groups responded with the popularization of a ritual that was previously limited to specific circumstances. The assembly put into practice the vision of the Holiness Code and made the sukka a ritual obligation upon Jews everywhere. The tannaim directed that the lulav be practiced everywhere for seven days, expanding the prior limitation to temple precincts. Again the program of the Holiness Code reached fruition in the widespread celebration of the festivals with popular agricultural rites. The period of Ezra, Nehemiah and "the scribes" is widely regarded as the precursor to rabbinic Judaism with its emphasis on scriptural authority and exegesis. The historical development of the Sukkot rituals supports this view and exemplifies the parallel dynamics at work.

In this way rabbinic Judaism experienced continuity and discontinuity with the Judaism of the second temple period. Continuity, because the same ritual objects were used and transferred to the system of rabbinic piety.[26] The destruction of the temple neither entailed a complete break with temple practice nor produced a total religious vacuum. Sacrifices were precluded but other elements of the cult could be incorporated into emerging rabbinic Judaism. It is significant that the lulav functioned as a means of "rejoicing," of expressing the cultic *simḥa* (joy) that found its primary fulfillment in the sacrificial meal. The

---

the standard practice in synagogue worship by force of popular custom, not a legislating authority. For example, a letter of Bar-Kochba requests the species for his army (Yadin, *Bar-Kochba*, 128-29). Whether Bar-Kochba was part of the rabbinic movement is debatable. His attempt to procure the species probably reflects the popularity of the ritual in the early second century CE. The *taqqana* of the Mishna could mean that R. Yohanan b. Zakkai and his colleagues accepted this practice happily.

[25]We need not overinterpret this edict to discover a hidden agenda of R. Yohanan b. Zakkai. He was neither seeking to replace the temple, nor to appropriate its status and authority. His goal was simply to continue a ritual practice that had been part of the religious life of the people.

[26]On different interpretations of the meaning of the Yavnean edicts, see J. Neusner, A *Life of Yohanan ben Zakkai, ca. 1-80 CE* (Leiden: Brill, 1970), 206-207, n. 3.

destruction did not preclude experience and expression of *simḥa*. Yet the discontinuity should not be minimized. Divorced from the temple context, the lulav's function and meaning inevitably changed. No longer linked to sacrifices and the expression of cultic joy, the ritual was reinterpreted and new understandings of its significance and symbolism developed.[27]

We turn now to the legal history of the sukka and lulav. What did rabbinic Judaism inherit from pre-destruction times? Which laws reflect rabbinic innovations? How did observance change within the tannaitic period itself? What do these changes reveal about the rabbis, their ideas and the meaning of Sukkot?

To assess rabbinic innovations it is necessary to determine the nature of the rituals prior to the rabbinic period. Much of this groundwork was covered in Chapter 2 where we examined the relevant sources from the second temple period. As with the temple rituals, rabbinic sources contain traditions about the laws of the lulav and the sukka that prevailed during temple times. These sources must be analyzed in conjunction with the second temple materials to attain as complete as possible an understanding of the legal development. Great methodological care needs to be taken, since the rabbinic sources are much later and reflect the rabbinic point of view. Nonetheless, they can inform our understanding of earlier times.

To chart historical development within the tannaitic period we must rely on the attributions of traditions to various sages. As Jacob Neusner has emphasized, attributions cannot be trusted absolutely.[28] In most cases there is no independent proof that a sage actually said what rabbinic sources attribute to him. Moreover, two rabbinic documents

---

[27]Much has been made of the "trauma" experienced by Jews following the destruction and the courageous "response" of the framers of the Mishna who insisted the connection between God and his people was unbroken; see B. Bokser, "Rabbinic Responses to Catastrophe: From Continuity to Discontinuity," *PAAJR* 50 (1983), 37-62; idem, *Origins*, 7-8, 89-93; Green, *Name*, 79 and Neusner, *Judaism*. The decision to take the lulav for seven days in conscious imitation of the temple practice reflects this courage and constitutes a powerful response to their theological crisis. However, S.J.D. Cohen, "Jacob Neusner, Mishnah, and Counter-Rabbinics: A Review Essay," *Conservative Judaism* 37 (1983), 57-58 questions the extent of this trauma. The tannaim may have been motivated less by trauma than by the attempt to base their observance on scripture and to preserve as much as possible from temple times without appearing to perpetuate the cult itself. The lulav had never been the exclusive prerogative of priests, so its continued practice arrogated no sacerdotal rite. When rabbinic worship replaced the temple liturgy, the tannaim resolved to take the lulav each day as had been done in the temple.
[28]See Chapter 3, I n. 1.

sometimes attribute the same tradition to different sages. Often a ruling is worded differently in two documents, making it difficult to determine the original statement. In his monumental study of the Mishna, Neusner partially overcomes these considerations by dividing all attributed rabbinic traditions into three historical periods. He collects traditions attributed to all sages who lived "before the wars," i.e., before 70 CE, "between the wars," from the destruction of the temple until the Bar-Kochba revolt of 132-135 CE, and "after the wars," from 135 CE onward.[29] Neusner demonstrates that the sages in each period focus on specific issues and legal questions, and that those of the later periods build on the conclusions reached in earlier generations. I have essentially adopted this approach, although I analyze traditions attributed to each tannaitic generation, as opposed to Neusner's three historical periods. I focus on the legal issues discussed, rather than the exact wording of the tannaitic statements, so the problem of *verbatim* transmission generally does not apply.[30] The results bear out the general validity of a division according to generation. Sages of a given generation direct their attention to a limited range of issues, and succeeding tannaitic generations build on the conclusions of their predecessors in an orderly progression.[31] While this argument is somewhat circular, any methodology involves some degree of circularity, because conclusions emerge from data analyzed according to certain assumptions. In this case I consider it unlikely that mere

---

[29] Neusner, *Judaism*, 18-22.

[30] Research on the reliability of material attributed to the amoraim has demonstrated that sayings were preserved with a great degree of accuracy, and we should expect the same of tannaitic traditions. See David Kraemer, "On the Reliability of Attributions in the Babylonian Talmud," *HUCA* 60 (1989), 175-90; Richard Kalmin, "Talmudic Portrayals of Relationships between Rabbis: Amoraic or Pseudepigraphic," *AJS Review* 17 (1992), 165-98; idem, "Collegial Interaction in the Babylonian Talmud," *JQR* 83 (1992), 384-415; idem, "Changing Amoraic Attitudes Toward the Authority and Statements of Rav and Shmuel: A Study of the Talmud as a Historical Source," *HUCA* 53 (1992), 83-106; idem, *The Redaction of the Babylonian Talmud: Amoraic or Saboraic?* (Cincinnati, Ohio: Hebrew Union College Press, 1989), 1-11, 43-57. Literary criticism of the Talmud demonstrates the amoraic portions are distinguished by form, language, terminology and other criteria. See David Goodblatt, "The Babylonian Talmud," *Aufstieg und Niedergang der römischen Welt* II, 19, 2 (Berlin and New York, 1979), 294-95; 300-301, 314-18 and references; David Kraemer, *Stylistic Characteristics of Amoraic Literature* (Dissertation, Jewish Theological Seminary, 1984); Richard Kalmin, "Quotation Forms in the Babylonian Talmud: Authentically Amoraic, or a Later Editorial Construct?," *HUCA* 49 (1988), 167-87.

[31] Cf. Neusner, *Judaism*, 17: "all units of thought in the Mishnah made intelligible statements, exhibiting a logic coherent with the document as a whole. Thus I could attempt to correlate what was said in a given name with the place, in the unfolding logic of the document, of what that named authority was made to say."

chance or deliberate retrojection is responsible for the coherent unfolding of law generation by generation.

II. The Four Species

Rabbinic sources exhibit a unanimous and undisputed tradition concerning the interpretation of Lev 23:40. All sources assume that the commandment consists of taking four species in the hand as a festival bouquet.[32] In all sources these species are identified as the citron *(etrog)*, palm branch *(lulav)*, myrtle and willow. While the Bible refers to branches of palms *(kapot temarim)* and to "willows of the brook" *('arvei naḥal)*,[33] the precise identification of the palm branches as the immature

---

[32] This must be noted since some have suggested Lev 23:40 does not unambiguously refer to a festal bouquet. According to Samaritan tradition, the Torah directs the species be used for building sukkot, not that they be carried in the hand. See S. Hanover, *Das Festgesetz der Samaritaner* (Berlin, 1904), 31, 50-51; S. Lowy, *The Principles of Samaritan Bible Exegesis* (Leiden: Brill, 1977), 310 n. 45. (The fruit should be hung for decorative purposes from the roof of the sukka.) Some scholars suggest Neh 8 reflects this interpretation and claim the ritual of a festal bouquet developed later. However, we noted that Neh 8 lends itself to other interpretations, and its silence does not prove the lulav was unknown. Most scholars explain the *sensus literalis* of Lev 23:40 as the taking of a festal bouquet and consider the rite of biblical provenance. See Chapter 2, I nn. 14 and 18. Rejoicing with festal wands is a primitive ritual that derives from the earliest stages of the festival.

[33] The willow identified by the rabbis was possibly not the same willow intended by the biblical author of Lev 23:40. Many scholars identify the biblical *'arava* as the Euphrates poplar (populus euphratica), not the willow (of the salix genus), and consider the *ṣafṣefa* of Ezek 17:5 as the willow. The rabbis were aware of the confusion, claiming that after the destruction of the temple the *'arava* and *ṣafṣefa* changed names: that which was once called *'arava* was then called *ṣafṣefa* and vice versa (bSuk 34a; bShab 36a). Other scholars believe *'arava* in the Bible refers to both the salix and the Euphrates poplar; see Zohary, *Plants*, 130-31. The baraitot of tSuk 2:7, bSuk 34a and ySuk 3:3, 53c prohibit the *ṣafṣefa* and certain types of *'arava*, but describe them in different ways. Another species of willow, the *ḥilpa gila* is permitted by Abaye (bSuk 34a). For an exhaustive (and exhausting) discussion on the identification of the *'arava* and *ṣafṣefa* see Y. Feliks, "Lezihui 'arava veṣafṣefa," *Hama'ayan* 10,3 (1969), 12-18 and the response by M. Kislev, "'Arava keshera, 'arava pesula veṣafṣefa," *Hama'ayan* 11, 1 (1970), 37-49. In sum: Feliks identifies the permitted *'arava* as any type of salix, the unfit *'arava* as the populus euphratica and the *ṣafṣefa* as the populus alba. Kislev suggests that in Babylonian sources the permitted *'arava* is the salix acmophylla and the *ṣafṣefa* is the salix alba. In Palestinian sources the permitted *'arava* is the same salix acmophylla, while the unfit *'arava* and *ṣafṣefa* are hybrid species of salix. Kislev identifies the *ḥilpa gila* as the populus euphratica; Feliks and Löw, *Flora*, 3:329 say it is salix alba. (Cf. Löw, *Flora*, 3:325-27; H.N. and A.L. Moldenke, *Plants of the Bible* [Waltham, Massachusetts: Chronica Botanica Co., 1952], 183 and I. Abrahams, *Festival Studies* [London, 1906], 119-23.) On the post-talmudic debate

palm fronds *(lulav)*[34] and the willows as particular species of willow reflects post-biblical interpretation. Of course the identifications of "the fruit of goodly trees" as the etrog, and the "boughs of leafy trees" as the myrtle are also rabbinic, a fact of which the rabbis were fully conscious.[35] Yet Mishna-Tosefta presupposes that the terms in Leviticus refer to these species. No dissenting opinion appears, nor is any prooftext adduced. *Sifra 'Emor* 16:4,6 (102d) provides halakhic midrashim proving that the scriptural references relate to the citron, myrtle and willow,[36] but the

---

among the medieval jurists see Löw, *Flora*, 3:323-32. Since the rabbis do not distinguish the *'arava* used in the circumambulations of the altar from that of the lulav cluster, and even link it to Lev 23:40 (bSuk 45b), the identification of that *'arava* is connected to this question. For botanical descriptions and pictures of these species see M. Zohary, *Flora Palestina* (Jerusalem: The Israel Academy of Science and Humanities, 1966), 1, 1, 24-30 and 1, 2, 24-30 (plates).

[34]In later stages of development the palm frond is called a *ḥaruta*. See Löw, *Flora*, 2:329-30.

[35]See *VR* 30:15 (712): "*Solomon's wisdom was great...He was the wisest of all men [...He discoursed about trees, from the cedar in Lebanon to the hyssop that grows out of the wall] (I Kgs 5:10-13).* He sat and wondered about these four species, as it says, *Three things are beyond me (Prov 30:18).* The paschal offering, the unleavened bread and the bitter herbs. *Four I cannot fathom.* These are the four species which he tried to understand. *Fruit of goodly trees (Lev 23:40).* Who says this is the etrog? All trees produce goodly fruit. *Branches of palms.* The Torah said to take two branches of the palm tree and to praise with them, yet he specifically takes the *lulav*, the heart of the palm. *Boughs of leafy trees.* Who says this is the myrtle? Behold, it says in another place, *Go out to the mountains and bring leafy branches of olive trees, pine trees, and myrtles (Neh 8:15).* And *Willows of the brook.* All trees grow beside water...These are the four species which each and every Israelite hurries to acquire to praise the Holy One, and while they seem like trivial matters to human beings, they are important to the Holy One. And who explained to Israel that these fours species are the etrog, lulav, myrtle and willow? The sages, as it says, *Yet they are the wisest of the wise (Prov 30:24).*" See too Maimonides, *The Guide of the Perplexed*, trans. S. Pines, intro. by L. Strauss (Chicago: The University of Chicago Press, 1963), 3:43 (572-73): "As for the four species that constitute a lulab, the Sages, may their memory be blessed, have set forth some reason for this in the manner of Midrashim whose method is well known by all those who understand their discourses. For these [namely the Midrashim] have, in their opinion, the status of poetical conceits; they are not meant to bring out the meaning of the text in question." That is, the sages did not learn the identification of the species from Lev 23:40. The midrashim they devised were simply poetical conceits or mnemonic aids, not true exegesis. Maimonides then launches into a discussion of the nature of midrashim in general. For him the identification of the four species was a paradigmatic case of the midrash not being the true source of the law!

[36]The *derashot* for the myrtle and willow are unattributed. Two *derashot* are provided for the etrog, one of which is attributed to Ben Azai. bSuk 35a attributes the *derasha* of Ben Azai of the *Sifra* to R. Abahu, and attributes a different *derasha* to Ben Azai. Parallels to the *derashot*: etrog: ySuk 3:5, 53d; *BR* 15:7 (140); *VR* 30:8

The Tannaitic Period: Legal and Ritual Developments

exegeses only link the accepted custom to scripture. They are not reactions to competing halakhic traditions nor intended to pre-empt alternative interpretations of the verse.[37] The tradition of the targums, the Aramaic translations of the Torah, is unanimous. Onqelos translates "the fruits of the trees, etrogs, lulavs, and myrtle branches, as well as willows of the brook," and the other targums are similar.[38] The sources are in no way polemical, and all concur.[39] In addition, a letter from Simon Bar-Kochba (Kosiba), leader of the second Jewish revolt of 132-135 CE, requests the four species by their Mishnaic names.[40] Lulavs and etrogs appear on coins from the first and second revolts, and the species depicted, as far as is possible to tell, are those of the Mishna.[41]

---

(706); *PRK* 27:8 (413); myrtle: bSuk 32b; y3:2, 53c; *VR* and *PRK* as above; willow: tSuk 2:7; b33b-34a; y3:3, 53c; *VR* and *PRK* as above.

[37]It is interesting that Maimonides, in his introduction to his commentary to the Mishna, cites the identification of the four species among his examples of explanations of the commandments of the Torah about which absolutely no disagreement exists. He explains the halakhic midrashim as examples of the "science of Torah" whereby even undisputed elements of the oral law can be derived from the written Torah.

[38]Onqelos: פירי אילנא אתרוגין לולבין והדסין וערבין דנחל. See Grossfeld, *Leviticus*, 53. Not only the term *etrogin*, but also *lulavin* and *hadasin* are rabbinic, not biblical. TY, TN and CTgF also spell out the rabbinic interpretations of the species. Thus TY, 147: ותיסבון מן דלכון ביומא קמאה דחגא פירי אילן משבח תרוגין ולולבין והדסין וערבין דמרביין על נחלין. TN 3:173: ותסבון לכון ביומא טבה קדמיה פירי אילן משבח תרוגין ולולבין והדס וערבה דנחלה. CTgF: ותסבון לכון ביומא קדמיה פירי אילן משבח תרוגין ולולבין והדס וערבה דנחל (P. Kahle, *Masoreten des Westens* [Stuttgart, 1930], 2:54 = *The Fragment Targums to the Pentateuch*, ed. M. Klein [Rome: Biblical Institute Press, 1980], 1:318). The Peshitta, however, has לבותא דדקלא, "hearts of the palm."

[39]tSuk 2:9 rules that if one does not have an etrog, he may not bring any other fruit as a substitute. There is no polemical intent here. The ruling simply precludes the taking of other fruit even in emergencies. Tannaitic sources specify what types of palm branches may be used, and what species of willow, but these basic identifications are unquestioned (t2:7).

[40]Two of the Bar-Kochba letters requisition Sukkot ritual items. An Aramaic letter, published by Yadin, *Bar-Kochba*, 128-29 orders a certain Yehuda bar Menashe to procure and send the four species to Bar-Kochba "since the army is big." Bar-Kochba and his army clearly took the festival obligations seriously. Even in the midst of war he went to great lengths to obtain the requisite species. He designates the species as ללבין ואתרוגין...הדסין וערבין, identical to rabbinic terminology. The Greek letter was published by B. Lifshitz, "Papyrus grecs du desert de Juda," *Aegyptus* 42 (1962), 240-48. D. Goodblatt, "A Contribution to the Prosopography of the Second Revolt: Yehudah bar Menasheh," *JJS* (1987), 52 n. 60 proposes a few corrections to Lifshitz's readings. On the letters, see now Hayim Lapin, "Palm Branches and Citrons: Notes on Two Letters From Bar Kosiba's Administration," *HUCA* 64 (1993), 111-136.

[41]See Y. Meshorer, *Jewish Coins of the Second Temple Period*, trans. I.H. Levine (Tel-Aviv: Am Hassefer, 196), #161 (from 69 BCE). See also, #162, 162A, 163, 163A (also from 69 BCE); 165, 178-180, 199 (from the Bar-Kochba revolt).

How early can we date the rabbinic tradition that identifies the citron, palm, willow and myrtle as the four species?[42] Was this the unique interpretation of rabbinic or proto-rabbinic circles, or the common practice the rabbis inherited from temple times? Of course the ritual could not have crystallized before the species were available in Palestine. Palms, willows and myrtles are native to Palestine, but citrons are not. Thus the earliest possible date depends on the spread and cultivation of the citron. Fortunately, S. Tolkowsky addressed this question is his comprehensive work on the history of citrus fruit.[43] Tolkowsky argues that the word '*etrog* derives from the Persian *torong*',[44] an etymology which points to the source whence the fruit spread to the Near East. Citrus fruits originated in the East Asian regions of China and Malaysia. Traders carried them through India and into Persia in the first millennium BCE. The first reference to citrus fruit in western sources appears in a fragment of the poet Antiphanes (early fourth century BCE) preserved by Athanaeus (second century CE.)[45] The Greek botanist Theophrastus, circa 310 BCE, provides a full description of the citron in a section of his *Enquiry into Plants* entitled "Of the trees and herbs special to Asia." His detailed information came from the Greek scientists who accompanied Alexander the Great on his journeys into Persia.[46] Theophrastus calls the citron, the "Medean" or "Persian apple," as do all early Greek writers. That subsequent Greek and Latin authors generally

---

[42]That Neh 8 lists different species is not decisive. The passage proves that the rabbinic tradition was not normative, not that it was unknown.
[43]Tolkowsky, *Peri ʿeṣ hadar* (Jerusalem: Bialik, 1966), 13-68. See too Tolkowsky, *Hesperides: A History of the Culture and Use of Citrus Fruits* (London: John Bale, Sons & Carnow, 1938).
[44]Tolkowsky, *Hadar*, 14-15. See H. Glidden, "The Lemon in Asia and Europe," *JAOS* 57 (1937), 381-95, who independently proposes this etymology; G. Dalman. *Arämdisch-neuhebräisches Handwörterbuch*[2] (Frankfurt a.M, 1922), 46 and Löw, *Flora*, 3:279. The "n" still appears in several of the Aramaic forms in the talmuds, e.g., bQid 70a, אתרוננא; ySuk 3:12, 54a, תרונייא; yGit 2:3, 44b, תרונגא, תרונא, [תרוגניה, תרונגה in a Geniza fragment]. Nor is the spelling with a n uniform: in yAZ 2:3, 41a the reading is 'איטרוג. See Löw, 3:280 and M. Sokoloff, *A Dictionary of Jewish Palestinian Aramaic of the Byzantine Period* (Ramat Gan: Bar Ilan University Press, 1990), 591. The dialects are illustrated nicely in bQid 70a: He [R. Nahman] said, "Will you eat an etronga?" He [R. Yehuda] replied, "Thus Shmuel said: 'Whoever says *etronga* is a third [puffed up] with arrogance. Either [say] *etrog*, as the rabbis call it, or *etroga*, as it is popularly called.'"
[45]The fragment is from Antiphanes's play "The Boeotian Women," preserved in Athanaeus, *The Deipnosophists*, 3:83-84 (LCL, trans. C.B. Gulick [London: William Heinemann, 1927], 1:357-63. See Hehn, *Kulturpflanzen*, 332.
[46]Theophrastus, *Enquiry into Plants*, IV, iv, 1-3 (LCL, trans. W.A. Hort [London: William Heinemann, 1916], 1:309-13); Hehn, *Kulturpflanzen*; 331-33; Tolkowsky, *Hadar*, 46-47.

The Tannaitic Period: Legal and Ritual Developments

rely on Theophrastus's description indicates that cultivation of the citron in Greece and Italy did not take place for several centuries.

When did the citron reach Syria and Palestine? Could the citron have spread to Palestine and the Near East before arriving in Greece and the West? Tolkowsky discounts this possibility. He observes that Theophrastus emphasized that the citron grew exclusively in Persia and Medea, not in the other provinces of the Persian empire. Tolkowsky concludes that in the fourth century BCE citron cultivation was still limited to Persia and Medea, and had not spread even to Babylonia, let alone Syria, Palestine or beyond.[47] He thus rejects the conjecture of earlier scholars that the Jews encountered the citron during the Babylonian exile and brought the custom back after the restoration under Cyrus.[48] He calculates that the citron only reached Babylonia in the fourth century BCE, and could not have reached Palestine until sometime in the second century BCE.[49] Now we might question whether Theophrastus's testimony concerning the geographic limitation of the citron is completely accurate. Many years after Theophrastus, in the first century CE, Pliny still claimed that "because of its [the citron's] great medicinal value various nations have tried to acclimatize it in their own countries...but it has refused to grow except in Medea and Persia."[50] At this time, however, cultivation of the citron was thriving in both Judea and Babylonia.[51] Yet such speculation, in my mind, should not compromise Theophrastus's observation that in the fourth century BCE the citron grew exclusively in Persia and Medea, nor the complete absence of attestation in western sources until the early fourth century BCE. This places us in the late Persian or early Hellenistic period as the earliest possible date for the presence of the citron in Palestine and the standardization of the four species.[52]

---

[47]Tolkowsky, *Hadar*, 48.
[48]Giovanni Battista Ferrari, *Hesperides sive De Malorum Aurorum Cultura et Uso Libri Quatuor* (Rome, 1646); Georges Gallesio, *Traite du Citrus* (Paris, 1811).
[49]Tolkowsky claims that *peri 'eṣ hadar* of Lev 23:40 refers to the *dar* tree, a cedar tree considered holy in India, and the fruit used was the cedar cone. Simon Maccabeus ordered that the cone be replaced with the citron because pagans used the cone in their rituals. This speculative thesis in no way impugns Tolkowsky's analysis of when the citron appeared in Palestine.
[50]*Natural History* 12, 16 (LCL, trans. H. Rackham [Cambridge: Harvard University Press, 1945], 4:13).
[51]That there was no shortage of citrons in talmudic times suggests that cultivation must have started in Babylonia long before then. See the story of R. Zera (mid-3rd century; but MS Munich has Rava and Vatican 111 has Rav Yehuda) who was pelted by etrogs in Mehoza, bQid 73a.
[52]E. Isaac, "Influence of Religion on the Spread of Citrus," *Science* 129 (1959), 179-86 proposes a competing theory for the spread of the citron. He argues that

Yet the actual practice of taking the etrog on Sukkot and its identification with Lev 23:40 may have occurred later. Mere availability of the citron does not guarantee its ritual use. To further pinpoint the date of the practice we must turn to our literary sources. The Septuagint translates Lev 23:40 without any hint of the citron or myrtle, but this only proves that the translators chose to translate literally in this case, not that the identifications were unknown. In our survey of the sources from the second temple period we noted that Jubilees, following biblical terminology, mentions willows and palms but not citrons or myrtles. 2 Maccabees only refers to bouquets in general terms. Pseudo-Philo is the earliest source to identify one of the species with his reference to the myrtle. He may mention the citron, but this is uncertain.[53] Josephus unambiguously mentions the four species. In *AJ* 3:244-47 he mentions "a bouquet composed of myrtle and willow with a branch of palm, along with citrons." In *AJ* 13:372 he relates that Alexander Jannaeus (103-76 BCE) was pelted with citrons on Sukkot, "it being a custom among the Jews that at the festival of Sukkot everyone holds wands of palm branches and of citrons – these we have described elsewhere." Note that Josephus does not explicitly mention the myrtle and willow, as he does in the first passage. But his own cross-reference indicates that his intention is not to provide a full description here. The wands include the

---

current botanical theory points to the origin of the citron in Arabia, not in East Asia, basing himself on W.T. Swingle, *The Citrus Industry*, ed. H.J. Webber and L.D. Batchelor (University of California Press: Berkeley and Los Angeles, 1943), 397. Isaac cites as evidence of the existence of the citron in the ancient Near East the depiction of "what is most probably the citron on an Assyrian sculpture," the finding of citron seeds in the ruins of old Nippur in Southern Mesopotamia from about the fourth millennium BCE, and references to the *'iltakku*, which, he claims, corresponds to the Hebrew *'etrog*, in Assyrian medical texts of the second millennium. (Tolkowsky, *Hesperides: A History of the Culture and Use of Citrus Fruits* [London: John Bale, Sons & Carnow, 1938], 43 claims the seeds come from assorted rare fruits of foreign provenance.) Extensive contacts existed between all Near East civilizations even in the fourth and third millennia, and it is virtually certain that seeds, fruit and grain were transferred as well. So there is "great likelihood that the citron was transmitted from its place of origin in Southern Arabia to Egypt and Palestine in the course of trade" (p. 181). Isaac conjectures the citron spread to the coastal planes of Palestine in the "period of the early kings of Judah and Israel." He concludes the *pri 'eṣ hadar* of Lev 23:40 indeed refers to the citron. The arguments in favor of this last point are weak. That the citron was considered holy in other cultures, "including India and China," proves nothing about the Israelites. Worse, Isaac adduces the insistence of rabbinic sources (and their "long oral tradition") that Lev 23:40 refers to the citron as further evidence the biblical verse refers to that fruit. Of course we would expect Lev 23:40 to specify the citron if it meant it. For additional discussion of the merits of each theory, see Rubenstein, *Dissertation*, 310-15.
[53] See Chapter 2, VIII text at n. 109.

The Tannaitic Period: Legal and Ritual Developments 197

willows and myrtle he has detailed earlier. The Jannaeus account places us in the early second century BCE. While Josephus may be citing an early source, the legendary quality of the story suggests that he is retelling a folktale of sorts. This raises the possibility that Josephus has retrojected the ritual current in his day to the age of Jannaeus. So Josephus can only be taken as evidence of the situation in his own time.

It seems most likely that the identification of the species became the standard practice at some point during the first century BCE or early first century CE. An earlier date is unlikely because of the lack of documentation in the sources and because some time must have passed after the introduction of the citron to Palestine in the fourth or third century BCE until cultivation became widespread. A later date is ruled out by the fact that use of the citron became so standardized that Josephus, rabbinic sources and perhaps Pseudo-Philo take it for granted. In the age of Josephus and in even the earliest recollection of rabbinic sources the four species were universally recognized as the festal ritual on Sukkot and the fulfillment of Lev 23:40. The Josephan passages and the coins from the first revolt demonstrate that the four species were the practice even outside rabbinic circles. The lulav, then, was no idiosyncratic ritual limited to the rabbis, nor a rabbinic innovation – the rabbis simply inherited what had become the common practice in temple times.

III. The Rabbinic Lulav Ritual

Apart from the account of the Men of Jerusalem who held their lulav throughout the day,[54] all rabbinic sources assume that the lulav is "taken" or "shaken" at specific times. The earliest source, a debate between the Houses of Shammai and Hillel, employs the verb "shake" (N'N'; mSuk 3:9). The issue concerns at what times the lulav should be shaken during the recitation of the Hallel. m3:15, an unattributed source, rules that "a minor who knows how to shake is obligated with respect to the lulav." "Shake" also occurs in unattributed traditions in m3:1, tHag 1:2 and tBer 3:19. The verb "take" (NṬL) is far more common. NṬL occurs in late biblical Hebrew with the sense of "to take" or "to carry," and, due to the influence of Aramaic, is the regular verb in Mishnaic Hebrew for biblical LQḤ.[55] Its use in connection with the lulav clearly

---

[54]Chapter 3, VI text to n. 190.
[55]Cf. Isa 40:15. For Mishnaic usage see mBM 1:1; Shab 1:1 etc. The identity of the biblical לקח and the Mishnaic נטל can be seen in *Sifra Mesora* 4:8 (73c): ולקחו אבנים [ויק׳ 14:42] יכול יטול אבנים מצד זה. Other such examples include *Sifre Ṣav, Miluim*, 1:29 (42b); *BR* 65:6-9 (725-6); 97:1 (1242, according to MS Vatican); *Sifre Deut.* §23 (33). See A. Ben-David, *Leshon miqra veleshon hakhamim* (Tel-Aviv: Devir, 1967-71),

derives from the biblical phrase "and you shall take" (*uleqaḥtem;* Lev 23:40).[56] It is interesting that *NṬL* only appears in unattributed statements.[57]

Tannaitic Sources assume that the ritual gestures are known and do not define them in detail. The only description of shaking the lulav appears in a baraita, y3:10, 53d, which instructs that "one must shake three times." The most informative description of "to take a lulav" appears in tBer 6:10, which rules that when one "takes" the lulav he recites the blessing "...on the taking of the lulav" (*'al netilat lulav*), and when one "makes" the lulav he recites the blessing "...who has kept us alive and sustained us and brought us to this occasion."[58] To take a lulav presumably involved lifting up the lulav and reciting a blessing. Tannaitic sources do not reveal whether the blessing-taking involved "shaking" as well.[59] Nor do the sources specify when the taking takes

---

1:352, 2:100 for these and other examples. The Mishnaic לקח generally means "to buy."
[56]See David Abudarham, *Sefer Abudarham*, (Jerusalem, 1958), 293.
[57]See mSuk 3:5, 3:9, 3:13, 4:4, Ned 2:2, Shevu 3:8, tNed 1:5. mSuk 3:12 (= mRH 4:4), cited above, where R. Yohanan b. Zakkai ordained that the lulav be "taken" for seven days, is anonymously transmitted. The formulation, including choice of verb, cannot be attributed to R. Yohanan b. Zakkai. (The verb *NṬL* appears in attributed traditions in other contexts.) Some manuscripts of mSuk 3:9 contain the verb *metarfin*, from the root *TRP*, in place of *mena'ne'in*. This verb also means "to shake" or "to move vigorously." See Fox, *Succah*, 102-106.
[58]The *shehekhianu*. In ySuk 3:4, 53d the blessing upon making the lulav is not the *shehekhianu* but *veṣivanu la'asot lulav*, while the *shehekhianu* is to be said when one prays with it. Cf. bSuk 46a.
[59]The silence of the sources suggests the taking did not include shaking at least in the early tannaitic period. Tosafot, bSuk 37b, s.v. *behodu* observe that only two sources pertain to this question. mSuk 3:15 states that "a minor who knows how to shake is obligated with respect to the lulav." The Tosafot explain that although the minor does not know how to recite the Hallel, he should nevertheless "shake" when he recites the blessing, i.e., when he "takes" the lulav. The second source, tBer 3:19, rules: "If one sets out on a journey early in the morning, they bring him a shofar and he sounds, or a lulav and he shakes, or a scroll [of Esther] and he reads it, and when the time for reciting the *shema'* arrives, he recites." According to the Tosafot, although he does not recite Hallel, he nonetheless takes the lulav and shakes it. (Tosafot cite the passage from bBer 30a where it appears in slightly different form.) Both of these sources are given to alternative interpretations. mSuk 3:15 may simply mean that a minor who knows how to shake at the appropriate points in the Hallel, or even to recite the Hallel, must shake the lulav. It need not relate to the "taking" at all. tBer 3:19 may mean that only if one will not have a lulav when he prays does he shake the lulav beforehand. It may even imply that he recites the entire Hallel and shakes at the appropriate times. Some rishonim realized that these sources were not conclusive. Thus Ibn Ghiyyat, *Sha'arei simḥa*, 1:110 notes that several Geonim rule that one shakes the lulav following the blessing, but suggests they would not have done so had it not been

place, whether immediately upon waking in the morning or prior to the Hallel during the morning service, the standard practice of post-talmudic times. The shaking occurred during the recitation of the Hallel. In any case, the tannaitic lulav ritual involved two separate components. Here too we see continuity from temple times as well as rabbinic innovation. The shaking during the Hallel derived from the temple liturgy, while the blessing for the commandment of taking the lulav, like all blessings for commandments, were rabbinic creations.[60]

Few traditions concerning the lulav other than those already cited date from temple times. The Houses dispute the fitness of a *demai* etrog for ritual use (m3:5). The question primarily concerns tithing, a principal interest of the Pharisees.[61] In Chapter 3, VI we discussed mSuk 4:4, which purports to describe the logistics of bringing the lulav to the temple, and questioned the historical accuracy of the tradition.[62] Yet the law behind the account, that on the first day of Sukkot one must use a lulav that one owns, does appear to be of considerable antiquity. While this law is spelled out in m3:13, an unattributed Mishna, the ruling is introduced with the phrase "for the sages have said..." Thus m3:13 cites an older law. In t2:11 and *Sifra 'Emor* 16:2 (102c) the same ruling is adduced in connection with a *ma'ase* (case) involving Rabban Gamaliel (of Yavneh). Even if the *ma'ase* is apocryphal, there seems to be sufficient

---

a "tradition" (*qabbala*) they received and a practice they observed among their elders. He cites tBer 3:19 as a "support" (*semikha*), the implication being that it is not decisive. See too Abraham b. Nathan of Lunel, *Sefer Hamanhig*, ed. Y. Raphael (Jerusalem: Rav Kook, 1978), Laws of Etrog, §31-33 (2:397-98) who cites a chain of Geonim as well as tBer 3:19. See also OG, Sukka, *teshuvot* §§117-126 to bSuk 39a (52-54). Still other rishonim considered the evidence even less compelling. Thus Hagahot Maimoniot n. ס to Maimonides, MT, Laws of Lulav 7:10, cites Rabenu Simha: "There is no proof that we shake along with the taking, neither in our Talmud, nor the Palestinian Talmud, nor in the Tosefta, but only [that one shakes] during the Hallel." R. Simha notes that tBer 3:19 cannot be taken as proof. He concedes that while the common practice is to shake when the lulav is taken, "it is astounding" that mSuk 3:1, which mentions the shaking during the Hallel, omits mention of shaking with the blessing.
[60] At least in the rabbinic form. See E. Qimron, "Times for Praising God: A Fragment of a Scroll from Qumran (4Q409)," *JQR* 80 (1990), 341-44 for evidence of blessings for the commandments at Qumran.
[61] Neusner, *Judaism*, 53-55.
[62] Text to n. 186. m4:4 is unattributed. Epstein, *Tannaim*, 351 claims this mishna indeed dates from temple times. He notes that it contradicts m3:13, and, following b43a, suggests that m4:4 dates from temple times, m3:13 from post-temple times. (He also points out that the entire fourth chapter deals with temple rituals.) However, the two mishnayot may simply derive from different post-temple sources. That the two are so similar may indicate that the contemporary practice was retrojected back to temple times.

evidence to assign the ruling to the first or second tannaitic generation, if not earlier.[63]

The second and third tannaitic generation define the lulav with greater precision. R. Eliezer (second generation) rules on a basic matter of definition by legislating that the etrog need not be in the same "band" ('aguda) as the palm, myrtles and willows.[64] This suggests a band of some sort was customarily used to keep the species together, an issue the third generation would also consider. R. Ishmael and R. Akiba debate the number of each species required in the bouquet.[65] R. Ishmael requires three myrtles, two willows, one palm and one citron; R. Akiba rules that one of each is sufficient. Apparently at this time the palm was adorned with any number of willows and myrtles, and perhaps multiple palms and etrogs were taken as well. The tannaim wished to determine a minimum number for each species. These disputes reveal an increasing concern for standardization of the ritual.

R. Ishmael and R. Tarfon dispute whether the myrtles need be in perfect condition or whether the tops may be broken off (m3:4). In *Sifra 'Emor* 16:4 (102d) R. Tarfon comments on the biblical phrase "branches (*kapot*) of palm," that "if they are separate he should bind them (*yikhptenu*)." That is, if the leaves of the palm have begun to separate and spread apart from each other, they should be bound together. t2:8 rules that the willow and myrtle must be three handbreadths long, and the lulav four. R. Tarfon comments that these handbreadths are five to a cubit. These rulings continue the interest in standardization and begin the issue of setting minimum and maximal sizes.

The fourth tannaitic generation (including the students of R. Akiba) took a greater interest in defining imperfections that render the species unfit. They rule on such matters as palm branches with separated leaves (m3:1), minimum and maximum sizes of the etrog (m3:7), a discolored etrog (m3:6), withered etrogs and desiccated species (t2:9).[66] m3:1-3 and

---

[63]The division of tannaitic generations follows H. Albeck, *Mavo lamishna* (Jerusalem: Bialik; Tel-Aviv: Devir, 1959), 222-33. The first generation includes R. Yohanan b. Zakkai, R. Dosa b. Hyrcanus and their associates; the second Rabban Gamaliel, R. Eliezer b. Hyrcanus, R. Yehoshua b. Hananiah and the later Yavneans; the third R. Ishmael, R. Akiba, R. Tarfon et al.; the fourth the students of R. Akiba: R. Meir, R. Shimon, R. Yehuda, R. Yose; the fifth includes R. Yehuda Hanasi and the later tannaim. The same division can be found in Strack, *Talmud*, 69-90, except Strack-Stemberger divide the second generation into an "older group" and a "younger group" (my third generation.)
[64]Baraita, bSuk 34b.
[65]mSuk 3:4, *Sifra 'Emor* 16:7 (102d).
[66]Several baraitot in the talmuds relate to these matters: b31b-32a; y3:1, 53c. An unattributed baraita, b33a permits a myrtle with dried leaves provided three green clusters remain (שלשה בדי עלין לחין).

5-6, which contain the bulk of such laws, can probably be assigned to this generation.[67] These are the first attributed sources that disqualify the species on account of physical imperfections.

A second issue debated in the fourth generation was whether the lulav must be bound together, and with what it may be bound.[68] R. Eliezer, we noted, had ruled the etrog need not be in the band with the other three species, which indicates that having a band was a common practice. R. Meir ruled the lulav required a band, and attempted to prove his position by adducing a precedent from the custom of the Men of Jerusalem who used to bind their lulavs with golden bands (t2:10). The issue was whether the band was merely a convenience, and hence optional, or whether it formed an intrinsic part of the bouquet.

Tannaim of the fourth generation also turned their attention to matters of the lulav and the Sabbath, an interest that parallels the detailed instructions for carrying out the temple rituals on the Sabbath, which runs through the fourth and fifth chapters of the tractate. The question arose as to whether the prohibition against carrying affected the lulav ritual. Now m4:2, which treats the lulav ritual of the temple, rules that the lulav was performed in the temple on a Sabbath that coincided with the first Festival-Day, but not if the Sabbath fell on an intermediate day. Worshippers deposited their lulavs in the temple before the Sabbath and reclaimed them on the morrow (m4:4).[69] m3:13 rules the same for the synagogue: on the first day of Sukkot that coincides with the Sabbath the lulav is placed there on Friday. By implication, if the Sabbath coincides with the intermediate days of Sukkot, the lulav should not be taken. This ruling appears explicitly in a baraita, *Sifra 'Emor* 16:3 (102d).[70] So the distinction between the first day and subsequent days was retained after the destruction, and, if the tradition of depositing the lulav at the temple is accurate, the post-temple solution was based on temple precedent as well.[71] The students of R. Akiba explored further ramifications of this decision. R. Yose rules that if one carries his lulav outside his house by accident on the first day of Sukkot that falls on the

---

[67]Most statements in these mishnayot are unattributed. R. Yehuda is mentioned in 3:1, and R. Meir in 3:6. The only other attributions are to the Houses of Hillel and Shammai in m3:5, but here the issue is the *demai* etrog, a question related to tithing, and probably transferred here from an earlier source.
[68]m3:8, t2:10, *Sifra 'Emor* 16:1 (102c). Cf. the baraita, bSuk 11b.
[69]See Chapter 3, VI text to n. 185. Because of the commotion that resulted in the temple when each attempted to reclaim his own lulav, it was later decided that the rite should be performed at home.
[70]The baraita also appears in b43a. Cf. y3:13, 54a and *TK*, 4:869.
[71]Note that the tradition concerning R. Yohanan b. Zakkai's decree also testifies that the first day was distinguished in temple times. For the exegetical basis to distinguish the first day from other days, see n. 6.

Sabbath he is exempt from punishment (m3:14). He also rules that once one has shaken the lulav on the Sabbath, he may no longer touch it (t2:11). R. Yehuda rules that the lulav may be returned to water on the Sabbath, the issue being whether this act constitutes a type of planting (m3:15).

This leaves the unattributed sources. t2:8 limits the lulav to the four species defined by Leviticus. It is not self-evident from Lev 23 that no more than four species are to be brought. Conceivably several types of "leafy boughs" could have been incorporated into the lulav, even if the myrtle and willow had to be included. The Tosefta rules out this possibility; one brings the four species, no more, no less.[72] Compared to scripture, tannaitic sources know the precise identification of the components of the lulav, and know that there are only four. An anonymous tanna rules that a minor who knows how to shake the lulav is obligated (m3:15).

A number of unattributed traditions pertain to the definition of fit and unfit species. As we noted, most of m3:1-3, 5-6 deals with this topic. t2:7 disqualifies a dried palm-branch (ḥaruta) and one with spread leaves (i.e. in later stages of development, cf. m3:1), permits willows from a private field or from mountains, defines and disqualifies the ṣafṣefa,[73] and concludes that a fit willow has a red stem and a long leaf while an unfit willow has a white stem and a circular leaf.[74] These disqualifications represent a more restrictive interpretation of the biblical text. "Palm branches" refers to immature fronds, not firm boughs, and "willows of the brook" does not include all willows. In a similar fashion, m3:1 rules that a type of palm, "thorn branches of the iron mountain," are fit, while a related baraita, y3:1, 53c defines which of these palms are fit, and which forbidden.[75] t2:8 rules that willows and myrtles with cut stalks are fit.[76] A baraita, b32b, rules that a myrtle that has lost a majority of its leaves is permitted, provided its "plaiting" remains.[77] t2:10 rules that one may not make a band for the lulav on the festival-day. Thus most of the

---

[72] *Sifra 'Emor* 16:8 (102d) and mMen 3:6 rule that the lack of one of the species prevents the fulfillment of the commandment (מעכבים זה את זה).
[73] See n. 33.
[74] The baraita, b34a, defines a fit willow as one with "a leaf drawn out like a brook." A second baraita excludes the ṣafṣefa since it grows in the mountains, not by the brook. (Although this seems to go against the reasoning of other baraitot that do not specifically require willows of the brook.") Unattributed baraitot of b34a and y3:3, 53c rule on permitted willows and the shape of their leaves.
[75] On the identification of the "iron mountain" see Löw, *Flora*, 2:312-13 and the references there.
[76] Precisely which part of the branch is meant is unclear. See *TK*, 4:859.
[77] *'Avuto*. The baraita of b36a lists a number of defects which disqualify an etrog. Other baraitot about the etrog: y3:5, 53d, 3:6, 53d; b35b.

unattributed traditions define imperfections which disqualify each species or identify fit and unfit subspecies (e.g. white-leafed willows). The concern for defining imperfections parallels that of the fourth generation, and the disqualification of subspecies is related. The ruling on the lulav band also reflects a fourth generation concern. It seems likely that these traditions derive from the students of R. Akiba, who first concentrated on these issues, or from their students, who explored the matters in greater depth.[78]

The halakhic development in the tannaitic period reveals a fairly orderly progression by which, over the course of about a century, the tannaim proceeded from basic issues of definition to detailed legislation. The identification, number of the species and basic conception of the ritual (i.e. that Lev 23:40 is fulfilled by holding species in the hand) are presupposed by rabbinic sources. When the temple was destroyed the rabbis adopted the temple practice of taking the lulav for seven days. Blessings, hallmarks of rabbinic piety, were formulated for the lulav and added a second dimension to the ritual. Third generation tannaim (R. Akiba et al.) debated the number of each species required for the bouquet, and introduced certain standards for the palm branch. The students of R. Akiba continued this process and promulgated more detailed rulings about minimum and maximum sizes and other types of imperfections. The matter of the lulav band was also debated in the fourth generation, as were certain matters of the lulav and the Sabbath. The unattributed traditions parallel the fourth generation debates in defining fit and unfit species. There are no laws of the lulav attributed to the last generation of tannaim.

IV. *Skhakh* (Sukka-roofing)

Scripture provides little information about the actual construction of a sukka. Lev 23:42 tersely rules "You shall live in sukkot seven days" but offers no description or definition of the sukka. Only one scriptural passage – the account of sukkot fashioned from the branches of trees in Neh 8 – sheds any light on how sukkot were actually built. The tannaim, however, did not take the Nehemian description as paradigmatic for their conception of the sukka. The only tannaitic source to cite Neh 8:15

---

[78]Cf. Neusner, *Judaism*, 19: "the anonymous sayings usually turned out to find a compendious place right where they should – in the history of ideas assigned to the authorities of the Mishnah. That is to say, they turned out to express the same principle as was in the name of a specific authority (usually an authority of the period after 140)." The "period after 140" corresponds to the period of the students of R. Akiba.

shows how negligibly the passage informed the tannaitic conception.[79] *Sifra 'Emor* 17:10 (103a) cites the commandment to dwell in sukkot (Lev 23:42) and comments "in sukkot [made] of any substance." The Sifra then asserts R. Yehuda ruled that sukkot must be made out of the four species of the lulav. His reasoning and a refutation of his position are given.[80] The passage continues by appealing to Neh 8:15: "And so Ezra says, *and that they must announce and proclaim throughout all their towns and Jerusalem as follows, 'Go out to the mountains and bring leafy branches of olive trees, pine trees, myrtles, palms and [other] leafy trees to make booths, as it is written.'*" Thus Neh 8:15 is cited as an ancillary proof for the interpretation of Lev 23:42 that sukkot can be fashioned from "any substance."[81] The types of foliage listed in the verse are not the *only* permitted substances, as one might have concluded. Rather the types of foliage are those the people happened to find; in theory they could have used "any substance." Neh 8:15 serves almost as an afterthought, a secondary support after the primary evidence – the interpretation of Lev 23:42 and the legal reasoning of both sides – has been cited.[82] Note that R. Yehuda's ruling cannot be harmonized with Neh 8:15, for that verse lists species other than the four mentioned in Lev 23:40.[83] His conception of the sukka is actually in tension with the Nehemian description.

More importantly, the Sifra has already presupposed the tannaitic conception of the sukka and read Neh 8:15 in that light. Neh 8:15

---

[79]In the amoraic discussion Rav Hisda cites Neh 8:15 as proof that skhakh must derive from the soil and must not be subject to impurity; bSuk 12a. See Burgansky, *Sukka*, 221.

[80]According to the Sifra, R. Yehuda reasons as follows: the lulav, which only is practiced during the day, may only be taken from the four species. Therefore the sukka, which is observed day and night, *a minori ad maius* may only be made up of the four species. The sages reject this argument on the grounds that "any legal deduction that initially results in a stringency but ends up producing a leniency is not a valid deduction." Here R. Yehuda initially rules stringently, that the sukka may be made only of the four species, but ends up with a leniency, for if one lacks the four species, he is then exempt from dwelling in the sukka.

[81]That is, any *foliage* substance.

[82]Of course if the Nehemian passage were really paradigmatic for the tannaitic conception of the sukka, they would require that the sukka (or at least the skhakh) be exclusively from the five species mentioned (just as the four species of the lulav must be those "mentioned" in Lev 23:40.)

[83]According to Tosafot, bSuk 37a, s.v. *vehavi'u*, R. Yehuda would explain that the myrtle and palm mentioned in Neh 8:15 were for the skhakh, and the other three species for the walls. (In the printed talmud this explanation occurs in the body of the text. But it does not appear in the MSS, and apparently entered from the margin. See *DQS* ad loc. n. נ. A similar interpretation appears in ySuk 3:4, 53d.) That R. Yehuda requires this forced interpretation proves that he did not base his model of the sukka on Neh 8.

describes the construction of the entire sukka from various types of foliage; the text itself makes no distinction between the roof and the walls. While the Sifra theoretically could be understood as relating to the entire sukka ("in sukkot [made] of any substance" or, according to R. Yehuda, the "sukka may be [made] only of the four species"), when viewed in the context of all tannaitic sources it becomes clear that the Sifra debate is more limited. The tannaim viewed the sukka in terms of two components, the roofing *(skhakh)* and the walls, and subjected each component to different laws. As we shall see, tannaitic sources hardly limit the materials that may be used for the walls of the sukka, so that cannot be the subject of the debate. Rather, the Sifra debate exclusively pertains to the skhakh, and thereby imposes the concept on the verse. The Sifra (and other tannaitic sources by implication) reads the term sukkot in Neh 8 to refer to the skhakh, not the whole sukka as one might expect.[84] The laws of skhakh are analyzed in this section, and the laws of the body of the sukka in the next.

Tannaitic sources generally call the roofing *sikukh* (סיכוך),[85] the verb being *sikekh* (סיכך, מסככין). I use "skhakh" because this became the common term in the amoraic and later periods. Scripture, we noted, does not know of this concept. Nor does the idea appear in Josephus, Jubilees or Philo. A hint of the concept perhaps can be detected in the Temple Scroll. The scroll describes beams and columns fixed upon the roof of the temple upon which the "sukkot" were to be built each year.[86] This must mean that a roofing was built annually upon these permanent skeletal frameworks. We have no information about what materials were used for the roofing, nor whether laws governed this matter at all. In contrast, the concept of skhakh appears in all rabbinic sources. Skhakh,

---

[84]Some Qaraites, on the other hand, accepted the *sensus literalis* of the verse and ruled the entire sukka should be built from foliage. See Ibn Ezra to Lev 23:40 and B. Revel, "Inquiry Into the Sources of Karaite Halakah," *JQR NS* 3 (1912-13), 387.
[85]m1:4, 1:9, 1:10, 1:11. The only other use of סיכוך relates to the prohibition of "covering over" plant species with the Greek gourd, on account of "forbidden mixtures" (tKil 1:6; cf. *TK*, 2:588-89.) However, MS Erfurt reads לסכך in place of סיכוך. Mishna-Tosefta uses סכך or סככה for branches, twigs or overhanging branches in the context of purity laws: סכך, tKel BM 3:3; סככה, mAh 8:2, tAh 9:3, mNaz 7:3, mNid 7:5. In mAh 8:2 סככה is defined as "overhanging branches" (אלו הן הסככות: אילן שהוא מיסך על הארץ). In tNid 9:13 סכך relates to a woven cloth; cf. mShab 7:2, המיסך. Thus tannaitic sources generally distinguish the covering of the sukka (סיכוך) from twigs or overhanging branches in other contexts (סכך, סככה). This distinction was lost in the amoraic period (and in baraitot that appear in the talmuds), where סכך and סככה are used regularly for the sukka roofing. See bSuk 6b, 17a; y1:6, 52b, 1:7, 52c.
[86]Yadin, *Scroll*, 2:179 (col 42, 11. 10-17). See Chapter 2, V.

then, is a legal category not documented outside of rabbinic literature, a unique element of the rabbinic interpretation of the festival.

The concept of skhakh probably emerged from the common manner of building sukkot, whether specifically for the festival or for other purposes.[87] The flimsy shelters were covered with convenient and accessible materials to provide some protection overhead. Branches, stalks, husks and other discarded plant products were readily available.[88] That, in essence, coheres exactly with the Nehemian description of the building of sukkot. After discovering the commandment to make sukkot, the people proceed to do so in standard manner: they collect leaves, branches and miscellaneous foliage to fashion a roofing.[89] Bedouins of nineteenth and twentieth century Palestine still constructed the roofs of their huts from cut branches and other foliage.[90] Presupposing the common manner of constructing sukkot, the tannaim standardized and defined the process with legislation. This process created a category of skhakh distinct from the rest of the sukka. Yet the amount of legislation concerning skhakh indicates that it took on a significance of its own and quickly became a central rabbinic symbol. The interest in the relationships between resident, skhakh and sky shows that the rabbis were concerned with more than the typical manner of building sukkot.

That the concept of skhakh is presupposed by all rabbinic sources, that no effort is made to adduce a prooftext, and that no dissenting opinion exists,[91] suggest that the concept dates to temple times. mSuk 2:8 reports that Shammai the Elder removed some plaster from the roof and placed skhakh over the bed of the child.[92] In m1:7, the Houses of Shammai and Hillel set limitations on permitted roofing:

---

[87]See Krauss, *Qadmoniot*, 1:224-235. Tannaitic sources mention various types of sukkot. See n. 135.

[88]The only description of skhakh for non-festival sukkot in tannaitic sources occurs in *Sifre Deut.* §317 (360). "It once happened (*ma'ase*) in Shihin that a mustard stalk had three twigs. They split off one of them and used it to cover (*sikekhu bo*) the sukka of artisans." This *ma'ase* functions in the *Sifre* as proof that in the future each grain of wheat will be as large as the two kidneys of a bull. The legendary tenor of the source does not impugn the underlying reality – that the sukka of artisans was covered with skhakh. Cf. tMa 2:21; bSuk 8b.

[89]Whether the materials were used for the walls and posts, as the text seems to imply, is a separate question.

[90]Dalman, *AuS*, 7:59-61; Krauss, *Qadmoniot*, 1:225.

[91]Tannaim debate precisely what can be used for skhakh, but all presuppose the concept.

[92]This tradition contradicts the law preceding it, that women, slaves and minors are exempt from the sukka. There is thus good reason to trust the tradition, since no motive for fabrication exists.

[A] A ceiling [*tiqra*] that has no plastering:
[B] R. Yehuda says in the name of the House of Hillel: he loosens or removes one beam between each two. And the House of Shammai says: he loosens and removes one beam between each two.
[C] R. Meir says: He removes one beam between each two, and does not need to[93] loosen the roofing.[94]

According to R. Yehuda, both Houses invalidate a ceiling that contains plaster. Both invalidate a ceiling without plaster but consisting of wooden beams. The issue is how to render such a ceiling fit. The House of Shammai requires both that the beams be loosened, so that they no longer resemble a typical ceiling, and that every other board be removed, so that the space can be covered with skhakh.[95] The House of Hillel requires one of the two acts: either the beams be loosened, so that they no longer resemble a typical ceiling, or that every other beam be replaced with fit skhakh, so that despite the remainder of the ceiling, there exists a comparable amount of special roofing.[96] For the House of Hillel the beams themselves serve as skhakh once they have been loosened and designated as skhakh, not as ceiling. R. Meir claims the Houses agree that one must remove every other beam and put down fit skhakh. Now we do not know what materials the Houses considered fit for skhakh, but they clearly had traditions to that effect. Both Houses prohibit the ordinary roofing of plaster covered by wooden beams. Even loosened beams are prohibited by both Houses according to R. Meir, and by the House of Shammai according to R. Yehuda, since that type of roofing resembles that of ordinary dwellings. They require a clear indication that

---

[93]The better manuscripts read אינו צריך לפפקפ. See Fox, *Succah*, 22-23.
[94]Neusner, *Pharisees*, 2:150-51, points out that R. Yehuda need not have cited the Shammaite position. He could simply have quoted the Hillelite opinion anonymously. This fact makes it more likely that the Houses' debate is authentic. Indeed, it may be possible to discern an even older halakha underlying the debate. If R. Yehuda's tradition is accurate, then the Houses disagree over the correct interpretation of an older law. The law was formulated מפקפק ונוטל אחד בינתיים. The Houses dispute whether the "ו" should be interpreted as "and" (Shammai) or "or" (Hillel). See Epstein, *MLH*, 1064; Halivni, *Meqorot*, 4:175 n. 3; E.Z. Melamed, *'Iyyunim besifrut hatalmud* (Jerusalem: Magnes, 1986), 58. If this reconstruction is correct the laws of skhakh would even antedate the Houses.
[95]The Mishna does not spell out that the space must be covered with appropriate skhakh. But it cannot be that the spaces are left empty, for what advantage is that over loosened beams?
[96]This explanation follows Maimonides (commentary to the Mishna ad loc. and *MT*, Laws of Sukka 5:8; cf. bSuk 15a). Both talmuds propose alternative explanations as well.

the roofing is specially constructed for the festival.[97] That the Houses dispute the nature of skhakh confirms the early dating of the concept. The tannaim inherited legislation from their precursors who lived in temple times.

The Houses appear in one other debate related to skhakh. The House of Hillel declares valid a sukka with skhakh so thick that the sun cannot be seen through it. The House of Shammai declares such a sukka invalid. Both agree that the stars need not be perceived. This disagreement occurs only in a baraita of b22b, not in any tannaitic document, but there is no reason to suspect that the baraita is a late fabrication.[98] The passage implies that normally skhakh was sufficiently sparse that the sun could be perceived. When it became so thick that it began to resemble a normal roof, the fitness of the skhakh was questioned. Thus these early sources take for granted the idea that skhakh is a unique part of the sukka governed by laws that do not apply to the walls.

Two early traditions concern the use of mats for skhakh. In m1:11 R. Eliezer and the sages debate whether large and small reed mats are fit for skhakh. They agree on the principle that if the mat is subject to impurity, it may not be used for skhakh.[99] In t1:10 R. Dosa, a contemporary of Rabban Yohanan ben Zakkai at Yavneh,[100] appears in a similar dispute. R. Eliezer is known for his conservative tendencies and predilection for the old halakha.[101] Again the sources indicate that the laws of skhakh date to temple times.

Most laws of skhakh are unattributed, a result of the scarcity of disagreements on the topic. Consequently the legal development within the tannaitic period cannot be determined with any certainty. In the following pages my purpose is to describe the overall tannaitic concept of skhakh, not to chart its historical development.

Objects susceptible to impurity are unfit for skhakh.[102] We noted that certain types of mats were judged unfit.[103] m1:3 invalidates a sukka

---

[97] According to R. Yehuda, the House of Hillel permits loosened beams, since the act of loosening the beams fashions anew the roofing with the intention that it serve for the sukka.

[98] m2:2 contains the ruling that the stars need not be perceived.

[99] The same idea appears in the baraitot of b20a and 20b. Cf. the baraita in y1:11, 52c.

[100] Hyman, *Toledot*, 323.

[101] See Gilat, *Eliezer*, 23-67.

[102] This principle appears to be stated explicitly in mSuk 1:4. Printed versions generally read: "what is susceptible to impurity or does not grow from the soil may not serve as skhakh; but what is not susceptible to impurity and grows from the soil may serve as skhakh." The manuscripts contain a plethora of variants. MS Parma 138, judged the most accurate by Fox and selected as the base text for

The Tannaitic Period: Legal and Ritual Developments   209

in which a sheet is placed under the skhakh to prevent the sun from striking the residents or the foliage from falling on them.[104] Subject to impurity, the sheet may not be used as skhakh. Processed flax-stalks and sheaves with more grain than straw are unfit for the same reason.[105] Spits for cooking and side pieces of a bed are likewise disqualified because of considerations of impurity (m1:8).[106]

---

his critical edition, reads: "This is the general rule: That which [is susceptible to] impurity, if it does not grow from the soil, one may not use it for skhakh" (דבר שהוא [מקבל] טומאה אם אין גידוליו מן הארץ אין מסככין בו). See Fox, *Succah*, 13, 16-18; Epstein, *MLH*, 1043; Albeck, *Mishna*, 2:473; B. Ratner, *'Ahavat ṣiyon virushalayim* (Vilna, 1901-7), 8:72-73. But this would imply that an object which is susceptible to impurity is fit for skhakh provided it grew from the soil, which contradicts m1:11, as well as m1:8, t1:5-6. Fox suggests reading אם as או (and some versions do not have אם, but simply a -ו, so the ואין can then be read as או אין), rendering: "This is the general rule: That which is susceptible to impurity or does not grow from the soil, one may not use it for skhakh." See his discussion and the variants. Several rishonim point out that this "general principle" (זה הכלל) differs from all other such principles in the Mishna, since the general principle does not relate directly to the preceding law. The problematic variants, the idiosyncratic use of the term, and the fact that the amoraim never refer to this clause, and, what is more, derive the rule in other ways oblivious to the unambiguous statement in the Mishna, have led Burgansky to suggest that this clause was not original to the Mishna. It is an amoraic baraita that was appended to m1:4. This compelling suggestion solves numerous difficulties. See Burgansky, *Sukka*, 201-206, 216, 221. And see tShab 2:4.

[103]For more on mats see t1:10 and the baraitot, b20a, 20b.

[104]So Rashi, b10a, s.v. *hanesher*, Ritba, ibid., s.v. *pires*. R. Tam in Tosafot, b10a, s.v. *pires* explains the sheet prevents the skhakh from withering in the sun or from falling off, which would leave the sukka with more shade than sun.

[105]t1:5-6. Cf. b12b on types of processed flax, and tShab 2:4 with *TK*, 3:28.

[106]Maimonides and Bertinuro explain that the Mishna deals with metal spits which are unfit because they do not derive from the soil. The juxtaposition with bedposts suggests a different explanation, supplied by the Mishna commentary *Tiferet Yisra'el, Boaz* n. 42 to m1:8. Both wooden spits and bedposts are questionable examples of vessels subject to impurity. (Metal spits are obviously unfit, being subject to impurity and not growing from the ground.) Wooden spits might be considered, "simple wooden vessels," פשוטי כלי עץ, which are generally not subject to impurity. On the other hand spits, if used as vessels, are subject to impurity. Bedposts, when disconnected from the bed, are "broken vessels," שברי כלים, and also are free from impurity (mKel 18:5). But the bedposts were formerly subject to impurity (and will be again if reconnected to the bed.) Because the law is not self-evident, the Mishna takes care to rule that spits and bedposts may not be used for skhakh. The same point is made in a baraita, bSuk 16a: "A mat of rushes or reed-grass, [having worn out], its remnants, even if reduced to less than the minimum amount [necessary to be subject to impurity] – one may not use them for skhakh." Since the remnants originally came from mats subject to impurity, they cannot be used even in their present condition. See *TK*, 4:839; bSuk 15b-16a.

A second type of substance unfit for skhakh is foliage still growing in the soil. One may not train vines, ivy or other such plants over a sukka.[107] For the same reason, branches of a tree that overhang a sukka do not count as skhakh (m1:2).

R. Yehuda and R. Meir dispute whether beams are fit for skhakh (m1:6). The issue recalls that of the debate of the Houses concerning the beamed ceiling. Beams of a certain size resemble a normal roof.[108] Although they meet the other requirements of skhakh, R. Meir disqualifies the beams so as to distinguish the sukka from a typical residence. The same Mishna rules that one may not sleep under a four handbreadth wide beam placed on top of the sukka. The concern is that the experience of sleeping under the skhakh not be the same as sleeping under the solid cover of a house.

Tannaitic sources do not specify what should be used as skhakh.[109] We noted that the Sifra permits skhakh "of any substance," meaning any type of vegetation, not only the four species.[110] The examples cited in tannaitic sources reveal that a wide variety of vegetation was used. Skhakh normally came from cut foliage, such as straw, wood and brushwood (m1:5); vines, gourds and ivy (once cut down; m1:4); sheaves of grain, stalks of flax, reeds and spears (t1:4-6); fiber ropes[111] or bundles

---

[107]m1:4. The law also appears in *Sifre Deut.* §140 (194). bSuk 11b interprets the *Sifre* to disagree with the Mishna. But this reading is by no means necessary. The *Sifre* has simply quoted the first portion of the Mishna and attached it to a prooftext. Cf. Halivni, *Meqorot*, 4:171-72. Plutarch relates that Jews build booths of vines and ivy (see Chapter 2, X). A type of vine provided shade for Jonah in his sukka, Jonah 4:6-7.

[108]Cf. the baraitot, t1:7, b14a-b and b14b. This explanation follows Rav, b14a and y1:7, 52b. Shmuel, b14a, limits the disagreement to boards between three and four handbreadths in width. Narrower beams are considered mere sticks, hence fit for skhakh, while larger beams are considered "places" in and of themselves, and resemble the ceiling of a house. The tannaim debate widths between three and four handbreadths: R. Meir worries that these too resemble a typical ceiling, while R. Yehuda does not. R. Yohanan offers a different explanation for the debate in y1:7, 52b. There the disagreement concerns beams planed down for use in building. In this case the debate concerns the question of impurity, since such beams are subject to impurity according to some opinions.

[109]The only exception is R. Yehuda who maintains that the skhakh may only come from the four species used in the lulav. The amoraim provide several definitions, bSuk 11b-12a.

[110]p. 205.

[111]There are two manuscript versions of t1:4: one permits ropes and one prohibits them. y1:4, 52b cites both variants and explains, "He who permits, deals with ropes of fiber. He who prohibits deals with ropes of flax." Fiber ropes retain their natural form, hence they are not defined as vessels, and not susceptible to impurity. Flax, however, loses its natural form during the process by which it becomes rope. See *TK*, 4:837.

of stubble (t1:4);[112] and, in general, the type of foliage that would drop leaves (m1:3).[113]

These laws and examples yield the following generalizations. Skhakh must be a natural, vegetable product.[114] It may no longer be living or attached to the ground. It may not be subject to impurity. Nor may it consist of the types of beams that typically form the ceilings of houses. Thus tannaitic law defined and standardized the common practice of covering sukkot with miscellaneous foliage and thereby created a ritual object, the skhakh. An attempt to gain further insight into the nature of skhakh from an anthropological approach is worthwhile. Skhakh appears to mediate between polarities. Skhakh is, in a way, both living and dead: living, because it derived from living vegetation; dead, because it no longer grows in the soil. That skhakh may not be subject to impurity rules out food and *kelim* – vessels, utensils and clothing. Vessels are the elements of culture.[115] Food is also a cultural entity, distinguished from the mass of vegetation in that it is designated for human consumption. While skhakh must provide shade, the shade is generally not solid enough to prevent the sun, and perhaps

---

[112]פקיעי עמיר. פקיע עמיר or פקיעי עמיר in tannaitic sources refers to hay, fenugrec, stubble or other such food for animals. See mShab 7:4, 24:2; tMa 2:20, tDem 1:21, tBM 8:4, tMe 1:22; *Sifra Qedoshim* 3:7 (88b). In tShev 2: 13 'amir refers to a pile of grain (*goren*; see *TK*, 2:508). 'Amir may be used for skhakh since it is not human food, hence not subject to impurity.

[113]tKel BM 3:3 discusses the purity of shears used to cut "skhakh." Lieberman comments to *Ḥesdai David* (ad loc., p. 92) that it was customary to cut off light branches with shears to use as skhakh for the sukka. However the skhakh here may simply be the overhanging branches of trees pruned for other reasons. See n. 85.

[114]The only example of non-vegetable material permitted appears in t1:6 where R. Yose b. R. Yehuda rules that worn out garments may be used for skhakh. Garments are subject to impurity until they have worn out and are no longer fit for human use – i.e., they are no longer "garments." This ruling does not seem to be universally agreed upon. It does not appear in the Mishna and appears in the Tosefta as an individual opinion. And MS London reads "worn out garments are *invalid."* In bSuk 15b-16a R. Aba bar Taviomi rules that worn out garments may not be used as skhakh. See *TK*, 4:839. It is possible that the garments came from flax or other vegetable products.

[115]"Ropes of fiber" and certain mats are possible exceptions to the prohibition against *kelim*. However, as Maimonides explains, the natural form of the fiber remains intact, hence they are not considered vessels (*MT*, Laws of Sukka 5:4; *TK*, 4:837. Concerning the "of fiber" see above, n. 111.) The mats were apparently "made" for use as skhakh, hence they are not considered vessels intended for normal use; mats made for sleeping would be subject to impurity and unfit for skhakh. Krauss, *Qadmoniot*, 1:230, sensed this implied prohibition against using vessels for skhakh. He writes concerning the mat, "this is an exceptional case among the articles listed (for use as skhakh), *for it is a fruit of human labor.*"

other celestial bodies, from being seen.[116] In structuralist terminology, skhakh mediates between the polarities of life/death, nature/culture and outside/inside. At the time of the autumn harvest, when crops were collected from the field to supply food for the coming year, when the onset of the rainy season and the equinox marked the beginning of the transition from summer to winter, and when, after the harvest, the seasonal work in the fields was completed and winter lodgings occupied, these polarities would be felt most poignantly.

V. Skhakh: The Essence of the Sukka

The tannaim carefully regulated skhakh in several other ways that demonstrate they considered skhakh the essence of the sukka. Skhakh had to be placed with the intention that it serve as the roofing for a sukka. Bundles of straw, wood and twigs are not fit for skhakh, since they are generally left on the roof in order to dry out, not with the specific intention that they be used as skhakh.[117] The same reason apparently explains m1:8, "If one hollows out [a space] in a stack of grain to make a sukka therein, it is no sukka."[118] The skhakh, formed by the grain that remains at the top of the cavity, results from the hollowing out process, not from a deliberate act of placement. This principle is first spelled out in a baraita attributed to R. Hiyya: *"You shall make [the Festival of Sukkot for seven days] (Deut 16:13). And not from what has been made."*[119] That is, the skhakh must be "made" specifically for the sukka,

---

[116]Although in such cases the sukka is fit. See m2:2 and above, p. 208.

[117]*Midrash Tannaim*, 94; bSuk 12b.

[118]*Midrash Tannaim*, 94; ySuk 1:8, 52c, according to R. Hiyya. A baraita, b16a, permits such a sukka, but BT interprets this baraita to pertain to a case mentioned by R. Huna, where there had been a space of a handbreadth prior to the hollowing out. In this case we assume the initial space was formed by the placement of the grain, and the placing was done with the intention it serve as skhakh.

[119]y1:8, 52c; *Midrash Tannaim*, 94; baraita, b11b. A slightly different formulation appears in *Sifre Deut*. §140 (194): *"You shall make (Deut 16:13)*. This excludes an old sukka. From here you say: If he trained a vine or a gourd or ivy upon it (the sukka) and spread skhakh upon them, it is not valid." ("From here" refers back to the verse, and is not related to the law of the old sukka.) This midrash-halakha (cited in bSuk 11b) disqualifies the vine, gourd and ivy (and skhakh subsequently placed upon them) based on the principle that skhakh must be placed with the intention that it serve as roofing for the sukka. The vine had been trained on the sukka beforehand, without the intention that it serve for skhakh. m1:4, however, disqualifies the vine because it still grows in the ground. Thus the Mishna and the Sifre appear to disagree over the reason for the prohibition against vines and suchlike. But several rishonim explain that the prohibition against the use of living foliage derives from this very principle, that skhakh must be placed with intention. So the contradiction between the Sifre and the Mishna is not as sharp

and not result from materials already in place. Despite this late documentation of the formulation of the principle, the idea itself appears to be much older, probably dating to the time of the Houses. In the debate of m1:7, recall that the House of Hillel (according to R. Yehuda) permitted beams of an ordinary roof to serve as skhakh once they had been loosened. Although the appearance of the roof does not change much, if at all, the act of loosening serves to (re-)place the beams with the intention that they serve as skhakh. A debate of the Houses to be examined below over the "old" sukka is essentially a question of whether the entire sukka must be built with the intention that it serve as a festival booth.[120] This serves as further evidence that intention was an important consideration in the time of the Houses.

The importance of intention in the Mishna has been stressed by both Jacob Neusner and Howard Eilberg-Schwartz.[121] Intention often determines whether an act has been completed, or how a situation should be construed, or the status of an object. Ritual acts performed with intention are often valid while those performed without intention (or with the incorrect intention) are frequently invalid. The requirement that skhakh be placed with intention, then, coheres with a general characteristic of tannaitic law, for which Neusner has provided a philosophical interpretation and Eilberg-Schwartz an anthropological explanation. While both approaches may be applied to the skhakh, there are specific reasons why intention should be a factor here. Sukkot were used for many other purposes,[122] and, in theory, by inhabiting any such sukka the biblical commandment to stay in sukkot could be fulfilled. The tannaim wished to avoid this possibility. There is a substantial difference between taking up residence in a sukka used throughout the year to store

---

as at first glance. See Ritba to bSuk 11b (119), s.v. *heikhi dami*. And see Halivni, *Meqorot*, 4:170-72; Albeck, *Mishna*, 2:473.

[120] See below, p. 218. Intention also determines the law in the debates of the Houses in mAh 7:3 and mBM 3:12, and in the baraita, bQid 42b. B.S. Jackson, "Liability for Mere Intention in Early Jewish Law," *Essays in Jewish and Comparative Legal History* (Leiden: Brill, 1975), 202-34 shows that intention and other mental processes determined liability in biblical, post-biblical and ancient law. See also S. Belkin, *The Alexandrian Halakah in Apologetic Literature of the First Century C.E.* (Philadelphia, 1936), 57-62, who cites among other examples the bold statement of Josephus, *CA*, 2:215-17: "As for doing wrong to one's parents or of impiety against God, even if he (only) intends (to do so), he shall immediately die."

[121] Neusner, *Judaism*, 271-81; H. Eilberg-Schwartz, *The Human Will in Judaism: The Mishnah's Philosophy of Intention* (Atlanta, Georgia: Scholars Press, 1986). The issue also appears in the rabbinic debates of whether the commandments require proper intention; see bPes 114b and parallels.

[122] See n. 136.

animal fodder or to house chickens, and moving into a sukka constructed specifically for the celebration of the festival. Subjectively the experiences are different. In the second case the sukka feels sacred, holy, set aside for a higher purpose. It lacks the mundane associations of a typical booth used for ordinary functions. We shall see that throughout the tannaitic period one school of thought indeed required that the entire sukka be built for the sake of the festival. A second school of thought, however, ruled that any sukka could be used. But all agreed that the roofing had to be placed with the intention that it serve as skhakh, for the covering of festival sukkot. The experience of building "for the sake of the festival," in other words, was "concentrated" in the skhakh.[123] And there is a certain logic to this: many sukkot and shelters probably had rudimentary walls or lacked walls completely, consisting of roofings suspended on posts. It was therefore the roofing, the skhakh, that was considered the "essence" of the sukka,[124] and the demand for intention focused there. Thus the fact that many types of sukkot were used explains the necessity of intention for skhakh. The law is not simply another example of a ritual act requiring proper intention, as with performing a sacrifice or tying the fringes of a garment. The law ensures that the festival sukka is for the sake of the festival, not for any other purpose, and distinguishes it from other types of sukkot. In this way, the demand for intention enhances the religious experience of building and residing in a sukka.

Another law that underscores the centrality of skhakh rules that skhakh "that extends from the sukka is considered like the sukka" (t2:3).[125] The exact intention of this law is unclear, but the general sense

---

[123]In fact, this law probably explains the opinion of those that ruled that any booth could be used for the festival. Since the skhakh would be placed "for the sake of the festival," they felt the festival booth was adequately distinguished from its mundane counterparts and procured a measure of sanctity.

[124]This is expressed nicely by Tosafot, b2a, s.v. *ki*: "...granted that we do not worry about the walls, whether one makes them permanent, nevertheless, with the skhakh – *because the essence of the [term] 'sukka' is on account of [its having] skhakh* – it is not fit..." And see Rashi, b8b, s.v. *'amar*: "even if we do not require a sukka be built for the sake of the festival, we require [that a sukka be built] for the sake of a sukka, and it is called a *sukka* on account of the shade, since it provides shelter *(mesukakh)* from the heat." Krauss, *Qadmoniot*, 1:228 and n. 2 notes that the Aramaic terms for the sukka *(matla, metalalta,* etc.) derive from the root ṬLL (= Hebrew ṢLL), which points to the centrality of shade. Of course *sukka* and *skhakh* derive from the same Hebrew root.

[125]Skhakh in this law is called waste-matter *(psal)*, a term that derives from the common practice of collecting skhakh from unwanted and leftover foliage. Thus the midrash-halakha in b12a claims that skhakh derives "from the waste matter *(psolet)* of the threshing-floor and winepress." The same term appears in baraitot of 14b and 18a.

is that the area under skhakh which extends over the walls on the "outside" of the sukka has the same status as the area within the walls.[126] The skhakh can therefore confer "sukka-ness" on areas beyond the interior of the sukka. Residing under the shade of the skhakh confers the essential experience of the sukka.

The importance of skhakh can be seen from a series of tannaitic laws that governs its quantity, placement and relationship to the inhabitant of the sukka. There must be enough skhakh to produce more shade than sun within the sukka.[127] If substances unfit for skhakh are placed on the roof along with fit skhakh, the fit skhakh must equal or better the amount of unfit material (m1:4, 1:7-8, t1:7). There may not be large gaps in the skhakh.[128] There can be no empty separation greater than three handbreadths between the skhakh and the walls. However, skhakh may be separated from the walls by up to four cubits if a solid substance such as bricks surrounds the skhakh.[129] These laws reveal the *raison d'être* of skhakh – to provide shade. Skhakh does not merely possess symbolic value but serves a functional purpose. If the skhakh is so sparse that it does not produce sufficient shade, or if other substances form a covering such that the skhakh does not produce shade, the sukka is invalid.

The relationships between the skhakh and the sky and between the resident of the sukka and the skhakh also illustrate this point. The sukka must be directly under the sky and the resident directly under the skhakh. Therefore a sukka within a house or under the branches of trees is invalid.[130] If one sukka has been built on top of another, the Mishna permits the upper sukka and disqualifies the lower.[131] A sheet spread

---

[126] Babylonian amoraim offer five different interpretations, b19a. Cf. y1:1, 52b and *TK*, 4:852-53.

[127] m1:1 rules that a sukka with more sun than shade is invalid. t1:2 explains that the Mishna refers to the roof. There must be skhakh sufficient to provide more shade than sunlight, but if the walls allow more sun than shade, the sukka is still fit. Cf. m2:2. Only R. Yoshia rules that the walls must provide more shade than sun, bSuk 7b. See below, p. 224.

[128] A baraita, b14b, disqualifies skhakh with gaps large enough for a goat to fit through. In b17a the amoraim rule that an air-space of three handbreadths invalidates the skhakh (so y1:10, 52c). The rishonim claim the space large enough for a kid to fit through amounts to three handbreadths. See Ritba to b14b, s.v. *leima*. (Some rishonim, however, interpret the baraita to forbid a gap in the walls, not in the skhakh.)

[129] m1:10; baraita, y1:10, 52c.

[130] m1:2; *Sifra 'Emor* 17:4 (102d); baraita, b9b.

[131] m1:2; *Sifra 'Emor* 17:4 (102d). R. Yehuda, however, rules that the lower sukka is fit if the upper one is not inhabited. He reasons that a sukka without occupants does not constitute an abode, hence it does not interpose between the lower sukka and the sky. In some versions of the Mishna R. Yehuda rules "even the

above the four posts of a bed interposes between the occupant and the skhakh, hence one may not sleep in such a state.[132] The same principle governs the debate between R. Yehuda and the sages whether one can sleep under a bed in the sukka. The sages view the bed as a structure in its own right, hence it interposes between the skhakh and the person sleeping beneath. R. Yehuda does not view the bed as a separation between the occupant and the skhakh.[133] These laws indicate that the tannaim considered dwelling in the shade of the skhakh the essence of the ritual. Skhakh was meant to create a specific experience that entailed a direct sense of the foliage overhead and the sky beyond, a sense of being in the shade of the skhakh. When objects interposed between the resident and the skhakh or the skhakh and the sky, then the skhakh did not produce the requisite experience of shade. Recall that the Sifra interpreted the term sukkot in Neh 8:15 to refer exclusively to skhakh. For the tannaim "sukka" and "skhakh" were almost synonymous; to perform the ritual of the sukka was to experience the skhakh directly. We will consider the nature and meaning of that experience in the discussion of aggadic material in the following chapter.

VI. The Sukka

Although the tannaim considered the skhakh the essence of the sukka, they were interested in other structural aspects as well. As with other biblical commandments, they explored and defined the legal contours with great precision. Scripture had commanded that each Israelite dwell in a sukka; in order to comply with the commandment, precisely what constituted a sukka had to be determined. Several issues required elucidation: out of what materials could sukkot be made?

---

lower is fit." See b9b-10a; y1:2, 52b; Fox, *Succah*, 8-9 and the citations there; Halivni, *Meqorot*, 4:168.

[132]m1:3. See the series of baraitot, b10b-11a, concerning various types of beds and canopies.

[133]See m2:1. Lieberman, *TK*, 4:846, 852 explains that according to R. Yehuda the bed was made to sleep upon, not to cover anything below it. Hence it is not viewed as a separation. A series of baraitot in b10b considers different types of beds. The baraita of b21b attributes the prohibition of sleeping under a bed to Rabban Gamaliel. In t1:11 R. Yose b. R. Yehuda in the name of R. Yose rules that "he who sleeps under a wagon is like he who sleeps under a bed." Again the question is whether the floor of the wagon interposes between the sleeper and the skhakh that has been placed above, presumably across the sides of the wagon. See too the baraita about sheets hung for decoration, ySuk 1:3, 52b, the amoraic comments and the parallel in b10a. Note that t1:7 rules that fruits, nuts and wreaths hung from the roof of the sukka do not invalidate that skhakh. These objects are hung for decorative purposes, so they are not considered separations or unfit skhakh.

Could sukkot be constructed in any shape – square, round, triangular, tent-like? How many walls did a sukka require? What were the maximum and minimum heights and sizes of the sukka?

Extra-rabbinic sources provide little information on these issues. Philo and Josephus transmit the commandment to reside in sukkot (*skēnai*) without any indication of the type, size or shape of the structure. Both allude to shelter as a reason for the commandment: Josephus appeals to the need for protection from the cold while Philo contrasts the protection of the sukka with the exposure of denuded fields.[134] These reasons suggest that in the conception of these authors festival sukkot were solid structures, rather than open-faced sheds or lean-tos. The Temple Scroll is the only source which provides more detail, prescribing the height of the sukkot of the utopian temple as eight cubits.[135] Rabbinic traditions, in contrast, contain detailed legislation concerning dimensions, size and structure.

More fundamental than these matters of definition was a basic conceptual question concerning the nature of the festival sukka. Did the Bible obligate one to dwell in a sukka on the festival or in a festival sukka? In other words, did one have to build a new, unused sukka specifically for the festival? Booths, after all, were common structures, used for storage, shelter, the protection of guards in the fields, and many other purposes.[136] Did these shelters qualify as festival sukkot in which one could fulfill the biblical commandment (assuming they were covered with the requisite skhakh)? Or did mundane use disqualify them from ritual use? Lev 23:42 directs that the Israelite reside in a sukka, not that a special sukka be built anew: "You shall dwell in sukkot for seven days." Thus Israelites are commanded to dwell in sukkot, not to *build* them. However, Neh 8 reports that the people rush out to make sukkot. Their building activity can be seen as mere necessity – there happened to be no available sukkot at that time. It can be understood, however, as a ritual in its own right and an indispensable element of the observance of the festival. The Bible, then, was ambiguous. We have seen that the Temple

---

[134]Philo, *Special Laws* 2:205-208; Josephus, *AJ* 3:244-47; see Chapter 2, VI and VIII.
[135]Col. 42:10-17; Yadin, *Temple*, 2:179-80. See Chapter 2, V.
[136]Krauss, *Qadmoniot*, 1:234-35 counts twelve types of sukkot mentioned in rabbinic literature: 1) the festival sukka, 2) an ordinary sukka used for miscellaneous purposes (mBes 4:2), 3) sukka of gentiles (this and the following are found in baraitot, bSuk 8b), 4) sukka of women, 5) sukka of cattle, 6) sukka of Samaritans, 7) sukka of shepherds, 8) sukka of guards of drying fruits (שומרי קייצים; see Rashi, ad loc.), 9) sukka of *burgnin* (city guards; see Krauss, 1:38), 10) sukka of guards of orchards, 11) sukka of artisans, 12) sukka of Genasar (Sea of Galilee, mMa 3:7).

Scroll mandates that sukkot be built anew each year, although the beams and columns upon which the covering rested were permanent fixtures.[137]

We have returned, then, to the question of intention and the commandments, an issue encountered in the discussion of the skhakh. Foliage does not count as skhakh unless placed upon the sukka with that intention in mind. Did a similar principle apply to the sukka?

This fundamental question seems to have been debated throughout the tannaitic period. The Houses first debate this issue in mSuk 1:1:

> [A] An old sukka: The House of Shammai declares it invalid. And the House of Hillel declares it valid.
> [B] And what is deemed an old sukka? Any that one made thirty days before the Festival.
> [C] But[138] if one made it for the sake of the festival, even from the beginning of the year, it is valid.

The House of Shammai rules that a sukka must be constructed specifically for the festival. Thus the sukka must be built either within thirty days of Sukkot [B], the presumption being that the builder intended it for festival use, or it must be built specifically with that intention in mind [C]. The House of Hillel allows any booth to be used.[139] bSuk 9a provides a midrash-halakha, similar to the midrash

---

[137]Col. 42:10-17; Yadin, *Temple*, 2:179-80. See Chapter 2, V.
[138]Some MSS have "and."
[139]On the structure of this Mishna, see Burgansky, *Sukka*, 88-98. This explanation reads the Mishna as a unified whole. However, it may be the case that B and C were added at a later time to A, the original disagreement of the Houses. B gives a temporal definition of the term "old sukka," which limits the disagreement to sukkot built more than thirty days before the festival. C can be understood independently of B, defining the term "old sukka" in terms of the purpose for which the sukka was built. Accordingly, a sukka built even one day before sukkot, but not for the sake of the festival, is unfit. A sukka built long before the festival, even "at the beginning of the year," is valid if built for the sake of the festival. Thus B and C, read independently of each other, offer different definitions of an "old sukka." If read in light of C, the thirty days of B function as an indication of purpose: we assume a sukka built within thirty days of Sukkot was built for its sake. As a whole, then, B and C frame the essential disagreement in terms of whether the sukka was made for the sake of the festival. If they are comments appended by later authorities, then the original dispute of the Houses may be other than as understood and construed by these appended clauses. Without B and C, for example, we might explain A as follows: The House of Shammai requires that a new sukka be built every year for the festival. The House of Hillel allows last year's sukka (the "old" sukka) to be reused. In this case both Houses agree the sukka must be built for the festival; the question is whether the sukka must be built exclusively for the upcoming Sukkot celebration. This explanation could be modified slightly and serve to explain A and B without C, and many other explanations could be given. But this is all speculation. In the absence of any countervailing evidence, I assume C gives the correct

requiring skhakh be "made" for the festival, to supply scriptural support for the House of Shammai: *"You shall make the Festival of Sukkot for seven days (Deut 16:13).* We require a sukka made for the sake of the festival."[140] This midrash derives from the anonymous talmudic editors (the stammaim), and cannot be attributed to the House of Shammai. But the principle of the midrash – that a sukka must be built for the festival – accurately expresses the Shammaite position.

The provision at [C] pertains exclusively to the House of Shammai, which may indicate that the compiler of the Mishna rules in accordance with their view. Indeed, this seems to be the opinion of most tannaitic sources. *Sifre Deut.* §140 (194) cites the Shammaite ruling anonymously, which creates the impression that the editor of the *Sifre* held this position to be the accepted law.[141] So too t1:4 follows the position of the House of Shammai, ruling that the sukkot of shepherds and of field workers, and a stolen sukka, are invalid. The sukkot of shepherds and field workers were constructed in order to provide shelter in the fields and pastures, not for the festival. The thief did not make the stolen sukka at all, so we cannot consider it made for the festival.[142] We even find the Shammaite view explicitly stated in Targum Pseudo-Jonathan to Lev 23:42. Among the copious halakhic additions in the targum appears the instruction to dwell in a "sukka made for the sake of the festival."[143]

The baraitot of the talmuds modified the Shammaite preference of the Mishna, Tosefta and Sifre in favor of the Hillelite position. t1:4 appears in somewhat different form in the talmuds: b8b contains two baraitot corresponding to the Toseftan baraita:

---

interpretation of the disagreement. For those who believe C is a later gloss that reinterprets the Houses' debate, then the subject of the ensuing discussion is not "the House of Shammai" but "an anonymous tanna who construed the ruling of the House of Shammai" in this way.

[140]Above, p. 212. The sugya advances two halakhic midrashim for the House of Shammai. This one interprets Deut 16:13, while the other expounds Lev 23:34. In some manuscripts the verses quoted are interchanged. See *DQS* ad loc.

[141]Cf. L. Finkelstein, "Influences of the House of Shammai on Sifre Deuteronomy," *Sefer 'Asaf*, eds. U. Cassuto et al. (Jerusalem, 1943), 415 (Hebrew) and S. Lieberman's notes there, pp. 424-26. Finkelstein fails to recognize that the editor was simply citing the accepted halakha of his time. He was not influenced specifically by the House of Shammai. For literature on the issue of tannaitic law in accord with Shammaite rulings and other examples, see Sussmann, *MMT*, 72 n. 237. This case is hardly exceptional.

[142]The stolen sukka appears in the baraitot in b31a, y3:1, 53c. These baraitot, and the ensuing discussion in the talmuds, disqualify the stolen sukka for different reasons, and permit certain types of stolen sukkot.

[143]מתעבדא לטולא לשם חגא.

> A sukka of GNB"K:[144] A sukka of gentiles, a sukka of women, a sukka of cattle, a sukka of Samaritans, a sukka of any type, is valid, as long as it is covered with skhakh according to the law.
>
> A sukka of RQB"S: A sukka of shepherds, a sukka of guards of drying fruit, a sukka of city guards, a sukka of guards of orchards, is valid, as long as it is covered with skhakh according to the law.[145]

The baraita appears in the y1:1, 52b as follows:

> The sukka of shepherds and the sukka of craftsmen are fit. The sukka of Samaritans: if it was made according to the law, it is fit. If made not according to the law, it is unfit.

The three baraitot basically follow the opinion of the House of Hillel. Sukkot "of any type," including those made to serve the needs of various groups or occupations, are generally acceptable. Although these sukkot were not constructed for the sake of the festival, but for other purposes, they are nevertheless valid. Because the sukkot were not built with considerations of the festival in mind, there is some likelihood that they do not conform to the requirements of the festival sukka. The BT baraitot warn that the sukkot must have the requisite skhakh, while the PT baraita cautions that the sukkot of Samaritans must be built according to law.[146] Particular care was required since Samaritan booths would not necessarily conform to rabbinic specifications.

Other baraitot seem to compromise between the rulings of the Houses. A baraita in y1:1, 52b comments on the Hillelite opinion in the

---

[144]GNB"K is a mnemonic for the four sukkot listed: *Goyim* (gentiles), *Nashim* (women), *Behemot* (cattle), *Kutim* (Samaritans). Similarly RQB"S stands for: *Ro'im* (shepherds), *Qaisim* (guards of drying fruit [Rashi]), *Burgnin* (city guards), *Shomrei peirot* (guards of orchards).

[145]For some discussion of the realia of these sukkot, see Krauss, *Qadmoniot*, 1:234-35. On sukkot in the fields see Isa 1:8; mKil 5:3 *(shomera)*. On sukkot for animals, see Gen 33:17; Dalman, *AuS*, 6:61. Halivni, *Meqorot*, 4:167 suggests that the two baraitot derived from a single source which subsequently splintered.

[146]The provision "as long as it is covered with skhakh according to the law" is problematic. Even if a sukka was made by a Jew for the sake of the festival, the sukka would be fit only "as long as it is covered with skhakh according to the law." Cf. Rashi, bSuk 8b, s.v. *mai*. But the provision is simply meant as a warning to check punctiliously in these cases. Halivni, *Meqorot*, 4:166-67 notes that the provision serves as "good advice," to check whether these sukkot are properly covered with skhakh and warns one not to assume that they were made according to law. See too Burgansky, *Sukka*, 97. A similar provision, "if they were made according to the law, they are fit, but if made not in according to law, they are unfit" occurs in a baraita, y1:1, 52a. The amoraim explain the baraita as a comment to the law specifying that two walls must be four by four handbreadths in size and the third at least one square handbreadth. The point is that the walls must be facing each other, not split apart in different directions. Thus this sort of cautionary advice is not unprecedented.

The Tannaitic Period: Legal and Ritual Developments 221

Mishna that: "One must make new *(lehadesh)* part of it." The baraita accepts that opinion as law, but adds a proviso: a sukka not made for the festival is fit only if one builds anew, modifies or touches up part of it. This minimal act of rebuilding indicates symbolically that the sukka has been "made" for the sake of the festival. The Shammaite position essentially has been concentrated in a symbolic act, a type of ritual metonymy, whereby part of the sukka stands for the whole.[147]

A sustained interest in the dimensions and structural requirements of a sukka continued throughout tannaitic times. Already the Houses of Hillel and Shammai debate the minimum size of the sukka (m2:7). The House of Hillel rules that a sukka must be large enough to contain one's head and the majority of one's body. In this case one is considered "in" the sukka. The House of Shammai requires that the sukka be large enough to contain a table as well.[148] R. Yehuda Hanasi rules that the

---

[147] A baraita in b8b modifies the Hillelite position in a different manner. Attributed to R. Levi in the name of R. Meir, the baraita rules that in the case of two sukkot of craftsmen, one built within the other, the outer sukka is fit, inner sukka is unfit. Consistent with the Hillelite position, the outer sukka is fit despite the fact that it is used throughout the year as a gallery for the craftsman's wares. The reason the inner sukka is unfit relates to the other datum of the baraita, that the inner sukka requires a mezuza, indicating that it is a habitation in its own right. Cf. Rashi, s.v. *penimit* and tMa 2:21. But this should not matter. If a sukka need not be built specifically for the festival, of what relevance is the fact that it forms the living quarters of the craftsman throughout the year? Thus Ritba, ad loc., (78): "Some raise the following difficulty: why is it not a sukka? As long as it is covered with skhakh according to the law, and we do not require that the sukka be made for the sake of the festival?" Rashi here suggests that one cannot "recognize" that the craftsman occupies the booth for the sake of the festival. And that is the crux. The baraita does not totally forgo the principle that a festival booth must be for the sake of the festival. However it has shifted the gauge of what makes a sukka 'for' the festival from the intention of the builder to the public recognition of the purpose served by the sukka. Because the craftsman lives in his sukka throughout the year, there is no indication that on Sukkot he inhabits the sukka specifically for the sake of the festival. The outer sukka, however, does not typically serve as a dwelling. If the craftsman moves in there, he clearly indicates that it serves as a festival sukka. Thus the question of building a sukka for the sake of the festival remained an issue throughout the tannaitic period and in later times. The Babylonian amoraim accepted the Hillelite ruling unquestionably. But some medieval jurists were influenced by PT and ruled that some part of the sukka should be "renewed" on an annual basis.

[148] The formulation of the Mishna is ambiguous, and may be interpreted to refer to the person, not the sukka. One who situates himself such that his head, body or table is outside the sukka, even in the case of a large sukka, has not fulfilled his obligation. bSuk 3a emends the Mishna such that it governs both the sukka and the person, whether the sukka is too small to contain the table or one perches himself at the border of a large sukka with his table outside. The original Mishna dealt only with the case of a small sukka. See Halivni, *Meqorot*, 4:155. Cf.

minimum size of a sukka is four by four cubits (t2:2).[149] The maximum acceptable height of a sukka was debated by the students of R. Akiba. The sages set the maximum height of the sukka at twenty cubits. R. Yehuda demurs, and seems to have no maximum height.[150] An unattributed Mishna sets the minimum height of the sukka at ten handbreadths, and the Tosefta adds that even a bed or tree ten handbreadths tall may serve as a valid sukka provided it has the requisite skhakh (m1:1, t1:3).

A dispute from the Yavnean stratum considers a tent-like sukka and a sukka that is propped up against the wall in the form of a lean-to (m1:11). R. Eliezer invalidates a structure of this type since "it has no roof." The sages, however, permit it. In t1:10, R. Eliezer concedes that if such a sukka has a roof of at least one handbreadth, or was raised from the ground by one handbreadth, it is valid. In these cases one can distinguish the walls from the roof.[151] Deliberations on structure are also found among later authorities. A round sukka is disqualified on the grounds that it has no corners.[152] R. Yehuda rules that a sukka must be able to stand on its own, while an unattributed opinion allows the sukka to be propped up beside the legs of a bed.[153] An unattributed Mishna permits a sukka placed on top of a wagon, ship, tree or camel.[154]

Epstein, *MLH*, 631. The rishonim conclude this minimum size amounts to seven handbreadths. The opinions of the Houses also appear in baraitot of b3a. The opinion of the House of Hillel is attributed to the sages in t2:2. That of the House of Shammai appears in the unattributed baraita of b14b.

[149]See the previous note. R. Yehuda Hanasi avoided a contradiction between his own position and those of the Houses in m2:7 by shifting the Houses dispute to the case of a person sitting below the edge of a large sukka. He would claim that both Houses agree with his position concerning the minimum size of the sukka. In t2:2, however, the sages disagree with R. Yehuda Hanasi, claiming a sukka is valid as long as it contains one's head and the greater part of the body. The sages in the Tosefta correspond with the House of Hillel in the Mishna.

[150]m1:1, t1:1. In the parallel baraita in b2b, R. Yehuda limits the maximum height to forty or fifty cubits. The baraita of R. Hiyya in y1:1, 51c preserves the same tradition. See *TK*, 4:835.

[151]On the different interpretations of these laws see *TK*, 4:844-45. Rav Yosef in b19b claims that this Mishna was transmitted by R. Natan. The sages, however, reverse the attribution of the opinions of R. Eliezer and his anonymous disputants such that R. Eliezer permits such sukkot while his opponents disqualify them. PT makes no such claim.

[152]Baraita, b7b.

[153]m2:2. In both y2:2, 52d and b21b a second reason is considered for R. Yehuda's position: that one may not put skhakh on an object that is subject to impurity. The PT rejects this reason. See *TK*, 4:851.

[154]m2:3. In a baraita, b23a, R. Yehuda prohibits a sukka built on top of an animal, while R. Meir permits it.

The fourth tannaitic generation systematically considered laws relating to the walls of the sukka. The students of R. Akiba debated the number of walls a sukka required.[155] The majority rule that a sukka must have two proper walls and a third wall of at least one handbreadth. R. Shimon requires three proper walls, and a fourth of at least one handbreadth. An unattributed opinion in m1:1 requires three walls and makes no mention of the handbreadth. R. Yaakov rules that four posts qualify as walls, provided they are of sufficient circumference that were they straightened out, they would cover an area of one handbreadth.[156] An unattributed baraita, y1:1, 51c, permits four reed-posts but makes no specification as to their width.[157] A minimalist position is attributed to the Men of Jerusalem, who are reported to have hung their beds out of the windows and placed skhakh above them, apparently dismissing the need for walls (t2:3).[158] The dimensions of the walls were debated too. m1:9 rules that a wall must be ten handbreadths high, measured from the ground. R. Yose permits a ten-handbreadth wall that descends from the roof, while the sages forbid it.[159] A baraita in b7a allows a wall to be constructed from reed posts, provided they are not separated from each other by more than three handbreadths, even if the net empty space is greater than the amount of wall.

Unlike the skhakh, few laws govern the materials from which the walls may be made.[160] Trees may function as walls, and even human beings may be counted as the third wall (m2:3, t1:8). R. Meir and R. Yehuda disagree whether an animal can form the wall of a sukka.[161] The pillars surrounding a courtyard may be considered walls (t1:8).[162] After the list of materials unfit for skhakh in m1:4-5, (ivy and vines still growing in the ground, and bundles of straw or twigs) the Mishna

---

[155]t1:12-13; see Epstein, *Tannaim*, 347. Fifth generation tannaim also debated the issue; t1:12, y1:1, 52a.
[156]t1:12-13; b4b.
[157]*Qorban ha'eda* ad loc. reads the baraita in terms of R. Yaakov's statement in the parallel baraita that the posts must be of a minimum circumference. This reading is based on his interpretation of the PT sugya. But other interpretations are possible; cf. *Mar'eh hapanim* to the parallel in yEruv 1:1, 18b. In any case the baraita requires no minimum circumference.
[158]Unless the Tosefta considers the sides of the bed to count as walls. The Tosefta points out that the beds were ten handbreadths high, thus complying with the minimum height established in m1:1.
[159]A baraita, b16b, rules that a mat seven handbreadths large can be considered a wall. Rashi, s.v. *besukka*, explains that the mat must be suspended three handbreadths from the top of the sukka, thus forming a partition ten handbreadths in all.
[160]As noted by Büchler, *Cabanes*, 188 n. 1.
[161]Baraita, b23a.
[162]So too the baraita, y1:1, 52a.

concedes "all these are fit for the walls." In fact, there appear to be no prohibitions whatsoever on materials that may be used for walls. And unlike skhakh, walls are fit even if they allow more sun than shade.[163]

The paucity of legislation concerning the walls and the fact that the extant legislation is both lenient and late can be attributed to the common pattern of building shelters in antiquity. Roofings suspended on mere posts probably served as rudimentary shelters for animals, guards, workmen in the fields and many other purposes. These crude structures were inexpensive and could be erected easily. In all likelihood, the number and nature of walls varied. Many had four walls, others had two or one, and some had none. The walls probably varied in dimension as well, some reaching to the roof, others rising only a foot or two. The case debated in t1:12, "If he erected four beams and placed skhakh upon them...," seems to describe a common practice.[164] Similarly, the Temple Scroll describes beams and columns fixed upon the roof of the temple upon which the sukkot were to be built annually.[165] The skhakh was placed each year upon the permanent frameworks. Thus the sukka of the Temple Scroll had no walls other than fixed columns, and parallels the Toseftan sukka formed by placing skhakh upon posts. Perhaps the sukkot described in Neh 8 were structures of this sort. Scholars generally claim that the entirety of the Nehemian sukkot were built of foliage, the only materials mentioned. But it is just possible that the author referred only to the foliage gathered for the roof, assuming the people placed it upon four beams or a crude framework.[166] Krauss describes nineteenth century Palestinian sukkot whose only walls were short partitions of brick, half a meter high, while wooden beams supported the roofing.[167] Dalman too witnessed this manner of building huts in his extensive investigations.[168]

At all events, the walls are not central to the tannaitic idea of the sukka. Skhakh was the essence of the sukka and had to conform to numerous and varied laws. Legislation governing the walls is basically limited to minimum standards: the number of walls required, the minimum height, and the maximum distances from the skhakh and the

---

[163]t1:2. Only R. Yoshia, b7b, insists the walls supply more shade than sun.
[164]Cf. the baraita, ySuk 1:1, 51c, noted above. R. Yoshia, Y.1:1, 51d, notes that the rich made the walls of their sukkot "thin" (*qalil*) so that cool winds could enter.
[165]See n. 86.
[166]This obviates the problem of interpreting "leaves of olive, leaves of wild-olive, leaves of myrtle..." (Neh 8:15) as "leaves [on *branches*] of olive..." Only if one assumes that the materials for constructing walls were mentioned would solid branches be needed.
[167]Krauss, *Qadmoniot*, 1:225.
[168]Dalman, *AuS*, 6:59-61 and illustration 15.

ground. The legislation concerning skhakh, on the other hand, is far more comprehensive, and regulates not only minimum measures, but also the materials, the intention of the placement and the relationships between the skhakh, the occupant and the sky. These facts have important ramifications for the meaning of the sukka to the tannaim. The sukka was an overhead shelter that provided protection from the heat of the sun. The essential characteristic of the sukka was that it cast shade from above. To experience that shade comprised the religious experience the laws aimed to create.

When one considers the sources chronologically, a limited historical development can be discerned. Two of the three early traditions involve basic issues of definition of the sukka. The debate of the Houses over the "old" sukka is a fundamental question concerning the nature of the festival booth. The Yavnean dispute over the tent and lean-to addresses the essential conception of the configuration of the sukka, whether a structure without identifiable roof and walls can be called a "sukka" at all. The other debate of the Houses, the dispute over the minimum area of the sukka, initiates a discussion of dimensions which would continue for several generations. In the fourth generation two issues receive further attention. First, there is more debate as to minimum and maximum measurements. Now height, in addition to area, becomes an issue. Second, the nature of the walls becomes a topic of interest. Students of R. Akiba debate the minimum height and number of walls. Several unattributed mishnayot and baraitot of the talmuds pertain to the material for the walls. Since only fourth generation scholars discuss the laws regulating the walls, it is likely that these unattributed sources derive from the last generations of tannaim.

In sum, questions about the nature and structure of sukkot received attention prior to the destruction of the temple or at Yavneh, but were debated throughout the tannaitic period.[169] The dispute over the "old" sukka continues from the Houses through the later baraitot, while the early dispute over the minimum size is still disputed by R. Yehuda Hanasi at the end of the tannaitic period. The students of R. Akiba continued the discussion, promulgating minimum and maximum dimensions. They raised the issue of the walls for the first time, and promulgated a number of rulings on this topic.

VII. Dwelling in the Sukka

Lev 23:42 commands "You shall dwell in booths seven days." The tannaim sought to define this commandment precisely. How did one

---

[169] R. Eliezer, who rules on the structural questions, is known for his conservative tendencies and predilection for the "old" halakha. See Gilat, *Eliezer*, 23-67.

fulfill the obligation to "dwell" in a sukka? Could one ever leave the sukka? Was everybody obligated unconditionally or were some people exempt under certain circumstances?

The biblical commandment lends itself to two interpretations. The meaning may be: "You must live in a sukka for seven days." That is, each Israelite is commanded to stay within a sukka for seven days. At any given moment throughout the seven day period, an absolute obligation to be in the sukka devolves upon the Israelite. Taken to the extreme, it would follow that an Israelite may never leave the sukka. But the verse may also be interpreted: "You must make the sukka your dwelling-place for seven days." That is, for seven days you shall treat the sukka as your home, and not regard your house as a home. The sukka is simply a substitute house. The routine activities one ordinarily does in a house are transferred to the sukka. How was Leviticus to be interpreted: that one must occupy the sukka or that one must treat the sukka as a house?

The general tannaitic understanding tended toward the second interpretation: the sukka was considered a surrogate house. For seven days, it became the primary dwelling place. Tannaitic sources do not express this principle as abstractly as formulated above, but the idea is implicit in the following traditions:

> *You shall dwell (Lev 23:42).* "You shall dwell" [means] in the way you reside [in your normal dwellings].
>
> From this they said. One eats in the sukka. One drinks in the sukka. One rejoices[170] in the sukka. One brings his utensils up to the sukka."
>
> *(Sifra 'Emor 17:5 [103a])*[171]
>
> All seven days one makes his sukka regular *(qeva')* and his house occasional *('arai)*.
>
> (mSuk 2:9)

The *Sifra* compares dwelling in a sukka to residing in a house: one dwells in a sukka in the same manner as one resides in a house. The second half of the baraita derives from this interpretation the activities to be done in the sukka, namely, the routine activities that take place in a residence. They are not specific ritual gestures like the shaking of the lulav or the sounding of the shofar. That is to say, the ritual of the sukka consists of

---

[170]*metayel.* A. Mirsky, "Perushei hamefaresh lelashon hapiyyut," *Sinai* 87 (1980), 221 demonstrates that the root טול often appears in piyyutim as a synonym for "joy," and collects numerous precedents from rabbinic literature. Here the meaning is not "travel," but "rejoice, enjoy one's self." See too Jastrow, *Dictionary,* 523, s.v. טול.

[171]bSuk 28b, y2:10, 53b.

performing everyday activities there, of spending time therein and treating it as a domicile. m2:9 expresses a similar idea. One "makes" or treats his sukka as his "regular" residence and the house as an "occasional" or secondary residence. Since the house will serve as a residence occasionally – under circumstances defined by other tannaitic sources – the sukka will not be occupied continuously. Moreover, since the sukka functions in place of the house as the primary residence, there will be times one need not dwell in the sukka, just as there are times one does not stay in the house.

No explicit formula prescribes when one is exempt from staying in the sukka, although an implicit principle can be detected. The test is whether, were it not Sukkot, one would normally be in the house, or perform the act in question in one's house. If so, then on Sukkot one must be in the sukka. This principle can be seen in the following examples.

> [A] Guards of the city who work by day are exempt from the sukka during the day, and obligated during the night.
> [B] Guards of the city who work by night are exempt [from the sukka] during the night, and obligated during the day.
> [C] Guards of the city who work day and night are exempt [from the sukka] both during the day and the night.
> [D] Travelers are exempt from the sukka during the day, and obligated during the night.
> [E] Guards of gardens and orchards are exempt [from the sukka] during the night, and obligated during the day.
>
> (tSuk 2:3)

City guards are exempt from the sukka when they are on duty, since they are busy at their posts, and would not be at home. Travelers journey throughout the day. They do not stop for shelter, but eat their meals on the road. Hence on Sukkot they are exempt from the sukka during the day. At night travelers typically stay over at an inn or seek shelter at someone's house.[172] On Sukkot, then, they are obligated to spend the

---

[172]One might argue that there are times when travelers sleep outside, for example, when they cannot find shelter or do not wish to delay their journey to search out a lodging. Therefore, they should be exempt from the sukka at night. The tannaim, however, take into account the norms of society. Normally travelers seek shelter during the night. On Sukkot, then, they are obligated to seek shelter in a sukka. For a full discussion of societal norms and how they affect law, see Eilberg-Schwartz, *Intention*, 64-91.

In bSuk 26a [= bAr 3b] the baraita appears in a more expanded form: "Travelers by day are exempt from the sukka during the day, but are obligated at night. Travelers by night are exempt from the sukka at night, but are obligated during the day. Travelers by day and night are exempt from the sukka during day and night." The explanation is straightforward.

night in a sukka. Guards of orchards and gardens only work during the night.[173] Spending the night in crude shelters out in the fields, they do not return to their homes until the next day. Therefore, on Sukkot, they are exempt from the sukka at night.

For the tannaim, eating and sleeping comprise the two essential acts of dwelling in the sukka. These activities are normally performed at home, so on Sukkot, by eating or sleeping in the sukka, one demonstrates that the sukka is one's primary residence.[174] m2:4 states the principle with respect to eating: "One eats and drinks *occasional* (*'arai*) [food] outside of the sukka." Occasional snacking is permitted outside the sukka, just as throughout the year one might snack outside of one's house. Full meals, however, must be consumed in the sukka, since throughout the year meals are eaten at home. The tannaim debated the maximum that may be eaten outside the sukka. Rabban Yohanan b. Zakkai and Rabban Gamaliel insisted that a taste of cooked food, two dates and a pail of water be brought to the sukka before they would eat,[175] yet R. Sadoq ate less than the bulk of an egg outside the sukka (m2:5). R. Yehuda Hanasi relates that he and R. Elazar b. R. Sadoq ate figs and grapes outside the sukka when paying a visit to R. Yohanan b. Nuri (t2:2).[176]

Mishna-Tosefta presupposes that one must sleep in a sukka at night.[177] m2:1 rules that "if one slept under a bed in the sukka he has not fulfilled his obligation," which assumes an obligation to sleep in the sukka. The Men of Jerusalem are reported to have hung their beds out the windows and covered them with skhakh, presumably because they found no room in standard sukkot (t2:3). A number of laws govern the details of how one properly sleeps in the sukka (m1:3; t1:8, 2:2, 2:4). In one respect the matter of sleeping is more stringent than eating. A baraita rules that one may "snack" but not "nap" outside the sukka.[178] A

---

[173] In bSuk 26a the baraita exempts guards of orchards from the sukka during both day and night. This ruling assumes the guards work during the day as well.
[174] The place where one plans to eat serves to establish a residence for the Sabbath. See e.g. mEruv 3:1-8; 6:6-7.
[175] See J. Neusner, *A Life of Yohanan ben Zakkai, ca. 1-80 C.E.* (Leiden: Brill, 1970), 60 n. 6 for discussion of the identity of Gamaliel.
[176] According to the sages, one is obligated to eat a meal in the sukka only on the first night of the festival (m2:6). On subsequent days, one may fast or suffice with snacks. R. Eliezer, however, obligates one to eat two meals in the sukka on each day of the festival. He construes the obligation to dwell in the sukka more strictly. See below.
[177] *Sifra 'Emor* 17:4 (103a) provides a halakhic midrash proving the obligation to reside in a sukka applies during the night. A different midrash is found in bSuk 43a.
[178] b26a. The ruling is attributed to R. Elazar in y2:5, 53a.

nap may turn into an extended sleep because one may not wake after a short while even if one intends to do so. In such cases the person has slept fully. However, throughout the year sleeping takes place at home, and on Sukkot must be done in the sukka. A snack is not prone to become a full meal, because the agent is awake and aware of his actions.[179]

While eating and sleeping are the primary expressions of "dwelling" in the sukka, the *Sifra* cited above expressed a wider conception, encouraging one to eat, drink, rejoice and bring all his utensils into the sukka. Every act that one would normally perform in the house is now done in the sukka. The sukka completely replaces the house as the abode in which one spends one's time. Thus the ritual experience of the sukka is of broader scope than eating and sleeping.

A comparison of several rulings of R. Eliezer with those of the sages helps to further illuminate the tannaitic conception of the commandment. A series of six baraitot in b27a-27b contain three debates between R. Eliezer and the sages and a number of other traditions of R Eliezer. The BT seems to have preserved an early source, a collection of R. Eliezer traditions, some of which are paralleled elsewhere in tannaitic literature. The unified composition, parallels, and the fact that the rulings cohere with R. Eliezer's general halakhic standpoint suggest that the traditions are authentic. The three disputes are as follow:

1. R. Eliezer rules that one may not go from sukka to sukka. One must spend the entire festival in the same sukka. Accordingly, R. Eliezer rules that one who has two sukkot and two wives in different places may not move from one to the other since "whoever goes from sukka to sukka negates the commandment of the first [sukka]." The sages rule that one may go from sukka to sukka.

2. R. Eliezer rules that one may not build a sukka on the intermediate days of the festival. The sages allow it.[180]

3. R. Eliezer rules that one does not fulfill his obligation in a sukka that belongs to another person. Each man must reside in his own

---

[179]This explanation coheres with that of the "Companions" (ḥevraya), y2:5, 53a: "A man tends to become entrenched in sleep." Similarly R. Ashi explains in b26a: "[One is prohibited to nap] lest one fall fast asleep [and not wake from his nap.]" Other explanations are offered in both talmuds.

[180]Cf. b9a. R. Eliezer concedes that if the sukka collapses, it may be rebuilt on the intermediate day (b27b). His reasoning is explained in y2:7, 53a (where the same baraita is brought.) R. Aḥa in the name of R. Ḥanina comments that R. Eliezer imposed a penalty (qenas) on one who did not build his sukka before the festival. He wished to provide additional incentive that the sukka be built at the proper time, prior to the festival. A collapsed sukka is not due to neglect of the appropriate preparation for the festival.

sukka. The sages permit one to reside in the sukka that belongs to another.[181]

These rulings underscore the different conceptions of the commandment. R. Eliezer posits a continuous, seven-day obligation to dwell in the sukka. This obligation may be compared to other positive commandments such as the sounding of the shofar or shaking the lulav. One may not interrupt the performance of these commandments. Once one begins to sound the shofar, he should not stop in the middle and sound a different shofar. For R. Eliezer, once one has begun to fulfill the commandment in a particular sukka, he must not interrupt and shift to another sukka, nor leave the sukka to embark on a journey.[182] One who neglects to build a sukka before the festival cannot build a sukka on the intermediate days because the ritual can no longer be performed for the requisite seven day period. Thus R. Eliezer is reported to have rebuked a colleague for paying him a visit on the festival;[183] the colleague should have remained in his own sukka. Now R. Eliezer does not push this position to the extreme and completely forbid leaving the sukka. But he construes the commandment in strict terms and applies the obligation to dwell in the sukka throughout the festival. On the other hand, the majority of the tannaim, as we have seen, conceive of the sukka as a surrogate house. Throughout the year, one may visit the house of another person. On Sukkot, then, one may visit a friend. A sukka may be built on the intermediate days in order to dwell there during the rest of the festival. Granted that one who did not reside in a sukka on the first day may have transgressed, this act of omission does not affect the remaining days, for there is no autonomous, seven-day obligation that cannot now be fulfilled.

---

[181]The other traditions in the collection: 1) A procurator asks R. Eliezer whether he may eat but one meal each day in the sukka, since that is his regular custom. R. Eliezer responds that such individuals should honor God by eating two festival meals. 2) R. Eliezer rebukes a colleague for paying him a visit on the festival and rules that one should not embark on a journey on a festival. (See t2:1 and y2:5, 53a. The BT comments that the event and rebuke occurred on the Sabbath.) 3) He refuses to answer the question whether a sheet can be spread on top of the sukka to keep out the sun. 4) It is reported that once his students asked him thirty questions relating to the sukka. In a separate baraita, b31a, R. Eliezer disqualifies a stolen sukka and one who places skhakh in public places, while the rabbis rule these fit. See too n. 176.
[182]R. Eliezer accounts of no import the fact that the ritual of the sukka lasts a full week, as opposed to the shofar or lulav that are completed rather quickly, nor the fact that one may leave the sukka if it rains. Seven days is simply the length of the ritual. (But note the lulav ritual as reflected in the tradition of the "Men of Jerusalem." See Chapter 3, VI text to n. 190.)
[183]bSuk 27b. See n. 181.

The dispute over whether one must own his sukka is not related to this difference in conception of the commandment. The *Sifre* derives R. Eliezer's reason from Deut 16:13: "*You shall make for yourself the Festival of Sukkot for seven days (Deut 16:13)* – from your own."[184] That is, one must own one's sukka. The sages, with their more flexible approach to the commandment, reject this exegesis.[185]

Two other types of exemptions reflect the rather lenient attitude of the tannaim towards the commandment. Those sent on a religious duty are exempt from residing in the sukka (m2:4, t2:1). Engaged in one act of piety, they are not required to seek out a sukka in which to eat and sleep. The exemption accords with a general rabbinic principle that one performing a commandment is exempt from other commandments. Yet the tannaim could have ruled that agents not be sent out on acts of piety during the festival, since this prevents them from observing the rituals. That they did not do so reflects a loose construction of the obligation.[186] To dwell in the sukka does not mean a complete disruption of ordinary activities.

The sick and even their attendants are exempt from the sukka (m2:4, t2:2). We would expect the sick to be exempt, in accord with general rabbinic principles, since matters of health take precedence over ritual obligations. But the fact that attendants are also exempt is surprising. Furthermore, a baraita of b26a rules that the exemption applies equally to those who are dangerously ill and those who are not dangerously ill, and even to those who have sore eyes or headaches. Rabban Shimon b. Gamaliel relates that when he had sore eyes R. Yose exempted him and his attendants from the sukka.[187] Even feelings of mild discomfort which pose no threat to life are grounds for exemption from the sukka. To contribute to the comfort of the ill person, even his attendants are exempt.

Other types of discomfort also serve as grounds for exemption from the commandment. m2:9 rules that rain annuls the obligation to dwell in the sukka.

---

[184]The midrash turns on the phrase *ta 'ase lakh*, literally, "you shall make *for yourself.*" It must be yours.
[185]*Sifre Deut.* § 140 (194). Cf. b27b. The same principle grounds another debate between R. Eliezer and the sages. A baraita, b31b, reads: "A stolen sukka or one who placed skhakh in a public domain: R. Eliezer declares it unfit, and the sages declare it fit." For R. Eliezer the sukka is unfit because it does not belong to the thief. See Gilat, *Eliezer*, 306-307. On sukkot in public domains see tBQ 6:28.
[186]Although t2:1 suggests that the sages disapproved of such missions on the festivals.
[187]t2:2. On R. Yose see *DQS* to b26a, n. ב and Lieberman, *TK*, 4:850 and 1:73, n. 2.

> [A] All seven days one makes his sukka regular (*qeva'*) and his house occasional (*'arai.*)
> [B] If rains descend, when is he permitted to empty [the sukka]?
> [C] When the porridge will spoil.
> [D] They made a parable. To what is the matter like? To a servant who came to mix a cup [of wine] for his master, and he poured the flagon in his face.[188]

This Mishna offers a parabolic justification for leaving the sukka when it rains. Like the master who calls for wine and then rejects it, rain indicates divine displeasure, that God no longer desires his commandment to be carried out.[189] Since God does not want the sukka to be occupied, one may return to the house. Clearly considerations of comfort motivate this law; to dwell in a sukka when it rains is an unpleasant experience. t2:4 even rules that if the rain subsequently stops, one need not return to the sukka until after he has finished his meal or awakened from his night's sleep.[190] This ruling eliminates the inconvenience of having to shift back to the sukka immediately. Some tannaim apparently did not accept this leniency. A baraita, y2:10, 53b relates that R. Eliezer and R. Gamaliel were more strict about returning to the sukka:

> Just as they clear out the sukka on account of rain, so too because of extreme heat or mosquitoes. R. Gamaliel enters and leaves all night. R. Eliezer enters and leaves all night.

R. Eliezer and R. Gamaliel considered themselves exempt from the sukka only while the rain fell. As soon as the rain stopped the obligation to reside in the sukka took force again. Despite the inconvenience of disrupted sleep, they returned to the sukka.[191] The importance of discomfort is also evident in the first half of the baraita. The tannaim ruled that discomfort due to extreme heat and mosquitoes, in addition to rain, is grounds for leaving the sukka.[192]

---

[188] According to mTa 1:1, rain on Sukkot is a sign of a curse.

[189] The parable has been given various explanations, beginning already with bSuk 29a. For a survey of interpretations see P. Culbertson, "'Who Splashed on Whom.' Textual Equivocality and Rabbinic Exegesis," *Proceedings of the Tenth World Congress of Jewish Studies* C/1 (1990), 17-24.

[190] b29a transmits several versions of the baraita.

[191] See *Qorban ha'eda* ad loc.

[192] Note that the parable does not apply as neatly to these cases. In rabbinic thought God alone is responsible for rain. The same cannot be said of mosquitoes and heat. While rabbinic theology would consider God responsible for them insofar as God is provident over the entire world and all that happens, heat and mosquitoes do not immediately reflect the work of God in the same way as does rain. Yet these inconveniences are grounds enough to suspend the obligation to dwell in the sukka.

The blessings for the sukka should be considered here. The Tosefta prescribes the following blessings:

[A] When he makes a sukka for himself he says, "Blessed [are you, Lord our God, king of the universe] who has brought us to this occasion."

[B] When he enters to dwell in it, he says, "Blessed [are you, Lord our God, king of the universe] who has sanctified us with his commandments and commanded us to reside in the sukka."

[C] Once he has made a blessing for it on the first day, he no longer needs to recite a blessing.

(tBer 6:9)

It is interesting that the Tosefta formulates a blessing for making a sukka. Lev 23:42 only commands that one dwell in a sukka, not that one make a sukka.[193] Neh 8, however, relates that the people "went out to *make* sukkot, as it is written." We have seen that sukkot constructed for other purposes are fit for the festival sukka, at least according to some tannaitic opinions. Thus one would not necessarily build a sukka every year. The blessing either pertains to those who do in fact build sukkot, or to the act of covering the sukka with skhakh, as all opinions require. The version of this baraita in bSuk 46a explains more clearly: "If he found a sukka already made and ready, if he can 'renew' something, he blesses, if not, when he enters to dwell therein he recites both blessings." That is, he says both blessings [A] and [B]. In any case, this baraita groups the sukka with the lulav, fringes, and tefillin, the objects for which blessings are prescribed when they are made (tBer 6:9-10). Reciting the blessing distinguishes the building of the sukka as a religious obligation and sensitizes the builder to the religious significance of his act.

The Tosefta prescribes an independent blessing for the actual performance of the commandment at the point when one first enters the sukka to "sit" or "dwell" there. [C] limits the blessing to the first day.[194] That is, the blessing is recited only the first time one enters the sukka. The talmuds explain that one only blesses the first time because one is obligated to dwell in the sukka day and night.[195] The same obligation lasts throughout the festival, hence only one blessing is appropriate. The lulav, however, may be performed only during the day. Nights interrupt the obligation. Hence each day a new obligation arises and a new

---

[193]See the struggles of the Qaraite Aaron ben Elijah to find biblical warrant for the commandment to make a booth; Nemoy, *Karaite*, 178-79.

[194]That is, the first night of the first day of the festival, when the first meal is eaten. Cf. yBer 3:3, 6b.

[195]yBer 3:3, 6b; bSuk 45b.

blessing must be said. This amoraic explanation notwithstanding,[196] it seems that the one blessing limit follows from the tannaitic conception of the commandment. There exists a general obligation to reside in the sukka, to treat the sukka as a surrogate house. But there is no independent, discrete obligation to perform a "dwelling" ritual each day in the same way as there is an obligation to take the lulav or sound the shofar. A blessing on the first night thus suffices.[197]

To gain perspective on the general tannaitic conception of the commandment to dwell in the sukka, let us postulate a hypothetical legal continuum. At one end of the spectrum is an absolute prohibition against residing in the house and an absolute requirement to dwell in the sukka. Such a strict prohibition would be connected to ideas that the house was temporarily taboo, dangerous or demonic, beliefs some scholars have suggested lie behind the origin of the ritual.[198] At the other end of the spectrum is an obligation to spend a limited period of time in the sukka or to perform a defined ritual act therein. Having performed that act, one has fulfilled his obligation completely and could return to his normal abode. The tannaitic conception lies somewhere between these extremes. There is no taboo or absolute prohibition against residing in the house, provided the proper circumstances obtain. One need not necessarily eat meals in the sukka. If one chooses not to eat, or to eat only occasional snacks, one need not enter the sukka. A journey, duty or work (e.g. keeping watch) or involvement in a religious act exempts one from the sukka. Sickness and the inconveniences of rain, mosquitoes and heat also suspend the commandment. On the other hand, no specific act or defined time exhausts the obligation. Throughout the festival all meals and sleeping should be performed in

---

[196]This explanation is problematic. PT raises the difficulty that one is obligated to study Torah day and night, yet a blessing is recited each morning when one commences study. So the fact that one is obligated to reside in the sukka day and night should not preclude a new blessing each day. The talmud suggests that one cannot avoid desisting from the study of Torah (since one must sleep) but one can never desist from the sukka (since one even sleeps in the sukka.) But one legitimately desists from the sukka if it rains, or if one embarks on a journey, or must stand watch, etc. B. Ratner, 'Ahavat ṣiyon virushalayim (Vilna, 1901-7), 1:79 emends PT and creates a somewhat more satisfying explanation, but lacks manuscript evidence for his proposed emendation. And see L. Ginzberg, Peirushim veḥidushim birushalmi (New York: Jewish Theological Seminary, 1941-61), 2:182 on Ratner's error and on the sugya in general, which he concludes requires further investigation.

[197]In b45b Shmuel rules like the Tosefta, but R. Yohanan rules that one blesses each day. Thus the present custom.

[198]Wensinck, New Year, 33-41; de Vaux, Israel, 500; W. Robertson Smith, Lectures on the Religion of the Semites³, ed. S.A. Cook (London: A & C Black, 1927), 484.

The Tannaitic Period: Legal and Ritual Developments

the sukka, as should all mundane activities. In contrast to the sages, R. Eliezer's view falls closer to the stricter side of the continuum. One must occupy the same sukka for seven days, and cannot build a sukka in the middle of the festival. If R. Eliezer's conception reflects the older halakha, as is often the case, then we have another example of legal development within tannaitic law.

VII. Conclusions

While it is difficult to document accurately the nature of the lulav and the sukka prior to the destruction of the temple, it appears that these rituals attained a fair degree of standardization. The identification of the four species took place in temple times. A ritual gesture, a type of shaking, was performed during the recitation of the Hallel Psalms. The ritual then developed significantly throughout the tannaitic period. The tannaim incorporated the lulav into the emerging rabbinic liturgy, transferring what had been a temple ritual to the synagogue service. They ruled that the six or seven-day practice of the temple should be normative in all places. They formulated a blessing for the "taking" of the lulav, thereby giving the general biblical commandment a concrete expression, and determined more precisely at what point in the recitation of the Hallel the lulav should be shaken. This represented a slight change from the temple practice, at least that of the Men of Jerusalem and perhaps other groups, who held the lulav throughout the day. For the tannaim, once one had shaken the lulav during the service, he could set it aside until the morrow. Much interest was devoted to further questions of standardization: how many of each species, minimum and maximum dimensions, and defining fit and unfit species.

The conception of skhakh as the *sine qua non* of the sukka and the requirement that it produce shade are unknown outside of rabbinic literature. Yet the debate of the Houses on certain laws of skhakh indicates that the concept dates back to temple times. The centrality of these concepts is reflected in the specification that the occupant be directly beneath the skhakh and that nothing interpose between the skhakh and the sky. The tannaim defined carefully what materials could be used for skhakh. The walls, on the other hand, were of secondary importance. As with the lulav, great attention was given to standardization: the minimum and maximum dimensions of the sukka, and the number and height of the walls. Tannaitic law also ruled on the nature of the commandment to reside in the sukka. Optimally all mundane activities, especially eating and sleeping, should be done in the sukka. But various circumstances provided exemptions from the obligation.

Although the history of tannaitic law cannot be charted precisely, a general picture of the development emerges from a close analysis of the traditions. The basic principles and ideas appear to date back to temple times. These include the identification of the four species, the lulav ritual, the concept of skhakh and the nature and structure of the sukka. In an almost organic manner, each generation of tannaim turned their attention to related areas. For example, already in temple times the skhakh, not the walls, was considered the essence of the sukka. The early tannaim debated the configuration of the sukka and its minimum and maximum sizes, considerations that further refine, but do not alter, this basic conception of the sukka. The students of R. Akiba provided further standardization by setting the minimum number of walls and their required dimensions.

Focusing only on the sukka and the lulav reveals a remarkable degree of continuity from temple times. The tannaim retained the basic contours of the rituals they inherited. They standardized, regulated, defined and set minimum and maximum dimensions, but refrained from major redefinitions of the rituals. Compare the Pesaḥ *seder* with its retelling of the exodus, the liturgical components and the highly developed symbolism. In this case, the tannaim replaced the sacrificial meal with a complex ritual of a fundamentally different character.[199] The Sukkot rituals, at least in terms of their external forms, display no such metamorphosis. Whether the content – the understanding of the meaning of the rituals – remained intact is a separate question. Yet we have seen that the lulav retained its function as a fertility symbol and rain-making device in the tannaitic period, content documented in Pseudo-Philo and strongly implied in earlier sources. At all events, the tannaim displayed considerable religious conservativism with regard to the ritual forms.

When we turn to the larger picture, however, we must recognize the extensive discontinuity in the overall character of the festival. First and most obvious, the cessation of the sacrifices, libations, SBH, the willow procession and other temple rituals obliterated the basic orientation and religious experience of Sukkot. The rabbinic sources that preserved narrative accounts of the temple rites reflect a degree of continuity in the theoretical conception of the festival but had little effect on the actual practice. Second, even the same rituals, the sukka and the lulav, produced different experiences in the post-temple world. To reside in a sukka among thousands of pilgrims in a crowded Jerusalem anticipating the cultic rites differed from dwelling in a sukka in a small Galilean

---

[199]On the difference between the *seder* and the sacrificial meal see Bokser, *Origins*, 51-76.

village. To shake the lulav as the priests circumambulated the altar while the Levitical choir sang the Hallel differed considerably from the shaking in the synagogue or *beit midrash* as the precentor intoned the service. This is not to rank the religious experience or spiritual power of either context, but to acknowledge a fundamental dissimilarity.

If Sukkot in the rabbinic period was not primarily a temple-festival, then what was it? The halakhic materials in and of themselves reveal mere inklings of the meaning of the rituals or the general understanding of the festival. What did the experience of dwelling directly under the skhakh mean to them? How did this contribute to the meaning of the festival? What did the lulav symbolize to the rabbis? To begin to answer these questions we must turn to the aggadic material.

6

Tannaitic Midrashim: The Clouds of Glory

The previous chapter presented a history of the legal development of the Sukkot rituals in the tannaitic period. Analysis of these halakhot, in and of themselves, provides limited insight as to the meaning of Sukkot to the tannaim. To discover the tannaitic understanding of the festival and the nature of their religious experience it is necessary to turn to midrashic literature. Unfortunately, little tannaitic aggadic material relevant to Sukkot is extant. The most important traditions link the sukka to the "clouds of glory." These midrashim are comprehensively analyzed here. After exploring the aggadic midrashim and the web of associations connected to the traditions I relate the aggadic motifs to certain halakhot, and show that the two are reflections of the same underlying religious experience. The clouds of glory which the sukka symbolized were associated with divine protection, love and intimacy, and these sentiments are connected with shade, the fundamental halakhic requirement of the sukka.

The motif of the "clouds of glory" (*'ananei kavod*) appears in a debate concerning the sukkot of the exodus in *Sifra 'Emor* 17:11 (103a-b):

> *In order that future generations may know that I caused the Israelites to live in sukkot when I brought them out of the land of Egypt (Lev 23:43).* R. Eliezer says: They were real sukkot. R. Akiba says: The sukkot were the clouds of glory.[1]

---

[1] bSuk 11b has the attributions reversed, with R. Akiba expounding *sukkot* as real booths, as does *Mekhilta RSBY*, 33 (cited below, p. 250.) The Sifra version of the attributions appears to be more reliable. It is consistent with the parallel debate of R. Eliezer and R. Akiba concerning the meaning of the place "Sukkot" of Exod 12:37 and 13:20 – whether the term refers to "real" sukkot (*sukkot mammash*) or to the clouds of glory – which appears in *Mekhilta Pisha* §14 (48) (cited below, p. 253), as well as *Mekhilta Beshalah, petihta* (80), and *Mekhilta RSBY*, 47. In *Sifre Deut.*

R. Eliezer interprets the sukkot in which God placed the Israelites as real, ordinary booths. R. Akiba interprets the sukkot as divine, preternatural shelters formed from "clouds of glory," the ethereal substance surrounding the presence of God.

The interpretation of sukkot as clouds of glory also appears in the targums, the Aramaic translations of the Pentateuch. Targum Onqelos translates Lev 23:43 as: "in order that your future generations should recognize that I made the Israelites *dwell under the sukka*[2] *of my cloud* when I brought them forth out of the land of Egypt." The Palestinian targums are similar: Neofiti reads "with the cloud of the glory of my presence in the form of booths"; Targum Pseudo-Jonathan reads "under the sukka of my cloud of glory" and the "Fragmentary Targum" reads "with clouds like booths."[3] The targumic traditions thus follow the opinion of R. Akiba in the Sifra.[4] These Aramaic translations suggest that the popular understanding of the exodus sukkot in both Palestinian and Babylonian circles followed Akiban tradition.

The disagreement between R. Akiba and R. Eliezer has a significant bearing upon the symbolism of the sukka. For R. Akiba ritual sukkot

---

§213 (246) R. Eliezer also employs the term *mammash* ("real"), whereas R. Akiba provides a midrashic explanation: ובכתה את אביה ואת אמה ירח ימים אביה ואמה ממש דברי רבי אליעזר. רבי עקיבה אומר אין אביה ואמה אלא עבודה זרה שנאמר אומרים לעץ אבי אתה. So too in *Mekhilta Neziqin* §8 (277) R. Eliezer comments to the verse with the term *mammash* (cf. bBQ 84a; but see the variants Horovitz cites in line 8; the term is not found in all manuscripts.) Thus tannaitic sources in three independent documents attribute the tendency to interpret the verse more literally *(mammash)* to R. Eliezer, while R. Akiba expounds a competing midrashic interpretation in both the Sifra and Sifre. On R. Eliezer's penchant for literal explanation, especially for halakhic purposes, see Gilat, *Eliezer*, 68-82. For parallels to the Sifra tradition see *Tan Bo* §9 (210); *ShR* 1:7. Only the Akiban position is cited in PRK, "Alternative Parsha," 457. And see C. Albeck, *Untersuchungen uber die halakischen Midraschim* (Berlin, 1927), 37-38.

[2]Onqelos employs the Aramaic *matla* which corresponds to the Hebrew *sukka*. The phrase can also be translated "under the shelter of My cloud."

[3]*CTgF*, published in P. Kahle, *Masoreten des Westens* (Stuttgart, 1930), 2:54 = *The Fragment Targums to the Pentateuch*, ed. M. Klein (Rome: Biblical Institute Press, 1980), 1:318. See Grossfeld, *Leviticus*, 53-55. A variant of Neofiti reads: "under clouds in the form of booths" (Diez Macho, *Neofiti*, 3:173, apparatus.)

[4]Note the variation between "cloud" and "clouds." On the relationship between Onqelos and R. Akiba, see A.E. Silverstone, *Aquila and Onkelos* (Manchester: Manchester University Press, 1931), 107-22; R. Le Déaut, "The Targumim," in *The Cambridge History of Judaism*, vol. 2, *The Hellenistic Age*, ed. W.D. Davies and L. Finkelstein, (Cambridge: Cambridge University Press, 1989), 576; and Grossfeld, *Leviticus*, 53 n. 12. bMeg 3a claims that Onqelos was directed in his translation by R. Eliezer and R. Joshua. Scholarly consensus, however, associates Onqelos with the school of R. Akiba. This is further evidence to trust the attributions of the Sifra (see n. 1.)

symbolize the clouds of glory, the miraculous sukkot of the wilderness period. The temporary shelters represent something much larger than themselves, the mythical sukkot of the exodus. For R. Eliezer no such symbolism exists.[5] The festival sukkot simply symbolize the sukkot in which the Israelites resided. These different symbolisms point to disparate religious experiences of dwelling in a sukka. For R. Eliezer the annual ritual *re-enacts* the exodus from Egypt. Just as the biblical Israelites resided in rudimentary shelters as they fled from Egypt, so the tannaim re-enact that event and occupy a similar shelter.[6] For R. Akiba the annual ritual does not *re-enact*, but rather *commemorates*, the exodus sukkot, the clouds of glory.

What provoked the interpretation of the sukkot of Lev 23:43 as the clouds of glory? Why did R. Akiba eschew the *sensus literalis* of the term sukkot?[7] First, apart from this verse, the Bible never states that the Israelites dwelled in booths during their desert sojourn. The actual narratives of the desert trek in Exodus, Numbers and Deuteronomy make no mention of booths, although they occasionally describe the Israelites residing in tents.[8] Why does Leviticus presuppose an institution that is never mentioned elsewhere? Second, the rabbis, although not always concerned with historical realism, perhaps realized that the assertion of Leviticus is highly implausible. They knew, both from experience and scripture, that desert travelers reside in tents, not

---

[5] At least none that derives from this passage. It is theoretically possible that R. Eliezer agrees that the sukka symbolizes the clouds of glory, based on other prooftexts, but nonetheless believes that the sukkot of the wilderness were real sukkot. Y. Epstein, ʿArukh hashulkhan, ʾOraḥ Ḥayyim §625 (reprint: Jerusalem, 1986), wrestles with this issue.

[6] Stern, *Reference*, 121, defines re-enactment as follows: "One gesture *re-enacts* another (i) only if the two are *replicas* of one another, i.e. only if they are performances (tokens) of the same type of ritual. But the re-enactment is also not simply a matter of performing another replica of past performances. Re-enactment also requires (ii) that the individual perform the ritual replica *aware* that his gesture *is* a replica of past performances, believing that the given performance belongs to a succession of parallel performances and that it falls within a historical tradition." The ritual dwelling in sukkot for R. Akiba fails the first criterion, for the ritual sukkot are not replicas of the exodus-sukkot.

[7] Tur-Sinai, *Halashon*, 78-86 argues that "sukkot" in Lev 23:43 actually means "clouds," that this is the *sensus literalis*. That a prominent scholar suggests the midrash captures the plain sense of the verse indicates that the rabbinic exegesis is plausible. I know of only one extra-rabbinic tradition that identifies the clouds of glory with sukkot – and that depends on a manuscript variant. The Vatican manuscript of Pseudo-Philo 13:7 reads "et nubem posui in umbraculum capitis eorum." However, the Phillips manuscript has "tabernaculum" for "umbraculum": "and he put a cloud for a tabernacle (sukka) for their heads." See *Pseudo-Philo's Liber-Antiquitatum Biblicarum*, ed. G. Kisch (Indiana, 1949), ad loc.

[8] Exod 16:16; 33:8,10; Num 11:10, 16:27, 24:5; Deut 1:27, 5:27.

booths.⁹ Booths were fashioned from wood, reeds, foliage and other substances unavailable in the desert. The claim of Leviticus that the Israelites dwelled in booths when they came out of Egypt was difficult to accept. Third – and this is more subtle – there is something odd about building a booth to commemorate a booth. Usually rituals commemorate miracles, other supernatural acts, tragedies or events of major historical importance. Yet the ritual of the sukka, according to the Lev 23:43, commemorates the fact that the Israelites stayed in ordinary booths. Why make a festival and a ritual practice out of this?

Fourth and most important, the verb *hoshavti*, "I caused to dwell," suggests that God provided the sukkot, and hence that they were supermundane.¹⁰ God presumably supplies something greater than ordinary shacks. A God who brought ten plagues, split the Sea of Reeds, and provided manna in the desert, should bestow commensurate, miraculous shelter. Now in several biblical passages the term *sukka* actually refers to a supernatural cloud. Isa 4:5-6 prophesies that God will cause a cloud to descend upon Zion. The cloud is described as a *ḥuppa* (canopy) and a sukka.¹¹ Ps 18:12 (= 2 Sam 22:12) calls the clouds the sukka of God: "Dense clouds of the sky were His sukka round about him."¹² Moreover, while the narrative of the exodus never mentions actual booths, it frequently describes clouds around the Israelite camp, namely the pillar of cloud and fire that guided the people in the desert and rested over the Tabernacle.¹³ Did the term sukka refer to the divine cloud-sukka or the mundane earth-sukka? Which meaning of sukka – cloud or booth – is most appropriate in Lev 23:43? Given the considerations above, especially the fact that God provided the sukkot, R. Akiba reasoned that the term *sukka* referred to the divine cloud-sukka.¹⁴

---

⁹See the previous note.
¹⁰Rashi to Lev 23:43 implies the interpretation of sukkot as clouds is the *pshat*. (Although Rashbam to Lev 23:43 disagrees.) E. Mizrahi on Rashi, ibid., explains that Rashi believed this was the *pshat* because the verb "I cause to dwell" indicates a divine act, hence a divine object, the clouds of glory. Ramban to Lev 23:43 provides a similar explanation. See too *Beit Yosef* to Tur, 'O.H. §625.
¹¹See below, p. 253.
¹²See too Job 36:29, Ps 105:39, 1 Kgs 8:12. Cf. Job 26:8-9, Sira 35:16 (220), 24:4 (145). In Lam 3:44, the verb *SKK* is used to describe God in the clouds: *sakota beʻanan*, "You have screened yourself off with a cloud" (cf. Ps 105:39). Thus clouds, like sukkot, *mesakekh* – provide cover. For discussion of the biblical passages see *TDNT*, 4:905-906 and Luzarraga, *Nube*, 15-37.
¹³Exod 13:21-22; 14:19 etc. See below.
¹⁴Daniel Boyarin, *Intertextuality*, 1-38 defines midrash as intertextuality, as interpreting any part of the text with any other part and filling in "gaps" in the text with other biblical verses. That is exactly the process here. The midrash read Lev 23:43 in light of other texts that refer to sukkot as clouds and in light of the repeated presence of the cloud in the desert camp.

Thus for one stream of tannaitic thought ritual sukkot symbolized the clouds of glory.[15] Dwelling in the sukka recalled the associations of the clouds of glory and evoked the feelings this imagined covering instilled. To apprehend that experience it is necessary to explore the associations of the clouds of glory in Jewish thought.[16] In the following discussion I cite sources from the Bible, Apocrypha and Pseudepigrapha which reflect patterns of thought inherited by the tannaim, as well as amoraic midrashim that develop associations documented in tannaitic texts. My purpose in citing the amoraic texts is both to bring to fuller expression the images and thinking of the tannaim and to explore notions of the clouds of glory in amoraic times. I do not claim on this basis that these complementary midrashim, documented first in amoraic texts, are necessarily tannaitic in origin – though this is a possibility. Given the paucity of tannaitic aggadic midrashim, I hope to attain a better sense of their conceptions through study of the legacy of their traditions.

I. The Biblical Background

In the biblical worldview clouds symbolize the celestial presence, residence and chariot of God. "Dense clouds are around him," sings the psalmist of God in His celestial abode.[17] This image derives from the

---

[15] This position appears to have been the dominant or at least majority opinion. As mentioned above, tannaitic sources attribute the interpretation of sukkot as clouds of glory to R. Akiba in *Sifra 'Emor* 17:11 (103a-b); *Mekhilta Pisḥa* §14 (48); *Mekhilta Beshalaḥ, petiḥta* (80) and *Mekhilta RSBY*, 47, while only *Mekhilta RSBY*, 33 attributes it to R. Eliezer (see n. 1.) That *TO* and the other targums preserve the same tradition confirms the fact that the clouds of glory is the Akiban tradition, since the targums reflect Akiban hermeneutics, and Akiba is thought to have had connections with Onqelos (see n. 4.) R. Eliezer is known for his idiosyncratic tendencies, while Akiba and his students became influential tannaim. And numerous amoraic midrashim continue the clouds of glory theme, while none exhibit a contrary opinion.

[16] The best studies of the clouds are Riesenfeld, *Jésus*, 130-145 and Luzarraga, *Nube*. See too Ulfgard, *Feast*, 124-27; Michaelis, *Skēnē*.

[17] Ps 97:2. Cf. Jgs 5:4, Ps 104:3, Ezek 1:4, 34:12, Isa 19:1, Joel 2:2, Zeph 1:15. See Ps 18:12 (= 2 Sam 22:12), cited above, where the cloud is described as a sukka, and Ps 105:39, 1 Kgs 8:12. For a full discussion of the biblical passages see *TDNT*, 4:905-906. In the ancient Near East, clouds are regularly associated with the gods. G.E. Mendenhall, *The Tenth Generation: The Origins of the Biblical Tradition* (Baltimore: Johns Hopkins University Press, 1973), 32-66, 210-13 explains the divine cloud in terms of the Akkadian *mellamu*, a type of splendid aura surrounding the deity which shared in his glory and power. *Mellamu* also masked the bodies of the gods in order that they not be seen. Mendenhall suggests that in Ugaritic texts ʿanan "designates something closely identified with divine beings: it is a substitute for their names or an aspect of their person" (p. 56). See too his

widespread conception of the sky and heavens as the divine realm. Atmospheric phenomena such as thunder, lightning and rainstorms are understood as results of God's actions on high. Clouds have the specific function of serving as the chariot of God, as in Ps 104:3: "He makes the clouds His chariot, moves on the wings of the wind."[18] The cherubim upon which God sits or rides reflect this original conception of a chariot of clouds.[19]

Clouds are characteristic elements of biblical theophanies. At Sinai God reveals himself amid thunder, lightning and a dense cloud.[20] In Isaian eschatology a cloud fixed upon Mt Zion symbolizes the eternal presence of God (Isa 4:5-6). The wilderness narratives portray the presence of God as the "pillar of cloud" that alternates with the "pillar of fire."[21] The pillar of cloud speaks with Moses, signals to the Israelites when to march and leads them through the desert.[22] These pillars are conspicuous symbols of the presence of God in the camp of the Israelites: "Now they [the inhabitants of the land] have heard that You, O Lord, are in the midst of this people; that You, O Lord, appear in plain sight when Your cloud rests over them and when You go before them in a pillar of cloud by day and in a pillar of fire by night" (Num 14:14). In other

---

discussion of *'anan* in the Bible (pp. 57-66), and see R.J. Clifford, *The Cosmic Mountain in Canaan and the Old Testament* (Cambridge: Harvard University Press, 1972), 125 for Canaanite parallels. In many religions clouds are associated with divinities or divine powers; e.g., the Greek goddess *nephelē*.

[18]Cf. Isa 19:1, "Mounted on a swift cloud, the Lord will come to Egypt"; Nah 1:3; Deut 33:26; Ps 68:5, 35. See Tur-Sinai, *Halashon*, 20-24; M. Haran, "Ha'aron vehakeruvim," *'Ereṣ Yisra'el* 5 (1963), 86-87.

[19]Tur-Sinai, *Halashon*, 20-24; Haran, ibid.; Kaufmann, *Toledot*, 2:350-54. Thus Ps 18:11: "He bent the sky and came down, thick cloud beneath his feet. He mounted a cherub and flew, gliding on the wings of the wind." For Ezekiel, the fiery *keruvim* serve as the chariot of God (see Ezek 9:3, 10:4, 18-19, 11:22.) Tur-Sinai points out that God also rides in a chariot of fiery horses (2 Kgs 2:11, 6:17, Hab 3:8, 15). The *keruvim* can be interchanged with other celestial creatures, given that they symbolize God riding upon the chariot in the clouds.

[20]Exod 19:16, Deut 5:19. See Jgs 5:4, Job 38:1.

[21]Exod 13:21-2, 14:19, 33:9-10, Num 12:5, 14:14, Deut 31:15, Ps 78:14, 99:7, Neh 9:12, 19. For a survey of theories concerning the origin of this image, as well as ancient Near East parallels, see T. Mann, "The Pillar of Cloud in the Reed Sea Narrative," *JBL* 90 (1971), 15-30. In Exod 14:24 there is one pillar, a "pillar of fire and cloud." G.E. Mendenhall, *The Tenth Generation: The Origins of the Biblical Tradition* (Baltimore: Johns Hopkins University Press, 1973), 32-66 proposes that this was the original tradition, which then developed into two pillars, a pillar of cloud by day and of fire by night.

[22]Exod 16:10, 33:9-11; 34:5, 40:34-36; Num 9:15-23, 12:5-6, 14:14, Deut 1:33, 31:15. In some passages the cloud, not the pillar of cloud, communicates: Num 11:25, 17:7.

theophanies, as in the revelation to Moses in the cleft of the rock, God simply descends in a cloud, not a pillar of cloud and fire.[23]

The "glory" (*kavod*) of God also appears in the form of a cloud.[24] A cloud fills Solomon's Temple after its dedication as a signal that God has taken his residence there (1 Kgs 8:10). The next verse identifies the cloud with the glory of God: "the priests were not able to stand and perform the service because of the cloud, for the glory of the Lord filled the House of the Lord" (1 Kgs 8:11).[25] The description of the theophany at Sinai also coordinates the glory and the cloud: "When Moses ascended the mountain, the cloud covered the mountain. The glory of the Lord abode on Mt Sinai and the cloud hid it for six days. On the seventh day He called Moses from the midst of the cloud" (Exod 24:15-16).[26] These accounts engendered the midrashic term, the "clouds of glory," as the designation for the presence or "glory" of God manifest as a cloud.[27]

II. The Clouds of Glory in the Midrashim

While the cloud, the pillar of cloud and the cloud appearing with the *kavod* are generally discrete images in the Bible,[28] the midrashim quickly assimilated the three. This amalgamation has some biblical precedent in that the Bible occasionally juxtaposes "cloud" with "pillar of cloud" and elsewhere has God reveal himself in a cloud without any mention of the glory.[29] Midrashim identify the cloud and pillar of cloud with the clouds

---

[23]Exod 34:5; and see Lev 16:2; Num 11:25, 14:14. See too M. Haran, "The Tent of Meeting," *Tarbiz* 25 (1957), 15-17 (Hebrew).

[24]The literature on the *kavod* = glory = *doxa* is enormous. See the bibliographical references in *TDNT*, 2:232-53.

[25]Cf. 1 Kgs 8:12-13 and 2 Chr 5:13-6:2. A parallel event signals that God occupies the Tabernacle: "The cloud covered the Tent of Meeting, and the glory of God filled the Tabernacle" (Exod 40:34).

[26]Cf. Exod 16:10, 40:34-38, Num 17:7 and Ezek 1:4, 1:28, 10:3-4 where the glory and the cloud appear together. The biblical authors are not in complete agreement as to the relationship between the glory and the cloud. See *TDNT*, 2:240-41; Luzarraga, *Nube*, 51ff.; Cross, *Canaanite*, 165 and 153 n. 30.

[27]The phrase "clouds of glory," ʿ*ananei kavod*, is not biblical. It first appears in the Tosefta and tannaitic midrashim. The LXX of Sira 50:7 reads "as a rainbow giving light in the *nephelais doksēs*" (the Hebrew has only *beʿanan.*) Although this would seem to translate "clouds of glory," the meaning of the phrase in context is "brilliant clouds." Thus Sira does not know of the midrashic concept. However, the LXX of 2 Chr 5:13 translates the MT ʿ*anan* as *nephelēs doksēs* (cloud of glory), which may relate to the tannaitic concept.

[28]Cross, *Canaanite*, 164-65 suggests the images all derive from the poetic descriptions of God manifested in a cloud.

[29]Num 10:34, 14:4 (where both a cloud and a pillar of cloud appear); Num 9:15-16 and Exod 40:38 (where a cloud and fire are mentioned, but no pillar); Num 12:5 and 12:10 (where God descends in the pillar of cloud, but then a cloud moves

of glory or conceive of the pillar of cloud as one of the clouds of glory.[30] Versions of a midrash in different documents often interchange the "pillar of cloud" and "clouds of glory" or simply "cloud."[31] Manuscript variants of the same source also exhibit free interchange.[32] Thus an analysis of the associations with the "clouds of glory" must include sources that speak of the "pillar of cloud" and "cloud."

---

from the tent); Exod 14:19-20. God generally speaks from a pillar of cloud (Num 11:25, 12:5, Deut 31:15, Ps 99:7) but occasionally from a cloud (Exod 16:10, Num 17:7-10).

[30]*SZ* 10:33 (266): "*The Lord's cloud kept above them by day* (Num 10:34); and it says, *The angel of God, who had been going ahead of the Israelite army, now moved and followed behind them; and the pillar of cloud...* (Exod 14:19); and it says, *For over the Tabernacle a cloud of the Lord* (Exod 40:38); and it says, *The pillar of cloud by day and the pillar of fire by night* (Exod 13:22); and it says, *The Lord went before them in a pillar of cloud* (Exod 13:21). This teaches that there are seven clouds of glory..." Thus the prooftexts for the clouds of glory are the verses which mention the pillar of cloud. tSot 4:2 describes seven clouds of glory with the "cloud of the *shekhina*" in the middle and the pillar of cloud leading the way. Cf. *Sifre Num.* §83 (79), *BMM* 14.1-4 (218). In *Sifre Num.* §84 (83), the cloud that surrounds the camp at rest seems to "fold up" when the march begins and become the pillar of cloud. The point of this midrash is to reconcile the images of a pillar of cloud with a cloud covering (cf. Ginzberg, *Legends*, 3:235 and Rashi to Num 10:35). *PRK* 4:5 (70-71) assumes the "cloud" from which God spoke to Moses (Num 11:25) and the pillar of cloud (Ps 99:7) are identical. And see bTan 9a: "When Aaron died the pillar of cloud disappeared, as it says, *And the Canaanite, the King of Arad heard* (Num 21:1). What did he hear? He heard that Aaron died and the cloud of glory disappeared." (So MS Munich; see *DQS* ad loc. and below, p. 248.) In *TY* to Exod 16:10 "cloud" becomes "cloud of glory ." And see *ShR* 4:5, bYom 4a-b, targum to Job 26:9 and *TY* to Num 9:15. The same amalgamation occurs in the targums. See e.g. *TY* and *TN* to Num 11:25; *TY* to Num 12:8-10. Most sources assume there are seven clouds of glory, although opinions of two, four, five and thirteen are found. See *SZ* and *Sifre Num.* ad loc. and §106 (105), tSot 4:2, *Mekhilta Beshalah, petihta* (81).

[31]Where *SZ* 10:33 (266) has "clouds of glory," *Sifre Num.* §83 (79) and *Mekhilta Beshalah, petihta* (81) have "clouds." *Mekhilta Vayasaʿ* §5 (173) and *Sifre Deut.* §305 (326) read "When Aaron died the pillar of cloud was taken away" (cf. tSot 11:1), while *SOR* 9 (39) reads "clouds of glory" (in some MSS; so *VR* 27:6 [636-37], *BR* 62:4 [676], *TY* to Deut 10:6). Among the ten descents of God, *ARNB* §37 (96-97) lists one in the cloud (Exod 34:5) and one in the pillar of cloud (Num 12:5) where *ARNA* §34 (102) lists only the descent in the pillar of cloud, but cites Num 11:25, which only mentions the cloud. See also *TO* to Deut 33:3 (ʿ*ananakh*) and *TY* there (ʿ*ananei yeqarakh*.) In general the tannaitic sources are more consistent than the amoraic and medieval midrashim, which substitute the terms freely. These later midrashim also interchange other expressions for the presence of God with the clouds of glory. See n. 36.

[32]*Sifre Num.* §84 (83), apparatus to line 9, "cloud" vs "pillar of cloud"; *Mekhilta Beshalah, petihta* (75), apparatus to line 10, "cloud" vs. "pillar of cloud"; *MM* 14.3 (109), "clouds of glory" vs. "the clouds"; *MM* 14.84 (119), "pillar of cloud" vs. "cloud." tSot 4:2 "clouds of glory" (MS Vienna) = "clouds" (MS Erfurt).

Tannaitic Midrashim: The Clouds of Glory

Midrashim continue the biblical tendency to symbolize the presence of God with the clouds of glory. *SZ* 11:10 (276) explains that when the cloud rose from the tent after Aaron and Miriam murmured against Moses (Num 12:10), "immediately the *shekhina* departed." Thus the cloud is understood as the *shekhina*, the presence of God.[33] One of the seven clouds of glory is called the ʿ*anan shekhina*, the "cloud of the presence" in several midrashim.[34] And parallel midrashim interchange "cloud" and *shekhina*, since both terms refer to the divine presence.[35] Abraham identified Mt Moriah as the intended place for the sacrifice of Isaac by the cloud hovering above it.[36] The mosaic of the Beit Alpha synagogue and the paintings of the Dura synagogue also symbolize the presence of God by a cloud.[37]

The dominant characteristic of the clouds of glory is protection.[38] According to the midrashim, the clouds surrounded the Israelite camp in the wilderness like an impenetrable shield. Here too there is some biblical precedent. While camped in the desert before the passage through the Sea of Reeds, Exod 14:19-20 narrates that the pillar of cloud moved from the front of the Israelite camp to the back to separate them from the Egyptians such that the two camps could not approach each other during the night.[39] The *Mekhilta* fleshes out the idea that the cloud formed a barrier, suggesting that the Egyptians "would shoot at them

---

[33]*SR* 45:4: "When Israel saw the pillar of cloud they knew that the *shekhina* revealed itself to Moses." See bSuk 5a, *TanB* 2:124, and targum to Song 3:1-2, where the Israelites search for the *shekhina* after the clouds of glory disappear. For Josephus, too, the cloud contains the presence of God, *AJ* 3:203. In Philo the cloud contains an angel or "a vision of the Godhead"; *Life of Moses* 1:166, 2:254; cf. Rev 10:1.

[34]tSot 4:2, *BMM* 14.5 (218), *SZ* 10:33 (266), *TanB* 4:12-13, targum to Song 1:4. See Goldberg, *Schekhinah*, 91-99 and *Mekhilta Pisha* §12 (41).

[35]Compare *SZ* 6:89 (254) with *Sifra, Vayiqra* 1:8 (3a =*Baraita derabi yishmaʿel* §8). And compare *Mekhilta Baḥodesh* §4 (216) with bSuk 4b-5a: the *kavod* becomes the *shekhina*, subsequently identified with a cloud. *SZ* replaces "cloud" with *shekhina*. Goldberg, *Schekhinah*, 42 and 475 comments that the *shekhina* is not identical to the cloud, but is thought to reside in the cloud. In later midrashim the cloud regularly represents the *shekhina*. See *SZ* 11: 10 (276) *SR* 45:4, *ARNA* §34 (102); cf. *Sifre Deut.* §296 (314). We also find such expressions as "the cloud of the glory of the *shekhina*" (*TanB* 4:12, *TN* to Lev 23:43). In *PRK* 4:5 (70-71) God speaks to Moses and Aaron from the cloud, and the homily endeavors to show that God likewise spoke to Samuel from the midst of a cloud.

[36]The cloud above Mt Moriah in *BR* 56:2 (595-96) becomes the "cloud of glory" in *TY*, *kavod hashekhina* in *PRE* §31 (70a-b) and *shekhina* in *Tan Vayera* §23 (77).

[37]Goodenough, *Symbols*, 1:247 (see also 10:135); M. Avi-Yonah, *Art in Ancient Palestine* (Jerusalem: Magnes Press, 1981), 292.

[38]See Riesenfeld, *Jésus*, 137; Luzarraga, *Nube*, 121-50.

[39]See Ps 105:39 and Wis. Sol. 19:6-7: "that the children might be guarded, unhurt, [as] a cloud shadowing the camp."

arrows and stones from their catapults, which the angel and the cloud intercepted."[40] As prooftexts the midrash cites Gen 15:1, Ps 18:3 and 18:31 where God is described as a shield *(magen)*. Thus the cloud was seen as a screen that protected the Israelites from attack. Indeed, the protective beneficence of the cloud extended to the individual Israelite: "If one of the Israelites was drawn away from the wings of the cloud, the cloud would be drawn with him, behind him, until he returned [to the camp.]"[41] The same source demonstrates that the clouds "protected" *(magen)* the Israelites but not the other nations of the world.[42] The clouds also protect Moses and Aaron from stones thrown at them during the incidents of the murmurings of the people.[43] When the fire on Mt Sinai scorched the Israelites during the revelation, God sent the clouds of glory to discharge a protective dew over the people.[44] Recall that Targum Onqelos translates *sukkot* of Lev 23:43 as "the shelter of my cloud."[45]

So secure were the Israelites within their retinue of clouds that the midrash attributes their vulnerability to attack to the temporary disappearance of the clouds:

> While Aaron was alive the pillar of cloud used to lead the Israelites. When Aaron died, what does it say? *And the Canaanite the King of Arad*

---

[40]*Mekhilta Beshalah* §4 (102); *Mekhilta RSBY*, 60-61. This idea may derive, in part, from Ps 105:39, "He spread a cloud for a screen" *(masakh)*.

[41]*Sifre Num.* §83 (79). See, too, *Mekhilta RSBY*, 135 to Exod 18:27: "[*The families of the scribes...] the Sucathites. (I Chr 2:55)."* They used to reside in sukkot. Another explanation: They sheltered Israel and protected them (שהיו סככים ומגינים על ישראל ד'א שהיו מסככים בסוכות.) The midrash reads the MT שוכתים as סוכתים. According to *PRE* §14 (33b), Adam and Eve were covered with a garment made from clouds of glory and a skin of nails (see *BHM* 2:52, 5:42.) See too *TY* to Gen 3:21. *DR* 7:11 (113) relates that the garments of the Israelites never wore out in the desert (Deut 8:4), because the cloud rubbed and whitened them.

[42]*TY* to Deut 32:10, which recalls the exodus, employs the same verb. The targum renders "[God] engirded him (the people), watched over him," as "they were protected by the seven clouds of his glory." See too the LXX and *PRK* 3 (35).

[43]Exod 16:1-10 and Num 14:1-10 as interpreted in *Mekhilta Vayasa* §2 (163) and *Mekhilta RSBY*, 108 to Exod 16:10. Later midrashim about the sedition provoked by the spies in Num 14 are more dramatic. Thus *BaR* 16:21: "*And the glory (kavod) of God was revealed in the Tent of Meeting (Num 14:10).* This teaches that they threw stones and the cloud intercepted them." So *Yalqut* §743. In Exod 16:10 and Num 16:19 the "glory" of God supports the leaders of the Israelites against murmurings and rebellion. The midrash again identifies the glory with the cloud: *ER* §29 (145) describes Moses and Aaron running under the clouds of glory to escape the stones. See *TanB* 4:69, bSot 35a, and Ginzberg, *Legends*, 6:96, n. 538. In *Midrash Tannaim*, 11, the people explain they wish to send spies because the clouds, which had been their "scouts" in the desert, would not enter the land with them. They felt defenseless and vulnerable.

[44]*Mekhilta Bahodesh* §9 (236). Cf. tAr 1:10.

[45]Above, n. 2.

who lived in the Negev heard... (Num 21:1). He said, "where has their scout gone, who straightened the land for them?"[46]

According to this midrash God gave the cloud on account of Aaron's merit, so when he died, the pillar of cloud temporarily disappeared from the camp.[47] Observing that the Israelites now lacked divine defenses, the Canaanite king attacked.[48] Prior to the death of Aaron, with the clouds of glory intact, the camp was inviolable. Similar thinking governs the midrashim about the attack of Amalek upon the "stragglers" at the rear of the camp (Deut 25:18). According to *Sifre Deut.* §296 (314), the Amalekites could assault only those "who 'straggled' from [obeying] God's ways and found themselves cast out from under the wings of the cloud."[49] For how could they attack the camp of the Israelites if the clouds of glory surrounded it? Only when the divine protection of the clouds was removed were sinners exposed to the dangers of their enemies. In a later version of the midrash, the Amalekites must trick the Israelites into leaving the enclosure of the clouds of glory before they can attack.[50] As long as the Israelites remain within the clouds of glory, they are immune to enemy onslaught.

Midrashim portray the structure of the clouds as a force-field that surrounded the camp.

---

[46] tSot 11: 1. MS Vienna reads: "Their scout has gone..." Cf. *ARNB* §25 (51); bRH 3a; *BaR* 19:20; *TK*, 8:719-20. The antiquity of this tradition can be seen from the similar tradition of Pseudo-Philo 20:8. The Tosefta suggests that God gave the clouds of glory because of the virtue of Aaron, the well on account of Miriam, and the manna on account of Moses. But in *ARNB* §37 (95) "the clouds" are reckoned among the ten things created "at twilight" (so *TY* to Num 22:28 of "the clouds of glory.") A later tradition asserts that God created the clouds of glory on the second day, *BHM* 6:38. On the cloud straightening the land, see tSot 4:2, cited below.

[47] The parallels state explicitly that when Aaron died the clouds disappeared. The clouds reappeared on account of the merit of Moses. See below where the clouds are given on account of the merit of Abraham. On these "merit" traditions see Luzarraga, *Nube*, 141-47.

[48] See *TK*, 8:719-20. *TY* to Num 21:1 reads: "...Aaron died, the pious man by whose merit the clouds of glory were defending Israel, and the pillar of cloud disappeared."

[49] See the version of *PRK* 3:12 (49-50): "*All the stragglers in your rear* (Deut 25:18). R. Yehuda, R. Nehemiah and the Rabbis differ. R. Yehuda said: Every one who desisted [from obeying God's commands] was left outside [of the cloud.] R. Nehemiah said: Every one whom the cloud expelled was left outside. The Rabbis said: It was the tribe of Dan whom the cloud expelled, for all the Danites worshipped idols." Cf. *Mekhilta RSBY*, 119 to Exod 17:8. *TY* to Exod 17:8 also relates that the cloud did not protect the tribe of Dan. See targum to Song 2:15 and Ginzberg, *Legends*, 6:24.

[50] *TanB* 5:41.

> By Abraham it is written, *Recline under the tree (Gen 18:4)*. So God gave to his children seven clouds of glory in the desert, one to their right, and one to their left, one before them, and one after them, and one above their heads, and one as the *shekhina* that was in their midst. And the pillar of cloud would precede them, killing snakes and scorpions, burning brush, thorns and bramble, reducing mounds and raising low places, and making a straight path for them, a continuous, ongoing highway, as it is said, *The ark of the covenant of the Lord traveled in front of them (Num 10:33)*.[51]

In return for the resting place Abraham offered the angels, God endowed his descendants with the seven clouds. Note again that the pillar of cloud is reckoned as one of the seven clouds of glory. It leads the way in the desert while six other clouds encompass the Israelites on all sides. The identification of one cloud as the "cloud of the *shekhina*" in the midst of the camp shows once more the understanding of the cloud as the divine presence.[52] Here the clouds protect the Israelites not from enemy attack but from the natural dangers of the desert. The divine escort ensured the safety of the camp and allowed it to journey easily through the most difficult terrain.[53]

The midrashic imagination sensed in the surrounding structure of the clouds of glory not only the proximity and protection of God, but also his love:

> *And the children of Israel went from Raamses towards Sukkot (Exod 12:37)*...
> Sukkot of clouds of glory came and settled upon the roofs of Raamses. They made a parable: What is this like? To a groom who brought a

---

[51] tSot 4:2 (MS Vienna). Cf. *Sifre Num.* §83 (79); *SZ* 10:33 (266); *Mekhilta RSBY*, 47 to Exod 13:20; *Mekhilta Beshalaḥ*, *petiḥta* (81, the clouds are termed "clouds of glory" in line 17) and many later parallels, including *PR* 14 (57a); *BaR* 19:22. And cf. *BR* 48:10 (487) and *BaR* 14:2 where the reward for Abraham is directly linked to sukkot.

[52] The continuation of this passage, tSot 4:6, correlates the fact that Abraham accompanied the angels when they departed for Sodom with the reward of the pillar of cloud and fire that led the Israelites for forty years. Thus the clouds are seen as a divine escort.

[53] *SZ* 10:33 (266), in a more modest variation of this theme, remarks that the clouds screened the Israelites from the sun and protected the soles of their feet so that they did not have to walk barefoot. Cf. 1 Cor 10:1, "They (our ancestors) were all of them protected by the cloud, and they all passed safely through the sea," and Justin Martyr, *Dialogue*, §131. In Pseudo-Philo 15:5 God relates that he "made their enemies melt away and set the angels beneath their feet and placed the cloud as a covering for their head." The flip side of the cloud's protective nature, an offensive, destructive capability, appears occasionally. See *Mekhilta Beshalaḥ* §5 (108). In Greek thought, too, the gods provide protection by sheltering men in a cloud or mist; *Iliad* 20:444; *Odyssey* 7:15, 41; 23:372.

canopy (*apiryon*) to the entrance of the house of his wife in order that she would come to him immediately.[54]

According to this midrash, the term sukkot of Exod 12:37 does not refer to the name of a place. When the Bible relates that Israel went from "Raamses towards Sukkot" it does not report the stopping-points of the journey but describes an encounter between Israel and God. At Raamses the Israelites entered the sukkot, the clouds of glory that God provided for them.[55] The clouds settle upon the rooftops because sukkot were regularly erected upon the flat tops of houses.[56] Imagining the divine "sukkot" of the exodus, the midrash projects them upon the rooftops of houses where festival sukkot were typically built. The clouds of glory are compared to the bridal canopy brought by an enthusiastic groom to the very doorstep of his bride. To consummate, as it were, his marriage to the people, God sends the clouds of glory. The image poignantly expresses love, harmony and intimacy. This midrash is particularly significant because it connects these sentiments not only to the clouds of glory but directly to the sukka. The author of the midrash evidently drew on the emotions he experienced when dwelling in sukkot. Residing in the sukka elicited a sense of the divine presence, love and intimacy.

The *Mekhilta* expresses the divine love connected with the clouds of glory through the metaphor of filial love:

> And the angel of God, going before the camp of Israel, moved and went behind them. And the pillar of cloud moved from before them and went behind them (Exod 14:19). R. Yehuda said: Here is a verse made rich in meanings by many passages. He made of it a parable; to what is the matter similar? To a king who was going on the way, and his son went before him. Brigands came to kidnap him from in front. He took him from in front and placed him behind him. A wolf came behind him. He took him from behind and placed him in front. Brigands in front and the wolf in

---

[54]*Mekhilta RSBY*, 33; MG 2:214, 2:251; cf. *TY* to Exod 13:20 and Num 33:5. This source ascribes to R. Eliezer the opinion that the sukkot were clouds of glory and to R. Akiba the explanation of sukkot as real booths. See p. 239 and n. 1.

[55]It seems that the reference of Lev 23:43 to sukkot in which God caused Israel to dwell provoked this exegesis of Exod 12:37. For outside of this toponym (also mentioned in Exod 13:20), the Book of Exodus does not contain the term *sukkot*. Cognizant of this fact, the midrash interprets Exod 12:37 as an allusion to the sukkot to which Leviticus refers. The exegesis is based in part on the juxtaposition of themes in Exod 13:20-21: "(20) They set out from Sukkot and encamped at Etham, at the edge of the wilderness. (21) The Lord went before them in a pillar of cloud by day, to guide them along the way, and in a pillar of fire by night..." The midrash takes v. 21 as an explanation of the term *sukkot* of v. 20: "sukkot" should be understood as the pillar of cloud, the cloud of glory.

[56]See Neh 8:16 and the description of sukkot in the Temple Scroll, col. 42:10-17; Yadin, *Temple*, 2:179-80.

back, he took him and placed him in His arms, for it says, *I taught Ephraim to walk,*[57] *taking them on My arms (Hos 11:3).*
The son began to suffer; He took him on his shoulders, for it is said, *In the desert which you saw, where the Lord, your God carried you (Deut 1:31).* The son began to suffer from the sun; He spread on him His cloak, for it is said, *He has spread a cloud as a curtain (Ps 105:39).* He became hungry; He fed him... He became thirsty, He gave him drink...[58]

The parable compares the relationship of the angel / cloud[59] and the Israelites in the desert to that of a king and his son on a journey. When dangers arise the king takes precautions to protect his son. When the son needs food or water, the king provides it. The parable is further enriched through the quotation of biblical passages which depict (or are so interpreted) God's relationship to the Israelites with similar images. The passage once again illustrates the consummate protection provided by the cloud (= angel, king, God.) But the parable goes further, expressing the protection specifically as filial love, as nurturing, cherishing devotion. The clouds of glory are not simply an impersonal screen, shield or barrier, but are associated with love and nurture. This sentiment also emerges from the Hosean prooftext where God holds Ephraim (= Israel) in His arms like a father doting upon his son. Two verses earlier in Hosea God relates how he "fell in love with Israel when he was still a child, and have called [him] My son ever since Egypt (Hos 11:1)." The clouds in the desert enveloping the Israelites on all sides are understood as the embrace of God's arms and his paternal love. That the king supplies the needs of his son, providing him food, water and shade, also expresses love in addition to mere protection

Later midrashim also understand the clouds of glory as expressions of divine love. *Bamidbar Rabba* 20:19, following Neh 9:18-20, insists that although the Israelites worshipped the molten calf, God "did not cease loving them. The clouds of glory accompanied them, and the well and the manna did not cease."[60] *Yalqut Shimoni, Shir Hashirim* §986 expresses a similar thought: "*His left hand is under my head (Song 2:6)* – that means the clouds that surrounded Israel from above and below." The midrash associates God's love for Israel as understood in the allegorical reading of the Song of Songs with the shelter of the clouds. The surrounding presence of the clouds has become a metaphor for God's tender embrace.

---

[57]JPS translates, "I have pampered Ephraim, taking them in My arms."
[58]*Mekhilta Beshalaḥ* §4 (101). The translation follows Boyarin, *Intertextuality*, 28 based on his forthcoming edition.
[59]According to Exod 14:19, both the angel and the pillar of cloud moved to the rear of the Israelite camp. The repetition is due to the conflation of sources: the angel is J, the pillar of cloud E. See Luzarraga, *Nube*, 101-102.
[60]According to the targum to Song 2:17, the cloud of glory did indeed depart when the Israelites built the calf.

Tannaitic Midrashim: The Clouds of Glory

In the targum to Song 2:6, the cloud that protected the people from below is compared to a nurse who carries a baby at her breast.

An eschatological dimension of the clouds of glory appears in Mekhilta Pisha §14 (48):

> [And the Children of Israel journeyed from Raamses] To Sukkot (Exod 12:37)...R. Akiba says: "Sukkot" only refers to the clouds of glory, as it is said: [The Lord will create over the whole shrine and meeting place of Mt Zion cloud by day and smoke with a glow of flaming fire by night;] for over all the glory shall hang a ḥuppa (canopy) (Isa 4:5). This only tells me about the past. Whence do I know about the future? Scripture says: Which shall serve as a sukka for shade...(Isa 4:6). And it also says: And the ransomed of the Lord shall return and come with singing into Zion, and everlasting joy shall be upon their heads (Isa 35:10).[61]

R. Akiba cites Isa 4:5-6 to substantiate his identification of sukkot with the clouds of glory. The prophet designates the cloud which serves as the divine shelter as a ḥuppa and a sukka. The cloud hangs "over all the glory," so the term sukka is synonymous with the "clouds of glory."[62] The midrash then adduces Isa 4:6 to demonstrate that clouds of glory will return in the future, focusing on the double description of the cloud as both ḥuppa and sukka. "Huppa" refers to the exodus sukkot and, in classic midrashic style, the "superfluous" term sukka is not taken as a synonym, but assumed to refer to a different entity, the eschatological cloud. This actually suits the context of the verse which refers not to the wilderness sojourn but to eschatological times.[63] The introduction of the motif of the messianic future adds another association to the clouds of glory and a corresponding dimension to the symbolism of the sukka. Just as the clouds of glory surrounded the Israelites during the desert sojourn, so they will once again shelter the people in messianic times. Festival sukkot, which symbolize the clouds of glory of the exodus, thus symbolize the eschatological clouds of glory, the divine sukka of the future, as well. They call to mind the divine presence and protection that will characterize the World to Come.[64]

---

[61] Cf. the parallel tradition in Mekhilta Beshalaḥ, petiḥta (80). Cf. Mekhilta RSBY, 47 to Exod 13:20; BR 48:10 (487); TY to Exod 12:37, 13:20, Num 33:5.
[62] In Job 36:29 sukka is used in parallel with 'av, cloud, from which God thunders. See also Ps 18:12, Lam 3:43-44.
[63] Clouds also carry eschatological overtones in the Bible through their connection to the Day of Judgment: Ezek 30:3, 38:9, Joel 2:2, Zeph 1:15, Isa 45:8 (and see LXX there.)
[64] In amoraic midrashim the righteous reside in sukkot in the World to Come. See Chapter 7, I.

Similar eschatological associations appear in the *Baraita d'Melekhet Hamishkan*.⁶⁵ This text defines the pillar of cloud as one of the clouds of glory and describes how it "was spread over all the sons of Judah like a sukka." This phrase, incidentally, suggests that the conception of the clouds of glory was modeled after the sukka. The midrash then relates that the clouds provided light for all the Israelites, even while it was dark outside, and claims that in the World to Come *(la'atid lavo)* they will do the same. Similarly, the *Mekhilta* asserts that God will redeem his people from their exile by means of clouds.⁶⁶ The clouds and their eternal light, then, are elements of messianic times. This eschatological role of the cloud may be seen already in 2 Macc 2:7-8:

> The place (where Jeremiah hid the fire, Tabernacle, ark and altar of incense) will be unknown until God will gather together his people and his mercy become evident. Then will the Lord reveal these things, and the glory of the Lord and his cloud will be seen, as it was shown in the time of Moses, and as at the time when Solomon prayed that the place be gloriously sanctified.

The passage carries forward the biblical image of the glory of God manifest as a cloud. Just as God signaled his occupation of Solomon's temple by filling the temple with a cloud, so in the eschatological future when the ark, Tabernacle, altar and sacred fire are returned to the temple the cloud and glory will descend once again.⁶⁷

A related stream of thought associates the Messiah with the cloud. Dan 7:13 relates: "One like a human being came with the clouds of heaven; he reached the Ancient of Days and was presented to him." The meaning of "one like a human being" is uncertain. Often translated as "Son of Man," the figure has long been seen as the Messiah. Inspired by this passage, the messianic figure in 4 Ezra 13:1-4 flies with the clouds of heaven.⁶⁸ This motif becomes prominent in New Testament eschatology. In the transfiguration scene of the Gospels, in which Jesus appears to his disciples as the Messiah arrayed in heavenly glory, a cloud overshadows them and a voice from a cloud proclaims Jesus the "beloved son."⁶⁹

---

⁶⁵The eschatological reference appears in several, but not all, the manuscripts. See *BMM* 14 (220), apparatus to lines 12-13.
⁶⁶*Mekhilta Beshalaḥ* §5 (108). The prooftext comes from Isa 60:8, "Who are these that float like a cloud, like doves to their cotes."
⁶⁷For eschatological associations with the sukka, see Riesenfeld, *Jesus*, 188-205; Daniélou, *Symbols*, 8-12.
⁶⁸In 1 En 14:8, clouds and mist call Enoch to heaven, and he ascends by means of winds.
⁶⁹Mark 9:2-8 = Mt 17:1-8 = Lk 9:28-36. There is some question as to the function of the cloud in this pericope. Some believe that the cloud simply marks the theophany of God. As in the exodus narratives where God spoke to Moses from the midst of a cloud, here God addresses Jesus and his companions from the

Elsewhere Jesus warns the high priest that he will see the Son of Man "coming with the clouds of heaven."[70] And in the final judgment, the Son of Man returns from heaven seated upon a cloud.[71]

Rabbinic traditions interpreted the figure in Daniel in similar terms.

> R. Joshua ben Levi raised a contradiction: It is written, *One like a human being came with the clouds of heaven (Dan 7:13)*. Elsewhere it is written, *Lowly, and riding upon an ass (Zech 9:7)*. If they are meritorious, [he will come] with the clouds of heaven; if they are not meritorious, lowly and riding upon an ass.[72]

This statement occurs in a long aggadic section that deals almost exclusively with the Messiah. R. Joshua ben Levi interprets the "One like a human being" as the Messiah who will make his appearance with the majestic clouds of heaven. Thus the clouds constitute a retinue for the Messiah. The obscure appellation of the Messiah *bar naflei* of bSanh 96b, explained there in light of Amos 9:11, " I will rebuild the fallen *(nofelet)* sukka of David," that is, the scion of the fallen Davidic monarchy, perhaps should be understood as *bar nephelē*, the "one from the cloud."[73] Consistent with these ideas, the targum translates the name *'anani* of 1 Chr 3:24 as "the King Messiah."[74] Clearly the targum presupposes a tradition associating the Messiah with a cloud.[75]

---

cloud. Still, the cloud covers Moses, Elijah and Jesus. Eschatological symbolism emerges from the appearance of these messianic figures among the clouds of heaven, as in Daniel and Esdras. This passage is doubly significant for Peter proposes building *skēnas*, which might refer to *sukkot*. On this question see Chapter 2,IX n. 133. In *Apocalpyse of Peter* 6, the cloud carries Jesus, Moses and Elijah to heaven.

[70]Mark 14:62 = Mt 26:64 (cf. Mark 13:26 = Mt 24:30 = Luke 21:27). Both Gospels allude unmistakably to Daniel. According to Acts 1:9 Jesus ascends to heaven by means of a cloud. Matt 25:31, 1 Thes 3:13, 4:16-17 also allude to Daniel.
[71]Rev 14:14-16; cf. Rev 1:7.
[72]bSanh 98a.
[73]See G. Dalman, *The Words of Jesus*, trans. D. Kay (Edinburgh: T. & T. Clark, 1902), 245-46; N. Wieder, *The Judean Scrolls and Karaism* (London: Horovitz, 1962), 47 n. 2. This could involve an exegesis of the "fallen *sukka*" in terms of the cloud.
[74]A proper name in context, *'anani* can be translated "my cloud."
[75]Thus TanB 1:140: "Who is *'anani*? This is the King Messiah, as it is written, *One like a human being came with the clouds of heaven (Dan 7:13)*." See the passages collected in H. Strack and P. Billerback, *Kommentar zum Neuen Testament aus Talmud und Midrasch* (Munich: Beck, 1922-28), 1:956-57. See too *TYG* to Exod 15:18: "Moses will come from the middle of the desert, and the King Messiah from the middle of Rome. This one speaks from the top of a cloud, and that one speaks from the top of a cloud." (Cf. Ginsberger's note, p. 82. But see G. Vermes, *Scripture and Tradition in Judaism* [Leiden: Brill, 1961], 217 for a different reading, and see *TN* to Exod 12:42 and Diez Macho's notes, p. 442.)

The limited eschatological associations with Sukkot that we noted among marginal groups in second temple times surface in the tannaitic conception of the sukkot as clouds.[76] For R. Akiba in the *Mekhilta*, the festival sukkot represent the divine cloud that will form a permanent presence in eschatological time. The experience of the ritual should also be understood in this light. Dwelling in a sukka acted out the messianic experience for which the tannaim longed, the time when the divine presence would once again reside over the Jerusalem temple. Within the confines of the sukka, the tannaim felt the continual presence of the clouds of glory, just as they believed would be the case in messianic times.

ShR 2:6 vividly expresses these interrelated associations.

> *His left hand is under my head* – that means the sukka. *And his right hand embraces me (Song 2:6)* – that means the cloud of the *shekhina* in the World to Come. As it is written, *No longer shall you need the sun for light by day, nor the shining moon for radiance. Who will provide light for you? For the Lord shall be a light to you forever (Isa 60:19).*[77]

The midrash coordinates the sukka with the *shekhina*. This tradition presupposes the symbolism of the sukka as the clouds of glory, here identified as the "cloud of the *shekhina*,"[78] which the Tosefta designated as the central cloud. That is, the understanding of the sukka in terms of the clouds of glory and its associated themes has become so ingrained that the term "clouds of glory" need not appear explicitly. The reference to the *shekhina* and the prooftext referring to the eschaton convey the nature of the experience of residing in the sukka. In the sukka the rabbis experienced the same protection and love of God for his people as expressed in their allegorical reading of the Song of Songs, and as they pictured in messianic times.

III. The Clouds of Glory and the "Desert Motif"

The associations of the clouds of glory, and hence the sukka, essentially cohere with those that characterize the idealization of the desert motif in biblical thought. In contrast to the generally unfavorable conception of the forty years of desert wanderings portrayed in the

---

[76]Chapter 2, text to nn. 41 and 153.

[77]Cf. the interpretation of the verse in *Yalqut Shir Hashirim* §986, above p. 252. The "cloud of the shekhina" recalls the eschatological cloud that will form a permanent cover over Zion, protecting the people from the sun (Isa 4:5-6). See too *Sifre Num.* §83 (80) and *SZ* 10:33 (266) where the cloud supplies light for the Israelites.

[78]See above n. 26, and Goldberg, *Schekhinah*, 324. And see *TY* to Lev 23:42-43 which links several laws about the construction of the sukka to the "sukkot of clouds of glory" which God gave the Israelites.

Tannaitic Midrashim: The Clouds of Glory

Pentateuch, certain prophets and Psalms picture the desert experience in a favorable light. The people faithfully followed their God into the desert, trusted in his benevolent care and loyally entered into a covenant. For forty years an unmitigated relationship of love bound the nation and their God. Prophets who propounded the "nomadic ideal," as the pioneer of this analysis, K. Budde, called it, also made their conception of the desert experience a model of hope for the future when God and Israel would be reconciled.[79] The idealized mutual devotion after the redemption from Egypt became a paradigm for eschatological deliverance from the troubles of the present. Now Talmon has judiciously warned against exaggerating the prominence of this theme in the Bible; the dominant biblical outlook imagines the wandering in the desert as marred by constant murmuring and transgression.[80] For our purposes, however, the crucial motif is not as much the loyalty of the Israelites as the manner in which God related to the people. Biblical authors who conceive of the Israelites as constantly rebelling in the desert often depict God as nurturing, loving and doting on his people. Moreover, our goal is not to provide a balanced evaluation of the biblical evidence as a whole, but to discern certain motifs that the tannaim garnered from their reading of the Bible. They appropriated this idealized view as one interpretation of the desert experience and, as we shall see, concretized the sentiments of divine nurture, love and devotion in their conception of the clouds of glory.[81]

The Song of Moses in Deut 32 pictures God protecting the people from the dangers of the desert through the metaphor of an eagle hovering over her young:

> He found him [Israel] in a desert region, in an empty howling waste. He engirded him, watched over him, guarded him as the pupil of His eye. Like an eagle who rouses his nestlings, gliding down to his young, so

---

[79] K. Budde, "The Nomadic Ideal in the Old Testament," *New World* 4 (1895), 726-45. S. Talmon, "The Desert Motif in the Bible and in Qumrun Literature," *Biblical Motifs: Origins and Transformations*, ed., A. Altmann (Cambridge: Harvard University Press, 1966), 31-62 traces the evolution of scholarship on this topic after Budde, and supplies copious bibliographical references.

[80] Talmon, ibid., 34-37, 46-63. Talmon points out that even the prophets who romanticize the desert wanderings desire a return to the desert as a means to an end, not as a goal in and of itself. Reliving the utter dependence of the desert will effect a reconciliation with God and restitution of a harmonious relationship in the normative agricultural setting. See too the comments of de Vaux, *Israel*, 13-14.

[81] Boyarin, *Intertextuality*, 46-47 demonstrates the tension in the tannaitic conception of the desert experience, and astutely connects it to the tension within the Bible itself. See also G.W. Coats, *Rebellion in the Wilderness* (Nashville: Abingdon Press, 1968).

did He spread His wings and take him, bear him along on His pinions (Deut 32:10-11).

In the utter desolation of the desert God completely "engirded" his people in order to guard them from harm. The eagle image suggests both maternal love as well as closeness and intimacy, recalling Exod 19:4, where God relates that he brought the people to him on "eagles' wings." Hosea also expresses the image of parental love: "When Israel was a child I loved him and called my son out of Egypt" (Hos 11:1). As a parent tends to the needs of his child, God "looked after you in the desert, in a thirsty land" (Hos 13:5).

Hosea and Jeremiah depict God's love for his people in the wilderness as the love of a husband for his wife. God plans to lead his wayward wife "through the wilderness, and speak to her tenderly." The wife will then "respond as in the days of her youth, when she came up from the land of Egypt" by calling God "my husband." Finally God "remarries" his wife: "I will espouse you forever; I will espouse you with righteousness and justice and with goodness and mercy. And I will espouse you with faithfulness; Then you shall be devoted to the Lord" (Hos 2:16-23). Here the relationship between Israel and God following the exodus is seen as mutually faithful. At that time Israel called God her husband and loyally followed him, not the Canaanite gods, her current adulterous pursuits. By forcing Israel to return to the desert God will rekindle that devotion and restore pristine harmony. With yet more glowing ardor Jeremiah recalls "the devotion of your youth, your love as a bride, how you followed Me in the wilderness, in a land not sown" (Jer 2:2-3). God responded in kind: "Eternal love I conceived for you then" (Jer 31:3) and promises to restore the loving relationship in the future (Jer 31).

Deutero-Isaiah models the imminent new redemption after the exodus from Egypt.[82] God clears a highway in the desert, leads his people through the wilderness and brings them into the promised land. Once again he protects the people from all dangers such that they proceed unharmed through water and fire and are sheltered from wind and sun (Isa 43:2-3).[83] God "who loves them will lead them"; indeed he has already "taken back his afflicted ones in love" (Isa 49:10,13).[84] Soon the glory *(kavod)* will appear, "and all flesh, as one, shall behold." That is, all will experience directly the presence of God as they did in the

---

[82]See Anderson, *Exodus*.
[83]See too Isa 41:13, 45:5, 54:11-17.
[84]So Isa 43:4-6, 49:14-18, 54:5-10.

desert (Isa 40:5). This eschatological vision recalls our familiar themes of divine protection, love and presence.[85]

The images used by the prophets to describe God's relationship to the Israelites in the desert parallel the midrashic view of the clouds of glory. Just as the clouds constituted the presence of God in the camp and guided them by day and night, so God hovered over his people and led them faithfully for forty years. The cloud protected the Israelites from heat, scorpions and enemy attack in the same way as God safeguarded the people, his beloved child. The clouds greeted the Israelites like "a groom who brought a canopy to the entrance of the house of his wife in order that she would come to him immediately."[86] With similar images the prophets portray the love of God and Israel in the desert. And the eschatological associations of the clouds dovetail with the eschatological conception of the new exodus. Thus the motif of the clouds of glory functions as a concretization of the idealized conception of the desert experience. They provide a tangible image, a concrete symbol, with which to express the sense of God as loving, intimate and protective.

Beyond these parallel associations linguistic and thematic evidence suggests that the clouds of glory were modeled after the idealized view of the desert. The highway God forges through the desert features prominently in Deutero-Isaiah.[87] The prophet exhorts, "Let every valley be raised, every hill and mount made low" (*kol gei yenase vekhol har vegiv'a yishpalu*; Isa 40:4). The *Mekhilta* and *Mekhilta RSBY* cite this very verse as prooftext for the enveloping structure of the clouds of glory.[88] tSot 4:2, cited above,[89] adapts the language of the prophet, relating that the pillar of cloud "would precede them, killing snakes and scorpions, burning brush, thorns and bramble, reducing mounds and raising low places (*mashpil lahem 'et hagavoah*), and making a straight path for them, a continuous, ongoing highway." With a clear allusion to the pillar of cloud, Deutero-Isaiah prophesies "For you will not depart in haste, nor will you leave in flight; for the Lord is marching before you, the God of Israel is your rear guard" (Isa 52:12). Recall that the pillar of cloud preceded the camp in the desert and swung to the back to protect the Israelites from the Egyptians.[90] Anderson remarks of this verse, "[t]he

---

[85]N. Wieder, *The Judean Scrolls and Karaism* (London: Horovitz, 1962), 35-47 connects the cloud to messianic redemption based on the "prophets who envisaged the Messianic salvation in terms of the exodus from Egypt and sojourn of the Israelites in the wilderness."
[86]Above, p. 251.
[87]Isa 40:3-5, 42:16, 43:19, 45:2, 49:11.
[88]*Mekhilta RSBY*, 47 to Exod 13:20; *Mekhilta Beshalaḥ*, petiḥta (81).
[89]p. 250.
[90]Exod 14:19; Anderson, *Exodus*, 183.

new event not only surpasses the old; it supersedes it in many respects."[91] Unlike their exodus from Egypt, the Israelites will not depart in haste but in triumphant glory. So too the midrashic conception of the clouds of glory surpasses the biblical view of the first exodus. Protection from snakes and scorpions in the desert, as in Deut 8:15, a sign of God's benevolent care, becomes the physical destruction of these menaces by the clouds in the Tosefta.

Midrashim and targums to these passages also establish the connections between the clouds and the idealized view of the desert. *Sifre Deut.* §313 (355) comments to Deut 32:10: "Everything was found and provided for them in the desert. The well rose up for them, Manna descended for them, clouds of glory surrounded them." In a similar vein Targum Pseudo-Jonathan understands "engirded" and "guarded" as God "protected them with the seven clouds of glory." Isa 35:10 has the exiles return "crowned with joy everlasting," which the targum interprets: "everlasting joy will be theirs, that does not cease, and a cloud of glory will cover their heads." The *Mekhilta* cites this very verse as proof that the clouds of glory will reappear in eschatological times.[92] Thus midrashim appropriate aspects of the idealized conception of the desert and concretize them in terms of the clouds of glory. The clouds of glory represent divine devotion, protection and intimacy, and the pristine harmony between God and his people.

The clouds of glory connect the idealized view of the desert period to the festival of Sukkot. Divine protection, care and love – the ideas with which the Prophets characterize the desert experience – are associated with the clouds of glory. The clouds serve as a symbol, as a vehicle for the conception of this idealized time. The sukka in turn evoked the associations of the clouds and the idealized view of the desert. The annual ritual of dwelling in the sukka actualized these emotions. For the tannaim, the sukka meant the protection and presence of God, and fostered a sense of divine love and immediacy. The sukka recalled the desert experience, when God was close at hand, surrounding his people with His glory, and when the Israelites faithfully followed their Creator in a "land not sown."

IV. The Halakha and the Aggada

The attempt to relate halakhic prescriptions to the aggada is a problematic endeavor. Rarely do legal sources self-consciously explain themselves in terms of midrashic conceptions or base themselves on mythic symbolism. Rarely do midrashim explicitly connect the

---

[91] Anderson, *Exodus*, 191.
[92] *Mekhilta Pisha* §14 (48). Cf. *Mekhilta Beshalah*, *petihta* (80). See above, p. 253.

homiletical point to legal considerations. Connections between these two realms can be conjectured, not proven. Yet to recoil from an opportunity to explore the connection would be most unfortunate. It is unlikely that the entire law evolved in a vacuum, self-perpetuating by some internal force, governed by a sort of mathematical logic, with no relation whatsoever to external conceptions. And even if this is true in some spheres of law, it is unlikely that it holds for Sukkot and the festivals where the ritual experiences defined by the laws were still part of the living religion. Moreover, the same rabbis who worked out the legal parameters that defined the sukka and the obligation to dwell therein also transmitted the aggadot that expressed its symbolism. Their legal traditions must reflect, to some extent, how they conceived of the ritual experience, and what they intended the ritual to mean to those performing it.

Two elements are central to the tannaitic legal discussion of the sukka: shade and skhakh.[93] No sukka is valid unless the skhakh casts more shade than sun.[94] The presence of shade thus defines a sukka.[95] The obligation is not merely to reside in a booth, but in a booth that produces shade. Tannaitic halakha also displays great concern that the resident of the sukka directly sense the shade cast by the skhakh. A sukka may not be built within a house, since in that case no shade is produced.[96] One may neither sleep under a bed, nor eat below a barrier, such as a sheet, for such obstructions interfere with the direct perception of the shade.[97] In these cases the sukka is valid since it produces the requisite amount of shade. But the resident fails to perform the ritual correctly since he does not dwell under that shade. Not only must shade be produced, but it must be experienced.

The law that a sukka may not be built under a tree is especially significant.[98] In this case the resident both dwells in a sukka and experiences shade. Indeed, the shade produced by the tree may be identical to shade produced by the branches, leaves and other foliage that form the skhakh. Yet this scenario is unlawful because the resident does not experience the shade produced by the skhakh. The sukka – the skhakh – must produce the shade, not any outside object.

---

[93] See Chapter 5, IV-V.
[94] mSuk 1:1, t1:2.
[95] That shade is the essence of the sukka is clear from its Aramaic translation, *metalalta*, the regular term in the targums and talmuds, which comes for the root ṬLL, shade.
[96] m1:2; *Sifra 'Emor* 17:4 (102d).
[97] m1:3, 2:1; b10b, 21b.
[98] m1:2, *Sifra 'Emor* 17:4 (102d).

Even the tannaitic disagreement concerning the maximum height of the sukka is explained by certain amoraim to stem from considerations of shade. The sages rule in mSuk 1:1 that twenty cubits is the maximum height of the sukka. R. Zera and R. Abahu in the name of R. Yohanan explain that when the roof reaches such a height, its shade does not extend to the ground, and hence one does not reside in the shade of the sukka.[99] In this case the shade comes from the walls, which are not considered the essence of the sukka.[100] These amoraic explanation presuppose that the resident experience the shade produced by the skhakh.

The extensive interest in skhakh is a reflex of the centrality of shade. A sukka requires a special type of roofing to create shade: a solid roof of plaster, bricks or even boards produces the "inside" of an abode, but not shade, any more than we would call the inside of a house a "shaded" place. Shade is essentially a comparative concept; it is the lesser brightness or heat caused by an object intercepting rays of light. To recognize shade involves an awareness of an area in which light is absent even as the sun is perceived in the environs. Hence a "thatched" roofing, which allows shade to be perceived, is imperative. The examples of materials used for skhakh – cut foliage, such as straw, wood or brushwood; vines, gourds and ivy; sheaves of grain, stalks or flax; ropes and bundles of stubble[101] – are precisely those that generally allow some light to penetrate and thereby create shade.

The demand for shade seems to be partially responsible for the laws defining skhakh as foliage. Skhakh must come from materials that "had roots in the soil," from vegetation of various sorts.[102] The law makes sense if we understand that shade is generally associated with trees and other vegetation. Of course a mountain or large rock produces shade, as does any object in theory, and one cannot say that the concept of shade is restricted to elements of the vegetable kingdom. Nonetheless, in biblical and midrashic usage shade seems to be most closely associated with trees, branches, shrubs and other organic materials.[103] These are the

---

[99] b2a (R. Zera); y1:1, 51d (R. Yohanan). See Burgansky, Sukka, 54-55. The reason given by Rabba is also apposite (b2a). Rabba explains that if the roof is higher than twenty cubits, one does not "know" that he is inside a sukka, that is, at such a height the resident is unaware of the skhakh above him. The concern is that one sense the skhakh above, that the skhakh be experienced. Shade also bears legal import in the context of laws of idolatry, sacrilege (me'ila) and corpse-impurity. See mAZ 3:8, bAZ 48b, mAh 8:2.
[100] tSuk 1:2; b7b.
[101] mSuk 1:4-5, tSuk 1:4-6.
[102] See Chapter 5, IV.
[103] Jgs 9:15, Jon 4:5-6, Ezek 17:23, 31:3-12, Hos 4:13, 14:8, Ps 80:11, Job 40:22. See, however, Jgs 9:36 and Isa 32:2 (hills and rocks.)

common cultural associations of shade in symbolism and, undoubtedly, experience. Other objects associated closely with shade, clouds and the wings of flying birds for example,[104] cannot be put to ritual use. These considerations, in part, explain why skhakh must derive from foliage. I do not mean to reduce all the laws of skhakh to matters of shade, nor do I claim that a desire to create shade accounts completely for the limitation of skhakh to organic materials. Other factors are clearly involved.[105] But the concern for creating shade shares some responsibility for the laws of skhakh.

The concern that the resident experience the shade can also be seen in the rulings that disqualify wooden beams from skhakh and prohibit the resident from sleeping under a beam of a certain size.[106] Such beams satisfy the requirements for skhakh: they derive from the soil, no longer grow in the ground, and are not subject to impurity. But they may not be used because they resemble the solid roofing of a house. That is, they do not create a shady environment. The tannaim made this exception and instituted a specific prohibition against beams to insure that the resident experience shade.

To understand the experience of the sukka it is necessary to explore what shade meant and symbolized in biblical and rabbinic culture.[107] Shade served as protection from the hot, Mediterranean sun. Jonah felt "extremely happy" as he reclined under the shade of the plant, and so uncomfortable when God destroyed it that he begged for death (Jon 4:5-9). From a physical and perhaps psychological point of view, shade brings relief, joy and delight.[108] In the Bible shade is used metaphorically for protection. Lot beseeches the Sodomites not to harm the strangers who have come under the "shade of my roof," that is, the protection of his domain.[109] This metaphor is widely applied to the protection a leader or king provides. Isaiah prophesies doom for those who dare: "To seek refuge with Pharaoh, To seek shelter under the shade (protection) of

---

[104]Isa 25:5, Ps 17:8, 36:8, 57:2, 63:8; see below.
[105]For example, foliage still growing in the ground cannot be used as skhakh, although it produces shade; m1:2, 1:4, *Sifre Deut.* §140 (194). This prohibition probably requires a different explanation. (Unless the reason is that such shade is considered to derive from an independent object – a living plant – and not from the skhakh.)
[106]mSuk 1:6-7. See Chapter 5, IV text to n. 107.
[107]See Riesenfeld, *Jesus*, 138-145 and Gierlich, *Lichtgedanke*, 85-87. Of course shade may have different associations in different cultures. See, for example, P. van der Horst, "Der Schatten im hellenistischen Volksglauben," *Studies in Hellenistic Religions*, ed. M.J. Vermaseren (Leiden: Brill, 1979), 27-36.
[108]Song 2:3, Hos 14:7-8, Gierlich, *Lichtgedanke*, 73. Cf. *Mekhilta Shira* §4 (168); bTa 5b.
[109]Gen 19:8. Cf. Isa 16:3-4, Jer 48:45.

Egypt. The refuge with Pharaoh shall result in your shame; the shelter under Pharaoh's shade in your chagrin" (Isa 30:2-3). The author of Lamentations bewails the Judean King: "The breath of our life, the Lord's anointed, was captured in their traps; he in whose shade we had thought to live among the nations" (Lam 4:20).[110] Shade appears in these passages as a synonym for "refuge" and "shelter."

The same metaphor extends to the protection of God. Thus Ps 121:5-7:

> The Lord is your guardian, the Lord is your shadow (shade) at your right hand. By day the sun will not strike you, nor the moon by night. The Lord will guard you from all harm, He will guard your life.

The psalmist expresses God's constant presence and protecting care as an ever-present shadow or shade – the Hebrew word ṣel is used for both. Like a shadow, God is always present, close to each and every human being. And like someone protected by shade throughout the day from burning sun, and at night from the moon, so the psalmist feels God's constant protection.[111] A similar metaphor that includes the same cluster of words for protection, guarding and refuge appears in Isa 25:4: "For you have been a refuge for the poor man, a shelter for the needy man in his distress – shelter from rainstorm, shade from heat." Again the psalmist expressed the protection God affords to the defenseless with the image of shade.

The most profound expression of the biblical symbolism appears in Ps 91:

> (1) O you who dwell in the shelter of the Most High and abide in the shade (ṣel) of Shaddai –
> (2) I say of the Lord, my refuge and stronghold, my God in whom I trust,
> (3) That He will save you from the fowler's trap, from destructive plagues
> (4) He will cover (yasekh) you with His pinions; you will find refuge under His wings; His fidelity is an encircling shield.
> (5) You need not fear the terror by night....
> (9) Because you took the Lord – my refuge, the Most High – as your haven,
> (10) No harm will befall you, no disease touch your tent.
> (11) For He will order his angels to guard you wherever you go.

---

[110]See Num 14:9, Jgs 9:15, Hos 14:7-8, Isa 32:2, Jer 48:45, Ezek 17:22-4; cf. Gen 19:8. E. Cassin, *La Splendeur Divine* (Paris: Mouton & Co., 1968), 126-33 and T. Gaster, *Myth, Legend and Custom in the Old Testament* (New York: Harper & Row, 1969), 827 discuss this metaphor in Mesopotamian literature.

[111]See too Isa 51:16; Ps 57:2, 91:1-4; Sira 34:17 (217). On the "right hand," see Ps 16:8 and 109:31.

(12) They will carry you in their hands, lest you hurt your foot on a stone.

To reside in the shade of God is to be within a divine "shelter," "refuge" and "stronghold." He who does so is protected from snares, diseases and plagues. The psalmist reassures his audience that a constant escort of angels protects him from harm. He feels an absolute sense of security such that he remains safe even while thousands die around him in wars, or even if he encounters snakes and lions (vv. 7,13). The psalmist uses the metaphor of the sheltering wings of a bird, an image which evokes a sense of maternal love in addition to protection. The Bible often expresses this metaphor more graphically as the "shade of God's wings,"[112] which evokes a sense of love as well: "How precious is Your faithful care, O God! Mankind shelters in the shade of your wings (Ps 36:8)."[113] Ps 91 combines the wings of God sheltering above with the angels bearing the human being on their palms from below (v. 12) to create an image of encircling spiritual defense – most reminiscent of the clouds of glory.[114] At the end of the Psalm God promises that he will answer his follower when called upon, and be with him in distress. That is, God will be immediately present, a faithful and loyal guardian.[115]

Finally, in biblical imagery clouds, too, provide shade: "The rage of strangers like heat in the desert; You subdued the heat with the shade of clouds" (Isa 25:5). Just as a cloud provides a cool respite from the heat of the sun, so God mellows the rage of strangers. Isaiah's eschatological vision of the reappearance of the divine cloud emphasizes that the cloud "shall serve as a sukka for shade from heat by day and as a shelter for protection against drenching rain" (Isa 4:6). This verse is particularly important since it portrays the cloud in terms of a sukka and focuses on shade as its protective function. All three elements – the cloud, sukka and shade – appear in tandem and reveal the same associations. Sira 43:26

---

[112]Ps 17:8, 36:8, 57:2, 63:8; Isa 31:5, 49:2. See Deut 33:12 and LXX; Ps 140:8 and LXX. See too Ps.-Sol. 11:5-6 and 1 Bar 5:5-7. Gierlich, *Lichtgedanke*, 104, connects the metaphor of the shade of God's wings to the wings of the *keruvim* which covered the ark; Exod 25:20, 37:9.

[113]See too Ps 17:8, 57:2.

[114]Verses 12-13, which assure that stones will never injure his feet, and that he will tread on snakes and asps, are a striking parallel to the clouds of glory which protected the feet of the Israelites from the hot sand and destroyed the snakes and scorpions that infested the desert.

[115]*Tan Naso* §23 (512) attributes the Psalm to Moses, who recited it upon the completion of the Tabernacle when he ascended Mt Sinai. That context, although historically impossible, is emotionally appropriate: the Psalm poignantly expresses the type of feelings Moses is imagined to have experienced during his encounter with God on Sinai. bShevu 15b calls this Psalm the "song [against] dangers" or the "song [against] plagues" (*shir shel pega'im*).

sees in clouds succor from the heat of the sun. Ps.-Sol. 11:5-6 and 1 Bar 5:6-8 associate the glory *(doxa)* of God with shade. Although the cloud is not explicitly mentioned, the identification of the glory with the cloud probably forms the background to these images. Wis. Sol. 19:6-7 refers to the "cloud shadowing the camp" to protect the Israelites.[116]

Midrashim carry forward the biblical associations with shade. Shade typically symbolizes the protection of God. According to *MTeh* 104:24 (447), "were it not for the shade of God that protects a human being, the demons *(meziqin)* would kill him." The following parable expresses a related idea:

> Whoever learns the Torah, Prophets and Writings, Mishna and midrash, halakhot and aggadot and serves the sages – God Himself guards him. They made a parable. To what is it similar? To a king who was walking with his son in the desert. When they encountered the sun and the burning heat, the father stood up in the sun and made shade for his son, so that he should not be touched by the sun and burning heat. Thus it is written, *The Lord is your guardian, the Lord is your shade at your right hand* (Ps 121:5).[117]

God guards the righteous just as a father protects his son from the desert heat. Shade symbolizes more than protection; it expresses the paternal care a loving father extends to his son, even interposing his own body if need be. The resemblance of this text to the *Mekhilta* passage cited above is particularly striking.[118] The *Mekhilta* invoked a similar parable, that of a king and his son on a journey, to express the relationship of the pillar of cloud and angel to the Israelites in the desert. When the son of the king suffers from heat the king spreads his garment to provide shade from the sun. That midrash cites Ps 105:39, "He has spread a cloud as a curtain *(masakh)*" as a prooftext illustrating the shelter God provides with his "garments," the clouds. Thus the king and the father in the parables, and the cloud and God as their analogs, all provide shade. I am hinting here, and will argue explicitly below, that the symbolism of clouds and shade shares a great deal in common.

The PT promises that "whoever engages in [the study] of Torah and acts of lovingkindness will sit in the shade of God."[119] This may refer

---

[116] See the LXX to Deut 33:12, Ps 140:8 and Gierlich, *Lichtgedanke*, 85-103.

[117] *ER* §18 (100). Deut 1:31 compares God carrying the Israelites in the desert to a father who carries his son on a journey. *TY*, as we might expect, interprets the verse in terms of the clouds of glory. See too *CTgF* in P. Kahle, *Masoreten des Westens* (Stuttgart, 1930), 2:56; *TY* to Exod 19:4; *PRK* 3:1 (35).

[118] p. 251.

[119] yMeg 3:7, 74b. The prooftext is Ps 36:8: "How precious is Your faithful care, O God! Mankind shelters in the shadow of your wings." Cf. *PRK* 16:1 (264); *RR* 5:4; yTa 4:1, 68a (=ySot 7:4, 21d).

either to an eschatological conception of the righteous dwelling under divine shelter or to an immediate experience of the presence of God. With a similar image the targum to Song 2:3 explains the phrase "I love to sit in his shade" as "When God revealed himself upon Mt Sinai... I longed to dwell in the shade of the *shekhina.*" The midrash portrays the emotional response to the revelation at Sinai, when God's presence was manifest and experienced in a most intense manner, as a longing to be close to God, which it expresses in terms of shade.[120] To "dwell in shade" – like the resident in the sukka – is to feel the divine presence and to draw near to God. Conversion to Judaism is expressed symbolically as entering under the shade of God.

> R. Abahu began: *Those who sit in his shade shall be revived (Hos 14:8).* These are the gentiles who come and take refuge in the shade of the Holy One, Blessed be He.[121]

The image for conversion, for "drawing near" to God, is that of entering under God's shade.[122]

Midrashim, like the Bible, associate clouds with shade and its symbolism. R. Yehuda interprets Ps 105:39, "He spread a cloud for a cover," to refer to a cloud which God spread over the Israelites when they began to suffer from the heat of the sun in the desert."[123] A cloud that provides shade serves as a metaphor for general protection. Targum Pseudo-Jonathan paraphrases Num 14:14, where Moses convinces God of the ignominy that would result from the destruction of the people "when your cloud rests over them," as "your cloud shades (shelters) them so that they may not be harmed by heat or rain."[124] The targum to Song 2:17 also expresses the protective shade provided by the cloud. The illustration of the verse "the shadows flee away" is "the clouds of glory that had shaded them departed, and they were left exposed and devoid [of the ability] to take up their arms." Shade here is synonymous with protection. As long as the cloud remains the people are secure under its shade. When it departs, due to the sin of the calf, the shade disappears

---

[120]*PRK* 12:10 (210) interprets the same verse as Israel's desire to approach Sinai when the other nations fled. See too *Yalqut* §273.

[121]*VR* 1:2 (6), *BaR* 8:1. *TY* translates Deut 23:16, the prohibition against returning a runaway slave, as a prohibition against delivering a gentile who desires "to be under the shade of My *shekhina*" back to idolatry. According to yTa 3:2, 68a (=ySot 7:4, 21d), whoever performs good deeds merits to sit in the shade of God. See too bAr 32b.

[122]See further *TY* to Deut 32:11. R. Yohanan, bSanh 99b, interprets Isa 51:16, "I have put My words in your mouth and sheltered you in the shadow of My hand," in terms of protecting the whole world from sin.

[123]*Mekhilta Beshalaḥ* §4 (101), *Mekhilta RSBY*, 60 to Exod 14:19.

[124]See *TY* to Num 10:34 and Gen 50:1.

and the Israelites become vulnerable. It is not surprising that several versions of the midrash which describe the protective function of clouds of glory in the desert mention specifically that the clouds sheltered the Israelites from heat and sun.[125] Apart from the other miraculous modes of protection – destroying scorpions, burning away thistles, smoothing the way, providing a base under their feet – the clouds of glory created a covering of shade as shelter from the desert sun.

Shade, therefore, bears the same associations as the clouds of glory. Both convey a sense of the protection of God. Shade is a metaphor for the sheltering divine presence,[126] while the cloud represents the tangible form of the presence. We noted two strikingly similar midrashim wherein clouds and shade occur in parallel. And clouds of course provide shade. Indeed, it appears that clouds are associated with protection by virtue of the fact that they produce shade, the outstanding symbol of shelter. All this suggests that *shade in the halakha parallels the clouds of glory in the aggada*.[127] The laws deeming a sukka valid only if

---

[125]*SZ* 10:33 (266) (cf. n. 53); *TY* to Num 14:14. See too Wis. Sol. 18:3; *Mekhilta Bahodesh* §9 (236); *CTgG* to Exod 15:13 (86).

[126]Shade unambiguously symbolizes the presence of God in *Tan Vayaqhel* §7 (337). The midrash explains that Exod 37:1 specifies that Bezalel himself fashioned the ark (rather than delegating the task to another) because "there [in the ark] resides the shade of God, who contracts his presence (*shekhina*) there. On this account he was named *besalel* (*beṣel 'el* = in the shade of God), since he made the shade of God between the *keruvim*, as it says, *Then I will meet with you, and I will impart to you – from above the cover, from between the two keruvim that are on top of the Ark of the Pact – all that I will command you concerning the Israelite people (Ex 25:22)*." The most concentrated locus of God's presence, that which dwells in the ark, manifests itself as shade. In another version of the midrash, cited in M. Kasher, *Torah shelema* (Jerusalem: Hatchiyah, 1964), 21:51, Bezalel makes the shade of God, "in order that all Israel can dwell in his shade." Cf. bBer 55a, *Tan Vayaqhel* §3 (332-33).

[127]Maharam to bSuk 2a, s.v. *'amar* sensed the connection between the shade, skhakh and the clouds of glory: הק' קרא בסוכות תשבו כדי שיזכרו דורותיכם היקף ענני כבוד שהיו במדבר וע' מה יזכרו היקף ענני כבוד? כשיראו ויסתכלו שיושבים בצל סכך הסוכה. *Beit Yosef* to *Tur*, 'Oraḥ Ḥayyim §625, end, also connects shade to the clouds of glory. See too 'Arukh hashulkhan, 'Oraḥ Ḥayyim §625:5 on sitting in the shade of God in the sukka. tSot 4:2 connects shade and the clouds by explaining that the clouds were given by God as a reward for Abraham offering the angels repose under the shade of a tree. Thus the shade of the tree parallels the shelter of the clouds. A version of the midrash in *ER* §13 (60) spells this out clearly: "As reward for the shade of the tree under which Abraham had the angels sit, God surrounded Israel with seven clouds of glory under which to dwell in the desert for forty years." In *BR* 48:10 (487), the rewards for Abraham's offer of the shady tree are the cloud, linked to the desert (Ps 105:39), sukkot linked to the inhabitation of the Land of Israel, and the eschatological cloud of Isa 4:5-6 linked to the World to Come. The midrash emphasizes that this cloud will be for shade. Two points emerge from this source. First, sukkot symbolize the cloud of the desert sojourn and the

there is more shade than sunlight parallel the symbolism of the sukka as a divine cloud. The laws that define the nature of skhakh and require that the resident dwell under its shade reflect the aggadic conception that the clouds enveloped the Israelites on all sides. Shade is the crucial element which links the "myth" – that the exodus generation dwelled within the clouds of glory – with its "ritual," the annual commandment to reside in the sukka. The succinct biblical idea that Israelites annually dwell in sukkot to commemorate the desert sukkot of their ancestors is expressed by the tannaim in terms of shade and the clouds of glory. Jews must dwell directly beneath the shade of the sukka just as their ancestors dwelled within the protective shelter of the clouds.[128]

At a deeper level, both the halakhic and aggadic traditions are expressions of, and central to, the tannaitic religious experience of the sukka. Residing in the shade of the sukka, the tannaim experienced a sense of divine protection, love and intimacy. To create that experience the sukka had to provide a sort of sheltering protection, and the resident had to sense that shelter directly. Tannaitic halakha therefore requires that the sukka produce shade and that the shade be experienced by the resident. The same experience is reflected in the midrashic understanding of the sukka as symbol of the clouds of glory. The laws concerning shade and skhakh should not be seen as merely definitional. They express the aggadic understanding of the sukka as a symbol of the

---

eschatological cloud. These three are equivalant motifs, the form varying in the different historical periods. Second, the clouds and the sukka serve to provide shade, as did Abraham's tree, and as Isa 4:5-6 explicitly states.

[128] I am not making historical claims here as to which came first, the midrashic understanding or the halakhot. The halakhot originally may have required shade for reasons unrelated to the midrashic interpretation. Indeed, the interpretation of the sukka as symbolizing clouds of glory may have developed out of the experience of residing in the shade prescribed by the halakha for those other reasons. My sense is that both the halakha and aggada derived from the experience of residing in sukkot, which were built according to common practice, and undoubtedly provided some shade. That experience eventually gave rise to laws requiring a majority of shade and led to the symbolic conception of the aggada. But my argument here is phenomenological: shade and the clouds of glory carry a similar set of associations, hence the halakha and aggada reflect and create the same religious experience. For discussion of this issue, see R. Lapidus, "Halakhah and Haggadah: Two Opposing Approaches to Fulfilling the Religious Law," *JJS* 44 (1993), 100-113 and the references to Zunz, Bialik, Heschel and others. And see D. Boyarin, *Carnal Israel: Reading Sex in Talmudic Culrure* (Berkeley and Los Angeles: University of California Press, 1993), 15-16. Boyarin adopts the method of "cultural poetics," which "recombines aggada and halakha, but in a new fashion...both the halakha and the aggada represent attempts to work out the same cultural, political, social, ideological, and religious problems."

divine clouds and create an environment where that understanding becomes a living experience.[129]

Conclusions

The tannaitic conception of the sukka as a symbol of the clouds of glory connects the festival to the exodus. Of course Lev 23:43 itself explained the sukka as a commemoration of the sukkot inhabited during the desert sojourn, so the rabbinic interpretation was not an innovation. As an explicit declaration of scripture, we must assume that the symbolism was recognized throughout the second temple period. Yet our sources rarely reveal an awareness of this idea. Of the sources surveyed in Chapter 2, only Josephus and Philo associate the sukka with the exodus. Jubilees, Maccabees, Pseudo-Philo and even the Nehemian account which directly alludes to Lev 23, reveal no such awareness. And Josephus and Philo seem to de-emphasize the connection. Philo offers this explanation as the second of three reasons why Jews stay in sukkot. Josephus perforce acknowledges the connection to the exodus in his paraphrase of the biblical legislation, but elsewhere declares that sukkot are built in honor of God.[130] Prior to the destruction Sukkot was primarily a temple celebration, so the understanding of the festival as a commemoration of the exodus was secondary. Indeed, to recall a time of wandering during the most joyous occasion of the year, while celebrating at the temple, the foundation of order and stability, probably seemed somewhat incongruous.[131]

After the destruction and the cessation of cultic rituals, the sukka became the focus of the festival. Sleeping and eating for seven days in the sukka makes one continuously aware of the ritual, and naturally

---

[129]I have not analyzed the liturgical uses of these motifs – a topic worthy of further investigation. Let me just mention that in the *Hashkiveinu* blessing of the evening service this same complex of symbols appears. The prayer requests that God "spread over us a sukka of peace," a clear petition for God's protection, as evident from the rest of the prayer, which solicits succor against enemies, plagues and hunger. The image then turns to the divine shade: "shelter us in the shade of your wings." The eulogy (every day in the Palestinian tradition; on Sabbaths and festivals in Babylonia) returns to a request for the "sukka of peace." The liturgy has appropriated the sukka and shade as outstanding metaphors for the presence and protection of God. How early this precise wording can be dated requires further study, but it may well be tannaitic. The eulogy is found already in a statement of R. Abun, yBer 4:5,8c, and in a midrash attributed to R. Levi in *VR* 9:9 (194). The entire prayer is known to Amram. See Elbogen, *Hatefila*, 78-80.
[130]Philo, *Special Laws*, 2:204-214; Josephus, *BJ* 1:73 = *AJ* 13:303-308; *BJ* 16:301. See Chapter 2, VIII.
[131]Sensitive to the discrepancy, Philo, *Special Laws*, 2:208-209 observes that in times of prosperity and joy it is most appropriate to recall earlier misfortunes.

leads to a conception of the festival that places the sukka at the fore. With the temple in ruins and, after the Bar-Kochba revolt of 132-135 CE, Jerusalem transformed into a pagan city, the tannaim experienced a sense of dislocation, and could relate well to the Israelites of the exodus. Just as God had protected their ancestors in the hostile desert, so God would protect his people in the current predicament. The rabbinic interpretation of the sukka as the clouds of glory thus indicates a shift in the orientation of the festival from earlier times. The temple festival became a commemoration of the intimate relationship between God and the Israelites that had prevailed during the exodus. The shade of the sukka reified the experience of divine protection, love and intimacy, and foreshadowed the eschatological future when God would again deliver his people.

7

Sukkot in the Amoraic Midrashim

This chapter investigates the symbolism of the lulav and the sukka and the themes associated with Sukkot in the amoraic midrashim, the traditions attributed to the rabbis of the talmudic period, from the second through seventh centuries CE. The goal is to continue our investigation into the meaning of Sukkot in rabbinic Judaism. Given the paucity of tannaitic midrashim, we must turn to these later sources. What were the amoraim celebrating when they observed the festival? Did the joy of the harvest, thanksgiving for the bounties of the land and other agricultural elements have the same power as in previous eras? Or did social change, economic development and urbanization reduce the importance of this dimension of Sukkot? To what extent did associations with the temple persist as the centuries passed? That the Bible explained Sukkot as a commemoration of the desert sojourn guaranteed that this interpretation endure, and mandated that the amoraim incorporate it into their understanding. The festival would always recall the booths occupied during the exodus, and, at least in part, re-create that experience. But the amoraic period provided ample time for new conceptions to develop. With what meanings was the festival invested in talmudic times? What did the lulav and the sukka symbolize to the amoraim?

I have employed the terms "symbols" and "associations." I use "symbol" in the conventional sense of an object which expresses more than its concrete representation and hence communicates a significance beyond its immediate function. By "associations" I mean that particular themes appear in sources that relate to the festival or its rituals. A tradition that the Messiah will arrive on Sukkot expresses an eschatological association. Strictly speaking, no symbolism operates here: the sukka does not symbolize the Messiah or resurrection or any other eschatological element. Rather the association of Sukkot with the time of the Messiah's arrival indicates that the festival played a role in messianic thought. The goal, then, is both to study the symbolic uses of the lulav and the sukka and to learn from the general associations of the festival the meaning of Sukkot in amoraic times.

The midrashim fall into two categories. The first includes the series of homilies collected in *Pesiqta d'Rav Kahana* 27 (henceforth *PRK*) and *Vayiqra Rabba* 30 (henceforth *VR*).[1] These homilies were probably preached in synagogues on Sukkot or served as outlines for preachers.[2] They contain themes which their composers deemed important to communicate to their audiences on the festival. By creating a certain mood and emphasizing a set of concerns, the homilists reveal their conceptions of Sukkot. Even if the homilies are literary creations never delivered in public, as some scholars conjecture, they still reveal the conceptions and understanding of their composers.[3] That these homilies were incorporated into amoraic midrashic collections suggests that they were not idiosyncratic, but were judged worthy of preservation and further study. Subsequently they influenced those who studied these texts and helped to shape their understanding of Sukkot.

---

[1] The entire Pisqa 27 for Sukkot appears in *VR* 30 with but minor variations. So close is the parallel that it is unlikely both drew on a common source. Material from one was simply transferred to the other. Scholars debate which source did the borrowing. C. Albeck, "Midrash Vayiqra Rabba," *Louis Ginzberg Jubilee Volume* (New York, 1946), Hebrew section, 25-44 claims the material is original to *VR*, from which *PRK* borrowed. Margoliot in his introduction to *VR*, xiii, claims that the same redactor edited both documents. I follow J. Heinemann, "Chapters of Doubtful Authenticity in Leviticus Rabba," *Tarbiz* 37 (1968), 339-345 (Hebrew), who convincingly argues that this chapter is original to *PRK*. Heinemann was anticipated by Buber, Theodor, Ish-Shalom and A. Epstein (sources quoted by Margoliot ad loc.) Recently J. Neusner, "Appropriation and Imitation: The Priority of Leviticus Rabbah over Pesiqta deRab Kahana" *PAAJR* 54 (1987), 1-28 has argued this Pisqa (and the other shared Pisqas) originated in *VR*. Neusner makes no effort to respond to Heinemann's arguments.

[2] Heinemann, *Proem*, 100-22.

[3] R.S. Sarason, "The Petihot in Leviticus Rabba: Oral Homilies or Redactional Constructions?," *JJS* 33 (1982), 557-67 argues that the homilies are more redactional compositions that oral discourses. On this question see Heinemann, *Proem*, 104-22; D. Stern, *Parables in Midrash* (Cambridge, Mass.: Harvard University Press, 1991), 159-60; Abraham Goldberg's review of Mandelbaum's edition of *PRK*, *Qiryat Sefer* 43 (1967), 68-79 (who denies the Pisqas are edited sermons) and H. Fox, "The Circular Proem," *PAAJR* 49 (1982), 1-31. Norman Cohen, "Leviticus Rabbah, Parasha 3: An Example of a Classic Rabbinnic Homily," *JQR* 72 (1982), 18-31 and idem, "Structure and Editing in the Homiletic Midrashim," *AJS Review* 6 (1981), 1-20 demonstrates sophisticated editing and unified themes characterize the homilies of *PRK* and *VR*. For additional bibliography and discussion see H.L. Strack and G. Stemberger, *Introduction to the Talmud and Midrash*, trans. M. Bockmuehl (Minneapolis: Fortress Press, 1992), 313-29.

The second category of midrashim includes the exegeses of disparate biblical verses. These were not composed as homilies to be delivered on Sukkot but emerged from general interpretive activity. Scattered among the myriad rabbinic traditions are many that mention Sukkot, the sukka or lulav. How these motifs function in the traditions shows how they were understood, what they meant, and with what they were associated. The midrashim reveal the web of associations and symbolisms – the meanings – of the festival.

Admittedly there are many unknowns in this type of study. We do not know whether the *PRK* homilies were created by a small cadre of rabbis or by popular preachers, whether they reflect the ideas of the elite or the thoughts of the masses. We do not know how widespread were the exegetical traditions that mention Sukkot. How great an impact they exerted on the life of the people and how deeply they contributed to, or emerged from, the religious experience of the people is unclear. At all events, the midrashim of both types did not emerge in a vacuum. They represent more than poetic conceits, playful exegeses devoid of content. I assume they derive from some religious experience or living symbolic conception. Whose religious experience, and precisely where and when, are questions that cannot be answered precisely.

This study does not focus on the question of dating the texts. The homilies of *PRK* and *VR* are generally dated to the fifth or sixth centuries. Even the latest traditions from the Babylonian Talmud are not much later than this period. Occasionally I have drawn on *Shir Hashirim Rabba* (= *ShR*), the midrash to the Song of Songs, and *Lamentations Rabba* (=*LamR*), dated slightly later, perhaps to the sixth or seventh century. I also refer to the "Alternative Parsha," an addition to *PRK* which postdates the body of the document but cannot be dated precisely, and to late collections such as *Midrash HaGadol* and *Mishnat Rabbi Eliezer* to illustrate trends and developments. Of course in any given case the individual traditions may be earlier than the editing of the document, so that even an exact redactional date provides limited help.

I. Eschatology

Eschatological symbolism and associations appear prominently in the amoraic midrashim. Let us start with the famous drama of bAZ 2a-3b.[4] The aggada is attributed to R. Hanina b. Papa (third generation

---

[4]As is characteristic of the BT, layers of later commentary, digressions, interpolations, and passages transferred from other sources have been grafted upon the original aggada and interrupt the flow of the narrative. Most of the additions are Aramaic, while the aggada itself is Hebrew, so the later strata can be identified without too much difficulty. Already Israel ibn Al-Nakawa, *Menorat*

amora) or R. Simlai (second generation) in most versions, although MS JTS has R. Shela, probably R. Shela of Kefar Tamarta (second generation.)[5] These are all Palestinian amoraim; if the attributions can be trusted we are dealing with a third century Palestinian creation. The aggada can be divided into three parts. In the first part God summons the nations to collect their reward for the study of Torah. Rome, Persia and the other nations present their accomplishments to God and are summarily dismissed. In the second part the nations plead their case, protesting the unfairness of the judgment and accusing Israel of unworthiness. In the third part God tests the nations with the commandment of the sukka, which they fail to observe.

The crux of the drama emerges from the contrast between the first and third parts. Proudly Rome and Persia boast of their achievements, eager to collect their rewards. The former celebrate their markets, bathhouses and money, the later claim bridges, conquests of cities and waging war. Bridges, cities, markets and bathhouses, all impressive architectural achievements, evoke images of splendor, permanence and luxury. They comprise the beauty and brilliance of antiquity. However, realizing that God has established Torah alone as the criterion for reward, the Romans and Persians ignore the inherent merits of their projects and claim that they engaged in these enterprises only so that Israel could study Torah. God rejects this plea and exposes the true motivation for the building: self-interest. Markets harbor prostitutes, bathhouses provide for self-indulgent pampering, bridges and cities generate taxes. Money and war, on the other hand, are determined by God, and confer no merit on their proponents. All these enterprises are thisworldly, pursued exclusively out of selfish motivations, hence no reward is forthcoming.

The third part of the aggada fully exposes these selfish interests. God agrees to give a "simple precept," that of the sukka, as a test.[6] If the

---

Hama'or, ed. H.G. Enelow (New York: Bloch, 1929), 3:212 quotes a purified (albeit abbreviated) Hebrew narrative, having eliminated the Aramaic interpolations. I.H. Weiss, *Davar 'al 'odot hatalmud 'im yakhol hu letargem kol ṣorkho* (Pressburg, 1885) and A. Hilvitz, "Leharkava shel derashat ha'aggada bereish masekhet 'avoda zara," *Sinai* 80 (1977), 119-40 separate the original aggada from its later accretions. See too R. Hammer, "Complex Forms of Aggadah and Their Influence on Content," *PAAJR* 48 (1981), 186 and n. 4. *Tan Shoftim* §9 (651-52) = *TanB* 5:31-32 contain a version of the aggada free of the Aramaic additions, and probably close to the original, although some differences appear.
[5]Rosenthal, *Cycle*, 146 makes this identification. He notes that R. Hanina b. Papa regularly transmits the traditions of R. Shela of Kefar Tamarta.
[6]The meaning of *misva qala* in this context is "a simple precept," for this underscores the irony. Sukkot are readily available and simple to construct. To observe the *misva* of sukka is extremely easy – one need only enter the sukka and

nations succeed in observing this one commandment, they too will receive a reward. Eagerly the nations build sukkot on their roofs. But God causes the sun to shine upon them, and, sweltering in the heat, they angrily kick their sukkot and leave. The image of the sukka – a mere shelter, constructed of wood, covered with branches and vegetation, exposed to wind and rain, stark, bare – contrasts sharply with bridges, cities, markets and bathhouses, all solid, well-constructed, elegant, enduring structures, and creates the irony that lies at the heart of the homily. Indeed, the sukka is not only the structural opposite, but also

---

be. No effort, no struggle, almost no action is demanded. Compared with the energy required to build bridges, conquer cities, wage war or administrate marketplaces, simply to sit in the sukka is effortless. And yet the nations fail miserably since no self-aggrandizement is possible. In the talmud a glossator interpolated, "And why did he call it a *misva qala?* Since it is inexpensive." This is one possible meaning of *misva qala* as evident from mHul 12:5, "A *misva qala* which [costs] about an isar." But the term occurs frequently in tannaitic and amoraic sources with a range of different meanings. See the discussion in Al-Nakawa, *Menorat Hama'or*, ed. H.G. Enelow (New York: Bloch, 1929), 3:404-405. The failure of the nations bothered the glossator: if God made it so hot that the nations were forced to abandon their sukkot, how could the sukka be considered a "simple" precept? He chose a secondary meaning imported from mHul. But this misses the point of the aggada and destroys the irony. Nor does this interpolation appear in the parallel at *Tan Shoftim §9.*
S. Lieberman, "Redifat bat yisra'el," *Salo Wittmayer Baron Jubilee Volume* (Jerusalem and New York: American Academy for Jewish Research, 1974), 118-26 acknowledges that the original sense of *misva qala* here is not "an inexpensive commandment." He comments on our aggada in the course of an attempt to explain why the Hadrianic persecutions omitted any restriction upon the celebration of religious festivals. He suggests that the Romans themselves celebrated in a manner similar to the Jews. "They offered praises with palm branches and shook myrtles during times of rejoicing and victory, and they made sukkot on their festivals as well." Lieberman then explains *misva qala* in the aggada as "a *misva* which you too are accustomed to practice when you celebrate festivals." As evidence that pagans built sukkot Lieberman refers to A. Deissmarm, *Light from the Ancient East: The New Testament Illustrated by Recently Discovered Texts of the Graeco-Roman World* (New York: Doran, 1927), 115-16. But Deissmann himself refers to only one inscription (on pagans and the waving of branches, see below.) Other scholars have cited more parallels (see Licht, *Sukkot,* 175, Riesenfeld, *Jesus,* 154 n. 51) but the fact remains that the custom of building sukkot was not as common as Lieberman suggests. Modern scholars may stumble on a few examples, but we cannot expect our Palestinian aggadist to have known of obscure Hellenistic cults.
Rabbi Shlomo Goren, "Ha'universaliut vehayihud haruhani shebehag hasukkot," *Mahanayim* 50 (1961), 8 writing on a somewhat different topic, comments: "The explanation of the Talmud, 'since it is an inexpensive misva' is incomprehensible. Do all the other Jewish festivals cost more than the commandments of Sukkot?... And there are other commandments which cost less than the commandment of the sukka."

the functional opposite, of these grand edifices. The sukka generates no taxes, houses no prostitutes and offers no opportunity for self-indulgence. It is completely otherworldly, serving only as a means to fulfill the commandment of God. Ironically those who construct the much more impressive markets and bridges cannot observe the simple precept of the sukka. The discomfort experienced in the sukka is unbearable to those preoccupied with the thisworldly comforts of the bathhouse. The contrast between the sukka and the other edifices is the difference between otherworldly dedication and thisworldly success, between worship of God and self-satisfaction, between vanity and Torah, between Israel and the nations.

At this point the implications for Sukkot and the sukka may be considered.[7] It is important to recognize that the vision of Zech 14 – the *haftara* recited in the synagogue on Sukkot[8] – resonates in the substructure of the aggada, although the aggadist has translated the prophetic temple-oriented worldview into the rabbinic Torah-centered vantage and replaced a vision of limited universalism with a particularistic eschatological triumph.[9] Where Zechariah charges the nations to perform a temple ceremony on Sukkot, "to bow low before the King Lord of Hosts,"[10] the homilist has them observe a commandment of

---

[7]This literary analysis should not lead to the conclusion that the aggada was exclusively a literary creation. Rosenthal, *Cycle*, 144-48, argues that this very aggada is one of the earliest extant examples of a homily preached in a synagogue in Palestine. He suggests the homily was delivered on Sukkot, due to the importance of the sukka in the drama, while the attributions to Palestinian amoraim leave no doubt as to its provenance. The theme of the aggada, the emphasis on the reward for the observance of commandments, suits the conclusion of the annual Torah cycle on *Simḥat torah*, which E. Fleischer, "A List of Early Holidays in a *Piyyut* by Qiliri," *Tarbiz* 52 (1983), 236-53 (Hebrew), argued was practiced even in Palestine. Rosenthal also observes that the *haftara* for Sukkot in the Palestinian cycle includes Isa 43:9, around which the aggada is structured. On this basis Rosenthal claims to have found evidence supporting Fleischer's claim of an annual Palestinian Torah cycle as early as the third century. Both Fleischer's evidence and Rosenthal's conclusion have been trenchantly criticized by Fox, *Insights*, 81-84, and especially n. 13. Yet Fox himself relates the homily to Sukkot, the assembly of nations deriving from the theme of *haqhel*. In either case, that the themes appear in an oral homily suggests that the eschatological associations were living and real.

[8]bMeg 31a.

[9]This transformation provides an interesting example of reinterpretation due to a different religious context. In the rabbinic, post-temple era, failure to perform a pilgrimage no longer resonated in the imagination as a heinous sin. Celebration of Sukkot now occurred in local communities. The aggadist adapts Zechariah's conception of failure to satisfactorily observe Sukkot to his historical context and portrays the nations as unable to dwell in sukkot atop their houses.

[10]Zech 14:16.

the Torah pertaining to the festival. Where the prophet promises bounteous rain in the eschatological era, the homilist assures an undefined reward in the World to Come. And while the visionary believes the remaining nations will comply and acknowledge the supremacy of God, the homilist extends the nations' rebellion to the bitter end. The crucial point is that in both cases Sukkot rituals serve a key function in eschatological times. For the aggadist, the function is to distinguish Israel from the gentiles: dwelling in the sukka proves Israel worthy to enter the World to Come. In amoraic times, residing in the sukka was associated with eschatogical reward.

The idea of eschatological reward for dwelling in the sukka comes to full expression in the "Alternative Parsha for Sukkot" of *PRK*:

> Therefore the Holy One will have compassion for them [Israel] in the World to Come,[11] as it says, *A sukka for shade from the heat of the day (Isa 4:6)*. R. Levi[12] said, "whoever fulfills the commandment of sukka in this world, God says, 'since he observed the commandment of sukka in this world, I will protect him from the fire of the Day to Come.'"[13]

R. Levi applies the classic rabbinic "measure-for-measure" principle *(mida keneged mida)*: those who observe the commandment of the sukka in this world will be rewarded with a protective sukka on the Day to Come. Those who neglected the sukka in this world, like the nations in the homily, remain unprotected and suffer divine punishment. The punishment is made even more explicit in the continuation of the passage:

> In the World to Come what does the Holy One do? He exposes these heavens, as it says, *The heavens shall be rolled up like a scroll (Isa 34:4)*, and takes it [the sun] out from under its sheath, and it will come forth in all its power and avenge the wicked, as it says, *Behold the Day to Come, burning like an oven. And the arrogant and all the doers of evil shall be straw, and the day that is coming shall burn them to ashes and leave of them neither stock nor boughs (Mal 3:19)*. At that time God will make a sukka for the righteous and protect them in it, as it says, *He will shelter me in his*

---

[11] *'atid*, literally, "in the future," usually refers to the eschaton. The bAZ homily begins: In the World to Come (*'atid*) the Holy One...

[12] R. Levi is a third generation Palestinian amora, which squares neatly with the attributions of the bAZ aggada to R. Hanina b. Papa or R. Hana b. Hanina or R. Simlai. But the statement is unparalleled, and the "Alternative Parsha" was not originally part of the *PRK*. See the following note.

[13] *PRK*, 452, *Yalqut* §653. Mandelbaum argues that the "Alternative Parsha" was not original to *PRK*, since its style is radically different. He suggests it was composed for the second day of the festival, and postdates the rest of *PRK*. The precise date of redaction is unknown.

pavilion (sukko) on an evil day (Ps 27:5), and so *And it serve as a sukka for shade from the heat of the day (Isa 4:6)*, from the fire of that "Day."[14]

The midrash finds a basis for the protective sukka in Ps 27:5, which speaks of God sheltering his people in a metaphoric pavilion *(sukko)*, and Isa 4:6, which prophesies an eschatological cloud-sukka. The author connects the "evil day" of Ps 27:5 and the "day" (= daytime) of Isa 4:6 to the "Day to Come" of Mal 3:19, and relates the two scenes to the fate of the two sides. While the wicked burn in the fires of judgment day (Mal 3:19), the righteous are protected in a divine sukka (Ps 27:5, Isa 4:6). Of critical importance is the idea that dwelling in the sukka not only gains future salvation, but concretely symbolizes the form of that salvation. Application of the measure-for-measure principle produces the notion that the reward for dwelling in the sukka is a divinely bestowed protective sukka. The sukka both merits and comprises eschatological reward, and thus prefigures an element of eschatological times. Moreover, it should be noted that the compiler of the "Alternative Parsha" cites these traditions after paraphrasing the bAZ homily, which neither defined Israel's reward nor detailed the punishment of the nations. By juxtaposing such traditions with the homily he extends the eschatological vision. Israel, who annually observes the commandment of the sukka, will be rewarded with the protective sukka. Conversely, the nations, who reject the commandment to reside in sukkot because of the intense heat, will suffer *real* heat in the World to Come – the punishing flames of judgment day. The sun not only causes the nations to abandon their sukkot, but also provides the means of punishment. The sukka not only marks the dedication of Israel to the Torah, but the form of her eschatological reward.

These traditions shed light on the origin of the conception of the eschatological sukkot. The idea developed from the tannatic interpretation of the sukkot symbolizing the clouds of glory. According to the tannaim, the clouds of glory not only sheltered the Israelites during their desert wanderings but would return in eschatological time.[15] Isaiah's prophecy of the eschatological cloud was interpreted to refer to the eschatological return of the clouds of glory. The amoraim made this idea more concrete, and made the symbolism more direct, by interpreting the eschatological clouds of glory as miraculous sukkot. God would bestow protective sukkot to shelter his people in the eschaton. The amoraim took their cue, in part, directly from Isa 4:6, which describes the cloud as a sukka. As the tannaitic notion of eschatological clouds of glory evolved into the amoraic concept of

---

[14]*PRK*, 452-53.
[15]*Mekhilta Pisḥa* §14 *(48)*. See Chapter 6, II text to n. 61.

protective divine sukkot, the symbolism of the festival sukkot would naturally develop in parallel.

The eschatological sukka appears in a different guise in the exegetical midrash found in bBB 75a:

> Rabba bar bar Hanna[16] in the name of R. Yohanan further stated: The Holy One in the World to Come will make a sukka for the righteous from the skin of Leviathan, for it is said, *Can you fill 'sukkot' with his skin (Job 40:31).*[17] If a man is worthy, a sukka is made for him; if he is not worthy [of this] a mere covering (*ṣilṣal*) is made for him, for it is said, *And his head with a fish covering (Job 40:31)...* The rest of Leviathan will be spread by the Holy One upon the walls of Jerusalem and its splendor will shine from one end of the world to the other.

The attribution to Rabba bar bar Hanna (third generation Babylonian amora) or R. Yohanan (second generation Palestinian amora) places the date of the tradition close to that of the bAZ homily. The midrash reads ŠKWT, "fishhooks," as an orthographic variation of SKWT, booths. God constructs a sukka out of the monster's skin for the most pious and fashions a *ṣilṣal*, perhaps interpreted as a diminutive of *ṣel*, "a little shade" or "slight covering," for the less righteous.[18] The sukka does not serve a practical function, such as protection from the fires of judgment, nor does the "measure for measure" principle appear here. The sukka simply identifies the most righteous and enables them to bask directly in the splendor of Leviathan's skin.[19]

The Alternative Parsha again appends the "measure for measure" principle: "R. Levi said: Whoever fulfills the commandment of sukka in this world, God causes him to dwell in the sukka of Leviathan in the World to Come, as it says, *Can you fill 'sukkot' with his skin (Job 40:31)."*[20] Mundane sukkot not only symbolize the sukkot fashioned from Leviathan's skin, but effect that reward.

---

[16]See *DQS* ad loc.

[17]שכות (fishhooks) is read as סכות.

[18]Kohut, *'Arukh*, 7:21 translates "schattige bedachtung." Jastrow, *Dictionary*, 1286 translates "shady covering." Some manuscripts have ṣel ṣel (two words.) See *DQS* ad loc.

[19]In other aggadot God kills Leviathan and feeds his flesh to the righteous at a messianic banquet (bBB 74b).

[20]*PRK*, 455. See too 454,24-455,2. "Whoever observes the commandment of sukka in this world, God gives them a portion in the World to Come in the sukka of Sodom." The sukka of Sodom was formed from the shade of seven different fruit trees. Cf. *BaR* 14:2 which considers the eschatological sukka as a reward for Abraham inviting the angels to recline in the shade of his tent.

The divine shelters bestowed upon the righteous in eschatological times are sometimes designated *ḥuppot*: "canopies" or "shelters."[21] A series of midrashim about Leviathan and the World to Come includes the following tradition:

> Rabba said in the name of R. Yohanan: In the World to Come (*'atid*) the Holy One, blessed be He, will build seven *ḥuppot* for each righteous person, as it is said, *And God will create over the whole shrine and meeting place of Mt Zion a sukka by day...a ḥuppa (Isa 4:5)*. This teaches that God will fashion a *ḥuppa* for each one according to his merit.[22]

The *ḥuppa* "according to his merit" recalls the sliding scale of coverings constructed from Leviathan's skin for the different levels of righteousness. In this tradition the Isaian prophecy, which describes the cloud as both a *sukka* and *ḥuppa*, proves each righteous individual will merit a *ḥuppa*. R. Levi employed the same verse in the midrash cited above to prove that the righteous will be protected in a *sukka*. In other midrashim God makes seven jeweled *ḥuppot* for the Messiah in addition to a *ḥuppa* for the righteous.[23] Several sources locate the eschatological *ḥuppot* in the garden of Eden.[24]

---

[21] The terms *ḥuppa* and *sukka* are extremely close in meaning. They appear in parallel in Isa 4:6, where the divine cloud is described as "a sukka for shade from heat by day and as a *ḥuppa* for protection against drenching rain." In *Mekhilta Pisha* §14 (48), R. Akiba proves from the term *ḥuppa* that the sukkot of the desert were clouds of glory, and proves from the term *sukka* that sukkot in the future will also take this form. See too BR 18 (161). Ḥuppa occurs three times in the Bible: Ps 19:6 and Joel 2:16, where it refers to the bridal canopy, and Isa 4:5. In rabbinic literature *ḥuppa* became a *terminus technicus* for the bridal chamber or marriage ceremony, but in aggadic contexts it retained a more general connotation.

[22] bBB 75a. How the prooftext indicates seven *ḥuppot* is explained by the commentaries in various ways. Rashi, (s.v *'anan*) divides the verse into seven words or phrases relating to the *ḥuppa*. (He offers two possible divisions.) Maharsha interprets the midrash in light of bAZ 2b-3a and suggests that the seven *ḥuppot* are the reward for dwelling in the sukka for seven days. Like R. Levi, he invokes a "measure for measure" principle.

[23] PR §37 (163a): "Thereupon, what will the Holy one blessed be He make for the Messiah? He will make seven *ḥuppot* of precious stones and pearls for him. As for each *ḥuppa*, out of it there will flow forth four rivers – one of wine, one of honey, one of milk, and one of pure balsam. And the Holy One blessed be He will embrace the Messiah in the sight of the righteous and bring him within the *ḥuppa* where all the righteous ones, the pious ones, the holy ones, the mighty men of Torah of every generation, will gaze upon him." The imagery derives from Ezekiel's description of the king of Tyre who is "covered" or "sheltered" (*mesukatekha*) with precious stones and located in Eden (28:11-19).

[24] So VR 25:2 (570): "R. Huna and R. Yermia in the name of R. Hiyya b. Aba: In the World to Come God will make shade and *ḥuppot* for *ba'alei misvot* alongside *ba'alei tora* in the garden of Eden." See the apparatus for variants, especially for the

The midrashim describing types of eschatological *ḥuppot* and sukkot are variations on the same theme: the righteous will reside in special shelters in the World to Come. Festival sukkot symbolized to the amoraim the splendid eschatological chambers that awaited them. Dwelling in the sukka "pre-enacted" dwelling in the divinely constructed shelters of the next world and undoubtedly added an important dimension to the experience. The eschatological dimension was deeper than that of specific commandments, or pious deeds in general, for which the rabbis also promised eschatological reward. To cite one of many examples: "whoever learns halakhot each day is certain to inherit the World to Come."[25] But here "learning halakhot" neither comprises the reward nor serves any function in the next world. With the sukka, on the other hand, the commandment parallels the reward, a miraculous sukka, while the ritual foreshadows the nature of existence in the World to Come. The significant element of the equation is the form of the reward, the eschatological sukka. A later Jewish prayer recited upon leaving the sukka on *Shmini ʿaseret* captures this sentiment: "May it be Your will, Lord our God and God of our Fathers, that just as I have been privileged to observe the commandment of dwelling in this sukka, so in the future may I be privileged to dwell in the sukka made from the skin of Leviathan." It is not (only) *because* one observes the commandment, but *just as* one resides in the sukka during the festival, so he hopes to dwell in the divine sukkot of messianic times.

The lulav and etrog, like the sukka, become eschatological symbols in the midrashim. This symbolism appears in the homily found in VR 30:2 (691-95).[26] Ps 16:11, "You will teach me the path of life. In your presence is fullness of joy, delights are ever in your right hand, " serves as the petiḥta-verse, the opening verse of the homily. The homilist interprets the first half of the verse as a question King David asked God

---

attributions. Several manuscripts and a geniza fragment read *ḥuppa*, not *ḥuppot*; see M. Margoliot, *Seridei vayiqra rabba* (Jerusalem, 1960), 78. See too ySot 7:4, 21d; QohR 7:11. Other midrashim relate that God constructed jeweled *ḥuppot* for Adam in the garden of Eden. This image constitutes a retrojection of the eschatological canopies to the original paradise. The righteous will dwell in the same majestic abodes Adam inhabited in the garden. See BR 18:1 (161); bBB 75a; PRK 4:4 (66-67); 26:1 (389); VR 20:2 (446); QohR 8:1; PR 14 (62a). RR 3:4 speaks of an individual *"canopy" (ginun;* the Aramaic for *ḥuppa,* as in the targum to Isa 4:5) prepared for the righteous in the World to Come. Cf. bShab 152a: *"But man sets out for his eternal abode (Qoh 12:5).* R. Isaac said: This teaches that every righteous person is given a chamber *(mador)* as befits his honor." And see bBM 83b, QohR 12:5; VR 18:1 (396) and Margoliot's notes; BR 96 (1237).
[25]bNid 73a.
[26]Parallel to PRK 27:2 (404-407). I cite VR because it reads more smoothly. See n. 29.

about how to gain entry to the World to Come. "Joy" in the second half of the verse is interpreted to refer to the joy of study. A second interpretation reads "fullness of joy" *(sovaʿ semaḥot)* as "seven joys" *(shevaʿ semaḥot)*, explained as the seven companies of the righteous to be received by the shekhina in eschatological times. The homily describes the magnificent radiance emanating from their faces and considers which company is most beloved. Thus the midrash focuses throughout on the World to Come: how to attain it, who will be there, how they will appear and in what order they will sit. At this point the homilist introduces Sukkot. The seven joys are interpreted as the seven festival commandments – the four species of the lulav, the sukka, and the *simḥa* and *ḥagiga* sacrifices.[27] The homily then turns to the third clause of the verse, reading the Hebrew *neṣaḥ* ("ever") as "victory": "Delights in your right hand are victory."

> *Delights in your right hand are victory (Ps 16:11).* R. Avin said, this is the lulav, like the one who is victorious and takes the palm *(bain)*. A parable: Like two who appear before a judge, and we do not know which one is the victor. When one carries off the palm *(bain)*, then we know that he is the victor. So, too, when Israel and the nations of the world[28] appear before the Holy One on Rosh Hashana, bringing charges against each other, we do not know which ones are victors. But when Israel departs from the presence of the Holy One with their lulavs and their etrogs in their hands, we know that Israel are the victors.[29]

R. Avin pictures Israel and the nations standing in court before God the judge on Rosh Hashana. God releases the verdict of the heavenly trial on Sukkot, revealing his true judgment, whatever the illusory situation on earth. In this world the nations appear to have prevailed over Israel, but in the heavenly spheres the opposite is the case. R. Avin compares the lulav with the *bais*, the later Greek term for the palm,[30] and interprets the ritual shaking of the lulav as a victory parade.[31] In Hellenistic and

---

[27]The *ḥagiga* is the festival sacrifice brought on the three pilgrimage festivals. The *simḥa* sacrifice was an additional peace offering brought to add to the joy *(simḥa)* of the occasion.
[28]*PRK* and some manuscripts of *VR* read "the heavenly counterparts *(sarei)* of the nations."
[29]The parallel at *PRK* 27:2 (406-407) connects R. Avin's statement to the question why both *simḥa* and *ḥagiga* offerings are necessary. But since the answer – R. Avin's parable – relates to the lulav, the answer does not address the question. See the classical commentaries and Margoliot's notes.
[30]The classical Greek term for palm is *phoenix*. Later sources use *bais* or *baion*, from a root borrowed from Egyptian. See P.-W. 20, 1, p. 386, s.v. *phoenix*.
[31]See *Targum Sheni* to Esther 3:8: "[the Jews] destroy the orchards, by breaking down the hedges and not taking care, and they make for themselves a *hoshaʿana*, saying, 'as does the king in his [triumphal] ceremonies, so do we.'" (*Hoshaʿana* here is a synonym for lulav, as found in other sources.)

Roman times palms were routinely given to victorious athletes,[32] so the palm became the outstanding symbol of victory in classical culture[33] and in Jewish-Hellenistic literature.[34] Although the trial is not set specifically in eschatological time, but seems to be an annual event, there is no doubt

---

[32]Pausanius, *Periegara* VII 48, 2, notes "At most games, however, [the victor] is given a crown of palm, and at all a palm is placed in the right hand of the victor" (LCL, trans. W.H.S. Jones [Cambridge, 1935], 4:137.) Suetonius, *Caligula* 32, 2, relates that Caligula, after killing a gladiator (who intentionally fell), "ran about with a palm branch as victors do" (LCL, trans. J.C. Rolfe [London, 1914].) According to Livy, *Ab Urba Condita* X 47,1-4, the Romans borrowed this custom from the Greeks: "This year (292 BCE) for the first time those who had been presented with crowns because of gallant behavior in the war wore them at the Roman games, and palms were then for the first time conferred upon the victors" (LCL, trans. B.O. Foster [London, 1926], 4:541.) Numerous imperial inscriptions dedicating games include a provision that the victors be rewarded palms. See e.g. *CIL* 6.2065, an inscription of Domitian, *"victores palmis et coronis argenteis honoravit."*

[33]Plutarch, *Quaes. Conv.* VIII 4, 723 B, relates a discussion in which his companions consider the question: "Why, at the various athletic festivals different kinds of wreaths are awarded, but the palm frond at all of them?" Various answers explain in different ways how the palm naturally symbolizes victory: "The fame of victors ought to remain unfading and exempt from old age, as far as is possible. Now the palm is one of the most long-lived plants...to it alone, practically, belongs a characteristic falsely attributed to many others, namely that of being firm-leaved and always in leaf...and it is this strength that it has which people particularly associate with the vigour that brings victory" (LCL; trans. F. Babbitt [Cambridge, 1927], 145). "Palm," in fact, became synonymous with victory in later classical literature. Cicero, *Rosc.* 6.17: *aliter plurimarum palmarum vetus ac nobilis gladiator habetur* ("The first is reputed to be a famous and experienced gladiator, who has won many victories [palms]"; LCL; trans. J.H. Freese [London, 1930], 6:137.) In races first place was called "first palm." Thus Vergil, *Aeneid*, 5:339: "Euralus darts by and, winning by grace of his friend takes first, and flies on amid favouring applause and cheers. Behind come Helymus and Diores, now third palm *(nunc tertia palma, Diores;* LCL; trans. H. Fairclough, [London, 1935.]) Apuleius, *Metamorphoses* 2, 4, calls the goddess of victory the "palm goddess": *attolerabant statuas palmeris deae facies.* During their triumphal processions the triumphator wore a tunic adorned with palm leaves, the *tunica palmata.* See Livy, *Ab Urba Condita* XXX 15, 12 and X 7, 9. The triumphator usually held a myrtle branch in his right hand during the triumphal procession. See Ehlers, *Triumphus*, 506-508. Thus the myrtle also served as a victory symbol.

[34]In 1 Macc 13:51, Simon celebrated the purification of the Akra with "praise and palm branches and harps and symbols and viols and hymns, and with songs." Similar celebrations are described in 2 Macc 10:7, which, apparently on account of the palm branches, makes the explicit comparison to Sukkot. "Bearing wands *(thyrsoi)* wreathed with leaves and fair boughs and palms, they offered hymns of praise to Him who had prospered the cleansing of his own place." Judith and the women rejoicing with her carried branches in their victory parade, although these are not specified as palms; Jud 15:12-13. In *Testament of Naphtali* 5:4 Levi receives twelve date palms as a symbol of power.

that the sense is eschatological. The annual trial rehearses the judgment that will become a reality in the eschaton. Then the victors reap their rewards and celebrate in reality that which the lulav ritual symbolizes annually.

Now the court setting recalls the juridical environment of the bAZ homily. The phrase "bringing charges" before God suits the nations' arguments, their accusation that Israel never fulfilled the Torah and is unworthy of the reward.[35] Where the homily depicts the Romans, Persians and other nations departing dejectedly, the midrash portrays Israel's victorious exit. While the homily illustrates the failure of the nations to reside in sukkot and their dismissal by God, R. Avin pictures Israel carrying lulavs as a sign of a divinely recognized victory. He essentially picks up where our homily leaves off. Both homilists deploy the festival symbols to express the same theme. The sukka proves the ground for Israel's reward, her fidelity to God against the revolt of the nations, while the lulav symbolizes that reward, her victory triumph in the World to Come.[36]

---

[35] In the homily Israel does not bring charges. The dialogue takes place exclusively between God and the nations. Here both Israel and the nations bring charges before God.

[36] Compare the expansion of this midrash in MTeh 17:5 (126): "What is the reason for *Delights in Your right hand are victory (Ps 16:11)*? Just as according to the custom of the world, when two charioteers race in the hippodrome, which of them receives a palm *(bain)*? The one who wins. Thus on RH all the people of the world come like contestants on parade and pass before God, and the children of Israel among all of the people of the world also pass before Him like troops. When the first day of Sukkot comes, however, all the children of Israel, adults and children, take up lulavs in the right hand and etrogs in their left, and then all people of the world know that in the judgment Israel was proclaimed victorious." In the Byzantine Empire races between charioteers representing different religions were indeed seen as symbolic of a struggle for superiority. See Dan Yaron, "Circus Factions (Blues and Greens) in Byzantine Palestine," *The Jerusalem Cathedra 1*, ed. Lee Levine (Jerusalem, 1981), 105-119: "When rivals were members of different religions, the victory of their chariots was viewed as a victory for their religion. Thus triumph also served as a valuable form of propaganda. In one race held in fourth century Gaza, a Christian named Italicus competed against a pagan who was one of the heads of the city government... The race, in effect, represented a struggle between paganism and Christianity. The victory of Italicus's chariot was considered a victory of Jesus over Marnas, the god of the city *(Marnas victus est a Christo)*. Malalas reports that in Neapolis, the victory of a Christian charioteer named Nicias over Samaraitan and Jewish entries so enraged Julianus, the leader of the Samaritan revolt (529), that he ordered Nicias be killed" (p. 107). On Jewish participation in chariot races see there p. 106 n. 4. Yaron also argues that the "Samaritan riots and rebellion at Caeserea very likely began during the chariot races, or at least were connected in one way or another with the hippodrome" (p. 117; the riots occurred in 555). The midrash beautifully incorporates this cultural symbolism into its promise of eschatological victory for

A different eschatological symbolism appears in *PRK* 27:3 (407-409). After expounding Ps 102:18 the passage attends to Ps 102:19, "May this be written down for a coming generation, that a people that will be created may praise the Lord." In the Psalm itself, "this" refers to the subsequent verses which relate that God looked down from heaven, released prisoners condemned to die, and was then praised and worshipped in Jerusalem. The homily understands the "coming generation" first as penitents, then as the generations of Hezekiah and Mordechai which experienced times of great danger like the condemned prisoners of the Psalm. "That a people that will be created may praise the Lord" means that God created those generations anew.[37] Thus the "coming generation" is not a future generation that will praise God on account of His salvific acts of the past, but a specific generation that was "created anew" when God delivered them from death. The passage continues:

> Another explanation: *May this be written down for a coming generation (Ps 102:19)*. These are the present generations which are on the verge of death. *A people that shall be created shall praise the Lord*. That in the World to Come (*'atid*) the Holy One shall create them new life. And what should we take up? A lulav and etrog to praise the Holy One. Hence Moses charges Israel, saying to them, *You shall take on the first day... (Lev 23:40)*.

Once again the homily focuses on the eschatological future. "Coming generation" (*dor aḥaron*) is perhaps understood in the sense of "days to come" (*aḥarit hayamim*), the "final" or "eschatological" generation. A mini-salvation history describes the deliverance of previous generations and culminates with the conviction that prayers of present generations ultimately will be heard.[38] The homilist does not explain why these

---

the Jews. In *PRK* 27:1 (401-404) the lulav is also associated with triumph over gentiles. The homilist compares the lulav to the hyssop with which God instructed the Israelites to paint their doorposts in Egypt. The hyssop is inexpensive, yet Israel was rewarded with the spoil of Egypt, King Og, and the thirty-one Canaanite kings they conquered in Palestine. How much more will they be rewarded for taking the expensive lulav! Thus the lulav brings victories over Israel's enemies and rich spoil.

[37] בראם הקב'ה בריאה חדשה.

[38] Mandelbaum suggests that the conclusion, "and what should we take?," should be connected to the section expounding the "coming generation" as penitents. God hears their prayer on RH and YK, and in response, "what should we take up? A lulav and etrog to praise God..." This interpretation is based on *MTeh* 102:3 (431) where the conclusion is specifically linked to repentance: "the generation who have sinned with evil deeds, and come and repent before You on RH and YK, and since they make anew their deeds, God creates them anew." Similarly, S. Buber in his edition of *PRK* (Lyck, 1868), 181a n. 55 suggests emending *PRK* (and *VR* 30:3!) on the basis of *MTeh* by adding this conclusion.

generations are close to death; presumably he means that they are mortal and destined to die. God will "create them new life" by bestowing upon them eternal life in the World to Come. The image of bodily resurrection comes to mind, but the new creation need not be understood in such corporeal terms. The appropriate response is to take the lulav to praise and give thanks to their savior. Yet the lulav is more than a token of praise; it symbolizes the new creation: the verdant boughs express the vitality and rejuvenation of life. In essence the archaic use of the lulav as a fertility symbol has been refracted through an eschatological lens. The concern is not vegetable life in the next year, but eternal life for the people in the next world.

The Alternative Parsha proposes a different eschatological symbolism for the lulav:

> I also told you to take a lulav and shake *(tena'an'u)* it before me. Even though you do so, you are not benefiting me, but paying a debt to me. Why? When I took you out of Egypt I made the mountains skip *(lena'nea')* before you, as it says, *The mountains skipped like rams* (Ps 114:4). So too in the World to Come I will do this for you, as it says, *The mountains and the hills will break forth before you singing* (Isa 55:12).[39]

Here the *gesture* performed with the lulav expresses the symbolism.[40] The ritual shaking of the lulav points back to the exodus, symbolizing the mountains that skipped with joy, and forward to messianic times, to their anticipated singing and dancing. Just as the sukka symbolizes both the sukkot of the exodus and those of eschatological times, so the lulav symbolizes miraculous phenomena of both periods.

In earlier chapters we traced the roots of the eschatological associations with Sukkot. In the second temple period eschatological motifs developed among marginal groups as a reflex of the connection between the festival and the temple. Zech 14 pictures a restored temple where Sukkot is universally observed. Christian Scriptures depict the heavenly worship of the eschatological temple in terms of Sukkot imagery. An independent eschatological thrust emerged in the tannaitic midrashim. The sukka symbolizes the clouds of glory, which would return in messianic times and provide shelter just as they did in the desert. This rabbinic idea is not connected to temple imagery but stems

---

Neither suggestion is tenable. One should not emend when all manuscripts of both midrashim are consistent. Nor is it the style of *PRK* to connect the conclusion to a brief lemma earlier in the Pisqa. The point of the Pisqa is straightforward. The lulav symbolizes the anticipated eschatological re-creation. It expresses messianic grace, not a response to forgiveness granted annually on the Days of Awe.

[39] *PRK*, 457.
[40] For a fascinating discussion of symbolic gestures, see Stern, *Reference*.

from the projection of the desert experience into the eschaton. The variety of eschatological symbolisms and associations which characterizes Sukkot in amoraic midrashim reflects both the second temple and tannaitic conceptions. That the festival sukka symbolizes the protective sukka of judgment day, the sukka of Leviathan's skin and other divine shelters developed out of a concretization of the clouds of glory symbolism. The form of the divine shelter of the World to Come would not be the clouds of glory but divinely fashioned sukkot. On the other hand, the eschatological symbolism of the lulav as an expression of victory in the heavenly trial and as praise for God who grants eternal life, as well as the general eschatological associations of Sukkot, require a different explanation. These cannot be derived from tannaitic conceptions of the clouds of glory.

I would suggest that these ideas derive from two sources: the impact of Zech 14 and the legacy of Sukkot as the paramount temple festival of second temple times. Zech 14 stands out as perhaps the clearest eschatological prophecy. As scripture, it would inevitably inform rabbinic eschatological thinking.[41] In addition, the prophecy was selected as the *haftara* for Sukkot.[42] Whether or not the rabbis appreciated Zechariah's reasons for placing Sukkot in his eschatological vision,[43] they inherited the eschatological association as part of their canon. To give Sukkot an eschatological role was simply to read scripture well. Yet the legacy of Sukkot as the leading temple festival also factored in this process. The wealth of rabbinic traditions and laws concerning temple matters show that the rabbis were heavily invested in the temple and its history. Two of the six orders of the Mishna are devoted almost exclusively to temple law, while major portions of the other orders pertain solely to the temple. In Tractate Sukka of the Mishna, Tosefta and both talmuds traditions about the temple celebrations of Sukkot are preserved and recalled in an idealized fashion. Tannaim and amoraim knew well that Sukkot was "the Festival," a name out of character with its contemporary mode of celebration. When the temple would be rebuilt Sukkot would be celebrated the way it was meant to be, with numerous sacrifices, water libations and willow processions.[44] Like various groups of the second temple period, the

---

[41]We noted that the prophecy underlies the eschatological drama found in bAZ 2a-3b; above, p. 278.
[42]bMeg 31a.
[43]See Chapter 2, II.
[44]To be sure Pesaḥ, Shavuot and other festivals could not be celebrated according to biblical law in a world without a temple. To a certain extent, then, we find eschatological associations with all the festivals, just as we find them in the daily liturgy and throughout the worldview of rabbinic Judaism. But the destruction

amoraim looked forward to eschatological times as the hope for the complete celebration of Sukkot.[45] In the midrashim the eschatological associations cluster around the sukka and the lulav rather than the cultic rituals because those were the rituals currently observed. The sukka was the locus for eating and sleeping, the focus of energy and thought for seven days. The sukka and lulav comprised the essence of the religious experience of Sukkot. Eschatological associations therefore developed in connection with these rituals, the practices which were foremost in the minds of the people. Homilists communicated their message most effectively by linking eschatological associations to the symbols and rituals experienced daily.

II. Rejoicing and Atonement: Sukkot, Rosh Hashana and Yom Kippur

In our survey of theories of the origin of Sukkot we noted that many scholars believe that the festivities that coalesced as Sukkot, Rosh Hashana and Yom Kippur all originated in the pristine Israelite autumnal festival. The beliefs and rituals that developed into three festivals initially found expression at various points over the course of the autumnal festivities. Later the autumnal festival complex "splintered" and three separate festivals took shape, each with an identity of its own.[46] Other scholars believe that RH and YK were always independent of Sukkot, but suggest that these days functioned as preparations for the great harvest celebration. This view also argues that the three festivals were connected in a substantive way. Tannaitic sources which place the determination of rain on Sukkot express the process in terms of "judgment" and "sentence," the theological processes that occur on RH and YK. Thus an overlap of certain aspects of the festivals is evident. Even if these theories of origins are mistaken, the calendrical proximity of the festivals naturally moved those who celebrated them to frame their experience in a larger perspective and to discern relationships between the festivals. Why do RH, YK and Sukkot

---

cut to the very essence of Sukkot, which had been connected with the temple in a much deeper way.

[45]Thus I believe that the same thought process which we saw in Zech 14 and the Christian Scriptures led the rabbis to associate Sukkot with eschatology. When the rabbis thought of worship in the rebuilt temple they thought of "The Festival," the libations, the willow ritual and SBH. I doubt that the rabbis inherited ideas directly from the groups responsible for Zech 14 and the Christian Scriptures. Rather the rabbis and these earlier circles came to similar conclusions about Sukkot based on their common situation: inability to worship properly in the temple, whether because of alienation and sectarian ideology or the fact of its destruction.

[46]Chapter 1, III, n. 22 and text thereto.

follow one another so closely? Are they completely independent or are they interconnected parts of a larger drama? These very questions probably engendered the concept of the "ten days of repentance" that connect RH to YK. The two days became parts of a larger drama, and the themes of atonement, repentance and the kingship of God became appropriate for both.

What role did Sukkot play in this festival complex? Midrashim express a substantive relationship between Sukkot, RH and YK in various ways. Sukkot is generally understood as a response to the events of the previous two festivals, especially the favorable divine judgment. A different conception portrays the rejoicing on Sukkot as celebration of the renewal of life which God bestows on RH and YK. At the same time, themes that characterize RH and YK become associated with Sukkot. The period of atonement is extended from the High Holidays to Sukkot, and so the ideas of sin, repentance and forgiveness are related to the festival.

PRK 27:4 (409) expresses the relationship between the three festivals as follows:

> *The fields rejoice (Ps 96:12).* This refers to the world, as it says, *And it happened when they were in the field (Gen 4:8). And all that is in it (Ps 96:12).* This refers to its creatures, as its says, *The earth is the Lord's and all that it holds [the world and its inhabitants] (Ps 24:1).*
>
> *All the trees of the forest shout for joy (Ps 96:12).* And it says, *The trees of the forest shout for joy (1 Chr 16:33).* R. Aha said: *The forest* refers to trees that produce fruit. *All the trees of the forest* refers to trees that do not produce fruit.
>
> Before whom? *Before the Lord.* Why? *For he comes.* On Rosh Hashana and Yom Kippur. To do what? *To judge the world justly and its peoples in faithfulness (Ps 96:13).*

The Pisqa interprets the rejoicing of the fields and their contents of Ps 96:12 as the exultation of the entire world and all living creatures, as the general exuberance of all nature. The second half of the verse, "all the trees of the forest" is juxtaposed with the parallel verse from Chronicles which lacks the word "all."[47] The homilist interprets the verses to refer to different types of trees: Ps 96:12 pertains to trees that do not bear fruit (*all* the trees, even those that produce no fruit); 1 Chr 16:33 relates to trees that bear fruit. Here the homilist alludes to the lulav, which consists of a palm and the etrog (trees which bear fruit) and willows and myrtles (which do not bear fruit.) The source of this image is a baraita, bMen 27a:

---

[47]This omission is clearly the textual irritant. Mandelbaum observes (*PRK*, 409, l. 10) that the manuscripts do not consistently quote the verses as in the MT.

> The four species of the lulav: two of them produce fruit, and two of them do not produce fruit. The ones that produce fruit require those that do not produce fruit, and the ones that do not produce fruit require those that produce fruit. Thus one does not fulfill his obligation until they are all in one band.

The baraita does not appear in the extant tannaitic midrashim, nor in the PT, but was apparently well known to the homilist. He does not mention the lulav explicitly, assuming the allusion to "trees that produce fruit" will be understood. Note that the next verse in Chronicles (1 Chr 16:34) is identical to Ps 118:1, the precise point in the Hallel at which the lulav is shaken.[48] This provides an additional hint that the "trees" allude to the lulav species. While the first half of the verse describes the rejoicing of the fields and the earth's creatures, the second half proclaims the rejoicing of Israel with the lulav.

The homilist then interprets the following verse, Ps 96:13, as the advent of God on RH and YK. Nature exults and Israel rejoices with the lulav when God comes to "judge" or "rule" the earth. At first reading the rejoicing seems to be an acclamation or salutation at God's approach – "before the Lord, for he comes." But since Sukkot follows YK we should understand the rejoicing as a response to God's arrival and translate: "Why? For he *came* on RH and YK." In either case the rejoicing of Sukkot is not linked to the harvest or the pilgrimage, but to the celebration of the kingship of God actualized during the previous festivals. Nature shouts for joy and worshippers rejoice with the lulav after God reestablishes divine order.[49]

This explanation of the rejoicing recalls *PRK* 27:2, in which the lulav served as a victory symbol signaling that Israel triumphed in the annual trial.[50] God judges Israel meritorious on RH, and then Israel expresses its success by taking the lulav on Sukkot. In *PRK* 27:4 the festival celebrates the cosmic joy at the ascent of God to the throne of judgment; in *PRK* 27:2 the national joy of Israel at the favorable outcome of that event.

A variation on this understanding of Sukkot as a response to RH and YK finds expression in *PRK* 27:7 (412-13).[51] The Pisqa compares Israel to a city which owed taxes to a king.

---

[48] Cf. the interpretation of R. Asher, §26 in his notes to bSuk chapter 3.
[49] It is interesting that Mowinckel identified Ps 96 as one of the enthronement Psalms. He interpreted the psalm as a description of YHWH's advent, the restoration of right order, and the concomitant rejuvenation of nature. Mowinckel would have been pleased with the compiler of this Pisqa. On this midrash see too Stern, *Reference*, 119-20.
[50] Above, p. 284
[51] *Tan 'Emor* §22 (465); *TanB* 3:101; *MG* 3:658. A related but independent tradition appears in MG 3:657, ll. 20-25.

Sukkot in the Amoraic Midrashim 293

> *On the first day (Lev 23:40).* [Sukkot falls] on the fifteenth day [of the month], yet you say on the first day! R. Mani of Sheav and R. Yehoshua of Sikhnin in the name of R. Levi: [A parable: it is like] a province that owed arrears to the king, and the king went to collect them. [When he came within] ten miles the notables of the province went forth and praised him, so he remitted one third of their taxes. Within five miles the councilors went forth and praised him, so he remitted one third of the taxes. When he entered the city all its inhabitants went forth and praised him. The king said, let bygones be bygones. From now on we begin the account [anew].
>
> So too Israel comes on RH and repents and the Holy One forgives one third of their sins.[52] During the ten days of repentance the pious ones fast and the Holy One forgives most of their sins. When he comes on YK all Israel fasts and the Holy One forgives all their sins...[53] Between YK and Sukkot all Israel are busy with the commandments: this one is busy with his sukka, and that one is busy with his lulav. On the first day of the Festival they take their lulavs and etrogs in their hands and praise God, and God says, "I already forgave you for the past, from now on reckon your sins." Therefore it says, *[And you shall take] on the first day (Lev 23:40).* What is *the first day?* The first day of the Festival is the first day of the reckoning of sins.

The textual irritant for the homily is the problematic phrase of Lev 23:40, "you shall take on the first *day*," since Sukkot falls on the fifteenth day of the month.[54] The homily explains the phrase as the first day of a new account of sins. This interpretation already connects Sukkot to YK through the themes of sin and forgiveness. But the power of the connection appears most clearly in the parable and its solution.

The parable itself draws on a noted institution (and favorite literary motif) of the Greco-Roman culture of late antiquity: the imperial *adventus*, the emperor's approach and entrance into a city escorted by his royal retinue.[55] The *adventus* was a highly ceremonial event observed with elaborate pomp and due festivity. Men, women and children,

---

[52] Some versions have "the leaders of the generation fast on the eve of RH" in place of "Israel comes on RH and repents." See the variants in Mandelbaum, 412, l. 10-11 and Buber, *PRK*, 183a, n. 91. On the versions and their relationship to popular customs, see D. Sperber, *Minhagei yisra'el* (2 vols; Jerusalem: Rav Kook, 1989-91), 2:217-18 and n. 45.

[53] The tradition of R. Aha appears here in certain manuscripts. See p. 295 and n. 60.

[54] See Chapter 5, I n. 6.

[55] Actually any important dignitary could receive an *adventus*. On the *adventus* see F. Millar, *The Emperor in the Roman World* (London, 1977), 31-40 (and further bibliography 31 n. 21.); S. MacCormack, continuity and Change in Late Antiquity: The Ceremony of the Adventus," *Historia* 21 (1972), 721-52; T.E.V. Pearce, "Notes on Cicero, In Pisonem," *Classical Quarterly* 64 (1970), 313-16; Cohen, *Alexander*, 45-49.

sometimes animals as well, and especially the leading citizens or chief priests, greeted the emperor far beyond the city limits. They often wore special robes or other ceremonial garb, bedecked their heads with crowns and wreaths, danced and sang hymns. Sacrifices were slaughtered, libations poured, incense offered and altars lit. The processional way and streets of the city were adorned with banners, decorations, wreaths and garlands. These occasions were extremely important to the city because they were opportunities to demonstrate political allegiance and homage to the emperor. For his part, the emperor was usually willing, perhaps even expected, to hear the petitions of the citizens, dispense largess, bestow privileges or grant favors, either to the city as a whole or to an enterprising individual who provided for the special needs of the emperor.[56] The protocol of the *adventus* was not unknown to the rabbis: yBer 3:1, 6a permits a Jew of priestly decent *(kohen)* to become impure to "see the king," i.e. participate in an *adventus*, and mentions that R. Hiyya b. Abba passed through the graveyard of Tyre to see Diocletian.[57]

In the parable the king approaches with the specific purpose of collecting the taxes owed him. The province's fealty has been called into question by their failure to send taxes, so the king advances to reassert his authority, presumably prepared to use force if necessary. In view of this possibility, delegations of townsmen greet the king far before his arrival and shower him with praise. This type of an *adventus* – a type of surrender – was not uncommon. When Alexander marched upon Babylon ready to attack, the citizens went forth to greet him, showed appropriate homage and opened the gates to their city.[58] In the parable the king reciprocates for the show of homage by forgiving a portion of the taxes owed. When the entire city applauds the king at his entrance he is both persuaded that the failure to pay taxes in the past was not a willful rejection of his authority and simultaneously moved by the unanimous praise to remit the very taxes that had served as the reason for his approach. The final scene leaves the king and his subjects together within the city, a beautiful illustration of the now restored relationship between the two.

The spatial-political dimensions through which the action unfolds in the parable become temporal-theological in the *nimshal*. The advent of the king is the "advent" of God on RH and YK, and he comes not to

---

[56] Suetonius, *Tiberius* 40, reports that Tiberius issued an edict that forbade petitions during his entrance to Capri. Herod was rewarded amply for the services he showed Octavian in 30 BCE. See *BJ* 1:394-95; *AJ* 15:194-201.
[57] Josephus's famous account of Alexander the Great's entrance to Jerusalem portrays a classic *adventus*. See Cohen, *Alexander*. The celebration for Judith was a triumph, a type of *adventus*; Jdt 15:12-13.
[58] Arrian, *Anabasis*, 3.16.3-5. Cited in Cohen, *Alexander*, 47.

collect taxes but to requite sins of the past year. Israel's failure to fulfill the commandments has called into question their fidelity to God, so he approaches to reassert his authority and "collect" what is due. By repenting Israel demonstrates their enduring obedience and loyalty to the covenant. At each period of atonement, on RH, the ten days of repentance and YK, God forgives one third of their sins. Note that the *nimshal* does not cohere precisely with each point of the parable, not an uncommon phenomenon, although some variants attempt to forge a better fit.[59] In any case, Sukkot marks the full reconciliation between Israel and God. By occupying themselves with the commandments of the festival Israel again demonstrates obedience, and by taking the lulav and etrog, they fully dramatize their faith. The lulav functions as a means of atonement, but because God has forgiven all sin on YK, there remain, strictly speaking, no sins left to forgive on Sukkot. Nevertheless, it is only when Israel takes the lulav and etrog that God fully "lets bygones be bygones" and begins a new reckoning.

This point is underscored in a tradition of R. Aha which appears near the end of the homily.[60] R. Aha suggests God puts forgiveness "in trust" in order that Israel remain uncertain as to her fate. God actually forgives on RH and YK, but intentionally delays his response in order to fill Israel with awe and motivate them assiduously to attend to their sukkot and lulavs. On Sukkot Israel demonstrates that their repentance on RH and YK was sincere, that they fully intend to obey the dictates of their king, so God begins the new reckoning.

In this homily Sukkot represents the final stage of a drama that began on RH. Sukkot signals the true culmination of the "Days of Awe," when consummate forgiveness restores an harmonious relationship between God and Israel. Just as the parable concludes with an image of the king among his loyal subjects inside the town, so God is felt to reside again within his community. The periods of repentance have narrowed the psychological distance such that Israel and God reunite. Sukkot, not the previous festivals, rings out the old and in the new, marking the new beginning. In contrast to the view of *PRK 27:4*, where Sukkot celebrates

---

[59]Two delegations approach the king in the parable but there are three occasions for atonement before Sukkot. The leading citizens precede the whole town in the parable but all Israel atones on RH. Thus some variants begin the *nimshal* with the "leaders of the generation" on the eve of RH. And see n. 52.

[60]The tradition of R. Aha appears in different positions in the manuscripts of both *PRK* and *VR* (see Mandelbaum's apparatus, p. 413 ll. 1-3 and 6-9; Margoliot's apparatus and note to line 7, pp. 705-706), indicating that the tradition was a marginal gloss later incorporated into the text. In some manuscripts where the tradition appears within the homily, it can be read as relating to the time between RH and YK, not between YK and Sukkot. See Buber, *PRK*, 183b n. 92.

the prior ascension of God on RH and YK, here greater overlap between the festivals appears. The period of judgment extends through to Sukkot, and atonement remains a concern of the community. However, when the lulav is taken up on the first day the mood does begin to shift toward rejoicing.

In the *nimshal* the lulav serves both as a means of atonement and praise, or praise intended as atonement, and corresponds to the praise bestowed by the townsmen in the parable. Here the homilist appears to have drawn on the common use of flora at the *adventus*. In most accounts the citizens greet the emperor bedecked with wreaths or crowns (*stephanoi*), and place wreaths on the town buildings and temples as well. Josephus mentions wreaths in his (fictional?) description of Alexander's adventus,[61] and the participants wore wreaths at Judith's triumph, while she and her women carried branches in their hands.[62] These crowns were usually made from laurel, but palm leaves were used as well.[63] In fact Jubilees prescribes that crowns be worn in conjunction with the commandment to take the species.[64] At the triumph, an institution closely related to the *adventus*,[65] the assembled crowds threw flowers before the triumphator's carriage, while he held a palm branch in his right hand to symbolize victory.[66] In 1 Macc 13:51 and John 12:13 the citizens of Jerusalem carry palms in their celebrations.[67] It seems likely that the homilist expected his audience to picture the citizens' praise of the king in the parable to include wreaths, flora and perhaps palms. Hearing the parable, they understood the lulav of the *nimshal* in this context. That the lulav was held and shaken during the Hallel assures that the lulav was associated with praise and acclamation. The homily suggests that the use of fronds for praise in Greco-Roman culture added a second dimension to the symbolism of the lulav in the amoraic period.

This overlap of praise and atonement associated with the lulav appears in two manuscript traditions of a homily attributed to R. Mani in *VR* 30:14.

---

[61] See Cohen, *Alexander*, 47 and n. 16. It is unclear whether the buildings alone were wreathed, or the people too.
[62] Jdt 15:12: *thyrsous* – a term also used for the Dionysian wand. See Chapter 2, VIII and X.
[63] See Pausanius, *Periegara*, VII 48.2 and the references above, n. 32; Ehlers, *Triumphus*, 505-507.
[64] Jub 16:30; see Chapter 2, III.
[65] The triumph was celebrated at the emperor's (or in earlier times, general's) home town upon his return from a military victory.
[66] Ovid, *Tristia* IV ii, 50. Later a laurel branch was held; Pliny, *Nat. Hist.* xv, 136-7.
[67] See n. 34.

> R. Mani opened: *All my limbs shall say, 'Lord, who is like you?' (Ps 35:10).* This verse refers exclusively to the lulav. The spine of the lulav resembles the spine of a man. The myrtle resembles the eye. The willow resembles the mouth. The etrog resembles the heart. David said: None of the other limbs are greater than these. And since these are as important as the whole body, it is fair to say, *All my limbs shall say.*[68]

The components of the lulav correspond to the parts of the human body. In light of the opening-verse the lulav symbolizes the movements of the whole body in ecstatic praise of God. This version offers no explicit allusion to atonement. However the Paris and Oxford B manuscripts add this conclusion:[69]

> When one sins with these four limbs, if he repents the Holy One forgives him by means of these four species.

The final comment completely changes the function of the lulav. The four components no longer express consummate praise but atone for sins committed with the four main parts of the body. This understanding of the lulav as a means for atonement stems in part from the conception of Sukkot as the culmination of RH and YK. However, the ritual use of the lulav and the accompanying liturgy were partly responsible. The lulav is shaken during the Hallel when Ps 118:25 is recited: "O Lord deliver us, O Lord, deliver us," and carried while the *hosha'anot* are recited to the refrain of "deliver us."[70] The petition may be for eschatological salvation; we have seen these motifs associated with the lulav. But "salvation" may also be understood in a more immediate sense. The lulav brings "salvation" by delivering its bearer from any punishment incurred through sin. Moreover, we noted the notion of divine judgment factors in the association between rain and sukkot. These midrashim seem to have transferred the communal judgment to the individual level. To assure a favorable outcome of the judgment, the lulav serves as a symbol of atonement for sin. The focus of the ritual becomes the

---

[68] *VR* 30:14 (711-12). The Carmoly manuscript of *PRK* 27:9 contains the same tradition; see p. 416, apparatus to line 10. Cf. MG 3:661. I. Abrahams, *Festival Studies* (London, 1906), 115 comments: "The citron atones for heart-sins, the palm for stiff-backed pride, the willows for unholy speech, the myrtle for the lusts of the eye. The comparison to the eye is particularly apt. Not only does the elongated oval leaf of some species resemble the eye, but when held up to the light, it looks not unlike the iris. This effect is produced by the little oil-dots in the leaf."

[69] In these manuscripts this passage appears slightly earlier in the compilation, after 30:12. See p. 710 and the apparatus to line 7. Note too that the order of the four species is different, and the willow represents the lips, not the mouth.

[70] Assuming this custom dates back to amoraic times. Heinemann, *Prayer*, 139-42 claims the *hosha'anot* date back even to temple times. But whether they were continued in the tannaitic and amoraic periods is unclear. See Chapter 5, I and V.

individual and his need for the annual forgiveness of his sins, not the nation or the world and its annual need for rain.

Themes of atonement appear in conjunction with the famous midrash which connects the seventy bulls sacrificed during the course of Sukkot with the seventy nations, and the single bull offered on SA with Israel.[71]

> [A] R. Alexandrai said: It is like a king who held a celebration. For the seven days of the feast the king's son was busy with the guests. After the seven days of feasting the king said to his son, 'My son. I know that for the seven days of the feast you were busy with the guests. Now you and I will rejoice together, and I will not trouble you much, just one chicken and one *litra* of meat.' Thus for the seven days of feasting Israel is busy with the sacrifices of the nations.
>
> [B] As R. Pinhas said: All those seventy bulls that Israel used to sacrifice on Sukkot correspond *(keneged)* to the seventy nations, since the world will never be empty of them. What is the reason? *They answer my love with accusation, and I must stand judgment (Ps 109:4).*[72] We are confidant of the judgment.
>
> [C] When the seven days of the festival are over, the Holy One says to Israel, 'My sons. I know that for the seven days of the festival you were busy with the sacrifices of the nations. Now I and you will rejoice together, and I will not trouble you except with one bull and one ram.'"[73]

Sections [A] and [C] form one unit, which [B] interrupts, indicating that is has been interpolated from elsewhere.[74] For R. Alexandrai, the sacrifices serve to include the nations in the Sukkot festivities. The nations participate, at least vicariously, in the cultic joy and temple celebrations throughout the festival. They are honored guests who participate and contribute to the king's celebration. In Zech 14 the nations make the pilgrimage to Jerusalem and bow before God, and here sacrifices are offered on their behalf. Thus the sacrifices are "of the nations" *(shel 'umot ha'olam)*, i.e., they are the responsibility (and privilege) of the nations. The parallels state that Israel brings the

---

[71] Num 29:12-34 details the sacrifices.
[72] The meaning of the verse is unclear. This seems to be the understanding of the midrash.
[73] PRK 28:9 (433).
[74] For another example of a similar type of interpolation, see D. Boyarin, "Hamidrash veham'ase ‒ 'al haheqer hahistori shel sifrut hazal," *Saul Lieberman Memorial Volume*, ed. S. Friedman (New York and Jerusalem: Jewish Theological Seminary, 1993), 106-110.

sacrifices "on behalf" of the nations.[75] Israel is a "nation of priests" enabling the community of nations to join together and worship God.

R. Pinhas [B], on the other hand, understands the nature of the sacrifices differently. His point is developed more clearly in the parallel, *Tanḥuma, Pinḥas,* §17 (602): "therefore they ought to love us. Not only do they not love us, but they hate us, as it says, *They answer my love with accusation (Ps 109:4)."* Although Israel makes the loving gesture of bringing sacrifices for other nations, those nations nevertheless despise Israel. The question "what is the reason" should be understood: "what is the reason Israel offers sacrifices for the nations, since the nations are so ungrateful, and even accuse Israel?" The redactor evidently was so astonished at the suggestion that Israel offers sacrifices for the nations that he interrupted R. Alexandrai's parable with an explanation. Israel acts virtuously despite the ingratitude of the nations, and confidently awaits her vindication in court. In this tradition the sacrifices atone for the nations, as stated explicitly in the parallel in *ShR* 4:1:

> Just as a dove atones for sins, so Israel atones for the nations. Since all those seventy bulls that they sacrifice on the Festival correspond to the seventy nations, for the world will never be empty of them.

Both R. Pinhas and *ShR* 4:1 recognize that the "world will never be empty" of the nations. They therefore require a means to expiate sin, and rely on the sacrifices Israel brings for them on Sukkot.[76]

The atoning function of the sacrifices is also found in bSuk 55b, which juxtaposes a variation of the parable[77] with a lemma of R. Yohanan: "Alas for the nations of the world who had a loss and know not what they lost. While the temple stood the altar atoned for them. Now what will atone for them?" The juxtaposition suggests that the sacrifices atoned for the seventy nations, and that the destruction of the temple precludes this means of atonement. Relating atonement to the

---

[75]*'al 'umot ha'olam* or *'al shivim 'umot; BaR* 21:24; *Tan Pinhas* §17 (602); *TanB* 4:156; *MTeh* 109:4 (465).
[76]The clause can be translated "in order that the world never be empty of them." That is, Israel offers the sacrifices for the nations in order that their sins be forgiven and they not be destroyed like the generation of the flood.
[77]R. Elazar said, "To what do these seventy bulls correspond? To the seventy nations. To what does the single bull correspond? To the special nation. A parable to a king who said to his servants, 'Prepare a great feast for me.' On the last day he said to his friend. 'Make me a small feast so that I may benefit from you.'"

rain-producing aspect of Sukkot, Rashi explains that the seventy bulls atone for the nations in order that rain will fall throughout the world.[78]

It appears that the correspondence between the seventy sacrifices and seventy nations was a widespread tradition, but the meaning of this correspondence was interpreted in different ways. R. Alexandrai construed the correspondence in light of the association of Sukkot with rejoicing such that the nations participate in the joy of the festival. They have a share in the sacrifices, which the rabbis considered the essence of festal joy *(simḥa).*[79] This complements the understanding of Sukkot as the time when all nature and all living creatures (even gentiles!) rejoice at the advent of God. On the other hand, R. Pinhas, *ShR* and the BT relate the correspondence to themes of atonement associated with Sukkot. Not only do the lulav and sukka atone for any remaining sins of Israel, but the sacrifices atone (would have atoned!) for the rest of humanity.

Pressing Sukkot into the penumbra of YK paves the way for an alternative understanding of the festival. What happens if God judges Israel guilty on YK? In that case it would be inappropriate to rejoice on Sukkot in the manner endorsed by the previous midrashim. The Alternative Parsha advances a conception of the relationship between Sukkot, RH and YK that allows for this eventuality:

> R. Elazar bar Maryom said: Why do we make a sukka after YK? To tell you this: You find that on RH God judges all human beings, and on YK he seals the sentence. It may be that the sentence of Israel will be exile. Accordingly they make a sukka and exile themselves from their homes to the sukka, and God counts it as if they were exiled to Babylon, as it says, *Writhe and scream, Fair Zion, like a woman in travail. For now you must leave the city and dwell in the country – And you will reach Babylon. There you shall be saved, there the Lord will redeem you from the hands of your foes* (Micah 4:10).[80]

As in *PRK* 27:4, Sukkot is understood as a response to the drama of RH and YK. In place of the celebration of the kingship of God and its expected blessings, R. Elazar bar Maryom considers the darker side of God sitting in judgment. In contrast to *PRK* 27:7, this tradition assumes that all sins may not be forgiven on YK. If God judges Israel unfavorably then a severe punishment awaits them. Sukkot is not an opportunity to begin a new reckoning, but an opportunity to pre-empt the penalty incurred on YK. Dwelling in the sukka dramatizes the potential punishment of exile and is considered equivalent to the actual experience

---

[78] bSuk 55b, s.v. *shivʿim*. This seems to be the understanding reflected in *MTeh* 109:4 (465): "On Sukkot we offer up seventy bulls for the seventy nations, and we pray that rain will come down for them."
[79] bPes 109a.
[80] *PRK*, 457-58.

of that punishment. The belief that a symbolic penalty may prevent actual punishment is not an uncommon religious idea and appears in the Jewish mystical tradition, but it is rare in classical rabbinic sources, and may reflect a diaspora setting.[81]

III. Protection and the Clouds of Glory

In tannaitic midrashim the sukka symbolizes the clouds of glory that surrounded Israel during their desert wanderings. We found that the clouds were associated with divine protection and intimacy, and that similar associations characterized shade. Amoraic parallels to the tannaitic midrashim demonstrate that this conception continued in amoraic times.[82] We also noted an amoraic extension of this idea in the metamorphosis of the clouds into the eschatological sukkot which protected Israel from the fires of judgment day.[83] In later midrashim (which certainly contain amoraic traditions) the sukka as a symbol of divine protection is expressed even more clearly. Thus the Alternative Parsha promises general divine protection to those who observe the commandment:

> Whoever observes the commandment of sukka in this world [God] protects *(meisikh)* them from evildoers *(meziqin)* so that they not harm him, as it says, *He covers (yasekh) you with his pinions [and you will find refuge under his wings] (Ps 91:4)*.[84]

---

[81]Cf. bSanh 37b: "R. Yehuda the son of R. Hiyya said, 'Exile atones for half of one's sins'... R. Yohanan said, 'Exile atones for everything.'" In bBer 56a this principle motivates Bar Hedya to exile himself voluntarily in order to atone before the curse uttered by Rava could take effect on him. See too bTa 16a: Resh Laqish explains that the congregation prays in the street on public fast days such that "our exile (from the *beit midrash)* will atone for us."
[82]See e.g. BR 48:10 (487-88), ShR 1:7 and the parallels listed in the notes to Chapter 6. Note too the formulation of the Alternative Parsha, PRK 457, ll. 15-18: "Why does Israel make a sukka? For the miracles that God did for them when they came forth from Egypt. The clouds of glory surrounded them and covered *(mesukekhot)* them, as it says, *because I caused Israel to dwell in Sukkot (Lev 23:43)*, and the targum states, 'because I caused Israel to dwell in sukkot of clouds.'" The passage explains the "reason for the commandment" of the sukka with the explicit statement that the sukka commemorates the clouds of glory in which the Israelites dwelled. The proof that the sukkot of Lev 23:43 were divine clouds derives from the targum. See Chapter 6, I text at n. 3.
[83]See p. 279.
[84]PRK, 454 ll. 22-23. See too *Tan 'Emor* §22 (466): "The Holy One said to Israel: In this world I told you to make sukkot to pay me for the good I did for you, as it says, *You shall live in sukkot seven days; all citizens in Israel shall live in sukkot, in order that future generations may know that I made the Israelite people live in sukkot (Lev 23:42-43)*. And I count it as if you do good for me. But in the World to Come I will appear in my dominion and protect you like a sukka, as it says, *Which shall*

In this case the reward for dwelling in the sukka is not deferred to the World to Come. Those who dwell in the *skhakh* of the sukka will be protected from baleful forces in the here and now. Both the *skhakh* of the sukka and the wings of God it symbolizes provide cover, hence protection. *Shmot Rabba* extends this idea by giving the sukka a concrete function rather than a mere basis for reward.

> You [Israel] are a vineyard, as it says, *For the vineyard of the Lord of Hosts is the House of Israel (Isa 5:7)*. Make a sukka for the guard so that He may guard you.[85]

The midrash picks up on the original function of the sukka as a protective shelter for guards or workers in the fields. Isaiah compares Israel to a vineyard and God to the owner or guard. In the midrashic extension of this image the festival sukka serves as the abode of God where he watches over his people. Just as the guard dwells in the sukka while he watches the vineyard, so God dwells in the festival sukka and protects his people. Ironically, while the agricultural sukka serves to protect the guard from sun and rain, God obviously needs no protection from the sukka. The festival sukka rather provides a symbolic space for God to dwell among his people. This interpretation is a variation of the conception of the sukka as a symbol of the clouds of glory, which in turn symbolize the presence of God, and of the sukka as symbol of the protective eschatological sukkot. Here the symbolism is reified: God actually resides in the festival sukka.

IV. Unity

Rabbinic sources debate whether the three plant species of the lulav are to be bound together with a band *('aguda)*.[86] Whether bound or not, the commandment is only fulfilled when the four are taken simultaneously, not if each is lifted or shaken sequentially.[87] The baraita cited above expressed this requirement poetically by categorizing the species in terms of their ability to produce fruit and asserting that both categories "required" each other.[88] Midrashim develop these ideas in

---

serve as a sukka for shade from heat (Isa 4:6)." The midrash uses the sukka as the outstanding symbol of protection. Divine protection in eschatological time will be as solid as the sense of protection experienced in the sukka.
[85]*SR* 34:3.
[86]In tSuk 2:10 R. Yehuda rules that a lulav must have a band; the sages that a lulav is fit whether it has a band or not. In bSuk 33a, a second baraita reads that it is proper *(miṣva)* to have a band, but a lulav is fit without, and this source is assigned to the sages.
[87]mMen 3:6.
[88]bMen 27a; see p. 292.

greater depth, thereby providing an interesting example of how halakhic considerations bring symbolic meanings in their wake. The species become a symbol of unity, an image of disparate elements bound together in a unified whole. The symbolism is achieved by coordinating the species with various types of Jews such that the taking of the four together symbolizes the unity of the Jewish people.

[A] *The fruit of goodly trees (Lev 23:40).* These are Israel. Just as an etrog has fragrance and food so Israel has men who are learned in Torah and perform good deeds.
[B] *Palm branches.* These are Israel. Just as the date tree has food but no fragrance, so Israel has men who are learned in Torah but do not perform good deeds.
[C] *Branches of leafy trees.* These are Israel. Just as the myrtle has fragrance but no taste, so Israel has men who performed good deeds but are not learned in Torah.
[D] *And willows of the brook.* These are Israel. Just as the willow has neither fragrance nor taste, so Israel has men who are neither learned in Torah nor performed good deeds.
[E] The Holy One says: It is unthinkable that I destroy them. Rather let them all form one band and atone for each other.
[F] And if you do this, at that moment I am exalted. Thus it is written, *Who built his chambers in heaven.* When is He exalted? When they form one band, as it is said, *And founded his band ('agudato) on earth (Amos 9:6).*[89]
[G] Therefore Moses admonishes Israel and says to them, *And you shall take..." (Lev 23:40).*[90]

The midrash defines each species with respect to two qualities, 1) giving off fragrance and 2) producing food ('okhel) or having taste (ta'am).[91] These two qualities are then identified with the virtues of Torah and good deeds. Since each of the four species possesses a different combination of the two qualities, each symbolizes a different type of Jew. The assembly of the four species expresses the unity of the four different types of Jews. The midrash concludes with the theme of atonement that we noted was often connected to the lulav. Because God does not wish

---

[89]This section appears in MS Oxford of *PRK* and in most MSS of the parallel at *VR* 30:12 (710). Cf. the exegesis of this verse in *Sifre Deut.* §346 (403) and §96 (158), *Midrash Tannaim*, 72.
[90]*PRK* 27:9 (416). Parallels: *VR* 30:12 (709-10); *MG* 3:661.
[91]See the variants, and see *VR* 30:12 (709) and the apparatus. In both *PRK* and *VR* some versions consistently play off "taste" with "fragrance," and do not mention "food." In *MG* 3:660 the species correspond to "scholars" and "householders." Householders depend on scholars to petition God to have mercy on them, while scholars depend on householders to "behave decently" toward them (לעשות נחת רוח.) *MG* cites a second tradition together with this midrash: "let the grapes pray for the leaves, for but for the leaves, the grapes could not exist."

to destroy those who lack religious merit he instructs all Israel to come together so that those with merit compensate for those without. Just as one cannot fulfill his obligation unless he brings all four species together, so Israel cannot survive unless they band together as a unified people. Section [F], which does not appear in all manuscripts, introduces the somewhat mystical notion that the effect of the lulav adds power to God in his heavenly realm.

The lulav as a symbol of the unity of the Jewish people appears to have developed from halakhic considerations of the tannaim and amoraim. The debate whether the species should be bound together with a band and the law that one requires all four species in order to fulfill the commandment probably inspired this symbolism. Now R. Yehuda reports that the "Men of Jerusalem" bound their lulavs together with "golden bands,"[92] which suggests that placing a band on the lulav was a popular custom; it certainly makes carrying the lulav more convenient. So we cannot discount the possibility that the symbolism was inspired by common practice, not by halakhic considerations. (Of course the halakhic debate itself may have evolved from the popular practice.) It is interesting to consider whether this symbolism builds on an ancient dimension of the symbolism of the lulav. The anthropologist Harvey Goldberg has suggested that the cluster of flora symbolizes the unity of the land.[93] The four types described in Lev 23:40 – fruit, palms, leafy boughs and willows – represent four main categories of Palestinian foliage. Carried together in celebration they express the unity of the different regions of the land under the dominion of God. The midrashim propose a national rather than agricultural understanding of the unity, but draw on the same basic symbolism.[94]

Here we should mention a midrash found in bSuk 32b which also suggests that the lulav symbolizes the Jewish people: "Just as the palm has only one heart, so Israel has only one heart for their father in heaven." This notion derives not from the assembly of the four species in

---

[92] tSuk 2:10.
[93] Private communication.
[94] The midrash also illustrates rabbinic reinterpretation of fertility symbols. In Chapter 1, IV we noted that some scholars understand the lulav as a rain charm, the four species being particularly dependent on rain. In rabbinic tradition God determines rain based on the merits of Israel, not on rain charms or fertility rites. The midrash accordingly interprets the species to represent Jews of different degrees of merit, the basis of the divine judgment in rabbinic tradition. Hopefully God will not withhold rain from any segment of the people (or on account of any segment of the people), just as the four diverse species expressed the hope that no portion of the vegetation would lack water. Cf. *Yefe to'ar* to *VR* 30:12. Yet another expression of unity develops in Qabbalistic tradition where the lulav symbolizes the unity of certain sefirot.

one band, but from the nature of the palm tree. The one "heart" of the palm symbolizes the "heart" of Israel, the complete fidelity of Israel to their God.[95] Thus the lulav expresses both the unity of the Jewish people and their faithfulness to God.

V. The Lulav as Sign

The previous symbolisms of the lulav have been relatively straightforward. Connections between the lulav and that which it symbolizes or expresses were readily understandable. The lulav as a victory symbol stems from the widespread practice of awarding palms to victorious athletes. The lulav as a means of atonement devolves from the liturgy recited during the ritual and from the relationship between the festival as a whole to RH and YK. The lulav as a symbol of unity, however, involves a more complicated symbolism. On the one hand, the facts that the species must be held simultaneously and that the palm, myrtle and willow were generally bound together naturally symbolize unity. On the other hand, the identification with different types of Jews – that the unity is that of the Jewish people – is less "natural." It requires that the species be categorized in terms of producing fruit and fragrance (a "natural" quality), and then entails a second move, that these qualities be understood in terms of the Torah and good deeds. We see the beginning of a trend in which the lulav functions less as "symbol" and more as "sign." As a symbol the connection between the lulav (the symbol) and its representation (atonement, victory, Israel) relates to an inherent quality of the lulav (it is green or fragrant) or to a recognized liturgical or cultural function (use in victory parades.) As a sign the connection between the lulav (the signifier) and its sign (the signified) is arbitrary. The lulav represents "x" because the homilist, or some authority, has decreed that the lulav denotes "x."[96] This phenomenon emerges in *PRK* 27:9 (414-15).[97]

> Rabbi Akiba says:
> [A1] *Fruit of goodly (hadar) trees (Lev 23:40).* This is the Holy One blessed be He, since it says about Him, *You are clothed in glory and majesty (hadar) (Ps 104:1).*
> [A2] *Palm branches.* This is the Holy One blessed be He, since it says about Him, *The righteous bloom like a palm (Ps 92:13).*

---

[95]Cf. *MTeh* 92:11 (409).
[96]The lulav as a victory symbol and other such symbolisms based on cultural functions are, strictly speaking, arbitrary. That is, convention alone determines that the lulav represents victory. My point is that the following cases contain no recognized cultural signification.
[97]*VR* 30:9 (707); *MG* 3:660-62; *Yalqut* §651.

[A3] *Branches of leafy trees.* This is the Holy One blessed be He, *And He stood among the myrtles (Zech 1:8).*

[A4] *Willows ('arvei) of the brook.* This is the Holy One blessed be He, since it says about Him, *Extol Him who rides the clouds ('aravot) (Ps 68:5).*

[B1] *Fruit of goodly (hadar) trees.* This is Abraham our forefather whom God adorned *(hidro)* with beautiful gray hair, as it says, *Abraham was old (Gen 24:1).*

[B2] *Palm branches (kapot).* This is Isaac our forefather who was tied *(kafut)* and bound on the altar.

[B3] *Branches of leafy trees.* This is Jacob our forefather. Just as a myrtle is thick with leaves, so Jacob was "thick" with children.

[B4] *Willows of the brook.* This is Joseph. Just as this willow is dried out and withered compared with the three species,[98] so Joseph died before his brothers.

Similarly the midrash connects the four species to the four matriarchs and to four components of the court: the Sanhedrin, the rabbis *(talmidei ḥakhamim),* the three rows in which the rabbis sat, and the two scribes.[99] The first section, attributed to R. Akiba, is one of two aggadic traditions concerning the lulav attributed to a tanna.[100] No tannaitic midrashic collection contains the midrash, so the attribution is uncertain.[101] Yet the mystical character of the midrash is consistent with mystical tendencies in the thought of R. Akiba and his disciples.[102] The subsequent midrashim about the patriarchs and matriarchs, however, are probably later imitations modeled on the Akiban tradition.

R. Akiba proposes the mystical notion that each of the four species symbolizes God.[103] Exactly what he means by this interpretation is

---

[98] That is, the willow is the first to wither. Cf. *MG* 3:661.

[99] Three myrtle branches correspond to three rows; two willows correspond to the two scribes.

[100] The other is R. Eliezer's explanation that the lulav entreats God for rain, bTa 2b.

[101] False attributions do not seem to be characteristic of *PRK*. In the entire *PRK* (excluding the additional fragments included in Mandelbaum, 460-72) only three other traditions are attributed to Akiba (Mandelbaum, pp. 146, 173, 241.) Of course more research is required on this point.

[102] See Joseph Dan, *Hamistiqa ha'ivrit haqeduma* (Tel Aviv, 1989), 51-52; S. Lieberman, "Mishnat shir hashirim," in G. Scholem, *Jewish Gnosticism, Merkabah Mysticism and Talmudic Tradition* (New York: Jewish Theological Seminary, 1960), 213-36; Scholem, ibid., 38-42.

[103] I am assuming that the midrash is not merely exegetical, i.e., that the interpretation pertains to the lulav actually held in the hand, and not exclusively to the text of scripture. This is *not* an example of that trend in later Qabbala which sought to show how each verse mystically encodes the name of the Godhead. However, attention must be called to the tendency of *PRK* (and other midrashim) to cite a scriptural phrase followed by "this is the Holy One Blessed

unclear. Does he suggest that by holding the lulav one adheres to God in a mystical union? Or, in the spirit of later Qabbala, that bringing the species together unifies different aspects of the Godhead? Or that holding the lulav either "supports" or arouses the Divinity?[104] We have seen an echo of this idea in the midrash cited above which suggests that God is "exalted" when the species are taken together.[105] We also noted that in temple times, during the circumambulations of the altar with willows, the worshippers recited Ps 118:25, "O Lord deliver us," or, according to R. Akiba's student R. Yehuda, "אני והו, deliver us."[106] The Palestinian amoraim explained that God participates in the suffering of Israel.[107] The liturgy recited upon concluding the ritual may also have mystical overtones.[108] Such traditions seem to point to a mystical experience of communion with God connected with the willow processions. After the destruction of the temple the liturgy and experience may have been transferred to the lulav and processions in the synagogue. R. Akiba's interpretation of the species as symbolizing God probably emerges from this background.

The hermeneutics of R. Akiba's tradition and of the subsequent interpretations reflect an important development. The scriptural proofs are highly literary, relying on wordplays, literary juxtapositions and other rabbinic exegeses. For example, the willow relates to God because in one biblical image God rides upon clouds, and the same term is used for "cloud" and "willow" ('arava). In this extended chain the cloud symbolizes God by metonymy, while willow is a homonym for cloud.[109]

---

be He" with a prooftext. See *PRK* 2:2, 2:6, 4:4, 4:10 (thrice), 5:17, 6:2, 9:11. In these cases the midrash is purely exegetical; the scriptural phrases do not relate to a ritual object practiced in rabbinic times such as the lulav. Since R. Akiba interprets the reference to the lulav, a contemporary ritual, I assume he expresses its symbolism.

[104]M. Idel, *Kabbalah: New Perspectives* (New Haven: Yale University Press, 1988), 156-172 discusses this type of theurgy in rabbinic literature. "Supporting the Holy One" was one explanation for the ritual in classical Qabbala. See *Zohar* 3:104a, 3:31b and I. Tishby, *The Wisdom of the Zohar*, trans. D. Goldstein (New York: Oxford University Press, 1987-89), 3:1249-50.

[105]Above, p. 303. The tradition (section [F]) appears in MS Oxford of *PRK* and in the parallel in *VR* 30:12.

[106]mSuk 4:5. See Chapter 3, I text to n. 30.

[107]y4 3, 54c. So R. Hananel, bSuk 45b.

[108]bSuk 45b.

[109]The palm symbolism appears to be more straightforward: God is elsewhere compared to a palm, hence the palm symbolizes God. But the prooftext from Ps 92:13 does not refer to God in context. Unless the homilist draws on a well-known interpretation of Ps 92:13, the "proof" is no better than the simple assertion that the palm should stand for God. That God gave Abraham gray hair presupposes *BR* 65:9 (717) where God makes Abraham look old.

Likewise, the relationship between the species and the patriarch to whom it refers depends entirely on the descriptive language adopted by the homilist. The palm refers to Isaac only because the homilist used the term *kafut* (tied) to describe an event in his life, and this word resembles the term *kapot* of Lev 23:40. Substitute a synonym for "tied" in the description – "Isaac was lashed down *(qashur)* on the altar" – and the connection collapses. The willow relates to Jacob only insofar as the language of "thickness" serves metaphorically for having many children. Each case has a unique, complicated chain of reference. Thus the four species refer to God and the patriarchs neither by means of any quality of the species, nor by any accepted cultural symbolism.

At first one is inclined to think that the connection depends on the fact that there are *four* species, and that this number evokes other sets of four. This is true of the matriarchs, but there is one God, three patriarchs, and no fixed number of components of the Sanhedrin or the authority it represents. So while the number of species determines the number of correspondences in each set, that number is technically irrelevant to the content of the set. Had there been five species, the homilist might have added Moses or included the "lesser Sanhedrin" (the court of twenty-three) as well. The species function more as *signs* than *symbols*. That is, the assignment between signifier (the individual species) and signified (God, the patriarch, the matriarch) is arbitrary. The homilist – or scripture as interpreted by the homilist – simply establishes an equation: the myrtle is a sign for Jacob.

How to assess this type of symbolism or signification is a complicated question. The complex hermeneutical connections between the species and the referents suggest literary creativity rather than living symbolism. At a certain point midrash becomes a force in its own right, an art, a kind of "play" in the anthropological sense of the term, without reference to the outside world.[110] Of course these complicated wordplays and literary allusions are typical of midrash in general. But our question is whether we may see the significations as related to the religious experience of those who shook the lulav. Did the homilist draw on a recognized convention in which the species represented the patriarchs, matriarchs and court, and then add scriptural "prooftexts" on his own initiative? And if no living symbolism is present, did the homilist nonetheless draw on specific themes commonly associated with the lulav? It is difficult to answer these questions affirmatively since there seems to be no plausible reason why these referents should be

---

[110] J. Kugel, "Two Introductions to Midrash," *Midrash and Literature*, ed. G. Hartman and S. Budick, (New Haven: Yale University Press, 1986), 95 aptly calls midrash a "kind of joking."

associated with the species. If the homily had only identified God with the species, we might conjecture that the midrash reflects a mystical, theosophic interpretation of Lev 23:40. The homilist shows how this verse, like every other verse in the Torah, contains God's mystical name, and draws on esoteric exegetical conventions, not on the associations of Sukkot. But even later mystics would not claim that the Torah mystically encodes the patriarchs, matriarchs and Sanhedrin as well. In any case this type of mystical exegesis probably postdates the talmudic period.

It seems most likely that the purpose of the homily is to create a series of *commemorations*.[111] While the Bible explains that various commandments commemorate concepts or historical events (e.g. the sukka), it provides no such explanation for the lulav. Our homilist wished to fill this void. Now many cases of symbolic commemoration are arbitrary; only the stipulation of scripture forges the link. For example, circumcision is a sign of the covenant only because scripture defines it as such. Here our homilist has ingeniously found indications of the concepts, figures or objects which Scripture intended the species to commemorate. That the homily was included in *PRK* suggests that the commemorative symbolism the homilist created was warmly received. Henceforth it would add another dimension to the symbolic meaning of the lulav.[112]

This tradition heralds a trend in which the symbolism of the lulav becomes progressively more removed from its natural and cultural symbolism. In later midrashim the fact that there are *four* species determines the content of the symbolism. The four species are made to represent common sets of four elements. Thus *Midrash HaGadol* 3:660-62 cites *PRK* 27:9[113] and continues:

---

[111]Stern, *Reference*, explains symbolic commemoration and the genesis of religious symbolism.
[112]The origin of the midrash may be sought in the *hoshaʿanot*. In one popular *hoshaʿana* form each line begins: *hoshaʿana lemaʿan*, "save for the sake of..." and provides a litany of items. Several *hoshaʿanot* of this form in fact begin with Abraham, Isaac and Jacob, followed by other leading figures. See e.g. *Maḥzor lesukkot*, ed D. Goldschmidt and Y. Frankel (Jerusalem, 1981), no. 17 (pp. 192-97), ג (p. 208), ה (pp. 211-12), and *'Ahavat qedumim*, *'El 'eḥad*, and *'Av hamon* in *Mahzor Vitry*, ed. S. Hurwitz (Berlin: H. Itzkowski, 1893), §386-87, 392 (447-49). Since the lulav was held as the *hoshaʿanot* were recited it may have become a code for the patriarchs, and for their sake – i.e. on account of their merit – the congregation entreats God. Perhaps R. Akiba's identification of the species with God reflects the same idea. The standard preamble for all the *hoshaʿanot* beseeches: "Deliver us for Your sake, our God. Deliver us for Your sake, our Creator. Deliver us, for Your sake our Redeemer. Deliver us for Your sake, our Provider." Holding the lulav entreats God to deliver the people for His own sake.
[113]*MG* omits the section on the Sanhedrin.

> Another explanation: The four species correspond to the four banners (*degalim*) that Israel comprised in the desert.
>
> Another explanation. Corresponding to the four creatures of the chariot.
>
> Another explanation. Corresponding to the four kingdoms that scatter Israel. If they plot evilly against Israel, these four species will annul their plans.
>
> Another explanation. Corresponding to the four seasons that govern the world.
>
> Another explanation. Corresponding to the four types of capital punishment. God says: If you bring before me the four species of the lulav I will atone for you for the four capital punishments...

And so forth. Note that the text makes no effort to connect the species to that which they signify. The midrash suffices with the assertion that the four species correspond to other sets of *four*. In this way the lulav has almost become a "sign," not a "symbol," a convention for the number four. Note further the mystical power attributed to the lulav, the ability to annul the evil plots of the enemies of Israel and the ability to atone for capital crimes. Yet a further development appears in *Mishnat Rabbi Eliezer*, where no less than twenty-five sets of four are coordinated with the species.[114]

This trend reveals the polysemous symbolism of the lulav. The symbolism of the sukka, in contrast, remained relatively defined and circumscribed. The function of the sukka as a dwelling place during the festival is probably responsible for its limited symbolic development. It could symbolize dwellings of various sorts – eschatological dwellings, cloud-like shelters, the Messiah's canopy – but little more. This symbolism is rich and varied, but limited nonetheless. Moreover, the Bible explained that festival sukkot represented the sukkot of the exodus and thus advanced an "authoritative" symbolism. The lulav, on the other hand, served no clear function and received no biblical explanation. Lev 23:40 simply instructs the Israelite to take the species and rejoice. In short, the lulav was a symbol with no obvious content. Later interpreters consequently had more latitude in explaining the purpose and meaning of the opaque ritual with its well-defined but unexplained components. They were not displacing any biblical, authoritative or functional explanation. Besides the common natural and cultural associations with plants and festive bouquets, other interpretations based on the most remote connection to the lulav itself developed. In this way the lulav could symbolize God, the patriarchs or any set of four. It is interesting to

---

[114]*The Mishnah of Rabbi Eliezer*, ed. H.G. Enelow (New York: Bloch, 1933), chapter 5, pp. 101-106.

note that early medieval halakhic compendia such as *Manhig*, *Abudarham* and *Sha'arei simha* cite numerous midrashim in the section on the laws of the lulav.[115] These midrashim stand out against the consistently halakhic character of the works; indeed the authors cite no aggadic midrashim in the sections on the sukka or matzah. Apparently the authors felt a need to explain the symbolism of the lulav as opposed to other rituals for which the Bible explained the symbolism. The same phenomenon is responsible for the genesis of multivalent symbolisms in the midrashim themselves. The absence of a clear and authoritative understanding of the lulav paved the way for diverse symbolisms to develop.

VI. Rain and Agriculture

In Chapter 4 we noted that R. Eliezer explains the function of the lulav to entreat God for rain: "These four species only come to obtain the favor [of God] about water. Just as it is impossible for these four species [to subsist] without rain, so it is impossible for the world [to subsist] without water."[116] The connection between the lulav and rain appears only sporadically in the amoraic midrashim. The clearest tradition appears in *VR* 30:13 (710-11).[117] The passage begins by noting that God has commanded many "takings" in order that Israel receive merit. After listing various commandments where the Bible utilizes the language of "taking," the passage concludes: "And now that I said to you, *And you shall take on the first day, (Lev 23:40)*, it is in order that you merit that rain descend for you." The folk proverb, "when you tie up your lulav, tie up your feet"[118] or "when you tie your lulav, tie your ship"[119] associates the lulav with rain. After Sukkot, when one puts away the lulav, one should not embark on a journey or board a ship because storms are imminent.[120] Even general associations like this between the festival and rain are sparse. In *ShR* 7:2 we find: "You close your work before me on Sukkot and I open and cause winds to blow, and raise clouds and bring rain and cause the sun to shine and plants to grow and fruits to fatten and set a

---

[115] Abraham b. Nathan of Lunel, *Sefer Hamanhig*, ed. Y. Raphael (Jerusalem: Rav Kook, 1978), 2:377-401; David Abudarham, *Sefer Abudarham* (Jerusalem, 1958), 294-95; Ibn Ghiyyat, *Sha'arei simha*, 94-95.

[116] bTa 2b. Cf. yTa 1:1, 63c. See Chapter 4, I for full context and parallels.

[117] *Yalqut* §652. Cf. *Tan 'Emor* §17 (463); *TanB* 3:98, *MG* 2:607.

[118] *BR* 6:17 (44); yShal 2:6, 5b. See Marmorstein, *Volkskunde*, 293 for discussion of related magical formulae.

[119] *QohR* 3:2

[120] Here setting aside the lulav essentially serves to define the time when one should cease travel. Not the function of the lulav, but the play on "tie" your lulav and "tie" you feet/ship relates the lulav to rain. It is not explicitly stated that performing the ritual produces rain.

table for each person's needs."[121] Two late examples: *Midrash Tehilim* 109:4 (465) suggests that on Sukkot Israel prays for rain on behalf of the gentile nations,[122] and *Midrash HaGadol* 3:657 interprets "the first day" of Lev 23:40 as "the first day of rainfall."[123] These sources are not insignificant, but we might expect more emphasis on a primary concern of the festival.

The liturgy and general conception of SA may be responsible for the paucity of rain associations in the amoraic period. We find in *PRK* 28:8 (432):

> During the seven days of Sukkot the Torah hints to Israel and says to them: Ask God for rain... Since they did not notice, the Torah set aside for them an additional day. Therefore scripture had to say, *On the eighth day (Num 29:35)*.

Because Sukkot is considered the appropriate time to request rain, the Torah hints to Israel to direct their prayers to God during the festival.[124] Because Israel did not understand the hint and neglected to petition God, the additional day of SA was designated for this purpose. This midrash recognizes that while the *raison d'être* of Sukkot stems from its impact on the supply of rain, that function shifted to SA.[125] Although formulated in the playful spirit of midrash, the homily reflects something of the historical development. While the temple stood the fertility rituals performed each day fostered a staunch connection between the festival and the rain supply. With the destruction of the temple and the cessation of libations the liturgy became the vehicle which expressed this connection. In the tannaitic period we saw different opinions as to when the liturgical "mention of rain" should be incorporated into the Eighteen Blessings. By the amoraic period it appears that the opinion of R. Joshua prevailed; the phrase was added for the first time in the additional

---

[121] Israel "closes" by completing the agricultural labors and celebrating the festival. See the poem in *MM* 9 ll. 38-41 (70) which Mirsky, *Piyyut*, 67 suggests may have been an early piyyut for rain.
[122] See above n. 78.
[123] See Chapter 4, III n. 37 for the full source.
[124] The hint comes from the exposition of superfluous letters in Num 29:12-28 to read *mym*, water, an allusion to the water libation. See *Sifre Num.* §150 (96).
[125] Cf. the tradition found in *MG* 3:657: it is fitting that rain begins to fall on the first day of Sukkot, but because this would inconvenience pilgrims at the temple, the rain is deferred until SA. See too the midrash found in *PRK* 28 (420), a later addition to the *PRK* for SA. God "closes off" the rain that He would otherwise bring on the festival so that the people can celebrate the festival in their sukkot. On SA God apparently ceases holding back the rain. (See Mandelbaum's note to line 9.) The midrash expresses the tension that while Sukkot is oriented toward rain, SA marks the period rain should begin to fall. And see *PRK* 28:3 (427) and 28:4 (428) that associate SA with rain.

service *(musaf)* on SA. The reason, of course, was that rain was not actually desired on Sukkot, lest it impede the ritual dwelling in sukkot.[126] As a result, SA, a festival of almost totally undefined character, developed strong associations with rain. As this conception of SA emerged, it tended to displace associations of rain and Sukkot.

Associations of Sukkot with the harvest, ingathering and agricultural cycle are also elusive. The Additional Parsha asks why the term "joy" *(simha)* appears thrice in the biblical legislation about Sukkot (Deut 16:14, 16:15; Lev 23:40) but only once in the sections relating to other festivals.[127] The answer given is twofold: first, since all souls were forgiven on YK, all wish to rejoice on Sukkot, and second, that the harvests of Pesah and Shavuot occur in the middle of the agricultural year, but Sukkot follows the final harvest when all the fruit has been gathered from the trees. The first answer draws once again on the relationship between Sukkot and YK: rejoicing on Sukkot is a response to a favorable judgment. The second answer conceives of the festival in terms of the fruit harvest. Sukkot is a particularly joyous time because it concludes the agricultural year. Here the midrash accurately expresses the biblical character of the festival. Connection to the ingathering also appears in MG 3:657:

> [And you shall take on the first day (Lev 23:40).] Why was it called "the first"? Because throughout the summer Israel is busy with their work, with the grain-harvest and the winnowing and the vintage and the olive-harvest, until the festival of Sukkot, as it says *The festival of ingathering (Exod 23:16)*. The Holy One, blessed be He, said to them. Have you not gathered in your work from the fields? Let this be the first day on which to engage in the study of Torah, since you have already prepared your food and drink.

Again the midrash reflects the ancient nature of Sukkot: the concluding festival of the year following the final agricultural activities. But the passage seizes upon the mention of "first day" in the verse and claims that Sukkot marks a beginning as well. Sukkot is the first day on which Israel is completely free to study Torah since their agricultural labors have now been completed. This notion, of course, conceives of the festival in terms of classical ideas of rabbinic piety. Sukkot is not a time for dancing, feasting and rejoicing over the harvested crops, but an opportunity to engage in the study of Torah.

The lack of interest in the agricultural associations of the festival may indicate a shift away from an agricultural economy to a more urban, commercial culture, at least among the rabbis (or whoever composed the

---

[126] mSuk 2:9. See Chapter 4, III for further discussion.
[127] *PRK*, 458.

homilies) and their audience. Communities in which the harvest, vintage and threshing ceased to be annual activities would have conceived of the festival in different terms, since the agricultural aspects of Sukkot no longer resonated with their experience. Among diaspora communities, separated from the climatic and agricultural cycles of the land of Israel, associations with the harvest and rain were naturally weaker. On the other hand, the sparseness of midrashim on this topic may imply that the agricultural conception was universally known. The homilists wanted to add other dimensions to the festival experience, and felt no need to rehearse familiar territory.

VII. Miscellaneous Traditions

The previous sections contain the dominant associations and symbolisms of Sukkot. A few other traditions will be summarized here. bSuk 38a reports that R. Aha b. Yaakov used to shake the lulav and say "this (the lulav) is an arrow in the eye of Satan." Elsewhere the same phrase expresses a confident, almost scoffing, attitude toward temptation.[128] R. Aha b. Yaakov apparently considered the lulav as a charm that warded off the demonic. Or, as Rashi understands him, a symbol that the bearer will never abandon God's commandments.

bSuk 37b-38a transfers a sugya from bMen 62a to interpret mSuk 3:7, which discusses the shaking of the lulav. mMen 5:6 rules that the loaves of bread offered on Shavuot must be waved "to and fro, up and down." The amoraim comment as follows:

> [A] R. Yohanan said: "to and fro" before him who commands the four winds; "up and down" before him who possesses the heavens and earth.
>
> [B] In the West (Palestine) they taught as follows: R. Hama bar Uqba said in the name of R. Yose the son of R. Hanina: "to and fro" to prevent[129] harmful winds; "up and down" to prevent harmful dews.
>
> [C] R. Yose b. R. Avin, some say R. Yose b. Zevida[130] said: This implies that even the dispensable elements of the commandments prevent disasters, since the waving is a dispensable element of the commandment, and yet it prevents harmful winds and harmful dews.
>
> [D] And Rava[131] said: And so with the lulav.

---

[128] bQid 30a and 81a.
[129] MS Munich to bMen 62a reads "to annul." See *DQS* ad loc.
[130] "Zevela" should be corrected to Zevida since these two Rabbi Yoses regularly appear in tandem; see Hyman, *Toledot*, 715, 718.
[131] MS M in *DQS* has Rabba here, but Rava in Menahot. The rishonim attest both readings. See *DQS*, bMen 62a, n. א.

The waving of the loaves in all directions acknowledges the sovereignty of God over the entire earth and heavens. According to the Palestinian tradition the waving magically wards off undesirable climatic phenomena. The connection to the lulav emerges from the comment of Rava. But the antecedent of this remark is unclear. If it is mMen 5:6, as seems most likely, then Rava means that the lulav too should be waved or shaken, "to and fro, up and down," but offers no interpretation.[132] If the antecedent is these amoraic explanations of the waving [A,B], which is chronologically difficult but not impossible, then Rava means the lulav too has these effects. In any case, the anonymous editors (stam) may have interpreted the shaking of the lulav in light of the waving of the loaves, and transferred the sugya to the discussion of mSuk 3:7 to promote this interpretation.[133] The effect on the weather, of course, recalls the lulav's function as a rainmaking device. In this case the lulav prevents baleful atmospheric forces.

Conclusions

The amoraic midrashim reveal that Sukkot possessed manifold associations in the amoraic period. The festival cannot be pigeonholed as the celebration of one well-defined subject or event. Sukkot communicated several meanings, each of which impacted the religious consciousness of the worshipper in different respects and fostered multiple religious experiences. In fact the biblical explanation of the festival as a commemoration of the desert sojourn during which the Israelites dwelled in Sukkot is surprisingly underemphasized in these sources.

The lulav and the sukka, the primary symbols of the festival, are mainly responsible for this phenomenon. Symbols, as contemporary study of religion likes to emphasize, are "polysemous" and "multivalent." They contain multiple values, evoke many feelings and operate simultaneously on different levels. It is precisely this quality that characterizes the most powerful and enduring religious symbols. This ability of the lulav and the sukka to absorb, foster and evoke new symbolisms enabled the festival as a whole to take on different meanings and communicate them effectively. Compare Shavuot, a festival almost entirely devoid of symbols, and consequently lacking manifold

---

[132]So Rashi, bSuk 38a s.v. *vekhen;* R. Hananel, 37b; Ritba, s.v. *'amar* (356), and most rishonim.

[133]Cf. Stern, *Reference,* 121 who suggests that "the structure of the talmudic discussion" relates the rituals such that they "allude" to one another. Medieval sources conclude from the sugya that the lulav has these powers. See David Abudarham, *Sefer Abudarham* (Jerusalem, 1958), 292.

associations. It celebrates the harvest, as in biblical times, and the revelation of the Torah, a post-biblical historical interpretation – and little more. *PRK* 12, the Pisqa for Shavuot, focuses throughout on Torah, rarely introducing other topics. Sukkot, in contrast, displays a varied, multidimensional character.

Eschatological associations appear consistently in the amoraic midrashim. The tannaitic conception that the sukkot of the desert period, the clouds of glory, will return in eschatological times made a strong impression on the amoraim. In amoraic sources this symbolism developed into the conception that Israel (or the righteous) will reside in protective, divine sukkot in the World to Come. Festival sukkot symbolized sukkot fashioned from the skin of Leviathan, jeweled canopies and miraculous *huppot*. The protective shade of the sukka foreshadowed the peace, protection and divine intimacy expected in messianic times. At the same time, the lulav developed into an eschatological symbol in its own right, symbolizing the ultimate triumph over the nations and the hills dancing with joy at the advent of the Messiah.

Amoraic meditations on the relationship between RH, YK and Sukkot contributed a great deal to the meaning of the festival. While in ancient times these festivals indeed may have been celebrated in tandem, the Bible itself obscures any thematic connection. Tannaitic sources struggled to reconcile the belief that a judgment for rain takes place on Sukkot with the idea that RH and YK determine the course of the coming year. This legacy emerges in two understandings of Sukkot in the amoraic period. The first views Sukkot as a response to the events of RH and YK, the climax of a tri-partite drama. Sukkot celebrates the advent of God as cosmic judge and invites all nature to rejoice before its master. Since Israel receives a favorable judgment, it is appropriate to rejoice enthusiastically. At the same time, the belief that rain is determined on Sukkot linked it to themes of atonement and repentence characteristic of RH and YK. The lulav, in particular, is understood as a means of atonement for sins of different parts of the body and for different types of Jews. Atonement brings forgiveness and salvation, which connect again with eschatological ideas. The festival anticipates the ultimate redemption from sin and the ultimate advent of God, not annually in cyclical time, but eschatologically in linear time.

Traditions that associate sukkot with the temple seldom appear in the amoraic midrashim.[134] While a few traditions interpret the seventy bulls sacrificed over the course of the festival, almost no mention is made

---

[134]See, however, *PR* 30 (138b); *BR* 56:10 (608); *MTeh* 76:3 (341); targum to Ps 76:3.

of the water libations, willow and other cultic rituals.[135] Both talmuds, however, comment on the Mishna's reports of the rituals and supply additional traditions, including some aggadic material. ySuk 5:1, 55a, for example, contains a midrash in which the prophetic spirit came upon Jonah while he celebrated at SBH. Clearly the amoraim were conscious of, and interested in, the cultic dimension of Sukkot. Yet the homiletical midrashim did not focus on the cultic legacy. Despite their powerful imaginations and exegetical abilities, the homilists made no effort to transform the libation flask or willow into a living symbol with new meanings. Now we should be cautious before jumping to conclusions based on this absence. Homilists generally focus on current religious practices and symbols rather than on relics of the distant past. It is easier to inspire, edify and entertain by relating to contemporary experience than ancient custom. The fact that the temple rituals are not explicitly mentioned in scripture results in a parallel absence of exegetical midrashim. Exegetes could interpret the verses that mention the sukka and the lulav, but no scripture serves as a starting point for reflection on the libation. Liturgical poetry from the seventh century onward frequently employs the sukka as a symbol for the temple and consistently alludes to the temple ceremonies, so the cultic dimension of Sukkot did not disappear from Jewish tradition.[136] Indeed, the varied eschatological associations in amoraic midrashim suggest that the rabbis understood that Sukkot was meant to be a temple festival, and projected its fulfillment and true celebration to eschatological times.

The other biblical associations of Sukkot never lost their power in the amoraic period. The autumnal harvest and rain feature intermittently in the midrashim. Later periods added new meanings and symbolisms to their inherited conceptions of the festival but never replaced them entirely. While the lulav came to symbolize unity, victory, God, the patriarchs and other ideas, the older understanding that taking the lulav entreats for rain remained potent. Of course we do not know precisely which ideas were most meaningful to a given community or individual. This must have fluctuated over time and depended on the most pressing concerns of the age. But throughout this period and in subsequent ages Sukkot imbued a spectrum of meanings to those who celebrated it.

---

[135]Ironically one midrash that mentions the libations, PRK 28:8 (432), partially quoted above, p. 312, suggests that the Israelites did not understand the Torah hinted at them to bring libations on Sukkot as a sign for rain, and therefore SA was instituted as the day to propitiate God for rain! So much for Sukkot as a temple festival – the people did not grasp what rituals they should perform.

[136]See J. Rubenstein, "Cultic Themes in Sukkot Piyyutim," PAAJR 52 (1993), 185-209.

8

Conclusions

In the second temple period the festival of Sukkot displayed a twofold character. Above all, Sukkot was a temple and cultic festival. Early extra-rabbinic sources and rabbinic traditions of the Sukkot temple celebrations consistently paint this picture. As in biblical times, Sukkot was *the* festival, the primary pilgrimage. Only in autumn when the agricultural season came to a close could the bulk of the population leave their farms and villages and journey to the temple. The autumnal festival celebrated in first temple times ceased with the demise of the monarchy, but the priestly hierarchy observed Sukkot in the second temple with due pomp. A series of cultic rituals focused attention on the temple as the source of fertility. The willow-procession decorated the altar with verdant boughs to promote a parallel rejuvenation of nature. Water libations set in motion the hydraulic processes that would produce copious rainfall in the ensuing year. Floral wands carried by the worshippers symbolized the restoration of fertility and expressed festive mirth. Attention centered on the high priest and the splendid garments in which he officiated, yet processions and other popular celebrations allowed everyone to participate actively in the cultic drama. Abundant sacrifices, nocturnal festivities, dance, games and song produced an experience of consummate joy.

The second aspect of Sukkot derived from the canonization of the Torah and the rise of movements that turned to scripture as the source of religious authority. The Holiness School prescribed the dwelling in booths, an ancient agricultural ritual, in accordance with its program of preserving popular festival customs. Invested with scriptural authority, a utilitarian practice was transformed into a sacred rite and religious obligation. The vision of the Holiness School became a reality at the outset of the second temple period when the community described in Neh 8 demonstrated their allegiance to the Torah by celebrating Sukkot as commanded, by building booths and dwelling in them for seven days. In this way an old and neglected ritual suddenly became an inherent part of the second temple Sukkot festival. Observed because scripture commanded it, the sukka depended less on the temple for its *raison d'être*. To dwell in the sukka involved no priest or cultic component. The Torah gave the ritual additional autonomy by explaining the sukka as a commemoration of the shelters which the Israelites inhabited during the exodus. The ritual dwelling could be equally observed in all places: Jerusalem, the outlying regions of the country and in the diaspora.

The temple remained the focus of the festival until the destruction. To dwell in booths could not compare with the majestic celebrations in the temple with pageantry, grandeur and cultic power. When people thought of Sukkot they thought of the temple, not the exodus. Ezra associates the resumption of worship in the second temple with Sukkot sacrifices. The letters preserved in 2 Maccabees model the festival commemorating the rededication of the temple after Sukkot. Jason of Cyrene portrays the dedication festivities as Sukkot rites. Jubilees sets the institutionalization of the priesthood on Sukkot. Of course the account of Solomon dedicating the festival at the autumnal celebration of ancient times served as the paradigm for these sources. But all depend on a deeper model: the reality of Sukkot as the temple festival *par excellence*.

The destruction of the temple gave Sukkot an identity crisis. The cultic rituals that comprised its essential content no longer made religious sense. They depended too heavily on the mythic conception of the temple as the source of fertility, as the point from which the fructifying subterranean waters flow forth to rejuvenate the earth. Post-destruction Judaism required a new conception of Sukkot.

At this point that secondary character of Sukkot, the rituals prescribed by the Holiness Code, rose in importance. The cultic orientation now defunct, the scriptural description of the festival determined its essential nature. The sukka no longer competed with temple celebrations for the focus of religious energy. While the Nehemian assembly resurrected the ritual dwelling in sukkot, the destruction of the temple made it central. The tannaitic decision to retain the lulav and practice the ritual for seven days in imitation of the temple custom constitutes a parallel development. Because scripture explicitly prescribed the lulav, the tannaim were loath to let the ritual fall into desuetude together with the water libations and other cultic rites. Although they recognized that the lulav primarily had been part of the cultic dimension of the festival, the tannaim incorporated it into their post-temple construction of Sukkot. In this respect the tannaim were the spiritual descendants of the Nehemian assembly.

Conclusions

Sukkot in the rabbinic period thus manifests both continuity and discontinuity when compared with the pre-destruction festival. When a temple festival loses its temple and cult, clearly discontinuity results. Yet the rabbinic festival was fashioned from older traditions and rituals, not from radical innovations. The sukka, lulav and Hallel were familiar, if not central, components of the temple festival. Perhaps it is more helpful to speak of *adaptation* than continuity or discontinuity. The tannaim adapted elements of the temple Sukkot festival in shaping their new construction. Ironically, with the Holiness School as its inspiration, the tannaitic festival perhaps resembled ancient rural autumnal celebrations of premonarchic times. Before the rise of the Jerusalem temple peasants celebrated in the booths from which the festival took its name and observed primitive agricultural rites such as the lulav. The ritual forms of the rabbinic festival therefore had deep roots in tradition.

The relationship of Sukkot to rain illustrates the adaptation of ancient components of the festival. Rabbinic Judaism inherited from ancient Israelite tradition the idea that the divine judgment of rain takes place on Sukkot. Where the cult performed water libations, willow-processions and other rain-making rites, the tannaim incorporated prayers for rain into the liturgy. The mechanism to ensure the continued fertility of the earth changed from cultic ritual to communal prayer, but the conception of Sukkot as the determinative time endured. That the tannaim understood the lulav as a means to propitiate God to send rain preserved the connection between the Sukkot rituals and the rain supply. To a certain extent, however, associations with rain spread to SA, as the liturgical request for rain entered the service on that day. This was a natural development, for SA always had a close relationship with Sukkot – not totally independent, yet possessing an identity of its own. The association of the festival and rain was thus developed more elaborately in the rabbinic construction. God determined the extent of rain on Sukkot and the festival rituals both symbolized the need for rain and exerted some theurgic effect, but explicit prayers for rain were deferred to SA so that rain would not preclude residing in the sukka. The conception of Sukkot as a rain festival remained in place, adapted to the structures and beliefs of rabbinic piety and the reality of the post-temple world.

The persistence of Sukkot's connection to rain is related to the endurance of the mythic temple worldview in rabbinic times. The destruction of the temple abolished sacrifices, the altar and other cultic rituals, but did not undermine their mythic underpinnings. Indeed, the richest mythic descriptions of the fertilizing powers of the temple, its role in the hydraulic structure of the cosmos and the workings of cultic rituals appear in rabbinic sources redacted long after the destruction. Without this mythic structure it is unlikely that Sukkot would have remained a rain festival. The conception of RH and YK as the annual days of judgment, as well as the idea that rain and other bounties of nature are rewards for obeying the commandments in general – a point explicitly articulated in the *Shema'* the rabbis recited twice daily – could well have supplanted the legacy of Sukkot as a rain festival. When we ponder the fate of a temple festival after the temple is destroyed, we must be aware of the fact that the temple lived on in myth. In such a case a temple festival retains much of its original character. The descriptions of the Sukkot temple rituals in the Mishna and Tosefta, which are transmitted in a narrative account of mythic character, are neither historical data of a defunct cult, nor a program for the utopian age, nor yet an attempt to perpetuate the lost past in conscious denial of reality. They emerge from the overall mythic worldview and reflect the continuity of the mythic-cultic legacy of the festival.[1]

The endurance of the mythic worldview is of considerable significance. If this is not an idiosyncratic rabbinic phenomenon but reflects a widespread characteristic of religion, then we have evidence of the power of myth and symbol to sustain itself despite the destruction of their original context. Sacred places, whether temples, sanctuaries, mountains or rocks, may not be as central to a religious tradition as one might have expected. Destruction of place need not undermine the related religious practices and beliefs because the place endures in myth.[2] Myths apparently retain their symbolic structure even when the referents of their symbols are destroyed. The true context of a religious practice or idea is less the geographical setting, the material environment or any other tangible element than the myths and symbols that give it

---

[1] Cf. Bokser, *Origins*, 84-94. However, Bokser appeals to the assumption that the "destruction of the temple in 70 CE and the paganization of the city in the second century undoubtedly led to a sense of despair" to explain the Mishna's description of the sacrificial protocol as a living reality (p. 89). He then discusses the Mishna in terms of psychological theories of "working through" trauma and coping with crisis (pp. 90-94). I think the endurance of myth explains these mishnaic narratives equally well without requiring speculation as to psychological states, crisis, despair and trauma. The Mishna simply narrates the myth of the temple and its worship that endured in rabbinic thought.

[2] J.Z. Smith, *To Take Place* (Chicago: University of Chicago Press, 1987) discusses the role of place in religion and ritual. See especially the final chapter where he illustrates how the "Christian myth / ritual" (i.e. the life and deeds of Jesus as recounted in the Christian liturgical year) transformed what had been rituals associated with places to "mental representations of the place" (p. 117). See too the conclusions of Jeremias, *Golgotha*, 108ff. as to where Golgotha is really located.

coherence.³ And symbols include words and ideas as much as physical objects. Studies of other religions are needed to test these suggestions and examine whether and in what manner myths survive catastrophe. But rabbinic Judaism, at least, embraced the myths of earlier times despite both historical vicissitudes and the emergence of new religious ideas.

The rabbinic conception of the sukka also illustrates the process of adapting older traditions to new contexts. The Holiness School already interpreted the ritual sukka as a symbol of the sukkot of the exodus. While some second temple sources acknowledge this tradition, others neglect it; for none is it a central concern. The tannaim accepted the symbolism but interpreted the sukkot of the exodus as the "clouds of glory." So in rabbinic times an earlier ritual became more prominent and received a new symbolism. The sukka symbolized a specific understanding of the exodus experience: God protected his people in the hostile wasteland, guarded them with his sheltering presence and cherished them lovingly. Tannaitic legislation reified the symbolism by requiring that the sukka have skhakh, that the skhakh produce shade and the resident directly experience the shade. The rabbinic sukka ritual was an adaptation of an older institution with a pronounced rabbinic slant.

The tannaim adapted the lulav ritual of the temple cult and incorporated it into the emerging system of rabbinic piety. By designating set points in the Hallel for shaking the lulav they carried over a temple practice. Formulating blessings for the "taking" that scripture prescribed constituted an additional dimension shared with other commandments. The identification of the four species as the etrog, palm, willow and myrtle was an inheritance from the second temple period. The tannaim then standardized the ritual with a great degree of specificity. They defined characteristics required by each species, prescribed the number of each that the band should include, determined maximum and minimum sizes, and catalogued imperfections that disqualified the species. In this way a rather general scriptural description of rejoicing with flora narrowed first during the second temple period as common custom restricted itself to four species, and subsequently during tannaitic times as rabbinic legislation defined the contours of the ritual precisely.

In contrast to the specificity with which the halakha defined the lulav, amoraic aggadic traditions display a remarkably broad symbolic

---

³Thus Clifford Geertz, "Religion as a Cultural System," *The Interpretation of Cultures* (New York: Basic Books, 1973), 87-125 defines religion as "a system of symbols..."

range. The Torah gave no clue as to the meaning of the ritual, other than the direction that the Israelites rejoice with the bouquet. The sukka commemorated the *sukkot* of the exodus and the unleavened bread symbolized the bread the ancestors consumed as they fled from the Egyptians, but the lulav received no such explanation. It was an undefined ritual, a symbol without meaning, and this gave the rabbis latitude to exercise their interpretive imaginations. In the tannaitic period R. Eliezer understood the lulav to symbolize the earth's need for rain. Amoraic midrashim make the lulav a symbol of eschatological victory over gentile nations, of joy upon receiving the favorable divine judgment, of praise at the advent of God, of atonement for sins of the body, and of the unity of all Israel. Eventually the lulav became a sign with the four species arbitrarily assigned to any four items. This polysemous character, the ability to absorb new symbolisms, made Sukkot relevant to the concerns of Jews throughout the rabbinic period. The festival had no single character, no one dimension, but acquired novel aspects through symbolic innovations. Perhaps the rigid halakhic specifications of the lulav is partly responsible for the proliferation of symbolism. With no concern that the ritual lose its integrity or basic form, the rabbis could take liberties with the content. In any case, the festival took on a multidimensional character in amoraic times.

Eschatological associations are particularly prominent in both tannaitic and amoraic midrashim relating to Sukkot and its rituals. The roots of this eschatological dimension can be detected among marginal groups of the second temple period. Alienated or disenfranchised by the Jerusalem temple institutions, these circles prophesied its replacement with an eschatological temple. They pictured eschatological worship as Sukkot celebrations because Sukkot was the primary temple festival of their experience. In tannaitic times the understanding of the sukka as the symbol of the "clouds of glory" reflects a different eschatological orientation. The tannaim believed that the clouds would envelop the entire people in the eschaton just as they had during the exodus.[4] Since the redemption from Egypt was paradigmatic of the future redemption, the sukka, which symbolized the clouds of glory of the exodus, came to symbolize the clouds of glory of the ultimate redemption. The amoraic midrashim transformed the tannaitic conception of the clouds of glory and thereby intensified the eschatological symbolism of the sukka. They picture God bestowing protective shelters, not protective clouds, upon

---

[4]The tannaim also believed that the clouds of glory would return in the eschaton and permanently hover above the future temple. So the tannaitic eschatological associations derive in part from notions of the eschatological temple, as in earlier times.

the righteous in the World to Come. Festival sukkot symbolized various types of eschatological sukkot, a more direct and immediate symbolism. The lulav also attracted eschatological symbolism as a symbol of Israel's victory in the eschatological trial and of life in the World to Come.

The development of Sukkot during second temple and rabbinic times does not lend itself to neat summaries or hard and fast generalizations. Sukkot was a complex, multifaceted festival that underwent a complex, multifaceted development. After the destruction of the temple the rabbis constructed a Sukkot celebration from the legacy of tradition. Adaptation of inherited rituals and beliefs to new circumstances characterizes the development better than radical change. There is a surprising resilience of ancient elements doggedly to endure. Although the conception of Sukkot as a temple festival faded somewhat as the centuries passed, the endurance of temple myths in rabbinic times preserved the connection. Numerous amoraic sources still expect the Sukkot temple rituals to set in motion the hydraulic system of the world. The new symbolisms that appear in amoraic midrashim supplement older conventions but do not totally displace them. This is not to minimize the discontinuity between the temple festival and its rabbinic counterpart, for similar elements built into different systems may produce vastly different experiences. The whole does not always equal the sum of its parts. But the continuity of ritual, symbol and belief that marks the rabbinic Sukkot festival should be appreciated.

A similar process of adaptation, I suspect, characterizes other rabbinic festivals, and perhaps aspects of rabbinic religion in general. Bokser's study of the Pesah seder, which I considered in the introduction, reflects a similar process at work. The cultic meal and other practices from temple times were combined with blessings, prayers and study to constitute a rabbinic ritual. In this way Bokser suggests the rabbinic seder "restructures" the pre-destruction practice.[5] So too the rabbinic Yom Kippur absorbed the *malkhuyot* and other prayers from the temple liturgy and carried over fasting and other atonement rites. In place of the temple ritual rabbinic liturgy narrated the high priest's routine and the offering of the scapegoat as practiced in temple times. These elements were placed in a new setting, the synagogue or Beit Midrash, and integrated into the rabbinic liturgy. This study of the rabbinic Sukkot festival may serve as a model for future studies of rabbinic religion as it developed from the Judaism of the second temple period.

---

[5]*Origins*, 77.

Bibliography

Works cited only once or twice are not listed here. Collected bibliography can be found in Jeffrey L. Rubenstein, *The History of Sukkot during the Second Temple and Rabbinic Periods: Studies in the Continuity and Change of a Festival* (Dissertation: Columbia University; Ann Arbor; University Microfilms, 1992), 526-564

Abbreviations of Journals and Series follow that of the *Society of Biblical Literature, Membership Directory and Handbook, 1992*, pp. 212-213.

Aalen, S. *Die Begriffe 'Licht' un 'Finsternis' im alten Testament, im Spätjudentum und im Rabbinismus.* Oslo, 1951.

Ackroyd, P.R. *I & II Chronicles, Ezra, Nehemiah.* London, 1973.

———. *The Chronicler in his Age.* Sheffield, England, 1991.

Albeck, H. *Das Buch der Jubiläen und die Halacha.* Berlin, 1930.

———, ed. *Shisha sidrei mishna.* Jerusalem and Tel Aviv, 1954-59.

Allon, G. "Leheqer hahalakha shel filon." *Tarbiz* 6 (1933/4): 457-59.

Alt, A. *Essays on Old Testament History and Religion.* Trans. R.A. Wilson. Oxford: Basil Blackwell, 1966.

Anderson, B.W. "Exodus Typology in Second Isaiah." *Israel's Prophetic Heritage: Essays in Honor of James Muilenburg.* Eds. B.W. Anderson and W. Harrelson. New York: Harper & Brothers, 1962.

ARNA, ARNB = 'Avot D'Rabbi Natan. Ed. S. Schechter. New York: Feldheim, 1967 [Vienna, 1887].

Attridge, H. "Historiography." *Jewish Writings of the Second Temple Period.* CRINT II/I. Ed. M. Stone. Philadelphia: Fortress, 1984. 157-84.

Auerbach, E. "Die Feste im Alten Israel." *VT* 8 (1958): 1-18.

Baumgarten, J.M. "4Q502, Marriage or Golden Age Ritual." *JJS* 34 (1983): 125-35.

———. *Studies in Qumran Law.* Leiden: Brill, 1977.

Beyerlin, W. *Origins and History of the Oldest Sinaitic Traditions.* Trans. S. Rudman. Oxford: Basil Blackwell, 1965.

BHM = *Beit Hamidrash.* Ed. A. Jellinek. 6 vols. Leipzig: F. Nies, 1853-77.

Blenkinsopp, J. *Ezra-Nehemiah.* Philadelphia: Westminster Press, 1988.

BMM = *Baraita D-Melekhet Ha-Mishkan: Critical Edition with Introduction.* Ed. R. Kirchner. Ann Arbor: University Microfilms, 1989.

Bokser, B. *The Origins of the Seder.* Berkeley and Los Angeles: University of California Press, 1984.

Börner, F. "Pompa." P.-W., vol. 21, 2: 1878-94.

Boyarin, D. *Intertextuality and the Reading of Midrash.* Bloomington: Indiana University Press, 1990.

BR = *Midrash Bereisheet Rabba.* Ed. J. Theodor and H. Albeck. 3 vols. Jerusalem, 1965 [1903-29].

Brown, R. *The Gospel According to John (i-xii).* AB 29. London, 1975.

Buber, S. *Pesiqta DeRav Kahana.* Lyck, 1868.

Büchler, A. "La fête des cabanes chez Plutarque et Tacite." *REJ* 37 (1898): 181-202.

Burgansky, I. *Masekhet sukka shel talmud bavli: meqoroteha vedarkei arikhata.* Dissertation: Bar-Ilan University, 1979.

Burkert, W. *Greek Religion.* Trans. J. Raffan. Cambridge: Harvard University Press, 1985.

Charlesworth, J.H., ed. *The Old Testament Pseudepigrapha.* 2 vols. Garden City, N.Y.: Doubleday, 1983-85.

Childs, B.S. *Introduction to the Old Testament as Scripture.* Philadelphia, Fortress Press, 1979.

———. *Myth and Reality in the Old Testament.* SBT 27. Naperville, Ill.: A.R. Allenson, 1960.

Cohen, S.J.D. "Alexander the Great and Jaddus the High Priest According to Josephus." *AJS Review* 7-8 (1982-3): 41-68.

Comblin, J. "La Liturgie de la Nouvelle Jérusalem." *ETL* 29 (1953): 5-40.

Cross, F.M. *Canaanite Myth and Hebrew Epic.* Cambridge: Harvard University Press, 1973.

Dalman, G. *Arbeit und Sitte in Palästina.* 7 vols. Gütersloh: C. Bertelsmann, 1928-42.

Daniélou, J. *The Bible and the Liturgy.* Notre Dame: University of Notre Dame Press, 1956.

_____. *Primitive Christian Symbols*. Trans D. Attwater. London: Burns & Oates, 1964.

Diamond, E. *A Model for a Scientific Edition and Commentary for Bavli Ta'anit, Chapter 1, with a Methodological Introduction*. Dissertation. The Jewish Theological Seminary, 1990. Hebrew.

Diez-Macho, A. *Neophyti I*. 5 vols. Madrid, 1968-78.

DQS = R. Rabbinovicz. *Diqduqei Sofrim. Variae Lectiones in Mischnam et in Talmud Babylonicum*. 12 vols. Reprint; New York, 1960.

DR = *Midrash Devarim Rabba*. Ed. S. Lieberman. Jerusalem: Wahrmann, 1964.

Draper, J. "The Heavenly Feast of Tabernacles: Revelation 7:1-17." *JSNT* 19 (1983): 133-47.

Ehlers, W. "Triumphus." P.-W. vol. 7A, 1:493-511.

Ehrlich, A.B. *Hamiqra kifeshuto*. New York: Ktav, 1969 [1900].

Ehrlich, E. *Die Kultsymbolik im Alten Testament und im nachbiblishen Judentum*. Stuttgart: Anton Hiersemann, 1959.

Eitrem, E. "Die Prozession." *Skrifter Utg. Av Videnskapselskapet*. 2 (1919): 56-108.

Elbogen, I. *Hatefila beyisra'el*. Ed. J. Heinemann. Tel Aviv, 1972.

Epstein, J.N. *Mavo lenusaḥ hamishna*. 2nd ed. Tel Aviv, 1964.

_____. *Mevo'ot lesifrut hatana'im*. Ed. E.Z. Melamed. Jerusalem: Magnes, 1957.

ER = *Seder Eliahu Rabba und Seder Eliahu Zuta (Tanna Debe Eliahu)*. Ed. M. Ish-Shalom. 3d ed. Jerusalem: Wahrmann, 1969 (1904].

Feuchtwang, D. "Das Wasseropfer und die damit verbundenen Zermonien." *MGWJ* 54, 55 (1910, 11); 535-52; 713-29; 43-63.

Fishbane, M. *Biblical Interpretation in Ancient Israel*. Oxford, 1985.

Fox, H. *A Critical Edition of Mishnah Tractate Succah with an Introduction and Notes*. Dissertation: Hebrew University, 1979.

_____. "Insights on the Palestinian Custom of *simḥat torah*, the Sabbath that coincides with the New Moon, and the Days of Awe." *Sinai* 103 (1989), 81-88. Hebrew.

_____. "Simḥat Beit Hasho'eva." *Tarbiz* 55 (1986): 173-216.

Gaster, T. *Thespis*. Connecticut, 1956.

Gierlich, A. *Der Lichtgedanke in Den Psalmen*. Feiburg im Breisgau: Herder, 1940.

Gilat, Y. *R. Eliezer Ben Hyrcanus – A Scholar Outcast*. Ramat-Gan, Israel: Bar-Ilan University Press, 1984.

Ginzberg, L. *Legends of the Jews*. 7 vols. Philadelphia: Jewish Publication Society, 1909-38.

Goldberg, A.M. *Untersuchungen über die Vorstellung von der Schekhina in der frühen rabbinischen Literatur*. Berlin: De Gruyter, 1969.

Goldstein, J.A. *I Maccabees*. AB 41. Garden City, New York: Doubleday, 1976.

_____. *II Maccabees*. AB 41A. Garden City, New York: Doubleday, 1983.

Goodenough, E.R. *Jewish Symbols of the Greco-Roman Period*. 13 vols. New York: Pantheon Books, 1953-68.

Green, W.S. "What's in a Name? – The Problematic of Rabbinic 'Biography'." *Approaches to Ancient Judaism: Theory and Practice*. Missoula, Montana: Scholars Press, 1978. 77-96.

Grossfeld, B. *The Targum Onqelos to Leviticus and Numbers*. The Aramaic Bible. Vol. 8. Wilmington, Delaware: Michael Glazier, 1988.

Grunwald, M. "Zur Vorgeschichte des Sukkothrituals." *Jahrbuch für jüdische Volkskunde* 25 (1923): 427-72.

Genneweg, A. *Nehemia*. KAT 19, 2. Gütersloh: Gerd Mohn, 1987.

Habicht, C. *2 Makkabäerbuch*. Jüdische Schriften aus hellenisch-römanischer Zeit. I/3. Güttersloh: Gerd Mohn, 1979.

Halivni, D. *Meqorot umesorot*. Vol 1. *Nashim*. Tel-Aviv: Devir, 1968. Vols 2-4. *Moʿed*. Jerusalem: The Jewish Theological Seminary, 1975-82.

Hanson, P.D. *The Dawn of Apocalyptic*. Philadelphia: Fortress, 1975.

Harrington, D.J. "Pseudo-Philo." In Charlesworth, *Pseudepigrapha*. 2:299-377.

Hehn, V. *Kulturpflanzen und Haustiere in ihrem Übergang aus Asien nach Griechenland und Italien sowie in das übrige Europa*. 8th ed. Berlin, 1911.

Heinemann, J. *Prayer in the Talmud: Forms and Patterns*. Trans. R. Sarason. Berlin, New York: De Gruyter, 1977.

_____. "The Proem in the Aggadic Midrashim: A Form-Critical Study." *ScrHier* 22 (1971): 100-122.

_____. *ʿIyyunei tefila*. Ed. A. Shinan. Magnes Press: Jerusalem, 1983.

Hengel, M. *Judaism and Hellenism*. Trans. J. Bowden. 2 vols. Philadelphia: Fortress, 1981.

Herzfeld, L. *Geschichte des Volkes Israel*. 3 vols. Braunschweig: G. Westermann, 1847-63.

Hochman, J. *Jerusalem Temple Festivities.* London: George Routledge, 1910.

Hoffmann, D. *Sefer vayiqra meforash.* Trans T. Shefer and A. Liberman. Jerusalem: Rav Kook, 1952.

Hooke, S., ed. *Myth and Ritual.* London: Oxford University Press, 1933.

Hyman, A. *Toledot tannaim ve'amoraim.* Jerusalem, 1916 [1987].

Ibn Ghiyyat, Isaac. *Sha'arei simḥa.* Ed. S. Halevi. Fürth, 1861-62.

In der Smitten, W. *Esra: Quellen, Überlieferungen und Geschichte.* Studia Semetica Neerlandica 15. Assen, 1973.

Jaffee, M. "The Taqqanah in Tannaitic Literature: Jurisprudence and the Construction of Rabbinic Memory." *JJS* 41 (1990): 204-25.

Jastrow, M. *A Dictionary of the Targumim, the Talmud Babli and Yerushalmi and the Midrashic Literature.* New York: Jastrow Publishers, 1967.

Jellinek, *Beit hamidrash.* See *BHM.*

Jeremias, J. "Golgotha und der Heilige Felsen." *Angelos* 2 (1926): 74-128.

Josephus, Flavius. *Works.* Eds. H.J. Thackeray, et al. 10 vols. Loeb Classical Library. London, 1926-65.

JPS = *Tanakh: The Holy Scriptures. The New JPS Translation according to the Traditional Hebrew Text.* Philadelphia: The Jewish Publication Society, 1988.

Jubilees = "Jubilees." Trans. O.S. Wintermute. In Charlesworth, *Pseudepigrapha.* 2:35-142.

Kapelrud, A.S. *Authorship in the Ezra-Narrative.* Oslo: Jakob Dybwab, 1944.

Kaufmann, Y. *Toledot ha'emuna hayisra'elit.* 4 vols. Jerusalem: Bialik, 1937-56.

Kellerman, U. *Nehemia: Quellen, Überlieferung und Geschichte.* Berlin: Alfred Töpelmann, 1967.

Knohl. I. "The Priestly Torah Versus the Holiness School: Sabbath and the Festivals." *HUCA* 58 (1987): 65-117.

Kohut, A., ed. *Ha'arukh.* By Nathan B. Yehiel of Rome. 8 vols. Vienna, 1878-92.

Kraus, H.J. *Worship in Israel.* Oxford: Blackwell, 1966.

Krauss, S. *Qadmoniot hatalmud.* 2 vols. Tel Aviv: Devir, 1923-25.

Levenson, J. *Creation and the Persistence of Evil.* San Francisco: Harper & Row, 1988.

———. *Sinai and Zion.* San Francisco: Harper & Row, 1985.

Licht, J. "Sukkot." *Mo'adei yisra'el.* Reprints from *Ha'enṣiqlopedia hamiqra'it.* Jerusalem: Bialik, 1988.

Liddell, H.G. and Scott, H. *A Greek-English Lexicon.* Reprint; Oxford: Clarendon Press, 1968.

Löw, I. *Die Flora der Juden.* 4 vols. Vienna and Leipzig: Kohut Foundation, 1924-34.

Luzarraga, J. *Las Tradiciones de la Nube en la Biblia y en el Judaismo Primitivo.* An Bib 54. Rome: Biblical Institute Press, 1973.

McKelvey, R.J. *The New Temple.* Oxford, 1969.

MacRae, G.W. "The Meaning and Evolution of the Feast of Tabernacles." *CBQ* 22 (1960): 251-76.

Malter, H. *The Treatise Ta'anit.* Philadelphia: Jewish Publication Society, 1967.

Mekhilta RSBY = *Mekhilta d'Rabbi Shimon Bar Yoḥai.* Ed. J.N. Epstein and E.Z. Melamed. Jerusalem, 1955.

Mekhilta =*Mekhilta d'Rabbi Ishmael.* Ed. H. Horovitz. Jerusalem, 1960.

Meyers, C.E. and E.M. *Zechariah 9-14.* AB 25C. New York: Doubleday, 1993.

MG = *Midrash HaGadol.* 5 Vols. Ed. M. Margolioth. Jerusalem: Rav Kook, 1947-1976. Vol. 3. *Sefer Vaqira.* Ed. A. Steinsalz. Vol. 4. *Sefer Bamidbar.* Ed. Z.M. Rabinowitz. Vol. 5. *Sefer Devarim.* Ed. S. Fisch.

Michaelis, W. "σκηνη." *TDNT,* 7:369-82.

Midrash Tannaim. Ed. D. Hoffmann. Berlin, 1909.

Milgrom, J. *Leviticus 1-16.* AB 3. New York: Doubleday, 1991.

MM = *Midrash Mishle.* Ed. B. Visotzky. New York: Jewish Theological Seminary, 1990.

Mowinckel, S. *The Psalms in Israel's Worship.* Trans. D.R. Ap-Thomas. Oxford: Blackwell, 1962.

_____. *PsSt* = *Psalmen-studien II. Das Thronbesteigungsfest Jahwes und der Ursprung des Eschatologie.* Amsterdam: P. Schippers, 1961 [1921-24].

_____. *Studien* = *Studien zu dem Buche Ezra-Nehemia III.* Skrifter Utgitt av Det Norske Videnskaps-Akademi I Oslo II. Hist-Filos. Klass. Ny Serie. No. 7. Oslo: Universitetsforlaget, 1965.

MTeh = *Midrash Tehillim.* Ed. S. Buber. Jerusalem, 1966 [Vilna, 1891].

Neusner, J. *Judaism, the Evidence of the Mishna.* Chicago: University of Chicago Press, 1981.

Bibliography

———. *The Rabbinic Traditions About the Pharisees Before 70.* Leiden: Brill, 1971.

Nilsson, M. *Geschichte der griechischen Religion.* Munich: C.H. Beck, 1940.

———. *Griechische Feste von Religiöser Bedeutung.* Stuttgart: B.G. Teubner, 1957.

———. "Die Prozessionstypen im griechischen Kult." *Jahrbuch des kaiserlich deutsches archäologischen Instituts* 31 (1916): 309-339.

Oesterly, W. "Early Hebrew Festival Rituals." *Myth and Ritual.* Ed. S. Hooke. London: Oxford University Press, 1933. 111-46.

OG = *Oṣar hageonim.* Thesaurus of the Gaonic Responsa and Commentaries following the order of the Talmudic Tractates. Ed. B. Lewin. 13 vols. Haifa and Jerusalem, 1928-43.

Ohler, A. *Mythologische Elemente im Alten Testament.* Düsseldorf: Patmos, 1969.

Otzen, B., Gottlieb, H. and Jeppensen, K. *Myths in the Old Testament.* Trans. F. Cryer. London: SCM Press, 1980.

P.-W. = *Paulys Real-encyclopaedie der klassischen Altertumwissenschaft.* Eds. A. Pauly and G. Wissowa. Stuttgart: J.B. Metzler, 1894-1959.

Parke, H.W. *Festivals of the Athenians.* Ithaca, N.Y.: Cornell University Press, 1977.

Patai, R. *Hamayim.* Tel Aviv: Devir, 1936.

———. *Man and Temple.* New York: Ktav, 1947.

Pedersen, J. *Israel, Its Life and Culture.* 2 vols. London: Oxford University Press, 1926-40.

Petuchowski, J.J. "'Hoshi'ah Na' in Psalm Cxviii 25." *VT* 5 (1955): 266-71.

Philo = *Philo with an English Translation.* Trans. F.H. Colson et al. Loeb Classical Library. Cambridge: Harvard University Press, 1949-56.

PR = *Pesiqta Rabbati.* Ed. Meir Ish-Shalom. Tel Aviv, 1963 [Vienna, 1880].

PRK = *Pesiqta DeRav Kahana.* Ed. B. Mandelbaum. New York: The Jewish Theological Seminary, 1987.

Riesenfeld, H. *Jésus Transfiguré.* Acta Seminarii Neotestamentici Upsaliensis. Copenhagen, 1947.

Rosenthal, D. "The Torah Reading in the Annual Cycle in the Land of Israel." *Tarbiz* 53 (1983): 144-48.

Rosenthal, E.S. *Lepeirusha shel masekhet taʿanit 1:1-2.* Yad Reʾem: Jerusalem, 1978.

Rubenstein, J.L. *The History of Sukkot during the Second Temple and Rabbinic Periods: Studies in the Continuity and Change of a Festival.*

Dissertation: Columbia University; Ann Arbor: University Microfilms 1992.

Ryle, H.E. *The Books of Ezra and Nehemiah.* Cambridge: Cambridge University Press, 1893.

Safrai, S. ʿAliya leregel biyemei bayit sheini. Tel-Aviv: Am Hasefer, 1965.

Schaefer, K.R. "The Ending of the Book of Zechariah: A Commentary." *RB* 100 (1993): 165-238.

―――――. "Zechariah 14 and the Composition of the Book of Zechariah." *RB* 100 (1993): 368-98.

Schnackenburg, R. *The Gospel According to St. John.* 2 vols. Trans. C. Hastings et al. New York: Herder & Herder, 1980.

Septuaginta. Ed. A. Rahlfs. 4th edition. 2 vols. Stuttgart: Privilegierte Württembergische Bibelanstalt, 1935.

Shaver, J.R. *Torah and the Chronicler's History Work.* Atlanta, Georgia: Scholars Press, 1989.

Sifra. Ed. I. Weiss. New York, 1946 [Vienna, 1862.]

Sifre Deut. = *Sifre Devarim.* Ed. L. Finkelstein. New York: Jewish Theological Seminary, 1979 [Berlin, 1940].

Sifre Num. = *Sifre ʿal sefer bamidbar veSifre Zuta.* Ed. H.S. Horovitz. Jerusalem: Wahrmann, 1966 [Leipzig, 1917].

Simon, E. *Festivals of Attica: an Archaeological Commentary.* Madison, Wis.: University of Wisconsin Press, 1983.

Sira = *Sefer ben sira hashalem.* Ed. M. Segal. Jerusalem: Bialik, 1953.

Snaith, N.H. *The Jewish New Year Festival.* London, 1947.

SOR = *Seder ʿOlam Rabba.* Ed. B. Ratner. Jerusalem, 1988.

Stern, J. "Reference Modes in the Rituals of Judaism." *RelS* 23 (1987): 109-28.

Stern, M., ed. *Greek and Latin Authors on Jews and Judaism.* 3 vols. Jerusalem: Israel Academy of Sciences, 1974-84.

Strack, H.L. and Stemberger, G. *Introduction to the Talmud and Midrash.* Trans. M. Bockmuehl. Minneapolis: Fortress Press, 1992.

SZ = *Sifre Zuta.* See *Sifre Num.*

TDNT = *Theological Dictionary of the New Testament.* Ed. R. Kittel. Trans. G.W. Bromiley. 10 vols. Michigan: Grand Rapids: Eerdmans, 1964-76.

Thackeray, H.J. *The Septuagint and Jewish Worship.* London: Oxford University Press, 1921.

TK = S. Lieberman. *Tosefta Kifshuta: A Comprehensive Commentary on the Tosefta*. 10 vols. Jerusalem: The Jewish Theological Seminary, 1955-1988.

TO = *The Bible in Aramaic: The Pentateuch According to Targum Onkelos*. Ed. A. Sperber. Leiden: Brill, 1959.

Tolkowsky, S. *Peri 'eṣ hadar*. Jerusalem: Bialik, 1966.

Tosefta = *The Tosefta*. According to Codex Vienna with Variants from Codex Erfurt, Genizah MSS, and Editio Princeps. Ed. S. Lieberman. 5 vols. New York: The Jewish Theological Seminary, 1955-88.

Tosefta = *Tosephta*. Based on the Erfurt and Vienna Codices. Ed. M. Zuckermandel. Jerusalem: Wahrmann, 1970.

TR = S. Lieberman. *Tosefet rishonim*. 4 vols. Jerusalem: Bamberger and Wahrmann, 1938.

Tur-Sinai, N.H. *Halashon vehasefer*. Vol. 3. Jerusalem: The Bialik Institute, 1955.

TY = *Targum Pseudo-Jonathan of the Pentateuch: Text and Concordance*. Ed. E.G. Clarke. Hoboken, N.J.: Ktav, 1984.

TYG = *Das Fragmententhargum (Targum Yerushalmi Latora)*. Ed. M. Ginsberger. Berlin: S. Calvary, 1899.

Ulfgard, H. *Feast and Future: Revelation 7:9-17 and the Feast of Tabernacles*. ConBNT 22. Stockholm: Almqvist & Wiksell, 1989.

Urbach, E. *The Sages: Their Concepts and Beliefs*. Trans. I. Abrahams. Jerusalem: Magnes, 1979.

Vaux, R. de. *Ancient Israel: Its Life and Institutions*. Trans. John McHugh. New York: McGraw-Hill, 1961.

Volz, P. *Das Neujahrsfest Jahwes*. Tübingen: Mohr, 1912.

VR = *Midrash Vayiqra Rabba*. Ed. M. Margoliot. 5 vols. Jerusalem, 1953-60.

Wacholder, B.Z. "The Letter from Judah Maccabee to Aristobolus: Is 2 Maccabees 1:10b-2:18 Authentic?" *HUCA* 49 (1978): 89-133.

Weinfeld, M. "Social and Cultic Institutions in the Priestly Source Against Their Ancient Near East Background." *Proceedings of the Eighth World Congress of Jewish Studies - 1981*. Panel Sessions: Bible Studies and Hebrew Language Section. (1983): 95-129.

Welch, A.C. *Post-exilic Judaism*. Edinburgh and London: William Blackwood and Sons, 1935.

Wellhausen, J. *Prolegomena to the History of Ancient Israel*. New York: Meridian Books, 1957 [1878].

Wensinck, A.J. *The Ideas of the Western Semites Concerning the Navel of the Earth.* Amsterdam: J. Müller, 1916.

_____. *Arabic New Year and the Feast of Tabernacles.* Amsterdam, 1925.

Wilamowitz-Möllendorff, U. *Der Glaube der Hellenen.* 2 vols. Stuttgart: Benno Schwabe, 1959 [1931].

Yadin, Y. *The Temple Scroll.* 3 vols. Jerusalem: Israel Exploration Society, 1983.

Zeitlin, S., ed. *The First Book of Maccabees.* Trans. S. Tedesche. New York: Dropsie College, 1950.

_____., ed. *The Second Book of Maccabees.* Trans. S. Tedesche. New York: Dropsie College, 1954.

Zohary, M. *The Plants of the Bible.* Cambridge: Cambridge University Press. 1982.

Index

Aaron, 53, 246-249

Abraham, 51-55, 72, 100-102, 116, 154, 182, 247, 249-250, 268-269, 274, 281, 306-307, 309

Akiba, 119, 122, 156, 158, 165-170, 173, 175-176, 178, 186, 200-201, 203, 222-223, 225, 236, 239-243, 251, 253, 256, 282, 305-307, 309

Albeck, H., 9, 37, 54, 73, 110, 115-116, 126, 132-133, 136, 171, 176, 183-184, 200, 209, 213, 240, 274

Allon, G., 73, 112, 121, 166, 183-184

altar, 2, 32-33, 44, 51-59, 62, 64, 79, 81-82, 89-93, 97, 99, 101-102, 107-118, 120-121, 125, 128, 130-131, 133, 137, 140, 142-143, 147, 152-154, 157, 159, 163, 175, 181-182, 185, 192, 237, 254, 299, 306-308, 319, 321

angel, 56, 114, 129, 246-248, 251-252, 266

'arava, see willow

art, 9, 57, 97, 99, 247, 308

atonement, 22, 35, 37, 134, 290-291, 295-300, 303, 305, 316, 324-325

band, 116, 200-203, 292, 302-305, 323

Bar-Kochba, 98, 188, 190, 193, 271

Baumgarten, J., 67-68, 105, 112-113, 131, 149-150, 152

beams, 65, 101, 205, 207-208, 210-211, 213, 218, 224, 263

blessings, 6, 16, 21, 23, 48, 124, 128, 166, 168-169, 171, 199, 203, 233, 300, 312, 323, 325

Boethusians, 66, 108, 110-111, 139

booth, see sukka

calendar, 13-14, 24, 51, 55, 62, 69, 110-111, 166

Christian Scriptures, New Testament, 8-9, 84-94, 97-98, 100-101, 254, 277, 288, 290

Chronicler, 19, 33-34, 40-42, 44-45, 47

circumambulation, 53-54, 89, 91-92, 111, 115-116

clouds of glory, cloud, 10, 28, 85, 92-93, 239-257, 259-260, 265-271, 280, 282, 288-289, 301-302, 307, 316, 323-324

coins, 97-98, 193, 197

commandments, 7, 34, 36, 40-41, 44-45, 56, 66, 72, 77, 98, 100, 156, 167, 179, 184, 193, 199, 213, 216, 218, 230-231, 233, 277-278, 283-284, 293, 295, 309, 311, 314, 322-323

commemoration, 4, 52, 59-60, 67, 77, 84, 142, 181, 270-271, 273, 309, 315, 320

covenant-renewal ceremony, 23-24, 27

dance, 21, 27, 54, 132, 134-135, 145-148, 150-151, 288, 313, 316, 319

Deep, tehom, 123-130, 138, 163

desert, 10, 18, 23, 28-30, 51, 67, 70-71, 76-77, 85, 90, 110, 128, 170, 193, 241-242, 244, 247-248, 250, 252-253, 255-260, 265-271, 273, 280, 282, 288-289, 301, 310, 315-316

diaspora, 2, 5, 71-73, 149, 183, 301, 314, 320

eating, 5, 26, 64-65, 107, 116, 134, 140, 184, 187, 194, 227-231, 234-235, 261, 270, 290

Eliezer, 69, 108, 112, 114, 128-130, 158, 170-178, 200-201, 208, 222, 225, 228-232, 235, 239-241, 243, 251, 275, 306, 310-311, 324

enthronement festival, 20, 22-25, 28, 50, 85, 164

Epstein, J.N., 9, 73, 106, 112, 140-143, 151, 171, 176, 183, 199, 207, 209, 222-223, 241, 274

equinox, 21, 69, 71-72, 139, 141, 178, 212

eschatology, 45-50, 85, 87, 90-94, 99-101, 124-125, 244, 253-257, 259-260, 265, 267-269, 271, 273, 275, 278-290, 297, 301-302, 310, 316-317, 324-325

etrog, citron, 17, 29, 73-75, 78, 82, 97-99, 101, 170, 188, 191-197, 199-202, 283, 287, 291, 295, 297, 303, 323

exodus, 18, 21, 23, 28, 52, 73, 76-77, 84-85, 90, 94, 181, 236, 239-242, 248, 251, 253-254, 258-260, 269-271, 273, 288, 310, 320, 323-324

Ezra, 9, 20, 29, 32-43, 45, 58, 77, 79, 99-100, 112, 188, 204-205, 254, 320

fertility, 1, 3, 16-17, 21, 23, 25, 28-29, 48, 50, 68, 98, 114, 117, 123-125, 127, 130, 159, 163-164, 182, 185, 236, 288, 304, 312, 319-321

Feuchtwang, D., 8, 122, 125, 127-128, 142

flute, 106, 132, 143-145, 147-149, 157

Fox, H., 8, 59, 107-108, 111-112, 132-133, 136, 140, 142, 145, 148-149, 152, 158, 198, 207-209, 216, 274, 278

garden of Eden, 94, 123-125, 282-283

gentile, 73, 267, 312, 324

Goodenough, E.R., 30, 46, 53, 69, 73, 97-99, 247

Halivni, David Weiss, 173-174, 176, 207, 210, 213, 216, 220-221

Hallel, 55, 86, 106, 111, 148, 150, 152, 155-159, 184-186,

197-199, 235, 237, 292, 296-297, 321, 323

Hanukka, 56-57, 60-62, 87-88, 141, 157

haqhel, 15, 23, 43-44, 79, 115, 278

harvest, ingathering, 2-4, 13-15, 17, 20-22, 25-28, 35-36, 39, 50, 70, 73, 76, 102, 125, 166, 212, 273, 290, 292, 313-314, 316-317

Hasmonean, 2, 4, 59-63, 81, 87

Hellenistic religion, 26, 53, 63, 72, 78, 82, 95-97, 113-114, 145-149, 151

high priest, 2, 22, 33, 57, 63-64, 80-81, 100, 115, 120, 126, 140, 178, 255, 319, 325

homily, 121, 172, 247, 274-275, 277-281, 283-284, 286-287, 293, 295-296, 309, 312, 314

Hosanna, 86-87, 159

huppa, 242, 253, 282-283, 316

intention, 56, 156, 196, 208, 212-214, 218, 221, 225, 227

Jesus, 28, 84-92, 94, 100, 105, 111, 139, 182, 254-255, 263, 277, 286, 322

Josephus, 2, 10, 31, 61, 63-64, 69, 72, 74-84, 100-101, 115, 119-122, 126, 137, 139, 154, 159-160, 182-185, 196-197, 205, 213, 217, 247, 270, 294, 296

joy, rejoicing, 4, 8, 14, 22, 27, 35-36, 51-54, 68, 71, 81, 103, 106, 112, 116-117, 131-132, 135, 138, 140-146, 148-149, 154, 156, 160, 182, 186, 188-189, 191, 226, 253, 260, 263,

270, 273, 277, 283-285, 288, 290-292, 296, 298, 300, 313, 316, 319, 323-324

Jubilees, 10, 31, 50-56, 82, 97, 100-102, 110-111, 116, 154, 156, 159-160, 168, 182, 184, 196, 205, 270, 296, 320

judgment, 22, 47, 49, 93, 164-169, 179, 253, 255, 276, 280-281, 284, 286, 289-292, 296-298, 300-301, 304, 313, 316, 321-322, 324

Knohl, I., 15-16, 18, 27, 65-66, 109, 163

Levenson, J., 22-23, 123-125, 127, 149, 164

Leviathan, 85, 127, 281-283, 289, 316

Lieberman, S., 17, 38, 53, 113, 118, 126, 133-134, 136, 155, 158, 166, 170, 211, 216, 219, 231, 277, 298, 306

love, 159, 179, 239, 250-252, 256-260, 265-267, 269, 271, 298-299

lulav, 10-11, 17, 25, 28-30, 38, 54-55, 63-64, 67-68, 73, 76-78, 82, 84, 86-87, 91, 96-102, 103, 106, 108-109, 115-117, 135-136, 141, 143, 152-160, 163, 169-171, 173-175, 178-179, 181-189, 191-192, 197-204, 210, 226, 230, 233-237, 273-275, 283-284, 286-293, 295-297, 300, 302-311, 314-317, 320-321, 323-325

Maimonides, 126, 135-136, 141, 143, 192-193, 199, 207, 209, 211

Men of Jerusalem, 154-156, 187, 197, 201, 223, 228, 230, 235, 304

messianism, 53, 84-85, 87-88, 90, 92, 97-98, 124, 253-256, 259, 273-274, 281-283, 288, 310, 316

Moses, 34-36, 58-60, 69-70, 72, 75-77, 85, 90, 151, 158, 244-249, 254-255, 257, 265, 267, 287, 303, 308

Mowinckel, S., 8, 20-23, 28, 35, 37-38, 40, 47-48, 117, 124, 131, 139, 148-149, 163-164, 292

Mt Zion, 1, 45, 48, 94, 123, 125-127, 244, 253, 282

myrtle, 38, 55, 67, 73-75, 101, 145, 158, 191-194, 196-197, 200, 202, 204, 224, 285, 297, 303, 305-306, 308, 323

myth, 1, 3, 6, 8, 20-23, 25, 28, 48, 50, 85, 94, 105, 123-125, 127-131, 139-140, 163-164, 179, 185, 260, 264, 269, 320-322

nations, 45-50, 63, 92, 169, 195, 248, 264, 267, 276-280, 284, 286, 298-300, 312, 316, 324

Nehemiah, 10, 33-34, 36-38, 40-43, 45, 57-60, 99-100, 188, 249

Neusner, J., 7, 9, 46, 103-105, 136-137, 184, 188-190, 199, 203, 207, 213, 228, 274

Patai, R., 8, 28, 30, 47, 114, 116-117, 122, 124, 127-130, 142-143

Pesaḥ, Passover, 2, 6, 27-28, 41-42, 46, 62, 64, 69, 71, 76-77, 84, 86-88, 110-111, 139, 144, 157, 165-166, 172-173, 187, 236, 289, 313, 325

Pharisees, 4, 8, 51, 54, 66, 104-105, 109, 121, 136, 139-140, 184-185, 187, 199, 207

Philo, 5, 10, 31, 69-73, 76, 95-96, 99-101, 139, 149-152, 159, 183-184, 205, 217, 247, 270

pilgrimage, 1-2, 4-5, 8, 14-15, 19-20, 22, 25, 27-28, 30, 42, 44, 46-50, 56, 64, 79, 83-84, 87, 91-93, 100, 130, 169-170, 184, 278, 284, 292, 298, 319

Plutarch, 94-97, 100-101, 116, 145, 151, 159, 210, 285

praise, 53, 55, 61, 66-67, 71-72, 113-114, 138, 156, 192, 285, 287-289, 293-294, 296-297, 324

prayer, 3, 9, 25, 30, 40, 68, 72, 81, 111, 114, 117, 130-131, 134, 139, 146-147, 149-151, 155, 157-159, 171-172, 174, 178-179, 185, 270, 283, 287, 297, 312, 321, 325

priest, 2, 22, 33, 40, 56-57, 63-64, 80-81, 94, 100, 110, 115, 118-121, 126, 135, 140, 143-144, 170, 178, 181, 255, 319-320, 325

procession, 21-22, 24-25, 50, 53-55, 66, 87, 92, 95-97, 101-102, 103, 106, 108-109, 111-112, 115-116, 120-121, 138, 142-149, 151-152, 157, 159, 181, 236, 285

protection, 25, 70, 75-77, 93, 181, 206, 217, 225, 239, 247, 249-250, 252-253, 256, 259-260, 263-271, 281-282, 301-302, 316

Psalms, 8, 20-23, 25, 28, 47-48, 55, 71, 86, 106, 111-112, 116, 131-132, 138-139, 148-152, 156-

Index

157, 159, 163-164, 166, 184-185, 235, 257, 265, 287, 292

Qaraites, 36, 38, 77, 205, 233

Qumran, 5, 10, 51, 64-69, 101-102, 104-105, 109-110, 113, 130, 149, 152, 159, 185, 199

rain, 3, 10, 16, 23, 28, 30, 46-49, 68, 70, 73-74, 76, 91, 93, 97, 102, 114, 117, 119, 121-124, 128-131, 138, 140, 158, 160-161, 163-179, 182, 231-232, 234, 265, 267, 277, 279, 282, 290, 297-298, 300, 302, 304, 306, 311-317, 321-322, 324

religious experience, 7, 11, 32, 214, 225, 236-237, 239, 269, 275, 308

Rosh Hashana, 21-22, 79, 165-168, 179, 284, 286-287, 290-297, 300, 305, 316, 322

Sabbath, 4, 7, 15, 55, 66, 68-69, 83-84, 87-88, 106-111, 115, 118, 120-121, 132, 144, 152-155, 187, 201-203, 228, 230

sacrifices, 1-3, 16, 18-19, 21, 24-25, 33-34, 38, 43-44, 50-51, 56-59, 64, 66-67, 72-73, 75, 78-79, 81-82, 99-101, 109, 116, 120, 146-147, 150, 175, 178, 181, 185, 188-189, 236, 284, 289, 294, 298-300, 319-321

Sadducees, 55, 104, 110, 121, 139

Safrai, S., 8, 109, 115, 132, 136, 183-184

Samaritan, 17, 33, 67, 114, 191, 217, 220, 286

shade, 70, 85, 93, 209-211, 214-216, 224-225, 235, 239, 252-253, 261-271, 279-282, 301-302, 316, 323

Shavuot, 2, 4, 27, 62, 84, 157, 165-166, 289, 313-316

shekhina, 246-247, 250, 256, 267-268, 284

Shmini 'aṣeret, 88-89, 91, 115, 121, 124, 172, 176, 179, 298, 312-313, 315, 321

Siloam, 89, 118-121, 142-145, 147, 152

simḥat beit hasho'eva, 59, 68, 103, 113, 131-132, 135-152, 157, 159-160, 179, 181, 186, 236, 290, 317

skhakh, 65, 203-225, 228, 230-231, 233, 235-237, 261-263, 268-269, 302, 323

sleeping, 27, 65, 134, 144, 210-211, 216, 227-229, 231-232, 234-235, 261, 263, 270, 290

Solomon, 7, 18-20, 33, 42-46, 53, 56, 58-60, 62, 78, 83, 119, 127, 130-131, 192, 245, 254, 320

sukka, 10, 14-15, 17, 24-29, 34-39, 42-44, 52-55, 65-66, 68-73, 75-77, 79, 84-85, 92, 95-97, 99-102, 172, 181-183, 188-189, 191, 203-237, 239-243, 250-256, 260-271, 273, 275-283, 286, 288-290, 293, 300-302, 310-313, 315-317, 320-321, 323-325

symbol, 6, 10, 18, 26, 30, 49, 85-87, 94, 98-99, 116-117, 122, 181-182, 185, 189, 206, 236, 240-241, 253, 255-256, 259-261, 263-264, 266-270, 273, 275, 280-281, 283, 285-289, 292, 296-297, 301-305, 307-311, 314, 316-317, 322-325 synagogue, 5, 40, 53, 99, 134, 136, 149, 153, 155, 158, 181, 188, 201, 235, 237, 247, 278, 307, 325

Talmon, S., 14, 20, 51, 105, 110, 257

targum, 16, 46, 58, 119-120, 138, 175, 219, 240, 246-249, 252-253, 255, 260, 267, 283-284, 301, 316

temple, 1-6, 8-10, 13-25, 29-30, 31-34, 36, 38-39, 41, 43-66, 68, 73, 75, 77-78, 80-81, 83-102, 103-106, 109-111, 113-114, 116-128, 130-146, 148-154, 156-160, 163-164, 168, 171-172, 175-179, 181-191, 193-194, 196-197, 199, 201, 203, 205-206, 208, 217-218, 224-225, 235-236, 245, 251, 254, 256, 270-271, 273, 278, 288-290, 297-299, 307, 312, 315-317, 319-325

thyrsos, 63, 78, 82, 96, 116

Tolkowsky, S., 17, 75, 194-196

transfiguration, 84-85, 254

trees, 16-17, 29-30, 35, 38, 52, 54-55, 63, 66-67, 70, 73-74, 78, 82, 86, 90, 97-98, 101, 107, 124, 131, 159, 165-166, 170, 192-195, 203-204, 210-211, 215, 222-223, 250, 261-262, 268-269, 281, 291-292, 303, 305-306, 313

trumpet, 16, 97, 107-108, 116-118, 120, 133, 142-144

vine, 32, 63, 95-98, 100, 125, 210, 212, 223, 262

walls, 204-206, 208, 214-215, 217, 220, 222-225, 235-236, 262, 281

water libation, 8, 55, 66, 89, 94, 97-98, 106, 114, 117, 119-123, 128, 130, 139, 142, 147, 167, 169-170, 175, 177-178, 186, 312

willow, 30, 54-55, 66, 73-75, 81, 96, 103, 106-108, 110-112, 114-117, 120-121, 130-131, 148, 153-154, 157, 159, 181, 185-186, 191-194, 196, 200, 202, 236, 289-290, 297, 303, 305-308, 317, 323

willow procession, 54, 96, 103, 106, 111, 115-116, 157, 181, 236

wine, 2, 14-15, 115, 118, 120, 128, 130-131, 145, 152, 175, 232, 282

World to Come, 85, 253-254, 256, 268, 279-284, 286-289, 301-302, 316, 325

Yom Kippur, 2, 21-22, 35, 38, 79, 95, 110, 126, 165-168, 287, 290-297, 300, 305, 313, 316, 322, 325

Zechariah, 9, 31, 45-49, 58, 90, 121, 124, 163, 168, 178, 278, 289

Source Index

Bible

Genesis
1..............164
2:6..........128, 129 n.101
3:21..........248 n.41
4:8..........291
7:11..........124
8:2..........124
9:12-17....124 n.76
15:1..........248
18:4..........250
19:8..........263 n.109, 264 n.110
24:1..........306
26:19........90 n.149
28............56 n.58
28:18........126 n.85
29:2-3......130 n.107
33:17........55, 220 n.145
40:20........141 n.138
49:25........124 n.79, 128 n.99
50:1..........127 n.94, 267 n.124

Exodus
12:8..........187
12:11........84 n.131
12:14........84 n.131
12:37........239 n.1, 250, 251, 253
12:42........255 n.75
13:20........239 n.1, 251 n.54, 253 n.61, 259 n.88
13:21........246 n.30, 251 n.54
13:21-22...242 n.13, 244 n.21
13:22........246 n.30
14:19........242 n.13, 244 n.21, 246 n.30, 251, 252 n.59, 259 n.90, 267 n.123
14:19-20...246 n.29, 247
14:19-21...112 n.28
14:24........244 n.21
15:1..........158
15:1-17....158 n.200
15:2..........158
15:3..........158
15:13........268 n.125
15:18........255 n.75
16:1-10....248 n.43
16:10........244 n.22, 245 n.26, 246 n.29
16:16........241 n.8
16:23........84 n.131
17:8..........249 n. 49
18:27........248 n.41
19:4..........258, 266 n.117
19:16........244 n.20
20:20........113 n.35
23:16........13, 313
23:5..........84 n.131
24:15-16...245
25:20........265 n.112
25:22........268 n.126
28:30........126 n.87
29:40........120 n.64
33:8..........241 n.8
33:9-10....244 n.21-2
33:10........241 n.8
34:5..........245 n.23, 246 n.31
34:22........13, 69, 139 n.133
37:1..........268 n.126
37:9..........265 n.112
40:34........245 n.25
40:34-38...245 n.26
40:38........245 n.29, 246 n.30

Leviticus
14:5..........90 n.149
14:42........197 n.55
14:50........90 n.149
14:51........90 n.149
14:52........90 n.149
15:13........90 n.149
16:2..........245 n.23
23............42 n.24
23:3..........84 n.131

23:9-14....110 n.22, n.23
23:15.......110 n.22, n.23
23:33-44...15, 75-76
23:34.......66 n.89, 84, 219 n.140
23:35.......172 n.37
23:36.......16 n.8
23:39-43...36-39
23:38.......110 n.22
23:40.......25, 29, 52-55, 63, 67, 73, 74, 78, 82, 101, 114, 115 n.42, 153 n.184, 154, 155, 182, 183 n.6, 191-192, 195-198, 202, 203, 204, 205, 287, 293, 303, 304, 305, 308, 309, 310, 311, 312, 313
23:41.......84 n.131
23:42.......29, 203-204, 217, 219, 225-6, 233
23:42-43...256 n.78, 301 n.84
23:43.......28 n.51, 71, 77, 239-42, 247, 248, 251 n.55, 270, 301 n.82
26:18.......53 n.47

Numbers
9:11.........187
9:15-16....245 n.26, 246 n. 30
9:15-23....244 n.22
10:33.......250
10:34.......245 n.29, 246 n.30, 267 n.124
10:35.......246 n.30
11:10.......241 n.8
11:25 .....244 n.22, 245 n.23, 246 n.29-31
12:5.........245 n.29, 246 n.29, n.31
12:5-6......244 n.22
12:8-10....246 n.30
12:10.......245 n.29, 247
12:25.......244 n.21
14:1-10....248 n.43
14:4.........245 n.29, 267, 268 n.125
14:9.........264 n.110
14:10.......248 n.43
14:14.......244, 245 n.23
16:10.......246 n.30
16:19.......248 n.43
16:27.......241 n.8
17:7.........244 n.22, 245 n.26, 246 n.29
21:1.........246 n.30, 249
21:6.........128 n.99
22:28.......249 n. 46
24:5.........241 n.8
28:7.........120 n.64
29:2.........16 n.8

29:8.........16 n.8
29:12-25...64
29:12-28...175
29:12-34...15-18, 33, 34 n.7, 72, 298 n.71
29:12-40...51
29:31.......175 n.46, n.47
29:35.......175 n.46, 312
29:36.......16 n.8
33:5.........251 n.54, 253 n.61

Deuteronomy
1:27.........241 n.8
1:31.........252, 266 n.117
1:33.........244 n.22
5:19.........244 n.20
5:27 ....241 n.8
8:4 ....248 n.41
8:7 ....124 n.79
8:15.........260
10:6.........246 n.31
11:13-17...179 n.62
16:13.......26 n.41, 66, 212, 219, 231
16:13-15...14-15, 39
16:14.......143 n.148, 313
16:15.......52 , 313
17:15.......115 n.45
23:16.......267 n.121
25:18.......249
27:7.........140 n.136
31 ....42 n.24
31:10.......43 n.28, 79
31:10-13...15, 23, 43 n.30, 115 n.45

Source Index

31:12.......43
31:15.......244 n.21-2, 246 n.29
32:10.......128 n.99, 248 n.42, 260
32:10-11...257-8
32:11.......267 n.122
33:3.........246 n.31
33:12.......265 n.112, 266
33:13.......124
33:26.......244 n.18

Joshua
18:26.......107 n.12
24............42

Judges
5:4...........243 n.17, 244 n.20
9:15.........262 n.103, 264 n.110
9:27.........14, 95 n.174
9:36 ....262 n.103
21............17
21:19.......95 n.174
21:19-21...14-15

1 Samuel
1:3...........14 n.4
1:14.........14 n.4
10:5.........149 n.168
12:17-18...178

2 Samuel
11:11.......24 n.28
14:4.........87 n.138
22:12.......242, 243 n.17

1 Kings
1:33.........119 n.58
1:40.........149 n.168
5:10-13 35

8.............18, 19 n.16, 43, 45 n.32, 53, 59 n.66, 78 n.121
8:2...........78 n.120
8:10.........245
8:11.........245
8:12.........242 n.12, 243 n.17
8:12-13 ....245 n.25
8:62-66 19
8:65.........19 n.15, 130 n.107
12:25-33...78 n.122
12:26-31...19
12:27.......78
12:32.......19, 79
18............178

2 Kings
2:11.........244 n.21
6:17.........244 n.21
10:19-20...16 n.8
19:19.......87 n.138
20:20.......119
23:22.......41
24:8-16 ....32 n.1
25:12.......32 n.1

Isaiah
1:8...........25 n.32, 220 n.145
1:13.........16 n.8
4:5...........92
4:5-6........93, 242 , 244, 253, 256 n.77, 268-9 n.127, 282
4:6...........25 n.32, 94 n.165, 265, 279-80, 302 n.84
4:14.........89 n. 146

5:7...........302
5:12.........149 n.168
6:35.........89 n.146
8:6...........119 n.58
11:15.......123 n.75
12............148 n.168
12:3.........141 n.141
16:3-4......263 n.109
18:11.......89 n.146
19:11.......243 n.17, 244 n.18
25:4.........264
25:5.........263 n.104, 265
28:1-5......53
28:16.......126 n.86
30:2-3......264
30:29.......148 n.168
31:5.........265 n.112
32:2.........262 n.103, 264 n.110
32:18.......49 n.41
33:20-24...123 n.74
34:4.........279
35............125
35:10.......253, 260
37:20.......87 n.138
40:3-5......259 n.87
40:4.........259
40:5.........259
40:15.......197 n.55
40:22.......113 n.35
41:13.......258 n.83
41:17-19...170
41:17-20...125 n.82
42:16.......259 n.87
43:2-3......258
43:4-6......258 n.84
43:19.......259 n.87
45:2.........259 n.87
45:5.........258 n.83
45:8.........253 n.61
48:21.......125 n.82

49:2.........265 n.112	17:23........262 n.103	*Nahum*
49:10.......125 n.82, 258	28:11-19...282 n.23	1:3..........244 n.18
49:11.......259 n.87	28:13-14...94 n.166	1:4..........123 n.75
49:13.......258	30:3.........253 n.63	*Habakkuk*
49:14-18...258 n.84	31:1-9......124 n.79	3:8..........244 n.18
51:3.........125 n.82	31:3-12....262 n.103	3:15.........244 n.18
51:9-10....123 n.75	34:12........243 n.17	*Zephaniah*
51:16.......264 n.111, 267 n.122	36:35........125	1:15.........243 n.17, 253 n.63
52:12.......259	45:25........18	
54:3.........89 n.146	47............89-90	*Haggai*
54:5-10....258 n.84	47:1-12....124 n.80, 125, 131	2:1-5........32 n.4
54:11-17...258 n.83	47:8-11....94 n.166	*Zechariah*
55:1.........89 n.146	*Hosea*	1:8..........306
55:10-13...170 n.28	2:16-23....258	9-14.........45
55:12.......288	4:13.........262 n.103	9:7..........255
60:8.........254 n.66	11:1.........252, 258	9:9..........87 n.140
60:19.......256	11:3.........252	13:1.........124 n.80
Jeremiah	13:5.........258	14............9, 20, 31, 45-50, 74,
2:2-3........258	14:8.........262 n.103, 267	89, 92, 93, 100, 102,
2:13.........90 n.149	14:7-8......263 n. 108	117, 121, 124, 159,
17:13........90 n.149	*Joel*	164, 165, 169, 179,
17:14........87 n.138	1:14.........16 n.8	278, 288, 289, 290
31............258	2:2..........243 n.17, 253 n.63	n.45, 298
31:7-14....125 n.82	2:15.........16 n.8	14:8..........90
48:45.......263 n.109, 264 n.110	2:16.........282 n.21	14:8-9......94 n.166
51:26.......126 n.85	2:21-27....16 n.8	14:8-21....124 n.80
Ezekiel	*Amos*	14:16-19...46
1:4..........243 n.17, 245 n.26	9:6..........68 n.97, 303	*Malachi*
1:28.........245 n.26	9:11.........255	3:19.........279, 280
8:16.........133 n.118	*Jonah*	*Psalms*
9:3..........244 n.19	4:5..........25	16:8.........264 n.111
10:3-4......245 n.26	4:5-6........262 n.103	16:11.......284, 286 n.36
10:4.........244 n.19	4:5-9........263	
10:18-19...244 n.19	4:6-7........210 n. 107	
11:22.......244 n.19	*Micah*	
16:14.......94 n.166	4:10.........300	
17:5.........191 n.33		
17:22-4....264 n.110		

Source Index

17:8.........263 n.104, 265 n.112, n.113
18:3.........248
18:12.......242, 243 n.17, 253 n.62
18:31.......248
19:6.........282 n.21
24:1.........291
27:5.........280
29 ....123 n.75
33:7.........123 n.75
33:15.......165
35:10.......297
36:8.........263 n.104, 265, 266 n.119
36:8-10 ....94 n.166, 123 n.74
36:133 .....123 n.74
42:8.........128, 129
46:2-4......124 n.76
46:4.........89 n.146
50:2.........94 n.166
57:2.........263 n.104, 265 n.112
57:9.........149 n.168
63:8.........263 n.104
68:5.........244 n.18, 306
68:35.......244 n.18
74:13-15...123 n.75
74:15.......124 n.77
76:3.........316 n.134
77:17-20...123 n.75
78:14.......244 n.21
78:15-6 ....89 n.146
80:11.......262 n.103
86:2.........87 n.138
89:10-11...123 n.75
91:1-4......264 n.111
91:1-12 264-5

91:4.........301
92:3.........149 n.168
92:13.......305, 307 n.109
93 ....123 n.75
96:12.......291
96:13.......291, 292
97:2.........243 n.17
99:7.........244 n.21, 246 n.29-30
102:18 287
102:19 287
104:1.......305
104:3.......243 n.17, 244
104:5-9 ....123 n.75
104:5-13...125 n.81
105:39 .....242 n.12, 243 n.17, 247 n.39, 248 n.40, 252, 265, 267, 268 n.127
105:40-41 89 n.146
106:9.......123 n.75
107:33-38 125 n.82
109:4.......298 , 299, 300
109:31 .....264 n.111
113-118....157
113:1.......159
114:1-8 ....123 n.75
114:4.......288
118..........116, 151 n.176, 156, 159
118:1.......292
118:25 .....86, 87 n.138, 91, 107 n.14,111, 297, 307
118:27 .....54, 55, 111

120-134....127, 138
121:5.......266
121:5-7 264
128:5-6 ....135, 151 n.176
134:1.......149 n.168, 151
134:2.......151 n.176
134:1-2 135
135-46 .....138 n.132
135:7.......129
136..........151 n.176
140:8.......265 n.112, 266 n.116

Proverbs
5:15.........89 n.146
9:4 ....89 n.146
18:4.........89 n.146
30:18.......192 n.35
30:24.......192 n.35

Job
26:8.........129 n.101
26:8-9......242 n.12
26:9.........246 n.30
26:12-13...124 n.75
27:18.......25 n.32
36:29.......242 n.12, 253 n.62
38:1.........244 n.20
38:8-9......129 n.101
38:8-11 ....124 n.75
40:22.......262 n.103
40:31.......281

Song of Songs
1:4 ....247 n.34
2:3 ....263 n.108, 267
2:6 ....252-3, 256
2:15.........249 n.49
2:17.........252 n.60, 267

3:1-2........247 n.33
4:15..........90 n.149
7:3 ....58 n.64

Lamentations
3:44..........242 n.12,
             253 n.62

Qohelet
2:5 ....120 n.59,
             131 n.110
12:5..........283 n.24

Esther
3:8 ....284 n.31
9:27-32 ....60 n.68

Daniel
7:13..........254, 255

Ezra
2:1-70......32 n.5
3..............20, 33-34, 43
3:1-6........41 n.21, 42-
             43, 79 n.123
3:2-4........58
3:12..........32 n.4
6:13-18 33
6:19-22 41
10 ....40 n.21

Nehemiah
2:1 ....34 n.9
7:72..........42, 43 n.25
8..............20, 34-36, 37
             n.16, 38
             n.19, 39-44,
             79, 100, 188,
             191, 192,
             194, 203,
             204, 205,
             216, 217,
             224, 233,
             251 n.56
8:1 ....120 n.61
8:9 ....38 n.18

8:12..........40 n.21
8:13-18 41
8:16..........65 n.88, 66
             n.89
8:18..........38 n.18
9:12..........244 n.21
9:18-20 252
9:19..........244 n.21
13:6-7......41 n.22
13:11........33

1 Chronicles
2:46..........107 n.12
2:55..........248 n.41
3:24..........255
16:33........291
16:34........292

2 Chronicles
5:2-7:10 ...18, 41, 45
             n.32, 47 n.37
5:3 ....19 n.15
5:13-6:2 ...245 n.25,
             n.27
7:8-10......19 n.15
7:9 ....19 n.17, 45
             n.32, 59 n.66
8:36-37 ....107 n.12
9:42-43 ....107 n.12
30 41
30:26........42
32:30........119
35:1-19 41
35:18........42

Qumran Scrolls

1QM
2:2-4........185 n.14
4Q266 113
4Q409 66-67
4Q500 .....131 n.109
4Q502 .....67-68, 149
             n.172

4QFlor....68 n.97

CD
3:14-15 ....51 n.44
7:10..........68 n.97
11:8..........68 n.97
11:17........110 n.22

Mishmerot A 68n.97

Mishmerot B 68n.97

Temple Scroll
(11QTemple)
Col.
11:13........64 n.82
17 ....64 n.84
17:1..........53 n.51
27:10-29:13 64
42:3-17 ....64 n.84, 65
42:10-17...64 n.82, 217
             n.135, 218
             n.137, 251
             n.56
44:6-10 65
44:6-16 ....64 n.82, n.84

Apocrypha and Pseudepigrapha

1 Baruch
5:5-7........265 n.112
5:6-8........266

Ben Sira
24:4..........242 n.12
24:19-21...89 n.146
24:30-33...89 n. 146
34:17........264 n.111
35:16........242 n.12
43:26........265
50:7..........245 n.27
51:23-4 ....89 n.146

1 Enoch
14:8..........254 n.68

Source Index

17 .... 125 n.83
18 .... 125 n.83
24-26 .... 125 n.83
26:1-6 .... 126 n.85

2 Enoch
28 .... 125 n.83, 129 n.102

1 Esdras
5:47-49 ..... 79 n.123
9 .... 40 n.21
9:37 .... 43 n.25

4 Esdras
13:1-4 254

Jubilees
6:32-35 ..... 51 n.44
8:12 .... 125 n.83
8:19 .... 125 n.83, 126 n.85
12:16-18 ... 168 n.20
16 .... 51-54, 116 n.46
16:30 .... 296 n.64
29 .... 116 n.46
31 .... 116 n.46
32 .... 51, 55, 56, 96
50 55

Judith
15:12 .... 63 n.77, 135 n.124, 296 n.62
15:12-13 ... 285 n.34, 294 n.57
15:13 .... 53 n.49

1 Maccabees
4:52-55 ..... 62 n.73
4:56 .... 61 n.72
10:21 .... 63-4, 80 n.123, 120 n.63
13:51 .... 61, 98, 154 n.188, 285 n.34, 296

2 Maccabees
1:18 .... 61 n.72
1:1-2:18 ... 57-60
2:7-8 254
10:5-8 ...... 61, 98, 182
10:6 .... 59 n.67, 87 n.137
10:7 .... 96, 285 n.34
10:7-8 116
10:8 .... 154 n.188

Psalms of Solomon
11:5-6 .... 265 n.112, 266

Testament of Naphtali
5:4 .... 285 n.34

Tobit
1:6-7 56

Wisdom of Solomon
18:3 .... 268 n.125
19:6-7 266

Christian Scriptures

Matthew
17:1-8 .... 84 n.133, 254 n.69
21:8 .... 86 n.137
21:33 .... 25 n.32
24:30 .... 255 n.70
25:31 .... 255 n.70
26:2 .... 86 n.134
26:64 .... 255 n.70

Mark
9:2-8 .... 84 n.133, 254 n.69
11:8 .... 86 n.137
11:11 .... 182 n.2
13:26 .... 255 n.70
14:1 .... 86 n.134
14:62 .... 255 n.70

Luke
9:28-36 .... 254 n.69
19:36 .... 86 n.137
21:27 .... 255 n.70
22:1-2 .... 86 n.134

John
2:1-11 .... 90 n.151
3:5-6 .... 90 n.151
4:10-14 .... 90 n.151
5:1-47 .... 88 n.141
6:1-71 .... 88 n.141
6:35 .... 90 n.141
7 .... 9 n.10, 74, 84, 102, 117, 121, 159
7:1-8:59 ... 87-89
7:37 111
7:37-38 94
7:37-40 .... 90 n.151
10:22-39 ... 88 n.141
12 86
12:13 .... 154 n.189, 182 n.2, 296
12:16 .... 87 n.140
19:34 .... 90 n.151

Acts
1:9 .... 255 n.70
2-6 84

1 Corinthians
10:1 .... 250 n.53

1 Thessalonians
3:13 .... 255 n.70
4:16-17 .... 255 n.70

Revelation
1:7 .... 255 n.71
4:2-11 .... 93 n.162, n.163

5:8-14......93 n.162
6:9..........93 n.163
7..............9 n.10
7:9..........154 n.189
7:9-17......91-94
8:3-6........93 n.163
9:13.........93 n.163
10:1.........247 n.33
11:1-3......93 n.163
11:15-19...93 n.162
12:10.......93 n.162
14:1-5......93 n.162, n.163
14:14-16...255 n.71
15:2-4......93 n.162
15:5-8......93 n.163
19:1-8......93 n.162
20:4-6......93 n.162
21:1-22:5..94 n.166
22:1-5......125 n.81
24...........9 n.10

Josephus

Antiquitates Judaicae
3:203.......247 n.33
3:246.......154 n.188
3:248.......76 n.115
3:244.......69 n.97, 72 n.102
3:244-47...75-6, 82, 182 n.1, 196, 217 n.134
4:209.......79 n.123
4:209-11...115 n.45
4:260-63...77 n.117
4:265.......77 n.117
4:266.......77 n.117
4:269.......77 n.117
4:275.......77 n.117
4:288.......77 n.117
8:100.......83, 160
11:75-78...79 n.123

11:154-58 79 n.123
13...........80
13:303-8...270 n.130
13:304.....76
13:372.....82, 96 n.177, 120 n.63, 121, 154 n.188, 182 n.1, 196
14:285-86 83 n.129
15:50.......81, 120 n.63
15:194-201 294 n.56
17:214.....184 n.9
17:254.....184 n.9
18:93-95...64 n.81
20:106.....184 n.9

Bellum Judaicum
1:73.........76 n.116, 80 n.124
1:88.........82 n.12
1:229-230 83 n.129
1:253.......184 n.9
1:394-95...294 n.56
1:73.........76
2:10.........2 n.1
2:128.......139 n.133
2:515.......83
2:517.......83 n.130
3:52.........126 n.86
5:140.......120 n.59
5:410.......119 n.59
6:301.......76
6:423-24...2 n.1
16:301.....270 n.130

Philo

The Contemplative Life
1..............152 n.181
Flaccus
116-24.....71-2, 96 n.176, 149 n.172

The Life of Moses
1:166.......247 n.33
1:180.......151
2:41.........72 n.104
2:254.......247 n.33
2:256.......151 n.178

On Flight and Finding
186..........72 n.103

On the Migration of Abraham
202..........72 n.103

Special Laws
1:69.........184 n.9
1:189-90...72
2:204-214 69-70, 270 n.130-1
2:205-208 217 n.134
2:206-207 76 n.114
2:155.......71

Pseudo-Philo

13:7.........73, 241 n.7
15:5.........250 n.53

Rabbinic Literature

Mishnah

Berakhot
5:2..........171 n.30
5:5..........132 n.114
Pe'a
8:1..........14 n.2
Kilayim
5:3..........220 n.145
Ma'aserot
3:7..........217 n.136

Source Index

Bikkurim
1:3 .... 166 n.11
3:2 .... 184 n.11
3:3 .... 53 n.49
3:3-4 .... 144 n.148

Shabbat
1:1 .... 197 n.55
7:4 .... 211 n.112
12:1 .... 136 n.128
24:2 .... 211 n.112

'Eruvin
3:1-8 .... 228 n.174
6:6-7 .... 228 n.174

Pesahim
1:5 .... 152 n.183
5:7 .... 157 n.193

Sheqalim
5:1 .... 132 n.113, 133 n.116
6:3 .... 120 n.61
8:4 .... 152 n.183

Yoma
1:1-8 .... 140 n.137
1:8 .... 133 n.116
2:5 .... 120 n.60
5:2 .... 126 n.84, n.86

Sukka
1:1 .... 215 n.127, 218, 222, 223 n.158, 261 n.93, 262
1:2 .... 210, 215 n.130-1, 261 n.96, n.98, 263 n.105
1:3 .... 96, 208, 211, 216 n.132, 228, 261 n.97
1:4 .... 205 n.85, 208 n.102, 210, 212 n.119, 215, 263 n.105
1:4-5 .... 223, 262 n.101
1:5 210
1:6 210
1:6-7 .... 263 n.106
1:7 .... 206-207, 213
1:8 .... 209, 212
1:9 .... 205 n.85, 223
1:10 .... 205 n.85, 215 n. 129
1:11 .... 205 n.85, 208, 209 n.102, 222
2:1 .... 216 n.133, 261 n.97
2:2 .... 208 n.98, 212 n.116, 215 n.127, 222 n. 153
2:3 .... 222 n. 154, 223
2:4 .... 228, 231
2:5 228
2:6 .... 89 n.145, 228 n. 176
2:7 .... 221, 222
2:8 206
2:9 .... 171 n.31, 226, 227, 231, 313
3:1 .... 197, 199 n.59, 201 n.67, 202
3:1-3 .... 200, 202
3:4 200
3:5 .... 198 n.57, 199, 201 n.67
3:5-6 202
3:6 .... 200, 201 n.67
3:7 .... 200, 314-15
3:8 .... 201 n.68
3:9 .... 55 n.56, 86 n.135, n.136, 91, 156, 197, 198 n.57
3:10 .... 159 n.203
3:12 .... 182-83, 198 n.57
3:13 .... 153, 197 n.57, 199, 201
3:14 .... 155 n.191, 202
3:15 .... 197, 198 n.59, 202
4:1 .... 106-7, 117, 142 n.144, 143, 144 n.149, 152
4:2 .... 54, 106 n.11, 201, 152, 153
4:3 106-9
4:4 .... 152, 153, 187 n.23, 198 n.57, 199, 201
4:5 .... 53 n.47, 54 n.53, 97 n.181, 108, 111-112, 116, 120
4:5-7 106-7
4:6 .... 109, 114-5, 153

4:7 11
4:8 ....89 n.145
4:9 ....89 n.144, 97,
119, 120,
121, 143
4:9-10 ......117-18, 143
n.147
4:10 153
5:1-4 132
5:1 ....135 n.122,
136 n.128,
141 n.138,
143
5:2 ....136 n.128,
144 n.148
5:3 ....135, 136
5:4 ....135, 144
n.148
5:5 ....97 n.181,
133, 138
n.133, 143,
151 n.180
5:6 ....143, 144
n.148

Besa
1:5 ....154 n.187
4:2 ....217 n.136

Rosh Hashana
1:2 ....165-167, 172
1:1-4 ....178 n.59
2:8-9 ....110 n.22
4:3 ....183 n. 5
4:4 ....198 n.57

Ta'anit
1:1 ....89 n.145,
171, 176,
177 n.55
1:1-3 ....177 n.56

1:2 ....89 n.145,
176 n.49,
n.50, 177
n.55
1:3 ....176, 177
n.55
2:2-3 ....184 n.11
2:5 ....117 n.52
2:7 184
3:1 ....117 n.52
3:3 ....117 n.52
4:2-3 ....178 n.59,
184
4:4 ....157 n.193,
185 n.12
4:8 ....135 n.124

Megila
3:6 ....184 n.11

Nedarim
2:2 ....198 n.57

Nazir
7:3 ....205 n.85

Ketubot
4:12 ....154 n.190

Sota
7:8 ....115 n.45
9:14 ....53 n.50
9:15 ....132 n.113

Gittin
4:2-7 ....137 n.128
4:9 ....137 n.128
5:5 ....137 n.128
9:4 ....137 n.128

Bava Mesia
1:1 ....197 n.55
3:12 ....213 n.120
8:6 ....177 n.54
10:5 ....136 n.128

Sanhedrin
4:5 ....166 n.13
7:5 113

Shevu'ot
3:8 ....198 n.57

'Eduyyot
1:13 ....137 n.128
7:9 ....137 n.128

'Avodah Zara
3:8 ....262 n.99

'Avot
3:15 ....166 n.13
3:16 ....136 n.128
5:5 140

Zevahim
6:2 ....120 n.64

Menahot
3:6 ....202 n.72,
302 n.87
5:6 314-15
10:3 ....110 n.23,
139 n.134

Hullin
12:5 ....277 n.6

'Arakhin
2:3 ....149 n.168,
157
2:6 ....132 n.115

Tamid
1:2 ....133 n.116
2:2 ....140 n.135
3:8 ....140, 149
7:4 ....132 n.115

Midot
2:5 ....132 n.115,
136 n.128
2:6 ....120 n.61
3:2 118

Source Index

4:6 .... 137 n.131

Kelim
1:8 .... 109 n.19
1:9 .... 109 n.19
18:5 .... 209 n.106

'Ahilot
8:2 .... 205 n.85, 262 n.99
7:3 .... 213 n.120

Para
3:2 .... 120 n.59

Nida
7:5 .... 205 n.85

Makhshirin
1:6 .... 154 n.190

Tosefta

Berakhot
3:19 .... 197, 198 n.59
6:9-10 233
6:10 198

Demai
1:21 .... 211 n.112

Kilayim
1:6 .... 205 n.85

Shevi'it
2:13 .... 211 n.112

Ma'aserot
2:20 .... 211 n.112
2:21 .... 206 n.88, 221 n.147

Shabbat
2:4 .... 209 n.102, n.105

'Eruvin
3:6 .... 153 n.185

Pesahim
10:7 .... 158 n.201

Sheqalim
2:14 .... 133 n.116, 154

Yoma
1:8 .... 140 n.137
1:14 .... 135 n.123
2:14 .... 126 n.86

Sukka
1:1 .... 222 n.150
1:2 .... 215 n.127, 261 n.94, 262 n.100
1:3 222
1:4 .... 211, 219
1:4-6 .... 210, 262 n.101
1:5-6 .... 209 n. 102, n.105
1:6 .... 211 n.114
1:7 .... 96, 210 n.108, 215, 216 n.133
1:8 .... 223, 228
1:10 .... 208, 209 n.103, 222
1:11 .... 216 n.133
1:12 224
1:12-13 ...... 223 n.155-6
2:1 .... 230 n.181, 231
2:2 .... 222, 228, 231
2:3 .... 154 n.190, 214, 223, 227, 228
2:4 .... 228, 232

2:7 .... 191 n.33, 193 n.36, n.39, 202
2:8 .... 200, 202
2:9 .... 193 n.39, 200
2:10 .... 154 n.190, 155, 201 n. 68, 202, 210, 302 n.86, 304 n.92
2:11 .... 199, 202
3:1 .... 66 n.89, 106 n.11, 108, 115
3:2 .... 157 n.193
3:3 .... 120 n.61
3:3-12 .... 131 n.110
3:8 .... 154 n.190
3:12 167
3:14 .... 118 n.53
3:14-15 ...... 118, 128
3:15 .... 130 n.108
3:16 .... 66 n.89, 118, 118 n.60, 121 n.67, 142 n.145, 145 n.151
3:18 .... 119, 121 n.67, 169, 165, 186 n.18
4:1 .... 135, 137
4:2-3 135
4:1 136
4:1-5 134
4:3 .... 136 n.126
4:4 136
4:5 .... 144 n.149
4:7 .... 149 n.168
4:7-9 .... 135, 138 n.132, 151
4:10 .... 143 n.147

5:1 ....141 n.138
6:2-3........158

Rosh Hashana
1:3 168
1:11.........165 n.5
1:12.........119 n.56,
         165-66, 169
1:13.........165-67
1:15.........111 n.23

Ta'anit
1:1 ....232 n.188
1:3 176
1:4 ....129 n.104
1:8 ....120 n.59

Hagiga
1:2 197

Yevamot
6:8 ....137 n.128

Ketubot
4:12.........154 n.190

Nedarim
1:5 ....198 n.57

Sota
4:2 ....246 n.30,
         n.32, 247
         n.34, 249
         n.46, 250
         n.51, 259
4:6 ....250 n.52
7:13-17....115 n.45
7:15.........154 n.190
11:1.........249 n.46
13:7.........140 n.135

Bava Qama
6:28.........231 n.185

Bava Mesia
8:4 ....211 n.112

Zevahim
6:11.........118 n.53

'Arakhin
1:10.........248 n.44
2:6 ....119 n.59

Me'ila
1:16.........130 n.108
1:22.........211 n.112

Kelim
BM 3:3....205 n.85,
         211 n.113

'Ahilot
9:3 ....205 n.85

Para
9:2 ....119 n.59

Tohorot
7:8 ....177 n.54

Nida
9:13 ....205 n.85

Palestinian Talmud

Berakhot
3:1 294
3:3 ....233 n.194-5
4:5 ....270 n.129

Bikkurim
3:3 ....53 n.49

Shabbat
2:6 ....311 n.118

'Eruvin
1:1 ....223 n.157

Yoma
5:3 ....178 n.60
5:4 ....125 n.84
6:3 ....140 n.135

Sukka
1:1 ....53 n.50, 215
         n.126, 220,
         222 n.150,
         223, 224
         n.164, 262
         n.99
1:2 ....216 n.131
1:3 ....216 n.132
1:4 ....210 n. 111
1:5 ....129 n.102
1:6 ....205 n.85
1:7 ....89 n.145,
         205 n.85,
         210 n. 108
1:8 ....212 n.118-9
1:10.........215 n.128-9
1:11.........208 n.99
2:2 ....222 n.153
2:5 ....228 n. 178,
         229 n.179,
         230 n.181
2:7 ....229 n.180
2:10.........226 n.171,
         232
3:1 ....200 n.66,
         202, 219
         n.142
3:2 ....193 n.36
3:3 ....191 n. 33,
         193 n.36,
         202 n.74
3:4 ....198 n.59,
         204 n.83
3:5 ....170 n.29,
         192 n. 36,
         202 n.77
3:6 ....202 n.77
3:11.........90 n.150
3:12.........194 n.44
3:13.........183, 201n.70
3:14.........155 n.190
4:1 ....186 n.19

Source Index

4:3 .... 107 n.12, n.13, 109 n.20, 112 n.30, 307 n.107
4:8 .... 120 n.63, 121 n.67
4:9 .... 118 n.54, n.55
4:17 .... 89 n.145

5:1 .... 144 n.148, 148 n.148, 317
5:2 .... 134 n.121, 135 n.123, 136 n.126, 144 n.148
5:3 .... 137 n.130
5:4 .... 135 n.125, 136 n.126
5:5 .... 138 n.133
5:6 .... 143 n.147

Besa
1:1 .... 53 n.49
3:9 .... 89 n.145

Rosh Hashana
1:3 .... 166 n.14, 167 n.16, 168 n.20, 186 n.18

Ta'anit
1:1 .... 170 n.25, 172-4, 311
1:2 .... 177 n.56
1:3 .... 128 n.99
3:2 .... 267 n.122
4:1 .... 266 n.119

Megila
3:7 .... 266 n.119

Hagiga
1:1 .... 120 n.59
2:10 .... 89 n.145

Moed Qatan
2:13 .... 89 n.145

Yevamot
15:2 .... 14 n.2

Sota
7:4 .... 266 n.119, 267 n.121, 283 n.24
9:16 .... 53 n.50

Gittin
2:3 .... 194 n.44

Sanhedrin
17:2 .... 126 n.87, 127 n.91

'Avodah Zarah
1:2 .... 113 n.36
2:3 .... 194 n.44

Babylonian Talmud

Berakhot
16a 167 n.17
26b 178 n.59
30a 198 n.59
55a 268 n.126
56a 301 n.81

Shabbat
152a 283 n.24

'Eruvin
19a 125 n.84, 128 n.95
45b 129 n.102

Pesahim
109a 140 n.137, 300 n.79
113a 155 n.190

114b 213 n.121
120a 187 n.22

Yoma
4a-b 246 n.30
20b 133 n.116
21a 130 n.105
21b 140 n.135
38a 140 n.135
39a 140 n.135
54a 140 n.135
54b 125 n.84

Sukka
2a 214 n.124, 262 n.99
2b 222 n.149
3a 221-2 n.148
4b 223 n.156
4b-5a 247 n.35
5a 247 n.33
6b 205 n.85
7a 223
7b 215 n.127, 222 n.152, 224 n.163, 262 n.100
8b 206 n.88, 214 n.124, 217 n.136, 219-21
9a 218, 229
9b 215 n.130
9b-10a 216 n.131
10a 209 n.104, 216 n.132
10b 261 n.97
10b-11a ... 216 n.132
11b .... 129 n.102, 201 n.68, 210 n.107, n.109, 212 n. 119, 239 n. 1

12a 204 n.80, 214 n.125	31b..........231 n.185	45a 107 n.12, n.13, n.17,
12b..........209 n.105, 212 n.117	31b-32a ...200 n.66	108 n.18,
	32a 115 n.42	111 n.26,
14a-b.......210 n.108	32b..........125 n.84, 193 n.36,	112 n.29,
14b..........214 n.125, 215 n.128, 222 n.148	202, 304	n.31, 116 n.47
	33a 200 n.66, 302 n.86	45b..........108, 114, 115 n.42,
15a 207 n.96	33b-34a ...193 n. 36	n.43, 192
15b-16a ...209 n.106, 211 n.114	34a 186 n.18,19, 191 n.33,	n.35, 233 n.195, 234 n.
16a ....209 n.106, 212 n. 118	202 n.74	197, 307
	34b..........200 n.63	n.107-8
16b..........223 n.161	35a 170 n.29	46a 198 n.59,
17a 205 n.85, 215 n.128	35b..........202 n.77	233
	36a 191 n.33, 202 n.77	46b..........116 n.47
18a ....214 n. 125	37a 158 n.199, 204 n.83	48b..........66 n.89, 118 n.53, 121
19a 215 n.126		n.67
19b..........222 n.151	37b..........158 n.199, 198 n.59	49a 128 n.95, n.96
20a 208 n.99, 209 n.103	37b-38a ...314, 315 n.132	50a 118 n.54, n.55, 142
20b..........208 n.99, 209 n.103	38b..........158 n.201, 159 n.203	n.144, 143 n.148
21b..........216 n.133, 222 n. 153, 261 n.97	39a 199 n.59	50b..........143 n.148, 148
	41b..........155, 156	
22b..........208	42a 143 n.148	51a 136 n.128, 186 n.21
23a 222 n.154, 223 n.161	43a 153 n.184, 183, 199	51b..........135 n.122, 136 n.128,
26a ....227 n.172, 228 n. 173, n.178, 229 n.179, 231	n.62, 201 n.70, 228 n.177	137, 140 n.135
	43b..........54 n.53, 109 n.19	52b..........135 n.123, 137
27a-b.......229-30	44a 109 n.20, 186	53a 113 n.35, 134 n.121,
27b..........69 n.97, 231 n.185	n.18,n.19, n.20	135 n.125, 136, 137
28b..........226 n.171	44b-45a ...152 n.183	n.130, 144
29a 232 n.189-90		n.149
30b-31a ...158 n.199		
31a 219 n.142, 230 n.181		

53a-b.......126 n.87,
          127 n.92,
          138 n.132
53b..........133 n.119,
          138 n.133
54a..........143 n.147
54b..........126 n.86
55b..........300 n.78

Rosh Hashana
3a...........249 n.46
16a..........165 n.6, n.8,
          n.10, 166
          n.11, n. 12,
          n.14, 167
          n.16, n.17,
          168 n.18

Ta'anit
2a...........172 n.36,
          173 n.40
2b 30 n.58, 170
          n. 24, 172-5,
          178 n.60,
          186 n.18,
          306 n.100,
          311 n.116
4a...........174 n.44
5b 263 n.108
6b 178 n.60
7a...........178 n.60
7b 178 n.60
8a...........178 n.60
9a...........246 n.30
9b 129 n.102
9b-10a.....130 n.105
10a 126 n.86,
          178 n.57
16a 301 n.81
25b..........128 n.97,
          129 n.105

Megila
3a............240 n.1

10b..........140 n.135
31a 278 n.8, 289
          n.41

Ketubot
111b-112a 125 n.82

Sota
35a 248 n.43
49b..........53 n.50

Qiddushin
30a 314 n.128
42b..........213 n.120
70a..........194 n.44
73a 121 n.68,
          195 n.51
81a 314 n.128

Bava Qama
84a 240 n.1

Bava Mesia
83b..........283 n.24
85a 178 n.60

Bava Batra
74b..........126 n.88,
          281 n.19
75a 281, 282
          n.22, 283
          n.24
99a 140 n.135

Sanhedrin
37b..........301 n.81
96b..........255
98a 255 n.72
99b..........267 n.112

Shevu'ot
15b..........265 n.115

'Avoda Zara
2a-3b.......275-281, 282
          n.22, 289
48b..........262 n.99

Menahot
27a 291-2, 302
          n.88
62a 314
65a-b.......11 n.23
69b..........102

'Arakhin
3b 227 n.172
10a 157 n.193
10b-11a ...140 n.135
32b..........42 n.24, 267
          n.122

Nida
73a 283 n.25

Midrash

Tannaitic Midrashim

Mekhilta
Pisha
12 ....247 n.34
14 ....239 n.1, 243
          n.15, 253,
          260 n.92,
          280 n.15

Beshalah, Petihta
(75).........246 n.31
(80).........239 n.1, 243
          n.15, 253
          n.61, 260
          n.92
(81).........246 n.30-1,
          250 n. 51,
          259 n.89

Beshalah, Shira
4.............248 n.40,
          252 n.58,
          263 n.108,
          267 n.123

5............127 n. 89,
          250 n.53,
          254 n.66

Beshalah, Vayasa
2.............248 n.43
5.............246 n.31

Bahodesh
4.............247 n.35
9.............248 n.44,
          268

Neziqin 8 240 n.1

Mekhilta Rabbi Shimon ben Yohai
33............239 n.1, 243
          n.15, 251
          n.54
47 ....239 n.1, 243
          n.15, 250
          n.51, 253
          n.61, 259
          n.88
60 ....267 n.123
60-61.......248 n.40
108..........248 n.43
119..........249 n.49
135..........248 n.41

Sifra

Vayiqra
1:8 ....247 n.35

Sav
1:29.........55

Qedoshim
3:7 ....211 n.112

Mesora
4:8 ....197 n.55

Emor
16:1.........201 n.67
16:2.........199

16:3.........153 n.184,
          183, 201
16:4.........200
16:4-6......192
16:6.........186 n.18
16:7.........200 n. 65
16:8.........202 n.68
16:9.........183
17:4.........215 n.120-1,
          228 n.177,
          261 n.96,
          n.98
17:5.........226
17:10.......204
17:11.......239, 243
          n.15

Sifre Numbers
83 ....246 n.30-1,
          248 n.41,
          250 n.51,
          256 n.77
84 ....246 n.30,
          n.32
106..........246 n.30
116..........154 n.190
150..........121 n.67,
          165 n.10,
          175, 186
          n.18, 312

Sifre Deuteronomy
23 ....197 n.55
37 ....126 n.86
40 ....165 n.10
96 ....303 n.89
140..........66 n.89, 210
          n.107, 212
          n.119, 219,
          231 n.185,
          263 n.105
213..........239-40 n.1
218..........154 n.190

296..........247 n.35,
          249
305..........246 n.31
313 260
317..........206 n. 88
346..........303 n.89
353..........128 n.99

Sifre Zuta
6:80.........247 n.35
10:33.......246 n.30-1,
          247 n.34,
          250 n.51,
          n.53, 256
          n.77, 268
          n.125
11:10.......247

Midrash Tannaim
11 ....248 n.43
72 ....303 n.89
94 ....212 n.117-9
103..........155 n.190

Amoraic and Post-Amoraic Midrashim

Avot deRabbi Natan, version A
12 ....136 n.126
34 ....246 n.31,
          247 n.35
35 ....120 n.59,
          140 n.135

Avot deRabbi Natan, version B
25 ....249 n.46
27 ....136 n.126
37 ....246 n.31,
          249 n.46

Bamidbar Rabba
8:1 ....267 n.121
14:2.........281 n.20

Source Index

16:21.......248 n.43
18:22.......126 n.88
19:20.......249 n.46
19:22.......250 n.51
20:19.......252
21:24.......299 n.75

Baraita demelekhet hamishkan
14...........254
14:1-4......246 n.30
14:5.........247 n.34

Beit Hamidrash
2:52.........248 n.41
5:42.........248 n.41
6:38.........249 n.46

Bereisheet Rabba
6:17.........311 n.118
10:6.........114 n.41
12:11.......129 n.102
13:10.......129 n.102
13:10-13...130 n.105
13:11.......129 n.102
13:13.......129 n.104
13:17.......128 n.99
15:7.........192 n.36
18 ....282 n.21
18:1.........283 n.24
32:7.........129 n.103
33:1.........127 n.89
40:17.......115 n.42
48:10.......250 n.51,
              268 n.127,
              301 n.81
55:7.........125 n.84
56:2.........247 n.36
56:10.......316 n.134
62:4.........246 n.31
65:6-9......197 n.55
65:9.........307 n.109
65:17.......140 n.136
70:8.........130 n.107

96 ....283 n.24
97:1.........97 n.55

Devarim Rabba
7:11.........248 n.41

Midrash HaGadol
1:508.......126 n.85
2:214.......251 n.54
2:251.......251 n.54
2:607.......311 n.117
3:586.......183
3:657.......172 n.37,
              292 n.51,
              312, 313
3:658.......292 n.51
3:660.......303 n.91
3:660-662 305 n.97,
              309
3:661.......297 n.68,
              303 n.90,
              306 n.98

Midrash Mishlei
14:3.........246 n.32
14.84.......246 n.32

Midrash Tehillim
17:5.........109 n.19,
              286 n.36
26:5.........109 n.19
76:3.........316 n.134
92:11.......305 n.95
102:3.......287 n.38
104:24 266
109:4.......299 n.75,
              300 n.78,
              312

Pesiqta d'Rav Kahana
2:2 ....307 n.103
2:6 ....307 n.103
3..............248 n.42
3:1 ....266 n.117
3:12.........249 n.49

4:4 ....283 n.24,
              307 n.103
4:5 ....246 n.30,
              247 n.35
4:10.........307 n.103
5:8 ....113 n.36
5:17.........307 n.103
6:2 ....307 n.103
9:1 ....127 n.89
9:11.........307 n.103
12 315
12:10.......267 n.120
16:1.........266 n.117
26:1.........283 n.24
27:1.........287 n.36
27:2.........284 n.29,
              292-3
27:3.........99 n.194,
              287
27:4.........291, 292,
              295, 300
27:7.........292, 300
27:8.........193 n.36
27:9.........297 n.68,
              303 n.90,
              305
28 ....312 n.125
28:8.........312, 317
              n.135
28:9.........298 n.73

Pesiqta d'Rav Kahana (alternative parsha)
409..........291 n.47
452..........279-80
454..........281 n.20,
              301 n.84
455 ....281 n.20
457..........240 n.1, 288
              n.39, 301
              n.82
457-58 .....300 n.80

458..........157 n.194,
            313 n.127

Pesiqta Rabbati
14 ....250 n.51,
            283 n.24
27 274
30 ....316 n.134
37 ....282 n.23

Pirqei d'Rabbi Eliezer
5..............129 n.100,
            n.102
10 ....125 n.84
14 ....248 n.41
31 ....247 n.37
35 ....125 n.84,
            126 n.85

Qohelet Rabba
3:2 ....311 n.119
7:11..........283 n.24
8:1 ....283 n.24
12:5..........283 n.24

Ruth Rabba
3:4 ....283 n.24
5:4 ....266 n.119

Seder Eliyahu Rabba
13 ....268 n.127
18 ....266 n.117
29 ....248 n.43

Seder Olam Rabba
9..............246 n.31

Shir HaShirim Rabba
1:7 ....240 n.1, 301
            n.82
2:6 256
4:1 299
4:5 ....246 n.30
7:2 311

Shmot Rabba
15:22 ....126 n.88
34:3..........302 n.85
45:4..........247 n.33,
            n.35

Tanhuma Vayera
23 ....247 n.36

Bo
9..............240 n.1

Vayaqhel
3..............268 n.126
7..............268 n.126

Qedoshim
8..............122 n.68
10 ....126 n.84,
            131 n.110

Emor
17 ....311 n.117
22 ....292 n.51,
            301 n.84

Naso
23 ....265 n.115

Pinhas
17 299

Shoftim
9..............276 n.4, 277
            n.6

Tanhuma Buber
1:140 ....254 n.75
2:124 ....247 n.33
3:101 ....292 n.51
3:77 ....122 n.68
3:78 ....126 n.84
3:98 ....311 n.117
4:12-13 ....247 n.34-5

4:69..........248 n.43
4:156........299 n.75
5:31-32 ....276 n.4

Vayiqra Rabba
1:2 ....267 n.122
9:9 ....270 n.129
18:1..........283 n.24
20:2..........283 n.24
25:2..........282 n.24
27:6..........246 n.31
30 274
30:2..........283
30:3..........287 n.38
30:7..........183 n.6
30:8..........170 n.29,
            192 n.36
30:9..........305 n.97
30:10.......117 n.51
30:12.......297 n.69,
            303 n.89-91,
            304 n.94,
            307 n.12
30:13.......311
30:14.......296, 297
            n.68
30:15.......192 n.35
37:2..........116 n.47

Yalqut Shimoni
273..........267 n.120
615..........122 n.68
651..........305 n.97
652..........311 n.117
653..........279 n.13
743..........248 n.42
986..........252, 256
            n.77

Source Index

Maimonides, Mishneh Torah

Lulav
7:10.........199 n.59
8:12.........136 n.128,
         143 n.148
8:12-15....141 n.140
8:13-4......135 n.124

Sukka
5:4..........211 n.115
5:8..........207 n.96

Daily and Additional Offerings
10:7-10....141 n.140

www.ingramcontent.com/pod-product-compliance
Lightning Source LLC
Chambersburg PA
CBHW020120240426
43673CB00038B/544